TWELFTH EDITION

MODERN MANAGEMENT

CONCEPTS AND SKILLS

Samuel C. Certo | S. Trevis Certo

Steinmetz Professor of Management
Roy E. Crummer Graduate School of Business
Rollins College

Dean's Council of 100 Scholars
W. P. Carey School of Business
Arizona State University

PRENTICE HALL

Boston   Columbus   Indianapolis   New York   San Francisco   Upper Saddle River   Amsterdam
Cape Town   Dubai   London   Madrid   Milan   Munich   Paris   Montréal   Toronto   Delhi
Mexico City   São Paulo   Sydney   Hong Kong   Seoul   Singapore   Taipei   Tokyo

Samuel C. Certo
To Mimi: My compass for right living

S. Trevis Certo
To the Certos in the desert: Melissa, Skylar, Lexie, and Landon

Editorial Director: Sally Yagan
Editor in Chief: Eric Svendsen
Acquisitions Editor: Kim Norbuta
Editorial Project Manager: Claudia Fernandes
Director of Editorial Services: Ashley Santora
Editorial Assistant: Carter Anderson
Director of Marketing: Patrice Lumumba Jones
Marketing Manager: Nikki Ayana Jones
Marketing Assistant: Ian Gold
Senior Managing Editor: Judy Leale
Sr. Production Project Manager/Supervisor:
Lynn Savino Wendel
Senior Operations Supervisor: Arnold Vila
Creative Director: Christy Mahon

Sr. Art Director/Design Supervisor: Janet Slowik
Art Director: Steve Frim
Interior and Cover Designer: Jill Lehan
Cover Art: fotolia
Manager, Rights and Permissions: Hessa Albader
Editorial Media Project Manager: Denise Vaughn
MyLab Product Manager: Joan Waxman
Media Project Manager: Lisa Rinaldi
**Full-Service Project Management and
Composition:** Integra
Printer/Binder: Courier/Kendallville
Cover Printer: Lehigh-Phoenix Color Hagerstown
Text Font: 11/12.5 Perpetua

Credits and acknowledgments borrowed from other sources and reproduced, with permission, in this textbook appear on the appropriate page within text (or on page 568).

Library of Congress Cataloging-in-Publication Data
Certo, Samuel C.
   Modern management: concepts and skills/Samuel C. Certo, S. Trevis Certo.—12th ed.
      p. cm.
   Includes bibliographical references and index.
   ISBN 978-0-13-217631-6
 1. Management. 2. Industrial management. 3. Social responsibility of business.
 4. Technological innovations.   I. Certo, S. Trevis. II. Title.
   HD31.C4125 2012
   658—dc22

                              2010034070

10 9 8 7 6 5 4 3 2 1

Prentice Hall
is an imprint of

www.pearsonhighered.com

ISBN 10:   0-13-217631-9
ISBN 13: 978-0-13-217631-6

Contents

Preface

Managers of today continue to face new opportunities and challenges. These opportunities include much publicized tasks like Florida's Universal Studios opening a new Harry Potter attraction and Apple encouraging technology innovation beyond the iPad and the iPhone. At the same time, other companies face intense challenges, such as BP's task of cleaning up an oil well leak in the Gulf of Mexico. Perhaps because these opportunities and challenges are so daunting, managers today arguably have the ability to earn higher financial rewards than at any other time in history.

This 12th edition of the *Modern Management Learning Package*, this text plus its ancillaries, continues a recognized and distinctive tradition in management education that has extended more than 30 years. As in all previous editions, this current edition of the *Modern Management Learning Package* has focused on a single objective: maximizing student learning of critical management concepts. All revisions reflect instructor and student feedback regarding ways to refashion the package to further enhance student learning. Starting with the text, the following sections explain each major component of this revision.

New to This Edition

Professors and students need and deserve textbooks that are modern. In this context, modern involves adding the latest concepts and empirical research as well as including the most recent examples of management in the business world. Modern also refers to how the text material is presented—the pedagogy used to help students learn the concepts. This edition of the *Modern Management Learning Package,* this text and its ancillaries, is undoubtedly modern in terms of *both* management concepts and pedagogy. Overall, this package includes:

- Substantial revision of Chapter 3 "Social Responsibility, Ethics, and Sustainability." We have added new coverage on sustainability.
- Substantial revision of Chapter 9 "Strategic Planning: Strategies, Tactics, and Competitive Dynamics." New coverage of competitive dynamics has been added.
- Half of the chapter-introductory Challenge Cases are new to this edition.
- Half of the chapter-ending Concluding Cases are new to this edition.
- We have added a new How Managers Do It feature. Each chapter includes at least three such features.
- Approximately half of the Research Highlights are new to this edition.
- A new Key Terms section has been added at the end of each chapter.
- Sequencing of pedagogical features like Target Skill, Learning Objectives, and Exploring Your Management Skill has been improved in all chapters to enhance student learning.
- Half of the VideoNet Exercises are new to this edition.

More detail on each of these new features is integrated within the following discussion.

Text: Theory Overview

Decisions about which concepts to include in this revision were difficult. Such decisions were heavily influenced not only by colleague and student feedback, but also by information from accrediting agencies such as The Association to Advance Collegiate Schools of Business (AACSB), professional manager associations such as the American Management Association (AMA), and academic organizations like the Academy of Management.

Overall, management theory in this edition is divided into the following six main sections: Introduction to Management, Modern Management Challenges, Planning, Organizing, Influencing, and Controlling. The following sections discuss the changes we made in this edition to continue the tradition of stressing the *modern* in *Modern Management*.

Part One: Introduction to Modern Management

This section contains the foundation concepts necessary to obtain a worthwhile understanding of management.

- Chapter 1, "Introducing Modern Management: Concepts and Skills" This chapter exposes students to what management is and gives insights about how to build their careers. This chapter also pinpoints management skills emphasized throughout the book and sets the stage for learning management concepts and developing related skills. Given high student interest, the chapter-opening case on Harry Potter and Universal Studios has been extensively revised. Also, new management compensation data has been added to give students a realistic view of recent management pay levels. A new extended example of achieving efficiency and effectiveness at Telstra, Australia's largest telecommunications company, was added to help students see the relevance of chapter concepts. A new experiential exercise was added at the end of the chapter to help students gain insight on gauging the progress of a career. A new VideoNet Exercise exploring management roles at azTeen Magazine was also added.

- Chapter 2, "Managing: History and Current Thinking" This chapter presents several fundamental, but different, ways managers can perceive their jobs. The work of management pioneers like Frederick W. Taylor, Frank and Lillian Gilbreth, and Henry L. Gantt is highlighted. Students are given insights into how to combine the work of management pioneers into a more comprehensive view of management. New discussion on the impact of Taylor's work on unions and product quality has been added. More depth on the work of the Gilbreths has also been added. A new extended illustration of how to build human relations into an organization is based on events at SAS, the world's largest privately held software company. Another illustration of how to track customer opinions focuses on ReviewPro, software that allows management to track and organize opinions of hotel customers. A new experiential exercise was added to help students better understand the impact of a time study job on career development. A new concluding case on present-day challenges at the *New York Times* has been added. A new VideoNet Exercise exploring the rewards and challenges of being a manager at Campus MovieFest was also added.

Part Two: Modern Management Challenges

This section helps students focus on understanding major challenges that modern managers face. Detail on each chapter in this section follows.

- Chapter 3, "Corporate Social Responsibility, Ethics, and Sustainability" This chapter discusses the responsibilities managers have to society and how business ethics applies to modern management. Major revision to this chapter is the addition of a new topic: *sustainability.* This chapter defines sustainability and a sustainable organization and discusses the triple bottom line, reasons why organizations should become sustainable, and steps to follow for building sustainable organizations. A new introductory Challenge Case on Verizon, a new Research Highlight on the impact of social responsibility on the organization's bottom line, and a new example of how PepsiCo builds sustainability have all been added to maximize chapter newness and freshness. A new career experiential exercise encourages students to explore how communicating about social responsibility activities can impact careers.
- Chapter 4, "Management and Diversity" This chapter defines diversity, explains the advantages of promoting diversity in organizations, outlines ways in which managers can promote it, and discusses some key challenges and dilemmas managers face in attempting to build a diverse workforce. A new Challenge Case on Siemens and global diversity has been added. Other new additions for this edition include coverage of Muslims in American society, an extended example of diversity in the legal profession, discussion of how Morgan Stanley highlights diversity information, and about how Walgreens Company actively hires workers with disabilities. A new experiential exercise focuses on gender bias and a woman's career. A new VideoNet Exercise on diversity in organizations was also added.
- Chapter 5, "Managing in the Global Arena" This chapter covers domestic versus international, multinational, and transnational organizations. The chapter also emphasizes expatriates, repatriation, and international market agreements. The introductory Challenge Case on Wal-Mart and Japan has been updated. New discussion regarding JP Morgan's attempts to target business in Brazil, China, and India has also been added. A new illustration of Kimberly-Clark controlling global operational costs also appears. Students will also see newly updated information regarding U.S. investment abroad—where investment in the United States has been originating and where U.S. investment in foreign countries has been focused. A new experiential exercise focuses on raising students' sensitivity to the types of topics they must study to build a global career. A new chapter-ending case on Jarden's global reach has also been added.
- Chapter 6, "Management and Entrepreneurship" This chapter focuses on the discovery, evaluation, and exploitation of business opportunities. We have added extensive examples describing entrepreneurial efforts in the agricultural, financial, and health and fitness industries. The Challenge Case on

Google has been updated to reflect some of the company's latest efforts. We have also included a new Research Highlight reviewing the primary reasons why entrepreneurs start new businesses. The chapter includes a new chapter-ending case on Heritage Auction Galleries, an entrepreneurial firm that sells collectibles all over the world. Finally, the chapter includes a new VideoNet exercise based on Boston Boxing and Fitness.

Part Three: Planning

This section elaborates on planning as a primary management function.

- Chapter 7, "Principles of Planning" This chapter details the primary concepts involved with planning. The chapter includes a new Challenge Case detailing the planning efforts at Quality Bicycle Products. The chapter also includes new examples illustrating the role of planning in a diverse set of companies including Target, ConocoPhillips, and MySpace. The chapter concludes with a new VideoNet exercise illustrating how managers plan at Kaneva.
- Chapter 8, "Making Decisions" This chapter details the primary concepts involved with decision making. The chapter begins with a new Challenge Case summarizing the decision that NBC executives made to replace Conan O'Brien with Jay Leno as host of "The Tonight Show." We also included a new Research Highlight examining how timely information improves decision making. We incorporate new content discussing the role of hubris and overconfidence in understanding executive decision making. Finally, the chapter includes new examples illustrating the role of decision making in the recycling and retailing industries.
- Chapter 9, "Strategic Planning: Strategies, Tactics, and Competitive Dynamics" This chapter was extensively revised to include the latest research on strategic planning. In addition to the chapter's existing coverage of strategies and tactics, this chapter now includes an in-depth discussion of competitive dynamics. This new section on competitive dynamics helps students understand how and why firms act and react when competing with their rivals. Specifically, we introduce the framework suggesting that a firm's awareness, motivation, and capabilities influence its competitive actions. We introduce an example of the rivalry between Amazon.com and Barnes & Noble to illustrate how these concepts influence competitive actions. The chapter includes a new Challenge Case detailing the role of strategic planning in understanding the success of Samsung Electronics. The chapter concludes with a new VideoNet Exercise on Nom Nom.
- Chapter 10, "Plans and Planning Tools" This chapter details the fundamental tools that help improve planning success. This chapter includes a new Challenge Case on Microsoft to help students better understand how planning tools can improve organizational effectiveness. We also included a diverse set of examples to illustrate how planning tools assist both non-profit organizations (e.g., Nationwide Children's Hospital) as well as more prominent companies such as H&M and Apple. The chapter concludes with a new VideoNet Exercise that describes how employees at Triple Rock Brewing employ planning tools.

Part Four: Organizing

This section discusses organizing activities as a major management function.

- Chapter 11, "Fundamentals of Organizing" This chapter details the key concepts involved with organization. The chapter includes new examples illustrating the importance of organization for companies such as General Electric, General Motors, and EnergySolutions. We also included in this chapter a new Research Highlight examining how organizational structure influences the ability of companies to mass customize their products for customers. This example also provides a discussion of the distinctions between organic versus mechanistic organizational structures. The chapter concludes with a new chapter-ending case describing the challenges involved with 3M's organizational structure.
- Chapter 12, "Responsibility, Authority, and Delegation" This chapter details the importance of responsibility, authority, and delegation in managerial effectiveness. The chapter begins with a new Challenge Case summarizing the roles of responsibility, authority, and delegation in understanding the quality challenges that recently troubled Toyota. The chapter also includes new examples illustrating how these important concepts influenced managerial effectiveness at Goldman Sachs and Johnson & Johnson.
- Chapter 13, "Human Resource Management" This chapter covers the primary concepts involved in understanding effective human resource management. New examples have been added to illustrate a variety of issues in human resource management. For instance, new examples highlight the

practices Intel uses to recruit new employees as well as the tactics used by Health South when laying off employees. We also included a new Research Highlight illustrating how the timing of a job offer (i.e., how soon after an interview a job offer was made to a candidate) influences the likelihood that a candidate accepts the offer. This chapter concludes with a new chapter-ending case describing how Raising Cane's employed social media to attract and hire new employees.

- Chapter 14, "Organizational Change: Stress, Conflict, and Virtuality" This chapter emphasizes ways in which managers change organizations and the stress-related issues that can accompany such action. Coverage also emphasizes building alternative work situations, communicating successfully in virtual offices, and handling change-related conflict. New extended examples of organizational change focus on changing a data technology system at University Health Systems, people change at Caterpillar, and identifying workplace bullying. New coverage has also been added on "storytelling" as a technique for initiating change. A new experiential exercise allows students to explore the role of change in career management. A new chapter-ending case focuses on change at P&G. A new VideoNet Exercise exploring change at homestarrunner.com was also added.

Part Five: Influencing

This section discusses ways managers should deal with people. Reflecting the spirit of AACSB guidelines, encouraging thorough coverage of human factors in business curriculum, the influencing section is quite comprehensive.

- Chapter 15, "Influencing and Communication" This chapter introduces the topic of managing people, defines interpersonal communication, and presents organizational communication as the primary vehicle managers use to interact with people. A new introductory Challenge Case was added. In addition, more coverage of emotional intelligence has been added. New extended examples on communication strategy at the White House and the use of podcasts for communication at Ericsson have also been newly added. New emphasis in this chapter explores informal communication during an economic downturn and the relationship between trust in a manager and the manager's credibility as a communicator. The new experiential exercise for this chapter focuses on the relationship between a manager's personal communication philosophy and his or her career. The end-of-chapter VideoNet Exercise focuses on communication at Zifty.com.
- Chapter 16, "Leadership" This chapter highlights more traditional concepts, such as the Vroom-Yetton-Jago leadership model, the path–goal theory of leadership, and the life-cycle theory of leadership. Coverage also includes more recently developed and evolving concepts such as servant leadership, transformational leadership, coaching, super-leadership, and entrepreneurial leadership. The new introductory Challenge Case for this chapter is on Sotoru Iwata, the president of Nintendo. New research coverage focuses on the relationship between leader traits and charismatic leadership, and leader flexibility and "quick wins." New extended examples feature transformational leadership at Ben & Jerry's and servant leadership at Zappos.com. We also added a new Research Highlight examining the role of transformational leadership in understanding group performance. The new career experiential exercise for this chapter helps students explore the role of leadership opportunities within an organization and choosing to take a job within that organization. The newly designed concluding case is "Oprah Leads an Empire."
- Chapter 17, "Motivation" This chapter defines motivation, describes the motivation process, and provides useful strategies managers can use in attempting to motivate organization members. Both content and process theories of motivation are discussed in detail. New extended examples of how American Airlines addresses pay inequity, how entrepreneur Bob Crane handles achievement motivation, and distributing incentives at Comarco are all included to help students see how chapter concepts can impact real managers. Research findings related to Theory X–Theory Y, the relationship between job satisfaction and economic recession, the findings of others that are seemingly consistent with Herzberg's ideas, job rotation, and communicating about incentive programs have been added to enrich chapter content. This chapter includes a new Research Highlight examining how goal-setting may influence the motivation—and performance—of individuals. The new career experiential exercise helps students explore the relationship between punishment and career development. The new case for this chapter is "Motivation at United Way."
- Chapter 18, "Groups and Teams" This chapter emphasizes managing clusters of people as a means of accomplishing organizational goals. Coverage focuses on managing teams. Coverage also focuses on groups versus teams, virtual teams, problem solving, self-managed and cross-functional teams, stages of team development, empowerment, the effectiveness of self-managed teams, and factors contributing to team effectiveness. An extended example of how committees function focuses on the committee for

recruitment at Red Robin Gourmet Burgers. Another such example focuses on building teams at Renaissance Executive Forums. New coverage discusses groupthink, the relationship between trust and team effectiveness, and integrating informal groups within formal organization structure. We also added a new Research Highlight that discusses how personality type may influence the extent to which an individual is able to influence group decision making. The new career-oriented experiential exercise for this chapter helps students explore the location of a first job and its impact on their careers. The newly designed concluding case for this chapter focuses on team building at Best Buy.

- Chapter 19, "Managing Organization Culture" The chapter opens with an extensively revised case on BP that focuses on an oil leak in the Gulf of Mexico and the company's attempt to establish an organization culture emphasizing safety. Major topics include defining organization culture, the importance of culture, and building a high-performance organization culture. Special discussion focuses on cultural artifacts: organizational values, myths, sagas, language, symbols, ceremonies, and rewards. New content includes comments on the difficulty in defining a particular culture, what beekeeping can teach us about building values within an organization, and the impact of economic turbulence on organizational socialization. New extended examples illustrate issues related to changing a code of conduct at Tocquigny and recruiting within a law firm to provide new employees who fit the organization culture. We also included a new Research Highlight discussing how aspects of organizational culture influence employee turnover. The new career experiential exercise for this chapter emphasizes the impact of organization culture on job choice. The new concluding case designed for this chapter explores organization culture and Cintas.

- Chapter 20, "Encouraging Creativity and Innovation" The chapter details new research on creativity and innovation and updates the efforts of the most innovative companies in America. The chapter also includes a new example illustrating the importance of creativity for Activision, a video game developer. We also added a new example illustrating how Amazon.com continues to innovate and change its overall business model. A new Research Highlight in this chapter highlights the important link between creativity and innovation in entrepreneurial firms. The chapter concludes with a new case describing the importance of innovation for Inventables.

Part Six: Controlling

This section presents control as a major management function. Major topics include fundamentals of control, controlling production, and information technology.

- Chapter 21, "Controlling, Information, and Technology" The chapter opens with a new Challenge Case discussing how Sperry Van Ness, a commercial real estate brokerage, employs controlling, information, and technology to improve operational efficiency and effectiveness. To better understand these concepts, we also include new examples illustrating how companies like Stein Mart and Sage use the latest information technologies to improve operations. We also include the most recent research available to expand our discussion of power in the organizational context. The chapter concludes with a new VideoNet Exercise demonstrating how Platinum Autobody uses information technology.

- Chapter 22, "Production and Control" We updated the Challenge Case in this chapter to reflect the control issues that surround Delta's recent merger with Northwest. We also included examples illustrating how Duke Energy, Chrysler, and Domino's implement controls to improve operational effectiveness. The chapter concludes with a new VideoNet Exercise illustrating the roles of production and control at Sound in Motion. We also included a new chapter-ending case to highlight how Michael's on East uses various controls to reduce costs.

Modern Management 12th edition: The Skills

From a pedagogy standpoint, the 12th edition of *Modern Management* continues its unique focus in the marketplace of developing students' management skills *across all of the primary management functions*. Each chapter opens by identifying a specific management skill on which the chapter focuses. The remainder of the chapter contains a number of purposefully placed features designed to help students develop that skill.

This focus on skill development is consistent with the Association to Advance Collegiate Schools of Business (AACSB), which provides higher education professionals with sound standards for maintaining excellence in management education. AACSB standards indicate that excellence in modern management education is achieved when students acquire both *knowledge* about management concepts and *skill* in applying that knowledge. According to these standards, management educators must help students understand and appreciate both the "why" of management as well as the "how" of management.

The following sections discuss pedagogical features in this text that help students learn management theory and how to apply it.

1. **Chapter Target Skill:** Each chapter opens by identifying and defining the target management skill emphasized in that chapter. By focusing on this target skill early in the chapter, students immediately have a context for learning chapter concepts. As an example of a chapter target skill, see the definition of corporate social responsibility skill on page 50.

2. **Learning Objectives:** For each chapter, a list of learning objectives follows the Chapter Target Skill. These objectives flow from the chapter target skills to help students further focus on learning critical chapter concepts. See page 2 for an example of how a chapter target skill and learning objectives work together to help students focus their learning on how to make decisions.

3. **Challenge Case:** Each chapter opens with an introductory Challenge Case. The purpose of a Challenge Case is to introduce students to real challenges faced by real managers and to demonstrate the usefulness of chapter concepts and related management skills in meeting those challenges. Each case summarizes a set of issues for a manager within a company and asks students how they would resolve the issues. Over half the cases in this edition are new or updated. New cases in this edition focus on companies such as Best Buy, United Way, and Harpo Productions. Turn to page 451 to see this edition's new introductory Challenge Case on BP.

4. **How Managers Do It:** New to this edition, each chapter contains two or three features called How Managers Do It. This feature shows students concrete steps practicing managers have actually taken that are consistent with chapter concepts. This feature focuses on companies such as 3M, Zappos, and Caterpillar. For a sample of this feature, see "Committee for Recruitment at Red Robin Gourmet Burgers" on page 428.

5. **Research and Class Discussion Highlights:** Each chapter includes a "Research Highlight" or "Class Discussion Highlight" that focuses on recent research related to chapter content. These highlights include specific questions to help students better understand the implications of recent management research on chapter content and management skills. These questions are designed primarily for in-class discussion but could be used for out-of-class study. Half of the highlights are new to this edition. New highlights cover such topics as organizational culture, recruiting tactics, and team decision making. For a sample of this feature, see "Modern Research and Human Resources Skill: The Timing of Job Offers" on page 308.

6. **You and Your Career:** Each chapter contains an Experiential Exercise that helps students understand the relationship between the targeted skill of the chapter and the development of their own careers. This feature includes a number of questions designed to help students appreciate the importance of managing their own careers. To see a sample You and Your Career exercise turn to page 23.

7. **Challenge Case Summary:** Each chapter ends with a Challenge Case Summary. This section provides extensive narrative on how chapter concepts relate to issues in the chapter-opening Challenge Case. To better understand this pedagogical feature, see the Challenge Case Summary for the BP introductory case on page 467.

8. **Management Skill Activities:** Each chapter ends with a rich array of learning activities that helps students better understand management concepts and develop skills in applying those concepts. Specific activities are listed and explained below.

    A. **Understanding Management Concepts:** This section helps students review and understand chapter concepts.

    1. **Know Key Terms** is a section in which key terms in a chapter are listed along with page numbers on which they are discussed. For an example Know Key Terms section, see key terms in the Strategic Planning chapter on page 220.

    2. **Know How Management Concepts Relate** is a section containing essay questions related to chapter material. These questions help students focus on the interrelationships of chapter concepts and how they relate to the management process. For the Influencing and Communication chapter, see a sample Know How Management Concepts Relate on page 362.

    B. **Developing Management Skills:** This chapter-ending section contains many activities that focus on helping students develop skills related to chapter content.

    1. **Exploring Your Management Skill: Part 1.** This exercise starts the Developing Management Skill section of each chapter. Taken before studying the chapter, Part 1 is a true-false, multiple-choice test (self-scored or electronically-scored) that helps students to assess their level of expertise in a chapter target skill *before* studying the chapter. The questions focus on how a manager in a Challenge Case might apply chapter content to organizational

issues. For an example of Exploring Your Management Skill: Part 1, check out page 266 in the Fundamentals of Organizing chapter.

2. **Exploring Your Management Skill: Part 2.** This exercise is actually repeating the same Exploring Your Management Skill: Part 1 test *after* studying the chapter. Students retake the test in Part 2 to see the impact of studying and to assess their learning as encouraged in AACSB guidelines on assurance of learning. For an example of Exploring Your Management Skill: Part 2, check out page 267 in the Fundamentals of Organizing chapter.

3. **Your Management Skills Portfolio.** An activity at the end of each chapter is specially designed to allow students to demonstrate management skill learned in that chapter. Instructors may choose to have students turn in hard or electronic copies of this assignment. In addition, instructors may ask students to present their completed portfolios in class. If completed online, a student can accumulate this evidence and print a portfolio covering as many chapters as desired, to help win a job during an employment interview. See "Delegating Basketball Duties at Texas A&M" on page 289 as an example of a Your Management Skills Portfolio.

4. **Experiential Exercises.** Each chapter concludes with two types of experiential exercises. *Type one* is specially designed to help students develop knowledge and skill related to chapter content. For an example of this type of experiential exercise, see Analyzing Study Results on page 419 of the Motivation chapter.

   Type two is an exercise that focuses on helping students use chapter content to better manage their own careers. These exercises are called You and Your Career. A sample of this type of experiential exercise, can be found on page 154 of the Management and Entrepreneurship chapter.

5. **Cases.** Each chapter concludes with two cases. The first concluding case is based on the chapter's introductory Challenge Case. Students are given a series of discussion questions that stimulate further discussion of the Challenge Case. Page 448 contains an example of such questions related to "Teamwork Spreads at Xerox," the Challenge Case for the Groups and Teams chapter.

   The second concluding case is specifically designed to illustrate real-life management issues and the steps necessary to face those issues. Half of these specially designed cases are new to this edition. An example of this type of case, new to this edition, is "Best Buy's Extreme Team Building" on page 448 of the Groups and Teams chapter.

6. **VideoNet Exercises.** Each chapter ends with a unique learning tool called a VideoNet Exercise. This exercise begins with students watching a video of an actual company and discussing chapter content as it relates to the company featured in the video. Next, students enrich what they've learned by completing an Internet activity—an *online* exploration of the company featured in the video. Half of the VideoNet Exercises are new to this edition. For a sample VideoNet exercise, see "Production and Control: Sound in Motion" on page 553 of the Production and Control chapter.

Modern Management: The Student Learning Process

Students often ask professors to suggest the best way to study to maximize learning. By using the components of *Modern Management* in a conscientious and systematic fashion, students can build their knowledge about management concepts and their skill to apply it. Although the components of *Modern Management* are flexible and can be used for many different study processes, one suggested study process is discussed below.

As shown in Figure 1, students can start chapter study by experiencing Exploring Your Management Skill: Part 1. This activity will introduce students to concepts and skills emphasized in the chapter and help them assess how much they know in these areas before studying the chapter.

Once students have been introduced via Exploring Your Management Skill: Part 1, they can start learning management concepts. They learn concepts by reading and studying the chapter and checking their progress in meeting the learning objectives stated at the beginning of the chapter as well as being able to answer essay questions at the end of the chapter. By checking their learning progress, students can pinpoint areas in which further study is needed before moving forward.

Once students are satisfied that they have learned chapter content, they can experience Exploring Your Management Skill: Part 2. This exercise will reemphasize the knowledge and skills focus in the chapter and give students feedback about how much they've learned in the chapter. If students are not satisfied with their feedback, they can restudy material to improve.

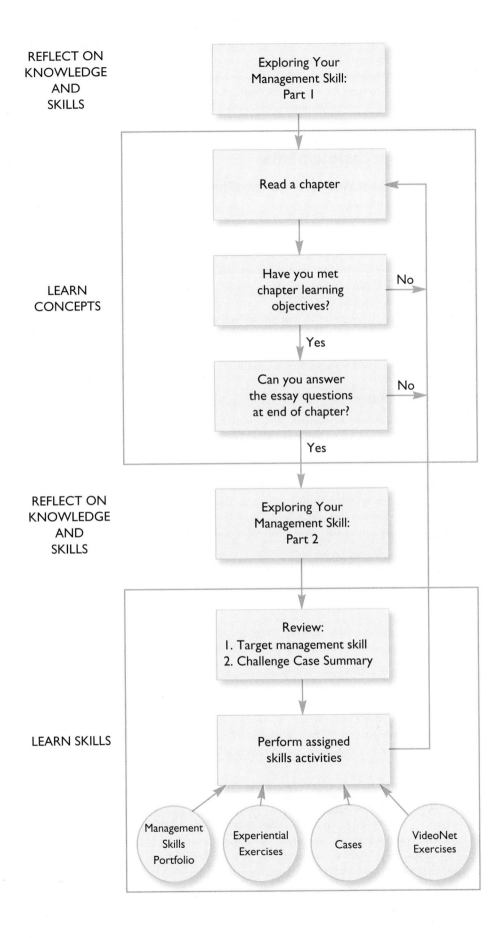

FIGURE 1
A systematic method for maximizing learning when studying *Modern Management*

When students are satisfied with this feedback, they can focus more on learning management skills related to chapter content. Students focus on learning how to apply management concepts by performing application exercises assigned by professors and referring to chapter content as often as necessary to further clarify concepts and how to apply them. Students might also work on exercises independently and do work not assigned by the professor. Application exercises can include the Management Skills Portfolio, Experiential Exercises, Cases, and VideoNet Exercises.

Instructor/Student Supplements

The *Modern Management* Web Site—New to This Edition

The *Modern Management* author Web site (www.twocertos.com) is new to this edition and a unique feature for principles of management textbooks. This site provides professors using *Modern Management* with a rich array of content aimed at making the text as close to real-time as possible. Content on the site includes features like experiential exercises, videos, podcasts, and research updates. By integrating this content with the text, professors can deliver courses that are content appropriate *and* current. The *Modern Management* Web site is maintained by the authors of the text, who personally choose and include the content that best complements and continuously updates text content.

Because instructors around the world teach courses and concepts at different times, the authors designed this site so instructors can quickly identify and use relevant content when they need it. The site allows instructors to search the entries by either chapter or content type. This design allows instructors to access content available for each teaching topic quickly and easily as needs arise.

Instructor Resource Center

At the Instructor Resource Center, www.pearsonhighered.com/irc, instructors can access a variety of print, digital, and presentation resources available with this text in downloadable format. Registration is simple and gives you immediate access to new titles and new editions. As a registered faculty member, you can download resource files and receive immediate access to and instructions for installing course management content on your campus server. In case you ever need assistance, our dedicated technical support team is ready to help with the media supplements that accompany this text. Visit http://247.pearsoned.com for answers to frequently asked questions and toll-free user support phone numbers.

The following supplements are available for download to adopting instructors:

- Instructor's Manual
- Test Item File
- TestGen (test-generating program)
- PowerPoint Slides

Videos on DVD—Video segments that illustrate the most pertinent topics in management today and highlight relevant issues that, demonstrate how people lead, manage, and work effectively. Contact your Pearson representative for the DVD.

CourseSmart eTextbook—CourseSmart is an exciting new choice for students looking to save money. As an alternative to purchasing the printed textbook, students can purchase an electronic version of the same content. With a CourseSmart eTextbook, students can search the text, make notes online, print out reading assignments that incorporate lecture notes, and bookmark important passages for later review. For more information, or to purchase access to the CourseSmart eTextbook, visit www.coursesmart.com.

PEARSON mymanagementlab MyManagementLab (www.mymanagementlab.com) is an easy-to-use online tool that personalizes course content and provides robust assessment and reporting to measure individual and class performance. All of the resources that students need for course success are in one place—flexible and easily adapted for your students' course experience. Some of the resources include an eText version of all chapters, quizzes, video clips, simulations, assessments, and PowerPoint presentations that engage your students while helping them study independently.

Acknowledgments

The overwhelming success of *Modern Management* has now continued for three decades. The *Modern Management Learning Package*, this book and its ancillaries, has become a generally accepted academic standard for high-quality learning materials in colleges and universities throughout the world. These materials have been published in special "country editions," serving the special needs of management students in countries like Canada and India. *Modern Management* has also been published in foreign languages including Portuguese and Spanish and is commonly used in professional management training programs.

Obviously, we have received much personal satisfaction and professional recognition for the success of this text over the years. In truth, however, much of the credit for this success continues to rightfully belong to many of our respected colleagues. Many key ideas for text development and improvement have come from others. We're grateful for the opportunity to recognize the contributions of these individuals and extend to them our warmest personal gratitude for their professional insights and encouragement throughout the life of this project.

For this edition, several colleagues made valuable contributions through numerous activities like reviewing manuscript and providing unsolicited ideas for improvement. These individuals offered different viewpoints that required us to constructively question our work. Thoughtful comments, concern for student learning, and insights regarding instructional implications of the written word characterized the high-quality feedback we received. These individuals are:

Helen Davis, Jefferson Community College–Downtown Louisville

E. Gordon DeMeritt, Shepherd University

Theresa Freihoefer, Central Oregon Community College

George Gannage, West Central Technical College

Wayne Gawlik, Joliet Jr. College

Ashley Geisewite, Southwest Tennessee Community College

Jon Matthews, Central Carolina Community College

Robert Morris, Florida State College of Jacksonville

Paul Robillard, Bristol Community College

Gisela Salas, Webster University, Barry University, St. Leo University, University of the Rockies

Duanne Schecter, Muskegon Community College

M. Smas, Kent State University

Paul Thacker, Macomb Community College

Bob Waris, University of Missouri Kansas City

Many colleagues have made significant contributions to previous editions of this project that are still impacting this 12th edition. A list of such respected colleagues includes:

Don Aleksy, Illinois Valley College

Karen Barr, Penn State University

Dan Baugher, Pace University

Wayne Blue, Allegany College of Maryland

Elise A. Brazier, Northeast Texas Community College

Michael Carrell, Morehead State University

Lon Doty, San Jose State University

Megan Endres, Eastern Michigan University

Joyce Ezrow, Anne Arundel Community College

William Brent Felstead, College of the Desert

Robert Freeland, Columbia Southern University

Adelina Gnanlet, California State University

Joseph Goldman, University of Minnesota

Heidi Helgren, Delta College

Jo Ann Hunter, Community College of Allegheny County

Steven E. Huntley, Florida Community College at Jacksonville

Robert E. Kemper, Northern Arizona University

Toni Carol Kind, Binghamton University

Dennis L. Kovach, Community College of Allegheny County

Loren Kuzuhara, University of Wisconsin

Gosia Langa, University of Maryland

Theresa Lant, New York University

Maurice Manner, Marymount College

Michelle Meyer, Joliet Junior College

Marcia Miller, George Mason University

Jennifer Morton, Ivy Tech Community College

Rhonda Palladi, Georgia State University

Donald Petkus, Indiana University

James I. Phillips, Northeastern State University

Richard Ratliff, Shari Tarnutzer, and their colleagues, Utah State University

Johnny Shull, Central Carolina Community College

Denise M. Simmons, Northern Virginia Community College

Joe Simon, Casper College

Randi L. Sims, Nova Southern University

Gregory Sinclair, San Francisco State University

L. Allen Slade, Covenant College

Charles I. Stubbart, Southern Illinois University Carbondale

Dr. Peter Szende, Boston University

Tom Tao, Lehigh University

Don Tobias, Cornell University

Larry Waldorf, Boise State University

Gloria Walker, Florida Community College at Jacksonville

Cindy W. Walter, Antelope Valley College

In addition, several colleagues have worked diligently on developing text ancillaries of only the highest quality. Such colleagues worked tirelessly to provide instructional aids to all of us and we thank them for their time and efforts. For this edition, we also thank Steve Stovall for his work on the end of chapter cases and Patricia Lanier for her work on the VideoNet exercises.

We will always owe Professor Lee A. Graf, Professor Emeritus, Illinois State University, a huge debt of gratitude for helping to build the success of *Modern Management* throughout the early years of this project. Dr. Graf's countless significant contributions in many different areas have certainly been instrumental in building the reputation and widespread acceptance of the *Modern Management Learning Package*. More important than our professional relationship, Dr. Graf is our friend.

Members of our Prentice Hall family deserve personal and sincere recognition. Our book team has been nothing but the best: Sally Yagan, Editorial Director; Kim Norbuta, Acquisitions Editor; Claudia Fernandes, Editorial Project Manager; Carter Anderson, Editorial Assistant; Lynn Savino, Production Project Manager; Judy Leale, Senior Managing Editor; and Nikki Jones, Marketing Manager. Needless to say, without our Prentice Hall colleagues, there would be no *Modern Management*.

Sam Certo would like to give special recognition to Craig McAllaster, Dean of the Crummer Graduate School of Business at Rollins College and Charles "Chuck" Steinmetz, entrepreneur extraordinaire. Personal and professional support demonstrated by these individuals over the years has helped to ensure the intensity, growth, and excitement necessary to maintain a vigorous, long-term writing schedule. Probably unknown to them, McAllaster and Steinmetz have been invaluable in the completion of this text.

Last and arguably most importantly, Sam Certo would like to thank his wife, Mimi, for her continual support throughout this revision. She constantly made personal sacrifices "beyond the call of duty" in support of the completion of this project. Thank you! Brian, Sarah and Andrew, Matthew and Lizzie, and Trevis and Melissa, continually but unknowingly help to build my confidence and focus. Thank you! To Skylar, Lexie, and Landon, a very special thanks. You guys always help "Pop" to remember that "adult things" aren't always as important as adults make them out to be.

Trevis Certo: I would like to thank my colleagues at Arizona State University for their continued support. I would also like to thank my wife Melissa for her patience with my writing schedule. I would also like to thank Skylar, Lexie, and Landon for humbling me every day. Finally, and most importantly, I would like to thank God for blessing me with a beautiful and healthy family.

Samuel C. Certo

S. Trevis Certo

About the Authors

Dr. Samuel C. Certo is presently the Steinmetz Professor of Management at the Roy E. Crummer Graduate School of Business at Rollins College. Over his career, Dr. Certo has received many prestigious awards including the Award for Innovative Teaching from the Southern Business Association, the Instructional Innovation Award granted by the Decision Sciences Institute, and the Charles A. Welsh Memorial Award for outstanding teaching.

Dr. Certo has written several successful textbooks including *Modern Management, Strategic Management: Concepts and Applications,* and *Supervision: Concepts and Applications.* His textbooks have been translated into several foreign languages for distribution throughout the world. Having received six different teaching awards in the last four years alone, Dr. Certo constantly focuses on crafting all of his books to facilitate both the instructional and student learning processes. Dr. Certo's numerous publications include articles in such journals as *Academy of Management Review, The Journal of Change Management, Business Horizons, The Journal of Experiential Learning and Simulation,* and *Training.*

A past chairperson of the Management Education and Development Division of the Academy of Management, he has been honored by that group's Excellence of Leadership Award. Dr. Certo has also served as president of the Association for Business Simulation and Experiential Learning, as associate editor for *Simulation & Games,* and as a review board member of the *Academy of Management Review.* His consulting experience has been extensive with notable experience on boards of directors in both private and public companies.

Dr. S. Trevis Certo is an associate professor and a Dean's Council of 100 Scholar in the W. P. Carey School of Business at Arizona State University. Dr. Certo holds a Ph.D. in strategic management from the Kelley School of Business at Indiana University. His research focuses on corporate governance, top management teams, initial public offerings (IPOs), and research methodology. Dr. Certo's research has appeared in the *Academy of Management Journal, Academy of Management Review, Strategic Management Journal, Journal of Management, California Management Review, Journal of Business Venturing, Entrepreneurship Theory and Practice, Business Ethics Quarterly, Journal of Business Ethics, Business Horizons, Journal of Developmental Entrepreneurship,* and *Across the Board.* Dr. Certo's research has also been featured in publications such as *BusinessWeek, New York Times, Wall Street Journal, Washington Post,* and *Money* magazine.

Dr. Certo is a member of the Academy of Management and the Strategic Management Society and serves on the editorial review boards of the *Academy of Management Journal, Journal of Management, Entrepreneurship Theory and Practice, Journal of Management and Governance,* and *Business Horizons.* Prior to joining the faculty at Arizona State, he taught undergraduate, MBA, EMBA, and Ph.D. courses in strategic management, research methodology, and international business at Indiana University, Texas A&M University, Tulane University, and Wuhan University (China).

Introducing Modern Management

CONCEPTS AND SKILLS

Target Skill

management skill: the ability to work with people and other organizational resources to accomplish organizational goals

objectives

To help build my *management skill*, when studying this chapter, I will attempt to acquire:

1. An understanding of the importance of management to society and individuals

2. An understanding of the role of management

3. An ability to define management in several different ways

4. An ability to list and define the basic functions of management

5. Working definitions of managerial effectiveness and managerial efficiency

6. An understanding of basic management skills and their relative importance to managers

7. An understanding of the universality of management

8. Knowledge of skills that help managers become successful

9. Insights concerning what management careers are and how they evolve

CHALLENGE CASE

UNIVERSAL OPENS HARRY POTTER THEME PARK

AFTER MONTHS OF MEDIA SPECULATION and then additional months in development, Universal Studios debuted its latest theme park, "The Wizarding World of Harry Potter." The park opened in June 2010 at the Universal Orlando Resort in Florida, in what Universal calls "a theme park within a theme park."[1]

The new park, developed as a partnership between Warner Bros. Entertainment Inc. and Universal Orlando Resort, creates the world's first fully immersive Harry Potter–themed environment based on the best-selling books by J. K. Rowling and wildly successful feature films from Warner Bros. The author worked with a creative team to make sure the park resembles her work.[2]

Pressure to build an attraction that is true to the Harry Potter brand was intense, as Universal's chairperson, Tom Williams, noted. However, early visitors to the park claim it has successfully captured the smells, sounds, and texture of Hogwarts Castle and the Forbidden Forest. Universal reportedly worked closely with Warner Bros. to ensure that marketing for the new park (launched in the form of advertising during the 2010 Super Bowl) aligned closely with the global Harry Potter brand. The 20-acre facility includes "meticulously re-created" versions of Hogwarts Castle and other settings from the series, along with amusements, dining, and shopping. Rides include Harry Potter and the Forbidden Journey, Flight of the Hippogriff, and a pair of high-speed roller coasters known as Dragon Challenge.[3]

The power of the Harry Potter brand is impressive. Rowling has sold more than 400 million Harry Potter books in more than 63 languages, and the movies have generated billions of dollars in revenues.[4] An estimated 8 out of 10 people already recognize the Harry Potter name, which is also an important draw for park visitors.[5]

Industry observers say the Harry Potter theme park is an attempt by Universal to better compete with Walt Disney World, the leading attraction in Orlando with more than 45 million visitors in a recent year—as compared with Universal's Orlando park figures of just over 11 million during the same period.[6]

Going from concept to the reality of operating a profitable enterprise, however, is a formidable challenge that rests squarely in the hands of management. Management must avoid classic mistakes such as recruiting the wrong employees, not creating a motivating work environment, and failing to keep the park's many systems operating properly. Competent managers will meet the challenge, whereas incompetent management will not. Only time will tell.

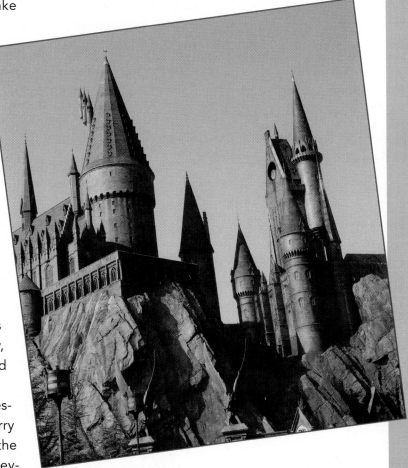

■ *Bringing a massive project like a new Harry Potter theme park to life requires many types of management skills at all levels of the organization.*

EXPLORING YOUR MANAGEMENT SKILL

You can explore your level of *management skill* **before** studying the chapter by completing the exercise "Exploring Your Management Skill: Part 1" on page 21 and **after** studying this chapter by completing the exercise "Exploring Your Management Skill: Part 2" on page 22.

THE MODERN MANAGEMENT CHALLENGE

The Challenge Case illustrates just a few of the challenges that face Universal Orlando management at its new Harry Potter theme park. The remaining material in this chapter explains the basic concepts of modern management and helps to develop the corresponding management skill you will need to meet such challenges throughout your career. After studying chapter concepts, read the Challenge Case Summary at the end of the chapter to help you to relate chapter content to meeting the management challenges at "The Wizarding World of Harry Potter."

THE IMPORTANCE OF MANAGEMENT

Managers influence all phases of modern organizations. Plant managers run manufacturing operations that produce the clothes we wear, the food we eat, and the automobiles we drive. Sales managers maintain a salesforce that markets goods. Personnel managers provide organizations with a competent and productive workforce. The "jobs available" section in the classified advertisements of any major newspaper describes many different types of management activities and confirms the importance of management (see Figure 1.1).

FIGURE 1.1
The variety of management positions available

SR. MANAGEMENT DEVELOPMENT SPECIALIST

We are a major metropolitan service employer of over 5,000 employees seeking a person to join our management development staff. Prospective candidates will be degreed with 5 to 8 years experience in the design, implementation, and evaluation of developmental programs for first-line and mid-level management personnel. Additionally, candidates must demonstrate exceptional oral and written communications ability and be skilled in performance analysis, programmed instruction, and the design and implementation of reinforcement systems.

If you meet these qualifications, please send your résumé, including salary history and requirements to:

Box RS-653

An Equal Opportunity Employer

BRANCH MGR

$30,500. Perceptive pro with track record in administration and lending has high visibility with respected firm.

Box PH-165

AVIATION FBO MANAGER NEEDED

Southeast Florida operation catering to corporate aviation. No maintenance or aircraft sales—just fuel and the best service. Must be experienced. Salary plus benefits commensurate with qualifications. Submit complete résumé to:

Box LJO688

DIVISION CREDIT MANAGER

Major mfg. corporation seeks an experienced credit manager to handle the credit and collection function of its Midwest division (Chicago area). Interpersonal skills are important, as is the ability to communicate effectively with senior management. Send résumé with current compensation to:

Box NM-43

ACCOUNTING MANAGER

Growth opportunity. Michigan Ave. location. Acctg. degree, capable of supervision. Responsibilities include G/L, financial statements, inventory control, knowledge of systems design for computer applications. Send résumé, incl. salary history to:

Box RJM-999
An Equal Opportunity Employer

THE MANAGEMENT TASK

In addition to understanding the significance of managerial work to themselves and society and its related benefits, prospective managers need to know what the management task entails. The sections that follow introduce the basics of the management task through discussions of the role and definition of management, the management process as it pertains to management functions and organizational goal attainment, and the need to manage organizational resources effectively and efficiently.

Our society could neither exist as we know it today nor improve without a steady stream of managers to guide its organizations. Peter Drucker emphasized this point when he stated that effective management is probably the main resource of developed countries and the most needed resource of developing ones.[7] In short, all societies desperately need good managers.

Management is important to society as a whole as well as vital to many individuals who earn their livings as managers. Government statistics show that management positions have increased from approximately 10 percent to 18 percent of all jobs since 1950. Managers come from varying backgrounds and have diverse educational specialties. Many people who originally trained to be accountants, teachers, financiers, or even writers eventually make their livelihoods as managers. Although in the short term, the demand for managers varies somewhat, in the long term, managerial positions can yield high salaries, status, interesting work, personal growth, and intense feelings of accomplishment.

Over the years, *Forbes* magazine has become well known for its periodic rankings of total compensation paid to top managers in the United States. Based on the 2009 *Forbes* compensation study, Table 1.1 shows the names of the 10 most highly paid chief executives, the company they worked for, and how much they earned. In the study, total compensation includes factors such as salary, bonuses, and stock options.

An inspection of the list of highest paid executives in Table 1.1 reveals that the executives are all men. Based on the results of a recent survey at the *Wall Street Journal*, Figure 1.2 illustrates a broad salary gap between men and women. According to Figure 1.2, while women and men make up roughly the same proportion of the workforce, men hold a disproportionate number of higher paying jobs. In addition, a recent study by the American Association of University Women indicated that the discrepancy between the pay of men versus women is a national phenomenon and is not isolated to a particular state or region.[8]

TABLE 1.1 The 10 Highest Compensated CEOs, 2009

Ranking	CEO Name	Company Name	Paid ($ millions)
1	Lawrence J. Ellison	Oracle	$556.98
2	Ray R. Irani	Occidental Petroleum	222.64
3	John B. Hess	Hess	154.58
4	Michael D. Watford	Ultra Petroleum	116.93
5	Michael G. Papa	EOG Resources	90.47
6	William R. Berkley	Berkley	87.48
7	Matthew K. Rose	Burlington Santa Fe	68.62
8	Paul J. Evanson	Allegheny Energy	67.26
9	Hugh Grant	Monsanto	64.60
10	Robert W. Lane	Deere & Co.	61.30

Source: "CEO Compensation," *Forbes*, April 22, 2009, http://www.forbes.com.

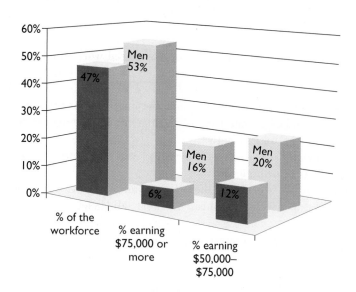

FIGURE 1.2

The salary gap between genders

Did Home Depot
Overpay Its CEO?

Predictably, concerns that certain managers are paid *too* much have been raised. For example, consider the notable criticism in recent years regarding the high salary paid to Robert R. Nardelli, former CEO of Home Depot.[9] Disapproval of the excessive compensation paid to Nardelli surfaced in the popular press as well as in statements by stockholders. An article in the *Wall Street Journal*, for example, questioned whether Nardelli was worth the amount he received.[10] Nardelli had been paid $63.5 million during a five-year period at Home Depot, while company shares lost 6 percent of their value. In the end, as with any manager, Nardelli's compensation should be determined by how much value he adds to the company. The more value he adds, the more compensation he deserves. As a result of the growing criticism about Nardelli's compensation and Nardelli's resistance to modify his compensation level, he was fired. ■

Some evidence suggests that societal concern about management compensation goes well beyond one manager at one company.[11] A recent Senate Commerce Committee meeting, for example, focused on justifying lavish pay programs for managers at companies such as Tyco International and American Airlines, whose companies were in financial trouble and laying off employees. Senators seemed unified in questioning the logic that justifies the average chief executive officer salary being more than 400 times higher than a production worker's wages. This Senate Committee meeting should be an important signal that managers who do not exercise judicious self-control about their salaries may face future legislative control.

The Role of Management

Essentially, the role of managers is to guide organizations toward goal accomplishment. All organizations exist for certain purposes or goals, and managers are responsible for combining and using organizational resources to ensure that their organizations achieve their purposes. Management moves an organization toward its purposes or goals by assigning activities organization members perform. If the activities are designed effectively, the production of each individual worker will contribute to the attainment of organizational goals. Management strives to encourage individual activity that will lead to reaching organizational goals and to discourage individual activity that will hinder the accomplishment of those goals. Because the process of management emphasizes the achievement of goals, managers must keep organizational goals in mind at all times.[12]

Defining Management

Students of management should be aware that the term *management* can be, and often is, used in different ways. For instance, it can refer simply to the process that managers follow in order to accomplish organizational goals. It can also refer to a body of knowledge; in this context, management is a cumulative body of information that furnishes insights on how to manage. The term *management* can also refer to the individuals who guide and direct organizations or to a career devoted to the task of guiding and directing organizations. An understanding of the various uses and related definitions of the term will help you avoid miscommunication during management-related discussions.

As used most commonly in this text, **management** is the process of reaching organizational goals by working with and through people and other organizational resources. A comparison of this definition with the definitions offered by several contemporary management thinkers indicates broad agreement that management encompasses the following three main characteristics:

1. It is a process or series of continuing and related activities.
2. It involves and concentrates on reaching organizational goals.
3. It reaches these goals by working with and through people and other organizational resources.

A discussion of each of these characteristics follows.

The Management Process: Management Functions

The four basic **management functions**—activities that make up the management process—are described in the following sections.

Planning Planning involves choosing tasks that must be performed to attain organizational goals, outlining how the tasks must be performed, and indicating when they should be performed. Planning activity focuses on attaining goals. Through their plans, managers outline exactly what organizations must do to be successful. Planning is essential to getting the "right" things done.[13] Planning is concerned with organizational success in the near future (short term) as well as in the more distant future (long term).[14]

Organizing Organizing can be thought of as assigning the tasks developed under the planning function to various individuals or groups within the organization. Organizing, then, creates a mechanism to put plans into action. People within the organization are given work assignments that contribute to the company's goals. Tasks are organized so that the output of individuals contributes to the success of departments, which, in turn, contributes to the success of divisions, which ultimately contributes to the success of the organization. Organizing includes determining tasks and groupings of work.[15] Organizing should not be rigid, but adaptable and flexible to meet challenges as circumstances change.[16]

Influencing Influencing is another of the basic functions within the management process. This function—also commonly referred to as *motivating, leading, directing,* or *actuating*—is concerned primarily with people within organizations.* Influencing can be defined as guiding the activities of organization members in appropriate directions. An appropriate direction is any direction that helps the organization move toward goal attainment. The ultimate purpose of influencing is to increase productivity. Human-oriented work situations usually generate higher levels of production over the long term than do task-oriented work situations, because people find the latter type less satisfying.

---

*In early management literature, the term *motivating* was commonly used to signify this people-oriented management function. The term *influencing* is used consistently throughout this text because it is broader and permits more flexibility in discussing people-oriented issues. Later in the text, motivating is discussed as a major part of influencing.

FIGURE 1.3
Classic mistakes commonly made by managers in carrying out various management functions

Planning
Not establishing objectives for all important organizational areas
Making plans that are too risky
Not exploring enough viable alternatives for reaching objectives

Organizing
Not establishing departments appropriately
Not emphasizing coordination of organization members
Establishing inappropriate spans of management

Influencing
Not taking the time to communicate properly with organization members
Establishing improper communication networks
Being a manager but not a leader

Controlling
Not monitoring progress in carrying out plans
Not establishing appropriate performance standards
Not measuring performance to see where improvements might be made

Controlling Controlling is the management function through which managers:

1. Gather information that measures recent performance within the organization.
2. Compare present performance to preestablished performance standards.
3. From this comparison, determine whether the organization should be modified to meet preestablished standards.

Controlling is an ongoing process. Managers continually gather information, make their comparisons, and then try to find new ways of improving production through organizational modification.

History shows that managers commonly make mistakes when planning, organizing, influencing, and controlling. Figure 1.3 shows a number of such mistakes managers make related to each function. Studying this text carefully should help managers avoid making such mistakes.

Management Process and Goal Attainment

Although we have discussed the four functions of management individually, planning, organizing, influencing, and controlling are integrally related and therefore cannot be separated in practice. Figure 1.4 illustrates this interrelationship and also indicates that managers use these activities solely for reaching organizational goals. Basically, these functions are interrelated because the performance

FIGURE 1.4
Relationships among the four functions of management used to attain organizational goals

of one depends on the performance of the others. For example, organizing is based on well-thought-out plans developed during the planning process, and influencing systems must be tailored to reflect both these plans and the organizational design used to implement them. The fourth function, controlling, involves possible modifications to existing plans, organizational structure, or the motivation system used to develop a more successful effort.

To be effective, a manager must understand how the four management functions are practiced, not simply how they are defined and related. Thomas J. Peters and Robert H. Waterman, Jr., studied numerous organizations—including Frito-Lay and Maytag—for several years to determine what management characteristics best describe excellently run companies. In their book, *In Search of Excellence,* Peters and Waterman suggest that planning, organizing, influencing, and controlling should be characterized by a bias for action; a closeness to the customer; autonomy and entrepreneurship; productivity through people; a hands-on, value-driven orientation; "sticking to the knitting"; a simple organizational form with a lean staff; and simultaneous loose–tight properties.

This brief introduction to the four management functions will be further developed in Parts 3 through 6 of this text.

Management and Organizational Resources

Management must always be aware of the status and use of **organizational resources**. These resources, composed of all assets available for activation during the production process, are of four basic types:

1. Human
2. Monetary
3. Raw materials
4. Capital

As Figure 1.5 shows, organizational resources are combined, used, and transformed into finished products during the production process.

Human resources are the people who work for an organization. The skills they possess and their knowledge of the work system are invaluable to managers. Monetary resources are amounts of money that managers use to purchase goods and services for the organization. Raw materials are ingredients used directly in the manufacturing of products. For example, rubber is a raw material that Goodyear would purchase with its monetary resources and use directly in manufacturing tires. Capital resources are machines used during the manufacturing process. Modern machines, or equipment, can be a major factor in maintaining desired production levels. Worn-out or antiquated machinery can make it impossible for an organization to keep pace with competitors.

Managerial Effectiveness
As managers use their resources, they must strive to be both effective and efficient. **Managerial effectiveness** refers to management's use of organizational resources in meeting organizational goals. If organizations are using their resources to attain their goals, the managers are said to be effective. In reality, however, managerial effectiveness can be measured by degrees. The closer an organization comes to achieving its goals, the more effective its managers are considered to be. Managerial effectiveness, then, exists on a continuum ranging from *ineffective* to *effective.*

FIGURE 1.5
Transformation of organizational resources into finished products through the production process

Managerial Efficiency **Managerial efficiency** is the proportion of total organizational resources that contribute to productivity during the manufacturing process.[17] The higher this proportion, the more efficient is the manager. The more resources wasted or unused during the production process, the more inefficient is the manager. In this situation, *organizational resources* refer not only to raw materials that are used in manufacturing goods or services but also to related human effort.[18] Like management effectiveness, management efficiency is best described as being on a continuum ranging from inefficient to efficient. *Inefficient* means that a small proportion of total resources contributes to productivity during the manufacturing process; *efficient* means that a large proportion of resources contributes to productivity.

As Figure 1.6 shows, the concepts of managerial effectiveness and efficiency are obviously related. A manager could be relatively ineffective—with the consequence that the organization is making little progress toward goal attainment—primarily because of major inefficiencies or poor utilization of resources during the production process. In contrast, a manager could be somewhat effective despite being inefficient if demand for the finished goods is so high that the manager can get an extremely high price per unit sold and thus absorb inefficiency costs. Thus a manager can be effective without being efficient, and vice versa. To maximize organizational success, however, both effectiveness and efficiency are essential.

how managers do it

Achieving Effectiveness at Telstra Corporation

As an example of achieving efficiency and effectiveness, consider Telstra Corporation, Australia's largest telecommunication company. Like its counterparts the world over, Telstra faces the challenges of a changing industry where mobile phones are fast becoming more popular than the landline business on which it built its fortunes. To survive, Telstra is scrambling to create a nimble management team and prune the bureaucracy that slows down decision making and internal operations. In a recent reorganization of his executive team, Telstra CEO David Thodey created four groups—customer sales and support, product and marketing innovation, operations, and corporate support—all focused on effectiveness, getting more competitive while also attracting and retaining customers.[19] ■

FIGURE 1.6
Various combinations of managerial effectiveness and managerial efficiency

THE UNIVERSALITY OF MANAGEMENT

Management principles are universal: That is, they apply to all types of organizations (businesses, churches, sororities, athletic teams, hospitals, etc.) and organizational levels.[20] Naturally, managers' jobs vary somewhat from one type of organization to another because each organizational type requires the use of specialized knowledge, exists in a unique working and political environment, and uses different technology. However, job similarities are found across organizations because the basic management activities—planning, organizing, influencing, and controlling—are common to all organizations.

The Theory of Characteristics

Henri Fayol, one of the earliest management writers, stated that all managers should possess certain characteristics, such as positive physical and mental qualities and special knowledge related to the specific operation.[21] B. C. Forbes emphasized the importance of certain more personal qualities, inferring that enthusiasm, earnestness of purpose, confidence, and faith in their own worthiness are primary characteristics of successful managers. Forbes described Henry Ford as follows:

> At the base and birth of every great business organization was an enthusiast, a man consumed with earnestness of purpose, with confidence in his powers, with faith in the worthwhileness of his endeavors. The original Henry Ford was the quintessence of enthusiasm. In the days of his difficulties, disappointments, and discouragements, when he was wrestling with his balky motor engine—and wrestling likewise with poverty—only his inexhaustible enthusiasm saved him from defeat.[22]

Fayol and Forbes can describe desirable characteristics of successful managers only because of the universality concept: The basic ingredients of successful management are applicable to all organizations.

MANAGEMENT SKILL: THE KEY TO MANAGEMENT SUCCESS

Thus far, the introduction to the study of management has focused on discussing concepts such as the importance of management, the task of management, and the universality of management. This section continues the introduction to management by defining management skill and presenting both classic and more contemporary views of management skills thought to ensure management success.

Defining Management Skill

No introduction to the field of management would be complete without a discussion of management skill. **Management skill** is the ability to carry out the process of reaching organizational goals by working with and through people and other organizational resources. Learning about management skill and focusing on developing it are of critical importance because possessing such skill is generally considered the prerequisite for management success.[23] Because management skills are so critical to the success of an organization, companies commonly focus on possible steps that can be taken to improve the skills of their managers.

Management Skill: A Classic View

Robert L. Katz has written perhaps the most widely accepted early article about management skill.[24] Katz states that managers' ability to perform is a result of their managerial skills. A manager with the necessary management skills will probably perform well and be relatively successful. One without the necessary skills will probably perform poorly and be relatively unsuccessful.

As an example illustrating how companies need to develop their managers' skills, consider the importance of preparing managers for working with people of other cultures. An increasingly global business world requires that managers who travel be aware of and grasp cultural differences in their dealings with coworkers, clients, and the public. Professionals at New York-based Dean Foster Associates, an intercultural consulting firm, provide cross-cultural training that helps businesspeople prepare for work overseas. For example, for a client heading to Japan, Foster conducted a five-hour session that included a traditional Japanese meal, coaching on Japanese dining etiquette, and information on business customs, socializing, and developing the proper mind set for working outside one's native country.[25] ■

Technical skills are among the types of skills necessary for successful management.

Katz indicates that three types of skills are important for successful management performance: technical, human, and conceptual skills.

- **Technical skills** involve the ability to apply specialized knowledge and expertise to work-related techniques and procedures. Examples of these skills are engineering, computer programming, and accounting. Technical skills are mostly related to working with "things"—processes or physical objects.

- **Human skills** build cooperation within the team being led. They involve working with attitudes and communication, individual and group interests—in short, working with people.

- **Conceptual skills** involve the ability to see the organization as a whole. A manager with conceptual skills is able to understand how various functions of the organization complement one another, how the organization relates to its environment, and how changes in one part of the organization affect the rest of the organization.

As one moves from lower-level management to upper-level management, conceptual skills become more important and technical skills less important (see Figure 1.7). The supportive rationale is that as managers advance in an organization, they become less involved with the actual production activity or technical areas, and more involved with guiding the organization as a whole. Human skills, however, are extremely important to managers at top, middle, and lower (or supervisory) levels.[26] The common denominator of all management levels, after all, is people.

Management Skill: A Contemporary View

More current thought regarding management skills is essentially an expansion of the classic view list of skills managers need to be successful. This expansion is achieved logically through two steps:

1. Defining the major activities that managers typically perform
2. Listing the skills needed to carry out these activities successfully

FIGURE 1.7
As a manager moves from the supervisory to the top-management level, conceptual skills become more important than technical skills, but human skills remain equally important

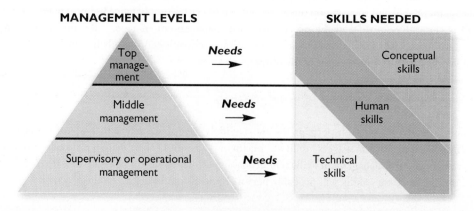

The major activities that modern managers typically perform are of three basic types.[27]

1. **Task-related activities** are management efforts aimed at carrying out critical management-related duties in organizations. Such activities include short-term planning, clarifying objectives of jobs in organizations, and monitoring operations and performance.

2. **People-related activities** are management efforts aimed at managing people in organizations. Such activities include providing support and encouragement to others, providing recognition for achievements and contributions, developing skill and confidence of organization members, consulting when making decisions, and empowering others to solve problems.

3. **Change-related activities** are management efforts aimed at modifying organizational components. Such activities include monitoring the organization's external environment, proposing new strategies and vision, encouraging innovative thinking, and taking risks to promote needed change.

Important management skills deemed necessary to successfully carry out these management activities appear in Figure 1.8. This figure pinpoints 12 such skills, ranging from empowering organization members to envisioning how to change an organization. Remember that Figure 1.8 is not intended as a list of *all* skills managers need to be successful, but as an important list containing many of the necessary skills. One might argue, for example, that skills such as building efficient operations or increasing cooperation among organization members are critical management skills and should have prominence in Figure 1.8.

Management Skill: A Focus of This Book

The preceding sections discussed both classic and contemporary views of management skills in modern organizations. A number of critical management skills were presented and related to top, middle, and supervisory management positions.

One common criticism of such management skill discussions is that although understanding such rationales about skills is important, skills categories—such as technical skill, human skill, and conceptual skill—are often too broad to be practical. Many management scholars believe that these broad skills categories contain several more narrowly focused skills that represent the more practical and essential abilities for successfully practicing management.[28] These more narrowly focused skills should not be seen as valuable in themselves, but as "specialized tools" that help managers meet important challenges and successfully carry out the management functions of planning, organizing, influencing, and controlling. Table 1.2 summarizes the management functions and challenges covered in this book and corresponding management skills that help address them.

Because management skill is generally a prerequisite for management success, aspiring managers should strive to develop such skill. In developing such skill, however, managers should keep

FIGURE 1.8
Skills for increasing the probability of management success

To increase the probability of being successful, managers should have competence in . . .

. . . Clarifying roles: assigning tasks and explaining job responsibilities, task objectives, and performance expectations

. . . Monitoring operations: checking on the progress and quality of the work, and evaluating individual and unit performance

. . . Short-term planning: determining how to use personnel and resources to accomplish a task efficiently, and determining how to schedule and coordinate unit activities efficiently

. . . Consulting: checking with people before making decisions that affect them, encouraging participation in decision making, and using the ideas and suggestions of others

. . . Supporting: acting considerate, showing sympathy and support when someone is upset or anxious, and providing encouragement and support when there is a difficult, stressful task

. . . Recognizing: providing praise and recognition for effective performance, significant achievements, special contributions, and performance improvements

. . . Developing: providing coaching and advice, providing opportunities for skill development, and helping people learn how to improve their skills

TABLE 1.2   Management Functions and Challenges Covered in This Text and Corresponding Management Skills Emphasized to Help Address Them

Introduction to Modern Management

Chapter 1—Management Skill: The ability to work with people and other organizational resources to accomplish organizational goals.

Chapter 2—Comprehensive Management Skill: The ability to collectively apply concepts from various major management approaches to perform a manager's job.

Modern Management Challenges

Chapter 3—Corporate Social Responsibility Skill: The ability to take action that protects and improves both the welfare of society and the interests of the organization.

Chapter 4—Diversity Skill: The ability to establish and maintain an organizational workforce that represents a combination of assorted human characteristics appropriate for achieving organization success.

Chapter 5—Global Management Skill: The ability to manage global factors as components of organizational operations.

Chapter 6—Entrepreneurship Skill: The identification, evaluation, and exploitation of opportunities.

Planning

Chapter 7—Planning Skill: The ability to take action to determine the objectives of the organization as well as what is necessary to accomplish these objectives.

Chapter 8—Decision-Making Skill: The ability to choose alternatives that increase the likelihood of accomplishing objectives.

Chapter 9—Strategic Planning Skill: The ability to engage in long-range planning that focuses on the organization as a whole.

Chapter 10—Planning Tools Skill: The ability to employ the qualitative and quantitative techniques necessary to help develop plans.

Organizing

Chapter 11—Organizing Skill: The ability to establish orderly uses for resources within the management system.

Chapter 12—Responsibility and Delegation Skill: The ability to understand one's obligation to perform assigned activities and to enlist the help of others to complete those activities.

Chapter 13—Human Resource Management Skill: The ability to take actions that increase the contributions of individuals within the organization.

Chapter 14—Organizational Change Skill: The ability to modify an organization in order to enhance its contribution to reaching company goals.

Influencing

Chapter 15—Communication Skill: The ability to share information with other individuals.

Chapter 16—Leadership Skill: The ability to direct the behavior of others toward the accomplishment of objectives.

Chapter 17—Motivation Skill: The ability to create organizational situations in which individuals performing organizational activities are simultaneously satisfying personal needs and helping the organization attain its goals.

Chapter 18—Team Skill: The ability to manage a collection of people so that they influence one another toward the accomplishment of an organizational objective(s).

Chapter 19—Organization Culture Skill: The ability to establish a set of shared values among organization members regarding the functioning and existence of their organization to enhance the probability of organizational success.

Chapter 20—Creativity and Innovation Skill: The ability to generate original ideas or new perspectives on existing ideas and to take steps to implement these new ideas.

Controlling

Chapter 21—Controlling Skill: The ability to use information and technology to ensure that an event occurs as it was planned to occur.

Chapter 22—Production Skill: The ability to transform organizational resources into products.

class discussion highlight

MODERN RESEARCH AND MANAGEMENT SKILL

Skills Needed to Manage in Vietnam

A study by Neupert, Baughn, and Dao investigated the skills necessary to be a successful manager in Vietnam. The researchers focused on the opinions of practicing managers in Vietnam in generating their list of skills for managerial success.

To gather their information, the researchers used the critical incident method. This method asked managers in an interview format to tell the story of their *worst nightmare* or *biggest challenge* in their management positions. The researchers also asked managers their opinion about what skills were necessary to be a successful manager in Vietnam. Through this critical incident process, a commonly used research technique, the researchers hoped to identify skills necessary to be a successful manager in Vietnam.

The researchers interviewed 50 local Vietnamese managers and 24 managers from other countries. Interviews lasted between 45 and 90 minutes and were conducted in English or Vietnamese, depending on manager preference. The managers interviewed were from a number of firms in various industries from two major Vietnamese business centers: Hanoi and Ho Chi Minh City.

Do you think that the local Vietnamese and foreign managers suggested the same skills for managerial success in Vietnam? Why? If not, how do you think the suggested skills differed? Why?

Source: Kent E. Neupert, C. Christopher Baughn, and Thi Thanh Lam Dao, "International Management Skills for Success in Asia: A Needs-Based Determination of Skills for Foreign Managers and Local Managers," Journal of European Industrial Training 29, nos. 2/3 (2005): 165–180.

in mind that the value of individual management skills will tend to vary from manager to manager, depending on the specific organizational situations faced. For example, managers facing serious manufacturing challenges might find the skill to encourage innovative thinking aimed at meeting these challenges is their most important skill. On the other hand, managers facing a disinterested workforce might find the skill of recognizing and rewarding positive performance is their most valuable skill. Overall, managers should spend time defining the most formidable tasks they face and sharpening skills that will help to successfully carry out these tasks.

MANAGEMENT CAREERS

Thus far, this chapter has focused on outlining the importance of management to society, presenting a definition of management and the management process, and explaining the universality of management. Individuals commonly study such topics because they are interested in pursuing a management career. This section presents information that will help you preview your own management career. It also describes some of the issues you may face in attempting to manage the careers of others within an organization. The specific focus is on career definition, career and life stages and performance, and career promotion.

A Definition of Career

A **career** is a sequence of work-related positions occupied by a person over the course of a lifetime.[29] As the definition implies, a career is cumulative in nature: As people accumulate successful experiences in one position, they generally develop abilities and attitudes that qualify them to hold more advanced positions. In general, management positions at one level tend to be stepping-stones to management positions at the next higher level. In building a career, an individual should be focused on developing skills necessary to qualify for the next planned job and not simply taking a job with the highest salary.[30]

Career Stages, Life Stages, and Performance

Careers are generally viewed as evolving through a series of stages.[31] These evolutionary stages—exploration, establishment, maintenance, and decline—are shown in Figure 1.9, which highlights the performance levels and age ranges commonly associated with each stage. Note that the levels and ranges in the figure indicate what has been more traditional at each stage, not what is inevitable. According to the Census Bureau, the proportion of men in the U.S. population age 65 and older who participated in the labor force in 2008 reached 17.8 percent. This participation rate was the highest since 1985. The proportion for women in this age group was 9.1 percent, the highest since 1975.[32] As more workers beyond age 65 exist in the workforce, more careers will be maintained beyond the traditional benchmark of age 65, as depicted in Figure 1.9.

Exploration Stage   The first stage in career evolution is the **exploration stage**, which occurs at the beginning of a career and is characterized by self-analysis and the exploration of different types of available jobs. Individuals at this stage are generally about 15 to 25 years old and are involved in some type of formal training, such as college or vocational education. They often pursue part-time employment to gain a richer understanding of what a career in a particular organization or industry might be like. Typical jobs held during this stage include cooking at Burger King, stocking at a Federated Department Store, and working as an office assistant at a Nationwide Insurance office.

Establishment Stage   The second stage in career evolution is the **establishment stage**, during which individuals about 25 to 45 years old start to become more productive, or higher performers (as Figure 1.9 indicates by the upturn in the dotted line and its continuance as a solid line). Employment sought during this stage is guided by what was learned during the exploration stage. In addition, the jobs sought are usually full-time jobs. Individuals at this stage commonly move to different jobs within the same company, to different companies, or even to different industries.

Maintenance Stage   The third stage in career evolution is the **maintenance stage**. In this stage, individuals who are 45 to 65 years old show either increased performance (career growth), stabilized performance (career maintenance), or decreased performance (career stagnation).

FIGURE 1.9
The relationships among career stages, life stages, and performance

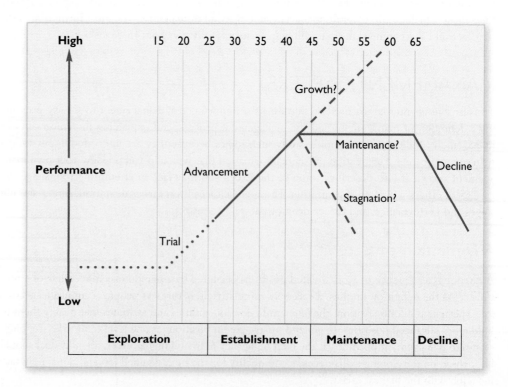

From the organization's viewpoint, it is better for managers to experience career growth than maintenance or stagnation. For this reason, some companies such as IBM, Monsanto, and Brooklyn Union Gas have attempted to eliminate **career plateauing**—defined as a period of little or no apparent progress in a career.[33]

Decline Stage The last stage in career evolution is the **decline stage**, which involves people about 65 years old whose productivity is declining. These individuals are either close to retirement, semi-retired, or fully retired. People in the decline stage may find it difficult to maintain prior performance levels, perhaps because they have lost interest in their careers or have failed to keep their job skills up-to-date.

As Americans live longer and stay healthier into late middle age, many of them choose to become part-time workers in businesses such as Publix supermarkets and McDonald's or in volunteer groups such as the March of Dimes and the American Heart Association. Some retired executives put their career experience to good social use by working with the government-sponsored organization Service Corps of Retired Executives (SCORE) to offer management advice and consultation to small businesses trying to gain a foothold in their market.

Promoting Your Own Career

Both practicing managers and management scholars agree that careful formulation and implementation of appropriate tactics can enhance the success of a management career.[34] Planning your career path—the sequence of jobs that you will fill in the course of your working life—is the first step to take in promoting your career. For some people, a career path entails ascending the hierarchy of a particular organization. Others plan a career path within a particular profession or series of professions. Everyone, however, needs to recognize that career planning is an ongoing process, beginning with the career's early phases and continuing throughout the career.

In promoting your own career, you must be proactive and see yourself as a business that you are responsible for developing. You should not view your plan as limiting your options. First consider both your strengths and your liabilities and assess what you need from a career. Then explore all the avenues of opportunity open to you, both inside and outside the organization. Set your career goals, continually revise and update these goals as your career progresses, and take the steps necessary to accomplish these goals.

Another important tactic in promoting your own career is to work for managers who carry out realistic and constructive roles in the career development of their employees.[35] Table 1.3 outlines what career development responsibility, information, planning, and follow-through generally include. It also outlines the complementary career development role for a professional employee.

Promoting your own career may require you to continually demonstrate your skills and abilities. These production managers in California are teleconferencing with project managers in India, although the time difference requires them to convene at 7:30 in the evening local time.

TABLE 1.3	Manager and Employee Roles in Enhancing Employee Career Development	
Dimension	**Professional Employee**	**Manager**
Responsibility	Assumes responsibility for individual career development	Assumes responsibility for employee development

Information	Obtains career information through self-evaluation and data collection:
	    What do I enjoy doing?
	    Where do I want to go?
		Provides information by holding up a mirror of reality:
		    How manager views the employee
		    How others view the employee
		    How "things work around here"

Planning	Develops an individual plan to reach objectives	Helps employee assess plan
Follow-through	Invites management support through high performance on the current job by understanding the scope of the job and taking appropriate initiative	Provides coaching and relevant information on opportunities

To enhance your career success, you must learn to be *proactive* rather than *reactive*.[36] That is, you must take specific actions to demonstrate your abilities and accomplishments. You must also have a clear idea of the next several positions you should seek, the skills you need to acquire to function appropriately in those positions, and plans for acquiring those skills. Finally, you need to think about the ultimate position you want and the sequence of positions you must hold in order to gain the skills and attitudes necessary to qualify for that position.

Special Career Issues

In the business world of today, countless special issues significantly affect how careers actually develop. Two issues that have had a significant impact on career development in recent years are:

1. Women managers
2. Dual-career couples

The following sections discuss each of these factors.

Women Managers Women in their roles as managers must meet the same challenges in their work environments as men. However, because they have more recently joined the ranks of management in large numbers, women often lack the social contacts that are so important in the development of a management career. Another problem for women is that, traditionally, they have been expected to manage families and households while simultaneously handling the pressures and competition of paid employment. Finally, women are more likely than men to encounter sexual harassment in the workplace.

Interestingly, some management theorists believe that women may have an enormous advantage over men in future management situations.[37]

They predict that networks of relationships will replace rigid organizational structures and star workers will be replaced by teams made up of workers at all levels who are empowered to make decisions. Detailed rules and procedures will be replaced by a flexible system that calls for judgments based on key values and a constant search for new ways to get the job done. Strengths often attributed to women—emphasizing interrelationships, listening, and motivating others—will be the dominant virtues in the corporation of the future.

Despite this optimism, however, some reports indicate that the proportion of men to women in management ranks seems to have changed little in the last 10 years.[38] This stabilized proportion can probably be explained by a number of factors. For example, perhaps women are not opting to move into management positions at a greater pace than men because of trade-offs they have to make, such as not having or delaying the birth of a baby. In addition, women often indicate that

TABLE 1.4	Seven Steps Management Can Take to Encourage the Advancement of Women in Organizations

1. *Make sure that women know the top three strategic goals for the company.* Knowing these goals will help women focus their efforts on important issues. As a result, they'll be better able to make a meaningful contribution to goal attainment and become more likely candidates for promotion.

2. *Make sure that women professionals in the organization have a worthwhile understanding of career planning.* Having a vision for their careers and a career planning tool at their disposal will likely enhance the advancement of women in an organization.

3. *Teach women how to better manage their time.* The most effective managers are obsessed with using their time in the most valuable way possible. Helping women know where their time is being invested and how to make a better investment should better ready them for promotion.

4. *Assign outstanding mentors to women within the organization.* Women continually indicate that mentors are important in readying themselves for promotion. Assigning outstanding leaders in an organization to women organization members should accelerate the process of readying women for management positions.

5. *Have career discussions with women who have potential as managers.* Career discussions involving both managers and women with the potential to be managers should be held regularly. Helping women to continually focus on their careers and their potential for upward mobility should help them to keep progressing toward management positions.

6. *Provide opportunities for women organization members to make contributions to the community.* In today's environment, managers must be aware of and contribute to the community in which the organization exists. Experience within the community should help ready women for management positions.

7. *Encourage women to take the initiative in obtaining management positions.* Women must be proactive in building the skills necessary to become a manager or be promoted to the next level of management. They should set career goals, outline a plan to achieve those goals, and then move forward with their plan.

it's more difficult for them to move into management positions than men because of the lack of female mentors and role models in the corporate world. Table 1.4 lists seven steps that management can take to help women advance in an organization.[39]

Dual-Career Couples With an increasing number of dual-career couples, organizations who want to attract and retain the best performers have found it necessary to consider how dual-career couples affect the workforce. Those in dual-career relationships even have a Facebook community devoted to their concerns.[40] The traditional scenario in which a woman takes a supporting role in the development of her spouse's career is being replaced by one of equal work and shared responsibilities for spouses. This arrangement requires a certain amount of flexibility on the part of the couple as well as the organizations for which they work. Today such burning issues as whose career takes precedence if a spouse is offered a transfer to another city and who takes the ultimate responsibility for family concerns point to the fact that dual-career relationships involve trade-offs and that it is difficult to "have it all."

How Dual-Career Couples Cope Studies of dual-career couples reveal that many cope with their career difficulties in one of the following ways.[41] The couple might develop a commitment to both spouses' careers so that when a decision is made, the right of each spouse to pursue a career is taken into consideration. Both husband and wife are flexible about handling home- and job-oriented issues. They work out coping mechanisms, such as negotiating child care or scheduling shared activities in advance, to better manage their work and their family responsibilities. Often, dual-career couples find that they must limit their social lives and their volunteer responsibilities in order to slow their lives to a manageable pace. Finally, many couples find that they must take steps to consciously facilitate their mutual career advancement. An organization that wants to retain an employee may find that it needs to assist that employee's spouse in his or her career development as well.

CHALLENGE CASE SUMMARY

The information just presented furnishes you, as the chief executive of Universal Orlando, with insights concerning the significance of your role as manager. That role is important not only to society as a whole but to you as an individual. As a manager, you contribute to creating the standard of living that we all enjoy, and you earn corresponding rewards. Universal Orlando is making societal contributions aimed at providing essentials such as food and clothing to people throughout the world. As its chief executive, you would be helping Universal Orlando in this endeavor. If you exert significant impact, the company's contribution to society, and your personal returns, will be heightened considerably.

The chapter emphasizes what management is and what managers do. According to this information, as chief executive at Universal Orlando, you must have a clear understanding of the company's objectives, and you must guide its operations in a way that helps the company reach those objectives. This guidance will involve you working directly with sales managers, other upper managers such as the vice president of human resources, and theme park personnel.

You must be sure that planning, organizing, influencing, and controlling are being carried out appropriately. You must be sure that jobs are designed to reach objectives, that jobs are assigned to appropriate workers, that workers are encouraged to perform their jobs well, and that you make any changes necessary to ensure the achievement of company objectives. As you perform these four functions, remember that the activities themselves are interrelated and must blend together appropriately. Your wise use of Universal's organizational resources is critical. Strive to make sure Universal managers are both effective and efficient, reaching company objectives without wasting company resources.

As is the case with managers of any company, the managers at Universal are at various stages of career development. As an example of how those stages might relate to managers at Universal, let us focus on one particular manager, Marsha Platt. Assume that Marsha Platt is a manager overseeing park visitor relations. She is 45 years old and is considered a member of middle management.

Platt began her career (exploration stage) in college by considering various areas of study and by working at a number of different types of part-time positions. She took phone orders for Domino's Pizza and worked for Menard's, a home-improvement retailer, as a cashier. She began college at age 18 and graduated at age 22.

Platt then moved into the establishment stage of her career. For a few years immediately after graduation, she held full-time trial positions in the retail industry as well as in the delivery industry. What she learned during the career exploration stage helped her choose the types of full-time trial positions to pursue.

At the age of 26, she accepted a trial position as an assistant park visitor relations manager at Universal Studios in Orlando, Florida. Through this position she discovered that she wanted to remain in the theme park industry and, more specifically, with Universal Orlando. From age 27 to age 45, she held a number of supervisory and management positions at Universal.

Now Platt is moving into an extremely critical part of her career, the maintenance stage. She could probably remain in her present position and maintain her productivity for several more years. However, she wants to advance her career. Therefore, she must emphasize a proactive attitude by formulating and implementing tactics aimed at enhancing her career success, such as seeking training to develop critical skills, or moving to a position that is a prerequisite for other, more advanced positions at Universal Studios.

In the future, as Platt approaches the decline stage of her career, it is probable that her productivity will decrease somewhat. From a career viewpoint, she may want to go from full-time employment to semiretirement. Perhaps she could work for Universal Orlando or another theme park business such as Disney World on a part-time advisory basis or even pursue part-time work in another industry. For example, she might be able to teach a management course at a nearby community college.

Focusing on developing management skills throughout a career would help any manager, including Marsha Platt, to ensure management success. Such skills include the ability to clarify organizational roles, encourage innovative thinking, and recognize worthwhile performance of organization members. Overall, such skills would help Platt to carry out task-, people-, and change-related activities.

MANAGEMENT SKILL ACTIVITIES

This section is specially designed to help you develop management skills. An individual's management skill is based on an understanding of management concepts and the ability to apply those concepts in various organizational situations. The following activities are designed to both heighten your understanding of management concepts and to develop the ability to apply those concepts in a variety of organizational situations.

UNDERSTANDING MANAGEMENT CONCEPTS

 To check your understanding and to practice using the concepts in this chapter, go to www.mymanagementlab.com and explore the material associated with Chapter 1.

Know Key Terms

Understanding the following key terms is critical to your understanding of chapter material. Define each of these terms. Refer to the page(s) referenced after a term to check your definition or to gain further insight regarding the term.

management **7**
management functions **7**
organizational resources **9**
managerial effectiveness **9**
managerial efficiency **10**
management skill **11**

technical skills **12**
human skills **12**
conceptual skills **12**
task-related activities **13**
people-related activities **13**
change-related activities **13**

career **15**
exploration stage **16**
establishment stage **16**
maintenance stage **16**
career plateauing **17**
decline stage **17**

Know How Management Concepts Relate

This section is comprised of activities that will further sharpen your understanding of management concepts. Answer essay questions as completely as possible. Also, remember that many additional true/false and multiple choice questions appear online at MyManagementLab.com to help you further refine your understanding of management concepts.

1. Explain the relationships among the four functions of management.
2. How can *controlling* help a manager to become more efficient?

3. What is the value in having managers at the career exploration stage within an organization? Why? The decline stage? Why?
4. Discuss your personal philosophy for promoting the careers of women managers within an organization. Why do you hold this philosophy? Explain any challenges that you foresee in implementing this philosophy within a modern organization. How will you overcome these challenges?
5. List and define five skills that you think you'll need as CEO of a company. Why will these skills be important to possess?

DEVELOPING MANAGEMENT SKILLS

Learning activities in this section are aimed at helping you develop management skill. Learning activities include Exploring Your Management Skill: Parts 1 & 2, Your Management Skill Portfolio Exercise, an Experiential Exercise, Cases, and a VideoNet Exercise.

Exploring Your Management Skill: Part 1

Before studying this chapter, respond to the following questions regarding the type of advice you would give to Universal Studios' chairperson, Tom Williams. Then address the management challenges he faces within the company. You are not expected to be a "management" expert at this point. Answering the questions now can help you focus on important points when you study the chapter. Also, answering the questions again after you study the chapter will give you an idea of how much you have learned.

Record your answers here or online at MyManagementLab .com. Completing the questions at MyManagementLab.com will

allow you to get feedback about your answers automatically. If you answer the questions in the book, look up answers in the Exploring Your Management Skill section at the end of the book.

FOR EACH STATEMENT CIRCLE:
• "Y" if you would give the advice to Williams.
• "N" if you would NOT give the advice to Williams.
• "NI" if you have no idea whether you would give the advice to Williams.

Mr. Williams, in meeting your management challenges at Universal, you should...

Before   After
Study   Study

1. make sure you understand how important management is in successfully marketing the new Harry Potter theme park.
Y, N, NI

2. keep in mind that launching "The Wizarding World of Harry Potter" may not be consistent with Universal's overall goals.
Y, N, NI

3. strive to manage people appropriately but understand that managing resources is generally not as important as managing people.
Y, N, NI

4. focus mainly on planning and organizing to meet management challenges at Universal.
Y, N, NI

5. use mainly the influencing function to make sure that people at Universal are managed appropriately.
Y, N, NI

6. use the planning, organizing, influencing, and controlling functions together to reach Universal's organizational goals.
Y, N, NI

7. use the management process to attain Universal's goals.
Y, N, NI

8. almost always be aware of the status and use of Universal's resources.
Y, N, NI

9. strive to be effective in reaching Universal's goals.
Y, N, NI

10. focus on being an efficient manager, one who reaches organizational goals.
Y, N, NI

11. ensure that an overabundance of managers in the exploration career stage is not involved in operating the new Harry Potter theme park.
Y, N, NI

12. as CEO, have more technical skill than conceptual skill in managing the launch of the Harry Potter theme park.
Y, N, NI

13. focus mainly on building conceptual skill in managing Universal.
Y, N, NI

14. rely on the universality of management principle as a worthwhile rationale for assigning only people with prior experience at Universal in managing the new theme park.
Y, N, NI

Exploring Your Management Skill: Part 2

As you recall, you completed Exploring Your Management Skill Part 1 before you started to study this chapter. Your responses gave you an idea of how much you initially knew about modern management and helped you focus on important points as you studied the chapter. Answer the Exploring Your Management Skill questions again now and compare your score to the first time you took it so that you get an idea of how much you learned from studying this chapter. Pinpoint areas for further clarification before you start studying the next chapter. Record your answers within the text or online at MyManagementLab.com. Completing the survey on MyManagementLab.com will allow you to grade and compare your test scores automatically. If you complete the test in the book, look up answers in the Exploring Your Management Skill section at the end of the book.

Your Management Skills Portfolio

Your Management Skills Portfolio is a collection of activities specially designed to demonstrate your management knowledge and skill. By completing these activities online at MyManagementLab .com, you will be able to print, complete with cover sheet, as many activities as you choose. Be sure to save your work. Taking your printed portfolio to an employment interview could be helpful in obtaining a job.

The portfolio activity for this chapter is Managing the Blind Pig Bar. Read the highlight about the Blind Pig and complete the activities that follow.

You have just been hired as the manager of the Blind Pig, a bar in Cleveland, Ohio.[42] The Blind Pig has a local bar feel with downtown style, has 42 beers on tap, and offers games such as darts, foosball, and Silver Strike Bowling. Also available is a DJ to provide music and encourage dancing. Thursdays are Neighborhood & Industry Appreciation nights with half-priced drinks for those living or working in the area.

Given your five years of managerial experience in a similar bar in Cleveland, you know that managing a bar or club is a high-profile job. You also know that even with 12 employees, as manager you'll sometimes have to do everything from carrying kegs of beer up flights of stairs to handling irate customers. Naturally, as manager, you'll be responsible for the smooth bar operations and bar profitability. You start your new job in two weeks.

To get a head start on managing the Blind Pig, you decide to develop a list of issues within the bar that you'll check upon your arrival. You know that for your list to be useful, it must include issues related to bar planning, organizing, influencing, and controlling. Fill out the following form to indicate issues related to each management function you'll check when you arrive at the Blind Pig.

PLANNING ISSUES TO INSPECT

Example: The type of scheduling system used

1. _____
2. _____
3. _____
4. _____
5. _____

Influencing Issues to Inspect

1. _____
2. _____
3. _____
4. _____
5. _____

Organizing Issues to Inspect

1. _____
2. _____
3. _____
4. _____
5. _____

Controlling Issues to Inspect

1. _____
2. _____
3. _____
4. _____
5. _____

Assuming you change the scheduling system used at the Blind Pig, explain how that change affects your organizing, influencing, and controlling activities.

_____
_____
_____
_____

Experiential Exercises

1 Assessing Inefficiency at Ryan Homes

Directions. Read the following scenario and then perform the listed activities. Your instructor may want you to perform the activities as an individual or within groups. Follow all of your instructor's directions carefully.

Ryan Homes is a home building company that has been building homes in more than 10 states in the northeastern part of the United States. The company has been in business since 1948 and has built major housing developments in Michigan, Ohio, Pennsylvania, and Virginia.

Your group, the newly established Ryan Homes Efficiency Team, is searching for ways to make your company more efficient. More specifically, you are to focus on making carpenters more efficient workers. In your company, the job of a carpenter is described as follows:

Carpenters are craftsmen who build things. The occupation rewards those who can combine precise detail work with strenuous manual labor. For Ryan, carpenters are involved with erecting and maintaining houses. Carpenters turn blueprints and plans into finished houses. Ryan's carpenters work with supervisors and construction managers on the production of houses containing different materials including fiberglass,

drywall, plastic, and wood. Carpenters use saws, tape measures, drills, and sanders in their jobs. The job of a carpenter can entail long hours of physical labor in sometimes unpleasant circumstances. The injury rate among carpenters is above average. Some carpenters work indoors and are involved in maintenance and refinishing; others are involved in the creation of frame and infrastructure.

Your team is to list five possible ways carpenters at Ryan homes might be inefficient. In addition, assuming that each of your possible ways is a reality, suggest a corresponding action(s) the company might take to eliminate this inefficiency.

2 You and Your Career

From the discussion of compensation in this chapter, you might conclude that a person's career progress can be gauged by his or her salary level; that is, the greater your salary, the more successful you are. Do you think a person's salary is a valid measure of career progress? Why? List three other factors that you should use as measures of your career progress. In your opinion, which is the most important factor in determining your progress? Why? How would you monitor changes in these factors as your career progresses?

VideoNet Exercise

Management Roles: azTeen Magazine

Video Highlights

azTeen Magazine is a newly created publication in the Arizona market. It is written by teenagers for teenagers. The video features company staff who discuss their managerial roles at azTeen and how the four functions of management—planning, organizing, leading, and controlling—are executed in an informal environment.

Discussion Questions

1. Describe the many roles of the azTeen management staff as discussed by Deb Rochford, Michelle Burgess, and Veronica Sherbina in the video.

2. What overall characteristics are important to azTeen Magazine when hiring teenaged interns?

3. What standards are used at azTeen Magazine to measure organizational performance?

Internet Activity

Browse the azTeen Magazine website at www.azteenmagazine .com. Roam around the site. Look at the different types of information and articles available to teens who visit the site. Click on the "About Us" and "Contact Us" links. What evidence do you see that emphasizes the company culture discussed by editor-in-chief Michelle Burgess in the video clip? Is the information presented on the Web site consistent with the video clip?

CASES

1 UNIVERSAL OPENS HARRY POTTER THEME PARK

"Universal Opens Harry Potter Theme Park" (p. 3) and its related Challenge Case Summary were written to help you better understand the management concepts contained in this chapter. Answer the following discussion questions about the introductory case to better understand how fundamental management concepts can be applied in a company such as Universal Orlando.

1. Do you think it will be difficult for you to become a successful manager? Explain.

2. What do you think you would like most about being a manager? What would you like least?

3. As the chief executive at Universal Studios, Tom Williams faces the multiple challenges of competing in a highly competitive industry; guiding the fortunes of a newly launched theme park; finding ways to attract visitors; and more. If you were Williams, list and describe five activities that you think you would have to perform as part of this job.

2 MANAGING ZINGERMAN'S COMMUNITY OF BUSINESSES

Read the following case and answer the questions. Studying this case will help you better understand how concepts relating to fundamental management concepts can be applied in a company such as Zingerman's Delicatessen.

In 1982, when Paul Saginaw and Ari Weinzweig opened Zingerman's Delicatessen in Ann Arbor, their goal was to make the best pastrami sandwich in Michigan—and beyond. "We wanted people to say about other sandwiches, 'This is a great sandwich, but it's not a Zingerman's,'" Saginaw says. By 1992, the deli was a popular Detroit Street destination, drawing crowds of food lovers to its historic brick building near the local farmers market. That year, one of the deli managers helped open Zingerman's Bakehouse to provide the deli with fresh-baked breads and desserts.

However, even with the new bakery, annual sales were stagnating at the $5 million mark, and Saginaw feared that management complacency would allow competitors to take a bigger bite out of Zingerman's future sales and profits. The cofounders were unsure whether to keep their business small and local or to pursue a growth strategy. Could they move beyond the deli's roots without sacrificing the quality, intense customer focus, employee commitment, and community spirit that had made Zingerman's successful?

Saginaw and Weinzweig spent two years debating their company's direction. Arguing for change, Saginaw wanted to try new things and expand, possibly by opening delis in other cities. His partner understood the business case for growth but resisted the chain approach because he believed that trying to replicate the original would dilute the deli's uniqueness. The two continued to discuss alternatives and finally settled on a long-term concept they called the Zingerman's Community of Businesses. They envisioned a group of 12 to 15 businesses located in and around Ann Arbor, offering goods and services related to, or in some way supporting, Zingerman's Deli. "The key was having partners who were real owners," Weinzweig notes. "We wanted people who had visions of their own. Otherwise, whatever we did would be mediocre, and the whole idea was to elevate the quality of each element of the company." After the cofounders announced their plan in a letter to all employees, they found that not everyone agreed with the new direction. Faced with major changes to the company's culture, structure, and expectations, 80 percent of Zingerman's managers left during the first 18 months.

Saginaw and Weinzweig persisted and today, the Zingerman's Community of Businesses rings up more than $20 million annually from proceeds of the deli and bakery plus a mail order/Internet sales unit, a catering unit, a creamery, a restaurant, a mobile sandwich stand, a coffee company, and a training business. After the initial exodus of managers, the firm began attracting talented managers interested in new challenges. Consider Maggie Bayless, who worked at Zingerman's when the deli first opened. She left to complete an MBA and became a training consultant to corporations, but she wasn't completely satisfied: "I missed feeling that what I did was making a difference."

In 1994, Bayless returned to help Saginaw and Weinzweig start Zingerman's Training (ZingTrain), which shares the founders' management and food-service expertise through seminars and consulting. ZingTrain offers courses such as "3 Steps to Great Service" and "5 Steps to Implementing Change" for internal managers and for outside customers as well. Bayless remains excited about her work because "the more we share, the more we learn." Many ZingTrain customers take one course, go back to their jobs to apply what they learn, and then enroll in another. "Every time I go, I'm reenergized and recharged," comments the training coordinator of Michigan's First National Bank, which distinguishes itself on the basis of personal service.

Zingerman's, which *Inc.* magazine recently declared "The coolest small company in America," has not stopped

growing. It currently employs more than 330 people and opens a new business approximately every 18 months. Just as important, Weinzweig and Saginaw are having fun and making money without compromising the principles that made their deli a regular stop for avid pastrami lovers all around Ann Arbor.

QUESTIONS

1. Which of the skills listed in Figure 1.8 did the cofounders apply when they made and implemented the decision to expand into the Zingerman's Community of Businesses?

2. Why was it important for Zingerman's to expand as a way to provide opportunities for employee and managers to develop their careers?

3. On which of the four types of resources do you think Saginaw and Weinzweig rely most heavily when planning a new business? Explain.

Endnotes

1. "Universal in Global Marketing Push for 'The Wizarding World of Harry Potter,'" *International Marketer's Blog,* February 8, 2010, http://blog. freedmaninternational.com.

2. Jim Ellis, "Harry Potter Theme Park Slated for 2009," *Dallas Morning News,* June 4, 2007, http://www.dallasnews.com.

3. Company Web site, http://www.universalorlando.com, accessed April 11, 2010; and "Universal in Global Marketing Push for 'The Wizarding World of Harry Potter,'" *International Marketer's Blog,* February 8, 2010, http://blog. freedmaninternational.com.

4. Barbara Liston, "Harry Potter Park Adds New Characters," *Reuters.com,* March 26, 2010, http://www.reuters.com.

5. Beth Kassab, "Universal to Spend up to $265 Million in Building Harry Potter 'Wizarding World,'" *Orlando Sentinel,* June 1, 2007.

6. James Luxford, "Harry Potter vs. Mickey Mouse," *Entertainmentwise.com,* June 4, 2007.

7. For an interesting discussion of how the World Bank is launching a pilot program to address the scarcity of well-trained managers in developing and transition countries, see "Improving Management in Developing Countries," *Finance & Development* 40, no.2 (June 2003): 5.

8. "For Women, Equal Pay? No Way," *Time* 169, no. 19 (May 7, 2007).

9. "Shareholders Win One at Home Depot: An Arrogant CEO's Exorbitant Pay Had No Relation to Sagging Stock Price," *Knight Ridder Tribune Business News,* January 15, 2007, 1.

10. Alan Murray, "A Gathering Consensus on CEO Pay," *Wall Street Journal,* March 15, 2006, A2.

11. Marcy Gordon, "Lawmakers Take Up Issue of Excessive Executive Pay," *The Orlando Sentinel,* May 21, 2003, C3.

12. John R. Schermerhorn Jr., *Management* (New York: John Wiley & Sons, Inc., 2005), 19.

13. Jacqueline McLean, "Making Things Happen," *The British Journal of Administrative Management* (October/November 2006): 16.

14. Gary Hamel and C. K. Prahalad, "Seeing the Future First," *Fortune,* September 5, 1994, 64–70; Paul J. Di Stefano, "Strategic Planning—Both Short Term and Long Term," *Rough Notes* 149, no. 8 (August 2006): 26.

15. T. L. Stanley, "Management: A Journey in Progress," *SuperVision* 67, no. 12 (December 2006): 15–18.

16. Jared Sandberg, "Office Democracies: How Many Bosses Can One Person Have?" *Wall Street Journal,* November 22, 2005, B1.

17. For an example of tactics taken by Chase Manhattan Corporation to enhance its efficiency, see Matt Murray, "Chase Combines International Units in Efficiency Move," *Wall Street Journal,* February 19, 1998, C17.

18. William Wiggenhorn, "Motorola U: When Training Becomes an Education," *Harvard Business Review* (July/August 1990): 71–83.

19. Mitchell Bingemann, "Telstra Rings in New Era with More Management Changes," *The Australian,* March 30, 2010, http://www.theaustralian.com; Almar Latour and Lyndal McFarland, "If You Don't Deliver Numbers Then You Aren't Doing Your Job," *Wall Street Journal,* March 15, 2010, http://online.wsj.com.

20. Wyatt Wells, "Concept of the Corporation," *Business History Review* 81, no. 1 (Spring 2007): 142.

21. Henri Fayol, *General and Industrial Management* (London: Sir Isaac Pitman & Sons, 1949).

22. B. C. Forbes, *Forbes,* March 15, 1976, 128.

23. Les Worrall and Cary Cooper, "Management Skills Development: A Perspective on Current Issues and Setting the Future Agenda," *Leadership & Organization Development Journal* 22, no. 1 (2001): 34–39.

24. Tanya Mohn, "Going Global, Stateside," *New York Times,* March 8, 2010, http://www.nytimes.com.

25. Robert L. Katz, "Skills of an Effective Administrator," *Harvard Business Review* (January/February 1955): 33–41.

26. Ruth Davidhizar, "The Two-Minute Manager," *Health Supervisor* 7 (April 1989): 25–29; for an article that demonstrates how important human skills are for middle managers, see also Philip A. Rudolph and Brian H. Kleiner, "The Art of Motivating Employees," *Journal of Managerial Psychology* 4 (1989): i–iv.

27. Gary Yukl, Angela Gordon, and Tom Taber, "A Hierarchical Taxonomy of Leadership Behavior: Integrating a Half Century of Behavior Research," *Journal of Leadership & Organizational Studies* 9, no. 1 (Summer 2002): 15–32.

28. Tim O. Peterson and David D. Van Fleet, "The Ongoing Legacy of R. L. Katz: An Updated Typology of Management Skills," *Management Decision* 42, no. 10 (2004): 1297–1308.

29. Don Hellriegel and John W. Slocum Jr., *Organizational Behavior,* 13th ed. (Mason, Ohio: Thomson SouthWestern, 2010), 6.

30. Perri Capell, "Why Increased Pay Isn't Always Best Reason to Accept Another Job," *Wall Street Journal,* December 19, 2006, B8.

31. John Ivancevich and Michael T. Matteson, *Organizational Behavior and Management* (Homewood, IL: BPJ/Irwin, 1990), 593–95.

32. Patrick J. Purcell, "Older Workers: Employment and Retirement Trends," *Monthly Labor Review* 123, no. 10 (October 2000): 19–30.

33. John W. Slocum Jr., William L. Cron, and Linda C. Yows, "Whose Career Is Likely to Plateau?" *Business Horizons* (March/April 1987): 31–38.

34. Joseph E. McKendrick Jr., "What Are You Doing the Rest of Your Life?" *Management World* (September/October 1987): 2; Carl Anderson, *Management: Skills, Functions, and Organizational Performance,* 2nd ed. (Boston: Allyn and Bacon, 1988).

35. Paul H. Thompson, Robin Zenger Baker, and Norman Smallwood, "Improving Personal Development by Applying the Four-Stage Career Model," *Organizational Dynamics* (Autumn 1986): 49–62.

36. Kenneth Labich, "Take Control of Your Career," *Fortune,* November 18, 1991, 87–90; Buck Blessing, "Career Planning: Five Fatal Assumptions," *Training and Development Journal* (September 1986): 49–51.

37. Thomas J. Peters Jr., "The Best New Managers Will Listen, Motivate, Support," *Working Woman* (September 1990): 142–143, 216–217.

38. Ann Pomeroy, "Peak Performances," *HR Magazine* 52, no. 4 (April 2007): 48–53.

39. Jan Torrisi-Mokwa, "The Seven Questions Firm Leaders Need to Ask to Advance Professional Women More Effectively," *CPA Practice Management Forum* 2, no. 12 (December 2006): 13–14.

40. Facebook, http://www.facebook.com, accessed March 25, 2010. For an interesting discussion of challenges of dual-career versus single-career couples, see David F. Elloy and Catherine R. Smith, "Patterns of Stress, Work-Family Conflict, Role Conflict, Role Ambiguity, and Overload Among Dual-Career and Single-Career Couples: An Australian Study," *Cross-Cultural Management* 10, no. 1 (2003): 55.

41. Sharon Meers and Joanna Strober, *Getting to 50/50: How Working Couples Can Have It All by Sharing It All* (New York: Bantam, 2000). For additional information, see Sue Shellenbarger, "For the Burseks, Best Parent Regimen Is Back-to-Back Shifts," *Wall Street Journal,* February 25, 1998, B1; Jacqueline B. Stanfield, "Couples Coping with Dual Careers: A Description of Flexible and Rigid Coping Styles," *Social Science Journal* 35, no. 1 (1998): 53–64; R. S. Hall and T. D. Hall, "Dual Careers—How Do Couples and Companies Cope with the Problems?" *Organizational Dynamics* 6 (1978): 57–77.

42. Information for this portfolio exercise is based on http://www. theblindpig.com.

chapter 2

Managing

HISTORY AND CURRENT THINKING

Target Skill

comprehensive management skill: the ability to collectively apply concepts from various major management approaches to perform a manager's job

objectives

To help build my *comprehensive management skill*, when studying this chapter, I will attempt to acquire:

1. An understanding of the classical approach to management

2. An appreciation for the work of Frederick W. Taylor, Frank and Lillian Gilbreth, Henry L. Gantt, and Henri Fayol

3. An understanding of the behavioral approach to management

4. An understanding of the studies at the Hawthorne Works and the human relations movement

5. An understanding of the management science approach to management

6. An understanding of how the management science approach has evolved

7. An understanding of the system approach to management

8. Knowledge about the learning organization approach to management

9. An understanding of how triangular management and the contingency approach to management are related

CHALLENGE CASE

HANDLING COMPETITORS AT BURGER KING

BURGER KING IS A FAST-FOOD HAMBURGER RESTAURANT. Recent reports indicate that the company owns or franchises a total of 11,129 restaurants in 65 different countries. Burger King restaurants feature flame-broiled hamburgers, chicken, and other specialty sandwiches. Overall, the menu consists of hamburgers, cheeseburgers, and chicken and fish sandwiches. The menu also includes french fries, onion rings, salads, and desserts. Burger King is also known for its array of breakfast items.

Burger King and other fast-food companies are facing new competition from unlikely rivals. Specifically, "quick casual" restaurants, including Subway Sandwiches, Chipotle Mexican Grill, Cosi, and Panera Bread, are offering healthier food at higher prices. This combination has helped restaurants in this category steal away traditional fast-food customers. Although executives in the fast-food industry initially believed that these new restaurants were attracting only older customers who could afford to pay higher prices, recent research reveals the quick casual concept appeals to individuals between 18 and 34 years old, a key demographic for the fast-food industry.

One way Burger King management is trying to better compete is to operate the company in a way that is consistent with concerns of customers in a modern society. For example, Burger King attacked this new competition by adding its own healthier food offerings. The Chicken Whopper and a new Veggie Burger are examples of healthier alternatives. More recently, the company is offering other more socially conscious choices to customers. For example, in what animal welfare advocates are describing as a "historic advance," Burger King, the world's second-largest hamburger chain, has begun buying eggs and pork from suppliers that do not confine their animals in cages and crates.[1]

John Chidsey was recently named CEO of Burger King. Chidsey understands that Burger King must compete ferociously to survive. Some of his future challenges will be more traditional, like building and maintaining store efficiency, while others will reflect more contemporary issues, such as managing the caloric content of the Burger King menu, and dealing with illegal immigrants.[2] For sure, Chidsey will have to meet these challenges by managing comprehensively, applying various management concepts collectively to management problems. For Burger King to be successful, Chidsey will have to successfully apply his comprehensive management skill.

■ *In the highly competitive fast-food market, Burger King managers use many management tools to attract and keep loyal customers, like these in Manhattan, New York.*

EXPLORING YOUR MANAGEMENT SKILL

You can explore your level of *comprehensive management skill* **before** studying the chapter by completing the exercise "Exploring Your Management Skill: Part 1" on page 44 and **after** studying this chapter by completing the exercise "Exploring Your Management Skill: Part 2" on page 45.

THE COMPREHENSIVE MANAGEMENT SKILL CHALLENGE

The Challenge Case illustrates many different comprehensive management skill challenges that management at Burger King must strive to meet. For Burger King to be successful, management must collectively apply insights from the classical, behavioral, management science, contingency, systems, and learning organization approaches to managing.

The remaining material in this chapter explains these approaches and helps you develop your comprehensive management skill. After studying chapter concepts, read the Challenge Case Summary at the end of the chapter to gain insights about using comprehensive management skill at Burger King.

Chapter 1 focused primarily on defining *management*. This chapter presents various approaches to analyzing and reacting to management situations, each characterized by a different method of analysis and a different type of recommended action.

Over the years, a variety of different approaches to management has popped up, along with wide-ranging discussions of what each approach entails. In an attempt to simplify the discussion of the field of management without sacrificing significant information, Donnelly, Gibson, and Ivancevich combined the ideas of Koontz, O'Donnell, and Weihrich with those of Haynes and Massie, and categorized three basic approaches to management:[3]

1. Classical approach
2. Behavioral approach
3. Management science approach

The following sections build on the work of Donnelly, Gibson, and Ivancevich in presenting the classical, behavioral, and management science approaches to analyzing the management task. The contingency approach is discussed as a fourth primary approach, while the system approach is presented as a recent trend in management thinking. The learning organization is continually evolving and is discussed as the newest form for analyzing management.

THE CLASSICAL APPROACH

The **classical approach to management** was the product of the first concentrated effort to develop a body of management thought. In fact, the management writers who participated in this effort are considered the pioneers of management study. The classical approach recommends that managers continually strive to increase organizational efficiency to increase production. Although the fundamentals of this approach were developed some time ago, contemporary managers are just as concerned with finding the "one best way" to get the job done as their predecessors were. To illustrate this concern, notable management theorists see striking similarities between the concepts of scientific management developed many years ago and the more current management philosophy of building quality into all aspects of organizational operations.[4]

For discussion purposes, the classical approach to management can be broken down into two distinct areas. The first, lower-level management analysis consists primarily of the work of Frederick W. Taylor, Frank and Lillian Gilbreth, and Henry L. Gantt. These individuals studied mainly the jobs of workers at lower levels of the organization. The second area, comprehensive analysis of management, concerns the management function as a whole. The primary contributor to this category was Henri Fayol. Figure 2.1 illustrates the two areas in the classical approach.

Lower-Level Management Analysis

Lower-level management analysis concentrates on the "one best way" to perform a task; that is, it investigates how a task situation can be structured to get the highest production from workers. The process of finding this "one best way" has become known as the *scientific method of management*,

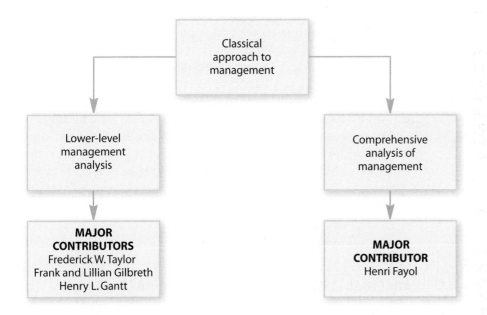

FIGURE 2.1
Division of classical approach to management into two areas and the major contributors to each area

or simply, **scientific management.** Although the techniques of scientific managers could conceivably be applied to management at all levels, the research, research applications, and illustrations relate mostly to lower-level managers. The work of Frederick W. Taylor, Frank and Lillian Gilbreth, and Henry L. Gantt is summarized in the sections that follow.

Frederick W. Taylor (1856–1915)

Because of the significance of his contributions, Frederick W. Taylor is commonly called the "father of scientific management." His primary goal was to increase worker efficiency by scientifically designing jobs. His basic premise was that every job had one best way to do it and that this way should be discovered and put into operation.[5]

WORK AT BETHLEHEM STEEL CO. Perhaps the best way to illustrate Taylor's scientific method and his management philosophy is to describe how he modified the job of employees whose sole responsibility was shoveling materials at Bethlehem Steel Company.[6] During the modification process, Taylor made the assumption that any worker's job could be reduced to a science. To construct the "science of shoveling," he obtained answers—through observation and experimentation—to the following questions:

1. Will a first-class worker do more work per day with a shovelful of 5, 10, 15, 20, 30, or 40 pounds?
2. What kinds of shovels work best with which materials?
3. How quickly can a shovel be pushed into a pile of materials and pulled out properly loaded?
4. How much time is required to swing a shovel backward and throw the load a given horizontal distance at a given height?

As Taylor formulated answers to these types of questions, he developed insights on how to increase the total amount of materials shoveled per day. He raised worker efficiency by matching shovel size with such factors as the size of the worker, the weight of the materials, and the height and distance the materials were to be thrown. By the end of the third year after Taylor's shoveling efficiency plan was implemented, records at Bethlehem Steel showed that the total number of shovelers needed was reduced from about 600 to 140, the average number of tons shoveled per worker per day rose from 16 to 59, the average earnings per worker per day increased from $1.15 to $1.88, and the average cost of handling a long ton (2,240 pounds) dropped from $0.072 to $0.033—all in all, an impressive demonstration of the applicability of scientific management to the task of shoveling.[7]

While Taylor's approach had a significant impact on productivity, his ideas were unpopular with unions and their workers, who feared that the reengineering of their jobs would ultimately lead to fewer workers. In addition, the heightened emphasis on productivity led to a lessening of quality.[8]

Managers continue to seek ways to improve organizational efficiency and productivity. Consulting firm Pace Productivity uses Taylor-like efficiency studies within its own organization. Using a Timecorder, the company's proprietary handheld electronic device, employees track their own time by pushing buttons associated with precoded work activities. When an employee presses a new button, time stops recording on the previous activity and begins recording on a new one. The Timecorder tracks how many times each activity occurs as well as how much time is cumulatively spent on each activity. Managers receive summary reports showing how many times work activities are performed, the time spent, and suggestions for improving worker efficiency based on the results. ■

Frank Gilbreth (1868–1924) and Lillian Gilbreth (1878–1972) The Gilbreths were also significant contributors to the scientific method. As a point of interest, the Gilbreths focused on handicapped as well as non-handicapped workers.[9] Like other contributors to the scientific method, they subscribed to the idea of finding and using the one best way to perform a job. The primary investigative tool in the Gilbreths' research was **motion study,** which consists of reducing each job to the most basic movements possible. Motion analysis is used today primarily to establish job performance standards. Each movement, or motion, that is used to do a job is studied to determine how much time the movement takes and how necessary it is to performing the job. Inefficient or unnecessary motions are pinpointed and eliminated.[10] In performing a motion study, the Gilbreths considered the work environment, the motion itself, and behavior variables concerning the worker. Table 2.1 shows many factors from each of the categories the Gilbreths analyzed.

TABLE 2.1 Sample Variables Considered in Analyzing Motions

Worker Variables

1. Anatomy
2. Brawn
3. Contentment
4. Habits
5. Health

Environmental Variables

1. Work clothes
2. Heat
3. Materials quality
4. Tools
5. Lighting

Work Motion Requirements of Job

1. Acceleration requirements
2. Automation available
3. Inertia to overcome
4. Speed necessary
5. Combinations of motions required

TABLE 2.2	Partial Results for One of Frank Gilbreth's Bricklaying Motion Studies		
Operation No.	The Wrong Way	The Right Way	Pick and Dip Method: The Exterior 4 Inches (Laying to the Line)
1	Step for mortar	Omit	On the scaffold, the inside edge of the mortar box should be plumb with the inside edge of the stock platform. On the floor, the inside edge of the mortar box should be 21 inches from the wall. Mortar boxes should never be more than 4 feet apart.
2	Reach for mortar	Reach for mortar	Do not bend any more than absolutely necessary to reach mortar with a straight arm.
3	Work up mortar	Omit	Provide mortar of the right consistency. Examine sand screen and keep it in repair so that no pebbles can get through. Keep tender on scaffold to temper up and keep mortar worked upright.
4	Step for brick	Omit	If tubs are kept 4 feet apart, no stepping for brick will be necessary on scaffold. On the floor, keep brick in a pile not nearer than 1 foot or more than 4 feet 6 inches from wall.
5	Reach for brick	Included in 2	Brick must be reached for at the same time the mortar is reached for, and picked up at exactly the same time the mortar is picked up. If it is not picked up at the same time, allowance must be made for operation.

Frank Gilbreth was born in Maine in 1868. After high school graduation, he qualified to be a student at the Massachusetts Institute of Technology but decided to work for a construction business in Boston.[11] He started as a bricklayer's apprentice and advanced to general superintendent. His experience as an apprentice bricklayer led him to do motion studies of bricklaying. He found that bricklayers could increase their output significantly by concentrating on performing some motions and eliminating others. Table 2.2 shows a simplified portion of the results of one of Gilbreth's bricklaying motion studies. For each bricklaying operation, Gilbreth indicated whether it should be omitted for the sake of efficiency and why. He reduced the five motions per brick listed under "The Wrong Way" to the one motion per brick listed under "The Right Way." Overall, Gilbreth's bricklaying motion studies resulted in reducing of the number of motions necessary to lay a brick by approximately 70 percent, consequently tripling bricklaying production.

Lillian Gilbreth, who began as her husband's collaborator, earned two doctorates and was awarded numerous honorary degrees. After Frank's death, she continued to research while also raising the twelve Gilbreth children and becoming the first woman professor at Purdue University. Lillian Gilbreth's work extended into the application of the scientific method to the role of the homemaker and to the handicapped.[12]

Much of the Gilbreths' work has broad application today for how to design jobs. However, the Gilbreths were also among the first to consider the employee as a productivity factor. Frank Gilbreth recognized that, for motion studies to best impact jobs, managers must communicate with employees about their jobs and develop their job related skills.[13]

Henry L. Gantt (1861–1919) The third major contributor to the scientific management approach was Henry L. Gantt. He, too, was interested in increasing worker efficiency. Gantt attributed unsatisfactory or ineffective tasks and piece rates (incentive pay for each product piece an individual produces) primarily to the fact that these tasks and rates were set according to what had been done by workers in the past or to someone's *opinion* of what workers could do. According to Gantt, *exact scientific knowledge* of what could be done by a worker should be substituted for opinion. He considered this task measurement and determination the role of scientific management.

Gantt's management philosophy is encapsulated in his statement that "the essential differences between the best system of today and those of the past are the manner in which tasks are 'scheduled' and the manner in which their performance is rewarded."[14] Using this rationale, he sought to improve systems or organizations through task-scheduling innovation and the rewarding innovation.

SCHEDULING INNOVATION The Gantt chart, the primary scheduling device that Gantt developed, is still the scheduling tool most commonly used by modern managers.[15] Basically, this chart provides managers with an easily understood summary of what work was scheduled for specific time periods, how much of this work has been completed, and by whom it was done.[16]

Special computer software such as MacSchedule has been developed to help managers more efficiently and effectively apply the concept of the Gantt chart today.[17] MacSchedule allows managers to easily monitor complicated and detailed scheduling issues such as the number of units planned for production during a specified period, when work is to begin and be completed, and the percentage of work that was actually completed during a period. (The Gantt chart is covered in much more detail in Chapter 10.)

REWARDING INNOVATION Gantt was more aware of the human side of production than either Taylor or the Gilbreths. He wrote that "the taskmaster (manager) of the past was practically a slave driver, whose principal function was to force workmen to do that which they had no desire to do, or interest in doing. The task setter of today under any reputable system of management is not a driver. When he asks the workmen to perform tasks, he makes it to their interest to accomplish them, and is careful not to ask what is impossible or unreasonable."[18]

In contrast to Taylor, who pioneered a piece-rate system under which workers were paid according to the amount they produced and who advocated the use of wage-incentive plans, Gantt developed a system wherein workers could earn a bonus in addition to the piece rate if they exceeded their daily production quota. Gantt, then, believed in worker compensation that corresponded not only to production (through the piece-rate system) but also to overproduction (through the bonus system).

Comprehensive Analysis of Management

Whereas scientific managers emphasize job design when approaching the study of management, managers who embrace the comprehensive view—the second area of the classical approach—are concerned with the entire range of managerial performance.

Among the well-known contributors to the comprehensive view are Chester Barnard,[19] Alvin Brown, Henry Dennison, Luther Gulick and Lyndall Urwick, J. D. Mooney and A. C. Reiley, and Oliver Sheldon.[20] Perhaps the most notable contributor, however, was Henri Fayol. His book, *General and Industrial Management,* presents a management philosophy that still guides many modern managers.[21]

Henri Fayol (1841–1925) Because of his writings on the elements and general principles of management, Henri Fayol is usually regarded as the pioneer of administrative theory. The elements of management he outlined—planning, organizing, commanding, coordinating, and control—are still considered worthwhile divisions under which to study, analyze, and affect the management process.[22] (Note the close correspondence between Fayol's elements of management and the management functions outlined in Chapter 1—planning, organizing, influencing, controlling.)

Benefits such as on-campus day care, a medical center, and a free 66,000-square-foot fitness center, reward SAS employees for their unsurpassed skill at devising a continuous stream of successful innovations for the company.

The general principles of management suggested by Fayol, still considered useful in contemporary management practice, are presented here in the order developed by Fayol, accompanied by corresponding defining themes:[23]

1. **Division of work**—Work should be divided among individuals and groups to ensure that effort and attention are focused on special portions of the task. Fayol presented work specialization as the best way to use the human resources of the organization.
2. **Authority**—The concepts of authority and responsibility are closely related. *Authority* was defined by Fayol as the right to give orders and the power to exact obedience. *Responsibility* involves being accountable, and is therefore naturally associated with authority. Whoever assumes authority also assumes responsibility.
3. **Discipline**—A successful organization requires the common effort of workers. Penalties should be applied judiciously to encourage this common effort.
4. **Unity of command**—Workers should receive orders from only one manager.
5. **Unity of direction**—The entire organization should be moving toward a common objective, in a common direction.
6. **Subordination of individual interests to the general interests**—The interests of one person should not take priority over the interests of the organization as a whole.
7. **Remuneration**—Many variables, such as cost of living, supply of qualified personnel, general business conditions, and success of the business, should be considered in determining a worker's rate of pay.
8. **Centralization**—Fayol defined *centralization* as lowering the importance of the subordinate role. *Decentralization* is increasing the importance. The degree to which centralization or decentralization should be adopted depends on the specific organization in which the manager is working.
9. **Scalar chain**—Managers in hierarchies are part of a chainlike authority scale. Each manager, from the first-line supervisor to the president, possesses certain amounts of authority. The president possesses the most authority; the first-line supervisor, the least. Lower-level managers should always keep upper-level managers informed of their work activities. The existence of a scalar chain and adherence to it are necessary if the organization is to be successful.
10. **Order**—For the sake of efficiency and coordination, all materials and people related to a specific kind of work should be assigned to the same general location in the organization.
11. **Equity**—All employees should be treated as equally as possible.
12. **Stability of tenure of personnel**—Retaining productive employees should always be a high priority of management. Recruitment and selection costs, as well as increased product-reject rates, are usually associated with hiring new workers.
13. **Initiative**—Management should take steps to encourage worker initiative, which is defined as new or additional work activity undertaken through self-direction.
14. **Esprit de corps**—Management should encourage harmony and general good feelings among employees.[24]

Fayol's general principles of management cover a broad range of topics, but organizational efficiency, the handling of people, and appropriate management action are the three general themes he stresses. With the writings of Fayol, the study of management as a broad, comprehensive activity began to receive more attention. Some modern management researchers seem to believe, however, that Fayol's work has not received as much acclaim as it deserves.[25]

Limitations of the Classical Approach

Contributors to the classical approach felt encouraged to write about their managerial experiences largely because of the success they enjoyed. Structuring work to be more efficient and defining the manager's role more precisely yielded significant improvements in productivity, which individuals such as Taylor and Fayol were quick to document.

The classical approach, however, does not adequately emphasize human variables. People today do not seem to be as influenced by bonuses as they were in the nineteenth century. It is generally agreed that critical interpersonal areas, such as conflict, communication, leadership, and motivation, were shortchanged in the classical approach.

THE BEHAVIORAL APPROACH

The **behavioral approach to management** emphasizes increasing production through an understanding of people. According to proponents of this approach, if managers understand their people and adapt their organizations to them, organizational success will usually follow.

The Hawthorne Studies

The behavioral approach to management calls for a broad understanding of the way in which different people behave, respond, and interact with one another in work situations like this circuit board factory meeting.

The behavioral approach is usually described as beginning with a series of studies conducted between 1924 and 1932, which investigated the behavior and attitudes of workers at the Hawthorne (Chicago) Works of the Western Electric Company.[26] Accounts of the Hawthorne Studies are usually divided into two phases: the relay assembly test room experiments and the bank wiring observation room experiment. The following sections discuss each of these phases.

The Relay Assembly Test Room Experiments The relay assembly test room experiments originally had a scientific management orientation. The experimenters believed that if they studied productivity long enough, under different working conditions (including variations in weather conditions, temperature, rest periods, work hours, and humidity), they would discover the working conditions that maximized production. The immediate purpose of the relay assembly test room experiments was to determine the relationship between intensity of lighting and worker efficiency, as measured by worker output. Two groups of female employees were used as subjects. The light intensity for one group was varied, while the light intensity for the other group was held constant.

The results of the experiments surprised the researchers: No matter what conditions employees were exposed to, production increased. They found no consistent relationship between productivity and lighting intensity. An extensive interviewing campaign was undertaken to determine why the subjects continued to increase production under all lighting conditions. The following are the main reasons, as formulated from the interviews:

1. The subjects found working in the test room enjoyable.
2. The new supervisory relationship during the experiment allowed the subjects to work freely, without fear.
3. The subjects realized that they were taking part in an important and interesting study.
4. The subjects seemed to become friendly as a group.

The experimenters concluded that human factors within organizations could significantly influence production. More research was needed, however, to evaluate the potential impact of this human component in organizations.

The Bank Wiring Observation Room Experiment The purpose of the bank wiring observation room experiment was to analyze social relationships in a work group. Specifically, the study focused on the effect of group piecework incentives on a group of men who assembled terminal banks for use in telephone exchanges. The group piecework incentive system dictated that the harder a group worked as a whole, the more pay each member of that group would receive.

The experimenters believed that the study would show that members of the work group pressured one another to work harder so that each group member would receive more pay. To their surprise, they found the opposite: The work group pressured the faster workers to slow down their work rate. The men whose work rate would have increased individual salaries were being pressured by the group, rather than the men whose work rate would have decreased individual salaries. Evidently, the men were more interested in preserving work group solidarity than in making more money. The researchers concluded that social groups in organizations could effectively exert pressure to influence individuals to disregard monetary incentives.[27]

Recognizing the Human Variable

Taken together, the series of studies conducted at the Hawthorne plant gave management thinkers a new direction for research. Obviously, the human variable in the organization needed much more analysis after showing that it could either increase or decrease production drastically. Managers began to realize that they needed to understand this influence so they could maximize its positive effects and minimize its negative effects. This attempt to understand people is still a major force in today's organizational research.[28] Hawthorne study results helped managers to see that understanding what motivates employees is a critical part of being a manager.[29] More current behavioral findings and their implications for management are presented in greater detail later in this text.

The Human Relations Movement

The Hawthorne Studies sparked the **human relations movement,** a people-oriented approach to management in which the interaction of people in organizations is studied to judge its impact on organizational success. The ultimate objective of this approach is to enhance organizational success by building appropriate relationships with people. To put it simply, when management stimulates high productivity and worker commitment to the organization and its goals, human relations are said to be effective; and when management precipitates low productivity and uncommitted workers, human relations are said to be ineffective. **Human relations skill** is defined as the ability to work with people in a way that enhances organizational success.

The human relations movement has made some important contributions to the study and practice of management. Advocates of this approach to management have continually stressed the need to use humane methods in managing people. Abraham Maslow, perhaps the best-known contributor to the human relations movement, believed that managers must understand the physiological, safety, social, esteem, and self-actualization needs of organization members. Douglas McGregor, another important contributor to the movement, emphasized a management philosophy built on the views that people can be self-directed, accept responsibility, and consider work to be as natural as play.[30] The ideas of both Maslow and McGregor are discussed thoroughly in Chapter 17. As a result of the tireless efforts of theorists such as Maslow and McGregor, modern managers better understand the human component in organizations and how to appropriately work with it to enhance organizational success.

Consistent with the human relations movement, SAS is dedicated to building a human-oriented work environment. Leaders at SAS, the world's largest privately held software company, believe that employees represent the company's most significant asset. SAS works to maintain this asset by providing generous benefits like subsidized cafeterias and daycare, a free health clinic for employees and their families, and a recreation and fitness center that boasts a pool, sauna, and massage facilities. By placing trust in its employees, SAS generates employee loyalty, productivity, and commitment. For 13 consecutive years, the company has been named to *Fortune* magazine's list of "100 Best Companies to Work For."[31] ∎

how managers do it

Building a "People" Environment at SAS

class discussion highlight

MODERN RESEARCH AND COMPREHENSIVE MANAGEMENT SKILL

Fostering Safe Behavior Among Construction Workers

The behavioral approach to management, presented as a major dimension of comprehensive management skill, emphasizes that managers should focus on solving organizational problems by incorporating a behavioral perspective into problem analysis and solution. This exercise focuses on the results of research relating to encouraging employees to act safely. Safe behavior is behavior that tends to keep employees from incurring injury while working. Although establishing a safe work environment admittedly contains classic, management science, contingency, and systems issues, this exercise focuses only on its behavioral issues.

A recent study by Teo, Ling, and Ong investigated various actions that construction-site managers can use to foster safe behavior among construction-site workers in Singapore. Many managers believe that workers "don't know" and "don't care" what safe behaviors are and how to perform them. Managers would like to encourage safe behavior of workers so that projects can more easily be completed on schedule and medical costs due to injuries can be minimized. Workers are commonly injured on construction sites by falling, being struck by objects, being burned by fire, and experiencing bodily harm through explosions.

The researchers surveyed opinions of contractors in Singapore to see what they believed to be the most effective ways to increase the safe behavior of construction workers. The survey focused on three possible tools to increase this safe behavior: (1) rewarding employees for safe behavior, (2) disciplining (punishing) employees for unsafe behavior, and (3) training employees in how to be safe on a construction site. In the survey, discipline involved administering an undesired consequence when an employee performs unsafe behavior. Punishments studied include (1) fining employees who perform unsafe behaviors, (2) temporarily suspending workers performing unsafe behaviors, and (3) demoting employees who perform unsafe behaviors.

Which of these possible punishments do you think contractors seemed to value most in encouraging safe behavior of workers? Why? Which punishment do you think they valued least? Why? Assuming your thoughts are accurate, what hints can this research give you about developing your comprehensive management skill?

Source: Evelyn Ai Lin Teo, Florence Yean Yng Ling, and Derrick Sern Yau Ong, "Fostering Safe Work Behavior in Workers at Construction Sites," *Engineering, Construction, and Architectural Management* 12, no. 4 (2005): 410–422.

THE MANAGEMENT SCIENCE APPROACH

Churchman, Ackoff, and Arnoff define the management science, or operations research (OR), approach as (1) an application of the scientific method to problems arising in the operation of a system and (2) the solution of these problems by solving mathematical equations representing the system.[32] The **management science approach** suggests that managers can best improve their organizations by using the scientific method and mathematical techniques to solve operational problems.

The Beginning of the Management Science Approach

The management science, or operations research, approach can be traced to World War II, an era in which leading scientists were asked to help solve complex operational problems in the military.[33] Scientists were organized into teams that eventually became known as operations research

(OR) groups. One OR group, for example, was asked to determine which gun sights would best stop German attacks on the British mainland. The term *management science* was actually coined by researchers of a UCLA–RAND academic complex featuring academic and industry researchers working together to solve operations problems.[34]

These early OR groups typically included physicists and other "hard" scientists who used the problem-solving method with which they had the most experience: the scientific method. The scientific method dictates that scientists:

1. Systematically *observe* the system whose behavior must be explained to solve the problem.
2. Use these specific observations to *construct* a generalized framework (a model) that is consistent with the specific observations and from which consequences of changing the system can be predicted.
3. Use the model to *deduce* how the system will behave under conditions that have not been observed but could be observed if the changes were made.
4. Finally, *test* the model by performing an experiment on the actual system to see whether the effects of changes predicted using the model actually occur when the changes are made.[35]

The OR groups proved successful at using the scientific method to solve the military's operational problems.

Management Science Today

After World War II, America again became interested in manufacturing and selling products. The success of the OR groups in the military had been so obvious that managers were eager to try management science techniques in an industrial environment. After all, managers also had to deal with complicated operational problems.

By 1955, the management science approach to solving industrial problems had proved effective. Many people saw great promise in refining its techniques and analytical tools. Managers and universities pursued these refinements.

By 1965, the management science approach was being used in many companies and applied to many diverse management problems, such as production scheduling, plant location, and product packaging.

In the 1980s, surveys indicated that management science techniques were used extensively in large, complex organizations. Smaller organizations, however, had not yet fully realized the benefits of using these techniques.

The widespread use of computers in the workplace and the introduction of the Internet have had a significant impact on organizations' use of management science techniques. In the twenty-first century, managers in organizations of all sizes now have ready access to a wealth of tools and other resources that enable them to easily apply the principles of management science to their business. Not only has the introduction of technology transformed how businesses operate, it enables leadership to automate and organize their company's systems for greater consistency—*and* it allows them to use the power of technology to aid in their decision making.[36]

Characteristics of Management Science Applications

Four primary characteristics are usually present in situations in which management science techniques are applied.[37] First, the management problems studied are so complicated that managers need help analyzing a large number of variables. Management science techniques increase the effectiveness of the managers' decision making in such a situation. Second, a management science application generally uses economic implications as guidelines for making a particular decision, perhaps because management science techniques are best suited for analyzing quantifiable factors such as sales, expenses, and units of production.

Third, the use of mathematical models to investigate the decision situation is typical in management science applications. Models constructed to represent reality are used to determine how the real-world situation might be improved. The fourth characteristic of a management science application is the use of computers. The great complexity of managerial problems and the sophisticated mathematical analysis of problem-related information required are two factors that make computers especially valuable to the management science analyst.

Today managers use such management science tools as inventory control models, network models, and probability models to aid them in the decision-making process. Later parts of this text will outline some of these models in greater detail and illustrate their applications to management decision making. Because management science thought is still evolving, more and more sophisticated analytical techniques can be expected in the future.

THE CONTINGENCY APPROACH

In simple terms, the **contingency approach to management** emphasizes that what managers do in practice depends on, or is contingent upon, a given set of circumstances—a situation.[38] In essence, this approach emphasizes "if–then" relationships: "If" this situational variable exists, "then" a manager probably would take this action. For example, if a manager has a group of inexperienced subordinates, then the contingency approach would recommend that he or she lead in a different fashion than if the subordinates were experienced.[39]

In general, the contingency approach attempts to outline the conditions or situations in which various management methods have the best chance of success.[40] This approach is based on the premise that, although there is probably no one best way to solve a management problem in all organizations, there probably is one best way to solve any given management problem in any one organization. Perhaps the main challenges of using the contingency approach are the following:

1. Perceiving organizational situations as they actually exist
2. Choosing the management tactics best suited to those situations
3. Competently implementing those tactics

The notion of a contingency approach to management is not novel. It has become a popular discussion topic for contemporary management thinkers. The general consensus of their writings is that if managers are to apply management concepts, principles, and techniques successfully, they must consider the realities of the specific organizational circumstances they face.[41]

THE SYSTEM APPROACH

The **system approach to management** is based on general system theory. Ludwig von Bertalanffy, a scientist who worked mainly in physics and biology, is recognized as the founder of general system theory.[42] The main premise of the theory is that to fully understand the operation of an entity, the entity must be viewed as a system. A **system** is a number of interdependent parts functioning as a whole for some purpose. For example, according to general system theory, to fully understand the operations of the human body, one must understand the workings of its interdependent parts (ears, eyes, and brain). General system theory integrates the knowledge of various specialized fields so that the system as a whole can be better understood.

Types of Systems

According to von Bertalanffy, the two basic types of systems are closed systems and open systems. A **closed system** is not influenced by, and does not interact with, its environment. It is mostly mechanical and has predetermined motions or activities that must be performed regardless of the environment. A clock is an example of a closed system. Regardless of its environment, a clock's wheels, gears, and other parts must function in a predetermined way if the clock as a whole is to exist and serve its purpose. The second type of system, the **open system,** is continually interacting with its environment. A plant is an example of an open system. Constant interaction with the environment influences the plant's state of existence and its future. In fact, the environment determines whether the plant will live.

Systems and "Wholeness"

The concept of "wholeness" is important in general system analysis. The system must be viewed as a whole and modified only through changes in its parts. Before modifications of the parts can be made for the overall benefit of the system, a thorough knowledge of how each part functions and the interrelationships among the parts must be present. L. Thomas Hopkins suggested the following six guidelines for anyone conducting system analysis:[43]

1. The whole should be the main focus of analysis, with the parts receiving secondary attention.
2. Integration is the key variable in wholeness analysis. It is defined as the interrelatedness of the many parts within the whole.
3. Possible modifications in each part should be weighed in relation to possible effects on every other part.
4. Each part has some role to perform so that the whole can accomplish its purpose.
5. The nature of the part and its function is determined by its position in the whole.
6. All analysis starts with the existence of the whole. The parts and their interrelationships should then evolve to best suit the purpose of the whole.

Because the system approach to management is based on general system theory, analysis of the management situation as a system is stressed. The following sections present the parts of the management system and recommend information that can be used to analyze the system.

The Management System

As with all systems, the **management system** is composed of a number of parts that function interdependently to achieve a purpose. The main parts of the management system are organizational input, organizational process, and organizational output. As discussed in Chapter 1, these parts consist of organizational resources, the production process, and finished goods, respectively. The parts represent a combination that exists to achieve organizational objectives, whatever they may be.

The management system is an open system—that is, one that interacts with its environment (see Figure 2.2). Environmental factors with which the management system interacts include the government, suppliers, customers, and competitors. Each of these factors represents a potential environmental influence that could significantly change the future of the management system.

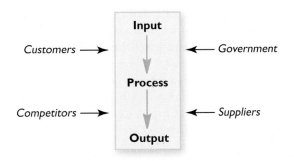

ENVIRONMENT

FIGURE 2.2
The open management system

Needless to say, tracking an environmental factor like customer opinion can be very time-consuming. The challenge of a hotel manager, for example, to accurately track what customers and others are saying about a hotel seems almost impossible. To help overcome this challenge, hotel managers can use a tool called ReviewPro to compile customer opinions. ReviewPro is a Web-based reputation management service for the hotel industry. It organizes, tracks, and analyzes hotel reviews and other hotel-related information on the Internet from a wide array of sites, including Facebook and Twitter. Overall, using a tool like ReviewPro helps hotel managers make better decisions about how to improve customer satisfaction.[44] ■

The critical importance of managers knowing and understanding their customers is perhaps best illustrated by the constant struggle of supermarket managers to know and understand their customers. Supermarket managers fight for the business of a national population that is growing by less than 1 percent per year. Survival requires that they know their customers better than the competition does. That is why many food retailers conduct market research to uncover customer attitudes about different kinds of foods and stores. Armed with a thorough understanding of their customers, gained from this type of research, they hope to win business from competitors who are not benefiting from the insights made possible by such research.[45]

Information for Management System Analysis

As noted earlier, general system theory supports the use of information from many specialized disciplines to better understand a system. Information from any discipline that can increase the understanding of management system operations enhances the success of the system. Although this statement is a fairly sweeping one, managers can get this broad information from the first three approaches to management outlined in this chapter.

Thus the information used to discuss the management system in the remainder of this text comes from three primary sources:

1. Classical approach to management
2. Behavioral approach to management
3. Management science approach to management

The use of these three sources of information to analyze the management system is referred to as **triangular management.** Figure 2.3 presents the triangular management model. The three sources of information depicted in the model are not meant to represent all the information that can be used to analyze the management system. Rather, these three types of management-related information are probably the most useful in analysis.

A synthesis of classically based information, behaviorally based information, and management science-based information is critical to effective use of the management system. This information is integrated and presented in subsequent parts of this book. These parts discuss management systems and planning (Chapters 7–10), organizing (Chapters 11–14), influencing (Chapters 15–20), and controlling (Chapters 21–22). In addition, a special part of the text focuses on modern challenges managers face when managing management systems (Chapters 3–6).

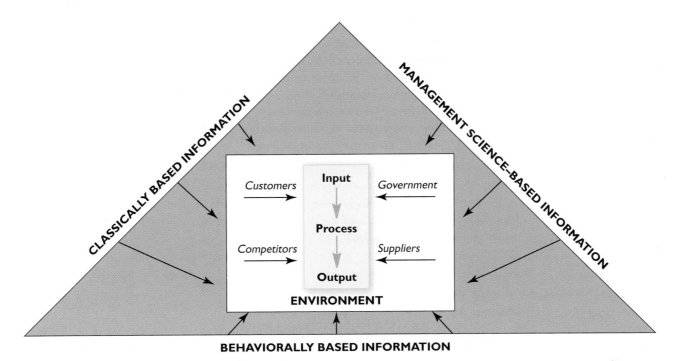

FIGURE 2.3 Triangular management model

LEARNING ORGANIZATION: A NEW APPROACH?

The preceding material in this chapter provides a history of management by discussing a number of different approaches to management that have evolved over time. Each approach developed over a number of years and focused on the particular needs of organizations at the time.

In more recent times, managers seem to be searching for new approaches to management.[46] Fueling this search is a range of new issues that modern managers face that their historical counterparts did not. These issues include a concern about the competitive decline of Western firms, the accelerating pace of technological change, the sophistication of customers, and an increasing emphasis on globalization.

A new approach to management that is evolving to handle this new range of issues can be called the *learning organization approach*. A **learning organization** is an organization that does well in creating, acquiring, and transferring knowledge, and in modifying behavior to reflect new knowledge.[47] Learning organizations emphasize systematic problem solving, experimenting with new ideas, learning from experience and past history, learning from the experiences of others, and transferring knowledge rapidly throughout the organization. Managers attempting to build a learning organization must create an environment conducive to learning and encourage the exchange of information among all organization members.[48] Honda, Corning, and General Electric are successful learning organizations.

The learning organization represents a specific, new *management paradigm,* or fundamental way of viewing and contemplating management. Peter Senge started serious discussion of learning organizations with his book, *The Fifth Discipline: The Art & Practice of the Learning Organization.*[49] Senge, his colleagues at MIT, and many others have made significant progress in developing the learning organization concept. According to Senge, building a learning organization entails building five features within an organization:

1. **Systems thinking**—Every organization member understands his or her own job and how the jobs fit together to provide final products to the customer.
2. **Shared vision**—All organization members have a common view of the purpose of the organization and a sincere commitment to accomplish the purpose.

3. **Challenging of mental models**—Organization members routinely challenge the way business is done and the thought processes people use to solve organizational problems.
4. **Team learning**—Organization members work together, develop solutions to new problems together, and apply the solutions together. Working as teams rather than as individuals will help organizations gather collective force to achieve organizational goals.
5. **Personal mastery**—All organization members are committed to gaining a deep and rich understanding of their work. Such an understanding will help organizations successfully overcome important challenges that confront them.

Overall, managers attempting to build learning organizations face many different challenges. One such challenge involves ensuring that an organization changes as necessary. Changes in the external environment, like an increasingly global marketplace, rapid technological advances, and growing pressure to do more with less, all require managers to implement needed change as they build their learning organization.[50]

CHALLENGE CASE SUMMARY

John Chidsey, the CEO of Burger King mentioned in the introductory case, could attempt to use a classical approach to management to stress organizational efficiency—the "one best way" to perform jobs at Burger King restaurants—to increase productivity. Focusing on efficiency could help Burger King reduce costs, which would also help the company contend with new competitors. To take a simplified example, Burger King's managers might want to check whether the dispenser used to apply mustard and ketchup is of the appropriate size to require only one squirt or whether more than one squirt is necessary to adequately cover a hamburger.

In the face of intense competition and the need to control costs, Chidsey could use motion studies to eliminate unnecessary or wasted motions by his employees. For example, are Whoppers, french fries, and drinks located for easy insertion into customer bags, or must an employee walk unnecessary steps during the sales process? Also, would certain Burger King employees be more efficient over an entire working day if they sat, rather than stood, while working?

The classical approach to management might also guide Chidsey to stress efficient scheduling. By ensuring that an appropriate number of people with the appropriate skills are scheduled to work during peak hours and that fewer such individuals are scheduled to work during slower hours, Burger King would maximize its return on labor costs.

Chidsey and other Burger King managers also might want to consider offering employees some sort of bonus if they reach certain work goals. Management should make sure, however, that the goals it sets are realistic; unreasonable or impossible goals tend to make workers resentful and unproductive. For example, management might ask that certain employees reduce errors in filling orders by 50 percent during the next month. If and when these employees reached the goal, Burger King could give them a free lunch as a bonus.

The comprehensive analysis of organizations implies that John Chidsey might be able to further improve success at Burger King by evaluating the entire range of managerial performance—especially with regard to organizational efficiency, the handling of people, and appropriate management action. For example, Chidsey should make sure that Burger King employees receive orders from only one source (be sure that one manager doesn't instruct an employee to serve french fries moments before another manager directs the same employee to prepare milkshakes). Along the same lines, Chidsey might want to make sure that all Burger King employees are treated equally—that fry cooks, for example, don't get longer breaks than order takers.

The behavioral approach to management suggests that Chidsey strongly encourages Burger King managers to consider the people working for them and evaluate the impact of their employees' feelings and relationships on the productivity of Burger King restaurants. A Burger King manager, for example, should try to make the work more enjoyable, perhaps by allowing employees to work at different stations (grill, beverage, cash register, etc.) each day. A Burger King manager might also consider creating opportunities for employees to become more friendly with one another, perhaps through a Burger King employee picnic. In essence, the behavioral approach to management stresses that managers recognize the human variable in their restaurants and strive to maximize its positive effects.

This chapter suggests that John Chidsey could enhance the success of Burger King by encouraging managers to use the management science approach to solve operational problems. According to the scientific method, a Burger King manager would first spend some time observing what takes place in a restaurant. Next, the manager would use these observations to outline exactly how the restaurant operates as a whole. Third, the manager would apply this understanding of Burger King's operations by predicting how various changes might help or hinder the restaurant as a whole. Before implementing possible changes, the manager would test them on a small scale to see whether they actually affected the restaurant as desired.

If Burger King's managers were to follow the contingency approach to management, their actions as managers would depend on the situation. For example, *if* some customers hadn't been served within a reasonable period because the equipment needed to make chocolate sundaes had broken down, *then* management probably would not hold employees responsible. But *if* management knew that the equipment had broken down because of employee mistreatment or neglect, *then* reaction to the situation would likely be different.

A Burger King manager could also apply the system approach and view a restaurant as a system, or a number of interdependent parts that function as a whole, to reach restaurant objectives. Naturally, a Burger King restaurant would be viewed as an open system—one that exists in and is influenced by its environment. Major factors within the environment of a Burger King restaurant would be its customers, suppliers, competitors, and the government. For example, if a Burger King competitor significantly lowered its price for hamburgers to a point well below what Burger King was asking for a hamburger, Burger King management might be forced to consider modifying different parts of its restaurant system in order to meet or beat that price.

Last, a Burger King manager could apply the learning organization approach. Using this approach, a restaurant manager, for example, would see the restaurant as an organizational unit that needs to be good at creating, acquiring, and transferring knowledge, and modifying behavior to reflect new knowledge. For example, all Burger King employees at a restaurant would be involved in gathering new thoughts and ideas about running the restaurant and be on a team with management in which they possess a significant voice in establishing how the restaurant exists and operates.

MANAGEMENT SKILL ACTIVITIES

This section is specially designed to help you develop comprehensive management skill. An individual's comprehensive management skill is based on an understanding of various approaches to management and the ability to apply that understanding to various management situations. The following activities are designed to both heighten your understanding of various approaches to management and to develop your ability to apply this understanding.

UNDERSTANDING MANAGEMENT CONCEPTS

 To check your understanding and to practice using the concepts in this chapter, go to www.mymanagementlab.com and explore the material associated with Chapter 2.

Know Key Terms

Understanding the following key terms is critical to your understanding of chapter material. Define each of these terms. Refer to the page(s) referenced after a term to check your definition or to gain further insight regarding the term.

classical approach to management **28**
scientific management **29**
motion study **30**
behavioral approach to management **34**
human relations movement **35**

human relations skill **35**
management science approach **36**
contingency approach to management **38**
system approach to management **38**
system **38**

closed system **38**
open system **39**
management system **39**
triangular management **40**
learning organization **41**

Know How Management Concepts Relate

This section is comprised of activities that will further sharpen your understanding of management concepts. Answer essay questions as completely as possible. Also, remember that many additional true/false and multiple choice questions appear online at MyManagementLab.com to help you further refine your understanding of management concepts.

1. How will you be able to use the classical approach to management in your job as a manager?

2. How does Henri Fayol's contribution to management differ from the contributions of Frank and Lillian Gilbreth?

3. Discuss the primary limitation of the classical approach to management. Would this approach be more significant to managers today than managers in the more distant past? Explain.

4. What is the "systems approach" to management? How do the concepts of closed and open systems relate to this approach?

5. Discuss the triangular management model as a tool for organizing how a manager should think about the management process.

DEVELOPING MANAGEMENT SKILLS

Learning activities in this section are aimed at helping you develop comprehensive management skill. Learning activities include Exploring Your Management Skill: Parts 1 & 2, Experiential Exercises, Cases, and a VideoNet Exercise.

Exploring Your Management Skill: Part 1

Before studying this chapter, respond to the following questions regarding the type of advice you would give to Burger King's CEO, John Chidsey, referenced in the Challenge Case. Then address the concerning comprehensive management skill challenges that he presently faces within the company. You are not expected to be a comprehensive management skill expert at this point. Answering the questions now can help you focus on important points when you study the chapter. Also, answering the questions again after you study the chapter will give you an idea of how much you have learned.

Record your answers here or online at MyManagementLab .com. Completing the questions at MyManagementLab.com will allow you to get feedback about your answers automatically. If you answer the questions in the book, look up answers in the Exploring Your Management Skill section at the end of the book.

FOR EACH STATEMENT CIRCLE:

- "Y" if you would give the advice to Chidsey.
- "N" if you would NOT give the advice to Chidsey.
- "NI" if you have no idea whether you would give the advice to Chidsey.

Mr. Chidsey, in meeting your comprehensive management skill challenges at Burger King, you should …

Before   After
Study   Study

1. keep in mind that there is probably "one best" way to do restaurant jobs.
   Y, N, NI

2. use motion study principles to manage lower-level jobs in restaurants, such as cooks, but not upper-level jobs, such as vice president of marketing.
   Y, N, NI

3. divide work among Burger King workers so that they can focus on special portions of tasks.
   Y, N, NI

4. not apply insights of the classical approach to management in concert with insights from the behavioral approach.
   Y, N, NI

5. focus on understanding how to increase production at Burger King through an understanding of people.
   Y, N, NI

6. not worry about some Burger King workers influencing other workers to disregard monetary incentives you offer.
   Y, N, NI

7. continually focus on building experience in determining what action to take at Burger King, depending on what events occur.
   Y, N, NI

8. see Burger King as a series of interdependent parts functioning as a whole.
   Y, N, NI

9. build an understanding of Burger King as a closed system.
   Y, N, NI

10. visualize Burger King system inputs as directly leading to system outputs.
    Y, N, NI

11. feel free to change Burger King system inputs after considering system outputs but not system process.
    Y, N, NI

12. continually monitor customers to determine ways to make the Burger King system more responsive to customer needs.
    Y, N, NI

13. use the triangular management model as a guideline for understanding comprehensive management skill.
    Y, N, NI

14. analyze Burger King as a group of interrelated parts that may or may not function as a whole.
    Y, N, NI

15. use systems thinking at Burger King as a foundation for building the company as a learning organization.
    Y, N, NI

Exploring Your Management Skill: Part 2

As you recall, you completed Exploring Your Management Skill before you started to study this chapter. Your responses gave you an idea of how much you initially knew about various approaches to management and helped you focus on important points as you studied the chapter. Answer the Exploring Your Management Skill questions again now and compare your score to the first time you took it. This comparison will give you an idea of how much you have learned from studying this chapter and pinpoint areas for further clarification before you start studying the next chapter. Record your answers within the text or online at MyManagementLab.com. Completing the survey at MyManagementLab.com will allow you to grade and compare your test scores automatically. If you complete the test in the book, look up answers in the Exploring Your Management Skill section at the end of the book.

Your Management Skills Portfolio

Your Management Learning Portfolio is a collection of activities especially designed to demonstrate your management knowledge and skill. By completing these activities online at MyManagementLab.com, you will be able to print, complete with cover sheet, as many activities as you choose. Be sure to save your work. Taking your printed portfolio to an employment interview could be helpful in obtaining a job.

The portfolio activity for this chapter is Comprehensive Management Skill at Crocs. Read this highlight about Crocs Inc. and perform the activities that follow.

Crocs Inc. started when three Boulder, Colorado-based founders decided to develop and market an innovative type of footwear called Crocs™ shoes. Originally intended as a boating/outdoor shoe because of its slip-resistant, nonmarking sole, by 2003 Crocs had become a bona-fide phenomenon, universally accepted as an all-purpose shoe for comfort and fashion.

During 2003–2004 Crocs focused on accommodating remarkable growth while maintaining control. The company expanded its product line, added warehouses and shipping programs for speedy assembly and delivery, and hired a senior management team. Today, Crocs are available all over the world and on the Internet as the company continues to significantly expand all aspects of its business.

Despite rapid success, Crocs still stands behind its core values. The company is committed to making a lightweight, comfortable, slip-resistant, fashionable, and functional shoe that can be produced quickly and at an affordable price.

Crocs has also developed products that focus on the needs of specific industries. The company offers specialized footwear products that support the needs of the health care, hospitality, restaurant, and transportation industries. The stylish closed-toe designs, made from patented material, are nonmarking, slip resistant, and odor resistant. Ergonomically certified, company shoes provide arch support with circulation nubs designed to stimulate your feet while you work. Crocs purports that its shoes improve health, safety, and overall well-being in the workplace.

Activity 1

You have just been appointed the new president of Crocs, Inc. To be successful, you will need to apply insights from many different approaches to management—your comprehensive management skill. Fill out the following form to help you organize your thoughts about how to examine Crocs, Inc., from a comprehensive management skill perspective.

PLANNING ISSUES TO INSPECT

Approach to Management	Issues to Be Examined at Crocs, Inc.
Behavioral Approach **(managing by focusing on people)**	**Do employees get along with management?** 1. _____ 2. _____ 3. _____ 4. _____
Systems Approach **(managing by viewing the organization as a whole)**	**What major parts of Crocs, Inc., function together to achieve goals?** 1. _____ 2. _____ 3. _____ 4. _____
Classical Approach **(managing by finding the "one best way" to do jobs)**	**Do people have the right tools to perform their jobs?** 1. _____ 2. _____ 3. _____ 4. _____

Activity 2

Assuming that you have gathered the information outlined in Activity 1, explain how the triangular management model would help you organize your thoughts for enabling Crocs to maximize success.

_____

_____

_____

_____

Experiential Exercises

1 Analyzing a Golf Swing

Directions. Read the following scenario and then perform the listed activities. Your instructor may want you to perform the activities as an individual or within groups. Follow all of your instructor's directions carefully.

Frank and Lillian Gilbreth recommended improving worker efficiency and effectiveness by searching for the "one best way" to perform work tasks. To discover this one best way, the Gilbreths would perform motion studies. A motion study would pinpoint those behaviors normally associated with a job well done and encourage workers to adopt those behaviors. As a result of one of the Gilbreths' motion studies, the number of motions needed to lay brick was reduced from 12 to 2.

Obviously, the effectiveness and efficiency of bricklayers were significantly increased as a result of the motion study.

To gain some experience in performing a motion study, find two photos on the Internet. One photo should show professional golfer Phil Mickelson's golf swing and follow-through. The other photo should show an amateur's golf swing and follow-through. The form and follow-through of the amateur do not lead to the same golf success that Mickelson attains.

Activity 1: Compare Phil Mickelson's follow-through and finish to that of the amateur. How are they the same? How are they different? Refer to specific behaviors in your comparison.

Activity 2: What advice would you give the amateur for improving his success in golf?

Activity 3: What are the strengths and limitations of your motion study results?

2 You and Your Career

Planning to Be President

You have just been offered a job as time study specialist in a company that manufacturers plumbing tools.[51] Your main job would be to figure out how hard people should be working—that is, how many activities of various sorts they should be performing per hour. Using a stopwatch and computer, you would measure what people do during a typical workday and make suggestions to their supervisors for how employees can improve. You would probably enjoy seeing how a piece of scrap metal is molded into a finished tool. On the other hand, you may not enjoy pushing people to work harder through the results of your studies. The salary and benefits seem fine to you. You've been with the company for two years and think that eventually you'd like to be president of this company. Would you take the job? Why? Why not?

Video Net Exercise

Rewards and Challenges of Being a Manager: Campus MovieFest

Video Highlights

Campus MovieFest (CMF) began in the Atlanta area as a student film club. It has expanded to hold festivals at more than 50 colleges and universities worldwide and is now the world's largest student film festival. On each campus location, CMF provides student teams all the equipment, training, and technical support needed to make their own five-minute movies, for one week. In the video, several managers discuss the beginnings of the company, managerial roles, communication, challenges, and rewards.

Discussion Questions

1. Describe the beginnings of Campus MovieFest as discussed by Vijay Makar in the video.
2. Describe the many roles of the managers in the video.
3. What do the managers say are the rewards and challenges of their jobs?

Internet Activity

Browse the Campus MovieFest site at www.campusmoviefest .com. Look around the site. Take the time to watch some of the featured student videos. Now click on the "About Us" link. Once there, read the statements listed about the organization's mission and goals. Are these statements consistent with the video clip? Use the management systems approach to describe the typical process of making a student video. If you were to make your own student video, what would it be about? Why?

CASES

1 HANDLING COMPETITORS AT BURGER KING

"Handling Competitors at Burger King" (p. 27) was written to help you better understand the management concepts contained in this chapter. Answer the following discussion questions about the Challenge Case to better understand how concepts relating to management history can be applied in a company such as Burger King.

1. Based on information in the introductory case, list three problems you think future Burger King managers will have to solve.
2. What action(s) do you think the managers will have to take to solve these problems?
3. From what you know about fast-food restaurants, how easy would it be to manage a Burger King restaurant? Why?

2 21ST CENTURY CHANGES FOR 160-YEAR OLD NEW YORK TIMES

Read the case and answer the questions that follow. Studying this case will help you better understand how the history of an organization impacts its current strategy. This case examines the New York Times.

The *New York Times* has been not only a fixture in New York City, but an American institution as well. Founded in 1851, it has covered the American Civil War, Custer's last stand, two world wars, moon landings, and even Lady Gaga. Few organizations in the United States are simultaneously as tenured and well-known as the *Times*. In its storied history, it has slowly and sometimes swiftly changed and evolved.

Some of the milestones it has achieved seem somewhat quaint today, but they were the latest in technology when they occurred. A few highlights from the organization's history read like the history of American society. As early as 1896, the paper began using photographs in its stories—now a ubiquitous component of papers all over the world. And in 1919, the *New York Times* sent a shipment of papers to London—by dirigible—thereby becoming the first trans-Atlantic delivery by air. Starting in 1980, news was being sent by satellite to printing presses across the country, enabling the paper to publish a national edition that would have universal appeal. Then, 16 years later, the *Times* made its debut on the Internet with its own Web site, nytimes.com.

But other changes are occurring at the *Times*. Venturing far away from its mainstay newspaper business, the paper is attempting to find new ways to maintain a profit. The *Times* is not alone in dealing with a generation that simply doesn't read the newspaper. Since 2000, readership of newspapers in general has been declining at the rate of about 700,000 per year. Advertising dollars from classified ads have dropped in half and employment ads are about one-quarter what they were just 10 years ago.[52]

So, what is a newspaper to do? How about offer a fine wine? Or a class on nursing? Or even a piece of the *Titanic*? The *New York Times* is doing all of these things—and more. According to Alice Ting, executive director of brand development with the paper, "Like a lot of newspapers, we were looking to expand into different verticals." In other words, offerings beyond the daily news. "If you think of the newspaper," she added, "we report on dining and food and home and health, so we've always looked at whether there was a way to extend the brand into those areas."[53] Thus, the New York Times Wine Club was a natural extension. Here, readers and nonreaders may order boutique wines directly from the *Times*. Customers may choose to have a shipment arrive once a month, every other month, or every three months. Along with their purchase, they receive tasting notes, recipes, and information about certain wine regions.[54]

In addition, through its "Knowledge Network," the *Times* offers online classes on art, cooking, nursing, paralegal studies, and numerous other topics. Students earn continuing education credits for taking classes directly from the *Times* or from various universities and colleges that partner with the paper. Collectibles are also available through the *Times*' Web site. One can order a piece of coal from the *Titanic* or a guitar signed by Willie Nelson. Jim Mones, director of the *Times*' online store said, "We started out with just photographs, and had great success. Then we extended to other kinds of content." That extension ties back to the *Times*' brand image. "We always look to see if it is a fit for the brand," added Ting. "And secondarily, is it something our readers would be passionate about? It's always brand first and then our customers."

Beyond unique offerings, the *Times* is at a major crossroads with regard to the access of their online content for news. Currently, subscribers and nonsubscribers can read news headlines on the *Times*' Web site at no cost. However, consideration is being given to charging for this access for those who do not have a paid subscription. With countless competing Web sites offering free news, this decision is one the *Times* is not taking lightly. The current plan is to permit free access to a predetermined number of articles per month—say, 10. Then, a fee would be assessed for any access beyond that number. Those who already have a paid subscription would have unlimited no-charge access. Arthur Sulzberger, Jr., chairman and publisher of the *Times*, sees this as a necessary step for the paper. "We believe this is where our world is going," Sulzberger said, "it's a journey."[55]

QUESTIONS

1. Assume you are a manager working at the *New York Times*' headquarters. Based on the current changes taking place at the newspaper, which of Henri Fayol's 14 principles of management would be most pertinent to you? Why?

2. With all the changes occurring at the *Times*, do you think the systems approach to management is applicable in this organization? Why or why not?

3. How do you think working conditions have changed at the *New York Times*? What do you imagine it was like to work there in 1851?

Endnotes

1. Andrew Martin, "Burger King Shifts Policy on Animals," *New York Times*, March 28, 2007, 1.
2. Thomas J. Lueck, "City May Ask Restaurants to List Calories," *New York Times*, October 30, 2006, B1; Charlie LeDuff, "Dreams in the Dark at the Drive-Through Window," *New York Times*, November 27, 2006, A12.
3. James H. Donnelly, Jr., James L. Gibson, and John M. Ivancevich, *Fundamentals of Management* (Plano, TX: Business Publications, 1987), 6–8; Harold Koontz, Cyril O'Donnell, and Heinz Weihrich, *Management*, 8th ed. (New York: McGraw-Hill, 1984), 52–69; W. Warren Haynes and Joseph L. Massie, *Management*, 2nd ed. (Upper Saddle River, NJ: Prentice Hall, 1969), 4–13.
4. David W. Hays, "Quality Improvement and Its Origin in Scientific Management," *Quality Progress*, May 5, 1994, 89–90.
5. For an article describing how Taylor's work has given rise to other types of modern production research, see Betsi Harris Ehrlich, "Service with a Smile," *Industrial Engineer* 38, no. 8 (August 2006): 40–44.
6. Frederick W. Taylor, *The Principles of Scientific Management* (New York: Harper & Bros., 1947), 66–71.
7. For more information on the work of Frederick Taylor, see Edward Rimer, "Organization Theory and Frederick Taylor," *Public Administration Review* 53 (May/June 1993): 270–272; Alan Farnham, "The Man Who Changed Work Forever," *Fortune*, July 21, 1997, 114; Hans Picard, "Quit Following Marx's Advice," *ENR* 246, no. 12 (March 26, 2001): 99.
8. "Date in Quality History," *Quality Progress* 43, no. 3 (March 2010): 14.
9. Franz T. Lohrke, "Motion Study for the Blinded: A Review of the Gilbreths' Work with the Visually Handicapped," *International Journal of Public Administration* 16 (1993): 667–668. For information illustrating how the career of Lillian Gilbreth is an inspiration for modern women managers, see Thomas R. Miller and Mary A. Lemons, "Breaking the Glass Ceiling: Lessons from a Management Pioneer," *S.A.M. Advanced Management Journal* 63, no. 1 (Winter 1998): 4–9.
10. Edward A. Michaels, "Work Measurement," *Small Business Reports* 14 (March 1989): 55–63. For information regarding the application of time studies in nursing home, see Greg Arling, Robert L. Kane, Christine Mueller, and Teresa Lewis, "Explaining Direct Care Resource Use of Nursing Home Residents: Findings from Time Studies in Four States," *Health Services Research* 42, no. 2 (April 2007): 827.
11. Dennis Karwatka, "Frank Gilbreth and Production Efficiency," *Tech Directions* 65, no. 6 (January 2006): 10.
12. Fariss-Terry Mousa and David J. Lemak, "The Gilbreths' Quality System Stands the Test of Time," *Journal of Management History* 15, no. 2 (2009): 198–215.
13. Ibid.
14. Henry L. Gantt, *Industrial Leadership* (New Haven, CT: Yale University Press, 1916), 57.
15. For more information on the Gantt chart, see Jeff Angus, "Software Speeds Up Project Management," *Informationweek*, September 8, 1997, 85–88; Mel Lofurno, "The Gantt Chart," *Compoundings* 52 (2002): 35.
16. Marc Puich, "The Critical Path," *Biopharm International* 20, no. 3 (March 2007): 28, 30.
17. Doug Green and Denise Green, "MacSchedule Has Rich Features at Low Price," *InfoWorld*, July 12, 1993, 88.
18. Gantt, *Industrial Leadership*, 85.
19. Chester I. Barnard, *Organization and Management* (Cambridge, MA: Harvard University Press, 1952).
20. Alvin Brown, *Organization of Industry* (Upper Saddle River, NJ: Prentice Hall, 1947); Henry S. Dennison, *Organization Engineering* (New York: McGraw-Hill, 1931); Luther Gulick and Lyndall Urwick, eds., *Papers on the Science of Administration* (New York: Institute of Public Administration, 1937); J. D. Mooney and A. C. Reiley, *Onward Industry!* (New York: Harper & Bros., 1931); Oliver Sheldon, *The Philosophy of Management* (London: Sir Isaac Pitman and Sons, 1923).

21. Henri Fayol, *General and Industrial Management* (London: Sir Isaac Pitman and Sons, 1949). See also David Frederick, "Making Sense of Management I," *Credit Management* (December 2000): 34–35.

22. Charles A. Mowll, "Successful Management Based on Key Principles," *Healthcare Financial Management* 43 (June 1989): 122, 124; Carl A. Rodrigues, "Fayol's 14 Principles of Management Then and Now: A Framework for Managing Today's Organizations Effectively," *Management Decision* 39 (2001): 880–889.

23. Fayol, *General and Industrial Management,* 19–42. For an excellent discussion of the role of accountability and organization structure, see Elliott Jaques, "In Praise of Hierarchy," *Harvard Business Review* 68 (January/February 1990): 127–133.

24. For an interesting discussion on how "chain of command" helps to minimize the negative impact of oil spills, see James Hunt, Bruce Carter, and Frank Kelly, "Clearly Defined Chain-of-Command Helps Mobilize Oil Spill," *Occupational Health & Safety* (June 1993): 40–45. For a discussion of the impact of remuneration on an organization, see Jeffrey Bradt, "Pay for Impact," *Personnel Journal* (January 1992): 76–79.

25. Lee D. Parker and Philip Ritson, "Fads, Stereotypes, and Management Gurus: Fayol and Follett Today" *Management Decision* 43, no. 10 (2005): 1335–1357.

26. For detailed summaries of these studies, see *Industrial Worker,* 2 vols. (Cambridge, MA: Harvard University Press, 1938); and F. J. Roethlisberger and W. J. Dickson, *Management and the Worker* (Cambridge, MA: Harvard University Press, 1939).

27. Stephen Jones, "Worker Interdependence and Output: The Hawthorne Studies Reevaluated," *American Sociological Review* (April 1990): 176–190.

28. Jennifer Laabs, "Corporate Anthropologists," *Personnel Journal* (January 1992): 81–91; Samuel C. Certo, *Human Relations Today: Concepts and Skills* (Burr Ridge, IL: Irwin, 1995), 4; Scott Highhouse, "Well-Being: The Foundations of Hedonic Psychology," *Personnel Psychology* 54, no. 1 (Spring 2001): 204–206.

29. Michael Wilson, "The Psychology of Motivation and Employee Retention," *Maintenance Supplies* 50, no. 5 (July 2005): 48–49.

30. A. H. Reylito Elbo, "In the Workplace," *BusinessWorld* (2002): 1.

31. David A. Kaplan, "SAS: A New No. 1 Best Employer," *CNNMoney.com,* January 22, 2010, http://money.cnn.com.

32. C. West Churchman, Russell L. Ackoff, and E. Leonard Arnoff, *Introduction to Operations Research* (New York: Wiley, 1957), 18.

33. Hamdy A. Taha, *Operations Research: An Introduction* (New York: Macmillan, 1988), 1–2; see also Scott Shane and Karl Ulrich, "Technological Innovation, Product Development, and Entrepreneurship in Management Science," *Management Science* 2 (2004): 133–145.

34. Kalyan Singhal, Jaya Singhal, and Martin K Starr, "The Domain of Production and Operations Management and the Role of Elwood Buffa in its Delineation," *Journal of Operations Management* 25, no. 2 (March 2007): 310.

35. James R. Emshoff, *Analysis of Behavioral Systems* (New York: Macmillan, 1971), 10.

36. For a discussion of management science in the twenty-first century, see Michael S. Hopkins, "Putting the Science in Management Science?" *MIT Sloan Management Review,* March 17, 2010, http://www.URL. An interesting discussion of the issues related to establishing a health information technology system for the United States are found in David J. Bailer, "Guiding the Health Information Technology Agenda," *Health Affairs* 29, no. 4 (April 2010): 586–594. See also H. J. Zimmermann, "Some Observations on Practicing Successful Operational Research," *The Journal of the Operational Research Society* 49, no. 4 (April 1998): 413–419.

37. The discussion concerning these characteristics is adapted from Donnelly, Gibson, and Ivancevich, *Fundamentals of Management,* 302–303; Efraim Turban and Jack R. Meredith, *Fundamentals of Management Science* (Plano, TX: Business Publications, 1981), 15–23.

38. Harold Koontz, "The Management Theory Jungle Revisited," *Academy of Management Review* 5 (1980): 175–187. For a practical application of the contingency approach to management, see Henri Barki, Suzanne Rivard, and Jean Talbot, "An Integrative Contingency Model of Software Project Risk Management," *Journal of Management Information Systems* 17, no. 4 (Spring 2001): 37–69.

39. For an application of the contingency approach to management in an information systems organization, see Narayan S. Umanath, "The Concept of Contingency Beyond 'It Depends': Illustrations from IS Research Stream," *Information & Management* 40 (2003): 551–562.

40. Don Hellriegel, John W. Slocum, and Richard W. Woodman, *Organizational Behavior* (St. Paul, MN: West Publishing, 1986), 22.

41. J. W. Lorsch, "Organization Design: A Situational Perspective," *Organizational Dynamics* 6 (1977): 2–4; Louis W. Fry and Deborah A. Smith, "Congruence, Contingency, and Theory Building," *Academy of Management Review* (January 1987): 117–132.

42. For a more detailed development of von Bertalanffy's ideas, see "General System Theory: A New Approach to Unity of Science," *Human Biology* (December 1951): 302–361.

43. L. Thomas Hopkins, *Integration: Its Meaning and Application* (New York: Appleton-Century-Crofts, 1937), 36–49.

44. Company Web site, http://www.reviewpro.com, accessed April 15, 2010; Marina Zaliznyak, "Hotel Reputation Management Service ReviewPro Has Big International Plans," *TechCrunch,* January 5, 2010, http://eu.techcrunch.com.

45. Joe Schwartz, "Why They Buy," *American Demographics* 11 (March 1989): 40–41.

46. Ken Starkey, "What Can We Learn from the Learning Organization?" *Human Relations* 51, no. 4 (April 1998): 531–546.

47. David A. Garvin, "Building a Learning Organization," *Harvard Business Review* 74, no. 4 (July 1993): 78. For more recent discussion of learning organizations, see Bente Elkjaer, "The Dance of Change: The Challenges of Sustaining Momentum in Learning Organizations," *Management Learning* 32, no. 1 (March 2000): 153–156.

48. For a study on the effectiveness of the learning organization approach, see Ashok Jashapara, "Cognition, Culture, and Competition: An Empirical Test of the Learning Organization," *The Learning Organization* 10 (2003): 31–50.

49. Peter Senge, *The Fifth Discipline, The Art & Practice of the Learning Organization* (New York: Doubleday/Currency, 1990). Used by permission of Doubleday, a division of Random House, Inc. For more background regarding learning organizations and innovation, see Li-Fen Liao, "A Learning Organization Perspective on Knowledge-Sharing Behavior and Firm Innovation," *Human Systems Management* 25, no. 4 (2006): 227.

50. Leonel Prieto, "Some Necessary Conditions and Constraints for Successful Learning Organizations," *Competition Forum* 7, no. 2 (2009): 513–520.

51. This exercise based on Edward V. Morandi, Jr., "On the Job, Time Study Supervisor," *Telegram & Gazette,* November 13, 2006, E1.

52. Harris, J. (2009). Newspapers are suffering. *Backbone,* 10. http://www.nytimes.com.

53. Fitzgerald, M. (2010). Oh, And We Sell Newspapers, Too. *Editor & Publisher, 143*(4), 32–35.

54. www.nytimes.com.

55. Saba, J. (2010). WWNYTD: What would 'The New York Times' do?. *Editor & Publisher, 143*(3), 7–2.

chapter

3

Corporate Social Responsibility, Ethics, and Sustainability

Target Skill

corporate social responsibility skill: the ability to take action that protects and improves both the welfare of society and the interests of the organization

objectives

To help build my *corporate social responsibility skill,* when studying this chapter, I will attempt to acquire:

1. A thorough understanding of the term *corporate social responsibility*

2. An ability to argue both for and against the assumption of social responsibilities by business

3. Useful strategies for increasing the social responsiveness of an organization

4. Insights into the planning, organizing, influencing, and controlling of social responsibility activities

CHALLENGE CASE

VERIZON'S COMMITMENT TO SOCIAL RESPONSIBILITY

VERIZON, A LEADING GLOBAL provider of wireless telecommunications services, has nearly 223,000 employees and recently posted $107 billion in revenues. Currently, more than 100 million customers use Verizon's network.

Verizon is committed to making the world a better place. To manage and implement its social responsibility mission, the company established the Verizon Foundation. Led by Patrick R. Gaston, the foundation concentrates its efforts in two areas: literacy and education and safety and health.

Verizon's emphasis on education stems from dismal national statistics: more than two-thirds of America's students score below proficiency levels in reading and math. To help, Verizon established Thinkfinity, an online storehouse offering a wealth of standards-based educational resources for home and classroom use at no charge.

Verizon also focuses on public safety, saying that one in four women, one in nine men, and more than 3 million children in America will experience domestic violence in their lifetime. Domestic violence is reportedly the single greatest cause of injury to women ages 15 to 44 in the United States, with the annual health-related costs of intimate partner violence totaling nearly $6 billion. Verizon provides wireless phones to not-for-profit organizations for the use of their clients, survivors, and victims of abuse. The company also helps maintain a directory of resources providing pro bono legal services to victims of domestic violence.

The company also encourages social responsibility among employees and retirees. Employees can obtain company assistance coordinating fundraising campaigns for their favorite charity, and employees who log 50 hours of volunteer time can register their charity for a $750 grant from Verizon. Retirees can double the impact of their contributions to higher education through Verizon's 1:1 matching program.

Verizon responded decisively after an earthquake devastated Haiti. Besides enabling employees and customers to make mobile text donations to the Red Cross, the company donated $50,000 each to World Vision and Food for the Poor to aid in relief efforts. In addition, to help those affected by the quake, Verizon waived all long-distance usage charges for calls from residential landlines and Verizon wireless phones to Haiti for several weeks following the quake. Calls were billed at zero cents per minute and, for customers whose calling plan includes monthly minutes, calls to Haiti did not accrue to their total.

■ *After an earthquake devasted Haiti, Verizon participated in relief efforts by enabling employees and customers to make mobile text donations to the Red Cross, in addition to donating $50,000 each to World Vision and Food for the Poor.*

As Verizon Foundation president Gaston said, "The passion to lead corporate philanthropy efforts and create a stronger, wiser, and healthier nation and world stands at the core of the Verizon Foundation's mission." Gaston attributed that passion to the "hearts, minds and hands" of Verizon employees and retirees and the not-of-profit agencies Verizon supports. Verizon has recently awarded $67.5 million to nonprofit organizations and was named to *Fortune* magazine's list of the world's most admired companies.[1]

EXPLORING YOUR MANAGEMENT SKILL

You can explore your level of corporate social responsibility skill **before** studying the chapter by completing the exercise "Exploring Your Management Skill: Part 1" on page 75 and **after** studying this chapter by completing the exercise "Exploring Your Management Skill: Part 2" on page 76.

THE CORPORATE SOCIAL RESPONSIBILITY CHALLENGE

The Challenge Case illustrates the social responsibility challenges that Verizon strives to meet. The remaining material in this chapter explains corporate social responsibility concepts and helps develop the corresponding corporate social responsibility skill you will need to meet such challenges throughout your career. Within the chapter, *ethics* is presented as a catalyst that spurs management into being socially responsible and *sustainability* is presented as an approach to social responsibility that emphasizes present and future resource use. After studying chapter concepts, read the Challenge Case Summary at the end of the chapter to help you relate chapter content to meeting social responsibility challenges at Verizon.

FUNDAMENTALS OF SOCIAL RESPONSIBILITY

The term *social responsibility* means different things to different people. For purposes of this chapter, however, **corporate social responsibility** is the managerial obligation to take action that protects and improves both the welfare of society as a whole and the interests of the organization. According to the concept of corporate social responsibility, a manager must strive to achieve societal as well as organizational goals.[2] This obligation is important for managers worldwide, including those in emerging economies.[3]

how managers do it

Managing Responsibly at Arch Chemicals

Michael E. Campbell is the top manager at Arch Chemicals.[4] Campbell recently explained how his company focuses on social responsibility through its production of water sanitization products. According to Campbell, water supplies are undergoing extreme swings in developed and underdeveloped countries across the globe due to violent storms and floods. Campbell believes water shortages are growing and in the near future will affect more than 450 million people. Also, according to Campbell, even when water is available, it is not unusual to find water sources that are too contaminated for people to drink without the risk of serious illness. Following the spirit of the social responsibility concept, Campbell pointed out that seeing both human need and, someday at least, profits, companies in the chemical industry have now begun developing a wide range of technologies that can help secure safe drinking water for the world's poor. ■

The amount of attention given to the area of social responsibility by both management and society has increased in recent years and probably will continue to increase.[5] The following sections present the fundamentals of social responsibility of businesses by discussing these topics:

1. The Davis Model of corporate social responsibility
2. Areas of corporate social responsibility
3. Varying opinions on social responsibility
4. Conclusions about the performance of social responsibility activities by business

The Davis Model of Corporate Social Responsibility

A generally accepted model of corporate social responsibility was developed by Keith Davis.[6] Stated simply, Davis's model is a list of five propositions that describe why and how business should adhere to the obligation to take action that protects and improves the welfare of society as well as that of the organization:

- **Proposition 1: Social responsibility arises from social power**—This proposition is derived from the premise that business has a significant amount of influence on, or power over, such critical social issues as minority employment and environmental pollution. In essence, the collective action of all businesses in the country primarily determines the proportion of minorities employed and the prevailing condition of the environment in which all citizens must live.

  Davis reasons that because business has this power over society, society can and must hold business responsible for social conditions that result from the exercise of this power. Davis explains that society's legal system does not expect more of business than it does of each individual citizen exercising personal power.

- **Proposition 2: Business shall operate as a two-way open system, with open receipt of inputs from society and open disclosure of its operations to the public**—According to this proposition, business must be willing to listen to what must be done to sustain or improve societal welfare. In turn, society must be willing to listen to business reports on what it is doing to meet its social responsibilities. Davis suggests that there must be ongoing, honest, and open communications between business and society's representatives if the overall welfare of society is to be maintained or improved.

A Home Depot assistant manager at work in Stratford, CT. One area of social responsibility for Home Depot includes convincing its suppliers to protect forests in countries like Chile and Indonesia.

Source: Courtesy of Douglas Healey/*The New York Times*/Redux Pictures.

- **Proposition 3: The social costs and benefits of an activity, product, or service shall be thoroughly calculated and considered in deciding whether to proceed with it**—This proposition stresses that technical feasibility and economic profitability are not the only factors that should influence business decision making. Business should also consider both the long- and short-term societal consequences of all business activities before undertaking them.

- **Proposition 4: The social costs related to each activity, product, or service shall be passed on to the consumer**—This proposition states that business cannot be expected to completely finance activities that may be socially advantageous but economically disadvantageous. The cost of maintaining socially desirable activities within business should be passed on to consumers through higher prices for the goods or services related to these activities.

- **Proposition 5: Business institutions, as citizens, have the responsibility to become involved in certain social problems that are outside their normal areas of operation**—This last proposition points out that if a business possesses the expertise to solve a social problem with which it may not be directly associated, it should be held responsible for helping society solve that problem. Davis reasons that because business eventually will reap an increased profit from a generally improved society, business should share in the responsibility of all citizenry to generally improve society.

Areas of Corporate Social Responsibility: Going Green

The areas in which business can act to protect and improve the welfare of society are numerous and diverse. Perhaps the most publicized of these areas are urban affairs, consumer affairs, community volunteerism, and employment practices. The one area that is arguably receiving the most recent attention is the area of ecology conservation, popularly called "going green."[7] An international effort sponsored by the United Nations is currently underway and growing to get large companies to start thinking seriously about ecosystems and how to maintain them. Companies are responding. For example, the Coca-Cola Company is exploring ways to maintain its bottling operation in India without using underground water; the Mohawk Home Company is developing a new line of bathroom rugs with all natural fibers;[8] and Kellogg's is developing environmentally sensitive products, such as its organic Rice Krispies.[9] Pressure groups are also springing up to persuade companies to "go green." One such group, The Center for Health, Environment, and Justice, was founded and is led by grassroots leader, Lois Gibbs.

Varying Opinions on Social Responsibility

Although numerous businesses are already involved in social responsibility activities, much controversy remains about whether such involvement is necessary or even appropriate. The following two sections present some arguments for and against businesses performing social responsibility activities.[10]

Arguments *for* Business Performing Social Responsibility Activities
The best-known argument for the performance of social responsibility activities by business was alluded to earlier in this chapter. This argument begins with the premise that business, as a whole, is a subset of society, one that exerts a significant impact on the way society exists. Because business is such an influential member of society, the argument continues, it has the responsibility to help maintain and improve the overall welfare of society.[11] If society already puts this responsibility on its individual members, then why should its corporate members be exempt?

In addition, some people argue that business should perform social responsibility activities because profitability and growth go hand-in-hand with responsible treatment of employees, customers, and the community. This argument says, essentially, that performing social responsibility activities is a means of earning greater organizational profit.[12]

Researchers continue to study the relationship between corporate social responsibility and revenue growth.[13] However, empirical studies have not yet demonstrated a definitive relationship between corporate social responsibility and profitability. In fact, several companies that have been acknowledged leaders in social commitment—including Control Data Corporation, Atlantic Richfield, Dayton-Hudson, Levi Strauss, and Polaroid—simultaneously experienced serious financial difficulties.[14] No direct relationship between corporate social responsibility activities and these financial difficulties was shown, however.

research highlight

DOES SOCIAL RESPONSIBILITY HELP A COMPANY'S BOTTOM LINE?

This chapter introduces social responsibility as a modern management challenge. For years, scholars have examined the influence of social responsibility on a company's financial performance. In an attempt to add more evidence to this debate, a recent study by Professors Brammer and Millington examined the influence of corporate donations on a company's bottom line.[15]

To examine this relationship in detail, the authors tracked 537 firms listed on the London Stock Exchange over 10 years. The authors classified the companies as making high, medium, or low levels of charitable donations. The authors then studied the short- and long-term financial performance of these three groups of firms. Do you think charitable donations led to better or worse short-term performance? What about long-term performance? Prepare to defend your answers in class.

Arguments *Against* Business Performing Social Responsibility Activities The best-known argument against business performing social responsibility activities has been advanced by Milton Friedman, one of America's most distinguished economists. Friedman argues that making business managers simultaneously responsible to business owners for reaching profit objectives and to society for enhancing societal welfare sets up a conflict of interest that could potentially cause the demise of business as it is known today. According to Friedman, this demise will almost certainly occur if business is continually forced to perform socially responsible actions that directly conflict with private organizational objectives.[16]

Friedman also argues that to require business managers to pursue socially responsible objectives may, in fact, be unethical, because it compels managers to spend money on some individuals that rightfully belongs to other individuals. Following Friedman's argument, a corporate executive is an employee of a business and is directly responsible to owners of the business. Overall, this responsibility is to conduct business in ways desired by the owners. Usually, owners desire to maximize profit while following the basic rules of society reflecting both laws and ethical customs. When managers reduce profit, they are spending owners' money. When managers raise prices of products they are spending customers' money.[17]

An example that Friedman could use to illustrate his argument is the Control Data Corporation. Former chairman William Norris involved Control Data in many socially responsible programs that cost the company millions of dollars—from building plants in the inner city and employing a minority workforce to researching farming on the Alaskan tundra. When Control Data began to incur net losses of millions of dollars in the mid-1980s, critics blamed Norris's "do-gooder" mentality. Eventually, a new chairman was installed to restructure the company and return it to profitability.[18]

Conclusions About the Performance of Social Responsibility Activities by Business

The preceding section presented several major arguments for and against businesses performing social responsibility activities. Regardless of which argument or combination of arguments particular managers embrace, they generally should make a concerted effort to do the following:

1. Perform all legally required social responsibility activities.
2. Consider voluntarily performing social responsibility activities beyond those legally required.
3. Inform all relevant individuals of the extent to which the organization will become involved in performing social responsibility activities.

Performing Required Social Responsibility Activities Federal legislation requires that businesses perform certain social responsibility activities. In fact, several government agencies have been established expressly to enforce such business-related legislation (see Table 3.1). The Environmental Protection Agency, for instance, has the authority to require businesses to adhere to certain socially responsible environmental standards. Examples of specific legislation requiring the performance of corporate social responsibility activities are the Equal Pay Act of 1963, the Equal Employment Opportunity Act of 1972, the Highway Safety Act of 1978, and the Clean Air Act Amendments of 1990.[19]

Voluntarily Performing Social Responsibility Activities Adherence to legislated social responsibilities is the minimum standard of social responsibility performance that business managers must achieve. Managers must ask themselves, however, how far beyond the minimum they should go.

Determining how far to go is a simple process to describe, yet it is difficult and complicated to implement. It entails assessing the positive and negative outcomes of performing social responsibility activities over both the short and the long terms, and then performing only those activities that maximize management system success while making a desirable contribution to the welfare of society.

TABLE 3.1   Primary Functions of Several Federal Agencies That Enforce Social Responsibility Legislation

Federal Agency	Primary Agency Functions
Equal Employment Opportunity Commission	Investigates and conciliates employment discrimination complaints that are based on race, sex, or creed
Office of Federal Contract Compliance Programs	Ensures that employers holding federal contracts grant equal employment opportunity to people regardless of their race or sex
Environmental Protection Agency	Formulates and enforces environmental standards in such areas as water, air, and noise pollution
Consumer Product Safety Commission	Strives to reduce consumer misunderstanding of manufacturers' product design, labeling, and so on, by promoting clarity of these messages
Occupational Safety and Health Administration	Regulates safety and health conditions in nongovernment workplaces
National Highway Traffic Safety Administration	Attempts to reduce traffic accidents through the regulation of transportation-related manufacturers and products
Mining Enforcement and Safety Administration	Attempts to improve safety conditions for mine workers by enforcing all mine safety and equipment standards

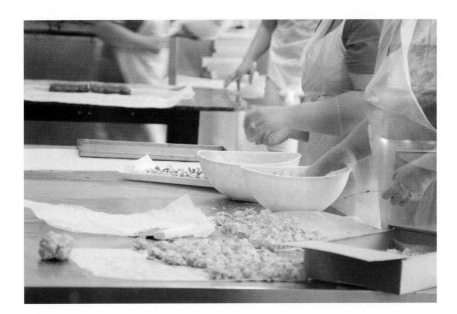

Sara Lee Bakery took voluntary action to help employees who were developing the painful symptoms of carpal tunnel syndrome. Following a thorough investigation, the company asked its own engineers to design new tools for the workers that soon eliminated the symptoms.

Events at the Sara Lee Bakery plant in New Hampton, Iowa, illustrate how company management can voluntarily take action to protect employees' health. Many employees at the plant began to develop carpal tunnel syndrome, a debilitating wrist disorder caused by repeated hand motions. Instead of simply having its employees go through physical therapy—and, as the principal employer in the town, watching the morale of the town drop—Sara Lee thoroughly investigated the problem. Managers took suggestions from factory workers and had their engineers design tools to alleviate the problem. The result was a virtual elimination of carpal tunnel syndrome at the plant within a short time.[20]

Communicating the Degree of Social Responsibility Involvement

Determining the extent to which a business should perform social responsibility activities beyond legal requirements is a subjective process. Despite this subjectivity, however, managers should have a well-defined position in this vital area and should inform all organization members of that position.[21] Taking these steps will ensure that managers and organization members behave consistently to support the position and that societal expectations of what a particular organization can achieve in this area are realistic.

Nike, the world-famous athletic-gear manufacturer, recently felt so strongly that its corporate philosophy on social responsibility issues should be clearly formulated and communicated that the company created a new position, vice president of corporate and social responsibility. Maria Eitelto, a former public-relations executive at Microsoft, was hired to fill that position and is now responsible for clearly communicating Nike's thoughts on social responsibility both inside and outside the organization.[22]

SOCIAL RESPONSIVENESS

The previous section discussed social responsibility, a business's obligation to take action that protects and improves the welfare of society along with the business's own interests. This section defines and discusses **social responsiveness**, the degree of effectiveness and efficiency an organization displays in pursuing its social responsibilities.[23] The greater the degree of effectiveness and efficiency, the more socially responsive the organization is said to be. The next three sections address the following issues:

1. Determining whether a social responsibility exists
2. Social responsiveness and decision making
3. Approaches to meeting social responsibilities

Determining Whether a Social Responsibility Exists

One challenge facing managers who are attempting to be socially responsive is to determine which specific social obligations are implied by their business situation. Managers in the tobacco industry, for example, are probably socially obligated to contribute to public health by pushing for the development of innovative tobacco products that do less harm to people's health than present products do, but they are not socially obligated to help reclaim shorelines contaminated by oil spills.

Clearly, management has an obligation to be socially responsible toward its stakeholders. A **stakeholder** is any individual or group that is directly or indirectly affected by an organization's decisions.[24] Managers of successful organizations typically have many different stakeholders to consider: stockholders, or owners of the organization; suppliers; lenders; government agencies; employees and unions; consumers; competitors; and local communities as well as society at large. Table 3.2 lists these stakeholders and gives a corresponding example of how a manager is socially obligated to each of them.

Social Responsiveness and Decision Making

The socially responsive organization that is both effective and efficient meets its social responsibilities without wasting organizational resources in the process. Determining exactly which social responsibilities an organization should pursue and then deciding how to pursue them are the two most critical decisions for maintaining a high level of social responsiveness within an organization.

Figure 3.1 is a flowchart that managers can use as a general guideline for making social responsibility decisions that enhance the social responsiveness of their organization. This figure implies that for managers to achieve and maintain a high level of social responsiveness within an organization, they must pursue only those responsibilities their organization possesses and has a right to undertake. Furthermore, once managers decide to meet a specific social responsibility, they must determine the best way to undertake activities related to meeting this obligation. That is, managers must decide whether their organization should undertake the activities on its own or acquire the help of outsiders with more expertise in the area.

Approaches to Meeting Social Responsibilities

Various managerial approaches to meeting social obligations are another determinant of an organization's level of social responsiveness. According to Lipson, a desirable and socially responsive approach to meeting social obligations does the following:[25]

TABLE 3.2	Stakeholders of a Typical Modern Organization and Examples of Social Obligations Managers Owe to Them
Stakeholder	**Social Obligations Owed**
Stockholders/owners of the organization	To increase the value of the organization
Suppliers of materials	To deal with them fairly
Banks and other lenders	To repay debts
Government agencies	To abide by laws
Employees and unions	To provide safe working environment and to negotiate fairly with union representatives
Consumers	To provide safe products
Competitors	To compete fairly and to refrain from restraints of trade
Local communities and society at large	To avoid business practices that harm the environment

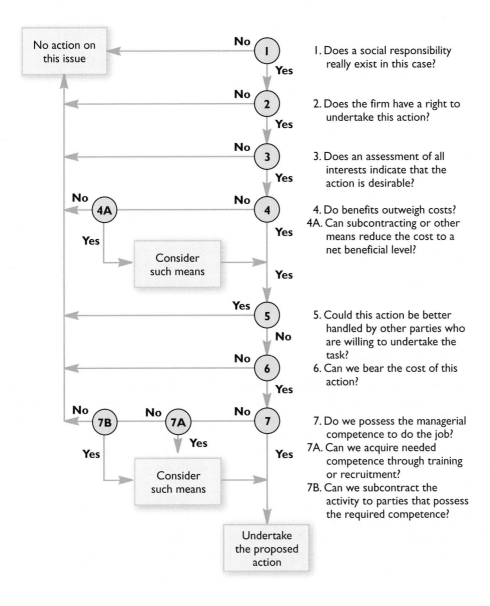

FIGURE 3.1
Flowchart of social responsibility decision making that generally will enhance the social responsiveness of an organization

1. Incorporates social goals into the annual planning process.
2. Seeks comparative industry norms for social programs.
3. Presents reports to organization members, the board of directors, and stockholders on social responsibility progress.
4. Experiments with different approaches for measuring social performance.
5. Attempts to measure the cost of social programs as well as the return on social program investments.

   S. Prakash Sethi presents three management approaches to meeting social obligations:[26]

1. Social obligation approach
2. Social responsibility approach
3. Social responsiveness approach

Each of these approaches entails behavior that reflects a somewhat different attitude toward performance of social responsibility activities by business. The **social obligation approach**, for example, considers business as having primarily economic purposes and confines social responsibility activity mainly to existing legislation. The **social responsibility approach** sees business as having both economic and societal goals. The **social responsiveness approach** considers business as having both societal and economic goals as well as the obligation to anticipate potential social problems and work actively toward preventing their occurrence.

Organizations characterized by attitudes and behaviors consistent with the social responsiveness approach are generally more socially responsive than organizations characterized by attitudes and behaviors consistent with either the social responsibility or the social obligation approach. And organizations that take the social responsibility approach usually achieve higher levels of social responsiveness than organizations that take the social obligation approach. In other words, as one moves along the continuum from social obligation to social responsiveness, one generally finds management becoming more proactive. Proactive managers do what is prudent from a business viewpoint to reduce liabilities regardless of whether such action is required by law.

SOCIAL RESPONSIBILITY ACTIVITIES AND MANAGEMENT FUNCTIONS

This section considers social responsibility as a major organizational activity subject to the same management techniques used in other major organizational activities, such as production, personnel, finance, and marketing. Managers have known for some time that to achieve desirable results in these areas, they must be effective in planning, organizing, influencing, and controlling. Achieving social responsibility results is no different. The following sections discuss planning, organizing, influencing, and controlling social responsibility activities.

Planning Social Responsibility Activities

Planning was defined in Chapter 1 as the process of determining how the organization will achieve its objectives, or get where it wants to go. Planning social responsibility activities, then, involves determining how the organization will achieve its social responsibility objectives, or get where it wants to go in the area of social responsibility. The following sections discuss how the planning of social responsibility activities is related to the organization's overall planning process and how its social responsibility policy can be converted into action.

The Overall Planning Process   The model presented in Figure 3.2 illustrates how social responsibility activities can be handled as part of the overall planning process of the organization. As shown in this figure, social trends forecasts should be performed within the organizational environment along with the more typically performed economic, political, and technological trends forecasts. Examples of social trends that organizations can forecast are societal attitudes toward water pollution, safe working conditions, and the national education system.[27] Each of the forecasts would influence the development of the organization's long-run plans, or plans for the more distant future, and short-run plans, or plans for the relatively near future.

Organizing Social Responsibility Activities

Organizing was discussed in Chapter 1 as the process of establishing orderly uses for all the organization's resources. These uses emphasize the attainment of management system objectives and flow naturally from management system plans. Correspondingly, organizing for social

FIGURE 3.2   Integration of social responsibility activities and planning activities

FIGURE 3.3 How ChevronTexaco Company includes social responsibility in its organization chart

responsibility activities entails establishing for all organizational resources logical uses that emphasize the attainment of the organization's social objectives that are consistent with its social responsibility plans.

Figure 3.3 shows how ChevronTexaco Corporation decided to organize for the performance of its social responsibility activities. The vice president for Health, Environment, and Safety has primary responsibility in the area of societal affairs and oversees the related activities of numerous individuals. This chart is intended only as an illustration of how a company might include its social responsibility area on its organization chart. Specific organizing in this area should always be tailored to the unique needs of a company.

Influencing Individuals Performing Social Responsibility Activities

Influencing was defined in Chapter 1 as the management process of guiding the activities of organization members to help attain organizational objectives. As applied to the social responsibility area, then, influencing is the process of guiding the activities of organization members to help attain the organization's social responsibility objectives. More specifically, to influence appropriately in this area, managers must lead, communicate, motivate, and work with groups in ways that result in the attainment of the organization's social responsibility objectives.

Controlling Social Responsibility Activities

Controlling, as discussed in Chapter 1, is making things happen as they were planned to happen. To control, managers assess or measure what is occurring in the organization and, if necessary, change these occurrences in some way to make them conform to plans. Controlling in the area of social responsibility entails the same two major tasks. The following sections discuss various areas in which social responsibility measurement takes place and examine the social audit, a tool for determining and reporting progress in the attainment of social responsibility objectives.

Areas of Measurement Measurements to gauge organizational progress in reaching social responsibility objectives can be taken in any number of areas. The specific areas in which individual companies decide to take such measurements will vary according to the specific social responsibility objectives to be met. All companies, however, should take social responsibility measurements in at least the following four major areas:[28]

1. **The economic function area**—A measurement should be made of whether the organization is performing such activities as producing goods and services that people need, creating jobs for society, paying fair wages, and ensuring worker safety. This measurement gives some indication of the economic contribution the organization is making to society.

2. **The quality-of-life area**—The measurement of quality of life should focus on whether the organization is improving or degrading the general quality of life in society. Producing high-quality goods, dealing fairly with employees and customers, and making an effort to preserve the natural environment are all indicators that the organization is upholding or improving the general quality of life. As an example of degrading the quality of life, some people believe that cigarette companies, because they produce goods that can harm the health of society overall, are socially irresponsible.[29]

how managers do it

Responding Responsibly to Stakeholders at Volcom, Inc.

As an example of how an organization chooses to improve the general quality of life, consider events at Volcom, Inc., the manufacturer of activewear for surfers, snowboarders, and skateboarders. Some time ago Volcom management recognized its commitment to behaving responsibly toward its stakeholders. The company introduced a line of apparel made of 100 percent organic cotton and launched an initiative focused on reusing items to reduce the environmental impact. For its employees, the company sponsored eco-friendly initiatives, such as an Earth Day picnic and beach cleanups. In addition to donating 1 percent of its sales to global environmental organizations, the company allocates a percentage of proceeds from certain products to community-based charities. Volcom also actively supports organizations that focus on reducing hunger and homelessness.[30]

3. **The social investment area**—The measurement of social investment deals with the degree to which the organization is investing both money and human resources to solve community social problems. Here, the organization could be involved in assisting community organizations dedicated to education, charities, and the arts.
4. **The problem-solving area**—The measurement of problem solving should focus on the degree to which the organization deals with social problems, such as participating in long-range community planning and conducting studies to pinpoint social problems.

The Social Audit: A Progress Report A **social audit** is the process of measuring the present social responsibility activities of an organization to assess its performance in this area. The basic steps in conducting a social audit are monitoring, measuring, and appraising all aspects of an organization's social responsibility performance. Although some companies that pioneered concepts of social reporting, such as General Electric, are still continuing their social audit efforts, other companies have been somewhat slow to follow but are now growing in noticeable number.

BUSINESS ETHICS

The study of ethics in management can be approached from many different directions. Perhaps the most practical approach is to view ethics as catalyzing managers to take socially responsible actions. The movement to include the study of ethics as a critical part of management education began in the 1970s, grew significantly in the 1980s, and is expected to continue growing in the twenty-first century. John Shad, chair of the Securities and Exchange Commission during the 1980s when Wall Street was shaken by a number of insider trading scandals, recently pledged a $20 million trust fund to the Harvard Business School to create a curriculum in business ethics for MBA students. Television producer Norman Lear gave $1 million to underwrite the Business Enterprise Trust, which will give national awards to companies and "whistle blowers ... who demonstrate courage, creativity, and social vision in the business world."[31]

The following sections define ethics, explain why ethical considerations are a vital part of management practices, discuss a workable code of business ethics, and present some suggestions for creating an ethical workplace.

A Definition of Ethics

The famous missionary physician and humanitarian Albert Schweitzer defined ethics as "our concern for good behavior. We feel an obligation to consider not only our own personal well-being, but also that of other human beings." This meaning is similar to the precept of the Golden Rule: Do unto others as you would have them do unto you.[32]

In business, **ethics** can be defined as the capacity to reflect on values in the corporate decision-making process, to determine how these values and decisions affect various stakeholder groups, and to establish how managers can use these observations in day-to-day company management.[33] Ethical managers strive for success within the confines of sound management practices that are characterized by fairness and justice.[34] Interestingly, using ethics as a major guide in making and evaluating business decisions is not only popular in the United States but also in the very different societies of India and Russia.[35]

Why Ethics Is a Vital Part of Management Practices

John F. Akers, former board chair of IBM, recently said that it makes good business sense for managers to be ethical. Unless they are ethical, he believes, companies cannot be competitive in either national or international markets. According to Akers:

> Ethics and competitiveness are inseparable. We compete as a society. No society anywhere will compete very long or successfully with people stabbing each other in the back; with people trying to steal from one another; with everything requiring notarized confirmation because you can't trust the other person; with every little squabble ending in litigation; and with government writing reams of regulatory legislation, tying business hand and foot to keep it honest.[36]

Although ethical management practices may not be linked to specific indicators of financial profitability, conflict is not inevitable between ethical practices and making a profit. As Akers's statement suggests, our system of competition presumes underlying values of truthfulness and fair dealing. The employment of ethical business practices can enhance overall corporate health in three important areas: productivity, stakeholder relations, and government regulation.

Productivity The employees of a corporation constitute one major stakeholder group that is affected by management practices. When management is resolved to act ethically toward stakeholders, then employees will be positively affected. For example, a corporation may decide that business ethics requires it to make a special effort to ensure the health and welfare of its employees. To this end, many corporations have established Employee Advisory Programs (EAPs) to help employees with family, work, financial or legal problems, or with mental illness or chemical dependency. These programs have even enhanced productivity in some corporations. For instance, Control Data Corporation found that its EAP reduced health costs and sick-leave usage significantly.[37]

Stakeholder Relations The second area in which ethical management practices can enhance corporate health is by positively affecting "outside" stakeholders such as suppliers and customers. A positive public image can attract customers who view such an image as desirable. For example, Johnson & Johnson, the world's largest maker of health care products, is guided by "Our Credo," addressed more than 60 years ago by General Robert Wood Johnson to the company's employees, stockholders, and members of its community (see Figure 3.4).

We believe our first responsibility is to the doctors, nurses and patients,
to mothers and fathers and all others who use our products and services.
In meeting their needs everything we do must be of high quality.
We must constantly strive to reduce our costs
in order to maintain reasonable prices.
Customers' orders must be serviced promptly and accurately.
Our suppliers and distributors must have an opportunity
to make a fair profit.

We are responsible to our employees,
the men and women who work with us throughout the world.
Everyone must be considered as an individual.
We must respect their dignity and recognize their merit.
They must have a sense of security in their jobs.
Compensation must be fair and adequate,
and working conditions clean, orderly, and safe.
We must be mindful of ways to help our employees fulfill
their family responsibilities.
Employees must feel free to make suggestions and complaints.
There must be equal opportunity for employment, development
and advancement for those qualified.
We must provide competent management,
and their actions must be just and ethical.

We are responsible to the communities in which we live and work
and to the world community as well.
We must be good citizens—support good works and charities
and bear our fair share of taxes.
We must encourage civic improvements and better health and education.
We must maintain in good order
the property we are privileged to use,
protecting the environment and natural resources.

Our final responsibility is to our stockholders.
Business must make a sound profit.
We must experiment with new ideas.
Research must be carried on, innovative programs developed
and mistakes paid for.
New equipment must be purchased, new facilities provided
and new products launched.
Reserves must be created to provide for adverse times.
When we operate according to these principles,
the stockholders should realize a fair return.

Government Regulation The third area in which ethical management practices can enhance corporate health is in minimizing government regulation. Where companies are believed to be acting unethically, the public is more likely to put pressure on legislators and other government officials to regulate those businesses or to enforce existing regulations. For example, in 1995, Texas state legislators held public hearings on the operations of the psychiatric hospital industry. These hearings arose, at least partly, out of the perception that private psychiatric hospitals were not following ethical pricing practices.[38]

A Code of Ethics

A **code of ethics** is a formal statement that acts as a guide for the ethics of how people within a particular organization should act and make decisions. Ninety percent of *Fortune* 500 firms, and almost half of all other firms, have ethical codes. Moreover, many organizations that do not already have an ethical code are giving serious consideration to developing one.[39]

Codes of ethics commonly address such issues as conflict of interest, competitors, privacy of information, gift giving, and giving and receiving political contributions or business. A code of ethics recently developed by Nissan of Japan, for example, barred all Nissan employees from accepting almost all gifts or entertainment from, or offering them to, business partners and government officials. The new code was drafted by Nissan president Yoshikazu Hanawa and sent to 300 major suppliers.[40]

According to a recent survey, the development and distribution of a code of ethics is perceived as an effective and efficient means of encouraging ethical practices *within* organizations.[41] Figure 3.5

Code of Ethics

I. Honest and Ethical Conduct

Netflix Parties are expected to act and perform their duties ethically and honestly and with the utmost integrity. Honest conduct is considered to be conduct that is free from fraud or deception. Ethical conduct is considered to be conduct conforming to accepted professional standards of conduct. Ethical conduct includes the ethical handling of actual or apparent conflicts of interest between personal and professional relationships as discussed in below.

II. Conflicts of Interest

A conflict of interest exists where the interests or benefits of one person or entity conflict or appear to conflict with the interests or benefits of the Company. While it is not possible to describe every situation in which a conflict of interest may arise, Netflix Parties must never use or attempt to use their position with the Company to obtain improper personal benefits. Any Netflix Party who is aware of a conflict of interest, or is concerned that a conflict might develop, is required to discuss the matter with a higher level of management or the General Counsel promptly. Senior Financial Officers may, in addition to speaking with the General Counsel, also discuss the matter with the Audit Committee.

III. Disclosure

Senior Financial Officers are responsible for ensuring that the disclosure in the Company's periodic reports is full, fair, accurate, timely and understandable. In doing so, Senior Financial Officers shall take such action as is reasonably appropriate to (i) establish and comply with disclosure controls and procedures and accounting and financial controls that are designed to ensure that material information relating to the Company is made known to them; (ii) confirm that the Company's periodic reports comply with the requirements of Section 13(a) or 15(d) of the Securities Exchange Act of 1934; and (iii) ensure that information contained in the Company's periodic reports fairly presents in all material respects the financial condition and results of operations of the Company.

Senior Financial Officers will not knowingly (i) make, or permit or direct another to make, materially false or misleading entries in the Company's, or any of its subsidiary's, financial statements or records; (ii) fail to correct materially false and misleading financial statements or records; (iii) sign, or permit another to sign, a document containing materially false and misleading information; or (iv) falsely respond, or fail to respond, to specific inquiries of the Company's independent auditor or outside legal counsel.

IV. Compliance

It is the Company's policy to comply with all applicable laws, rules and regulations. It is the personal responsibility of each Netflix Party to adhere to the standards and restrictions imposed by those laws, rules and regulations, and in particular, those relating to accounting and auditing matters.

Any Netflix Party who is unsure whether a situation violates any applicable law, rule, regulation or Company policy should discuss the situation with the General Counsel.

V. Internal Reporting

Netflix Parties shall take all appropriate action to stop any known misconduct by fellow Netflix Parties that violate this Code. To this end, Netflix Parties shall report any known or suspected misconduct to the General Counsel or, in the case of misconduct by a Senior Financial Officer, also to the Chair of the Company's Audit Committee. In addition, Netflix Parties are encouraged to use the Company's confidential internal reporting system to report breaches of this Code. Information

FIGURE 3.5
Netflix's Code of Conduct

Source: http://files.shareholder.com/ downloads/NFLX/991705948x0x17642/ ccfbe9a7-f0a5-4c16-a3a4- 9471252b4144/73.pdf

(continued)

FIGURE 3.5 (Continued)

concerning the Company's confidential internal reporting system can be located on the Company's Intranet. The Company will not retaliate or allow retaliation for reports made in good faith.

VI. Accountability

Any violation of this Code may result in disciplinary action, including termination, and if warranted, legal proceedings. This Code is a statement of certain fundamental principles, policies and procedures that govern the Netflix Parties in the conduct of the Company's business. It is not intended to and does not create any rights in any employee, customer, supplier, competitor, shareholder or any other person or entity. The General Counsel and/or the Audit Committee will investigate violations and appropriate action will be taken in the event of any violation of this Code.

VII. Waivers and Amendments of the Code

The Company is committed to continuously reviewing and updating our policies and procedures. Therefore, this Code is subject to modification. Any amendment or waiver of any provision of this Code must be approved in writing by the Company's Board of Directors and promptly disclosed pursuant to applicable laws and regulations. Any waiver or modification of the Code by a Senior Financial Officer will be promptly disclosed to stockholders if and as required by law or the rules of the stock exchange or over the counter trading system on which Netflix's stock is traded or quoted.

contains an excerpt from the code of conduct used at Netflix to encourage ethical practices within the company.

Managers cannot assume that merely because they have developed and distributed a code of ethics, organization members have all the guidelines they need to determine what is ethical and to act accordingly. It is impossible to cover all ethical and unethical conduct within an organization in one code. Managers should view codes of ethics as tools that must be evaluated and refined periodically so that they will be comprehensive and usable guidelines for making ethical business decisions efficiently and effectively.[42]

Creating an Ethical Workplace

Managers commonly strive to encourage ethical practices, not only to be morally correct, but to gain whatever business advantage lies in projecting an ethical image to consumers and employees.[43] Creating, distributing, and continually improving a company's code of ethics is one common step managers can take to establish an ethical workplace.

Another step many companies are taking to create an ethical workplace is to appoint a chief ethics officer. The chief ethics officer has the job of ensuring the integration of organizational ethics and values into daily decisions at all organizational levels. Such officers recommend, help implement, and reinforce strategies aimed at integrating appropriate conduct throughout all phases of company operations. Figure 3.6 lists a few characteristics that a person should have to be a successful chief ethics officer.

Another way to promote ethics in the workplace is to furnish organization members with appropriate training. General Dynamics, McDonnell Douglas, Chemical Bank, and American Can Company are examples of corporations that conduct training programs aimed at encouraging ethical practices within their organizations.[44] Such programs do not attempt to teach managers what is moral or ethical, but to give them criteria they can use to help determine how ethical a certain action might be. Managers can feel confident that a potential action will be considered ethical by the general public if it is consistent with one or more of the following standards:[45]

1. **The golden rule**—Act in a way you would expect others to act toward you.
2. **The utilitarian principle**—Act in a way that results in the greatest good for the greatest number of people.

1. The ability to be objective
2. The ability to understand the structure of an organization
3. The ability to know and maneuver within an organization's culture
4. The ability to communicate clearly and concisely
5. The ability to deal with conflict
6. The ability to keep matters confidential

*For more discussion of such skills see www.eoa.org.

FIGURE 3.6
Skills needed to be a successful chief ethics officer*

3. **Kant's categorical imperative**—Act in such a way that the action taken under the circumstances could be a universal law, or rule, of behavior.
4. **The professional ethic**—Take actions that would be viewed as proper by a disinterested panel of professional peers.
5. **The TV test**—Managers should always ask, "Would I feel comfortable explaining to a national TV audience why I took this action?"
6. **The legal test**—Is the proposed action or decision legal? Established laws are generally considered minimum standards for ethics.
7. **The four-way test**—Managers can feel confident that a decision is ethical if they can answer "yes" to the following questions: Is the decision truthful? Is it fair to all concerned? Will it build goodwill and better friendships? Will it be beneficial to all concerned?

Finally, managers can take responsibility for creating and sustaining conditions in which people are likely to behave ethically and for minimizing conditions in which people might be tempted to behave unethically. Two practices that commonly inspire unethical behavior in organizations are to give unusually high rewards for good performance and unusually severe punishments for poor performance. By eliminating such factors, managers can reduce any pressure on employees to perform unethically in organizations.

Following the Law: Sarbanes–Oxley Reform Standards

Outrageous management practices were recently discovered at several companies including Enron, WorldCom, and Tyco that seemed aimed at unjustifiably maximizing the personal wealth of top managers to the detriment of the well-being of other organizational stakeholders. As an example, many of these managers used inaccurate accounting reports to deceive employees, shareholders, legal authorities, the media, and the general public. These reports grossly overstated the level of company performance, allowing top managers to justify inflated salaries. Some employees were personally outraged by the deceitful management practices, and others experienced personal financial disaster after being encouraged to invest in worthless company stock and company retirement programs. Needless to say, managers involved in such deceitful practices were prosecuted to the full extent of the law.

Amid outcries of public outrage over such practices, the Sarbanes–Oxley Act of 2002 was passed to try to prevent such future deception in publicly owned companies. The general thrust of this legislation focuses on promoting ethical conduct.[46] Areas covered include maintaining generally accepted accounting practices, evaluating executive compensation, monitoring fundamental business strategies, understanding and mitigating major risk, and ensuring company structure and processes that enhance integrity and reputation.

Managers who do not follow stipulations of the Sarbanes–Oxley Act face significant jail time. Infractions such as securities fraud, impeding a financial investigation by regulators, and mail fraud can result in up to 25 years of imprisonment. The Sarbanes–Oxley Act and related significant infraction penalties create hope that grossly unethical behavior will be significantly discouraged in the future.

The Sarbanes–Oxley Act seems to support whistle-blowing as a vehicle for both discouraging deceptive management practices while encouraging ethical management practices. **Whistle-blowing** is the act of an employee reporting suspected misconduct or corruption believed to exist within an organization. A **whistle-blower** is the employee who reports the alleged activities. Whistle-blowers can make their reports in a number of different ways, including reporting suspected organizational wrongdoings to proper legal authorities and/or proper management authorities. The Sarbanes–Oxley Act prohibits retaliation by employers against whistle-blowers.

One of the most famous whistle-blowers of modern times is Sherron Watkins, former vice president of Enron Corporation.[47] Watkins testified to Congress that she was extremely alarmed by information she received about Enron's finances, and warned then-chairman Kenneth Lay that investors were being duped by inflated profit statements. Watkins attempted, with no success, to persuade Lay to restate and reissue corporate financial statements after eliminating accounting misrepresentations. Enron, once the seventh largest corporation in the United States, declared bankruptcy in December 2001. The bankruptcy cost thousands of employees their jobs and retirement pensions and investors lost millions of dollars. Perhaps mostly based on Watkins's testimony, Lay was charged and found guilty on six criminal counts of fraud. Lay died at age 64 awaiting sentencing for his Enron conviction.[48]

Ethics abuses at major corporations and other highly publicized business missteps have highly sensitized Americans to greed and corporate corruption. Business scholars see ethics remaining a hot topic for years to come.[49]

SUSTAINABILITY

Thus far, this chapter has focused on a manager's job by discussing corporate social responsibility as a society-based management obligation and ethics as a catalyst spurring management to pursue corporate social responsibility activities. This section discusses sustainability as an approach to corporate social responsibility that emphasizes present and future resource needs of society.

In recent decades, there has been an undeniable growing interest in sustainability.[50] This interest focuses on topics like how organizations can better conserve natural resources, reduce organizational waste, recycle used resources, and preserve the environment by protecting threatened plant and animal species.[51] The following sections define sustainability, define a sustainable organization, discuss why managers should build sustainable organizations, and outline steps that managers can use to help build sustainable organizations.

Defining Sustainability

Traditionally, the term *sustainability* has been used within management literature to describe the ability of a company to maintain a steady and improving stream of earnings. More recently, however, the term is often used in a much different way. In this section, reflecting this newer, different use of the term, **sustainability** is the degree to which a person or entity can meet its present needs without compromising the ability of other people or entities to meet their needs in the future.[52]

To illustrate the meaning of sustainability, assume that as part of its normal production process, an entity rids itself of contaminated waste by dumping it into a river. If this dumping renders the river toxic and unusable for fishing or recreation, the entity would be considered unsustainable. On the other hand, if the entity purifies the waste before dumping it to protect the cleanliness of the river, the entity would be considered sustainable. Overall, the more an entity increases its ability to meet present needs without compromising the ability of others to meet their needs in the future, the more sustainable the entity.

Defining a Sustainable Organization

Building upon the above definition of sustainability, a **sustainable organization** is an organization that has the ability to meet its present needs without compromising the ability of future generations to meet their needs. In building a sustainable organization, management should strive to make the organization sustainable in three areas: the economy, the environment, and society. In terms of the economy, the sustainable organization focuses on performing behaviors such as minimizing waste by not overproducing goods and generating a fair profit for stakeholders. Regarding the environment, the sustainable organization emphasizes performing behavior akin to protecting natural resources like air, water, and land. In terms of society, the sustainable organization stresses performing behavior such as maintaining the well-being and protection of the communities in which it does business.[53]

how managers do it
Building a Sustainable Organization at PepsiCo

For example, consider recent events at PepsiCo, with its billion-dollar portfolio of food and beverage brands. After measuring the carbon footprint of its Tropicana orange juice brand, managers discovered that more than one-third of Tropicana's carbon emissions—the single largest source—came from the use of fertilizers during the growing process. As a result, Tropicana partnered with two manufacturers of low-carbon fertilizers and one of its orange growers, SMR Farms in Bradenton, Florida, to conduct long-term tests of the fertilizers and identify an alternative to reduce Tropicana's carbon emissions. The study will last at least five years, to match the maturity cycle of orange trees, and its findings could impact global best practices in agriculture. Adopting behaviors that protect the world's natural resources will help PepsiCo achieve its sustainability goals.[54] ■

Managers have historically focused on the yardstick of profit, or the *bottom line*, as the primary gauge for evaluating organizational performance. In more recent times, managers are evaluating organizational performance by examining three sustainability gauges: the economy (which includes profit), the environment, and society. All three sustainability gauges for organizational performance considered collectively are commonly referred to as the **triple bottom-line**.[55]

The term *triple bottom-line* emphasizes that managers should focus on building organizations that are sustainable in economic, environmental, and societal activities. Essentially, the overall degree of sustainability achieved by any organization is judged by collective accomplishments in all three of these areas. If any one area is lacking in sustainability, the organization as a whole is lacking in sustainability. Being able to answer 'yes' to questions like the following would indicate that an organization is operating in a manner that is consistent with the triple bottom-line standard:

Is the organization providing a fair return to its stakeholders? (economic area)

Is the organization protecting or improving the natural environment through its work methods? (environmental area)

Is the organization protecting or improving the overall quality of life in the communities in which it does business? (societal area)

Why Sustainability?

Some people ask if building sustainable organizations is worthwhile. Management theorists and practicing managers alike outline many sound reasons why managers should build sustainable organizations. The following sections discuss a few such reasons.

Increased Profit Perhaps the most often used reason why managers should build sustainable organizations is that increased sustainability commonly results in more profitable organizations. History shows that sustainability doesn't have to be a burden on profit.[56] According to Brian Walker, the CEO of Herman Miller, achieving a position of leadership in sustainability can boost product demand. Walker found that customers are reluctant to buy from a company simply because of a worthwhile history of sustainability and probably won't pay a premium for its products.[57] However, a sustainable company is the type of company with which modern day customers like to do business.[58]

Increased Productivity Another reason commonly given why managers should strive to build sustainable organizations relates to employee productivity.[59] Many management theorists and practitioners claim that increased labor productivity is commonly the most immediate payoff of sustainability. According to this line of reasoning, a sustainable organization builds its workplace to include features like temperature control, clean air, noise control, and appropriate lighting. Workers in such workplaces have been shown to be as much as 16 percent more productive than workers in workplaces without features like temperature control, clean air, noise control, and appropriate lighting.

Increased Innovation A third reason commonly given why managers should pursue sustainability is that such a pursuit serves as a catalyst for innovation.[60] Management researchers are now finding that a byproduct of pursuing sustainability is a flood of valuable organizational and technological innovations that help organizations become more successful.[61]

To illustrate, consider recent events at Sam's Club, a discount retail division of Wal-Mart that specializes in the sale of products like jewelry, clothes, and food. Management at Sam's Club decided to pursue increasing sustainability by decreasing energy costs. One solution to decreasing energy costs was quite an innovation, a new milk jug. According to Doug McMillon, CEO of Sam's Club, the new jug increased the shelf life of milk in stores. Because of this greater shelf life, the new jug actually helped to reduce energy costs by eliminating the need for more than 10,000 milk truck deliveries to various stores. This milk jug innovation at Sam's Club was an outcome of an effort to increase sustainability and resulted in not only making the organization more sustainable, but also more successful.

Steps for Achieving Sustainability

The actual steps that managers take to increase organizational sustainability can vary drastically from organization to organization. For example, to increase sustainability, a chemical company might take steps to reduce hazardous waste, a shoe manufacturer might take steps to reduce energy consumption, and a food products company might take steps to buy food products only from suppliers who grow food using approved fertilizers.

Overall, to have a successful sustainability effort, a manager must understand the unique characteristics of a particular organization and the industry within which that organization exists. Based on this understanding, management must tailor sustainability activities and processes that best meet the needs of individual organizations.

Despite the fact that many of management's steps to achieve sustainability can vary significantly from organization to organization, there are some steps that a manager can take to help build a sustainable organization regardless of his or her organization. These steps include:

Setting sustainability goals. Management should set goals that clearly outline what the organization is attempting to accomplish in the area of sustainability. Such goals provide organization members with clear targets on which they can focus their sustainability efforts. Such targets provide a vehicle that management can use to ensure organization members have a unified, collective impact on organizational sustainability.

Consider the following sustainability goal set by Marks & Spencer, one of the largest retailers in the United Kingdom: Becoming the first major retailer to ensure that six key raw materials—

palm oil, soya, cocoa, beef, leather, coffee—come from sustainable sources that do not contribute to deforestation, one of the biggest causes of climate change.

Marks & Spencer's sustainability goal gives clear direction in announcing that the company will enhance its own sustainability by supporting suppliers who are focused on enhancing their own sustainability. In essence, Marks & Spencer's sustainability goal is to help eliminate deforestation by doing business with suppliers with the same goal. By establishing this goal and making sure all organization members understand it, Marks & Spencer is guiding its buyers to do business with only those suppliers who will help make Marks & Spencer a more sustainable organization.

Hiring organization members who can help the organization become more sustainable. A primary key to accomplishing any worthwhile activity in an organization is having appropriately talented people perform that activity. If an organization does not have appropriately talented people to accomplish an activity, individuals should be recruited and hired who possess the talent. Such recruiting and hiring will normally increase the probability that the activity is performed successfully.

Following the reasoning outlined above, hiring appropriately talented people can also be a primary key for ensuring that necessary sustainability activities are successfully performed in organizations. For example, many organizations have sustainability projects that focus on improving the use of energy and materials through new building construction or remodeling. Such projects typically explore topics like energy efficiency, materials selection, water savings, and indoor environmental quality. The U.S. Green Building Business Council runs a program called LEED (Leadership in Energy and Environmental Design) that is an ecology oriented certification program that rates the ecology impact of buildings of all types. Hiring individuals who understand the LEED program could help ensure that sustainability oriented construction or remodeling projects will be performed successfully in an organization.

As another example, Weis Markets, a regional grocery store chain headquartered in Pennsylvania, recently made a special hire to help with the company's sustainability efforts.[62] The company hired Patti Olenick, a sustainability specialist from the Pennsylvania Department of Environmental Protection. Olenick has extensive experience in waste management, recycling, and composting. She is expected to help the company develop a more systematic and coordinated approach to Weis Market sustainability programs.

Rewarding employees who contribute to an organization's sustainability goals. In all organizations, managers must encourage the performance of appropriate behavior, behavior that contributes to the accomplishment of organizational goals. In the sustainability area, managers should reward organization members who contribute to the accomplishment of sustainability goals. The purpose of the reward is to recognize organization members for what they've accomplished in the area of sustainability and to increase the probability that such organization members will continue to make contributions toward accomplishing organizational sustainability goals in the future.

The Colorado Department of Health and Public Environment provides an excellent illustration of how management can use rewards to encourage organization members to contribute to the attainment of sustainability goals. Management has designed and implemented an awards program that provides employees who excel in pursuing sustainability activities with a cash reward at a banquet held at the Denver Museum of Nature and Science. All employees are encouraged to nominate individuals to receive the award who have implemented a new sustainability program, have demonstrated innovation in sustainability solutions, or have displayed leadership in protecting the environment.

Tracking progress in reaching sustainability goals. As stated previously, setting sustainability goals is a critical component of an organization's sustainability effort. Such goals set clear targets on which all organization members can focus. However, simply setting such goals is not enough. Managers must also track an organization's progress in reaching such goals. Knowing if an organization is on schedule, behind schedule, or ahead of schedule in reaching sustainability goals is critical to ensuring the organization will ultimately reach those goals. If an organization is not on track for reaching sustainability goals, adjustments should be made to get the organization on track.

FIGURE 3.7

Chart DuPont uses to track progress in reaching 2010 energy consumption goal.

Source: DuPont Sustainability Progress Report, 2008, p. 4.

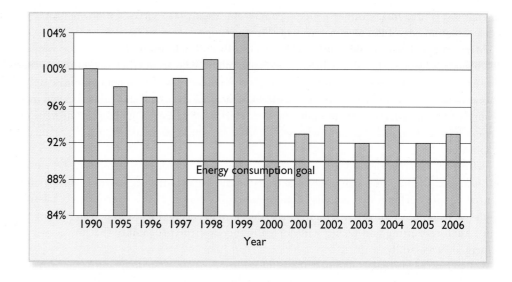

DuPont is a science-based company that focuses on creating problem solutions that contribute to a better, safer, and healthier human life. Well-known products offered by DuPont include a material used to coat cooking utensils called Teflon, a component of bulletproof vests called kevlar, and a solid surface material for making kitchen counter tops called Corian. In late 1999, DuPont established an energy goal for 2010 of holding energy consumption at its 1990 level.[63] The company did not simply establish the sustainability goal, but has also been tracking company progress in reaching the goal. Data acquired through such tracking tells DuPont management if activities aimed at reaching its 2010 energy consumption goal are working or if a new or modified approach to reaching the goal should be instituted. Overall, history shows that the company seems on track to achieve its 2010 energy consumption goal and has attained an overall reduction of 7 percent in energy consumption since establishing the goal.

CHALLENGE CASE SUMMARY

Social responsibility is the obligation of management to take action that protects and improves the welfare of society in conjunction with the interests of the organization. Based on the Challenge Case, Verizon protects and improves its communities through the use of its advanced telecommunication networks to improve the quality of life. Verizon presently makes substantial contributions in applying this technology in many different areas of community life and concern. According to Keith Davis's social responsibility model, making such investments in the welfare of society is essential to being a good business citizen. Corporations, however, must also take steps to protect their own interests while making social investments. For example, by helping to improve the educational level of citizens throughout the world, Verizon is simultaneously protecting its interests by preparing these citizens to be better able to use Verizon technology products in the future.

Following Davis's model of social responsibility further, Verizon should commit to benefiting society because of the vast power the company possesses in creating such benefit. It should be remembered, however, that the costs of social responsibility activities can be passed to consumers, and action should be taken only if it is financially feasible. For Verizon to invest in social responsibility activities to its own financial detriment would be socially irresponsible given the company's commitment to employees and stockholders.

Verizon could become involved in many different areas of social responsibility. Currently, however, the company targets two specific areas of concern: literacy and education and safety and health. In addition, it provides financial support to other not-for-profit organizations supported by its employees. No matter how much Verizon does in pursuing social responsibility goals, however, it will no doubt be criticized by someone for not doing enough. At this point, Verizon's activities in the area of social responsibility appear to be highly significant.

Anything Verizon does within the sphere of social responsibility could result in a short-run profit decrease simply because of the costs. Although, at first glance, such action might seem unbusinesslike, performing social responsibility activities could significantly improve Verizon's public image and could be instrumental in generating increased sales.

Some social responsibility activities are legislated and therefore *must* be performed by businesses. Most of the legislated activities, however, are aimed at larger companies like Verizon. Such legislation has to do with required levels of product safety and employee safety. Because Verizon is not required by law to support things such as education or campaigns to end domestic violence, whatever it might contribute to such areas would be strictly voluntary. In making a decision about how to support society, Verizon management should assess the positive and negative outcomes of such support over both the long and short terms, and then establish whatever support, if any, would maximize its success and offer some desirable contribution to society. Verizon should communicate to all organization members, as well as society, those areas it will support and why. The use of its Web site could greatly facilitate this communication.

Verizon should strive to maintain a relatively high level of social responsiveness in pursuing its social responsibility activities. To do this, management should make decisions focusing on Verizon's established social responsibility areas and approach meeting those responsibilities in appropriate ways. In terms of supporting education, for example, management must first decide if Verizon has a social responsibility to become involved, through the design and application of its products or efforts, in society's education issues. Assuming it was decided that Verizon *has* such a responsibility, it must then determine how to accomplish the activities necessary to meet it. For example, Verizon might employ its expertise to expand the online offerings of Thinkfinity.org, its Web site repository of free educational materials. Making appropriate decisions will help Verizon meet social obligations effectively and efficiently.

In terms of implementing an approach to meeting social responsibilities that will increase Verizon's social responsiveness, management should try to view the company as having both societal and economic goals. In addition, management should attempt to anticipate social problems and actively work to prevent them. Managers at Verizon should know that pursuing social responsibility objectives is a major management activity. Therefore, they must plan, organize, influence, and control Verizon's social responsibility activities if the company is to be successful in reaching social responsibility objectives.

Regarding the planning of these activities, management should determine how Verizon will achieve its objectives. By incorporating social responsibility planning into Verizon's overall planning process, social trends forecasts can be made along with economic, political, and technological trends forecasts. In turn, these forecasts would influence the development of plans and, ultimately, the action taken by Verizon in the area of social responsibility.

Management also must be able to turn Verizon's social responsibility policy into action. To convert a goal into action, management should first communicate the policy to all organization members. Next, it must determine the best way to achieve the goal. Finally, management should make sure everyone at Verizon is committed to meeting related objectives and that lower-level managers are allocating funds and establishing appropriate opportunities for organization members to help implement this policy.

In addition to planning social responsibility activities at Verizon, management must organize, influence, and control them. To organize these activities, orderly use of all resources at Verizon must be established to carry out the company's social responsibility plans. Developing an organization chart that shows the social responsibility area with corresponding job descriptions, responsibilities, and specifications for the positions would be an appropriate step for management to take.

To influence social responsibility activities, organization members should be guided in directions that will enhance the attainment of Verizon's social responsibility objectives. Management must lead, communicate, motivate, and work with groups in ways that are appropriate for meeting those objectives.

To control, management must make sure that social responsibility activities occur as planned. If they do not, changes should be made to ensure that activities will be handled properly in the near future. One tool that can be used to check Verizon's progress in meeting social responsibilities is the social audit. The audit will enable management to check and assess system performance in such areas as economic functions, quality of life, social investment, and problem solving.

Assuming management at Verizon is ethical, its decisions would focus on enhancing the well-being of all company stakeholders. In essence, management should follow the Golden Rule by acting in a way that it would expect others to act toward it. Decisions at Verizon will always be ethical if they are truthful and fair to all concerned, if they build goodwill and better friendships, and if they are beneficial to all concerned.

Verizon would want its corporate decisions to be sustainable—that is, able to meet the company's present needs without compromising the needs of others in the future. It would be up to Verizon management to determine the steps the company must take to achieve organizational sustainability. For example, it may be necessary to hire additional staff with unique expertise to help Verizon achieve sustainability.

To measure the level of sustainability at Verizon, managers could use the triple bottom-line approach. Under this yardstick, managers would assess Verizon's activities in economic, environmental, and societal terms. For example, they would ask the questions:

Is Verizon performing profitably and providing a fair return to stakeholders? (economic)

Is Verizon reducing its carbon footprint, minimizing energy use, or otherwise improving the natural environment through its work methods? (environmental) Is Verizon enhancing the overall quality of life in the communities in which it does business? (societal)

Answers to the above questions will help Verizon management determine whether its policies are sustainable.

MANAGEMENT SKILL ACTIVITIES

This section is specially designed to help you develop corporate social responsibility skill. An individual's corporate social responsibility skill is based on an understanding of social responsibility concepts and the ability to apply those concepts in management situations. The following activities are designed to both heighten your understanding of social responsibility concepts and to develop the ability to apply those concepts in a variety of management situations.

UNDERSTANDING CORPORATE SOCIAL RESPONSIBILITY CONCEPTS

 To check your understanding and to practice using the concepts in this chapter, go to www.mymanagementlab.com and explore the material associated with Chapter 3.

Know Key Terms

Understanding the following key terms is critical to your understanding of chapter material. Define each of these terms. Refer to the page(s) referenced after a term to check your definition or to gain further insight regarding the term.

corporate social responsibility **52**	social responsiveness approach **59**	whistle-blower **68**
social responsiveness **57**	social audit **62**	sustainability **68**
stakeholder **58**	ethics **63**	sustainable organization **69**
social obligation approach **59**	code of ethics **64**	triple bottom-line **69**
social responsibility approach **59**	whistle-blowing **68**	

Know How Management Concepts Relate

This section is comprised of activities that will further sharpen your understanding of management concepts. Answer essay questions as completely as possible. Also, remember that many additional true/false and multiple choice questions appear online at MyManagementLab.com to help you further refine your understanding of management concepts.

1. What are the five propositions of the Davis Model of corporate social responsibility? Which proposition would be the most valuable to you as a manager in guiding your social responsibility focus in an organization? Explain.

2. What is your personal position about businesses performing social responsibility activities now that you have studied the arguments "for" and "against" as presented in the chapter?

3. As a manager, would you use the social obligation, the social responsibility, or the social responsiveness approach in meeting your organization's social responsibilities? Why?

4. How can society help business meet social obligations?

5. What's the relationship between social responsibility and ethics?

6. Do you think it's worthwhile for managers to build sustainable organizations? Why? How would you do it?

DEVELOPING MANAGEMENT SKILLS

Learning activities in this section are aimed at helping you develop social responsibility skill. Learning activities include Exploring Your Management Skill: Parts 1 and 2, Experiential Exercises, Cases, and a VideoNet Exercise.

Exploring Your Management Skill: Part 1

Before studying this chapter, respond to the following questions regarding the type of advice you would give to Verizon Foundation's president Patrick R. Gaston, referenced in the Challenge Case. Then address the concerning social responsibility challenges that he presently faces. You are not expected to be a social responsibility expert at this point. Answering the questions now can help you focus on important points when you study the chapter. Also, answering the questions again after you study the chapter will give you an idea of how much you have learned.

Record your answers here or online at MyManagement Lab.com. Completing the questions at MyManagementLab.com will allow you to get feedback about your answers automatically. If you answer the questions in the book, look up answers in the Exploring Your Management Skill section at the end of the book.

FOR EACH STATEMENT CIRCLE
- "Y" if you would give the advice to Gaston.
- "N" if you would NOT give the advice to Gaston.
- "NI" if you have no idea whether you would give the advice to Gaston.

Mr. Gaston, in meeting your social responsibility challenges at the Verizon Foundation, you should...

Before After
Study Study

1. pass the costs of social responsibility activities on to the consumer.
Y, N, NI

2. be willing to have managers perform activities that result in good for society even though these activities might be outside the managers' normal area of expertise.
Y, N, NI

3. require managers to perform most social responsibility activities required by law.
Y, N, NI

4. normally require the performance of only a few social responsibility activities that benefit society but not Verizon.
Y, N, NI

5. monitor the Occupational Safety and Health Administration to keep current regarding safety and health legislation regarding conditions in nongovernmental workplaces.
Y, N, NI

6. be socially responsible toward Verizon's stakeholders.
Y, N, NI

7. be careful to determine whether Verizon has a social responsibility in a particular community before formulating and implementing programs to meet the needs of that community.
Y, N, NI

8. put more focus on effectiveness than efficiency in carrying out social responsibility activities.
Y, N, NI

9. determine whether the costs of performing social responsibility activities outweigh the benefits gained by performing them.
Y, N, NI

10. implement a special planning process to focus only on formulating and implementing social responsibility activities.
Y, N, NI

11. include environmental forecasts in determining future social responsibility activities of Verizon.
Y, N, NI

12. determine Verizon's short-run social responsibility plans before determining Verizon's long-run social responsibility plans.
Y, N, NI

13. periodically perform a social audit to monitor Verizon's social responsibility progress.
Y, N, NI

14. make sure that you control social responsibility activities by making sure that they happen as planned.
Y, N, NI

15. normally not worry about motivating Verizon employees to perform social responsibility activities since "doing good works" will be enough reward.
Y, N, NI

16. do not have to be concerned with the 'triple bottom-line' standard.
Y, N, NI

Exploring Your Management Skill: Part 2

As you recall, you completed Exploring Your Management Skill before you started to study this chapter. Your responses gave you an idea of how much you initially knew about social responsibility and helped you focus on important points as you studied the chapter. Answer the Exploring Your Management Skill questions again now and compare your score to the first time you took it. This comparison will give you an idea of how much you have learned from studying this chapter and pinpoint areas for further clarification before you start studying the next chapter. Record your answers within the text or online at MyManagementLab.com. Completing the survey at MyManagementLab.com will allow you to grade and compare your test scores automatically. If you complete the test in the book, look up answers in the Exploring Your Management Skill section at the end of the book.

Your Management Skills Portfolio

Your Management Learning Portfolio is a collection of activities especially designed to demonstrate your management knowledge and skill. By completing these activities online at MyManagementLab.com, you will be able to print, complete with cover sheet, as many activities as you choose. Be sure to save your work. Taking your printed portfolio to an employment interview could be helpful in obtaining a job.

The portfolio activity for this chapter is Identifying Corporate Social Responsibilities. Read this highlight about the Bugaboo Strollers Company, and answer the questions that follow.

Bugaboo is the brainchild of Dutch designer Max Barenburg and his physician brother-in-law Eduard Zanen. Together they wanted to invent a baby stroller that was functional, fashionable, appealing to both fathers and mothers, and able to function on different types of surfaces.

Their initial product was the Bugaboo Frog. Introduced in Holland in 1999, and named for its "frog-like" suspension wheels that "jump" over obstacles in its path, the Frog became the "must have" stroller of celebrities and parents who wanted this elite stroller for their babies.

After years of customer feedback and further testing and development on the Frog, the pair realized parents wanted more options and that different parents have different needs. In September of 2005, the pair introduced to the world the Bugaboo Cameleon, Bugaboo Gecko, and the Bugaboo Bee strollers to offer customers more choices.

Management of a company such as Bugaboo must clearly keep in mind the responsibilities that it has to society as a result of its business operations. The following list shows the four categories in which companies commonly have social responsibilities because of business operations. For each category, list the responsibilities to society that you believe Bugaboo has as a result of the products that it offers.

PLANNING ISSUES TO INSPECT

Category

**Social responsibilities related to the product itself
Bugaboo's Responsibilities to Society**

1. _____
2. _____
3. _____
4. _____
5. _____

Social responsibilities related to corporate philanthropy

1. _____
2. _____
3. _____
4. _____
5. _____

Social responsibilities related to marketing practices

1. _____
2. _____
3. _____
4. _____
5. _____

Social responsibilities related to employees

1. _____
2. _____
3. _____
4. _____
5. _____

Experiential Exercises

1 The Environmental Impact Team

Directions. Read the following scenario and perform the listed activities. Your instructor may want you to perform the activities as an individual or within groups. Follow all of your instructor's directions carefully.

You are the head of a major British newspaper, *Guardian Unlimited,* and have just completed a social audit of your organization's business activities. Your company produces a progressive, enlightened newspaper and a Web site, and writes regularly about corporate social responsibility topics. You conducted your social audit to make sure your company measures up to the high standards your editorials expect of other companies. In the past, your company has won several social responsibility awards in areas such as encouraging diversity, innovation in social reporting, and employee giving to social responsibility causes.

Based on the results of your audit, you have set a new social responsibility goal for your newspaper for the upcoming three-year period. This goal is simple: to persuade your readers to have a positive impact on the environment.

You have established a new team called the Environmental Impact Team to help you outline how your new goal will be accomplished. You are presently meeting with this new team for the first time. Lead your group in outlining plans, organization features, an influence system, and a control mechanism, all aimed at achieving this new goal.

2 You and Your Career

The preceding information implies that managers should communicate to other organization members the extent to which their organizations will be involved in performing social responsibility activities. Could the lack of such communication hinder your career success as a manger? Explain. As president of the school in which you are presently enrolled taking this management class, what would you say to professors and students regarding the overall position on social responsibility that *you* would like for the school to embrace? What specific activities should be pursued corresponding to this position?

VideoNet Exercise

Social Responsibility at TerraCycle

Video Highlights

CEO Tom Szaky, self-proclaimed "eco-capitalist," gives us the scoop on starting his quickly growing company, which "manufactures potent, organic products that are not only made from waste, but are also packaged entirely in waste. TerraCycle Plant Food™ is made by feeding premium, organic waste to millions of worms. The worm poop is then liquefied into a powerful organic plant food and bottled directly in used soda bottles. This story gives the phrase 'earth-friendly' a whole new meaning" (www.terracycle.net). Tom debunks the myth that doing the right thing costs more and explains how TerraCycle is different from other green businesses.

Discussion Questions

1. What argument does Tom Szaky use for his business performing socially responsible activities?

2. Using the Davis Model, discuss which of the five propositions of corporate responsibility you think are most applicable to TerraCycle.

3. Which management approach to meeting social obligations is being used by Szaky and TerraCycle?

Internet Activity

Go to the TerraCycle Web site at www.terracycle.net. Read the information on Ecocapitalism presented in the "Our Revolution" section, as well as the biography of Tom Szaky presented in the "Careers" section. Based on his theories and actions, do you see Szaky as a socially responsible manager? Overall, are his positions on social responsibility enhancing company success? Explain.

CASES

1 VERIZON'S COMMITMENT TO SOCIAL RESPONSIBILITY

"Verizon's Commitment to Social Responsibility" (p. 51) and its related Challenge Case Summary were written to help you better understand the management concepts contained in this chapter. Answer the following discussion questions about the Challenge Case to better understand how concepts relating to corporate social responsibility and business ethics can be applied in a company such as Verizon.

1. Do you think Verizon has a responsibility to support education and safety in the communities in which it does business? Explain.

2. Assuming Verizon has such a responsibility, in what instances would it be relatively easy for the company to be committed to living up to it?

3. Assuming Verizon has such a responsibility, in what instances would it be relatively difficult for the company to be committed to living up to it?

2 GAP GOES PUBLIC ON SOCIAL RESPONSIBILITY

Read the case and answer the questions that follow. Studying this case will help you better understand how concepts relating to corporate social responsibility and business ethics can be applied in a company such as Gap Inc.

Shortly after Paul Pressler became CEO of Gap Inc., his teenage daughter asked him, "Doesn't Gap use sweatshops?" The new CEO wasn't surprised by her question. Despite all the news coverage about the company's ups and downs, he realized that many customers, investors, and other stakeholders knew little about Gap's progress in monitoring and improving factory conditions. Gap operates 3,000 Gap, Banana Republic, and Old Navy stores in five countries, ringing up $16 billion in annual sales revenue. To keep its racks full of fashions, Gap's merchandise managers buy clothing and accessories from thousands of factories spread across North and South America, Eastern and Western Europe, Africa, India, Asia, and the Middle East.

Gap was going through a difficult time when Pressler came aboard. The company had lost money during the previous year and sales were stalled amid a sluggish economy. What's more, the stores were stuffed with inventory, markdowns were squeezing profit margins, and competition among clothing retailers was fiercer than ever. To turn Gap around, the CEO and his management team carefully researched their customers, changed both stores and merchandise to sharpen distinctions among the three chains, and began using special software to support their pricing decisions.

In addition to these urgent challenges, Pressler knew that Gap had been wrestling with allegations that some of its suppliers mistreated workers, employed children, and tolerated other violations. Gap's senior management first developed labor, health, and safety standards for company suppliers to follow in 1992. Over the next decade, its executives toughened the rules, hired dozens of inspectors to visit factories, and investigated whether Gap's standards were being met. By the time Pressler became CEO, the company had created an independent Global Compliance department and was spending millions of dollars checking up on suppliers, then taking action. For example, in 2003 alone, Gap stopped buying from 136 overseas factories that repeatedly violated its rules.

Gap had been posting some information about factory standards on its company Web site for a few years. Now the CEO gave the go-ahead to publish a more comprehensive social responsibility report. The initial 40-page report noted that Gap had made progress in helping suppliers improve factory conditions and in forging ties with nongovernmental organizations to build momentum for sustainability. Candidly, the report admitted that Gap still had a way to go in achieving "transparency" and getting the entire industry to address factory conditions. In pushing for more transparency, the company invited representatives of several stakeholder groups to comment on its social responsibility results and suggest improvements. Rather than keeping this feedback private, Gap reported both the compliments and the criticisms. It also printed its four social responsibility goals for the coming year, opening the door to closer stakeholder scrutiny of Gap's future performance in those areas.

While praising the company for going public with its results, some activists told the news media that Gap should be doing more to address factory conditions—and doing it more quickly. "We recognize and embrace our duty to take a leadership role" in promoting such changes, Pressler said in the report. He also mentioned the year's other social responsibility accomplishments, including donating $60 million to nonprofit groups, recycling 20,000 tons of cardboard and paper, and giving employees time off to volunteer 22,000 hours helping worthy causes.

Under Pressler, Gap returned to profitability and set ambitious financial goals for the future. Asked about Gap's ability to continue building sales and profits, Pressler recently said, "We don't take yesterday's success as a guarantee for tomorrow." That's also true on the social responsibility side. No one company can overhaul conditions in every supplier's factories overnight, but Pressler is committed to making a difference in the lives of thousands of workers. Is the message getting out to Gap's stakeholders—and to his daughter?

QUESTIONS

1. Should Gap publicly report its social responsibility results in detail, even if every objective hasn't been completely achieved?

2. Do you think Gap's conversion of social responsibility policies into action is in phase 1, phase 2, or phase 3? Explain.

3. Is Gap's approach to social responsibility based on obligation, responsibility, or responsiveness? Support your answer.

Endnotes

1. Corporate Web site, http://www.verizonfoundation.com, accessed June 15, 2010; organization Web site, http://thinkfinity.org, accessed June 15, 2010; "Verizon Publishes Its Corporate Responsibility Report," *Ethical Performance*, May 17, 2010, http://www.ethicalperformance.com; "Verizon Is Top Telecommunications Company in *Fortune* Magazine's 2010 List of World's Most Admired Companies," *Trading Markets*, March 9, 2010, http://www.tradingmarkets.com; "Verizon's Commitment to Corporate Responsibility Recognized by Corporate Responsibility Magazine," *AllBusiness*, March 5, 2010, http://www.allbusiness.com; "Company Broadens Haitian Relief by Connecting Family and Friends with Earthquake Victims," *PR Newswire*, January 20, 2010, http://www.prnewswire.com.

2. For a good discussion of many factors involved in the modern meanings of social responsibility, see Frederick D. Sturdivant and Heidi Vernon-Wortzel, *Business and Society: A Managerial Approach*, 4th ed. (Homewood, IL: Irwin, 1990), 3–24. "The definition of corporate social responsibility" is adapted from Keith Davis and Robert L. Blomstrom, *Business and Society: Environment and Responsibility*, 3rd ed. (New York: McGraw-Hill, 1975), 6. For illustrations of how social responsibility makes good economic sense, see Ernest Beck, "Body Shop Founder Roddick Steps Aside as CEO," *Wall Street Journal*, May 13, 1998, B14; Gerard J. J. M. Zwetsloot, "From Management Systems to Corporate Social Responsibility," *Journal of Business Ethics* 44 (2003): 201–208; see also Christine Hemingway and Patrick Maclagan, "Managers'

Personal Values as Drivers of Corporate Social Responsibility," *Journal of Business Ethics* 50 (2004): 33.

3. Bindu Arya and Gaiyan Zhang, "Institutional Reforms and Investor Reactions to CSR Announcements: Evidence from an Emerging Economy," *Journal of Management Studies* 46, no. 7 (May 14, 2009): 1089–1112.

4. Patricia L. Short, "Keeping It Clean," *Chemical & Engineering News* 85, no. 17 (April 23, 2007): 13.

5. Peter L. Berger, "New Attack on the Legitimacy of Business," *Harvard Business Review* (September/October 1981): 82–89.

6. Keith Davis, "Five Propositions for Social Responsibility," *Business Horizons* (June 1975): 9–24. For additional comments supporting social responsibility activities, see Lois A. Mohr, Deborah J. Webb, and Katherine E. Harris, "Do Consumers Expect Companies to Be Socially Responsible? The Impact of Corporate Social Responsibility on Buying Behavior," *Journal of Consumer Affairs* 35, no. 1 (Summer 2001): 45–72.

7. Virginia Gewin, "Industry Lured by the Gains of Going Green," *Nature*, July 14, 2005, 173.

8. ——— "Mohawk Going Green in Bath Rugs," *Home Textiles Today* 28, no. 7 (February 26, 2007): 12.

9. Kate Arthur, "Going Green: Simple Changes Make Vast Improvements on the Environment," *Knight Ridder Tribune Business News*, Washington: March 2, 2007, 1.

10. For extended discussion of arguments for and against social responsibility, see William C. Frederick, Keith Davis, and James E. Post, *Business and Society: Corporate Strategy, Public Policy, Ethics,* 6th ed. (New York: McGraw-Hill, 1988), 36–43.

11. For discussion in favor of corporate social responsibility, see Jane Fuller, "Banking on a Good Reputation: Companies Should Look at Corporate Social Responsibility on a Cost–Benefit Approach, Not by Whatever Campaign Is in the News," *Financial Times* (2003): 6.

12. For comments on a new way of exploring the relationship between the financial performance of an organization and its social responsibility activities, see Sandra A. Waddock and Samuel B. Graves, "Finding the Link Between Stakeholder Relations and Quality of Management," *Journal of Investing* 6, no. 4 (Winter 1997): 20–24.

13. For discussions of two research studies that identify the relationship between corporate social performance and financial performance, see John Peloza, "The Challenge of Measuring Financial Impacts from Investments in Corporate Social Performance," *Journal of Management* 35, no. 6 (December 2009): 1518–1541; and Baruch Lev, Christine Petrovits, and Suresh Radhakrishnan, "Is Doing Good Good for You? How Corporate Charitable Contributions Enhance Revenue Growth," *Strategic Management Journal* 31, no. 2 (September 2009): 182–200.

14. J. B. McGuire, A. Sundgren, and T. Schneeweis, "Corporate Social Responsibility and Firm Financial Performance," *Academy of Management Journal* (December 1988): 854–872; Vogel, "Ethics and Profits Don't Always Go Hand in Hand," *Los Angeles Times,* December 28, 1988, 7.

15. This feature is based on Stephen Brammer and Andrew Millington, "Does it Pay to be Different? An Analysis of the Relationship between Corporate Social and Financial Performance," *Strategic Management Journal* 29 (2008): 1325–1343.

16. For Friedman's view, see "Freedom and Philanthropy: An Interview with Milton Friedman," *Business and Society Review* (Fall 1989): 11–18.

17. Milton Friedman, "Does Business Have Social Responsibility?" *Bank Administration* (April 1971): 13–14.

18. Eric J. Savitz, "The Vision Thing: Control Data Abandons It for the Bottom Line," *Barron's,* May 7, 1990, 10–11, 22.

19. For a discussion of radical environmentalism, see Jeffrey Salmon, "We're All 'Corporate Polluters' Now," *Wall Street Journal,* July 2, 1997, A14.

20. Joan E. Rigdon, "The Wrist Watch: How a Plant Handles Occupational Hazard with Common Sense," *Wall Street Journal,* September 28, 1992, 1.

21. For insights regarding SC Johnson Wax's position on social responsibility involvement, see Reva A. Holmes, "At SC Johnson Wax Philanthropy Is an Investment," *Management Accounting* (August 1994): 42–45.

22. Bill Richards, "Nike Hires an Executive from Microsoft for New Post Focusing on Labor Policies," *Wall Street Journal,* January 15, 1998, B14.

23. Samuel C. Certo and J. Paul Peter, *The Strategic Management Process,* 3rd ed. (Chicago: Irwin, 1995), 219; Marianne M. Jennings, "Manager's Journal: Trendy Causes Are No Substitute for Ethics," *Wall Street Journal,* December 1, 1997, A22.

24. Carlo Wolff, "Living with the New Amenity," *Lodging Hospitality* (December 1994): 66–68; for an article demonstrating the importance of stakeholders' opinions in social responsibility, see David Wheeler, Barry Colbert, and Edward Freeman, "Focusing on Value: Reconciling Corporate Social Responsibility, Sustainability and a Stakeholder Approach in a Network World," *Journal of General Management* 28 (2003): 1.

25. S. Prakash Sethi, "Dimensions of Corporate Social Performance: An Analytical Framework," *California Management Review* (Spring 1975): 58–64.

26. For information on the growing trend for business to make contributions to support education, see Joel Keehn, "How Business Helps the Schools," *Fortune,* October 21, 1991, 161–171.

27. Frank H. Cassell, "The Social Cost of Doing Business," *MSU Business Topics* (Autumn 1974): 19–26.

28. Donald W. Garner, "The Cigarette Industry's Escape from Liability," *Business and Society Review* 33 (Spring 1980): 22.

29. Meinolf Dierkes and Ariane Berthoin Antal, "Whither Corporate Social Reporting: Is It Time to Legislate?" *California Management Review* (Spring 1986): 106–121.

30. Mike Lewis, "Volcom Launches Sustainability and Corporate Social Responsibility Program," *Transworld Business,* June 9, 2010, http://business.transworld.net.

31. For an interesting discussion of the ethical dilemma of fairly allocating an individual's time between work and personal life, see Paul B. Hoffmann, "Balancing Professional and Personal Priorities," *Healthcare Executive* (May/June 1994): 42.

32. Archie B. Carroll, "In Search of the Moral Manager," *Business Horizons* (March/April 1987): 7–15.

33. For an article outlining the relationship between ethics and management, see Elliott Jaques, "Ethics for Management," *Management Communication Quarterly* 17 (2003): 136.

34. Sundeep Waslekar, "Good Citizens and Reap Rewards," *Asian Business* (January 1994): 52. See also Genine Babakian, "Who Will Control Russian Advertising?" *Adweek* [Eastern Edit.], August 1, 1994, 16.

35. Natalie M. Green, "Creating an Ethical Workplace," *Employment Relations Today* 24, no. 2 (Summer 1997): 33–44.

36. "Helping Workers Helps Bottom Line," *Employee Benefit Plan Review,* July 1990.

37. Sandy Lutz, "Psych Hospitals Fight for Survival," *Modern Healthcare,* May 8, 1995, 62–65.

38. Patrick E. Murphy, "Creating Ethical Corporate Structures," *Sloan Management Review* (Winter 1989): 81–87; Louis J. D'Amore, "A Code of Ethics and Guidelines for Socially and Environmentally Responsible Tourism," *Journal of Travel Research* (Winter 1993): 64–66.

39. James B. Treece, "Nissan Rattles Japan with Tough Ethics Code," *Automotive News,* May 4, 1998, 1, 49.

40. Richard A. Spinell, "Lessons from the Salomon Scandal," *America,* December 28, 1991, 476–477; Touche Ross, *Ethics in American Business* (New York: Touche Ross & Co., January 1988). For a view on developing a code of ethics for the workplace, see O. C. Ferrell, "An Assessment of the Proposed Academy of Marketing Science Code of Ethics for Marketing Educators," *Journal of Business Ethics* 19, no. 2 (April 1999): 225–228.

41. For additional insights on how and why to create an ethical workplace, see Curt Smith, "The Ethical Workplace," *Association Management* 52, no. 6 (June 2000): 70–73.

42. For an interesting study of ethics codes, see Lawrence Chonko, Thomas Wotruba, and Terry Loe, "Ethics Code Familiarity and Usefulness: Views on Idealist and Relativist Managers Under Varying Conditions of Turbulence," *Journal of Business Ethics* 42 (2003): 237.

43. Alan L. Otten, "Ethics on the Job: Companies Alert Employees to Potential Dilemmas," *Wall Street Journal,* July 14, 1986, 25.

44. Gene R. Laczniak, "Framework for Analyzing Marketing Ethics," *Journal of Macromarketing* (Spring 1983): 7–18. See also Patricia Haddock and Marilyn Manning, "Ethically Speaking," *Sky* (March 1990): 128–31.

45. Saul W. Gellerman, "Managing Ethics from the Top Down," *Sloan Management Review* (Winter 1989): 73–79. For an interesting discussion of what management should do when charged with unethical actions see John A. Byrne, "Here's What to Do Next, Dow Corning," *BusinessWeek,* February 24, 1992, 33.

46. "Special Report: SEC Follows Up on Sarbanes–Oxley Reform Standards," *Directors & Trustees Digest* 62, no. 3 (March 2003): 1.

47. John Schwartz, "Playing Know and Tell," *New York Times,* June 9, 2002, 4.2.

48. ———, "Enron Ruling to Stand," *New York Times,* November 22, 2006, 6.

49. Stephen M. Paskoff, "Ten Ethics Trends for 2010," *Workforce Management,* December 2009, http://www.workforce.com.

50. David A. Lubin and Daniel C. Esty, "The Sustainability Imperative," *Harvard Business Review* 88, no. 5 (May 1, 2010).

51. Jeffrey Pfeffer, "Building Sustainable Organizations: The Human Factor," *Academy of Management Perspective* (February 2010): 34–45.

52. United Nations, *Report of the World Commission on Environment and Development,* United Nations General Assembly Resolution 42/187, December 1987. For a different viewpoint on the importance of sustainability, see John A. Vucetich and Michael P. Nelson, "Sustainability: Virtuous or Vulgar?" *BioScience* 60, no. 7 (July/August 2010).

53. Vince Luchsinger, "Strategy Issues in Business Sustainability," *Business Renaissance Quarterly* 4, no. 3 (Fall 2009): 163–174.

54. "PepsiCo Launches Groundbreaking Pilot Program to Reduce Carbon Footprint of Tropicana," *CSRWire,* May 18, 2010, http://www.csrwire.com.

55. Mark Hollingworth, "Building 360 Organizational Sustainability," *Ivey Business Journal Online* (November/December 2009).

56. Ram Nidumolu, C. K. Prahalad, and M. R. Rangaswami, "Why Sustainability Is Now the Key Driver of Innovation," *Harvard Business Review* (September 2009): 1.

57. Josette Akresh-Gonzales, "Herman Miller CEO Brian Walker on Meeting Sustainability Goals – With Customer Help," *Harvard Business Review* (December 2009): 1.

58. Michael S. Hopkins, "What Executives Don't Get about Sustainability (and Further Notes on the Profit Motive)," *MIT Sloan Management Review* 51, no. 1 (Fall 2009): 40.

59. Michael S. Hopkins, "8 Reasons Sustainability Will Change Management," *MIT Sloan Management Review* 51, no. 1 (Fall 2009): 27–30.

60. Daniel C. Esty and Andrew S. Winston, *Green to Gold: How Smart Companies Use Environmental Strategy to Innovate, Create Value, and Build Competitive Advantage* (New Haven, CT: Yale University Press), 2006.

61. Nidumolu, Prahalad, and Rangaswami, "Why Sustainability Is Now the Key Driver of Innovation," p. 2.

62. "Weis Markets Adds Sustainability Specialist," *Ecology, Environment & Conservation Business,* May 8, 2010, p. 93.

63. DuPont Company, "2008 Sustainability Report," p. 4.

chapter 4

Management and Diversity

Target Skill

diversity skill: the ability to establish and maintain an organizational workforce that represents a combination of assorted human characteristics appropriate for achieving organizational success

objectives

To help build my *diversity skill,* when studying this chapter, I will attempt to acquire:

1. A definition of diversity and an understanding of its importance in the corporate structure

2. An understanding of the advantages of having a diverse workforce

3. An awareness of the challenges facing managers within a diverse workforce

4. An understanding of the strategies for promoting diversity in organizations

5. Insights into the role of the manager in promoting diversity in the organization

CHALLENGE CASE

SIEMENS FOCUSES ON GLOBAL DIVERSITY

AT A TIME WHEN OTHER COMPANIES are looking for ways to trim costs, Germany-based Siemens AG, one of Europe's largest engineering conglomerates, is investing heavily in global diversity. The 160-year-old company markets technology and equipment for medical imaging, power generation, and transportation in 190 countries, serving 2 million customers daily.

Siemens has built global dominance through innovation. Its most recent skygazing led senior leadership to identify three "megatrends" that it believes will impact business and drive innovation well into the future: urbanization, demographic change, and climate change. To stay ahead of the curve, Siemens needs to attract and retain high-quality candidates.

And with its global reach, the company is committed to reflecting the same diversity in its workforce of approximately 405,000. (Currently, its population represents 140 nationalities.)

Demonstrating its commitment to diversity, in 2008, Siemens appointed its first Global Diversity Officer (GDO). Jill Lee earlier had served as Chief Financial Officer for Siemens in her native Singapore—the first woman to hold the position—as well as in China, Korea, Taiwan, and Hong Kong before accepting the GDO position.

Lee's charge: to ensure that Siemens builds a diverse, high-quality workforce. This would be accomplished not by quotas, rather, by continuing Siemens' long-standing policy of recruiting, hiring, and retaining top performers.

Lee used new and existing networks to create links between people of different backgrounds and different demographics: young with old, from different countries, men with women, and so forth.

She also launched GLOW, or *Glow Leadership Organization of Women*, a network designed to increase the numbers of women managers at Siemens (which stood at 7 percent when Lee assumed her role). Lee also created an enterprise-wide communication infrastructure and launched her own blog to stimulate global dialogue. The diversity initiative, according to Lee, is not a "nice-to-have" but rather a "must-have" if Siemens is to maintain its global dominance.

Other management demographics continue to be assessed. For example, although 83 percent of its business is conducted outside Germany and two-thirds of the company's employees work outside Germany, still two-thirds of Siemens management is German.

Global diversity, for Siemens, is an ongoing goal and one that creates competitive advantage.[1]

■ *Siemens' diverse workforce represents various nationalities and backgrounds, like these young engineers at a budget meeting.*

EXPLORING YOUR MANAGEMENT SKILL

You can explore your level of diversity skill **before** studying the chapter by completing the exercise "Exploring Your Management Skill: Part 1" on page 101 and **after** studying this chapter by completing the exercise "Exploring Your Management Skill: Part 2" on page 102.

THE DIVERSITY CHALLENGE

The Challenge Case illustrates the diversity challenge that Siemens management strives to meet. The remaining material in this chapter explains diversity concepts and helps develop the corresponding diversity skill that you will need to meet such challenges throughout your career. After studying chapter concepts, read the Challenge Case Summary at the end of the chapter to help you relate chapter content to building diversity at Siemens.

DEFINING DIVERSITY

Diversity refers to characteristics of individuals that shape their identities and the experiences they have in society. This chapter provides information about workforce diversity and discusses the strengths and problems of a diverse workforce. Understanding diversity is essential for managers today because managing diversity will undoubtedly constitute a large portion of the management agenda well into the twenty-first century.[2]

This chapter describes some strategies for promoting social diversity in organizations. It also explains how diversity is related to the four management functions. Given the nature of this topic, you will probably find yourself reflecting on diversity as you study future chapters. For example, you will reflect on diversity as you study the legal foundation for developing an inclusive workforce—affirmative action and Equal Employment Opportunity (EEO), discussed in Chapter 13, and ideas about organizational change, discussed in Chapter 14.

The Social Implications of Diversity

Workforce diversity is not a new issue in the United States. People from various other regions and cultures have been immigrating to these shores since colonial times, so the American population has always been a mix of races, ethnicities, religions, social classes, physical abilities, and sexual orientations.[3] These differences—along with the basic human differences of age and gender—comprise diversity. The purpose of exploring diversity issues in a management textbook is to suggest how managers might include diverse employees equally, accepting their differences and utilizing their talents.[4]

Majority and Minority Groups Managers must understand the relationship between two groups in organizations: majority groups and minority groups. **Majority group** refers to that group of people in the organization who hold most of the positions that command decision-making power, control of resources and information, and access to system rewards. **Minority group** refers to that group of people in the organization who are fewer or who lack critical power, resources, acceptance, and social status. Together, the minority and majority group members form the entire social system of the organization.

However, the majority group is not always the group that is larger in number: sometimes, in fact, the minority group is actually greater in number. For example, women are seen as a minority group in most organizations because they do not have the critical power to shape organizational decisions and control resources. Moreover, they have yet to achieve full acceptance and social status in most workplaces. In most health care organizations, for instance, women outnumber men. Although men are numerical minorities, however, they are seldom denied social status because white males hold most positions of power in the health care system hierarchy, such as physician and health care administrator.

ADVANTAGES OF DIVERSITY IN ORGANIZATIONS

Managers are becoming more dedicated to seeking a wide range of talents from every group in American culture because they now realize that distinct advantages come from doing so.[5] For one thing, as you will see in Chapter 18, group decisions often improve the quality of decision making. For another, work groups or teams that can draw on the contributions of a multicultural membership gain the advantage of a larger pool of information and a richer array of approaches to work problems.

Ann Morrison carried out a comprehensive study of 16 private and public organizations in the United States. In the resulting book, *The New Leaders: Guidelines on Leadership Diversity in America,* she outlines the several other advantages of diversity, each of which is discussed here.[6]

Gaining and Keeping Market Share

Today managers must understand increasingly diverse markets. Failure to discern customers' preferences can cost a company business in the United States and abroad. Some people argue that one of the best ways to ensure that the organization is able to penetrate diverse markets is to include diverse managers among the organization's decision makers.[7]

Diversity in the managerial ranks has the further advantage of enhancing company credibility with customers. Employing a manager who is of the same gender or ethnic background as customers may imply to those customers that their day-to-day experiences will be understood. One African American female manager found that her knowledge of customers paid off when she convinced her company to change the name of a product it intended to sell at Wal-Mart. "I knew that I had shopped for household goods at Wal-Mart, whereas the CEO of this company, a white, upper-middle-class male, had not. He listened to me and we changed the name of the product."

Morrison cites a case in which one company lost an important opportunity for new business in a southwestern city's predominantly Hispanic community. The lucrative business ultimately went to a competitor that had put a Hispanic manager in charge of the project who solicited input from the Hispanic community.

onsider how Safeway gained market share through diversity. One of North America's largest food retailers, with about 1,700 grocery stores, Safeway faced increasingly stiff competition from companies such as Target and Wal-Mart. In response, Safeway initiated a program to position itself as an employer of choice. In addition, with 70 percent of its customers being women, Safeway also wanted to expand its workforce diversity to be more consistent with its customer base. Safeway recognized that a diverse workforce would help the company better understand and respond to customer needs and create a competitive edge in the marketplace. With industry leadership traditionally being male, Safeway's initiative supporting women leaders broke from the norm. Today, management openly credits its past diversity efforts as the foundation for present levels of diversity and profitability.[8]

how managers do it

Profiting Through Diversity at Safeway

Cost Savings

Companies incur high costs in recruiting, training, relocating, and replacing employees and in providing competitive compensation packages. According to Morrison, Corning Corporation's high turnover among women and people of color was costing the company an estimated $2 million to $4 million a year. Many managers who were questioned for her study felt that the personnel expenses associated with turnover—often totaling as much as two-thirds of an organization's budget—could be cut by instituting diversity practices that would give nontraditional managers more incentive to stay. When nontraditional managers remain with the organization, nontraditional employees at lower levels feel more committed to the company.

In addition to the personnel costs, executives are distressed by the high legal fees and staggering settlements resulting from lawsuits brought by employees who feel they have been discriminated against. For example, $17.7 million in damages was awarded to a woman employed by Texaco who claimed she had been passed over for a management promotion because of her gender. Executives are learning that such sums would be better spent on promoting diversity.

Increased Productivity and Innovation

Many executives quoted in Morrison's study believe productivity is higher in organizations that focus on diversity. These managers find that employees who feel valued, competent, and at ease in their work setting enjoy coming to work and perform at a high level.

Morrison also cites a study by Donna Thompson and Nancy DiTomaso, which concluded that a multicultural approach has a positive effect on employees' perception of equity. This, in turn, positively affects employees' morale, goal setting, effort, and performance. The managers in Morrison's study also saw innovation as a strength of a diverse workforce. In essence, diversity becomes the spark that ignites innovation.[9]

Better-Quality Management

Morrison also found that including nontraditional employees in fair competition for advancement usually improves the quality of management by providing a wider pool of talent. According to the research she cites, exposure to diverse colleagues helps managers develop breadth and openness.

The quality of management can also be improved by building more effective personnel policies and practices that, once developed, will benefit all employees in the organization, not just minorities. According to Morrison's study, many of the programs initially developed for nontraditional managers resulted in improvements that were later successfully applied throughout the organization. Ideas such as adding training for mentors, upgrading techniques for developing managers, and improving processes for evaluating employees for promotion—all concepts originally intended to help nontraditional managers—were later adopted for wider use. (See Table 4.1 for more information on the advantages of a diverse workforce.)

At first glance, the advantages of diversity to an organization seem undeniable. In a recent survey focusing on small to medium-sized enterprises, however, more managers surveyed disagreed that diversity contributed to performance than agreed.[10] These findings, however, do not dispute the overall conclusion that diversity contributes to organizational performance. Instead, the findings seem to indicate that many managers still need to be convinced of the benefits that accrue to an organization through diversity.

TABLE 4.1   Advantages of a Diverse Workforce
Improved ability to gain and keep market share
Cost savings
Increased productivity
A more innovative workforce
Minority and women employees who are more motivated
Better quality of managers
Employees who have internalized the message that "different" does not mean "less than"
A workforce that is more resilient when faced with change

knowledge base. Alternatively, the manager might choose to tie organizational rewards to the development of diversity competencies. Examples of such rewards are giving employees public praise or recognition and providing workers with opportunities to use their diversity skills on desirable work assignments.

Controlling

Overseeing compliance with the legal stipulations of EEOC and affirmative action is one aspect of the controlling function in the area of diversity. According to Chapter 1, controlling is the set of activities that make something happen as planned. Hence the evaluation activities necessary to assess diversity efforts are part of the controlling role managers play in shaping a multicultural workforce.

Managers may find this function the most difficult one of the four to execute. It is not easy to evaluate planned-change approaches in general, and it is particularly hard to do so in the area of diversity. Many times the most successful diversity approaches reveal more problems as employees begin to speak openly about their concerns. Moreover, subtle attitudinal changes in one group's perception of another group are difficult to measure. What *can* be accurately measured are the outcome variables of turnover; representation of women, minorities, and other underrepresented groups at all levels of the company; and legal problems stemming from inappropriate or illegal behaviors (e.g., discrimination and sexual harassment).

Managers engaged in the controlling function in the area of diversity need to continually monitor their units' progress with respect to diversity goals and standards. They must decide what control measures to use (e.g., indicators of productivity, turnover, absenteeism, or promotion) and how to interpret the information these measures yield in light of diversity goals and standards.

For example, a manager may need to assess whether the low rate of promotions for African American men in her department is due to subtle biases toward this group or group members' poor performance compared to others in the department. She may find she needs to explore current organizational dynamics, as well as create effective supports for this group. Such supports might include fostering greater social acceptance of African American men among other employees, learning more about the African American male's bicultural experience in the company, making mentoring or other opportunities available to members of this group, and providing them with some specific job-related training.

Management Development and Diversity Training

Given the complex set of managerial skills needed to promote diversity, it is obvious that managers themselves will need organizational support if the company is to achieve its diversity goals. One important component of the diversity strategy of a large number of companies is diversity training.[34] **Diversity training** is a learning process designed to raise managers' awareness and develop their competencies to deal with the issues endemic to managing a diverse workforce. More and more, managers are recognizing that a diverse workforce is critical to the exploration of new ideas and the creation of innovation in organizations, and diversity training is a valuable tool in achieving this diversity.[35] Figure 4.4 shows the array of diversity training programs that McDonald's offers its managers.

Basic Themes of Diversity Training   Training is the process of developing qualities in human resources that will make those employees more productive and better able to contribute to organizational goal attainment. Some companies develop intensive programs for management and less intensive, more generalized programs for other employees. Such programs are discussed further in Chapter 13 and generally focus on the following five components or themes:

1. Behavioral awareness
2. Acknowledgment of biases and stereotypes
3. Focus on job performance
4. Avoidance of assumptions
5. Modification of policy and procedure manuals

FIGURE 4.4

Diversity training programs offered to McDonald's employees

Source: http://www.mcdonalds. com/corp/values/people/diversity/ education.html.

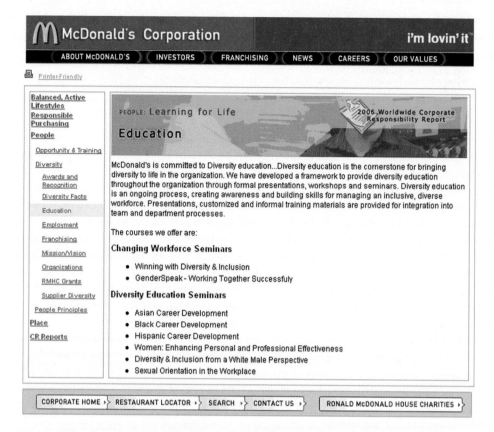

Stages in Managing a Diverse Workforce Donaldson and Scannell, authors of *Human Resource Development: The New Trainer's Guide,* have developed a four-stage model to describe how managers progress in managing a diverse workforce.[36] In the first stage, known as "unconscious incompetence," managers are unaware of behaviors they engage in that are problematic for members of other groups. In the second stage, "conscious incompetence," managers go through a learning process in which they become conscious of behaviors that make them incompetent in their interactions with members of diverse groups.

The third stage is one of becoming "consciously competent." Managers learn how to interact with diverse groups and cultures by deliberately thinking about how to behave. In the last stage, "unconscious competence," managers have internalized these new behaviors and feel so comfortable relating to others different from themselves that they need to devote little conscious effort to doing so. Managers who have progressed to the "unconscious competence" stage will be the most effective with respect to interacting in a diverse workforce. Effective interaction is key to carrying out the four management functions previously discussed.

Table 4.2 summarizes our discussion of the challenges facing those who manage a diverse workforce. Managers, who are generally responsible for controlling organizational goals and outcomes, are accountable for understanding these diversity challenges and recognizing the dynamics described here. In addition to treating employees fairly, they must influence other employees to cooperate with the company's diversity goals.

Understanding and Influencing Employee Responses Managers cannot rise to the challenge of managing a diverse workforce unless they recognize that many employees have difficulties coping with diversity. Among these difficulties are natural resistance to change, ethnocentrism, and lack of information and outright misinformation about other groups, as well

TABLE 4.2 Organizational Challenges and Supports Related to Managing a Diverse Workforce

Organizational Challenges	Organizational Supports
Employee's Difficulties in Coping with Cultural Diversity	**Educational Programs and Training to Assist Employees in Working Through Difficulties**
Resistance to change	**Top-Down Management Support for Diversity**
Ethnocentrism	Managers who have diversity skills and competence
Lack of information and misinformation	Education and training
Prejudices, biases, and stereotypes	Awareness raising
Reasons Employees Are Unmotivated to Understand Cultural Differences	Peer support
Lack of time and energy and unwillingness to assume the emotional risk necessary to explore issues of diversity	Organizational climate that supports diversity
	Open communication with manager about diversity issues
Absence of social or concrete rewards for investing in diversity work	Recognition for employee development of diversity skills and competencies
Interpersonal and intergroup conflicts arising when diversity issues are either ignored or mismanaged	Recognition for employee contributions to diversity goals
Work Group Problems	Organizational rewards for managers' implementation of organizational diversity goals and objectives
Lack of cohesiveness	
Communication problems	
Employee stress	

as prejudices, biases, and stereotypes. Some employees lack the motivation to understand and cope with cultural differences, which requires time, energy, and a willingness to take some emotional risks.

Another problem is that employees often receive no social rewards (e.g., peer support and approval) or concrete rewards (e.g., financial compensation or career opportunities) for cooperating with the organization's diversity policies.

For all these difficulties, managers cannot afford to ignore or mismanage diversity issues because the cost of doing so is interpersonal and causes intergroup conflicts. These conflicts often affect the functioning of the work group by destroying cohesiveness and causing communications problems and employee stress.

Managers who are determined to deal effectively with their diverse workforce can usually obtain organizational support. One primary support is education and training programs designed to help employees work through their difficulties in coping with diversity. Besides recommending such programs to their employees, managers may find it helpful to enroll in available programs themselves.

Getting Top-Down Support Another important source of support for managers dealing with diversity issues is top management. Organizations that provide top-down support are more likely to boast the following features:

1. Managers skilled at working with a diverse workforce
2. Effective education and diversity training programs
3. An organizational climate that promotes diversity and fosters peer support for exploring diversity issues
4. Open communication between employees and managers about diversity issues
5. Recognition for employees' development of diversity skills and competencies
6. Recognition for employee contributions to diversity goals
7. Organizational rewards for managers' implementation of organizational diversity goals and objectives

CHALLENGE CASE SUMMARY

An organization such as Siemens that uses the diverse talents of a multicultural workforce can reap many rewards. Some experts believe that one of the best ways for a company such as Siemens to capture a diverse customer base is to make sure that its decision makers are a diverse group. Promoting a diverse group of decision makers will ensure sensitivity to such issues, giving Siemens a better chance of establishing restaurants characterized by such diversity. In the United States, the Siemens diversity infrastructure resembles a matrix: a Diversity Board links all local diversity activities horizontally, across its U.S. operating companies. The board also links diversity activities vertically, from their respective local diversity councils all the way up to the President's council. Not only does this type of arrangement enable Siemens to be nimble and responsive, it also permits the sharing of best practices throughout the enterprise

Diversity activity takes many forms at Siemens operating companies in the United States. Its Siemens Teacher Scholarships encourage minority students to consider science as a teaching career—an area where minorities are traditionally underrepresented. It recently gifted a number of historically African American colleges with software worth $1.2 million. Siemens supports the Carnegie Mellon Summer Academy, a program that gives minority students "a leg up." In Chicago, Siemens encourages graduates of public high schools to go to college by helping them visit historically black colleges and universities to get a sense of academic life.

The progress of a company such as Siemens in its diversity program will enhance the productivity of its diverse workforce. An organization's diversity programs will help a diverse workforce feel valued and at ease in their work setting, thereby performing better than workers who feel their organization has little respect for them as people. As a result of its required diversity training, Siemens can retain employees, thereby lowering personnel costs related to recruiting and training.

Legislation and government involvement cannot provide complete direction for building diversity in organizations. Siemens management understands that organizations should not wait for laws and government to provide guidelines for building a diverse organization. Instead, management should recreate the company to reflect the markets in which it operates. For example, given demographics reflecting population trends, Siemens will probably be recruiting and hiring a greater proportion of Asian and Hispanic employees.

If an organization such as Siemens increases the proportion of Asian and Hispanic employees, company diversity training programs should be modified to include sensitivity toward factors relevant to the Asian and Hispanic cultures. This training should emphasize factors such as religion, values, and behavioral norms specific to these two groups. Such modification of diversity training at Siemens would be aimed at eliminating ethnocentrism within the company relating to these two demographic groups.

When management is committed to diversity, diversity programs are normally successful. In turn, by virtue of its financial investment in global diversity, Siemens demonstrates its commitment to building a world-class organization—a fact that is not lost on current and future employees. A reputation for diversity makes Siemens more attractive as an employer—and enables Siemens to attract and retain high-performing employees. In turn, top performers are typically best at innovation and productivity—areas where Siemens needs to excel if it is to hold competitive advantage in the marketplace.

In terms of the organizational diversity continuum, Siemens' commitment to diversity seems broad based. This broad-based commitment is reflected in company-wide practices related to recruiting, hiring, and training a diverse workforce. The broad-based commitment is also evident through Siemens' building of minority representation within influential company groups such as the board of directors. Consistent with diversity initiatives in most organizations, Siemens managers are given extensive diversity training. Managers in a company such as Siemens who know how to interact with people of different cultures will be the most successful in building productive multicultural teams in organizations. Overall, diversity training for managers at Siemens is aimed to help managers become more sensitive to other cultures and thereby more capable of using planning, organizing, influencing, and controlling skills to help organizations meet diversity goals.

In addition to managers, nonmanagers within organizations can be a focus of specially designed diversity training.

MANAGEMENT SKILL ACTIVITIES

This section is specially designed to help you develop diversity skill. An individual's diversity skill is based on an understanding of diversity concepts and the ability to apply those concepts in management situations. The following activities are designed to both heighten your understanding of diversity concepts and to develop the ability to apply those concepts in a variety of management situations.

UNDERSTANDING DIVERSITY CONCEPTS

To check your understanding and to practice using the concepts in this chapter, go to www.mymanagementlab.com and explore the material associated with Chapter 1.

Know Key Terms

Understanding the following key terms is critical to your understanding of chapter material. Define each of these terms. Refer to the page(s) referenced after a term to check your definition or to gain further insight regarding the term.

diversity **82**
majority group **82**
minority group **82**
demographics **85**
ethnocentrism **86**
prejudice **86**

stereotype **86**
discrimination **86**
tokenism **87**
gender-role stereotypes **87**
bicultural stress **88**
role conflict **88**

role overload **88**
reverse discrimination **92**
pluralism **93**
diversity training **97**

Know How Management Concepts Relate

This section is comprised of activities that will further sharpen your understanding of management concepts. Answer essay questions as completely as possible. Also, remember that many additional true/false and multiple choice questions appear online at MyManagementLab.com to help you further refine your understanding of management concepts.

1. When managing people, describe the significance of understanding both "minority" and "majority" groups as they exist in an organization.

2. Explain how average annual percentages changes in the U.S. population by race from 1995–2050 should influence today's diversity planning for organizations of the future.

3. Assume you are ethnocentric. List three specific beliefs about your own culture that you might possess. Would such beliefs be a hindrance or a help in you becoming a successful manager? Explain.

4. Pinpoint five ways that discrimination might negatively affect an organization.

5. List five ways you would promote diversity in an organization. How would you control your efforts to make sure they were successful?

DEVELOPING MANAGEMENT SKILLS

Learning activities in this section are aimed at helping you develop diversity skill. Learning activities include Exploring Your Management Skill: Parts 1 & 2, Your Management Skill Portfolio, Experiential Exercise, Cases, and a VideoNet Exercise.

Exploring Your Management Skill: Part 1

Before studying this chapter, respond to the following questions regarding the type of advice you would give to the CEO of Siemens AG. Then address the concerning diversity challenges he presently faces. You are not expected to be a diversity expert at this point. Answering the questions now can help you focus on important points when you study the chapter. Also, answering the questions again after you study the chapter will give you an idea of how much you have learned.

Record your answers here or online at MyManagementLab. com. Completing the questions at MyManagementLab.com will

allow you to get feedback about your answers automatically. If you answer the questions in the book, look up answers in the Exploring Your Management Skill section at the end of the book.

FOR EACH STATEMENT CIRCLE:

- "Y" if you would give the advice to the CEO.
- "N" if you would NOT give the advice to the CEO.
- "NI" if you have no idea whether you would give the advice to the CEO.

In meeting your diversity challenges at Siemens, you should . . .

Before   After
Study   Study

1. study the structure of minority and majority employee groups at Siemens.

2. emphasize diversity at Siemens as a vehicle to gain, but not necessarily keep, market share.
   Y, N, NI

3. be willing to sacrifice some productivity at Siemens to build a diverse organization.
   Y, N, NI

4. be aware that Hispanics will likely have a higher percentage growth than blacks during 2010–2020 within the U.S. population.
   Y, N, NI

5. avoid ethnocentrism.
   Y, N, NI

6. use the "glass ceiling" to your advantage at Siemens.
   Y, N, NI

7. focus on eliminating stereotyping of older workers at Siemens.
   Y, N, NI

8. use the strategy of improving mostly the skills of Siemens managers to improve company diversity.
   Y, N, NI

9. be careful of reverse discrimination at Siemens—employees' discrimination against managers.
   Y, N, NI

10. achieve excellent diversity at Siemens by using EEOC policies as guidelines for action, thereby reducing the need for diversity training of managers.
    Y, N, NI

11. control for diversity at Siemens by making sure that diversity efforts materialize as planned.
    Y, N, NI

12. follow the "Golden Rule" for business: "He who has the gold makes the rules."
    Y, N, NI

13. don't forget that at Siemens you may have to eliminate resistance to change for diversity efforts to be successful.
    Y, N, NI

14. make sure you are not being influenced by conscious incompetence in trying to build a pro-diversity climate at Siemens.
    Y, N, NI

15. organize your diversity efforts by offering incentives employees will receive if they follow Siemens' diversity guidelines.
    Y, N, NI

Exploring Your Management Skill: Part 2

As you recall, you completed Exploring Your Management Skill before you started to study this chapter. Your responses gave you an idea of how much you initially knew about diversity and helped you to focus on important points as you studied the chapter. Answer the Exploring Your Management Skill questions again now and compare your score to the first time you took it. The comparison will give you an idea of how much you have learned from studying this chapter and pinpoint areas for further clarification before you start studying the next chapter. Record your answers within the text or online at MyManagementLab.com. Completing the survey at MyManagementLab.com will allow you to grade and compare your test scores automatically. If you complete the test in the book, look up answers in the Exploring Your Management Skill section at the end of the book.

Your Management Skills Portfolio

Your Management Learning Portfolio is a collection of activities specially designed to demonstrate your management knowledge and skill. By completing these questions online at MyManagementLab.com, you will be able to print, complete with cover sheet, as many activities as you choose. Be sure to save your work. Taking your printed portfolio to an employment interview could be helpful in obtaining a job.

The portfolio activity for this chapter is Assessing Diversity at TECO Energy. Read this highlight about TECO Energy and answer the questions that follow.

TECO Energy is an energy company headquartered in Tampa, Florida. TECO Energy's five business units include (1) Tampa Electric, a regulated electric utility serving more than 635,000 customers in West Central Florida, (2) Peoples Gas System, Florida's largest natural gas distribution utility, (3) TECO Coal, producer of conventional coal and synthetic fuel, (4) TECO Transport, river and ocean waterborne transportation provider, and (5) TECO Guatemala, owner of two power plants in Guatemala. (You can learn more about the company by visiting www.tecoenergy.com). Over the years, TECO management has focused on building a diverse workforce. Management recently reported the results of a diversity study aimed at monitoring its diversity efforts by ascertaining the present characteristics of its workforce. Part of the results of that study appears in Exhibits 1, 2, and 3.

2 You and Your Career

Possible Negative Impact on Careers of Women

This chapter described how women may be negatively affected in their organizational lives simply because of their gender. A recent survey of professional women working in accounting companies seems to confirm this observation.[37] According to

the survey, 59 percent of the respondents indicated that they were negatively affected by gender bias. Respondents believed that to an influential extent they were either given or not given their jobs because of their gender.

Could such gender bias affect your career if you are a woman? If you are a man? Could such bias have an impact on the success of an organization? Explain each answer fully. Summarize what you have learned about gender bias and building your career in an organization.

Videonet Exercise

Promoting Diversity in Organizations: Progressive Redevelopment, Inc. and CaringWorks

Video Highlights

CaringWorks is the social services affiliate of Progressive Redevelopment, Inc. President Carol S. Collard and director of operations Wanda Rainey-Reed discuss how they manage the not-for-profit organization. The first three minutes of the video set the context for the focus in the last seven minutes on leadership and diversity. Both Collard and Rainey-Reed mention values, excellence, and integrity, and emphasize the role of intrinsic rewards when extrinsic monetary rewards are not always available. The end of the video addresses diversity. Rainey-Reed discusses why she considers workplace diversity to be valuable.

Discussion Questions

1. If you were employed at CaringWorks, would you be happy to receive a Care Free Day card instead of a monetary bonus?

2. Describe CaringWorks' hiring process.
3. Why did Rainey-Reed say CaringWorks desires to employ a diverse workforce? How committed is CaringWorks to creating a diverse organization? In what ways is this commitment demonstrated?

Internet Activity

Browse the CaringWorks Web site at www.caringworksinc.org. Explore the site. Look at the services offered. Now click on the "About Us" link. Read the organization's mission statement. Is this mission statement consistent with the video clip? Why or why not? Next, read some of the stories of those who have benefitted from the work of this organization under the "Stories" link. Make a link between these individual experiences and the organizational mission statement. Explain your answer.

CASES

1 SIEMENS FOCUSES ON GLOBAL DIVERSITY

The case that introduces this chapter, "Siemens Focuses on Global Diversity," and its related Challenge Case Summary were written to help you better understand the management concepts contained in this chapter. Answer the following discussion questions about the Challenge Case to better understand how concepts relating to management and diversity can be applied in an organization such as Siemens.

1. How important is it to Siemens to have a diverse workforce? Discuss fully.
2. How would you control diversity activities at Siemens if you were top management?
3. As Siemens' top management, what steps would you take to build commitment for diversity throughout the organization? Be as specific as possible.

2 THE U.S. POSTAL SERVICE PUTS ITS STAMP ON DIVERSITY

Read the case and answer the questions that follow. Studying this case will help you better understand how concepts relating

to management and diversity can be applied in a company like the U.S. Postal Service.

One of the largest U.S. employers is also one of the best at managing workforce diversity. With 780,000 employees and $68 billion in annual revenues, the U.S. Postal Service (USPS) is responsible for delivering mail to the country's homes and businesses. Over the years, the federal agency has become a leader in promoting diversity up and down the hierarchy. Its success has been recognized by a listing in *Fortune* magazine's "50 Best Companies for Diversity" ranking for five consecutive years.

The drive for diversity started in 1992. Top management carefully analyzed the demographic shifts within the United States and the USPS's growing involvement in global commerce, then created a Diversity Development department within the human resources function. The purpose was "to increase employees' awareness of and appreciation for ethnic and cultural diversity, both in the postal workplace and among customers," says Murry E. Weatherall, vice president of diversity development. Next, the USPS began training diversity specialists in career development and coaching skills so they could support and encourage diversity on the local level. The agency also initiated an Affirmative Employment Program to attract minority and female applicants as well as people with disabilities. In 1996, the USPS launched a

National Awards Program for Diversity Achievement, inviting employees to nominate colleagues and teams that have made outstanding contributions to promoting diversity.

As a result of these activities, the composition of the USPS workforce reflects more diversity. In 1991, 34 percent of the workforce was female; by 2004, 38 percent was female. The proportion of minorities in the workforce has increased, from 32 percent in 1991 to nearly 37 percent in 2004. Now 59 percent of newly hired employees are members of minority groups and 24 percent of the top-salaried managers are members of minorities. No glass ceiling here: Women hold 42 percent of first-line management jobs, 31 percent of middle management jobs, and 27 percent of senior management jobs at the USPS.

The USPS keeps its diversity specialists up to date on the latest techniques and trends through National Diversity Network meetings and educational programs led by headquarters staff. A special events committee provides internal support for diversity-related programs such as National Hispanic Heritage month, Black History month, and National Asian Pacific American Heritage month. And to gauge internal reaction to diversity initiatives, the agency has an outside firm conduct a confidential survey of 25 percent of its employees every three months. The surveys ask for comments on discrimination, harassment, fairness, and other issues, providing feedback on how the workforce views the diversity situation.

Despite its success in managing diversity, the USPS must deal with a number of serious challenges. First, it is facing stronger competition from FedEx, UPS, and other domestic and international delivery firms. Second, relations between management and union members have been strained at times as the agency seeks ways to cut costs and as it keeps streamlining

operations through new technology. Third, USPS managers must remain responsive to their customers' needs and priorities—while simultaneously complying with a complex set of government rules and regulations that limit their alternatives in making decisions about rates, facilities, transportation, and other key areas.

As the Postmaster General told a public hearing not long ago, "the status quo won't do" if the USPS is to operate both efficiently and effectively in the rapidly changing business environment. He is seeking the power to change the organization and "modernize with a vision of what America needs, not just today, but 10 to 15 to 30 years from now." Diversity plays such a vital role in shaping the USPS's future that top management has switched responsibility for succession planning from the human resources department to the diversity development department. Now "our corporate succession process is very inclusive and gives everybody—whether a minority or a woman—an opportunity to be considered," notes Murry Weatherall.

QUESTIONS

1. Describe the USPS's approach to pluralism, based on the information in this case study. Does this approach appear to be effective? Explain.

2. Of the challenges listed in Table 4.2, which do you think might be the most serious threats to the USPS's ability to manage its diverse workforce?

3. Would you recommend that the USPS strive to have its workforce mirror the demographic composition of the U.S. population? Why?

Endnotes

1. Company Web site, "Diversity," http://www.siemens.com, accessed April 15, 2010; Kellye Whitney, "Jill Lee: Taking Inclusion International at Siemens," *Diversity Executive*, January 17, 2010, http://www.diversity-executive.com; Heidi Brown, "Diversity Does Matter," *Forbes*, July 21, 2009, http://www.forbes.com.

2. *Fortune* Magazine annually publishes its list, "100 Best Companies to Work For," and provides a data cut of the rankings by percentage of minority employees. For the most recent list, see "100 Best Companies to Work For: Minorities," *Fortune*, http://money.cnn.com, accessed April 23, 2010. For a discussion of companies well-known for their positive work in the area of diversity, see Roy S. Johnson's seminal article, "The 50 Best Companies for Asians, Blacks and Hispanics," *Fortune* 138, no. 3 (August 3, 1998): 94–96.

3. Liz Winfeld and Susan Spielman, "Making Sexual Orientation Part of Diversity," *Training & Development* (April 1995): 50–51.

4. For an article describing the benefits of diversity management, see Mary Salomon and Joah Schork, "Turn Diversity to Your Advantage," *Research Technology Management* 46 (2003): 37.

5. Judith C. Giordan, "Valuing Diversity," *Chemical & Engineering News*, February 20, 1995, 40.

6. Ann M. Morrison, "Leadership Diversity as Strategy," in *The New Leaders: Guidelines on Leadership Diversity in America* (San Francisco: Jossey-Bass, 1992), 11–28.

7. Prem Benimadh, "Adding Value through Diversity," *Canadian Business Review* (Spring 1995): 6–11; Tara Parker-Pope, "Inside P&G, a Pitch to Keep Women Employees," *Wall Street Journal*, September 9, 1998, B1.

8. Ann Pomeroy, "Cultivating Female Leaders," *HR Magazine* 52, no. 2 (February 2007): 44–51.

9. Frans Johansson, "Masters of the Multicultural" *Harvard Business Review* 83, no. 10 (October 2005): 18–19.

10. Jonathan Moules, "Benefits of Ethnic Diversity Doubted," *Financial Times*, February 20, 2007, 4.

11. For a detailed look at the potential pitfalls of diversity management, see C. Von Bergen, Barlow Soper, and Teresa Foster, "Unintended Negative Effects of Diversity Management," *Public Personnel Management* 31 (2002): 239–252.

12. William B. Johnston and Arnold E. Packer, "Executive Summary," *Workforce 2000: Work and Workers for the Twenty-First Century* (Indianapolis: Hudson Institute, June 1987), xiii–xiv.

13. Roosevelt Thomas, "Affirmative Action or Affirming Diversity," *Harvard Business Review* (1990): 110.

14. "The Five Groups That Experience the Most Discrimination in the Workplace," *Libel.com*, October 22, 2009, http://www.libel.com; Roosevelt Thomas, "Stereotyping Muslims? Know Your Facts," *Knight Ridder Tribune Business News*, June 17, 2006, 1.

15. Michele Himmelberg, "Age Discrimination Alleged," *Knight Ridder Tribune Business News*, April 14, 2007.

16. Rosabeth Moss Kanter, *Men and Women of the Corporation* (New York: Basic Books, 1977).

17. American Bar Association, "Legal Outreach Is Model for Diversity Pipeline Success," press release, February 6, 2010, http://www.abanow.org.

18. Rosabeth Moss Kanter, "Numbers: Minorities and Majorities," in *Men and Women of the Corporation* (New York: Basic Books, 1977), 206–244. For a closer look at the effects of gender-role stereotypes, see N. Lane and N. Piercy, "The Ethics of Discrimination: Organizational Mindsets and Female Employment Disadvantage," *Journal of Business Ethics* 44 (2003): 313.

19. Ann M. Morrison, *Breaking the Glass Ceiling: Can Women Reach the Top of America's Largest Corporations?* (Reading, MA: Addison Wesley, 1992).

20. Annelies van Vianen and Agneta Fischer, "Illuminating the Glass Ceiling: The Role of Organizational Culture Preferences," *Journal of Occupational and Organizational Psychology* 75 (2002): 315.

21. Susan Webb, *Step Forward: Sexual Harassment in the Workplace* (New York: MasterMedia, 1991); Susan B. Garland, "Finally, a Corporate Tip Sheet on Sexual Harassment," *BusinessWeek*, July 13, 1998, 39; see also Maureen O'Connor, Barbara Gutek, Margaret Stockdale, Tracey Geer, and Renee Melancon, "Explaining Sexual Harassment Judgments: Looking Beyond Gender of the Rater," *Law and Human Behavior* 28 (2004): 69.

22. Ella Bell, "The Bicultural Life Experience of Career Oriented Black Women," *Journal of Organizational Behavior* 11 (November 1990): 459–478.

23. Tina Vasquez, "New Morgan Stanley Program Focuses on Diversity—Despite Tough Economic Climate," *GlassHammer.com*, March 31, 2010, http://www.theglasshammer.com.

24. For insights on how to manage older employees, see Carol Hymowitz, "Young Managers Learn How to Bridge the Gap with Older Employees," *Wall Street Journal*, July 21, 1998, B1.

25. Department of Labor Statistics, "Civilian Labor Force by Age, Sex, Race, and Hispanic Origin—1992, 2002, and Projected 2012," February 11, 2004.

26. Anonymous, "Time to Start Focusing on Attracting Older Workers," *HR Focus* 81, no. 2 (February 2004): 13–14.

27. ———, "Companies May Lose Older Workers with Shortsighted Policies," *PR Newswire,* May 29, 2007.

28. Jeffrey Sonnenfeld, "Dealing with the Aging Workforce," *Harvard Business Review* 56 (1978): 81–92.

29. Company Web site, "Walgreens Recognized as Private-Sector Employer of the Year for People with Disabilities," press release, April 15, 2010, http://news.walgreens.com.

30. William B. Johnston and Arnold E. Packer, "Executive Summary," *Workforce 2000: Work and Workers for the Twenty-First Century* (Indianapolis: Hudson Institute, June 1987): xii–xiv.

31. Jean Kim, "Issues in Workforce Diversity," Panel Presentation at the First Annual National Diversity Conference (San Francisco, May 1991).

32. *The Holy Bible,* Authorized King James Version (Nashville: Holman Bible Publishers, 1984).

33. J. Stewart Black and Hal B. Gregersen, "Serving Two Masters: Managing the Dual Allegiance of Expatriate Employees," *Sloan Management Review* (Summer 1992): 61–71.

34. Gwendolyn Combs, "Meeting the Leadership Challenge of a Diverse and Pluralistic Workplace: Implications of Self-Efficacy for Diversity Training," *Journal of Leadership and Organizational Studies* 8 (2002): 1.

35. Richard Lowther, "Embracing and Managing Diversity at Dell," *Strategic HR Review* 5, no. 6 (September/October 2006): 16–19.

36. Les Donaldson and Edward E. Scannell, *Human Resource Development: The New Trainer's Guide,* 2nd ed. (Reading, MA: Addison-Wesley, 1986), 8–9.

37. Charles B. Eldridge, Paula Park, Abbee Phillips, and Ellen Williams, "Executive Women in Finance," *The CPA Journal* 77, no. 1 (January 2007): 58–60.

chapter 5

Managing in the Global Arena

Target Skill

global management skill: the ability to manage global factors as components of organizational operations

objectives

To help build my *global management skill,* when studying this chapter, I will attempt to acquire:

1. An understanding of international management and its importance to modern managers

2. An understanding of what constitutes a multinational corporation

3. Insights concerning the risk involved in investing in international operations

4. Insights into those who work in multinational corporations

5. Knowledge about managing multinational corporations

6. Knowledge about managing multinational organizations versus transnational organizations

7. An understanding of how ethics and the preparation of expatriates relate to managing internationally

CHALLENGE CASE

WAL-MART FACING GLOBAL PROBLEMS IN JAPAN

WHEN SAM WALTON OPENED the first Wal-Mart store in 1962, it was the beginning of an American success story that has become famous throughout the world. As evidence of the success of Wal-Mart, the company recently ranked in the top 10 on *Fortune* magazine's list of "The World's Most Admired Companies," a list compiled by surveying industry executives as well as Wall Street analysts. Today, Wal-Mart has more than 8,300 stores scattered throughout the 50 states and 14 foreign countries. The company is the nation's largest private employer, with more than 1.4 million associates.[1]

Through Walton's experience in operating variety stores in small towns in Arkansas and Missouri, he was convinced that consumers would be drawn to a discount store offering a wide variety of merchandise that was accompanied by friendly service. Walton was absolutely correct.

In a few decades, Wal-Mart has become the world's number-one retailer. Company growth has come not only from the success of the original Wal-Mart concept, but also from diversified concepts such as the availability of grocery products to customers in Wal-Mart Supercenters and general merchandise being offered in countries such as Brazil, Argentina, and China. Also, Sam's Clubs (a subsidiary of Wal-Mart) has undoubtedly aided company growth.

Upon Sam Walton's death in 1992, many company analysts were concerned that Wal-Mart was coming on hard times. Analysts believed that Sam Walton was the personification of Wal-Mart's positive corporate culture and that without him it would erode. Time has shown, however, that the culture does not seem to have eroded, and indeed appears as strong or even stronger now than ever. Store openings are still conducted with high enthusiasm and operating stores look better than ever. The company cheer is still done regularly at store openings and meetings—the only difference is that now the cheer is done in many different countries and in many different languages.

Needless to say, Wal-Mart's CEO Lee Scott has approached global expansion with much excitement and enthusiasm. Today, Wal-Mart serves more than 200 million customers a year in 15 countries worldwide including Chile, China, India, and Japan. Recent news, however, seems to cast doubt on Wal-Mart's ability to manage its Japanese stores.[2] Seiyu, Wal-Mart's Japanese brand, posted losses five times greater in the first half of 2006 than in the same period in 2005. Management, however, says that it remains committed to its more than 350 stores in Japan.[3] This news from Japan is especially ominous after the company pulled out of South Korea and Germany because of lagging sales, labor market obstacles, and local competition.

■ *Wal-Mart has many challenges managing operations across the globe in countries like Japan, Argentina, and China. This crowded store in Shanghai reflects Wal-Mart's success in meeting many such challenges.*

EXPLORING YOUR MANAGEMENT SKILL

You can explore your level of global management skill **before** studying the chapter by completing the exercise "Exploring Your Management Skill: Part 1" on page 131 and **after** studying this chapter by completing the exercise "Exploring Your Management Skill: Part 2" on page 132.

THE GLOBAL MANAGEMENT CHALLENGE

The Challenge Case illustrates not only several steps Wal-Mart has taken to maintain its growth over the years, but also the problem that the company currently faces regarding its operations in Japan. The global management challenge for a manager such as Lee Scott at Wal-Mart includes understanding the need to manage internationally, managing a multinational corporation and its workforce, understanding management functions and multinational corporations and transnational organizations, and following through on special issues like maintaining ethics in international management situations and preparing expatriates for foreign assignments. After studying chapter concepts, read the Challenge Case Summary at the end of the chapter for added help in relating chapter content to meeting global management challenges at Wal-Mart.

MANAGING ACROSS THE GLOBE: WHY?

Most U.S. companies see great opportunities in the international marketplace today.[4] Although the U.S. population is growing slowly but steadily, the population in many other countries is exploding. For example, it has been estimated that in 1990, China, India, and Indonesia together had more than 2 billion people, or 40 percent of the world's population.[5] Obviously, such countries offer a strong profit potential for aggressive businesspeople throughout the world.

This potential does not come without serious risk, however. Managers who attempt to manage in a global context face formidable challenges. Some of these challenges are the cultural differences among workers from different countries, different technology levels from country to country, and laws and political systems that can vary immensely from one nation to the next.

The remaining sections of this chapter deal with the intricacies of managing in a global context by emphasizing the following:

1. Fundamentals of international management
2. Categories of organizations by international involvement
3. Management functions and multinational corporations
4. International management: Special issues

FUNDAMENTALS OF INTERNATIONAL MANAGEMENT

International management is simply the performance of management activities across national borders.[6] It entails reaching organizational objectives by extending management activities to include an emphasis on organizations in foreign countries.[7] The trend toward increased international management, or *globalization*, is now widely recognized. The primary question for most firms is not *whether* to globalize, but *how* and *how fast* to do so and how to measure global progress over time.[8]

International management can take several different forms, from simply analyzing and fighting competition in foreign markets to establishing a formal partnership with a foreign company. AMP, Inc., for example, has been vigorously fighting competition in a foreign market. This company, a manufacturer of electrical parts, headquartered in Harrisburg, Pennsylvania, has achieved outstanding success by gaining significant control over a portion of its multinational market. The company built factories in 17 countries because experience showed management that competitors could best be beaten in foreign markets if AMP actually produced products within those markets. A message recently sent to AMP stockholders by company president William J. Hudson indicates that the company is continuing to make good progress in the international arena. Hudson has promised to persist in his efforts to develop AMP into a "globe-able" organization.[9]

JP Morgan Chase is an example of a bank involved in international management. JP Morgan Chase, the second-largest bank in the United States, is one of the latest financial institutions to launch a global banking business, targeting such rapidly growing economies as Brazil, China, and India. The bank will sell loans and commercial banking services to multinational organizations in an effort to expand its business outside the United States and reduce its dependence on the U.S. economy.[10] Although JP Morgan Chase is the focus of this example, many other U.S. banks are pursuing similar international management activities. ■

how managers do it

Going Global at JP Morgan Chase

The notable trend that already exists in the United States and other countries toward developing business relationships in and with foreign countries is expected to accelerate even more in the future. As Figure 5.1 illustrates, U.S. investment in foreign countries and investment by foreign countries in the United States have grown since 1996 and are expected to continue growing, with slowdowns or setbacks in recessionary periods. The figure also shows that more recently, investments by foreign countries in the United States and U.S. investments in foreign countries continue to increase as a notable pace. As an interesting side note, Figure 5.2 shows that in 2008, U.S. foreign investments have focused most heavily in the United Kingdom and the Netherlands. This 2008 snapshot is equivalent to several years preceding 2008 and expected to be equivalent to

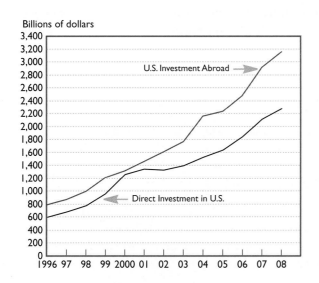

FIGURE 5.1

U.S. investment in foreign countries versus foreign investment in the United States

Source: U.S. Bureau of Economic Analysis.

FIGURE 5.2
U.S. direct investment abroad by country for 2008

Source: U.S. Bureau of Economic Analysis.

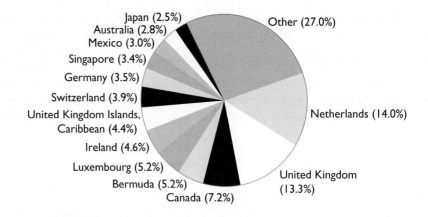

several years after. Figure 5.3 shows that European countries are by far the most significant foreign investors in the United States in 2008. This data also is equivalent to several years preceding 2008 and expected to be equivalent to several years after. Information of this nature has spurred both management educators and practicing managers to insist that knowledge of international management is necessary for a thorough understanding of the contemporary fundamentals of management.[11]

CATEGORIZING ORGANIZATIONS BY INTERNATIONAL INVOLVEMENT

A number of different categories have evolved to describe the extent to which organizations are involved in the international arena. These categories are domestic organizations, international organizations, multinational organizations, and transnational or global organizations. As Figure 5.4 suggests, this categorization format actually describes a continuum of international involvement, with domestic organizations representing the least and transnational organizations the most international involvement. Although the format may not be perfect, it is useful for explaining primary ways in which companies operate in the international realm.[12] The following sections describe these categories in more detail.

Domestic Organizations

Domestic organizations are organizations that essentially operate within a single country. These organizations normally not only acquire necessary resources within a single country but

FIGURE 5.3
Foreign direct investment in the United States by region for 2008

Source: U.S. Bureau of Economic Analysis.

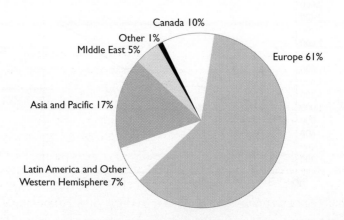

LEVEL 1 Domestic organizations	LEVEL 2 International organizations	LEVEL 3 Multinational organizations	LEVEL 4 Transnational organizations

(No or Low Involvement) → (High Involvement)

FIGURE 5.4   Continuum of international involvement

also sell their goods or services within that same country. Although domestic organizations may occasionally make an international sale or acquire some needed resource from a foreign supplier, the overwhelming bulk of their business activity takes place within the country where they are based.

Although this category is not determined by size, most domestic organizations today are quite small. Even smaller business organizations, however, are following the trend and becoming increasingly involved in the international arena.

International Organizations

International organizations are organizations that are based primarily within a single country but have continuing, meaningful international transactions—such as making sales and purchases of materials—in other countries. Nu Horizons is an example of a small company that can be classified as an international organization. This distributor of electronic goods made mainly by some 40 U.S. manufacturers has about 5,000 customers and is the fastest-growing company in Melville, New York. Nu Horizons is an international organization because an important part of its business is to act as the primary North American distributor of electronic components made by Japan's NIC Components Corp.[13]

In summary, international organizations are more extensively involved in the international arena than are domestic organizations, but less so than either multinational or transnational organizations.

Multinational Organizations: The Multinational Corporation

The *multinational organization,* commonly called the *multinational corporation (MNC)*, represents the third level of international involvement. This section of the text defines the multinational corporation, discusses the complexities involved in managing such a corporation, describes the risks associated with its operations, explores the diversity of the multinational workforce, and explains how the major management functions relate to managing the multinational corporation.

Defining the Multinational Corporation

The term *multinational corporation* first appeared in American dictionaries about 1970, and has since been defined in various ways in business publications and textbooks. For the purposes of this text, a **multinational corporation** is a company that has significant operations in more than one country. Essentially, a multinational corporation is an organization that is involved in doing business at the international level. It carries out its activities on an international scale that disregards national boundaries, and it is guided by a common strategy from a corporation center.[14]

Neil H. Jacoby explains that companies go through six stages to reach the highest degree of multinationalization. As Table 5.1 indicates, multinational corporations can range from slightly multinationalized organizations that simply export products to a foreign country to highly

With more than 30,000 restaurants in over 100 countires, McDonald's is a good example of a mulitnational corporation (MNC). This is its restaurant in the Plaza Flamingo shopping mall, Cancun, Mexico.

TABLE 5.1	Six Stages of Multinationalization				
Stage 1	**Stage 2**	**Stage 3**	**Stage 4**	**Stage 5**	**Stage 6**
Exports its products to foreign countries	Establishes sales organizations abroad	Licenses use of its patterns and know-how to foreign firms that make and sell its products	Establishes foreign manufacturing facilities	Multinationalizes management from top to bottom	Multinationalizes ownership of corporate stock

multinationalized organizations that have some of their owners in other countries. According to Alfred M. Zeien, CEO of Gillette Company, it can take up to 25 years to build a management team with the requisite skills, experience, and abilities to mold an organization into a highly developed multinational company.[15]

In general, the larger the organization, the greater the likelihood it participates in international operations of some sort. Companies such as General Electric, Lockheed, and DuPont, which have annually accumulated more than $1 billion from export sales, support this generalization. You will find exceptions, of course.

how managers do it

Building Global Market Share at BRK Electronics

In some industries, even small businesses can prosper in the global marketplace. For example, BRK Electronics, a small firm in Aurora, Illinois, holds a substantial share of world sales in smoke detectors. The company has created an advantage with its reputation for high-quality smoke alarms, carbon monoxide alarms, and fire extinguishers. BRK's market share has grown through its local distributors in countries like Australia, Mexico, and New Zealand.[16] As noted earlier, an increasing number of smaller organizations such as BRK Electronics are undertaking international operations. ■

Complexities of Managing the Multinational Corporation

From the discussion so far, it should be clear that international management and domestic management are quite different. Classic management thought indicates that international management differs from domestic management because it involves operating:[17]

1. Within different national sovereignties
2. Under widely disparate economic conditions
3. Among people living within different value systems and institutions
4. In places experiencing the industrial revolution at different times
5. Often over greater geographical distance
6. In national markets varying greatly in population and area

Figure 5.5 shows some of the more important management implications of these six variables and some of the relationships among them. Consider, for example, the first variable. Different national sovereignties generate different legal systems. In turn, each legal system implies a unique

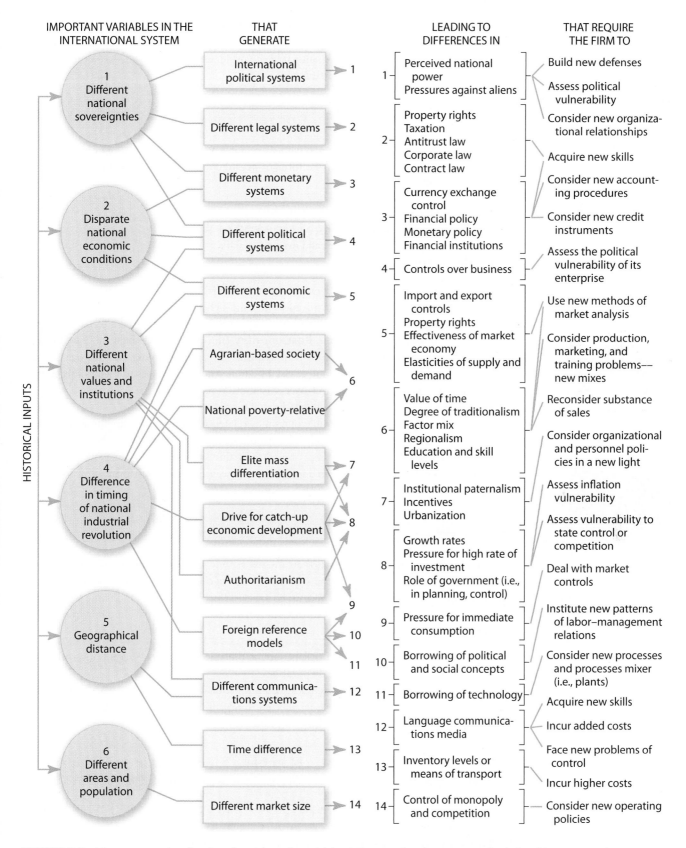

FIGURE 5.5   Management implications based on six variables in international systems and relationships among them

set of rights and obligations involving property, taxation, antitrust (control of monopoly) law, corporate law, and contract law. In turn, these rights and obligations require the firm to acquire the skills necessary to assess the international legal considerations. Such skills are different from those required in a purely domestic setting.

Risk and the Multinational Corporation

Developing a multinational corporation obviously requires a substantial investment in foreign operations. Normally, managers who make foreign investments expect that such investments will accomplish the following:[18]

1. Reduce or eliminate high transportation costs
2. Allow participation in the rapid expansion of a market abroad
3. Provide foreign technical, design, and marketing skills
4. Earn higher profits

Unfortunately, many managers decide to internationalize their companies without having an accurate understanding of the risks involved in making such a decision.[19] For example, political complications involving the **parent company** (the company investing in the international operations) and various factions within the **host country** (the country in which the investment is made) could prevent the parent company from realizing the desirable outcomes just listed. Some companies attempt to minimize this kind of risk by adding standard clauses to their contracts stipulating that in the event a business controversy cannot be resolved by the parties involved, they will agree to mediation by a mutually selected mediator.[20]

The likelihood of achieving desirable outcomes related to foreign investments will probably be somewhat uncertain and will certainly vary from country to country. Nevertheless, managers faced with making a foreign investment must assess this likelihood as accurately as possible. Obviously, a poor decision to invest in another country can cause serious financial problems for the organization.

The Workforce of Multinational Corporations

As organizations become more global, their members tend to become more diverse. Managers of multinational corporations face the continual challenge of building a competitive business team made up of people of different races who speak different languages and come from different parts of the world. The following sections perform two functions that should help managers build such teams:

1. They furnish details and related insights about the various types of organization members generally found in multinational corporations.
2. They describe the adjustments members of multinational organizations normally must make to become efficient and effective contributors to organization goal attainment, and they suggest how managers can facilitate these adjustments.

Types of Organization Members Found in Multinational Corporations   Workers in multinational organizations can be divided into three basic types:

* **Expatriate**—An organization member who lives and works in a country where he or she does not have citizenship[21]

* **Host-country national**—An organization member who is a citizen of the country in which the facility of a foreign-based organization is located[22]

* **Third-country national**—An organization member who is a citizen of one country and works in another country for an organization headquartered in still another country

Organizations that operate globally may employ all three types of workers. The use of host-country nationals, however, is increasing because they are normally the least expensive to employ. Such employees, for example, do not need to be relocated or undergo training in the culture, language, or tax laws of the country where the organization is doing business. Both expatriates and third-country nationals, on the other hand, would have to be relocated and normally undergo such training.

Workforce Adjustments Working in a multinational corporation requires more difficult adjustments than working in an organization that focuses primarily on domestic activities. Probably the two most difficult challenges, which pertain to expatriates and third-country nationals rather than to host-country nationals, are adjusting to a new culture and repatriation.[23]

Adjusting to a New Culture Upon arrival in a foreign country, many people experience confusion, anxiety, and stress related to the need to make cultural adjustments in their organizational and personal lives.[24] From a personal viewpoint, food, weather, and language may all be dramatically different, and driving may be done on the "wrong" side of the road. As an example of personal anxiety that can be caused by adjusting to a new culture, a U.S. expatriate recently working in Sao Paulo, Brazil, drove out of a parking lot by nudging his way into a terrible traffic jam. When a Brazilian woman allowed him to cut in front of her, the expatriate gave her the "ok" signal. To his personal dismay, he was told that in the Brazilian culture, forming a circle with one's first finger and thumb is considered vulgar.[25]

From an organizational viewpoint, workers may encounter different attitudes toward work and different perceptions of time in the workplace. To illustrate, the Japanese are renowned for their hard-driving work ethic, but Americans take a slightly more relaxed attitude toward work. On the other hand, in many U.S. companies, working past quitting time is seen as exemplary, but in Germany, someone who works late is commonly criticized.

Members of multinational corporations normally have the formidable task of adjusting to a drastically new organizational situation. Managers must help these people adjust quickly and painlessly so they can begin contributing to organizational goal attainment as soon as possible.[26]

Offices built out of shipping containers, in Baghdad Iraq, where sandbags offer some protection from mortar and missile attacks.

class discussion highlight

MODERN RESEARCH AND GLOBAL MANAGEMENT SKILL

Expectations about Leaders in Multinational Corporations

A recent study by Sergio Matviuk investigated expectations that individuals in multinational corporations have regarding how their leaders should behave. The researcher studied such expectations held by Mexicans versus Americans, all of which were managers of a multinational corporation with production plants in the northern U.S. and central Mexico. Both groups were similarly represented by male and female members, managers from various organizational levels, age, and education.

The researcher conducted the study to help leaders in multinational corporations be more successful. The researcher reasoned that, if all other things are equal, leaders who behave as followers should have a better chance of overall success than leaders who do not act as followers expect. As a result, leaders in multinational corporations should know whether managers from different countries might have different expectations about how leaders should behave and what those expected differences are.

Leader expectations explored were quite specific. Managers filled out a survey asking the extent to which they expect leaders to (1) challenge existing processes, (2) inspire others to accomplish a shared vision, (3) enable others to act, (4) be a role model, and (5) encourage the "hearts" of others to do a good job.

Do you believe that study results showed that Mexican and American managers have different expectations about how a leader should act? If "yes," how might they differ? If "no," why not? If you were a Mexican manager in this company, would you want to know how American managers expected leaders to act? Why?

Source: Sergio Matviuk, "Cross-Cultural Leadership Behavior Expectations: A Comparison between United States Managers and Mexican Managers," *Journal of American Academy of Business* 11, no. 1 (March 2007): 253–260.

Repatriation **Repatriation** is the process of bringing individuals who have been working abroad back to their home country and reintegrating them into the organization's home-country operations.[27] Repatriation has its own set of adjustment problems, especially with people who have lived abroad for a long time. Some individuals become so accustomed to the advantages of an overseas lifestyle that they greatly miss it when they return home. Others idealize their homeland so much while they are abroad they become disappointed when it fails to live up to their expectations when they return. Still others acquire foreign-based habits that are undesirable from the organization's viewpoint and that are hard to break.[28]

Managers must be patient and understanding with repatriates. Some organizations provide repatriates with counseling so they will be better prepared to handle readjustment problems. Others have found that providing employees, before they leave for foreign duty, with a written agreement specifying what their new duties and career path will be when they return home reduces friction and facilitates the repatriate's adjustment.

The advantages of having organization members participate in an international experience in business are well known and growing. Organization members who have succeeded in the global environment are valuable assets to their organizations. One of the significant challenges to organizations is retaining these highly sought-after individuals through a successful repatriation process after they complete their overseas assignments.[29]

MANAGEMENT FUNCTIONS AND MULTINATIONAL CORPORATIONS

The sections that follow discuss the four major management functions—planning, organizing, influencing, and controlling—as they occur in multinational corporations.

Planning in Multinational Corporations

Planning was defined in Chapter 1 as determining how an organization will achieve its objectives. This definition is applicable to the management of both domestic and multinational organizations, but with some differences.

The primary difference between planning in multinational and domestic organizations is in the plans' components. Plans for the multinational organization include components that focus on the international arena, whereas plans for the domestic organization do not. For example, plans for multinational organizations could include the following:

1. Establishing a new salesforce in a foreign country
2. Developing new manufacturing plants in other countries through purchase or construction
3. Financing international expansion
4. Determining which countries represent the most suitable candidates for international expansion

Components of International Plans

Although planning for multinational corporations varies from organization to organization, the following four components are commonly included in international plans:

- Imports/Exports
- License agreements
- Direct investing
- Joint ventures

This section discusses these four components as well as the responses of multinational corporations to international market agreements.

Imports/Exports

Imports/exports planning components emphasize reaching organizational objectives by **importing** (buying goods or services from another country) or **exporting** (selling goods or services to another country).

Organizations of all sizes import and export. On one hand, companies such as Auburn Farms, Inc., a relatively small producer of all-natural, fat-free snack foods, imports products to be resold. Auburn Farms is the exclusive U.S. importer of Beacon Sweets & Chocolates of South Africa. Auburn sees its importing activities as a way of expanding and diversifying.[30] On the other hand, extremely large and complex organizations, such as Eastman Kodak, export their products to a number of foreign countries.[31]

License Agreements

A **license agreement** is a right granted by one company to another to use its brand name, technology, product specifications, and so on, in the manufacture or sale of goods and services. The company to which the license is extended pays some fee for the privilege. International planning components in this area involve reaching organizational objectives through either the purchase or the sale of licenses at the international level.

For example, the Tosoh Corporation recently purchased a license agreement from Mobil Research and Development Corporation to commercialize Mobil's newly developed process for extracting mercury from natural gas. Tosoh, a Japanese firm, will use its subsidiaries in the United States, Japan, the Netherlands, Greece, Canada, and the United Kingdom as bases of operations from which to profit from Mobil's new process.[32]

Upon entering into a license agreement, both companies should make absolutely sure they understand the terms of the agreement. Some companies end up in litigation as a means of settling disagreements regarding specifics of the contents of a license agreement. Naturally, the cost of such litigation can be high and end up significantly diminishing the advantages that both companies thought they would gain as a result of entering into the agreement.[33]

Direct Investing

Direct investing uses the assets of one company to purchase the operating assets (e.g., factories) of another company. International planning in this area

Licensing agreements allow one company to use another's brand name or images to manufacture products, like these Mickey Mouse toys being made in China, in exchange for a fee.

emphasizes reaching organizational objectives through the purchase of the operating assets of another company in a foreign country.

A number of Japanese firms have recently been making direct investments in the United States. In fact, many people believe that a new wave of direct Japanese investment in the United States is building. Several large Japanese companies have announced plans to expand their U.S. production facilities. These planned direct investments are focused on building competitive clout for Japanese companies in such core industries as automobiles, semiconductors, electronics, and office products. Lower manufacturing wages and lower land costs in the United States are key attractions for the Japanese firms. For example, because the cost of building a factory was 30 percent cheaper in the United States than in Japan, Ricoh Company decided to spend $30 million to start making thermal paper products near Atlanta, Georgia. One of the largest Japanese direct investments in the United States was Toyota Motor Company's $900 million expansion of its Georgetown, Kentucky, plant. The lower costs associated with expanding and operating the Georgetown plant were the key reason Toyota decided to make this investment.[34]

Joint Ventures   An **international joint venture** is a partnership formed by a company in one country with a company in another country for the purpose of pursuing some mutually desirable business undertaking.[35] International planning components that include joint ventures emphasize the attainment of organizational objectives through partnerships with foreign companies. For example, joint ventures between car manufacturers are becoming more and more common as companies strive for greater economies of scale and higher standards in product quality and delivery.

Planning and International Market Agreements   In order to plan properly, managers of a multinational corporation, or any other organization participating in the international arena, must understand numerous complex and interrelated factors present within the organization's international environment. Managers should have a practical grasp of such international environmental factors as the economic and cultural conditions, and the laws and political circumstances, of foreign countries within which their companies operate.

One international environmental factor that affects strategic planning has lately received significant attention: An **international market agreement** is an arrangement among a cluster of countries that facilitates a high level of trade among these countries. In planning, managers must consider existing international market agreements as they relate to countries in which their organizations operate. If an organization is from a country that is party to an international market agreement, the organization's plan should include steps for taking maximum advantage of that agreement. On the other hand, if an organization is from a country that is *not* party to an international market agreement, the organization's plan must include steps for competing with organizations from nations that are parties to such an agreement. The most notable international market agreements are discussed here.

The European Union (EU) The **European Union (EU)** is an international market agreement established in 1994 dedicated to facilitating trade among member nations. To that end, the nations in the EU have agreed to eliminate tariffs among themselves and work toward meaningful deregulation in such areas as banking, insurance, telecommunications, and airlines. More recently, the nations are trying to develop a set of standardized accounting principles that will help facilitate business transactions among members.[36] Long-term members of the EU include Denmark, the United Kingdom, Portugal, the Netherlands, Belgium, Spain, Ireland, Luxembourg, France, Germany, Italy, and Greece. Member businesses are particularly excited about the EU because they are sure membership will ultimately boost exports and encourage foreign investment from other member nations. The significance of the EU as an international environmental factor can only increase, since the number of member countries is expected to continue growing.[37]

Figure 5.6 identifies countries that are presently members of the EU as well as membership-candidate countries and applications-pending countries. Applications-pending countries are countries more in the initial stages of obtaining EU membership. Candidate countries are countries that have applied and have been chosen by the EU for more serious membership consideration.

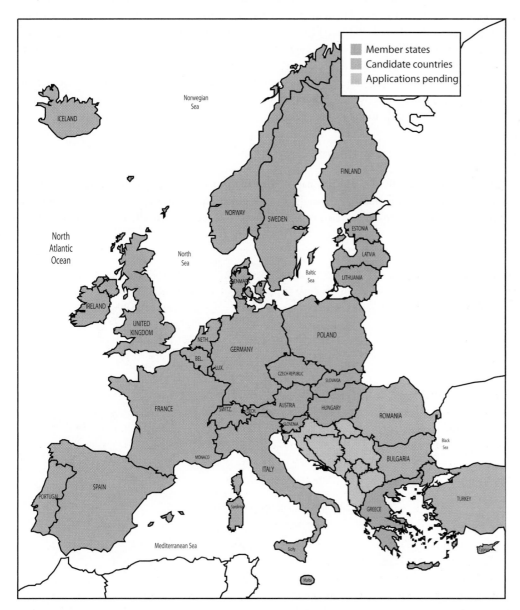

FIGURE 5.6
The European Union: Members, candidates, and applicants

North American Free Trade Agreement (NAFTA) The **North American Free Trade Agreement (NAFTA)** is an international market agreement aimed at facilitating trade among member nations. Current NAFTA members are the United States, Canada, and Mexico.[38] To facilitate trade among themselves, these countries have agreed to such actions as the phasing out of tariffs on U.S. farm exports to Mexico, the opening up of Mexico to American trucking, and the safeguarding of North American pharmaceutical patents in Mexico.

NAFTA has had significant impact since its implementation in January 1994. Recent figures show that since the agreement went into effect, U.S. exports to Mexico increased 30 percent and Mexican exports to the United States increased 15 percent. Trade between the United States and Canada exploded since NAFTA took effect. As with the EU, the significance of NAFTA as an international environmental factor can only grow in the future as other countries in the Caribbean and South America apply for membership.[39]

Asian-Pacific Economic Cooperation (APEC) APEC was established in 1989 to further the economic growth and prosperity of the Asia-Pacific community. Since its beginning, APEC has worked to reduce tariffs and other trade barriers across the Asia-Pacific region. APEC is based on the concept that free and open trade creates greater opportunities for international trade and related prosperity among member nations. The organization works diligently to create an environment in which goods can be transported safely and efficiently among countries. APEC has 21 members, including Canada, the People's Republic of China, Indonesia, and the United States. APEC entire country membership is depicted in Figure 5.7. Comparison of APEC and EU member countries shows that EU member countries are concentrated in Europe, while APEC member countries are spread throughout the globe.

To sum up, numerous countries throughout the world are already signatories to international market agreements. Moreover, the number of countries that are parties to such agreements should grow significantly in the future.

Organizing Multinational Corporations

Organizing was generally defined in Chapter 1 as the process of establishing orderly uses for all resources within the organization. This definition applies equally to the management of domestic and multinational organizations. Two organizing topics as they specifically relate to multinational

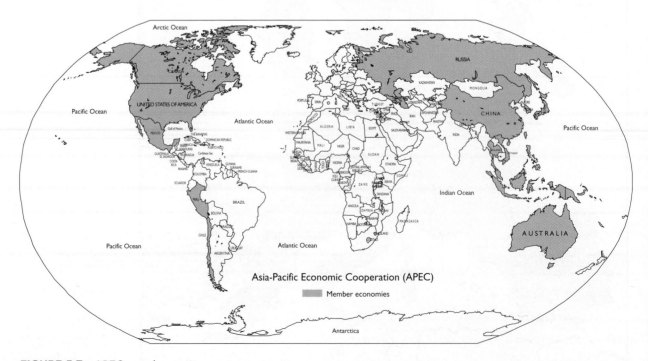

FIGURE 5.7 APEC member nations

corporations, however, bear further discussion. These topics are organization structure and the selection of managers.[40]

Organization Structure

Basically, *organization structure* is the sum of all established relationships among resources within the organization, and the *organization chart* is the graphic illustration of organization structure.

Figure 5.8 illustrates several ways in which organization charts can be designed for multinational corporations. Briefly, multinational organization charts can be set up according to major business functions the organization performs, such as production or marketing; major products the organization sells, such as brakes or electrical parts; or, geographic areas within which the organization does business, such as North America or Europe. The topic of organization structure is discussed in much more detail in Chapter 11.

As with domestic organizations, there is no one best way to organize a multinational corporation. Instead, managers must analyze the multinational circumstances that confront them and develop an organization structure that best suits those circumstances.

Selection of Managers

For multinational organizations to thrive, they must have competent managers. One characteristic believed to be a primary determinant of how competently managers can guide multinational organizations is their attitude toward how such organizations should operate.

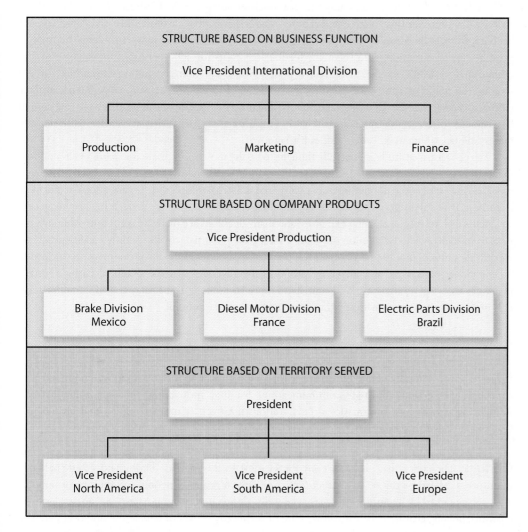

FIGURE 5.8
Partial multinational organization charts based on function, product, and territory

Managerial Attitudes Toward Foreign Operations Over the years, management theorists have identified three basic managerial attitudes toward the operation of multinational corporations: ethnocentric, polycentric, and geocentric. The **ethnocentric attitude** reflects the belief that multinational corporations should regard home-country management practices as superior to foreign-country management practices. Managers with an ethnocentric attitude are prone to stereotype home-country management practices as sound and reasonable and foreign management practices as faulty and unreasonable. The **polycentric attitude** reflects the belief that because foreign managers are closer to foreign organizational units, they probably understand them better, and therefore foreign management practices should generally be viewed as more insightful than home-country management practices. Managers with a **geocentric attitude** believe that the overall quality of management recommendations, rather than the location of managers, should determine the acceptability of management practices used to guide multinational corporations.[41]

Modern managers should continually monitor ethnocentric, polycentric, and geocentric attitudes that exist in organizations to make sure they are consistent with global aspirations of the organization. One example of this monitoring involves the Coca-Cola Company where management constantly monitors its Chinese Web site. The purpose of this monitoring is to examine how Coca-Cola, the number one brand in the world, is using its Web site to communicate with management as well as the public in the world's largest market, China. Management wants to make sure the site appropriately integrates ethnocentric and polycentric views in supporting the Chinese segment of the company's global strategy.[42]

Advantages and Disadvantages of Each Management Attitude It is extremely important to understand the potential advantages and disadvantages of these three attitudes within multinational corporations. The ethnocentric attitude has the advantage of keeping the organization simple, but it generally causes organizational problems because it prevents the organization from receiving feedback from its foreign operations. In some cases, the ethnocentric attitude even causes resentment toward the home country within the foreign society. The polycentric attitude permits the tailoring of foreign organizational segments to their cultures, which can be an advantage. Unfortunately, this attitude can lead to the substantial disadvantage of creating numerous foreign organizational segments that are individually run and rather unique, which makes them difficult to control.

The geocentric attitude is generally thought to be the most appropriate for managers in multinational corporations. This attitude promotes collaboration between foreign and home-country management and encourages the development of managerial skills regardless of the organizational segment or country in which managers operate. An organization characterized by the geocentric attitude generally incurs high travel and training expenses, and many decisions are made by consensus. Although the risks from such a wide distribution of power are real, the potential payoffs—better-quality products, worldwide utilization of the best human resources, increased managerial commitment to worldwide organizational objectives, and increased profit—generally outweigh the potential harm. Overall, managers with a geocentric attitude contribute more to the long-term success of the multinational corporation than managers with an ethnocentric or polycentric attitude.

Influencing People in Multinational Corporations

Influencing was generally defined in Chapter 1 as guiding the activities of organization members in appropriate directions through communicating, leading, motivating, and managing groups. Influencing people in a multinational corporation, however, is more complex and challenging than in a domestic organization.

Culture The factor that probably contributes most to this increased complexity and challenge is culture. **Culture** is the set of characteristics of a given group of people and their environment. The components of a culture that are generally designated as important are norms, values, customs, beliefs, attitudes, habits, skills, state of technology, level of education, and religion. As a manager moves from a domestic corporation involving basically one culture to a multinational corporation involving several, the task of influencing usually becomes more difficult.

To successfully influence employees, managers in multinational corporations should:

1. **Acquire a working knowledge of the languages used in countries that house foreign operations**—Multinational managers attempting to operate without such knowledge are prone to making costly mistakes.

2. **Understand the attitudes of people in countries that house foreign operations**—An understanding of these attitudes can help managers design business practices that are suitable for unique foreign situations. For example, Americans generally accept competition as a tool to encourage people to work harder. As a result, U.S. business practices that include some competitive aspects seldom create significant disruption within organizations. Such practices could cause disruption, however, if introduced into either Japan or the typical European country.

3. **Understand the needs that motivate people in countries housing foreign operations**—For managers in multinational corporations to be successful at motivating employees in different countries, they must present these individuals with the opportunity to satisfy personal needs while being productive within the organization. In designing motivation strategies, multinational managers must understand that employees in different countries often have quite different personal needs. For example, the Swiss, Austrians, Japanese, and Argentineans tend to have high security needs; whereas Danes, Swedes, and Norwegians tend to have high social needs. People in Great Britain, the United States, Canada, New Zealand, and Australia tend to have high self-actualization needs.[43] Thus, to be successful at influencing, multinational managers must understand their employees' needs and mold such organizational components as incentive systems, job design, and leadership style to correspond to these needs.

Hofstede's Ideas for Describing Culture
One of the most widely accepted methods for describing values in foreign cultures was developed by Geert Hofstede.[44] According to Hofstede's research, national cultural values vary on five basic dimensions:

1. Power Distance. *Power distance* is the degree to which a society promotes an unequal distribution of power. Countries that highly promote power distance have citizenry that tends to emphasize, expect, and accept more autocratic than democratic leadership. According to Hofstede's research, Mexico and France are examples of countries that tend to value more autocratic leadership while the United States is an example of a country that tends to value more democratic leadership.

2. Uncertainty Avoidance. *Uncertainty avoidance* is the extent to which a society feels threatened by uncertain or unpredictable situations. Countries that are high in uncertainty avoidance prefer being in more defined and predictable situations. Based on Hofstede's research, Greece and Japan feel more threatened by uncertainty than the United States and Canada. Correspondingly, citizenry in Greece and Japan would be less able to tolerate risk and uncertainty in their lives than citizenry in the United States.

3. Individualism and Collectivism. *Individualism–Collectivism* is the degree to which people in a society operate primarily as individuals or within groups. People operating as individuals tend to focus on meeting their own needs. People in this situation tend to be self-reliant and succeed by competing with others. On the other hand, people who operate collectively tend to build relationships among others and downplay individualism. Business success is pursued through relationships and cooperation among group members. According to Hofstede's research, China and South Korea are examples countries that emphasize collectivism while Australia, Canada, and the United States are examples of countries that emphasize individualism.

4. Masculinity and Femininity. *Masculinity–Femininity* is the extent to which a culture emphasizes traditional masculine or feminine values. Traditional masculine values place a high worth on factors like competitiveness, assertiveness, success, and wealth. Traditional feminine values place a high worth on factors like caring for and nurturing others and increasing the quality of life. According to Hofstede's research, the Scandinavian countries tend to value more traditional feminine values while Japan and the United States tend to value more traditional masculine values.

5. Short-Term and Long-Term Orientation. *Short Term–Long Term Orientation* is the degree to which a culture deemphasizes short-run success to achieve long-run success. Cultures that focus more on long-run success emphasize activities like planning, education, rewarding long-run results, and keeping a future oriented perspective. Conversely, cultures that focus more on short-run success emphasize training to enable one do a job now, rewarding short-run results, and maintaining a day-to-day perspective. Given Hofstede's research, Asian societies generally are among the countries most focused on long-term success. Pakistan is an example of a country valuing a short-term orientation.

The broad appeal and acceptance of Hofstede's work over recent decades is undeniable.[45] As a general rule, managers faced with doing business within different countries should understand the cultural values within those countries. Based on this understanding, to increase the probability of organizational success, management should strive to design and implement action consistent with those values. Hofstede's research provides worthwhile insights for how managers can define values in foreign cultures and react appropriately to them. Fortunately, management scientists continue to examine Hofstede's work to further refine its worth to modern managers.[46]

Controlling Multinational Corporations

Controlling was generally defined in Chapter 1 as making something happen the way it was planned to happen. As with domestic corporations, control in multinational corporations requires that standards be set, performance be measured and compared to standards, and corrective action be taken if necessary. In addition, control in such areas as labor costs, product quality, and inventory is important to organizational success regardless of whether the organization is domestic or international.

---

how managers do it

Controlling Costs at Kimberly-Clark

Kimberly-Clark Corporation is a U.S. multinational corporation that produces mostly paper-based consumer products. Kimberly-Clark brand name products include "Kleenex" facial tissue, "KimWipes" scientific cleaning wipes, and "Huggies" disposable diapers. One of Kimberly-Clark's challenges in being a multinational corporation is controlling purchasing costs. To help meet this challenge, the company recently established a *global* procurement function that will direct all purchasing for the company. By handling all purchasing activities in one spot rather than in many different places throughout the world, this change should help the company minimize the number of people needed in the purchasing function. As a result, this change is expected to save Kimberly-Clark as much as $500 million by 2013.[47] ■

Special Difficulties Control of a multinational corporation involves certain complexities. First, to deal with the problem of different currencies, management must decide how to compare profits generated by organizational units located in different countries and therefore expressed in terms of different currencies. Another complication is that organizational units in multinational corporations are generally more geographically separated. This increased distance normally makes it difficult for multinational managers to keep a close watch on operations in foreign countries.

Improving Communication One action successful managers take to help overcome the difficulty of monitoring geographically separated foreign units is carefully designing the communication network or information system that links them. A significant part of this design requires all company units to acquire and install similar computer equipment in all offices, both foreign and domestic, to ensure the likelihood of network hookups when communication becomes necessary. Such standardization of computer equipment also facilitates communication among all foreign locations and makes equipment repair and maintenance easier and therefore less expensive.[48]

Transnational Organizations

A **transnational organization,** also called a *global organization,* takes the entire world as its business arena.[49] Doing business wherever it makes sense is primary; national borders are considered inconsequential. The transnational organization transcends any single home country, with ownership, control, and management being from many different countries. Transnational organizations represent the fourth, and maximum, level of international activity as depicted on the continuum of international involvement presented earlier in this chapter. Seeing great opportunities in the global marketplace, some MNCs have transformed themselves from home-based companies with worldwide interests into worldwide companies pursuing business activities across the globe and claiming no singular loyalty to any one country.

Perhaps the most commonly cited transnational organization is Nestlé.[50] Although Nestlé is headquartered in Vevey, Switzerland, its arena of daily business activity is truly the world. Nestlé has a diversified list of products that include instant coffee, cereals, pharmaceuticals, coffee creamers, dietetic foods, ice cream, chocolates, and a wide array of snack foods. Its recent acquisition of the French company Perrier catapulted Nestlé into market leadership in the mineral water industry. Nestlé has more than 210,000 employees and operates 494 factories in 71 countries worldwide, including the United States, Germany, Portugal, Brazil, France, New Zealand, Australia, Chile, and Venezuela. Of Nestlé's sales and profits, about 35 percent come from Europe, 40 percent from North and South America, and 25 percent from other countries. As with most transnational organizations, Nestlé has grown by acquiring companies rather than by expanding its present operations.[51]

INTERNATIONAL MANAGEMENT: SPECIAL ISSUES

The preceding section of this chapter discussed planning, organizing, influencing, and controlling multinational corporations. This section focuses on two special issues that can help to ensure management success in the international arena: maintaining ethics in international management, and preparing expatriates for foreign assignments.[52]

Maintaining Ethics in International Management

As discussed in Chapter 3, *ethics* is a concern for good behavior and reflects an obligation that forces managers to consider not only their own personal well-being, but that of other human beings as they lead organizations. Having a manager define what ethical behavior is can indeed be challenging. Defining what behavior is ethical becomes increasingly challenging as managers consider the international implications of management action. What seems ethical in a manager's home country can be unethical in a different country.

The following guidelines can help managers ensure that management action taken across national borders is indeed ethical. According to these guidelines, managers can ensure that such action is ethical by the following:

> **Respecting core human rights**—This guideline underscores the notion that all people deserve an opportunity to achieve economic advancement and an improved standard of living. In addition, all people have the right to be treated with respect. Much effort has been made recently by major sporting goods companies, including Nike and Reebok, to ensure that this guideline is followed in business operations they are conducting in other countries.[53] These companies have joined forces to crack down on child labor, establish minimum wages comparable to existing individual country standards, establish a maximum 60-hour work-week with at least one day off, and support the establishment of a mechanism for inspecting apparel factories worldwide. These companies have also committed themselves to the elimination of forced labor, harassment, abuse, and discrimination in the workplace.

Respecting local traditions—This guideline suggests that managers hold the customs of foreign countries in which they conduct business in high regard. In Japan, for example, people have a long-standing tradition that those individuals who do business together exchange gifts. Sometimes, these gifts can be expensive. When U.S. managers started doing business in Japan, accepting a gift felt like accepting a bribe. As a result, many of these managers thought that the practice of gift giving might be wrong. As U.S. managers have come to know and respect this Japanese tradition, most have come to tolerate, and even encourage, the practice as ethical behavior in Japan. Some managers even set different limits on gift giving in Japan than they do elsewhere.

Determining right from wrong by examining context—This guideline suggests that managers should evaluate the specifics of the international situation confronting them in determining whether a particular management activity is ethical. Although some activities are wrong no matter where they take place, some that are unethical in one setting may be acceptable in another. For instance, the chemical EDB, a soil fungicide, is banned from use in the United States. In hot climates, however, it quickly becomes harmless through exposure to intense solar radiation and high soil temperatures. As long as the chemical is monitored, companies may be able to use EDB ethically in certain parts of the world.

Most managers and management scholars agree that implementing ethical management practices across national borders enhances organizational success. Although following the guidelines just described does not guarantee that management action taken across national borders will be ethical, it should increase the probability.

Preparing Expatriates for Foreign Assignments

The trend of U.S. companies forming joint ventures and other strategic alliances that emphasize foreign operations is increasing. As a result, the number of expatriates being sent from the United States to other countries is also rising.[54]

The somewhat casual approach of the past toward preparing expatriates for foreign duty is being replaced by the attitude that these managers need special tools to be able to succeed in difficult foreign assignments.[55] To help expatriates adjust, home companies are helping them find homes and high-quality health care in host countries. Companies are also responding to expatriate feelings that they need more help from home companies on career planning related to foreign assignments, career planning for spouses forced to go to the foreign assignment country to look for work, and better counseling for the personal challenges they will face during their foreign assignment.[56]

Many companies prepare their expatriates for foreign assignments by using special training programs. Specific features of these programs vary from company to company, depending on the situation. Most of these programs, however, usually contain the following core elements:

* **Culture profiles**—Here, expatriates learn about the new culture in which they will be working.

* **Cultural adaptation**—Here, expatriates learn how to survive the difficulties of adjusting to a new culture.

* **Logistical information**—Here, expatriates learn basic information, such as personal safety, who to call in an emergency, and how to write a check.

* **Application**—Here, expatriates learn about specific organizational roles they will perform.

Expatriates generally play a critical role in determining the success of an organization's foreign operations. The tremendous personal and professional adjustments that expatriates must make, however, can delay their effectiveness and efficiency in foreign settings. Sound training programs can lower the amount of time expatriates need to adjust and can thereby help them become productive more quickly.[57]

CHALLENGE CASE SUMMARY

As the Challenge Case shows, Wal-Mart is an organization heavily involved in international management. The company now operates in countries such as China and Brazil, and recently expanded into Japan. Manager Lee Scott will be performing international management activities in a number of countries and, given today's trend toward greater foreign investment, Wal-Mart is likely to continue to emphasize global expansion. In addition, it is likely that foreign companies will attempt to compete with Wal-Mart in the United States.

As Wal-Mart continues its international expansion it will become—and perhaps already is—more of a multinational corporation: an organization with significant operations in more than one country. In any company, management under international circumstances is a complex matter. As Wal-Mart continues to grow internationally, the complexity is related to the necessity for managing within different foreign countries that are separated by significant distances and that are characterized by different economic conditions, people, levels of technology, market sizes, and laws. Wal-Mart's success with foreign expansion illustrates the potential rewards to managers who can handle the complexity of doing business in other countries.

Management at Wal-Mart is attempting to minimize risk in its decisions to make foreign investments. Few managers would see expansion into a country such as Japan as too risky. This country is considered to be economically stable and safe for foreign investors, whereas expansion into a country characterized by civil upheaval and military action would certainly be risky.

The United States has normal trading relationships with Japan, and Wal-Mart may have much to gain by being successful merchandisers in Japan. Management must be aware, however, that the political situation between the United States and other countries can change rapidly. As a result, the company should constantly monitor the political relationship between the United States and the countries in which it does business, to enable a quick response to any changes.

Wal-Mart management has apparently decided that foreign investment in Japan represents a tolerable amount of risk when weighed against the prospect of increased return from operations in Japan. Actual operation in Japan, however, is more recently furnishing feedback indicating that the decision might be riskier than they first thought.

Perhaps the most important variable in building the success of Japanese Wal-Marts is probably the people it employs. The company must establish the best combination of people to run the stores—expatriates, host-country nationals, or third-country nationals. Whatever blend of human resources is decided on, management must be sensitive in helping individuals adjust both personally and organizationally to the Japanese culture. In addition, if expatriates are involved in running the stores, Wal-Mart should be sensitive to helping them adjust when they are repatriated.

Planning is equally valuable to both domestic and international companies. The primary difference between planning for Wal-Mart as a domestic company and as an international company would be reflected in components of company plans. As an international corporation, Wal-Mart would have planning components that focus on the international sector, whereas a totally domestic organization would not. Such components could include establishing a partnership with a Japanese construction company to build Wal-Mart stores throughout Japan, building nearby training facilities that could provide well-trained employees for Japanese stores and stores in nearby countries, choosing additional store locations in other countries, and selling the rights to a foreign company to use the Wal-Mart name in mass merchandising.

In organizing a company such as Wal-Mart along international lines, organization structure generally should be based on one or more of the variables of function, product, territory, customers, or manufacturing process. Wal-Mart managers must consider all the variables within the situations that confront them and then design the organization structure that is most appropriate for those situations. Wal-Mart might organize internationally on a geographic basis, for example, with a CEO for its European division.

Over the long term, management at Wal-Mart should try to fill the international positions with managers who possess geocentric attitudes, as opposed to polycentric or ethnocentric attitudes. Such managers would tend to build operating units in other countries, would use the best human resources available, and would be highly committed to the attainment of organizational objectives.

As Wal-Mart becomes more multinational, influencing people within the company will become more complicated. The cultures of people in countries such as Japan and other countries in which Wal-Mart does international business must be thoroughly understood. Managers of foreign operations who may be U.S. citizens must have a working knowledge of the languages spoken in the host country and an understanding of the attitudes and personal needs that motivate individuals within the foreign workforce. If motivation strategy is to be successful for Wal-Mart as a whole, rewards used to motivate Japanese workers may need to be much different from the rewards used to motivate U.S. workers.

The control process at Wal-Mart should involve standards, measurements, and needed corrective action, just as it should within a purely domestic company. The different currencies used in countries such as Japan, however, tend to make control more complicated for an international organization than for a domestic one. The significant distance of countries such as Japan from the United States would also tend to complicate the issue of control at Wal-Mart.

Based on this information, managers at Wal-Mart should be concerned with promoting ethical behavior in the company's foreign operations, which include actions that respect the core human rights of foreign citizens, accommodate foreign local traditions, and reflect what is "right" in the particular foreign context. Examples of ethical behavior could be forbidding foreign children to be hired as employees, paying a fair wage that reflects foreign national wage levels, and eliminating abuse and discrimination in Wal-Mart stores.

In addition, Wal-Mart must properly prepare expatriates who are going to work in countries like Japan if these individuals are to be as productive as possible as quickly as possible. The company should take steps to help expatriates find appropriate housing and health care, to explain how the assignment impacts the expatriates' long-term career at Wal-Mart, and to provide counseling for personal problems the expatriates could face simply by living in Japan or elsewhere. Formal training of expatriates going to Japan should include a description of the Japanese culture; steps that expatriates can take to adapt to that culture; basic information about logistics of life in Japan, such as whom to call in case of emergency; and specifics about the job they will be performing.

MANAGEMENT SKILL ACTIVITIES

This section is specially designed to help you develop global management skill. An individual's global management skill is based on an understanding of global management concepts and the ability to apply those concepts in management situations. The following activities are designed to both heighten your understanding of global management concepts and to develop the ability to apply those concepts in a variety of management situations.

UNDERSTANDING MANAGEMENT CONCEPTS

 To check your understanding and to practice using the concepts in this chapter, go to www.mymanagementlab.com and explore the material associated with Chapter 5.

Know Key Terms

Understanding the following key terms is critical to your understanding of chapter material. Define each of these terms. Refer to the page(s) referenced after a term to check your definition or to gain further insight regarding the term.

international management 110
domestic organizations 112
international organizations 113
multinational corporation 113
parent company 116
host country 116
expatriate 116
host-country national 116

third-country national 116
repatriation 118
importing 119
exporting 119
license agreement 119
direct investing 119
international joint venture 120
international market agreement 120

European Union (EU) 121
North American Free Trade Agreement (NAFTA) 122
ethnocentric attitude 124
polycentric attitude 124
geocentric attitude 124
culture 124
transnational organization 127

Know How Management Concepts Relate

This section is comprised of activities that will further sharpen your understanding of management concepts. Answer essay questions as completely as possible. Also, remember that many additional true/false and multiple choice questions appear online at MyManagementLab.com to help you further refine your understanding of management concepts.

1. Discuss three similarities and three differences of international versus transnational organizations.

2. What are the risks and rewards of operating a multinational organization?

3. List and define the three types of organization members found in multinational organizations. Discuss the contribution that each type can bring to building the success of the organization.

4. What knowledge must a manager have to successfully influence organization members of multinational corporations?

Would it be easy for a manager to acquire such knowledge? Why? How should the manager acquire the knowledge?

5. Is the preparation of expatriates more important than their repatriation? Explain fully.

6. Discuss the role of "examining context" in maintaining ethical practices in international management situations.

DEVELOPING MANAGEMENT SKILLS

Learning activities in this section are aimed at helping you to develop global management skill. Learning activities include Exploring Your Management Skill: Parts 1 & 2, Your Management Skill Portfolio, Experiential Exercise, Cases, and a VideoNet Exercise.

Exploring Your Management Skill: Part 1

Before studying this chapter, respond to the following questions regarding the type of advice you would give to Wal-Mart's CEO Lee Scott, referenced in the Challenge Case. Then address the questions concerning global management challenges that he presently faces within the company. You are not expected to be a global management expert at this point. Answering the questions now can help you focus on important points when you study the chapter. Also, answering the questions again after you study the chapter will give you an idea of how much you have learned.

Record your answers here or online at MyManagement Lab.com. Completing the questions at MyManagementLab. com will allow you to get feedback about your answers automatically. If you answer the questions in the book, look up answers in the Exploring Your Management Skill section at the end of the book.

FOR EACH STATEMENT CIRCLE:
- "Y" if you would give the advice to Lee Scott.
- "N" if you would NOT give the advice to Lee Scott.
- "NI" if you have no idea whether you would give the advice to Lee Scott.

Mr. Scott, in meeting your global management challenges at Wal-Mart, you should . . .

Before After
Study Study

1. shy away from having Wal-Mart make direct foreign investment.
   Y, N, NI

2. start by building Wal-Mart into a transnational company and grow it into an international company.
   Y, N, NI

3. become familiar and react to various value systems of the citizens of countries in which Wal-Mart operates.
   Y, N, NI

4. not be concerned with physical distances among Wal-Mart's global business unit operations.
   Y, N, NI

5. remember that different laws in foreign countries may require different management responses from Wal-Mart managers regarding the same issue.
   Y, N, NI

6. train Wal-Mart host-country nationals more thoroughly than expatriates in local customs of a country such as Japan in which foreign operations exist.
   Y, N, NI

7. build an effective repatriation process at Wal-Mart to help retain returning expatriates.
   Y, N, NI

8. help Wal-Mart's newly located expatriates deal with confusion, anxiety, and stress related to their new culture.
   Y, N, NI

9. consider market agreements when designing plans for Wal-Mart's foreign operations.
   Y, N, NI

10. focus on building an organization structure for Wal-Mart that primarily highlights foreign operations from either business function or territory viewpoints, but not both.
    Y, N, NI

11. usually avoid having an ethnocentric attitude, a feeling that home country policies and practices are superior to those of foreign countries.
    Y, N, NI

12. build systems to motivate Wal-Mart's organization members in foreign operations that consider the specific needs of individuals within host countries.
    Y, N, NI

13. thoroughly educate yourself in understanding the customs of foreign countries in which Wal- Mart does business.
    Y, N, NI

14. prepare Wal-Mart expatriates for foreign assignments through programs that emphasize how to adapt to a new culture more than how to perform their new jobs.
    Y, N, NI

15. emphasize expatriate preparation for foreign assignments at Wal-Mart slightly more than repatriation.
    Y, N, NI

Exploring Your Management Skill: Part 2

As you recall, you completed Exploring Your Management Skill: Part 1 before you started to study this chapter. Your responses gave you an idea of how much you initially knew about global management and helped you focus on important points as you studied the chapter. Answer the Exploring Your Management Skill questions again now and compare your score to the first time you took it. This comparison will give you an idea of how much you have learned from studying this chapter and pinpoint areas for further clarification before you start studying the next chapter. Record your answers within the text or online at MyManagementLab.com. Completing the survey at MyManagementLab.com will allow you to grade and compare your test scores automatically. If you complete the test in the book, look up answers in the Exploring Your Management Skill section at the end of the book.

Your Management Skills Portfolio

Your Management Learning Portfolio is a collection of activities especially designed to demonstrate your management knowledge and skill. By completing these activities online at MyManagementLab.com, you will be able to print, complete with cover sheet, as many activities as you choose. Be sure to save your work. Taking your printed portfolio to an employment interview could be helpful in obtaining a job.

The portfolio activity for this chapter is Managing a Business in Japan. Study this information and complete the exercises that follow.

You are an American-educated manager who believes in Western management philosophies. You have just accepted a job as a middle manager in a Toyota manufacturing plant in Tahara, slightly south of Osaka in Japan. The plant manufactures Toyota's new Lexus hybrid sedan. For your entire career, 10 years, you have worked as a middle manager in a General Motors plant in the United States and followed traditional American management practices. Toyota was clear, however, about expecting you to fit into its culture and following its management practices that have built company success. You know little about Japanese management practices and start to read as much as you can about how Japanese companies operate.

Based upon your study, you reach the following summary points about the differences between the way Japanese and American companies are structured*:

1. U.S. companies tend to have a well-defined organization structure while Japanese firms tend to be more loosely structured.

2. U.S. companies tend to have a number of people involved in making decisions while decisions made in Japanese firms tend to be made by one or a few people.

3. U.S. firms tend to value making profit in the short run while Japanese firms tend to value building long term growth.

4. Management of Japanese firms tends to be more centralized while management of U. S. firms tends to be more decentralized.

5. Job descriptions in Japanese firms tend to be broader and less precise than in U.S. firms.

This discussion is based upon: Michael Backman, *Asian Eclipse: Exposing the Dark Side of Business in Asia* (New York: John Wiley Publishers, 2001), 78.

Exercise 1: Overall, based on the information given, list three major challenges you will face as a manager at Toyota and steps you will take to meet these challenges.

Challenge 1: _____

What I will do to meet Challenge 1: _____

_____

_____

Challenge 2: _____

What I will do to meet Challenge 2: _____

_____

Challenge 3:

What will I do to meet Challenge 3:

Exercise 2: Based on the information given, to be successful in Japan, you will probably have to somewhat change the way you plan, organize, influence, and control. List the changes for each management function you probably will have to make.

Changes to the way I will plan in Japan:

Changes to the way I will organize in Japan:

Changes to the way I will influence people in Japan:

Changes to the way I will control in Japan:

Exercise 3: Do you think you would be successful in this job as manager at Toyota? Why?

Exercise 4: Overall, what did you learn from this experience?

Experiential Exercises

1 Building a Global Management Curriculum

Directions. Read the following scenario and then perform the listed activities. Your instructor may want you to perform the activities as an individual or within groups. Follow all of your instructor's directions carefully.

You are the president of Fiat Lux, a small liberal arts school in Denver, Colorado. In recent years you have tried to provide leadership in building more of a business emphasis into your curriculum. Reflecting your lead, your faculty over the past four years has been developing courses in organizational studies that focus primarily on managing people in organizations as well as how to organize and plan. Although you are pleased with the progress the school is making, you realize that the school's offerings should be expanded even more to offer a new major called Global Management.

Based on your feelings, you've asked a few global business leaders from the community to help you develop a list of eight courses that could comprise this new major. Your goal is to propose this new major and its related courses to your faculty as a vehicle they can use to prepare your undergraduate students for careers in global management.

You are presently leading a meeting of this business advisory group. Introduce your task for the group and lead a discussion concerning what the eight courses should be. Be sure to get course titles as well as descriptions of what the courses should include and rationales for why the courses should be included in the new major. When completed, your eight courses should provide your students with the essential knowledge to begin and be successful in entry-level positions that include global management responsibilities.

2 You and Your Career

You have just accepted a job with Nestlé and will soon be working in China as the manager of a plant with 300 employees making a new type of dog food. You know that Nestlé as a whole has about 250,000 employees, is made up of 100 different nationalities, and your China position looks to be a place where you can build an exciting international career.

You know that in your new job you will be managing mostly Chinese nationals. As such, you have read many articles about the Chinese culture and have found out the following:[58]

- Personal relationships are extremely important to the Chinese.
- The Chinese prefer working with friends.
- The Chinese avoid punishment and embarrassment.
- In China, gifts are used to build and strengthen personal relationships.
- Chinese businesses are built around family.
- The Chinese shy away from confrontational and direct conversation.

1. Is what you have found out about the Chinese culture important in building your career at Nestlé? Explain.
2. Would the way you manage in China change based on your new understanding of the Chinese culture? How?
3. Would it be easy for you to make such changes? Why?

VideoNet Exercise

Global Business at KPMG

Video Highlights

KPMG spends hundreds of thousands of dollars sending interns on overseas assignments to ensure their potential future employees are globally savvy. Hard to believe it's a cost-effective practice, but they are the accounting experts after all. Aidan Walsh, Head of Global Mobility for KPMG, explains why interns and employees need global exposure to be effective in the financial services industry. How could a cultural misunderstanding potentially send ripples through the global economy? What are the biggest challenges of managing a global company in a global business environment?

Discussion Questions

1. Is KPMG an international or multinational corporation? What are some of the complexities associated with managing this type of organization?
2. How does KPMG's Global Mobility program help in the organization of their corporation?
3. Discuss three managerial challenges of linking more than 100,000 employees in 150 countries. How would you meet each challenge?

Internet Activity

Go to the KPMG Web site at www.kpmg.com. How is KPMG organized? What is the structure of this large multinational organization? How is this organization governed?

CASES

1 WAL-MART FACING GLOBAL PROBLEMS IN JAPAN

"Wal-Mart Facing Global Problems in Japan" (p. 109) and its Challenge Case Summary were written to help you better understand the management concepts contained in this chapter. Answer the following discussion questions about the Challenge Case that relate to managing in the global arena and how it can be applied in a company like Wal-Mart.

1. Do you think that at some point in your career you will become involved in international management? Explain.
2. Assuming that you are involved in managing a Wal-Mart store in Japan, what challenges do you think will be the most difficult for you in improving Japanese store success? Why?
3. Evaluate the following statement: Wal-Mart can learn to manage its U.S. operations better by studying how successful competitive operations are managed in other countries.

2 JARDEN EXTENDS ITS GLOBAL REACH

Read the case and answer the questions that follow. Studying this case will help you better understand how concepts relating to global expansion can be applied in a company such as Jarden Corporation.

Though most people are unfamiliar with Jarden Corporation, they are probably very aware of many of its brands. From Bicycle playing cards to Coleman lanterns and from Mr. Coffee to Seal-a-Meal, Jarden has built a business of easy-to-recognize brands and taken that company worldwide.

Founded in 1991 and based in Rye, New York, the firm employs more than 20,000 people around the globe in offices, distribution centers, and manufacturing facilities. The company changed its name to Jarden in 2003 to reflect a new image for the company. "Jar" for Ball canning jars (one of the company's brands) and "den" to add a homey touch—as in the den of a home.

Helmed by CEO Martin Franklin, in 2009 Jarden's sales were $5.1 billion and outside the United States, growth included a global presence in Canada, Latin America, Asia, and Europe with more than 100 distinct brands. Currently, more than 30 percent of Jarden's sales are from customers in countries other than the United States.[59] In addition, Franklin is determined to bring innovation to the growing line of products. It is estimated that one-third of sales is derived from products launched by Jarden in only the last three years. This focus on new product development is key to the company's success.

Another important facet to the firm's expansion is acquisitions, especially those that extend Jarden's global reach. In April 2010, Jarden acquired French-based Mapa Spontex—a company that manufactures infant care products such as baby bottles and pacifiers. Valued at approximately half a billion dollars, the acquisition provides Jarden with entry into the infant care market. But, Mapa Spontex has a strong presence in Europe, Brazil, and Argentina, which means Jarden garners a

solid footing in these markets as well.[60] According to Franklin, "We don't have the infrastructure in place [in Europe] to launch products there now as well as they can."[61] Therefore, Mapa Spontex readily gives Jarden a marketing network to untapped customers.

Mapa Spontex's corporate office is located in Paris, France and approximately two-thirds of its sales are from European customers. Of course, taking a large company such as Mapa Spontex and placing it under the Jarden umbrella is no easy task. But Franklin remains optimistic. He states that Jarden has been "able to actively pursue operating and revenue synergies" and that Mapa Spontex "is folding seamlessly into Jarden."[62] Merging organizations requires melding logistics, communications, processes, and of course, distinct corporate cultures.

This acquisition is in line with prior steps Jarden has taken in building a portfolio of global businesses. In 2007, the company acquired K2 and Pure Fishing in separate transactions. K2 makes skiing and snowboarding equipment, while Pure Fishing produces a variety of fishing gear under the brand names of Shakespeare, Berkley, Penn, and others. And in prior years, acquisitions have included Pine Mountain, Holmes, American Household, and United States Playing Card Company. Growth through acquisitions is just one piece of Jarden's strategy. It also includes cutting costs and developing new products.

To keep costs in check while remaining an innovative company, Jarden conducts a significant amount of business in China. In fact, Jarden is the 15th largest U.S. importer from China. This, along with a significant amount of debt the company has incurred, has led to some criticism of Jarden. More than a few of the brands acquired are quite old and some critics believe they have lost their luster. Brands such as Oster and Sunbeam, which were once ubiquitous on store shelves, have had to be carefully managed by Jarden to develop interest among a new generation of consumers. However, Franklin is not deterred. He recognizes that each acquisition is carefully evaluated and if costs are contained, acquisitions can experience a renaissance through new product development. "I don't believe in having a business for the sake of it," Franklin states. "You have to have a reason for things."[63] The reason for acquiring Mapa Spontex is clear—extend Jarden's global reach while attracting European customers to other Jarden brands.

QUESTIONS

1. As Jarden continues to expand globally, what challenges do you envision for the company in maintaining quality control over the products produced?
2. If Martin Franklin asked your advice on how to assist in adjusting employees of Mapa Spontex to Jarden's organizational culture, what would you suggest?
3. What are the pros and cons of growing a multinational business through acquisitions?

Endnotes

1. "World's Most Admired Companies," *Fortune,* March 4, 2010, http://money.cnn.com.

2. Company Web site, "Helping People Live Better," http://www.walmartstores.com, accessed May 3, 2010; Jonathan Birchall, "International Sales Lift Wal-Mart," *Financial Times,* November 15, 2006, 30.

3. Company Web site, "Japan Fact Sheet," http://www.walmartstores.com, accessed May 3, 2010; William Hoffman, "Wal-Mart Losses Mount in Japan," *TrafficWorld,* August 22, 2006, 1.

4. For insights regarding ethical issues related to business opportunities in China see: Krueger, Davis A., "Ethical Reflections on the Opportunities and Challenges for International Business in China," *Journal of Business Ethics* 89 (November 2009): 145.

5. "Dossier: Telecommunications in Asia, Malaysia, Thailand," *International Business Newsletter* (June 1993): 12.

6. Jean J. Boddewyn, Brian Toyne, and Zaida L Martinez, "The Meanings of International Management," *Management International Review* 44, no. 2 (Second Quarter 2004): 195–212.

7. For a summary of recent developments in international management, see Steve Werner, "Recent Developments in International Management Research: A Review of 20 Top Management Journals," *Journal of Management* 28 (2002): 277.

8. Robert N. Lussier, Robert W. Baeder, and Joel Corman, "Measuring Global Practices: Global Strategic Planning Through Company Situational Analysis," *Business Horizons* 37 (September/October 1994): 56–63. For a detailed look at Hitachi Maxell, a successful internationally managed company, see Ray Moorcroft, "International Management in Action," *British Journal of Administrative Management* (March/April 2001): 12–13.

9. Alyssa A. Lappen, "Worldwide Connections," *Forbes,* June 27, 1988, 78–82.

10. Natasha Gural, "JP Morgan Goes Global with Corporate Banking," *Forbes,* January 29, 2010, http://www.forbes.com.

11. Ben J. Wattenberg, "Their Deepest Concerns," *Business Month* (January 1988): 27–33; American Assembly of Collegiate Schools of Business, *Accreditation Council Policies, Procedures, and Standards* (St. Louis, MO: Assembly Collegiate School of America, 1990–1992).

12. For additional information regarding various forms of organization based on international involvement, see Arvind Phatak, *International Dimensions of Management* (Boston: Kent, 1993).

13. "Nu Horizons Electronics," *Fortune,* June 13, 1994, 121. For an empirical study assessing the mobility of knowledge within a multinational corporation, see Anil K. Gupta and Vijay Govindarajan, "Knowledge Flows within Multinational Corporations," *Strategic Management Journal* 21, no. 4 (April 2000): 473–496.

14. U.S. Department of Commerce, *The Multinational Corporation: Studies on U.S. Foreign Investment* (Washington, D.C. Government Printing Office).

15. Benjamin Gomes-Casseres, "Group versus Group: How Alliance Networks Compete," *Harvard Business Review* 72 (July/August 1994), 62–74.

16. Company Web site, http://www.brkelectronics.com, accessed May 2, 2010.

17. This section is based primarily on Richard D. Robinson, *International Management* (New York: Holt, Rinehart & Winston, 1967), 3–5. For a focus on complexity related to differing ethical values of various societies, see Paul F. Buller, John J. Kohls, and Kenneth S. Anderson, "When Ethics Collide: Managing Conflicts Across Cultures," *Organizational Dynamics* 28, no. 4 (Spring 2000): 52–65.

18. 1971 Survey of National Foreign Trade Council, cited in Frederick D. Sturdivant, *Business and Society: A Managerial Approach* (Homewood, IL: Richard D. Irwin, 1977), 425.

19. Barrie James, "Reducing the Risks of Globalization," *Long Range Planning* 23 (February 1990): 80–88.

20. "NCR's Standard Contract Clause," *Harvard Business Review* 72 (May/June 1994): 125; for additional information on mediation, see: Freund, James C., "Three's a Crowd-How to Resolve a Knotty Multi-Party Dispute Through Mediation," *The Business Lawyer* 64, no. 2 (February 2009): 359.

21. For a discussion of family adjustments as a major factor in expatriate failure, see Sandra L. Fisher, Michael E. Wasserman, and Jennifer Palthe, "Management Practices for On-Site Consultants: Lessons Learned from the Expatriate Experience," *Consulting Psychology Journal: Practice and Research* 59, no. 1 (March 2007): 17.

22. For an interesting article discussing the work relationship between expatriates and host-country nationals, see Charles M. Vance and Yongsun Paik, "Forms of Host-Country National Learning for Enhanced MNC Absorptive Capacity," *Journal of Managerial Psychology* 20, no. 7 (2005): 590–606.

23. Jan Selmer, "Cross-Cultural Training and Expatriate Adjustment in China: Western Joint Venture Managers," *Personnel Review* 34, no. 1 (2005): 68–84.

24. For a look at challenges facing women expatriates, see Babita Mathur-Helm, "Expatriate Women Managers: At the Crossroads of Success, Challenges and Career Goals," *Women in Management Journal* 17 (2002): 18.

25. Brenda Paik Sunoo, "Loosening Up in Brazil," *Workforce* 3 (May 1998): 8–9.

26. For a discussion of the challenges associated with cross-cultural work assignments and the competencies required to meet the challenges, see Lynn S. Paine, "The China Rules," *Harvard Business Review,* June 2010; and Mansour Javidan, Mary Teagarden, and David Bowen, "Managing Yourself: Making It Overseas," *Harvard Business Review,* April 2010.

27. For a review of the possible effects of repatriation, see Jobert E. Abueva, "Many Repatriations Fail, at Huge Cost to Companies," *New York Times,* May 17, 2000, E1; Margaret Linehan and Hugh Scullion, "The Repatriation of Female International Managers: An Empirical Study," *International Journal of Manpower* 23 (2002): 649.

28. For an interesting discussion of repatriation in a Spanish context, see: Vidal, Ma Eugenia Sánchez, Raquel Sanz Valle, and Ma Isabel Barba Aragón "Analysis of the Repatriation Adjustment Process in the Spanish Context," *International Journal of Manpower* 31, no. 1 (2010): 21.

29. David C. Martin and John J. Anthony, "The Repatriation and Retention of Employees: Factors Leading to Successful Programs," *International Journal of Management* 23, no. 3 (September 2006): 620–631.

30. Roberta Maynard, "Importing Can Help a Firm Expand and Diversify," *Nation's Business* (January 1995): 11.

31. Karen Paul, "Fading Images at Eastman Kodak," *Business and Society Review* 48 (Winter 1984): 56.

32. G. Sam Samdani, "Mobil Develops a Way to Extract Hg from Gas Streams," *Chemical Engineering* 102 (April 1995): 17.

33. Leonard Berkowitz, "Supreme Court Says You Can License and Sue," *Research Technology Management* 50, no. 2 (March/April 2007): 9.

34. Robert Neff, "The Japanese Are Back—But There's a Difference," *BusinessWeek,* Industrial/Technology Edition, October 31, 1994, 58–59.

35. For insights on adding organizational value through international joint ventures, see Iris Berdrow and Henry Lane, "International Joint Ventures: Creating Value through Successful Knowledge Management," *Journal of World Business* 38 (2003): 15; see also Lifeng Geng, "Ownership and International Joint Ventures' Level of Expatriate Managers," *Journal of American Academy of Business* 4 (2004): 75.

36. Shyam Sunder, "Uniform Financial Reporting Standards," *The CPA Journal* 77, no. 4 (April 2007): 6, 8–9.

37. Francisco Granell, "The European Union's Enlargement Negotiations with Austria, Finland, Norway, and Sweden," *Journal of Common Market Studies* 33 (March 1995): 117–141; Jim Rollo, "EC Enlargement and the World Trade System," *European Economic Review* 39 (April 1995): 467–473. For a history surrounding the formation of NAFTA, see Richard N. Cooper, "The Making of NAFTA: How the Deal Was Done," *Foreign Affairs* 80, no. 3 (May/June 2001): 136.

38. For an interesting article discussing how NAFTA countries settle disputes among themselves, see John H. Knox, "The 2005 Activity of the NAFTA Tribunals," *The American Journal of International Law* 100, no. 2 (April 2006): 429–442.

39. Jim Mele, "Mexico in '95: From Good to Better," *Fleet Owner* (January 1995): 56–60; William C. Symonds, "Meanwhile, to the North, NAFTA Is a Smash," *BusinessWeek,* February 27, 1995, 66; Robert Selwitz, "NAFTA Expansion Possibilities," *Global Trade & Transportation* (October 1994): 17.

40. For an interesting account of organizing to go global, see Regina Fazio Maruca, "The Right Way to Go Global: An Interview with Whirlpool CEO David Whitwam," *Harvard Business Review* 72 (March/April 1994): 134–145.

41. Howard V. Perlmutter, "The Tortuous Evolution of the Multinational Corporation," *Columbia Journal of World Business* (January/February 1969): 9–18; Rose Knotts, "Cross-Cultural Management: Transformations and Adaptations," *Business Horizons* (January/February 1989): 29–33.

42. Yan Tian, "Communicating with Local Publics: A Case Study of Coca-Cola's Chinese Web Site," *Corporate Communications* 11, no.1 (2006): 13–22.

43. Geert Hofstede, "Motivation, Leadership, and Organization: Do American Theories Apply Abroad?" *Organizational Dynamics* 9 (Summer 1980): 42–63.

44. Geert Hofstede, *Geert Culture's Consequences: International Differences in Work-Related Values* (Beverly Hills, California: Sage, 1980); Hofstede, *Geert Culture's Consequences: Comparing Values, Behaviors, Institutions, and Organizations Across Nations,* 2nd ed. (London, England: Sage, 2001).

45. Vas Taras, Bradley L. Kirkman, and Piers Steel, "Examining the Impact of Culture's Consequences: A Three-Decade, Multilevel, Meta-Analytic Review of Hofstede's Cultural Value Dimensions," *Journal of Applied Psychology* 95, no.3 (2010): 405–439.

46. Robert J. House, Paul J. Hanges, Mansour Javidan, and Peter Dorfman, *Culture, Leadership, and Organizations: The GLOBE Study of 62 Societies* (Thousand Oaks, California: Sage, 2004).

47. Jake Kanter, "Procurement at Kimberly-Clark Goes Global," *Supply Management.com,* March 23, 2010, http://www.supplymanagement.com.

48. Walter Sweet, "International Firms Strive for Uniform Nets Abroad," *Network World,* May 28, 1990, 35–36.

49. For further information about developing global organizations, see Philip Harris, "European Challenge: Developing Global Organizations," *European Business Review* 14 (2002): 416; see Jonathon Cummings, "Work Groups, Structural Diversity, and Knowledge Sharing in a Global Organization," *Management Science* 50 (2004): 352.

50. To gain a feel for the broad range of activities occurring at a transnational company such as Nestlé, see Joel Chernoff, "Advancing Corporate Governance in Europe," *Pensions & Investments,* June 12, 1995, 3, 37; E. Guthrie McTigue and Andy Sears, "The Safety 80," *Global Finance* (May 1995): 62–65; Robert W. Lear, "Whatever Happened to the Old-Fashioned Boss?" *Chief Executive* (April 1995): 71; Claudio Loderer and Andreas Jacobs, "The Nestlé Crash," *Journal of Financial Economics* 37 (March 1995): 315–339.

51. Byeong-Seon Yoon, "Who Is Threatening Our Dinner Table? The Power of Transnational Agribusiness," *Monthly Review* 58, no. 6 (November 2006): 56–64.

52. This section is mainly based on Thomas Donaldson, "Values in Tension: Ethics Away from Home," *Harvard Business Review* 74, no. 5 (September/October 1996): 48–62.

53. Anabelle Perez, "Sports Apparel Goes to Washington: New Sweatshop," *Sporting Goods Business* 30, no. 7 (May 12, 1997): 24.

54. Edward M. Mervosh and John S. McClenahen, "The Care and Feeding of Expats," *Industry Week* 246, no. 22 (December 1, 1977): 68–72.

55. Valerie Frazee, "Research Points to Weaknesses in Expat Policy," *Workforce* 3, no. 1 (January 1998): 9.

56. A number of Web sites are now dedicated to the subject of expatriate life and provide different viewpoints through blogs, articles, reports, tips for pursuing the expatriate life, and more. Examples include Expat Exchange, and Future Expats Forum.

57. For a different view of the long-term value expatriates bring to organizational performance, see Yulin Fang, Gul-Liang Frank Jiang, Shige Makino, and Paul W. Beamish, "Multinational Firm Knowledge, Use of Expatriates, and Foreign Subsidiary Performance," *Journal of Management Studies* 47, no. 1 (January 2010): 27–54.

58. Min-Huei Chien, "A Study of Cross Culture Human Resource Management in China," *The Business Review* 6, no. 2 (December 2006): 231–237.

59. www.jardencorp.com

60. Ibid.

61. Miel, R. (2010). Jarden to buy Total baby, home care unit. *Rubber & Plastics News*, *39*(12), 19.

62. See note 59 above.

63. Demos, T. (2008). The new king of brand names. *Fortune*, *158*(1), 86–90.

chapter 6

Management and Entrepreneurship

Target Skill

entrepreneurship skill: involves the identification, evaluation, and exploitation of opportunities

objectives

To help build my *entrepreneurship skill*, when studying this chapter, I will attempt to acquire:

1. An understanding of the three stages of entrepreneurship

2. An overall appreciation for the opportunity concept and an understanding of the primary types of entrepreneurial opportunities

3. An ability to distinguish between opportunity identification, evaluation, and exploitation

4. Insights regarding the various types of financing available to entrepreneurs

5. An appreciation for how existing organizations use corporate entrepreneurship

6. An understanding of and appreciation for the role of social entrepreneurship in society

CHALLENGE CASE

GOOGLE ENTREPRENEURS WIN BIG

LARRY PAGE AND SERGEY BRIN were two typical computer science graduate students at Stanford University.[1] Their reputations—and fortunes—changed dramatically, however, when they incorporated Google in 1998. Today, the company has proven so successful that many people refer to online searching as *googling.*

Google's founders challenged the conventional wisdom regarding Internet search by changing the way in which their search engine processed search requests. In particular, Google based search results on how many other pages linked to a particular Web page and how popular those Web pages were. If, for example, no other pages linked to the page with 20 instances of "automobile tires" and many pages linked to the page with one instance of "automobile tires," Google would provide higher search results for the latter and lower search results for the former.

Page and Brin also differentiated their company by changing the way they approached search. While other companies such as Yahoo! used their search engine primarily as a way to obtain new visitors to their Web sites, Google focused its efforts on search alone. Yahoo!, for example, used its search engine to draw visitors to its Web site that also includes news, entertainment, and weather information. In contrast, Google offers a simple Web site that focuses strictly on search and does not include other information that might distract search.

Even though the intense focus on search may seem curious at first, it is the search process that provides Google with its revenues and profits. When users enter search terms, Google places small text advertisements next to the search results. Each time users click on these small advertisements, Google receives money from the advertisers. Given these incentives for profits, Google continues to constantly improve the search process. This continuous improvement helps explain why Google maintains approximately 64 percent of the market share for searches in the United States; this 64 percent is nearly three times as large as Google's biggest competitor, Yahoo! In other parts of the world, Google's market share is even higher.

Google's dominance in the search business has led to astounding performance. Although the company is just over 10 years old, it recently had revenues of approximately $24 billion and profits of more than $8 billion.

Taken together, then, Google's founders identified an opportunity while they were graduate students at Stanford. After they evaluated the opportunity, they decided to start their own company. Just as IBM dominated mainframes and Microsoft dominated personal computer software, today Google has the potential to rule the Internet. How Page and Brin approach these next several years will largely determine Google's place in Internet—and corporate—history.

■ *Google founders Larry Page (left) and Sergey Brin. Their exclusive focus on the search functions of their site has helped it garner a commanding market share.*

EXPLORING YOUR MANAGEMENT SKILL

You can explore your level of entrepreneurship skill **before** studying the chapter by completing the exercise "Exploring Your Management Skill: Part 1" on page 152 and **after** studying this chapter by completing the exercise "Exploring Your Management Skill: Part 2" on page 153.

THE ENTREPRENEURSHIP CHALLENGE

The Challenge Case illustrates different entrepreneurship challenges that Google strives to meet. The remaining material in this chapter explains entrepreneurship concepts and helps develop the corresponding entrepreneurship skill you will need to meet such challenges throughout your career. After studying the chapter concepts, read the Challenge Case Summary at the end of the chapter to help you relate chapter content to meeting entrepreneurship challenges at Google.

FUNDAMENTALS OF ENTREPRENEURSHIP

Entrepreneurship can be defined in a variety of ways. Most people believe that entrepreneurship entails an individual starting a new business to make money, but the meaning of the term is actually much broader. For our purposes, **entrepreneurship** refers to the identification, evaluation, and exploitation of opportunities.[2] Figure 6.1 illustrates this process. Opportunities, in a general sense, are appropriate or favorable occasions.[3] In the entrepreneurship context, though, the definition of *opportunity* is slightly different from this general definition. Specifically, an **entrepreneurial opportunity** is an occasion to bring into existence new products and services that allow outputs to be sold at a price greater than their cost of production.[4] In other words, entrepreneurial opportunities exist when individuals are able to sell new products and services at a price that produces a profit.

Although entrepreneurship has a broad definition, the term still involves starting new businesses. Understanding entrepreneurship is important; a recent survey reports that, on average, 460,000 people start new businesses in the United States each month.[5] Other studies suggest that somewhere between 20 to 50 percent of all individuals engage in entrepreneurial behaviors.[6] Despite these new businesses, the evidence suggests that entrepreneurs find it difficult to keep their businesses alive. Research reports, for example, that 34 percent of new businesses do not survive the first two years, 50 percent do not survive four years, and 60 percent do not survive six years.[7] Table 6.1 displays the results of some studies examining the failure rates of some new businesses.

Consistent with our framework, an **entrepreneur** is an individual who identifies, evaluates, and exploits opportunities. Many associate the term *entrepreneur* with one individual starting a new business, but it is not always the case. In fact, research suggests that approximately 75 percent of new organizations are started by entrepreneurial teams.[8] In other words, many entrepreneurs work with others when identifying, evaluating, and exploiting entrepreneurial opportunities. In fact, research suggests that organizations started by entrepreneurial teams tend to perform better than those started by individual entrepreneurs working by themselves.[9] Many attribute this "team advantage" to the combination of diverse skills, experiences, and relationships of the entrepreneurial team members.[10] In addition, as new organizations grow, they require leaders with new skills. Consequently, assembling a team makes it easier for entrepreneurs to add team members with these new skills as the venture expands.[11]

It is clear that entrepreneurship represents an important fabric of society. Taken together, then, these high business formation rates and high failure rates suggest that understanding the fundamentals of entrepreneurship represents an important activity. In the following sections, we highlight the primary issues as they pertain to identifying, evaluating, and exploiting entrepreneurial opportunities.

FIGURE 6.1
Stages of the entrepreneurship process

TABLE 6.1 A Summary of Entrepreneurial Failure Rates

Operation No.	Failure Rate
Restaurants	Approximately 51% of new restaurants failed within the first 5 years.
New Businesses	Approximately 60% of new businesses failed within the first 6 years.
New Chemical Plants	Approximately 80% of new chemical plants failed within the first 10 years.

Sources: Based on data from Matthew Hayward, Dean Shepherd, and Dale Griffin, "A Hubris Theory of Entrepreneurship," *Management Science* 52, no. 2 (2006): 160–172; H. G. Parsa, John Self, David Njite, and Tiffany King, "Why Restaurants Fail," *Cornell Hotel and Restaurant Administration Quarterly* 46, no. 3 (2005): 304–322; and Scott A. Shane, "Failure Is a Constant in Entrepreneurship," *New York Times*, July 17, 2009, http://boss.blogs.nytimes.com.

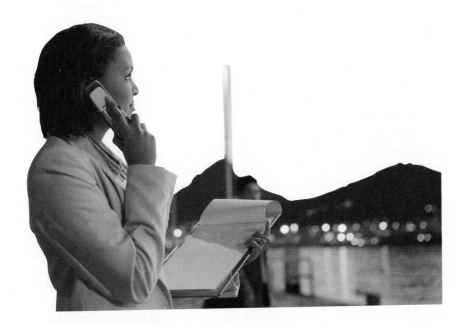

Entrepreneurs are characterized by their ability to identify and exploit information pinpointing concrete business opportunities that others fail to see or capitalize on.

class discussion highlight

MODERN RESEARCH AND ENTREPRENEURSHIP SKILL

Why Do Entrepreneurs Start New Ventures?

The preceding discussion highlighted the fact that most new businesses tend to perform poorly. In fact, history suggests that many new businesses fail within a short period of time. Given this record of poor performance, why then do so many individuals decide to start new ventures?

Professors Townsend, Busenitz, and Arthurs examined this question in detail. They proposed that two factors primarily determined an entrepreneur's decision to start a new venture: (1) The entrepreneur's confidence in his/her ability to perform entrepreneurial tasks and (2) The entrepreneur's expectations about the new venture's success in the future. They sampled 316 entrepreneurs to understand the relative influence of these two factors on their decisions to start new ventures. Which factor do you think most influenced entrepreneur's decisions to start new ventures? Why? If you were a researcher studying this issue, what other factors would perhaps influence such decisions?

Source: This research highlight is based on D. M. Townsend, L. W. Busenitz, and J. D. Arthurs, "To Start or Not to Start: Outcome and Ability Expectations in the decision to start a new venture," *Journal of Business Venturing*, 25 (2010), 192–202.

OPPORTUNITIES

In the previous section, we defined entrepreneurship in terms of opportunities. In the following sections, we describe the different types of opportunities. In addition, we describe how entrepreneurs identify, evaluate, and exploit these opportunities.

Types of Opportunities

Not everyone can invent a new medical device or diagnostic technology. But entrepreneurial opportunities in the field of health care are broad, and they include the work or persuading doctors to use new discoveries to improve patient outcomes.

In his classic formulation of opportunities, Schumpeter described five different types of opportunities.[12] First, opportunities arise from the creation of new products or services. When a new type of medical device is created, for example, an opportunity exists in the form of convincing doctors to use the new device in their practices. The invention of the heart stent became an entrepreneurial opportunity for companies like Boston Scientific and Abbott Laboratories. Stents help doctors to clear a patient's arteries and keep them open, in some cases enabling the patient to avoid open-heart surgery altogether. Today, an estimated 1 million Americans per year undergo the stent procedure.[13]

Second, opportunities arise from the discovery of new geographical markets in which new customers will value the new product or service. As an example, suppose an individual has exclusive rights to produce and distribute action figures based on a popular movie within the United States. After saturating the domestic market, the individual might begin to distribute the action figures in China. This scenario would represent an opportunity arising from the discovery of a new geographical market.

Third, opportunities may arise from the creation or discovery of new raw materials or after discovering alternative uses for existing raw materials. For example, ethanol, which can be produced from corn, represents a new use for corn. Although farmers typically sell corn to manufacturers of food products, ethanol provides farmers with another use for the corn they grow.

Fourth, opportunities may emerge from the discovery of new methods of production. According to Schumpeter, new methods of production allow entrepreneurs to produce goods or services at lower costs, which allows the entrepreneurs to satisfy the needs of customers more effectively. Finally, opportunities may arise from new methods of organizing. The emergence of the Internet provides an example of opportunities that arose from new methods of organizing. Specifically, the Internet allowed entrepreneurs to reach consumers without physical retail locations that required bricks and mortar.[14] The Internet allowed Netflix to offer customers a new way to rent DVDs and video games. Instead of driving to a retail outlet like Blockbuster, Netflix users order their DVDs and video games online.

In sum, then, five different types of opportunities arise from the creation of new products or services, the discovery of new geographical markets, the discovery of new raw materials, the discovery of new methods of production, and the discovery of new methods of organizing. Table 6.2 summarizes and provides examples for each of these different types of opportunities. In the following sections, we describe in detail how entrepreneurs identify, evaluate, and exploit these opportunities.

TABLE 6.2 Types of Opportunities

Operation No.	Example
New Product or Service	Nintendo developing and marketing the Wii gaming system
New Geographical Markets	Citibank providing services in China
New Raw Materials or New Uses for Raw Materials	Under Armour's use of microfiber-based materials to make sports apparel
New Method of Production	Tyson Chicken raising chickens without antibiotics
New Method of Organizing	Amazon.com using the Internet to sell books

Opportunity Identification

Although an opportunity may exist, entrepreneurs will not be able to take advantage of this opportunity unless they are able to first identify the opportunity. Research suggests, though, that opportunities do not appear in a prepackaged form, and individuals differ in their ability to identify opportunities.[15] Intuitively, these differences in discernment make sense. If all individuals were equally able to identify opportunities, all individuals might rush to exploit the same opportunities.

Which factors help determine whether individuals are able to identify opportunities? In the remainder of this section, we describe four factors that influence the ability of individuals to identify opportunities: entrepreneurial alertness, information asymmetry, social networks, and the ability to establish means-ends relationships.

First, individuals vary in terms of **entrepreneurial alertness**, which refers to an individual's ability to notice and be sensitive to new information about objects, incidents, and patterns of behavior in the environment.[16] When individuals have high levels of entrepreneurial alertness, they are more likely to identify potential entrepreneurial opportunities. In contrast, when individuals have low levels of entrepreneurial alertness, they are more likely to dismiss or ignore new information and overlook potential opportunities.

Entrepreneurial alertness helped Pennsylvania farmers Amos and Jacob Miller identify a valuable opportunity. Years ago, from conversations with their customers, 32-year-old Amos and his dad Jacob spotted a trend in the making: Americans' interest in nutrient-dense food was growing. As a result, the Millers began expanding their farm's product line to include such foods—for example, grass-fed beef, milk-fed pork, and fermented vegetables. At a time when it's become more difficult to make a living from farming, Miller Farm revenues have topped $1.8 million. The key: recognizing a trend and acting on it.[17] ∎

how managers do it

Identifying Opportunities at Miller Farm

Second, individuals vary in terms of the information to which they have access, which is known as **information asymmetry**. This variation in information involves both new information and old information, and no two people share all of this information at the same time.[18] Two individuals, for example, may gain new market information regarding a potential entrepreneurial opportunity. Despite the fact that both of these individuals have gained access to this new information, only one of these individuals has access to additional information suggesting that other competitors are already moving to exploit this opportunity. As such, only one of these individuals will correctly identify this opportunity.

Third, individuals vary in terms of their **social networks**, which represent individuals' patterns of social relationships. Some individuals have extended social networks (i.e., many social relationships), while other individuals have narrow social networks (i.e., few social relationships). Research suggests that individuals with extended networks are more likely to identify potential entrepreneurial opportunities than those with more narrow social networks.[19] Moreover, the *type* of social network may influence opportunity identification. An individual with entrepreneurial family members, for example, may be better able to identify opportunities than an individual with family members who are not entrepreneurial.[20]

Fourth, individuals will vary in terms of their ability to assess means-ends relationships. In this context, the ability to assess means–end relationships refers to the ability of entrepreneurs to understand how to turn a new technology into a product or service that will be valued by consumers. For example, individuals may have access to technology, but they are unable to understand the potential commercial applications associated with the technology.

FIGURE 6.2
Determinants of opportunity
identification

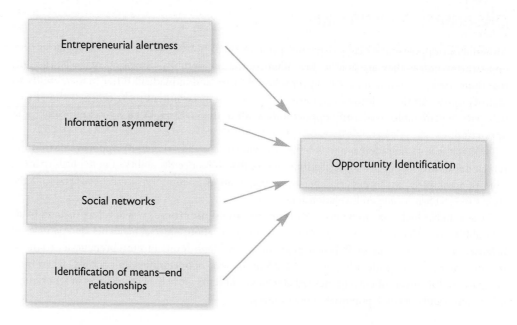

When individuals are unable to see these relationships, they are unable to identify the opportunity. In an effort to help establish these means-ends relationships, several universities are working with individuals and researchers to help in identifying the commercial applications associated with new technologies.[21]

Taken together, a number of different factors influence opportunity identification. Figure 6.2 summarizes theses different factors.

Opportunity Evaluation

In the previous section, we discussed opportunity identification, which is the first step of the entrepreneurship process. In this section, we discuss the second stage of this process: opportunity evaluation. Opportunity evaluation occurs when an entrepreneur decides whether he or she has just a good idea or a viable opportunity that will provide the desired outcomes.[22] The evaluation step is "where the rubber meets the road," and it often presents a difficult challenge. When evaluating opportunities, entrepreneurs must be honest with themselves.[23] If not, the entrepreneurs may purposely ignore or accidentally overlook important factors that will limit the potential success of the opportunity.

To evaluate ideas, entrepreneurs will often engage in **feasibility analysis**, which is analysis that helps entrepreneurs understand whether an idea is practical.[24] In such a study, entrepreneurs will study customer demands, the structure of the industry, and the entrepreneur's ability to provide the new product or service. Although entrepreneurs have many ideas, not all of them are feasible; this analysis helps them to better understand the likelihood that their opportunity will provide the resources required.

Even if an idea is feasible, opportunities are associated with some risk. One of the central factors that entrepreneurs will examine in the evaluation stage is the opportunity's **entrepreneurial risk**, which is the likelihood and magnitude of the opportunity's downside loss. In this context, **downside loss** refers to the resources (i.e., money, relationships, etc.) the entrepreneur could lose if the opportunity does not succeed. All else being equal, entrepreneurs are more likely to pursue opportunities with lower levels of entrepreneurial risk and less likely to pursue opportunities with higher levels of entrepreneurial risk.

Research suggests that two factors may adversely influence the accuracy of an entrepreneur's risk perceptions.[25] First, an entrepreneur's belief in the law of small numbers decreases the risk he or she perceives with an opportunity. The **law of small numbers** occurs when individuals rely on a small sample of information to inform their decisions. Because individuals are more likely to obtain good information (i.e., the success stories of other entrepreneurs) and less likely to obtain bad information (i.e., stories about the failures of other entrepreneurs), small samples of information are likely biased positively. Such beliefs tend to be common among entrepreneurs, because most entrepreneurs do not have access to large databases.[26] As such, the extent to which individuals believe in the law of small numbers helps determine whether they are likely to obtain biased information and thus associate lower levels of risk to their ideas.

Second, the control that an entrepreneur feels with respect to the opportunity's outcome may influence perceptions of the idea's risk. **Illusion of control** exists when entrepreneurs overestimate the extent to which they can control the outcome of an opportunity.[27] The outcomes of some opportunities rely more on luck than entrepreneurial skill. In these situations, believing that one can control the outcomes is problematic.

Taken together, when entrepreneurs evaluate opportunities, they pay careful attention to entrepreneurial risk—and savvy entrepreneurs work to reduce risk before engaging in substantial commitments of capital.[28] It is important that entrepreneurs do not fall victim to the law of small numbers or the illusion of control when evaluating opportunities, because these two factors may negatively influence the accuracy of risk perceptions. In the following section, we discuss the final stage in the entrepreneurship process: opportunity exploitation.

Opportunity Exploitation

The third step in the entrepreneurship process involves exploiting an opportunity. **Exploitation** refers to the activities and investments committed to gain returns from the new product or service arising from the opportunity.[29] Simply stated, exploitation occurs when an entrepreneur (or group of entrepreneurs) decides that an opportunity is worth pursuing. When an entrepreneur, for example, decides that customers would highly value a new product, exploitation entails all of those activities (i.e., marketing, production, etc.) needed to sell the new product to consumers.

Entrepreneur Bryan Green successfully exploited an opportunity he identified. Unlike most Americans, Green had always enjoyed exercising. The realization that Americans, in general, are out of shape was the opportunity and impetus Green needed to launch Advantage Fitness Products, a company that designs, supplies, and services fitness facilities worldwide. Green designs home gyms for celebrities as well as for professional teams like the San Francisco 49ers and New York Mets. Green says that once he exploited his opportunity, the keys to his success were to "stay flexible and execute flawlessly."[30]

how managers do it

Exploiting Opportunities at Advantage Fitness Products

Several factors can help entrepreneurs decide whether they should exploit an opportunity.[31] First, entrepreneurs are more likely to exploit an opportunity when they believe that customers will value their new product or service. When customers value a new product or service, they provide market demand. This market demand, in turn, helps individuals earn the resources (i.e., profits) necessary to support the opportunity exploitation.

Second, entrepreneurs are more likely to exploit an opportunity when they perceive that they have the support of important stakeholders. Stakeholders refer to groups such as employees, suppliers, investors, and other suppliers of capital (i.e., banks) who directly or indirectly influence organizational performance. When individuals perceive that these groups will provide support, they are more likely to exploit the opportunity. This tendency makes sense intuitively,

FIGURE 6.3
Factors influencing opportunity exploitation

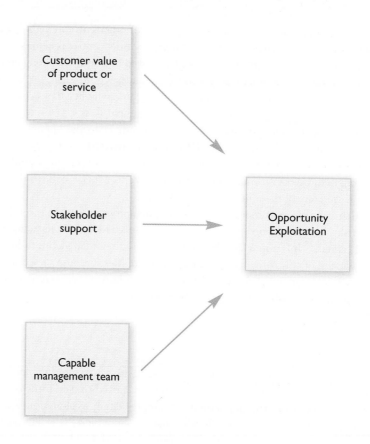

because these stakeholders will help ensure the success of the entrepreneur pursuing the opportunity. Conversely, it will likely prove difficult for entrepreneurs to succeed if they do not have the support of important stakeholders.

Finally, entrepreneurs are more likely to exploit opportunities when they perceive that their surrounding management team is capable. Qualified management teams will bring resources (i.e., ability, knowledge, information) to the opportunity, which will presumably enhance the prospects of the opportunity.[32] In contrast, when entrepreneurs feel as if their management teams are incapable, they are less likely to exploit the opportunity, because they feel they do not have access to the resources needed to ensure high levels of organizational performance.

In sum, several factors influence an entrepreneur's ability to exploit opportunities. Figure 6.3 summarizes these relationships.

Financing Exploitation

When entrepreneurs decide that an opportunity is worth exploiting, they often lack the capital (i.e., money) needed to exploit the opportunity. Although some entrepreneurs fund their operations with their own money or with credit cards, most entrepreneurs require at least some external money to fund operations. In this section we review three primary sources of external capital for entrepreneurs: angel investors, venture capitalists, and bank financing.

Angel investors are wealthy individuals who provide capital to new companies.[33] Angel investors may include an entrepreneur's family and friends, but angel investors are also private individuals who did not know the entrepreneur prior to funding the opportunity. Angel investors have existed for centuries. In fact, in 1903, five angel investors helped Henry Ford launch his auto company with a total of $41,500. Within 15 years, those angels' investment was worth a whopping $145 million.[34] Today, approximately 140,000 angel investors provide about $9 billion in capital to nearly 25,000 new ventures each year.[35]

Wealthy individuals who act as "angel" investors number about 400,000 today. Their financial backing helps some 50,000 companies get off the ground each year. What do you think "angels" would want to know about a firm they were considering financing?

Venture capitalists are firms that raise money from investors and then use this money to make investments in new firms. Many prominent companies such as Intel and Microsoft received investments from venture capitalists in their early days. The companies then used these funds to help acquire the resources (i.e., employees, equipment, etc.) that eventually made them the companies they are today. Although the use of venture capital in the United States peaked at about $100 billion during the dot-com frenzy of 1998–2000, the venture capital industry today totals nearly $18 billion.[36]

It is important to note that both angel investors and venture capitalists provide money to entrepreneurs and in return receive a portion of the firm's equity. In other words, in return for their investment (money) in the entrepreneur's firm, the entrepreneur gives them partial ownership of the firm. As such, when the entrepreneur's firm does well and increases in value, the value of the investor's investment also increases. Likewise, when the entrepreneur's firm does poorly and decreases in value, the value of the investor's investment also decreases.

Although similar, angel investors and venture capitalists differ in a number of significant ways. In contrast to angel investors, venture capitalists make fewer investments, but these investments are often larger than the investments made by angel investors. In fact, the average investment of venture capitalists is approximately $4 million, whereas the average investment of angel investors is about $75,000.[37] In addition, venture capitalists typically focus on a small number of industries. In contrast, angel investors tend not to focus on particular industries. Finally, venture capitalists typically invest in firms after the initial start-up stage. In other words, angel investors typically provide the initial financing to start-up ventures, and venture capitalists tend to provide more capital as the new venture becomes more established.

In sum, angel investors and venture capitalists are sources that entrepreneurs may use to fund new ventures. Whether an entrepreneur obtains funding from an angel investor or venture capital firm, however, it is important to note that such relationships present unique challenges and must be entered into with care.[38]

Bank financing occurs when an entrepreneur obtains financing from a financial institution in the form of a loan. It is important to note that unlike angel investors or venture capitalists, banks are not investors. Instead, banks make loans to entrepreneurs and in return expect repayment of the loans with interest. As such, banks are not concerned with the long-term potential for returns. Instead, these banks are more interested in ensuring that the entrepreneur's opportunity will survive long enough to ensure repayment. In other words, investors typically seek risk, but banks are more likely to minimize risk.

CORPORATE ENTREPRENEURSHIP

Until now, we have focused on entrepreneurial opportunities pursued by individuals or teams of individuals. It is important to note, though, that existing corporations can also identify, evaluate, and exploit opportunities. **Corporate entrepreneurship**, which refers to such activities, is the process in which an individual or group of individuals in an existing corporation create a new organization or instigate renewal or innovation within that corporation.[39] Although corporate entrepreneurship often involves establishing new organizations, these new organizations leverage the parent corporation's assets, market position, or other resources.[40] In other words, when corporate entrepreneurship results in new companies, these new companies often continue to work closely with the parent company.

It is important to recognize that corporate entrepreneurship does not necessarily require creating a new organization. Corporate entrepreneurship, for example, also involves creating new products, services, or technologies. At 3M, engineers can spend as much as 15 percent of their time on projects of their own design. The company believes this flexibility will provide the motivation needed for engineers to innovate successfully, possibly leading to new products or services— or new organizations altogether.[41] This flexibility may result in new products, services, or new organizations altogether.

Corporate entrepreneurship can be classified into four general types.[42] First, **sustained regeneration** occurs when firms develop new cultures, processes, or structures to support new product innovations in current markets as well as with existing products into new markets. Sustained regeneration, which refers to product innovation, is the most frequently used type of corporate entrepreneurship.

Second, **organizational rejuvenation** involves improving the firm's ability to execute strategies and focuses on new processes instead of new products. GE, for instance, successfully rejuvenated itself by changing policies and procedures within the company to support innovation.

Third, **strategic renewal** occurs when a firm attempts to alter its own competitive strategy. Unlike introducing a new product or service, strategic renewal occurs when the firm tries to offer a new strategy altogether. Of course, it remains quite difficult for a firm to change strategies. Wal-Mart, for example, is facing tremendous difficulties in trying to alter its strategy to focus on more affluent customers.[43]

Fourth, **domain definition** occurs when a firm proactively seeks to create a new product market position that competitors have not recognized. When pursuing domain definition, firms hope to become the first competitor in a market segment. In such situations, firms will enjoy the benefits of having no competitors. Amazon.com, for example, was one of the first companies to realize the potential of selling books online. It is important to note, though, that first movers do not always succeed. Apple's Newton, for example, was the first personal digital assistant (PDA), but this product no longer exists. Moreover, Apple's iPod was not the first digital music player on the market, but today the iPod dominates the marketplace.

In sum, there are several general types of corporate entrepreneurship. Despite its importance, not every organization can support corporate entrepreneurship. The success of corporate entrepreneurship efforts will depend on many factors, including the organization's culture, practices, and even its tolerance level for uncertainty.[44]

SOCIAL ENTREPRENEURSHIP

The discussion of entrepreneurship so far in this chapter involves individuals or corporations that pursue entrepreneurial opportunities for the purposes of generating sales and profits, which we call **commercial entrepreneurship**. In recent years, researchers have begun to examine entrepreneurship in a social context. **Social entrepreneurship** involves the recognition, evaluation, and exploitation of opportunities that create social value as opposed to personal or shareholder wealth.[45] In this context, **social value** refers to the basic long-standing needs of society and has little to do with profits. Basic long-standing needs might include providing water, food, and shelter to those individuals in need. Social value might also refer to more specific needs such as providing playground equipment to needy school districts or seeing-eye dogs for those who are blind.

Recent reports suggest that the growth in nonprofit organizations has increased at a faster pace than new businesses.[46]

how managers do it

Helping Third-World Entrepreneurs at Grameen Bank

Muhammed Yunus, an economist turned social entrepreneur, launched one of the world's most successful nonprofits: Grameen Bank, a microfinance organization. Yunus launched Grameen when he realized that small loans can make a huge difference in the life of an entrepreneur in an underdeveloped country. Grameen Bank makes these loans—and relatively low interest rates—because it is more interested in improving lives than in making money. The winner of the 2006 Nobel Peace Prize, Yunus recently received the Presidential Medal of Freedom, the highest civilian honor in the United States, awarded to those whose work has changed the world.[47] ■

How Do Commercial and Social Entrepreneurship Differ?

Although the two concepts share some similarities, substantive differences distinguish commercial entrepreneurship from social entrepreneurship. In the remainder of this section, we detail three differences with respect to mission, resources, and performance measurement.

Perhaps the most fundamental difference between commercial and social entrepreneurship involves the entrepreneur's mission or purpose. The purpose of the commercial entrepreneurship is to create profits, while the purpose of social entrepreneurship is to create value for the public. Despite this difference in focus, it is important to note that social entrepreneurs cannot totally ignore issues surrounding sales and costs. If social entrepreneurs did ignore such important concepts they likely would not have the money needed to continue their pursuit of social value. As such, the goal of social entrepreneurship does not involve profits, but social entrepreneurs still need to monitor profit-oriented measures, including revenues and costs. In this sense, then, profits remain somewhat important, but social value dominates the goal structure of social entrepreneurs.[48]

A second primary distinction between commercial and social entrepreneurship involves the availability of resources such as funding and employees. Unlike commercial entrepreneurship, social entrepreneurs face more difficulties attracting capital from angel investors, venture capitalists, or banks. Instead, most social entrepreneurs rely on donations as sources of funding. Also, social entrepreneurs often face difficulties in the form of hiring and compensating employees. Because social entrepreneurs often do not have the capital necessary to pay attractive salaries, they must focus on hiring employees who share the organization's purpose. When employees are able to share the organization's purpose, they may be more likely to work for lower salaries. In fact, many social entrepreneurs rely on volunteers to help their organizations fulfill their missions.

Commercial and social entrepreneurship also differ in terms of performance measures. Commercial entrepreneurs, for example, focus on quantitative measures such as profits, shareholder wealth, revenues, and costs. In contrast, social entrepreneurs focus on less quantitative performance measures that are not related to money. For example, a soup kitchen needs to monitor costs, but the primary performance measure would deal with the number of meals served. In addition, though, a free meal may help the emotional state of someone who is homeless; this outcome is difficult to quantify.

Winner of the 2004 Nobel Peace Prize and Kenyan environmental activist Wangari Maatha helps to plant a valley oak in Capitol Park as part of the organization's social entrepreneurship effort. Like most such efforts, the project is driven by a desire to provide social value, but within an acceptable ratio of revenues and costs.

Success Factors in Social Entrepreneurship

Although the topic of social entrepreneurship is fairly new from a research perspective, some studies look at the factors that influence the performance of social entrepreneurs.[49] In the remainder of this section, we describe three factors that influence the performance of social entrepreneurs: their networks of relationships, their capital bases, and the public's acceptance of the new venture.

Previously in this chapter, we described the importance of entrepreneurs' social networks. These networks are also important for social entrepreneurs. Large networks provide social entrepreneurs with potential sources of capital to fund their social missions. In addition, large social networks can help social entrepreneurs identify potential employees and volunteers. In sum, large social networks improve the performance of social entrepreneurs.

Similar to commercial entrepreneurship, an organization's capital base is also important for social entrepreneurs. At the same time, capital is perhaps even more important for social entrepreneurs, because they do not have access to the venture capital and bank financing available to commercial entrepreneurs. Consequently, the capital raised through donations and other funding sources is extremely important for the success of social entrepreneurs.

Finally, the acceptance of a particular social entrepreneur's social value influences the performance of his organization. When a large segment of society supports a social entrepreneur's cause, the social entrepreneur is likely to gather the funds and employees or volunteers needed for success. In contrast, when only a small segment of society supports the social entrepreneur's cause, it is more difficult to gather the necessary resources. For example, the National Association of Parents of the Visually Impaired Children in Israel faced difficulties raising the necessary resources because so few members of society found the organization worthy of support.[50]

CHALLENGE CASE SUMMARY

The Challenge Case describes how Larry Page and Sergey Brin incorporated Google in 1998 and turned the company into the world's leading search engine. The story of Google provides an example of how entrepreneurship fundamentally changed an industry. Prior to Google, search engines operated by searching the text of Web pages on the Internet. If a Web page contained many instances of the search term, most search engines such as Yahoo! would give that Web page high search grades.

Page and Brin, however, thought that this method of searching was not ideal, which provided them with an opportunity. In other words, the situation represented an opportunity to bring a new service into the industry that customers would value. They believed they could build a search engine that would produce revenues that would exceed their cost of providing the new search engine. The founders believed that this new search engine would produce profits.

Page and Brin changed the search process by focusing more on Web page popularity than on the number of times a given search term appeared on a Web page. They then linked search advertisements to these search results, which led in turn to extraordinary profits. By changing the nature of the search process, in retrospect it is clear that Page and Brin identified a valuable opportunity. Successful opportunity identification is not always the case, however, because research suggests that most new businesses fail.

According to Schumpeter's classic formulation of opportunities, Google would represent an opportunity that arose from a new product or service. The introduction of their new searching service has served many customers, but it is not the company's only new service. Google also provides Scholar Google, a Web site that allows academics and researchers to search for academic publications such as books, dissertations, and journal articles. Google also offers free software that allows users to complete basic tasks using word processing, spreadsheet, and presentation software.

When Google introduces international versions of its search engine, it is pursuing Schumpeter's second type of opportunity that arises from the discovery of new geographical markets. A modification of its search engine, for example, allows Google to enter markets in China. Of course, this market entry also allows Google to earn profits from selling advertisements in China. Today, Google offers a wide array of services to consumers. As the company progresses, it will continue to search for Schumpeter's other types of opportunities.

It is important to note that Page and Brin proceeded through the three steps of the entrepreneurial process when starting Google. First, the founders identified the opportunity; they understood that the search process could be improved, and they believed that they had the resources necessary to improve the process. It is clear that as graduate students, they had high levels of entrepreneurial alertness. In other words, they were able to notice and be sensitive to new information about objects, incidents, and patterns of behavior in the Internet environment.

After identifying the opportunity, Page and Brin also evaluated the opportunity. Specifically, they likely went through a process that helped them understand whether their idea was practical. For their analysis, they likely gathered information on the industry's current competitors and the functionality of their search engines to determine whether they could compete with the existing competitors. In addition, they almost certainly took note of the rapidly increasing usage of the Internet in the late 1990s; this information confirmed for them that they could potentially have a large customer base.

It was also important for Page and Brin to understand the entrepreneurial risk associated with their new search engine. In this case, the cost of creating Google was the cost of developing the new search engine. Other computer software companies face similar costs. If the search engine did not work effectively, they would largely lose the time they invested in the new project.

The potential loss for Google was dramatically different from starting a new company to compete with Lowe's and Home Depot, for example. If a new company wanted to compete with Lowe's and Home Depot, it would need to purchase or lease buildings throughout the world to sell its products. In addition, it would need to purchase all of the inventory needed to stock the shelves in these stores. Google, on the other hand, did not require such enormous expenditures, which helped Page and Brin limit the downside risk.

After identifying and evaluating the opportunity, Page and Brin decided to exploit the opportunity. Stated differently, the first two stages of the process convinced the two founders that the idea was worth pursuing. To finance their exploitation, they first relied on an angel investor in the form of one of their professors at Stanford, who wrote them a check for $100,000. With this check in hand, they were able to raise another $900,000 from family members, friends, and acquaintances. A year later, Page and Brin needed more money, and they were able to raise $25 million from two of Silicon Valley's most prominent venture capital firms. Taken together, then, Google raised millions of dollars from both angel investors and venture capitalists; without such investors it is unlikely Google would have succeeded.

Although the company started small, today Google is worth hundreds of *billions* of dollars. As such it is difficult to think of Page and Brin as entrepreneurs today; instead they are leaders of one of the world's largest and most influential companies. Nonetheless, entrepreneurship remains important at Google, particularly corporate entrepreneurship. Instead of individuals pursuing opportunities, today Google as a corporation pursues opportunities. This culture of entrepreneurship has helped Google maintain the diverse opportunities it pursues today. For example, today the company offers—among others—movie making software, picture editing software, mapping software, and social networking Web sites. In addition, Google even has an interface designed to respond to text message-based search queries from cell phones. It is this spirit of corporate entrepreneurship that Google will need to continue and thrive in an extremely competitive industry.

Finally, it is also important to note that Google developed Google.org to oversee the company's social entrepreneurship programs. The three broad missions of Google.org include addressing climate change, global public health, and economic development and poverty. To address climate change, Google.org is sponsoring initiatives to support alternative forms of transportation. Regarding global public health, Google.org has assembled the technology needed to more effectively communicate information regarding natural health disasters and other public health emergencies. To facilitate economic development and eliminate poverty, Google.org has provided grant money to support entrepreneurship programs in Africa and other parts of the world. Taken together, the company has donated millions of dollars to support these initiatives.

MANAGEMENT SKILL ACTIVITIES

This section is specially designed to help you develop entrepreneurship skill. An individual's management skill is based on an understanding of management concepts and the ability to apply those concepts in management situations. As a result, the following activities are designed both to heighten your understanding of entrepreneurship concepts and to help you gain facility in applying these concepts in various management situations.

UNDERSTANDING ENTREPRENEURSHIP CONCEPTS

 To check your understanding and to practice using the concepts in this chapter, go to www.mymanagementlab.com and explore the material associated with Chapter 6.

Know Key Terms

Understanding the following key terms is critical to your understanding of chapter material. Define each of these terms. Refer to the page(s) referenced after a term to check your definition or to gain further insight regarding the term.

Know How Management Concepts Relate

This section is comprised of activities that will further sharpen your understanding of management concepts. Answer essay questions as completely as possible. Also, remember that many additional true/false and multiple choice questions appear on-line at MyManagementLab.com to help you further refine your understanding of management concepts.

1. Describe the main components of entrepreneurship.
2. Distinguish between the different types of opportunities.

3. Describe the differences between opportunity identification and opportunity exploitation.
4. Describe the main components of social entrepreneurship, and describe how social entrepreneurship differs from commercial entrepreneurship.
5. Describe the different types of corporate entrepreneurship and provide examples.

DEVELOPING MANAGEMENT SKILLS

Learning activities in this section are aimed at helping you develop your entrepreneurship skill. Learning activities include Exploring Your Management Skill: Parts 1 & 2, Your Management Skills Portfolio, Experiential Exercises, Cases, and a VideoNet Exercise.

Exploring Your Management Skill: Part 1

Before studying this chapter, respond to the following questions regarding the type of advice you would give to Google's Larry Page and Sergey Brin, referenced in the Challenge Case. Then address the concerning entrepreneurship challenges that they presently face within the company. You are not expected to be an entrepreneurship expert at this point. Answering the questions now can help you focus on important points when you study the chapter. Also, answering the questions again after you study the chapter will give you an idea of how much you have learned.

Record your answers here or online at MyManagementLab.com. Completing the questions at MyManagementLab.com will allow you to get feedback about your answers automatically. If you answer the questions in the book, look up answers in the Exploring Your Management Skill section at the end of the book.

FOR EACH STATEMENT CIRCLE:
- "Y" if you would give the advice to Page and Brin.
- "N" if you would NOT give the advice to Page and Brin.
- "NI" if you have no idea whether you would give the advice to Page and Brin.

Messrs. Page and Brin, in meeting your entrepreneurship challenges at Google, you should . . .

Before Study   After Study

1. understand that because Google has become so large, they are no longer entrepreneurs and entrepreneurship concepts do not matter any longer to Google.
   Y, N, NI

2. recognize that entrepreneurship involves the identification, evaluation, and exploitation of opportunities.
Y, N, NI

3. recognize that, on average, entrepreneurial ventures succeed, particularly in the United States.
Y, N, NI

4. understand that, on average, entrepreneurial ventures started by teams of entrepreneurs tend to outperform entrepreneurial ventures started by solo entrepreneurs.
Y, N, NI

5. recognize that five broad types of opportunities exist, and Google must continue to monitor these potential opportunities.
Y, N, NI

6. understand that Google employees will be able to identify future opportunities equally.
Y, N, NI

7. understand that social networks influence ability to identify opportunities in the future.
Y, N, NI

8. require Google employees to use feasibility analysis when evaluating new opportunities.
Y, N, NI

9. understand the role of small numbers, which suggests that a small number of entrepreneurial ventures will succeed.
Y, N, NI

10. recognize that Google will most likely require angel investors if the company is to continue to succeed in the future.
Y, N, NI

11. understand that the objectives of venture capitalists, angel investors, and banks are all similar.
Y, N, NI

12. communicate to Google employees the value of sustained regeneration and its importance as the most common form of strategic entrepreneurship.
Y, N, NI

13. understand that *commercial entrepreneurship* and *social entrepreneurship* are two terms that have the same meaning.
Y, N, NI

14. evaluate Google's social entrepreneurship activities without considering revenues and costs.
Y, N, NI

15. recognize that corporate entrepreneurship is the most likely set of entrepreneurship activities to influence Google because it is a large company.
Y, N, NI

Exploring Your Management Skill: Part 2

As you recall, you completed Exploring Your Management Skill before you started to study this chapter. Your responses gave you an idea of how much you initially knew about entrepreneurship and helped you focus on important points as you studied the chapter. Answer the Exploring Your Management Skill questions again now and compare your score to the first time you took it. This comparison will give you an idea of how much you have learned from studying this chapter and pinpoint areas for further clarification before you start studying the next chapter. Record your answers within the text or online at MyManagement Lab.com. Completing the survey at MyManagementLab.com will allow you to grade and compare your test scores automatically. If you complete the test in the book, look up answers in the Exploring Your Management Skill section at the end of the book.

Your Management Skills Portfolio

Your Management Learning Portfolio is a collection of activities especially designed to demonstrate your management knowledge and skill. By completing these activities at MyManagementLab.com, you will be able to print, complete with cover sheet, as many activities as you choose. Be sure to save your work. Taking your printed portfolio to an employment interview could be helpful in obtaining a job.

The portfolio activity for this chapter is Serving up Drinks at BK. Study the information given here and complete the exercises that follow.[51]

Top management at Burger King has contacted you to help them enhance their business. In particular, top management has noticed a trend in the marketplace that the company is not capturing. Specifically, executives at Burger King are not sure the company is making enough profits from sales of drinks due to its focus on food.

Given the success of companies such as Starbucks, some of Burger King's competitors are changing their menus to compete more effectively. McDonald's, for example, has begun marketing and selling drinks to compete with Starbucks. In fact, McDonald's claims its new line of espresso drinks represents the most significant menu change for the company since it started serving breakfast in the 1970s. Sonic also started selling coffee-based beverages in addition to the many shakes and fruit slushes already on the menu.

Burger King would like you to help identify, evaluate, and form methods of exploitation for the company regarding drinks. In the following sections, answer the questions pertaining to the entrepreneurship process.

1. Identify a specific opportunity in the marketplace regarding drinks. It could be a new drink, a new line of drinks, a new type of retail outlet, or another type of opportunity.

2. Evaluate your opportunity using feasibility analysis. In particular, focus on how *customers* might respond to the new opportunity, how other *industry competitors* are already exploiting this opportunity, and describe Burger King's *ability to exploit* this opportunity.

3. How do you suggest Burger King exploit this opportunity? Does the company have enough money to easily follow your suggestion(s), or should the company pursue other financing options? (Use the company's Web site to obtain more information if necessary.)

Experiential Exercises

1 Identifying a Social Entrepreneurship Opportunity

Directions. Read the following scenario and then perform the listed activities. Your instructor may want you to perform the activities as an individual or within groups. Follow all of your instructor's directions carefully.

The president of your institution has contacted your group in an effort to improve its outreach programs. In particular, the president would like your group to make a short presentation describing the concept of social entrepreneurship. In addition, the president would like your group to identify three potential social entrepreneurship opportunities that your institution can evaluate and potentially exploit. These opportunities might involve only the local community, but they might also apply to other portions of the country or world.

2 You and Your Career

Earlier in the chapter, we discussed how many new businesses begin operations each day. Think about the role of entrepreneurship in your career. Have you given any thought to owning your own business one day? If you have not previously thought about being an entrepreneur, do the concepts in this chapter help you to identify potential entrepreneurial opportunities? How do the risks of being an entrepreneur compare to the risks of being a manager in a larger company? Finally, if you are planning to interview for a position in an established company, do you think your entrepreneurial ambitions may influence the company's perceptions of you as a potential employee? Why or why not?

Videonet Exercise

Entrepreneurship: Boston Boxing and Fitness

Video Highlights

Boston Boxing and Fitness is a boxing gym located in Allston, Massachusetts. Customers for Boston Boxing are individuals who seek to challenge themselves both physically and mentally far beyond the point to which ordinary fitness programs extend. The gym focuses on boxing, but the proprietor stresses that all of Boston Boxing's programs offer a level of total-body physical fitness that cannot be matched elsewhere. The video is narrated by the owner, who provides a description of the highly personalized service that Boston Boxing provides. The owner of Boston Boxing effectively relates the original idea that served as the genesis of his business, the risks he and his partner took to get the business off the ground, and his ongoing concerns, hopes, and plans for the future of the business.

Discussion Questions

1. How would you characterize the mission and goals of Boston Boxing and Fitness?

2. Does Boston Boxing and Fitness qualify as an entrepreneurial venture? Explain why or why not.

3. What is the essence of Boston Boxing and Fitness, in the eyes of owner Ed LaVache? What does he think he is selling to his customers? Explain. What challenges and risks does he describe?

Internet Activity

Browse the Boston Boxing and Fitness site at www.bostonboxing.com. Click around the site. Look at the classes and services offered. In the video clip, owner LaVache states that Boston Boxing is a "one-stop shop" for total fitness. Does the Web site reflect this statement? What type of customers do you think would be attracted to the services offered by Boston Boxing? Now click on the "About Us" link. Is the information presented consistent with what you've already learned about the company? Why or why not?

CASES

1 GOOGLE ENTREPRENEURS WIN BIG

"Google Entrepreneurs Win Big" (p. 139) and its Challenge Case Summary were written to help you better understand the management concepts contained in this chapter. Answer the following discussion questions about the Challenge Case that relate to entrepreneurship and how it can be applied in a company such as Google.

1. Do you think Google will be able to maintain its entrepreneurial culture in spite of its recent growth and increased size? Why or why not?

2. In your opinion, what were the key factors in determining the success of Google's entrepreneurial founders?

3. As you look into the future, what do you think represents a bigger threat to Google: established companies like Microsoft or smaller, entrepreneurial companies? Explain.

2 TURNING A HOBBY INTO A MULTIMILLION DOLLAR BUSINESS

Read the case and answer the questions that follow. Studying this case will help you better understand how concepts relating to entrepreneurship can be applied in a company such as Heritage Auction Galleries.

Heritage Auction Galleries sells history—all types of history. In recent years, the company has auctioned off virtually everything imaginable, from a fully articulated dinosaur skeleton to the derringer that the gangster John Dillinger was carrying when he was arrested in Tucson, Arizona more than 75 years ago. In 2010, Heritage gained worldwide attention when it sold a 1913 Liberty-head nickel for $3.73 million. And two years earlier, a sword belonging to Ulysses S. Grant went for $1.7 million. Big-ticket auctions like this have helped the Dallas-based firm become the largest collectibles auctioneer and third largest auction house in the world.

Heritage is an example of a multimillion dollar company that emerged from one man's boyhood hobby. When he was 9 years old, Steve Ivy was thrilled when he looked at a group of Indian-head cents minted in the 1890s. "From that point," Ivy said, "I was hooked." Immediately, he began asking his mother to take him to banks and stores to buy rolls of coins so that he could search through them. Within just a couple of years, he had begun selling his duplicates and buying still more coins with the profits. By the time he was in the 8th grade, he was running advertisements in national coin magazines. "I had to use my father's name because they wouldn't accept ads from a 14-year old," Ivy recalled. Even before he finished high school, he was already buying and selling coins at major collecting shows—some requiring extensive travel and overnight stays.

His passion for collectable coins never waned. His fledgling coin business was growing rapidly and he continued to buy and sell even while pursuing a law degree in college. By the time he was a junior, he was making $40,000 per year selling coins. Soon, he gave up the promise of practicing law and opened an office in Dallas for the purpose of selling coins. "The office was only 15 feet by 10 feet, but I was on the 16th floor of a downtown high rise, and I felt like I had really made it." In 1971, he had his first million-dollar year. Within 9 years, the business grew to become the second largest coin company in the United States with more than 80 employees and grossing over $70 million. But, the late-1970s also brought recession, and Ivy's coin business was hit hard. "I had to make some tough decisions and take some drastic actions," Ivy said. "We cut expenses by 50 percent and I had to let go of half my staff." It was a tough period of time for Ivy, but he persevered and by 1982 had once again turned the company around. A year later, he merged with his biggest competitor and took on the name Heritage Auction Galleries.

As Ivy's business ebbed and flowed with the nation's economy, a significant development began to take shape in the mid-1990s that would have a profound effect on Heritage even to this day. The Internet was just catching on and Ivy decided to learn as much as he could about it and how it could impact his business. "We decided to be an early adapter," Ivy said. "We had always been at the forefront of our business from an innovation standpoint and this was an easy decision for us." At this point, Heritage transitioned from a mail-order company to an Internet auction site. "Internet bidding propelled us to the number one spot," he added. "And soon we had almost 100,000 registered users." Simultaneously, the number of collectors was growing. The Internet helped foster a collecting craze because information was readily available and online bidding sped up the process of making a purchase (prior to this, collectors sent their bids and orders through the mail).

With the success of Internet coin auctions, other collectibles soon followed. Comic books, rare manuscripts, and more were being offered by Heritage. Today, Heritage has 29 different collecting categories and well over half a million registered bidders. Its Web site, ha.com, receives more than 30,000 unique visitors every day. Taking care of all these activities are 400 people employed in 5 different countries. According to Ivy, "Our goal is to become the number one auction company in the world. We also hope to reach the $1 billion mark in sales in the next couple of years."

QUESTIONS

1. What are the risks of managing a business like Heritage Auction Galleries?

2. How would you evaluate Steve Ivy's opportunity identification and opportunity exploitation?

3. Think about a hobby you enjoy. Can you identify an entrepreneurial opportunity associated with your hobby?

Endnotes

1. This challenge case was based on Ed Welles, "Maggie Overfelt," *Fortune Small Business* 12, no. 7 (September 2002): 24–32; "Inside the Googleplex," *The Economist,* September, 1, 2007, 53.

2. Scott Shane and S. Venkataraman, "The Promise of Entrepreneurship as a Field of Research," *Journal of Management* 25, no. 1 (2000): 217–226.

3. *Webster's College Dictionary* (New York: Random House, 1996).

4. Scott Shane, "Prior Knowledge and the Discovery of Entrepreneurial Opportunities," *Organization Science* 11, no 4 (2000): 448–469. See also, J.C. Short, D. J. Ketchen, J. R., C. L. Shook, & R. D. Ireland, "The Concept of 'Opportunity' in Entrepreneurship Research: Past Accomplishments and Future Challenges," *Journal of Management* 36 (2010): 40–65.

5. Robert Fairlie, "Kaufman Index of Entrepreneurial Activity," *Ewing Marion Kauffman Foundation* (2005).

6. Scott Shane and S. Venkataraman, "The Promise of Entrepreneurship as a Field of Research," *Journal of Management* 25, no. 1(2000): 217–226.

7. Matt Hayward, Dean Shepherd, and Dale Griffin, "A Hubris Theory of Entrepreneurship," *Management Science* 52, no. 2 (2006): 160–172.

8. A. C. Cooper and C. M. Daily, "Entrepreneurial Teams," in D. L. Sexton and R. W. Smilor (Eds.), *Entrepreneurship* (Chicago: Upstart Publishing Company, 2000), 127–150.

9. G. N. Chandler and S. H. Hanks, "An Examination of the Substitutability of the Founds' Human and Financial Capital in Emerging Business Ventures," *Journal of Business Venturing* 13 (1998): 353–369.

10. D. Ucbasaran, A. Lockett, M. Wright, and P. Westhead, "Entrepreneurial Founder Teams: Factors Associated with Member Entry and Exit," *Entrepreneurship Theory & Practice* (2003): 107–128.

11. C. M. Beckman, M. D. Burton, and C. O'Reilly, "Early Teams: The Impact of Team Demography on VC Financing and Going Public," *Journal of Business Venturing* 22 (2007): 147–173.

12. This discussion is based on J. Schumpeter, *Capitalism, Socialism, and Democracy* (New York: Harper & Row, 1934).

13. Joanne Silberner and Renee Montagne, "Coronary Stent Procedures Very Common," National Public Radio, transcript, February 12, 2010, http://www.nrp.org; A. Weintraub, "Heart Trouble," *BusinessWeek*, October 29, 2007, 54.

14. Jonathan Eckhardt and Scott Shane, "Opportunities and Entrepreneurship," *Journal of Management* 29, no. 3 (2003): 333–349.

15. Scott Shane, "Prior Knowledge and the Discovery of Entrepreneurial Opportunities," *Organization Science* 11, no 4 (2000): 448–469; S. Venkataraman, "The Distinctive Domain of Entrepreneurship Research: An Editor's Perspective," in J. Katz and R. Brockhaus (Eds.), *Advances in Entrepreneurship, Firm Emergence, and Growth* (Greenwich, CT: JAI Press, 1999).

16. Alexander Ardichvili, Richard Cardozo, and Sourav Ray, "A Theory of Entrepreneurial Identification and Development," *Journal of Business Venturing* 18 (2003): 105–123.

17. David E. Gumpert, "An Amish Entrepreneur's Old-Fashioned Approach," *BusinessWeek,* April 20, 2010, http://www.businessweek.com.

18. Alexander Ardichvili, Richard Cardozo, and Sourav Ray, "A Theory of Entrepreneurial Identification and Development," *Journal of Business Venturing* 18 (2003): 105–123; Scott Shane and S. Venkataraman, "The Promise of Entrepreneurship as a Field of Research," *Journal of Management* 25, no. 1 (2000): 217–226.

19. G. Hills, G.T. Lumpkin, and R. P. Singh, "Opportunity Recognition: Perceptions and Behaviors of Entrepreneurs," *Frontiers of Entrepreneurship Research* (Wellesley, MA: Babson College, 1997), 203–218. For a more detailed discussion of opportunity recognition, see J. Pierre-Andre and I. P. Vaghely, "Are opportunities recognized or constructed?: An information perspective on entrepreneurial opportunity identification," *Journal of Business Venturing* 25, no. 1 (2010): 73–86.

20. Alexander Ardichvili, Richard Cardozo, & Sourav Ray, "A Theory of Entrepreneurial Identification and Development," *Journal of Business Venturing* 18 (2003): 105–123.

21. Scott Shane, "Selling University Technology: Patterns from MIT," *Management Science* 48, no. 1 (2002): 122–137.

22. Andrew Corbett, "Experiential Learning Within the Process of Opportunity Identification and Exploitation," *Entrepreneurship Theory & Practice* (2005): 473–491.

23. M. Csikszentmihalyi, *Creativity* (New York: HarperCollins, 1996).

24. For more information on feasibility analysis, see R. G. Wyckham and W. C. Wedley, "Factors Related to Venture Feasibility Analysis and Business Plan Preparation," *Journal of Small Business Management* 28 (1990): 48–59.

25. This section based on H. T. Keh, M. D. Foo, and B. C. Lim, "Opportunity Evaluation Under Risky Conditions: The Cognitive Processes of Entrepreneurs," *Entrepreneurship Theory & Practice* (2002): 125–148.

26. For an exception, see L. W. Busenitz and J. B. Barney, "Differences between Entrepreneurs and Managers in Large Organizations: Biases and Heuristics in Strategic Decision Making," *Journal of Business Venturing* 12, no. 1 (1997): 9–30.

27. E. J. Langer, "The Illusion of Control," *Journal of Personality and Social Psychology* 32, no. 2 (1975): 311–328.

28. Clark G. Gilbert and Matthew J. Eyring, "Beating the Odds When You Launch a New Venture," *Harvard Business Review,* May 2010, http://hbr.org.

29. Young Rok Choi and Dean Shepherd, "Entrepreneurs' Decisions to Exploit Opportunities," *Journal of Management* 30, no. 3 (2004): 377–395.

30. Kara Ohngren, "Business Spotlight: Advantage Fitness Products," *Entrepreneur,* February 26, 2010, http://blog.entrepreneur.com.

31. This discussion is based on Young Rok Choi and Dean Shepherd, "Entrepreneurs' Decisions to Exploit Opportunities," *Journal of Management* 30, no. 3 (2004): 377–395.

32. For a review of top management teams, see S.T. Certo, R. H. Lester, C. M. Dalton, and D. R. Dalton, "Top Management Team Demographics, Strategy, and Financial Performance: A Meta-Analytic Review," *Journal of Management Studies* 43 (2003): 813–839.

33. Stephen G. Morrissette, "A Profile of Angel Investors," *Journal of Private Equity* 10, no. 3 (2007): 52–66.

34. R. J. Gaston, *Finding Private Venture Capital for Your Firm: A Complete Guide* (New York: John Wiley, 1989).

35. "Finding Venture Capital or Angel Investors," *About.com* Small Business Information, November 9, 2009, http://sbinformation.about.com; University of New Hampshire Center for Venture Research, "Angel Investor Market Declines in First Half of 2009," press release, October 27, 2009, http://wsbe.unh.edu.

36. PriceWaterhouseCoopers/National Venture Capital Association, "Total U.S. Investments by Year Q1 1995 - Q1 2010," April 16, 2010, http://www.nvca.org.

37. Stephen G. Morrissette, "A Profile of Angel Investors," *Journal of Private Equity* 10, no. 3 (2007): 52–66.

38. William Kerr, "Venture Financing and Entrepreneurial Success," *Harvard Business Review,* May 12, 2010, http://blogs.hbr.org. For an interesting discussion on what entrepreneurs must do to build credibility with investors in the absence of a track record of past accomplishments, see Quy Huy and Christoph Zott, "Trust Me," *MIT Sloan Management Review,* November 30, 2009, http://sloanreview.mit.edu.

39. P. Sharma and J. J. Chrisman. "Toward a Reconciliation of the Definitional Issues in the Field of Corporate Entrepreneurship," *Entrepreneurship Theory & Practice* 23, no. 3 (1999): 11–27.

40. R. C. Wolcott and M. J. Lippitz, "The Four Models of Corporate Entrepreneurship," *MIT Sloan Management Review* (2007): 75–82.

41. R. C. Wolcott and M. J. Lippitz, "The Four Models of Corporate Entrepreneurship," *MIT Sloan Management Review* (2007): 75–82.

42. The discussion of these forms of corporate entrepreneurship are based on J. G. Covin and M. P. Miles, "Corporate Entrepreneurship and the Pursuit of Competitive Advantage,"

Entrepreneurship Theory & Practice 23, no. 3 (1999): 47–63; G. D. Dess, R. D. Ireland, S. A Zahra, S. W. Floyd, J. J Janney, and P. J. Lane, "Emerging Issues in Corporate Entrepreneurship," *Journal of Management* 29, no. 3 (2003): 351–378.

43. M. Troy, "Wal-Mart Tries on Fashionable New Look," *DSN Retailing Today* 45, no. 7 (April 10, 2006): 3–4.

44. Claran Heavey, Zeki Simsek, Frank Roche, and Aidan Kelly, "Decision Comprehensiveness and Corporate Entrepreneurship: The Moderating Role of Managerial Uncertainty Preferences and Environmental Dynamism," *Journal of Management Studies* 46, no. 8 (August 2009): 1289–1314.

45. J. Austin, H. Stevenson, and J. Wei-Skillern, "Social and Commercial Entrepreneurship: Same, Different, or Both?" *Entrepreneurship Theory & Practice* (2006): 1–22.

46. Ibid.

47. Company Web site, "Professor Yunus Receives Presidential Medal of Freedom," http://www.grameen-info.org, accessed May 5, 2010.

48. A. M. Peredo and M. McLean, "Social Entrepreneurship: A Critical Review of the Concept," *Journal of World Business* 41 (2006): 56–65.

49. M. Sharir and M. Lerner, "Gauging the Success of Social Ventures Initiated by Individual Social Entrepreneurs," *Journal of World Business* 41 (2006): 6–20.

50. M. Sharir and M. Lerner, "Gauging the Success of Social Ventures Initiated by Individual Social Entrepreneurs," *Journal of World Business* 41 (2006): 6–20.

51. Company Web site, http://www.burgerking.com; and Jena McGregor, "Room & Board Plays Impossible to Get," *Business Week*, October 1, 2007, 80.

chapter

7

Principles of Planning

Target Skill

planning skill: the ability to take action to determine the objectives of the organization as well as what is necessary to accomplish these objectives

objectives

To help build my *planning skill,* when studying this chapter, I will attempt to acquire:

1. A definition of planning and an understanding of the purposes of planning

2. Insights into how the major steps of the planning process are related

3. An understanding of the relationship between planning and organizational objectives

4. A knowledge of the areas in which managers should set organizational objectives

5. An appreciation for the potential of a management-by-objectives (MBO) program

6. A knowledge of how the chief executive relates to the planning process

7. An understanding of the qualifications and duties of planners and how planners can be evaluated

CHALLENGE CASE

QUALITY BICYCLE PRODUCTS PLANS FOR THE FUTURE

BLOOMINGTON, MINN.-BASED QUALITY BICYCLE Products (QBP) was riding high. A leading distributor for over 5,000 independent bicycle dealers across the United States, QBP supplies bicycles, bicycle parts and accessories, and even apparel. Its family of bicycle brands includes All City, Civia, Salsa Cycles, and Surly. In addition, QBP is the exclusive U.S. distributor of Ridley, the Belgian manufacturer of road, mountain, and cyclocross bikes. It offers a comprehensive array of products and services, including a 1,700-page catalog, an online ordering system, merchandising programs for retail stores, a custom-wheel service, and a program for building specialty bikes.

QBP's business in the Southwest and Pacific Northwest was growing rapidly. Senior leadership saw that an expansion strategy was a critical element of QBP's business planning. In considering locations for that expansion, the company soon recognized that Ogden, Utah would represent an ideal location for its next facility.

With a population of more than 82,000, Ogden, Utah is a popular destination for sports enthusiasts and anyone else with a passion for the great outdoors. Located a short drive from Salt Lake City, the northwestern Utah city serves as a gateway to several ski resorts. Besides skiing and snowboarding, Ogden offers a full array of outdoor pleasures ranging from camping, hiking, and biking to horseback riding and golf.

Building its next facility—an 85,000-square-foot warehouse—in Ogden, would allow QBP to offer enhanced customer service in the form of speedy ground-based shipping to customers in the western United States. While building the warehouse, QBP leased building space nearby and engaged about 50 workers to run the business. After the warehouse is completed, the company plans to double the size of its staff. QBP offered a generous relocation package to those considering a move to Ogden and made a commitment to Ogden's city government to pay 125 percent of the county's average wage.

Ogden's dedication to the environment struck a chord with QBP, whose commitment to sustainability played a prominent role in the company's decision to build its warehouse according to standards set by Leadership in Energy and Environmental Design (LEED). The design of the new warehouse makes optimal use of such environmental elements as storm runoff, drought-resistant native plantings, and natural light. Other features include innovative wastewater technologies, high-efficiency appliances, and energy generation from a solar panel array.

QBP president Steve Flagg said the company chose Ogden because of the wide variety of recreational opportunities it offered. "The city attracted us with its core group of recreational industries and its strong commitment to bikes for commuting and

■ *Quality Bicycle Products operates a spacious, climate-controlled warehouse that boasts 36-foot-high ceilings and 27,000 types of parts, such as the sprocket shown here.*

recreation. We're really excited about getting to know the people of Ogden and being an active member of the community."

Locating the new facility in Ogden required a great deal of planning for QBP's top managers.

Over the next several years, these managers will learn whether the plans in Ogden will reach the organization's objectives.[1]

EXPLORING YOUR MANAGEMENT SKILL

You can explore your level of planning skill **before** studying the chapter by completing the exercise "Exploring Your Management Skill: Part 1" on page 174 and **after** studying this chapter by completing the exercise "Exploring Your Management Skill: Part 2" on page 175.

THE PLANNING CHALLENGE

The Challenge Case focuses on events at Quality Bicycle Products (QBP). The case ends with the implication that sound planning is necessary to successfully resolve the issues associated with managing the ongoing growth of the business. Material in this chapter will help managers like those at QBP understand why planning is so important not only for ensuring future successful business growth but for carrying out any other organizational activity. The fundamentals of planning are described in this chapter. More specifically, this chapter (1) outlines the general characteristics of planning, (2) discusses steps in the planning process, (3) describes the planning subsystem, (4) elaborates on the relationship between organizational objectives and planning, (5) discusses the relationship between planning and the chief executive, and (6) summarizes the qualifications of planners and explains how planners can be evaluated.

GENERAL CHARACTERISTICS OF PLANNING

The first part of this chapter is a general introduction to planning. The sections in this part discuss the following topics:

1. Definition of planning
2. Purposes of planning
3. Advantages and potential disadvantages of planning
4. Primacy of planning

Defining Planning

Planning is the process of determining how the organization can get where it wants to go, and what it will do to accomplish its objectives. In more formal terms, planning is "the systematic development of action programs aimed at reaching agreed-upon business objectives by the process of analyzing, evaluating, and selecting among the opportunities which are foreseen."[2]

Planning is a critical management activity regardless of the type of organization being managed. Modern managers face the challenge of sound planning in small and relatively simple organizations as well as in large, more complex ones, and in nonprofit organizations such as libraries as well as in for-profit organizations such as General Motors.[3]

Purposes of Planning

Over the years, management writers have presented several different purposes of planning. For example, a classic article by C. W. Roney indicates that organizational planning has two purposes: protective and affirmative. The protective purpose of planning is to minimize risk by reducing the uncertainties surrounding business conditions and clarifying the consequences of related management actions. The affirmative purpose is to increase the degree of organizational success.[4]

W hole Foods Market, a leading provider of natural and organic foods, relies on affirmative purpose in its planning. The company uses planning to ensure success as measured by the systematic opening of new stores. Currently, Whole Foods has more than 270 stores in the United States, Canada, and the United Kingdom. Whole Foods' CEO, John Mackey, believes that increased company success is not an accident, but a direct result of careful planning.[5]

how managers do it

Affirmative Planning
at Whole Foods Market

Another purpose of planning is to establish a coordinated effort within the organization. Where planning is absent, coordination and organizational efficiency are also often absent. Still another purpose of planning is to ensure integration among an organization's various business units, otherwise managers of these units might seek to maximize their own objectives.[6] ■

The fundamental purpose of planning, however, is to help the organization reach its objectives. As Koontz and O'Donnell put it, the primary purpose of planning is "to facilitate the accomplishment of enterprise and objectives."[7] All other purposes of planning are spin-offs of this fundamental purpose.

Planning: Advantages and Potential Disadvantages

A vigorous planning program produces many benefits. First, it helps managers be future-oriented. They are forced to look beyond their everyday problems to project what situations may confront them in the future.[8] Second, a sound planning program enhances decision coordination. No decision should be made today without some idea of how it will affect a decision that might have to be made tomorrow. The planning function pushes managers to coordinate their decisions. Third, planning emphasizes organizational objectives. Because organizational objectives are the starting points for planning, managers are continually reminded of exactly what their organization is trying to accomplish.[9]

Overall, planning is advantageous to an organization, particularly in the creation of new ventures.[10] According to an often-cited survey, as many as 65 percent of all newly started businesses are not around to celebrate a fifth anniversary. This high failure rate seems primarily a consequence of inadequate planning. Successful businesses have an established plan, a formal statement that outlines the objectives the organization is attempting to achieve. Planning does not eliminate risk, of course, but it does help managers identify and deal with organizational problems before they cause havoc in a business.[11]

The downside is that if the planning function is not well executed, planning can have several disadvantages for the organization. For example, an overemphasized planning program can take up too much managerial time. Managers must strike an appropriate balance between time spent on planning and time spent on organizing, influencing, and controlling. If they don't, some activities that are extremely important to the success of the organization may be neglected.[12]

Overall, the advantages of planning definitely outweigh the disadvantages. Usually, the disadvantages of planning result from using the planning function incorrectly.

Primacy of Planning

Planning is the primary management function—the one that precedes and is the basis for the organizing, influencing, and controlling functions of managers. Only after managers have developed their plans can they determine how they want to structure their organization, place their people, and establish organizational controls. As discussed in Chapter 1, planning, organizing, influencing,

class discussion highlight

MODERN RESEARCH AND PLANNING SKILL

The Influence of Team Plans

A recent study by Mathieu and Schulze examined the influence of planning skills on performance in the team context. The study's authors used teams of business school students to better understand the influence of planning skills on team performance. Specifically, the teams all took part in a simulation that helped determine their grade in a course. In this particular simulation, each group represented a simulated firm's top management team. Team members occupied different functional roles (i.e., marketing, accounting, etc.), and the team collectively made decisions. Presumably, the better the decisions each team made, the better would be the team's performance in the simulation as compared to the other student teams.

Prior to the simulation, each team created a formal plan outlining the steps needed to ensure success in the simulation. The authors then examined the relationship between the quality of the pre-simulation plan and the group's performance in the simulation. The authors then attempted to find a relationship between the quality of the plan and performance in the simulation. Do you think the study's results suggest that quality of the plan helped in understanding team performance? Why? Assuming that you are correct, what guidance can this research give you about developing your planning skill?

Source: This exercise was based on J. E. Mathieu and W. Schulze, 2006, "The influence of team knowledge and formal plans on episodic team process—performance relationships," *Academy of Management Journal* 3, 605–619.

and controlling are interrelated. Planning is the foundation function and the first one to be performed. Organizing, influencing, and controlling are all based on the results of planning. Figure 7.1 shows this interrelationship.

STEPS IN THE PLANNING PROCESS

The planning process consists of the following six steps. It is important to note, though, that the planning process is dynamic; in other words, effective planners will continuously revisit the planning process.

1. **State organizational objectives**—Because planning focuses on how the management system will reach organizational objectives, a clear statement of those objectives is necessary before planning can begin. Often planners examine important elements of the environment of their organizations, such as the overall economy or competitors, when forming objectives. In essence, objectives stipulate those areas in which organizational planning must occur.[13]

FIGURE 7.1

Planning as the foundation for organizing, influencing, and controlling

2. **List alternative ways of reaching objectives**—Once organizational objectives have been clearly stated, a manager should list as many available alternatives as possible for reaching those objectives.

3. **Develop premises on which to base each alternative**—To a large extent, the feasibility of using any one alternative to reach organizational objectives is determined by the premises, or assumptions, on which the alternative is based. For example, two alternatives a manager could generate to reach the organizational objective of increasing profit might be to (a) increase the sale of products presently being produced, or (b) produce and sell a completely new product. Alternative (a) is based on the premise that the organization can gain a larger share of the existing market. Alternative (b) is based on the premise that a new product would capture a significant portion of a new market. A manager should list all of the premises for each alternative.

4. **Choose the best alternative for reaching objectives**—An evaluation of alternatives must include an evaluation of the premises on which the alternatives are based. A manager usually finds that some premises are unreasonable and can therefore be excluded from further consideration. This elimination process helps the manager determine which alternative would best accomplish organizational objectives. The decision making required for this step is discussed more fully in Chapter 8.

5. **Develop plans to pursue the chosen alternative**—After an alternative has been chosen, a manager begins to develop strategic (long-range) and tactical (short-range) plans.[14] More information about strategic and tactical planning is presented in Chapters 9 and 10.

6. **Put the plans into action**—Once plans that furnish the organization with both long-range and short-range direction have been developed, they must be implemented. Obviously, the organization cannot directly benefit from the planning process until this step is performed. Figure 7.2 shows the sequencing of the six steps of the planning process.

FIGURE 7.2
Elements of the planning process

arget Corporation is an example of a company that has made charitable giving a significant element in its strategic plan. Since its founding in 1962, Target has allocated 5 percent of company revenues—more than $3 million a week—to programs that serve the communities in which it operates. Consistent with its concern for the health and safety of its communities, Target earmarked $50,000 to aid the National Wildlife Foundation in cleanup efforts following the explosion of the Deepwater Horizon oil rig in the Gulf of Mexico.[15] ■

THE PLANNING SUBSYSTEM

Once managers thoroughly understand the basics of planning, they can take steps to implement the planning process in their organization. Implementation is the key to a successful planning process. Even though managers might be experts on facts related to planning and the planning process, if they cannot transform this understanding into appropriate action, they will not be able to generate useful organizational plans.

One way to approach implementation is to view planning activities as an organizational subsystem. A subsystem is a system created as part of the overall management system. Figure 7.3 illustrates the relationship between the overall management system and a subsystem. Subsystems help managers organize the overall system and enhance its success.

Figure 7.4 presents the elements of the planning subsystem. The purpose of this subsystem is to increase the effectiveness of the overall management system by helping managers identify, guide, and direct planning activities within the overall system.[16]

Obviously, only a portion of organizational resources can be used as input in the planning subsystem. This input is allocated to the planning subsystem and transformed into output through the steps of the planning process.

FIGURE 7.3
Relationship between overall management system and subsystem

FIGURE 7.4 The planning subsystem

ORGANIZATIONAL OBJECTIVES: PLANNING'S FOUNDATION

The previous section made the point that managers start planning by stating or formulating organizational objectives. Only after they have a clear view of organizational objectives can they appropriately carry out subsequent steps of the planning process. Organizational objectives serve as the foundation on which all subsequent planning efforts are built. The following sections focus on organizational objectives, a critical component of the planning process:

1. Defining organizational objectives
2. Pinpointing areas in which organizational objectives should be established
3. Illustrating how managers work with organizational objectives
4. Discussing management by objectives, an approach to management based mainly on organizational objectives

Definition of Organizational Objectives

An **organizational objective** is a target toward which the open management system is directed. Organizational input, process, and output—topics discussed in Chapter 2—all exist to reach organizational objectives (see Figure 7.5). Properly developed organizational objectives reflect the purpose of the organization—that is, they flow naturally from the organization's mission. The **organizational purpose** is what the organization exists to do, given a particular group of customers and customer needs. Table 7.1 contains several statements of organizational purpose, or mission, as developed by actual companies.[17] If an organization is accomplishing its objectives, it is accomplishing its purpose and thereby justifying its reason for existence.

Organizations exist for various purposes and thus have various types of objectives. A hospital, for example, may have the primary purpose of providing high-quality medical services to the community. Therefore, its objectives are aimed at furnishing this assistance. The primary purpose of a business organization, in contrast, is usually to make a profit. The objectives of the business organization, therefore, concentrate on ensuring that a profit is made. Some companies, however, assume that if they focus on such organizational objectives as producing a quality product at a competitive price, profits will be inevitable.

Such is the case at Lincoln Electric Company. Although profitability is essential for all profit-oriented businesses, management at Lincoln Electric attracted attention when it seemed to diminish the role of profit in the company's organizational objectives:[18]

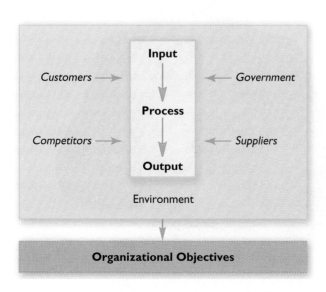

FIGURE 7.5
How an open management system operates to reach organizational objectives

TABLE 7.1	Examples of Statements of Organizational Purpose
Campbell Soup Company	Together we will build the world's most extraordinary food company.
Eli Lily & Company	We provide customers "Answers That Matter" through innovative medicines, information, and exceptional customer service that enable people to live longer, healthier, and more active lives.
Nike	To bring inspiration and innovation to every athlete in the world.
Charles Schwab	Our mission is to provide the most useful and ethical financial services in the world.
Wendy's	Our mission is to deliver superior quality products and services for our customers and communities through leadership, innovation, and partnerships.

> The goal of the organization must be this—to make a better and better product to be sold at a lower and lower price. Profit cannot be the goal. Profit must be a by-product. This is a state of mind and a philosophy. Actually, an organization doing this job as it can be done will make large profits which must be properly divided between user, worker, and stockholder. This takes ability and character.

In a 1956 article that has become a classic, John F. Mee suggested that organizational objectives for businesses can be summarized in three points:[19]

1. Profit is the motivating force for managers.
2. Service to customers by the provision of desired economic values (goods and services) justifies the existence of the business.
3. Managers have social responsibilities in accordance with the ethical and moral codes of the society in which the business operates.

Deciding on the objectives for an organization, then, is one of the most important actions managers take. Unrealistically high objectives are frustrating for employees, while objectives that

After suffering financial losses, Jeff Bezos, CEO of Amazon.com, earned a profit by improving customer service—with small changes such as anticipating demands and improving shipping.

are set too low do not push employees to maximize their potential. Managers should establish performance objectives that they know from experience are within reach for employees, but not within *easy* reach.[20]

Areas for Organizational Objectives

Peter F. Drucker, one of the most influential management writers of modern times, believed that the survival of a management system was endangered when managers emphasized only the profit objective because this single-objective emphasis encourages managers to take action that will make money today with little regard for how a profit will be made tomorrow.[21]

Managers should strive to develop and attain a variety of objectives in all areas where activity is critical to the operation and success of the management system. Following are the eight key areas in which Drucker advised managers to set management system objectives:

1. **Market standing**—Management should set objectives indicating where it would like to be in relation to its competitors.
2. **Innovation**—Management should set objectives outlining its commitment to the development of new methods of operation.
3. **Productivity**—Management should set objectives outlining the target levels of production.
4. **Physical and financial resources**—Management should set objectives regarding the use, acquisition, and maintenance of capital and monetary resources.
5. **Profitability**—Management should set objectives that specify the profit the company would like to generate.
6. **Managerial performance and development**—Management should set objectives that specify rates and levels of managerial productivity and growth.
7. **Worker performance and attitude**—Management should set objectives that specify rates of worker productivity as well as desirable attitudes for workers to possess.
8. **Public responsibility**—Management should set objectives that indicate the company's responsibilities to its customers and society and the extent to which the company intends to live up to those responsibilities.

According to Drucker, the first five goal areas relate to tangible, impersonal characteristics of organizational operation, and most managers would not dispute their designation as key areas. Designating the last three as key areas, however, could arouse some managerial opposition because these areas are more personal and subjective. Regardless of this potential opposition, an organization should have objectives in all eight areas to maximize its probability of success.

Increasing shareholder value represents an additional planning consideration for many publicly traded companies. For example, global oil producer ConocoPhillips recently unveiled plans to sell $10 billion in assets over a two-year period. Proceeds from the sale, the company said, would be used to pay down debt and increase shareholder value.[22]

Working with Organizational Objectives

Appropriate objectives are fundamental to the success of any organization. Theodore Levitt noted that some leading U.S. industries could be facing the same financial disaster as the railroads faced years earlier because their objectives were inappropriate for their organizations.[23]

Managers should approach the development, use, and modification of organizational objectives with the utmost seriousness. In general, an organization should set three types of objectives:[24]

1. **Short-term objectives**—targets to be achieved in one year or less
2. **Intermediate-term objectives**—targets to be achieved in one to five years
3. **Long-term objectives**—targets to be achieved in five to seven years

The necessity of predetermining appropriate organizational objectives has led to the development of a management guideline called the **principle of the objective**. This principle holds that before managers initiate any action, they should clearly determine, understand, and state organizational objectives.

Planning for the future often requires an organization to revisit its original objectives. For example, consider recent planning efforts at MySpace. The social networking site once led the industry but has recently experienced a decline in users. In charting a new path, MySpace management revisited the site's original business objectives and its key differentiator—self-expression—to make a comeback. As a result, MySpace dropped portal-like features such as horoscopes, job boards, and the weather and returned the emphasis to entertainment, with MySpace users sharing their thoughts and interests.[25] ■

Developing a Hierarchy of Objectives In practice, an organizational objective must be broken down into subobjectives so that individuals at different levels and sections of the organization know what they must do to help reach the overall organizational objective.[26] An organizational objective is attained only after the subobjectives have been reached.

The overall organizational objective and the subobjectives assigned to the various people or units of the organization are referred to as a hierarchy of objectives. Figure 7.6 presents a sample hierarchy of objectives for a medium-sized company.

Suboptimization is a condition wherein subobjectives are conflicting or not directly aimed at accomplishing the overall organizational objective. Suboptimization is possible within the company whose hierarchy of objectives is depicted in Figure 7.6 if the first subobjective for

FIGURE 7.6 Hierarchy of objectives for a medium-sized organization the finance and accounting department clashes with the second subobjective for the supervisors. This conflict would occur if supervisors needed new equipment to maintain production and the finance and accounting department couldn't approve the loan without the company's borrowing surpassing 50 percent of company assets. In such a situation, in which established subobjectives are aimed in different directions, a manager would have to choose which subobjective would better contribute to obtaining overall objectives and should therefore take precedence.

Controlling suboptimization in organizations is part of a manager's job. Managers can minimize suboptimization by developing a thorough understanding of how various parts of the organization relate to one another and by ensuring that subobjectives properly reflect these relations.

Guidelines for Establishing Quality Objectives

The quality of goal statements, like that of all humanly developed commodities, can vary drastically. Here are some general guidelines that managers can use to increase the quality of their objectives:[27]

1. **Let the people responsible for attaining the objectives have a voice in setting them**—Often the people responsible for attaining the objectives know their job situation better than managers do and can therefore help make the objectives more realistic. They will also be better motivated to achieve objectives that they have had a say in establishing. Work-related problems that these people face should be thoroughly considered when objectives are being developed.[28]
2. **State objectives as specifically as possible**—Precise statements minimize confusion and ensure that employees have explicit directions for what they should do.[29] Research shows that when objectives are not specific, the productivity of individuals attempting to reach those objectives tends to fluctuate significantly over time.
3. **Relate objectives to specific actions whenever necessary**—In this way, employees do not have to infer what they should do to accomplish their goals.
4. **Pinpoint expected results**—Employees should know exactly how managers will determine whether an objective has been reached.
5. **Set goals high enough that employees will have to strive to meet them, but not so high that employees give up trying to meet them**—Managers want employees to work hard but not to become frustrated.
6. **Specify when goals are expected to be achieved**—Employees must have a time frame for accomplishing their objectives. They then can pace themselves accordingly.
7. **Set objectives only in relation to other organizational objectives**—In this way, suboptimization can be kept to a minimum.
8. **State objectives clearly and simply**—The written or spoken word should not impede communicating a goal to organization members.

MANAGEMENT BY OBJECTIVES (MBO)

Some managers find organizational objectives such an important and fundamental part of management that they use a management approach based exclusively on them. This approach, called management by objectives (MBO), was popularized mainly through the writings of Peter Drucker. Although mostly discussed in the context of profit-oriented companies, MBO is also a valuable management tool for nonprofit organizations such as libraries and community clubs. The MBO strategy has three basic parts:[30]

1. All individuals within an organization are assigned a specialized set of objectives that they try to reach during a normal operating period. These objectives are mutually set and agreed upon by individuals and their managers.[31]
2. Performance reviews are conducted periodically to determine how close individuals are to attaining their objectives.
3. Rewards are given to individuals on the basis of how close they come to reaching their goals.

FIGURE 7.7
The MBO process

The MBO process consists of five steps (see Figure 7.7):

1. **Review organizational objectives**—The manager gains a clear understanding of the organization's overall objectives.
2. **Set worker objectives**—The manager and worker meet to agree on worker objectives to be reached by the end of the normal operating period.
3. **Monitor progress**—At intervals during the normal operating period, the manager and worker check to see whether the objectives are being reached.
4. **Evaluate performance**—At the end of the normal operating period, the worker's performance is judged by the extent to which the worker reached the objectives.
5. **Give rewards**—Rewards given to the worker are based on the extent to which the objectives were reached.

Factors Necessary for a Successful MBO Program

Certain key factors are essential to the success of an MBO program. First, top management must be committed to the MBO process and set appropriate objectives for the organization. Because all individual MBO goals will be based on these overall objectives, if the overall objectives are inappropriate, individual MBO objectives will also be inappropriate and related individual work activity will be nonproductive. Second, managers and subordinates together must develop and agree on each individual's goals. Both managers and subordinates must feel that the individual objectives are just and appropriate if each party is to seriously regard them as a guide for action. Third, employee performance should be conscientiously evaluated against established objectives. This evaluation helps determine whether the objectives are fair and if appropriate means are being used to attain them. Fourth, management must follow through on employee performance evaluations by rewarding employees accordingly.

If employees are to continue striving to reach their MBO program objectives, managers must reward those who do reach, or surpass, their objectives more than those whose performance falls short of their objectives. It goes without saying that such rewards must be given out fairly and honestly. Managers must be careful, though, not to conclude automatically that employees have produced at an acceptable level simply because they have reached their objectives. The objectives may have been set too low in the first place, and managers may have failed to recognize it at the time.[32]

MBO Programs: Advantages and Disadvantages

Experienced MBO managers claim that the MBO approach has two advantages. First, MBO programs continually emphasize what should be done in an organization to achieve organizational goals. Second, the MBO process secures employee commitment to attaining organizational goals. Because managers and subordinates have developed objectives together, both parties are sincerely interested in reaching those goals.

MBO managers also admit that MBO has certain disadvantages. One is that the development of objectives can be time consuming, leaving both managers and employees less time to do their actual work. Another is that the elaborate written goals, careful communication of goals, and detailed performance evaluations required in an MBO program increase the volume of paperwork in an organization.

On balance, however, most managers believe that MBO's advantages outweigh its disadvantages. Therefore, they find MBO programs beneficial.[33]

PLANNING AND THE CHIEF EXECUTIVE

More than two decades ago, Henry Mintzberg pointed out that the top managers—the chief executives—of organizations have many different roles to perform.[34] As organizational figureheads, they must represent their organizations in a variety of social, legal, and ceremonial situations. As leaders, they must ensure that organization members are properly guided toward achieving organizational goals. As liaisons, they must establish themselves as links between their organizations and factors outside their organizations. As monitors, they must assess organizational progress. As disturbance handlers, they must settle disputes between organization members. And as resource allocators, they must determine where resources should be placed to benefit their organizations best.[35]

Final Responsibility

In addition to these many varied roles, chief executives have the final responsibility for organizational planning. As the scope of planning broadens to include a larger portion of the management system, it becomes increasingly important for chief executives to get involved in the planning process.

As planners, chief executives seek answers to the following broad questions:[36]

1. In what direction should the organization be going?
2. In what direction is the organization going now?
3. Should something be done to change this direction?
4. Is the organization continuing in an appropriate direction?

Keeping informed about social, political, and scientific trends is of utmost importance in helping chief executives answer these questions.

Planning Assistance

Given the necessity to participate in organizational planning while performing other time-consuming roles, more and more top managers have established the position of organization planner to obtain the planning assistance they require. Just as managers can ask others for help and advice in making decisions, so can they involve others in formulating organizational plans.[37]

The chief executive of a substantial organization almost certainly needs planning assistance.[38] The remainder of this chapter assumes that the organization planner is an individual who is not the chief executive of the organization, but rather a manager inside the organization who is responsible for assisting the chief executive on organizational planning issues.[39] Where the planner and the chief executive are the same person, however, the following discussion of the planner can, with slight modifications, be applied to the chief executive.

THE PLANNER

The planner is probably the most important input in the planning subsystem.[40] This individual combines all other inputs and influences the subsystem process so that its output is effective organizational plans. The planner is responsible not only for developing plans but also for advising management on what actions should be taken to implement those plans. Regardless of who

Richard Branson, CEO and founder of the innovative Virgin Atlantic Airways, has continued to expand in new business directions. While some planners have their hands full managing one type of business, Branson has achieved success in widely different business ventures due to his superb planning skills.

actually does the planning or what organization the planning is being done in, the qualifications, duties, and evaluations of the planner are all important considerations for an effective planning subsystem.

Qualifications of Planners

Planners should have four primary qualifications:

- First, they should have considerable practical experience within their organization. Preferably, they should have been executives in one or more of the organization's major departments. This experience will help them develop plans that are both practical and tailor-made for the organization.

- Second, planners should be capable of replacing any narrow view of the organization they may have acquired while holding other organizational positions with an understanding of the organization as a whole. They must know how all parts of the organization function and inter-relate. In other words, they must possess an abundance of the conceptual skills mentioned in Chapter 1.

- Third, planners should have some knowledge of and interest in the social, political, technical, and economic trends that could affect the future of the organization. They must be skillful in defining those trends and possess the expertise to determine how the organization should react to the trends to maximize its success. This qualification cannot be overemphasized.[41]

- The fourth and last qualification for planners is that they be able to work well with others. Their position will inevitably require them to work closely with several key members of the organization, so it is essential that they possess the personal characteristics necessary to collaborate and advise effectively. The ability to communicate clearly, both orally and in writing, is one of the most important of these characteristics.[42]

Evaluation of Planners

Planners, like all other organization members, should be evaluated according to the contribution they make toward helping the organization achieve its objectives.[43] The quality and appropriateness of the planning system and the plans that the planner develops for the organization are the primary considerations in this evaluation. Because the organizing, influencing, and controlling functions of managers all vitally depend on the fundamental planning function, an accurate evaluation of the planner is critically important to the organization.

Objective Indicators Although the assessment of planners is necessarily somewhat subjective, several objective indicators can be used. The use of appropriate techniques is one objective indicator. A planner who uses appropriate techniques is probably doing an acceptable job. The degree of objectivity displayed by the planner is another indicator. The planner's advice should be largely based on a rational analysis of appropriate information.[44] The assessment of this indicator is not to say that planners should abandon subjective judgment altogether, only that their opinions should be based chiefly on specific and appropriate information.

Malik suggests that a planner is doing a reputable job if the following objective criteria are met:[45]

1. Organizational plan is in writing.
2. Plan is the result of all elements of the management team working together.
3. Plan defines present and possible future business of the organization.
4. Plan specifically mentions organizational objectives.
5. Plan identifies future opportunities and suggests how to take advantage of them.
6. Plan emphasizes both internal and external environments.
7. Plan describes the attainment of objectives in operational terms whenever possible.
8. Plan includes both long- and short-term recommendations.

These eight criteria furnish objective guidelines for evaluating the performance of planners. However, management's evaluation of planners should never be completely objective. Important subjective considerations include how well planners get along with key members of the organization, the amount of organizational loyalty they display, and their perceived potential.

CHALLENGE CASE SUMMARY

It seems apparent from facts in the introductory case that QBP managers must focus heavily on planning if the company's new strategy is to be successful. Such a process should help determine issues such as what types of new equipment must be purchased to implement the new plan, who maintains the equipment once purchased, and how to change the organization's culture to focus on the addition of a new location for the company's operations. This process should also focus on how to maintain the quality of QBP's service.

Because of the many related benefits of planning, QBP managers should make certain that the planning process is thorough and comprehensive, one particularly notable benefit of which is the probability of increased profits. To gain the benefits of planning, however, QBP managers must be careful that the planning function is well executed and not overemphasized.

QBP management should also keep in mind that planning is the primary management function. Thus managers should not begin to organize, influence, or control until planning for this new strategy is completed. Planning is the foundation management function on which all other management functions at QBP should be based.

Managers like those at QBP who are refocusing their strategies should use their planning process to produce a practical plan for the activities. The process of developing this plan should consist of six steps. It should begin with a statement of an organizational objective to successfully design the plan and end with guidelines for putting the new plans into action. In this case, the ultimate organizational objective involves refocusing the company to build on its historical strengths.

To implement a planning process, managers should view planning as a subsystem that is part of the process of the overall management system. Thus, they should use a portion of all the organizational resources available for the purpose of their planning. In this example, the output of this subsystem would be the actual plans to be used to deliver two-day ground shipping to customers in the Southwest and Pacific Northwest regions. Naturally, a comprehensive planning effort at QBP would focus on many other organizational areas such as obtaining needed funds and improving overall service delivery.

Planning at QBP, as at any other company, begins with a statement of organizational objectives, the targets at which the overall organization is aiming. These targets should be consistent with the purpose of QBP, the reason the company exists. Objectives for a company such as QBP normally include profit targets, service quality targets, and social responsibility targets. Other organizational objectives would normally focus on market standing, innovation, productivity, and worker performance and attitude. Overall objectives for a company such as QBP should be of three basic types: short-term objectives that are to be achieved in a year or less; intermediate objectives to be achieved in one to five years; and long-term objectives to be achieved in five to seven years. Additionally, QBP and companies like it would normally develop a hierarchy of objectives so that individuals at different levels of the organization know what they must do to help reach organizational targets.

Planning for QBP's entry into this new geography should emphasize how to implement activities to help reach various organizational targets. Overall, QBP's planning, as it pertains to its product lines, should focus on enhancing the accomplishment of its short-term, intermediate-term, and long-term objectives that exist throughout the company's hierarchy of objectives.

Planning activities at a company such as QBP tend to be more valuable the higher the quality of the organizational objectives. To increase the quality of objectives at QBP, managers can take steps that allow people responsible for attaining objectives to have a voice in setting them, that state objectives as clearly and simply as possible, and that pinpoint results expected when objectives are achieved.

Management at QBP might be so committed to managing via organizational targets that MBO becomes the primary management approach within the company. Such an approach would involve QBP management monitoring the progress workers are making in reaching established objectives and using rewards and punishments to hold workers accountable for actually reaching the objectives. An MBO program might be advantageous to QBP because it would continually emphasize what needs to be accomplished to reach organizational targets. On the other hand, an MBO program might be disadvantageous to QBP because the process itself can be time-consuming.

Technically, QBP's president is responsible for planning for the organization as a whole and for performing such related time-consuming functions as keeping abreast of internal and external trends that could affect the future of the company. Because planning requires so much time, and because QBP's president has many other responsibilities within the company, he might want to consider appointing a director of planning.

The director of planning at QBP would need certain qualities. Ideally, the planner should have some experience at the company, be able to see it as an entire organization, have some ability to gauge and react to major trends that probably will affect the company's future, and be able to work well with others. The planner must oversee the planning process, evaluate developed plans, and solve planning problems. An evaluation of the QBP organization planner would be based on both objective and subjective appraisals of his or her performance. Perhaps the first issue that a new company planner at QBP should address is the company's entry into Ogden, Utah.

MANAGEMENT SKILL ACTIVITIES

This section is specially designed to help you develop management skill. An individual's planning skill is based on an understanding of management concepts and the ability to apply those concepts in management situations. As a result, the following activities are designed both to heighten your understanding of principles of planning and to help you gain facility in applying these concepts in various management situations.

UNDERSTANDING PLANNING CONCEPTS

 To check your understanding and to practice using the concepts in this chapter, go to www.mymanagementlab.com and explore the material associated with Chapter 7.

Know Key Terms

Understanding the following key terms is critical to your understanding of chapter material. Define each of these terms. Refer to the page(s) referenced after a term to check your definition or to gain further insight regarding the term.

planning **160**
organizational objective **165**

organizational purpose **165**
suboptimization **168**

Know How Management Concepts Relate

This section is comprised of activities that will further sharpen your understanding of management concepts. Answer essay questions as completely as possible. Also, remember that many additional true/false and multiple choice questions appear online at MyManagementLab.com to help you further refine your understanding of management concepts.

1. Summarize the primary advantages and disadvantages regarding planning. In your opinion, what is the most prominent advantage of planning? What is the largest disadvantage of planning?

2. Describe the various stages involved in the planning process. Use an example to illustrate these stages.
3. Explain the characteristics of effective objectives. Relying on these characteristics, provide an example of an effective objective for a not-for-profit organization of your choice.
4. Describe the relationship between planning and the other general functions of management (organizing, controlling, and influencing). In your opinion, which of the four functions is most important?
5. Describe the concept of a hierarchy of objectives. Why is developing such a hierarchy important for managers?

DEVELOPING MANAGEMENT SKILLS

Learning activities in this section are aimed at helping you to develop diversity skill. Learning activities include Exploring Your Management Skill: Parts 1 and 2, Your Management Skill Portfolio, Experiential Exercises, Cases, and a VideoNet Exercise.

Exploring Your Management Skill: Part 1

Before studying this chapter, respond to the following questions regarding the type of advice that you would give to QBP president Steve Flagg. Then address the concerning planning challenges that he presently faces within the company. You are not expected to be a planning expert at this point. Answering the questions now can help you focus on important points when you study the chapter. Also, answering the questions again after you study the chapter will give you an idea of how much you have learned.

Record your answers here or online at MyManagementLab.com. Completing the questions at MyManagementLab.com will allow you to get feedback about your answers automatically. If you answer the questions in the book, look up answers in the Exploring Your Management Skill section at the end of the book.

FOR EACH STATEMENT CIRCLE:
• "Y" if you would give the advice to Steve Flagg.
• "N" if you would NOT give the advice to Steve Flagg.
• "NI" if you have no idea whether you would give the advice to Steve Flagg.

Mr. Flagg, in meeting your planning challenges at QBP, you should…

Before   After
Study   Study

1. understand that there are only advantages—and no disadvantages—to planning at QBP.
   Y, N, NI

2. encourage QBP's employees to spend more time organizing, influencing, and controlling as opposed to planning.
   Y, N, NI

3. establish broad and ambiguous objectives so it will be difficult to tell whether QBP reached the objectives.
   Y, N, NI

4. formulate both alternatives and premises when establishing plans for QBP.
   Y, N, NI

5. begin the planning process by establishing QBP's organizational objectives.
   Y, N, NI

6. focus more on long-term objectives than short-term or intermediate-term objectives.
   Y, N, NI

7. establish objectives that are related only to QBP's profitability rather than those related to areas such as innovation, productivity, and public responsibility.
   Y, N, NI

8. create objectives alone and resist the opinions of other employees in QBP.
   Y, N, NI

9. pinpoint expected results so that QBP employees will understand when an objective is or is not reached.
   Y, N, NI

10. form unreachable objectives, because higher goals always lead to higher performance.
    Y, N, NI

11. specify a timeline for achieving the objectives.
    Y, N, NI

12. realize the potential effectiveness of MBO programs for QBP, because MBO programs work only in for-profit organizations.
    Y, N, NI

13. understand the importance of giving rewards in improving the effectiveness of MBO programs.
    Y, N, NI

14. understand that as QBP's president, you are responsible for determining the overall direction of the firm.
    Y, N, NI

15. appreciate the fact that as QBP's central planner, no one will review your planning performance.
    Y, N, NI

Learning activities in this section are aimed at helping you develop planning skill. Learning activities include Exploring Your Management Skill: Part 2, Experiential Exercises, Cases, and a VideoNet Exercise.

Exploring Your Management Skill: Part 2

As you recall, you completed Exploring Your Management Skill before you started to study this chapter. Your responses gave you an idea of how much you initially knew about planning and helped you focus on important points as you studied the chapter. Answer the Exploring Your Management Skill questions again now and compare your score to the first time you took it. This comparison will give you an idea of how much you learned from studying this chapter and pinpoint areas for further clarification before you start studying the next chapter. Record your answers within the text or online at MyManagementLab.com. Completing the survey at MyManagementLab.com will allow you to grade and compare your test scores automatically. If you complete the test in the book, look up answers in the Exploring Your Management Skill section at the end of the book.

Your Management Skills Portfolio

Your Management Learning Portfolio is a collection of activities especially designed to demonstrate your management knowledge and skill. By completing these activities at MyManagement Lab.com, you will be able to print, complete with cover sheet, as many activities as you choose. Be sure to save your work. Taking your printed portfolio to an employment interview could be helpful in obtaining a job.

The portfolio activity for this chapter is Developing Your Planning Skills. Read the following highlight about Darden Restaurants, and answer the questions that follow.

Darden Restaurants Inc., which operates chains such as Red Lobster, Olive Garden, and Bahama Breeze, is one of the largest casual dining restaurant companies in the world. Darden is exploring potential opportunities for growth, and you have been hired to develop a new restaurant concept for the company. Executives at Darden are particularly interested in concepts that are consistent with the company's mission, which is "To nourish and delight everyone we serve." Darden has committed the funds necessary to test your new concept restaurant in an area around your school. If the new concept works well in your area, Darden may seek to expand the concept in a larger geographical area.

Your mission involves establishing a plan to introduce this new concept restaurant. After deciding on your new concept restaurant, Darden wants you to work through the first five steps of the planning process: (1) state organizational objectives; (2) list alternative ways of reaching objectives; (3) develop premises on which to base each alternative; (4) choose the best alternative for reaching objectives; and (5) develop plans to pursue the chosen alternative. In the space provided here, respond to the following inquiries regarding the first five steps of the planning process.

1. Briefly describe the most important characteristics of your new concept for Darden.

2. Develop three organizational objectives for your new restaurant.

3. Choose one of the three objectives to explore in more detail. List three alternative ways to reach this objective.

4. Develop premises to evaluate each of these three alternatives.

5. Based on these premises, choose the alternative that is most likely to reach the objective.

6. As you think about this alternative, list the significant steps needed to implement this alternative.

Experiential Exercises

1 Developing Objectives for the Don Cesar

Directions. Read the following scenario and then perform the listed activities. Your instructor may want you to perform the activities as an individual or within groups. Follow all of your instructor's directions carefully.

You have just been hired as the new assistant manager at the Don Cesar Beach Resort (www.doncesar.com) in St. Petersburg, Florida. This resort, which opened in 1928, has a storied history. Nonetheless, the manager of the resort has assigned you and your team the task of identifying new objectives for the resort. He thinks that your fresh perspective might help the organization thrive for the next 100 years. Lead your group by outlining five objectives for the resort. Then, use the "Guidelines for Establishing Quality Objectives" listed on page 169 to better understand the quality of the five objectives your team developed. Based on these guidelines, which objective was the best? Which objective was the worst? Why?

2 You and Your Career

Planning Skill and Your Career

The previous section discusses the role of objectives in the planning process. Understanding the importance of objectives will help you further develop your planning skill. As you think about your academic career thus far, describe the role of your own objectives in determining your course grades. Do you have objectives regarding your course grades? Now, think about your career in the future. Do you think employers will find your planning skills attractive? Thinking longer term, how do you think your planning skills will influence your career progression?

Videonet Exercise

Planning and the Control Process: Kaneva

Video Highlights

Kaneva is a start-up company that has built a virtual world to empower a community of customers to create their own realities. Despite the high-tech sheen, the company still must focus on raising revenue, group decision making, and its control process. Chief revenue officer Jeff Longoria describes how Kaneva monetizes its virtual world. Kaneva is an example of how even an up-to-date technology company depends on revenue to survive. Finally, Longoria describes the role of management by objectives (MBO) in the control process.

Discussion Questions

1. Why would a company ever give any of its product away for free?

2. How does management by objectives impact Kaneva's planning process? Describe why Kaneva's daily meeting is a stand-up meeting.

3. At the end of the video, CEO Chris Klaus says that Kaneva employees can spend 20 percent of their time on projects outside of the scope of the "roadmap." What does this mean? Do you approve or disapprove?

Internet Activity

Browse the Kaneva Web site at www.kaneva.com. Explore the site. Take a look at some of the press releases in the "Press Center" link. One of the articles describes Kaneva by stating "online games meet social networking." Do you think this statement accurately describes the Kaneva product? Why or why not? While some of Kaneva's services are free, others are offered at a premium price. Can you name some other examples of Web sites that offer some free usage and then sell premium services?

CASES

1 SOUND PLANNING AT QBP?

"Quality Bicycle Products Plans for the Future" (p. 159) was written to help you better understand the management concepts contained in this chapter. Answer the following discussion questions about the Challenge Case to better understand how principles of planning can be applied in a company like QBP.

1. What special challenges would QBP face in expanding its business by building a warehouse in Ogden, Utah? What steps would you take to meet these challenges?

2. Would you have the QBP president or an appointed planning executive do the planning for the new warehouse? Why?

3. List three criteria that you would use to evaluate the planning for the new QBP warehouse. Explain why you chose each criterion.

2 HSBC PLANS TO MAKE A DIFFERENCE

Read the case and answer the questions that follow. Studying this case will help you better understand how principles of planning can be applied in a company such as HSBC.

Founded as a small Hong Kong bank in 1865, HSBC Holdings has followed a series of growth plans to emerge today as one of the world's largest financial services firms. The London-based company serves 110 million customers through 9,500 offices in 79 countries, offering an extensive array of banking, investment, insurance, and credit services. Under a five-year strategic plan launched in 1998, HSBC enjoyed a number of outstanding financial accomplishments, including increasing corporate profits by 41 percent between 2002 and 2003. In 2002, the company also introduced a five-year plan to protect the environment by donating $50 million to conservation causes and lending 2,000 employees to work on ecological projects. Despite careful planning, however, some HSBC divisions weren't always able to overcome severe economic pressures or other adverse conditions to achieve the intended results throughout the five-year period. For example, the investment banking unit's performance was so disappointing in 2001 that management did not give bankers and analysts any bonuses that year.

Now Sir John Bond, HSBC's chairperson, is challenging corporate, division, and unit managers to set more ambitious objectives in line with a five-year "Managing for Growth" strategic plan initiated in 2003. This long-term plan builds on the foundation laid by the previous plan and establishes broad organizational priorities in key areas such as revenues and expenditures, customer service, shareholder return, competitive standing, productivity through teamwork, and corporate responsibility. In turn, these priorities guide objective-setting at all levels so managers can formulate and implement plans that will make a difference in the company's future, in its communities, and in the natural environment.

In their quest to secure the market leadership position that HSBC's mission envisions, Bond and his managers are applying each division's resources and strengths, which include sophisticated technology, human resources talent, customer knowledge, financial and risk management, and enduring business relationships. In the course of the previous strategic plan, corporate planners identified certain markets as especially promising for growth. Now they are coordinating divisional objectives and plans to make the most of profitable opportunities. For example, HSBC acquired or started banks as part of its lucrative expansion in the United States, Mexico, and France. Looking ahead, management is opening or buying more banks to serve consumers and business customers in these areas.

At the operational level, HSBC's country managers and branch managers are supporting corporate and divisional objectives by setting objectives for opening new accounts and other banking activities. HSBC Bank Malaysia's one-year objectives, as an example, are to issue 20 percent more credit cards and increase deposits by 20 percent. Similarly, the Hong Kong unit wants to expand its credit card base by 10 percent within a year—but "It's not just about competing in terms of the number of cards; profitability is more important," notes that unit's general manager. In Thailand, the local HSBC unit is targeting more affluent people in a short-term drive to open 300 new accounts within three months. And in the United States, the corporation applied for a national bank charter as one step in a long-term campaign to open dozens of new branches and bring in millions of dollars in deposits.

In addition, HSBC executives are developing measurement and reporting mechanisms so they can monitor the company's environmental impact and formulate appropriate long-and short-term objectives for greenhouse gas emissions, water consumption, energy consumption, and recycling. They are also examining interim results of HSBC's unprecedented $50 million environmental philanthropy project, designed to achieve objectives such as saving endangered plants, battling water pollution, preserving forests, and educating the public about the importance of conservation. Social responsibility objectives and plans are not easy to formulate or achieve, but the HSBC workforce is excited about the commitment. "The environment is something that people feel very strongly about, and the reality is that we can make some difference there because of our scale," says the HSBC manager in charge.

QUESTIONS

1. What are the arguments for and against HSBC managers making public their short-term and intermediate-term objectives, unit by unit or division by division?

2. Would you recommend that HSBC use the MBO process to reward investment bankers and analysts according to results, even though key factors influencing performance can't be precisely predicted or controlled? Explain.

3. Which stakeholders might be affected by HSBC's plan to invest $50 million in environmental conservation? Should the company continue this plan, regardless of short-term financial performance?

Endnotes

1. Company Web site, "QBP to Host Groundbreaking Ceremony for New Utah Distribution Center," April 13, 2010, http://www.qbp.com; "Distributors Choose Ogden; Bike Company Plans to Open Center in November," *Standard-Examiner*, March 3, 2010, http://www.standard.net; Ryan Shelton, "MN Firm Picks Ogden for Distribution Center," *The Enterprise*, November 9, 2009, http://www.slenterprise.com; Company Web site, "QBP Selects Site for New Distribution Center in Ogden, Utah," November 2, 2009, http://www.qbp.com; "Ogden Lures Warehouse for Bicycle Distributor," *Associated Press*, November 1, 2009, http://www.ksl.com.

2. Harry Jones, *Preparing Company Plans: A Workbook for Effective Corporate Planning* (New York: Wiley, 1974), 3; Richard G. Meloy, "Business Planning," *The CPA Journal* 63, no. 8 (March 1998): 74–75.

3. Robert G. Reed, "Five Challenges Multiple-Line Companies Face," *Market Facts* (January/February 1990): 5–6. For an article on minimizing risk, see "Prior Planning Is Key to Averting a Crisis," *Investor Relations Business*, July 23, 2001, 8.

4. C. W. Roney, "The Two Purposes of Business Planning," *Managerial Planning* (November/December 1976): 1–6; Linda C. Simmons, "Plan. Ready. Aim," *Mortgage Banking* 56, no. 5 (February 1996): 95–96. For an interesting account of the planning function in an international setting, see Gabriel Ogunmokun, "Planning: An Exploratory Investigation of Small Business Organizations in Australia," *International Journal of Management* 15, no. 1 (March 1998): 60–71.

5. Company Web site, http://www.wholefoodsmarket.com, accessed May 15, 2010; Wendy Zellner, "Moving Tofu into the Mainstream," *BusinessWeek*, May 25, 1992, 94.

6. Paula Jarzabkowski and Julia Balogun, "The Practice and Process of Delivering Integration through Strategic Planning," *Journal of Management Studies* 46, no. 8 (August 2009): 1255–1288.

7. Harold Koontz and Cyril O'Donnell, *Management: A Systems and Contingency Analysis of Management Functions* (New York: McGraw-Hill, 1976), 130.

8. For an interesting discussion on how the importance of planning relates to even day-to-day operations, see Teri Lammers, "The Custom-Made Day Planner," *Inc.* (February 1992): 61–62.

9. For other benefits of planning, see Scott Ransom, "Planning Is Vital New Skill for Physician Executives," *Physician Executive* 29 (2003): 59.

10. A study on the impact of business planning on new ventures is described in Andrew Burke, Stuart Fraser, and Francis J. Greene, "The Multiple Effects of Business Planning on New Venture Performance," *Journal of Management Studies* 47, no. 3 (May 2010): 391–415. For a discussion of how planning can yield the advantage of improved quality in organizations, see Z. T. Temtime, "The Moderating Impacts of Business Planning and Firm Size on Total Quality Management Practices," *The TQM Magazine* 15 (2003): 52; see also Anita Lee, "Early Planning for Hazards Bring Benefits to Biloxi," *Planning* 70 (2004): 51.

11. Kenneth R. Allen, "Creating and Executing a Business Plan," *American Agent & Broker* (July 1994): 20–21.

12. For a discussion of how improper planning might result in a competitive disadvantage, see Yolanda Sarason and Linda Tegarden, "The Erosion of the Competitive Advantage of Strategic Planning: A Configuration Theory and Resource-Based View," *Journal of Business and Management* 9 (2003): 1.

13. For a discussion of U.S. shortsightedness in planning, see Michael T. Jacobs, "A Cure for America's Corporate Short-Termism," *Planning Review* (January/February 1992): 4–9. For a discussion of the close relationship between objectives and planning, see "Mistakes to Avoid: From a Business Owner," *Business Owner* (September/October 1994): 11.

14. For an overview of strategic planning, see Bryan W. Barry, "A Beginner's Guide to Strategic Planning," *The Futurist* 32, no. 3 (April 1998): 33–36.

15. Company Web site, "Target Donates $50,000 to Support Oil-Spill Cleanup Efforts," May 7, 2010, http://pressroom.target.com.

16. For an example of a subsystem, see Sherry D. Ryan and David A. Harrison, "Considering Social Subsystem Costs and Benefits in Information Technology Investment Decisions: A View from the Field on Anticipated Payoffs," *Journal of Management Information Systems* 16, no. 4 (Spring 2000): 11–40.

17. For an excellent resource on mission statements, see Jeffrey Abrahams, *101 Mission Statements from Top Companies* (Berkeley, CA: Ten Speed Press, 2007).

18. James F. Lincoln, "Intelligent Selfishness and Manufacturing," *Bulletin* 434 (New York: Lincoln Electric Company).

19. John F. Mee, "Management Philosophy for Professional Executives," *Business Horizons* (December 1956): 7.

20. David J. Campbell and David M. Furrer, "Goal Setting and Competition as Determinants of Task Performance," *Journal of Organizational Behavior* 16, no. 4 (July 1995): 377–390.

21. Peter F. Drucker, *The Practice of Management* (New York: Harper & Bros., 1954), 62–65, 126–129. For an interesting discussion on objectives and innovation, see Barton G. Tretheway, "Everything New Is Old Again," *Marketing Management* 7, no. 1 (Spring 1998): 4–13. For a recent tribute to Drucker, see A. J. Vogo, "Drucker, of Course," *Across the Board* 37, no. 10 (November/December 2000): 1.

22. "ConocoPhillips to Shed Half of Lukoil Stake," *Forbes.com,* March 24, 2010, http://www.forbes.com.

23. Charles H. Granger, "The Hierarchy of Objectives," *Harvard Business Review* (May/June 1964): 64–74; Richard E. Kopelman, "Managing for Productivity: One-Third of the Job," *National Productivity Review* 17, no. 3 (Summer 1998): 1–2. Reprinted with the permission of American Management Association International. New York, NY. All rights reserved; see also Robert Kaplan and David Norton, "How Strategy Maps Frame an Organization's Objectives," *Financial Executive* 20 (2004): 40.

24. Geoffrey Moore, "To Succeed in the Long Term, Focus on the Middle Term," *Harvard Business Review* 85, no. 7/8 (2007): 84–91. For another excellent review underscoring the importance of time when forming objectives, see Piers Steel and Cornelius J. Konic, "Integrating Theories of Motivation," *The Academy of Management Review* 31, no. 4 (2006): 889–913.

25. Dawn C. Chmielewski and Jessica Guynn, "MySpace Looks to the Past for Its Future," *Los Angeles Times,* March 10, 2010, http://www.latimes.com.

26. See also Mike Deblieux, "The Challenge and Value of Documenting Performance," *HR Focus* (March 1994): 3. To better understand the role of setting objectives in compensation plans, see William J. Liccione, "Effective Goal Setting: A Prerequisite for Compensation Plans with Incentive Value," *Compensation & Benefits Management* 13, no. 1 (Winter 1997): 19–25.

27. Robert L. Mathis and John H. Jackson, *Personnel: Human Resource Management* (St. Paul, MN: West Publishing, 1985), 353–355.

28. Harry Levinson, "Management by Whose Objectives?" *Harvard Business Review* 81 (2003): 107.

29. For an interesting examination of goal specificity, see Gerard H. Seijts, Gary P. Latham, Kevin Tasa, and Brandon W. Latham, "Goal setting and goal orientation: An integration of two different literatures," *Academy of Management Journal* 47, no. 2 (2004): 227–239.

30. Robert Rodgers and John E. Hunter, "Impact of Management by Objectives on Organizational Productivity," *Journal of Applied Psychology* (1991): 322–335; Jerry L. Rostund, "Evaluating Management Objectives with the Quality Loss Function," *Quality Progress* (August 1989): 45–49; Peter Crutchley, "Management by Objectives," *Credit Management* (May 1994): 36–38; William J. Kretlow and Winford E. Holland, "Implementing Management by Objectives in Research Administration," *Journal of the Society of Research Administrators* (Summer 1988): 135–141.

31. MBO deals with objectives that are designed based on input from both managers and workers. Nonetheless, some workers may have some subconscious objectives that are not known to managers. For an interesting examination of such goals, see Alexander D. Stajkovic, Edwin A. Locke, and Eden S. Blair, "A First Examination of the Relationships Between Primed Subconscious Goals, Assigned Conscious Goals, and Task Performance," *Journal of Applied Psychology* 91, no. 5 (2006): 1172–1180.

32. Charles H. Ford, "Manage by Decisions, Not by Objectives," *Business Horizons* (February 1980): 17–18. For an interesting description of how firms in Sweden employ MBO, see Terry Ingham, "Management by Objectives—A Lesson in Commitment and Cooperation," *Managing Service Quality* 5, no. 6 (1995): 35–38.

33. For a different viewpoint on the management by objectives (MBO) approach, see Harry Levinson, "Management by Whose Objectives?" *Harvard Business Review* (Summer 2010): 28–38.

34. Henry Mintzberg, "A New Look at the Chief Executive's Job," *Organizational Dynamics* (Winter 1973): 20–40. For a recent interview with Mintzberg, see Stephen Bernhut, "In Conversation: Henry Mintzberg," *Ivey Business Journal* 65, no. 1 (September/October 2000): 18–23.

35. Another aspect of planning involves understanding who might become the firm's next CEO, a process that is known as CEO succession planning. For an interesting article examining CEO succession planning in entrepreneurial firms, see James P. Marshall, Ritch Sorenson, Keith Brigham, Elizabeth Wieling, Alan Reifman, and Richard S. Wampler, "The paradox for the family firm CEO: Owner age relationship to succession–related processes and plans," *Journal of Business Venturing* 21, no. 3 (2006): 348–368.

36. For similar questions focusing on strategic planning, see Hans Hinterhuber and Wolfgang Popp, "Are You a Strategist or Just a Manager?" *Harvard Business Review* (January/February 1992): 105–113. For an example of how a CEO plans organizational change, see Peter Spiegel, "Old Dog, New Tricks?" *Forbes,* June 1, 1998, 47.

37. James M. Hardy, *Corporate Planning for Nonprofit Organizations* (New York: Association Press, 1972), 37. For an interesting article that describes how CEOs gain assistance from their boards of directors, see David Ravasi and Alessandro Zattoni, "Exploring the Political Side of Board Involvement in Strategy: A Study of Mixed–Ownership Institutions," *Journal of Management Studies* 43, no. 8 (2006): 1671–1702.

38. For a better understanding of how chief executives interact with other members of a top management team, see Stephen A. Miles and Michael D. Watkins, "The Leadership Team: Complementary Strengths or Conflicting Agendas?" *Harvard Business Review* 85, no. 4 (2007): 90–98.

39. For a discussion of outside consultants who develop plans for business clients, see Donald F. Kuratko and Arnold Cirtin, "Developing a Business Plan for Your Clients," *National Public Accountant* (January 1990): 24–27.

40. In many organizations, individuals holding the title of either *president* or *chief operating officer (COO)* also have planning responsibilities. For an intriguing study examining the role of these individuals in the planning process, see Yan Zhang, "The presence of a separate COO/president and its impact on strategic change and CEO dismissal," *Strategic Management Journal* 27, no. 3 (2006): 283–300; and Nathan Bennett and Stephen Miles, "Second in Command: The Misunderstood Role of the Chief Operating Officer," *Harvard Business Review* 84, no. 5 (2006): 70–79.

41. John Chong and Jaesun Park, "National Culture and Classical Principles of Planning," *Cross Cultural Management* 10 (2003): 29.

42. The section "Qualifications of Planners" is adapted from John Argenti, *Systematic Corporate Planning* (New York: Wiley, 1974), 126. For an interesting look at the role of power and politics in the planning process, see Renee Berger, "People, Power, Politics," *Planning* 63, no. 2 (February 1997): 4–9.

43. Michael Muckian and Mary Auestad Arnold, "Manager, Appraise Thyself," *Credit Union Management* (December 1989): 26–28.

44. Edward J. Green, *Workbook for Corporate Planning* (New York: American Management Association, 1970).

45. Z. A. Malik, "Formal Long–Range Planning and Organizational Performance," Ph.D. diss. (Rensselaer Polytechnic Institute, 1974).

chapter 8

Making Decisions

Target Skill

decision-making skill: the ability to choose alternatives that increase the likelihood of accomplishing objectives

objectives

To help build my *decision-making skill,* when studying this chapter, I will attempt to acquire:

1. A fundamental understanding of the term *decision*

2. An understanding of each element of the decision situation

3. An ability to use the decision-making process

4. An appreciation for the various situations in which decisions are made

5. An understanding of probability theory and decision trees as decision-making tools

6. Insights into groups as decision makers

CHALLENGE CASE

MAKING DIFFICULT DECISIONS AT NBC UNIVERSAL

WAS IT "SIMPLY BUSINESS"—or a classic example of poor decision making? The tale of NBC Universal's recent late-night programming debacle—moving Jay Leno to a prime-time slot while anointing Conan O'Brien the new host of "The Tonight Show," then reversing itself—actually started in 2004.

At that time, O'Brien was 12 years into hosting the show that followed "The Tonight Show" on NBC. Concerned that O'Brien might be considering a move to another network, NBC management decided to make him a promise: in 2009 O'Brien would be able to succeed Jay Leno as host of "The Tonight Show." Presumably at that point, Leno would retire.

But a lot can happen in five years. Fast-forward to 2009: Jay Leno announced he had no interest in retiring from "The Tonight Show." To keep Leno from jumping ship, NBC and CEO Jeff Zucker concocted a solution: it would launch a new program, "The Jay Leno Show," for a prime-time slot—10 pm Eastern, 9 pm Central—while moving Conan into the Tonight Show seat. Making this double switch, NBC brass reasoned, would help the network in several ways. It would make good on their promise to Conan, enable NBC to hold on to both late-night stars, and also save the network money. Reportedly, it would cost about $300,000 to produce an hour-long Leno program versus $3 million for an hour-long drama.

But NBC's decision soon fell apart. The problem: low ratings. The new Leno show failed to impress critics and, as a result, could not deliver viewers in significant numbers to the reconstructed Tonight Show starring O'Brien. Meanwhile, the flame-haired comedian had problems of his own. Although his show attracted viewers in the coveted 28-to-49 age group, O'Brien still regularly came in third against David Letterman and ABC's "Nightline."

In its next move, NBC revisited its programming decisions, canceling the prime-time Leno show and reinstalling Leno at "The Tonight Show." Miffed at being replaced, O'Brien refused the alternatives offered by NBC and used his position to castigate the network, including CEO Zucker, and accuse Jay Leno of helping to oust him. Ultimately, O'Brien accepted a $40 million severance package plus several millions in severance for his staff. He then launched a several-city comedy tour to further capitalize on his NBC experience before signing a contract with the Turner Broadcasting System (TBS).[1]

Looking back, managers at NBC would probably like a "do over" on some of their previous decisions regarding "The Tonight Show." As time passes, NBC executives will learn more about the wisdom of their final decision to let go of O'Brien.

■ *Jay Leno—was he innocent in the Leno-O'Brien debacle?*

EXPLORING YOUR MANAGEMENT SKILL

You can explore your level of decision-making skill **before** studying the chapter by completing the exercise "Exploring Your Management Skill: Part 1" on page 197 and **after** studying this chapter by completing the exercise "Exploring Your Management Skill: Part 2" on page 198.

THE DECISION-MAKING CHALLENGE

The Challenge Case focuses on events at NBC Universal. The information in this chapter discusses specifics surrounding a decision-making situation and provides insights about the steps that NBC management might have taken in making these decisions. This chapter discusses (1) the fundamentals of decisions, (2) the decision-making process, (3) various decision-making conditions, (4) decision-making tools, and (5) group decision making. These topics are critical to managers and other individuals who make decisions.

FUNDAMENTALS OF DECISIONS

Definition of a Decision

A **decision** is a choice made between two or more available alternatives. *Decision making* is the process of choosing the best alternative for reaching objectives. Decision making is covered in the planning section of this text, but because managers must also make decisions when performing the other three managerial functions—organizing, influencing, and controlling—the subject requires a separate chapter.

We all face decision situations every day. A decision situation may involve simply choosing whether to spend the day studying, swimming, or golfing. It does not matter which alternative is chosen, only that a choice is made.[2]

Managers make decisions affecting the organization daily and communicate those decisions to other organization members.[3] Not all managerial decisions are of equal significance to the organization. Some affect a large number of organization members, cost a great deal of money to carry out, or have a long-term effect on the organization. Such significant decisions can have a major impact, not only on the management system itself, but on the career of the manager who makes them. Other decisions are fairly insignificant, affecting only a small number of organization members, costing little to carry out, and producing only a short-term effect on the organization.

Types of Decisions

Decisions can be categorized according to how much time a manager must spend making them, what proportion of the organization must be involved in making them, and the organizational functions on which they focus. Probably the most generally accepted method of categorizing decisions, however, is based on computer language; it divides all decisions into two basic types: programmed and nonprogrammed.[4]

A **programmed decision** is routine and repetitive, and the organization typically develops specific ways to handle such decisions. A programmed decision might involve determining how products will be arranged on the shelves of a supermarket. For this kind of routine, repetitive problem, standard-arrangement decisions are typically made according to established management guidelines.

In contrast, a **nonprogrammed decision** is typically a one-shot decision that is usually less structured than programmed decisions. An example of the type of nonprogrammed decision that more and more managers are having to make is whether to expand operations into the "forgotten continent" of Africa.[5] Another example is deciding whether a supermarket should

TABLE 8.1	Traditional and Modern Ways of Handling Programmed and Nonprogrammed Decisions		
	Decision-Making Techniques		
Types of Decisions	**Traditional**	**Modern**
Programmed: Routine, repetitive decisions Organization develops specific processes for handling them	1. Habit 2. Clerical routine: 　Standard operating procedures 3. Organization structure: 　Common expectations 　A system of subgoals 　Well-defined information channels	1. Operations research: 　Mathematical analysis models 　Computer simulation 2. Electronic data processing
Nonprogrammed: One-shot, ill-structured, novel policy decisions Handled by general problem solving processes	1. Judgment, intuition, and creativity 2. Rules of thumb 3. Selection and training of executives	1. Heuristic problem-solving techniques applied to: 　Training human decision makers 　Constructing heuristic computer programs

carry an additional type of bread. The manager making this decision must consider whether the new bread will merely stabilize bread sales by competing with existing bread carried in the store or actually increase bread sales by offering a desired brand of bread to customers who have never before bought bread in the store. These types of issues must be dealt with before the manager can finally decide whether to offer the new bread. Table 8.1 shows traditional and modern ways of handling programmed and nonprogrammed decisions.

Programmed and nonprogrammed decisions should be thought of as being at opposite ends of the decision programming continuum, as illustrated in Figure 8.1. As the figure indicates, however, some decisions are neither programmed nor nonprogrammed, falling somewhere between the two. One of the key distinctions between programmed versus nonprogrammed decisions is that programmed decisions typically require less time and effort as compared to nonprogrammed decisions.

The Responsibility for Making Organizational Decisions

Many different kinds of decisions must be made within an organization—such as how to manufacture a product, how to maintain machines, how to ensure product quality, and how to establish advantageous relationships with customers. Because organizational decisions are so varied, some type of rationale must be developed to stipulate who within the organization has the responsibility for making which decisions.

One such rationale is based primarily on two factors: the scope of the decision to be made and the levels of management. The **scope of the decision** is the proportion of the total management system that the decision will affect. The greater this proportion, the broader the scope of the decision is said to be. *Levels of management* are simply lower-level management, middle-level

FIGURE 8.1
Decision programming continuum

FIGURE 8.2
Level of managers responsible for making decisions as decision scope increases from A to B to C

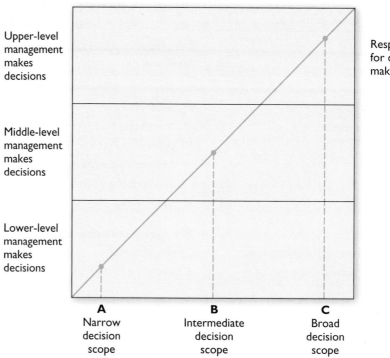

Upper-level management makes decisions

Middle-level management makes decisions

Lower-level management makes decisions

Responsibility for decision making

A
Narrow decision scope

B
Intermediate decision scope

C
Broad decision scope

management, and upper-level management. The rationale for designating who makes which decisions is that the broader the scope of a decision, the higher the level of the manager responsible for making that decision. Figure 8.2 illustrates this rationale. ■

how managers do it

Making Business Decisions at Green Queens

To better understand the role of delegation in different contexts, consider the decisions facing sisters Heather Castagna and Holly Rand, the owners of Lubbock, Texas–based Green Queens, a recycling company. An uptick in residential business and several new commercial contracts required Castagna and Rand to make major decisions about their firm's future, including a possible location change and the need to hire additional employees. As small-business owners, Castagna and Rand are responsible for making such decisions; they cannot delegate them to others.[6] ■

It is important to point out that the manager who is responsible for making a particular decision can ask the advice of other managers or subordinates before settling on an alternative. In his article "Moon Shots for Management," business thinker Gary Hamel observes that senior-level decision making is often marked by "executive hubris, unstated biases, and incomplete data." Hamel suggests that employees closest to a situation are often in the best position to evaluate alternatives or weigh in on the issues that will affect the decision.[7] Consistent with this idea, some managers prefer to use groups and input from other employees to make certain decisions.

Consensus is one method a manager can use in getting a group to arrive at a particular decision. **Consensus** is an agreement on a decision by all the individuals involved in making that decision. It usually occurs after lengthy deliberation and discussion by members of the decision group, who may be either all managers or a mixture of managers and subordinates.[8]

The manager who asks a group to produce a consensus decision must bear in mind that groups will sometimes be unable to arrive at a decision. Lack of technical skills or poor interpersonal relations may prove insurmountable barriers to arriving at a consensus. When a group is stalemated, a manager needs to offer assistance in making the decision or simply make it herself.

Decisions arrived at through consensus have both advantages and disadvantages. One advantage of this method is that it focuses "several heads" on the decision. Another is that employees are more likely to be committed to implementing a decision if they helped make it. The main disadvantage of this method is that it often involves time-consuming discussions relating to the decision, which can be costly to the organization.

Elements of the Decision Situation

Wilson and Alexis isolate several basic elements in the decision situation.[9] Five of these elements are defined and discussed in this section.

The Decision Makers Decision makers, the first element of the decision situation, are the individuals or groups who actually make the choice among alternatives. According to Ernest Dale, weak decision makers usually have one of four orientations: receptive, exploitative, hoarding, and marketing.[10]

Decision makers who have a *receptive* orientation believe that the source of all good is outside themselves, and therefore they rely heavily on suggestions from other organization members. Basically, they want others to make their decisions for them.

Decision makers with an *exploitative* orientation also believe that the source of all good is outside themselves, and they are willing to steal ideas as necessary to make good decisions. They build their organizations on others' ideas and typically hog all the credit, extending little or none to the originators of the ideas.

The *hoarding* orientation is characterized by the desire to preserve the status quo as much as possible. Decision makers with this orientation accept little outside help, isolate themselves from others, and are extremely self-reliant. They are obsessed with maintaining their present position and status.

Marketing-oriented decision makers look on themselves as commodities that are only as valuable as the decisions they make. Thus they try to make decisions that will enhance their value, and they are highly conscious of what others think of their decisions.

Store manager Gary Rains (right) leads Wal-Mart employees in the company cheer at the end of the regular morning staff meeting. Such actions are aimed at helping the manager build commitment to implementing decisions the manager and the team have made together.

The ideal decision-making orientation emphasizes the realization of the organization's potential as well as that of the decision maker. Ideal decision makers try to use all of their talents when making a decision and are characterized by reason and sound judgment. They are largely free of the qualities of the four undesirable decision-making orientations just described.[11]

how managers do it

Trusting Employees to Make Decisions at ShopRite

For an example of an ideal decision maker, consider Jeff Brown, whose chain of ShopRite supermarkets operates in economically depressed communities in Pennsylvania and New Jersey—communities that other grocery chains reject as too risky. Brown, whose company was recently named one of the region's top employers, entrusts his employees with authority to make major store decisions and the freedom to learn from their mistakes without fear of reprisal. Union leaders say Brown encourages their union members—his employees—to think creatively and try new ideas. In their many years of dealing with Brown, the union claims, no case ever went to arbitration.[12] ■

Goals to Be Served The goals that decision makers seek to attain are another element of the decision situation. In the case of managers, these goals should most often be organizational objectives. (Chapter 7 discussed the specifics of organizational objectives.)

Relevant Alternatives The decision situation is usually composed of at least two relevant alternatives. A **relevant alternative** is one that is considered feasible for solving an existing problem and for implementation. Alternatives that will not solve an existing problem *or* cannot be implemented are irrelevant and should be excluded from the decision-making situation.

Ordering of Alternatives The decision situation requires a process or mechanism for ranking alternatives from most desirable to least desirable. This process can be subjective, objective, or some combination of the two. Past experience of the decision maker is an example of a subjective process, and the rate of output per machine is an example of an objective process.

Choice of Alternatives The last element of the decision situation is the actual choice between available alternatives. This choice establishes the decision. Typically, managers choose the alternative that maximizes long-term return for the organization.

The Rational Decision-Making Process

A decision is a choice of one alternative from a set of available alternatives. The **rational decision-making process** comprises the steps the decision maker takes to arrive at this choice. The process a manager uses to make decisions has a significant impact on the quality of those decisions. If managers use an organized and systematic process, the probability that their decisions will be sound is higher than if they use a disorganized and unsystematic process.[13]

A model of the decision-making process that is recommended for managerial use is presented in Figure 8.3. In order, the decision-making steps this model depicts are as follows:

1. Identify an existing problem.
2. List possible alternatives for solving the problem.
3. Select the most beneficial of these alternatives.

FIGURE 8.3
Model of the decision-making process

4. Implement the selected alternative.
5. Gather feedback to find out whether the implemented alternative is solving the identified problem.

The paragraphs that follow elaborate on each of these steps and explain their interrelationships.[14]

This model of the decision-making process is based on three primary assumptions.[15] First, the model assumes that humans are economic beings with the objective of maximizing satisfaction or return. Second, it assumes that within the decision-making situation all alternatives and their possible consequences are known. Its last assumption is that decision makers have some priority system to guide them in ranking the desirability of each alternative. If each of these assumptions is met, the decision made will probably be the best possible one for the organization. In real life, unfortunately, one or more of these assumptions is often not met, and therefore the decision made is less than optimal for the organization.

Identifying an Existing Problem

Decision making is essentially a problem-solving process that involves eliminating barriers to organizational goal attainment. The first step in this elimination process is identifying exactly what the problems or barriers are, for only after the barriers have been adequately identified can management take steps to eliminate them.

how managers do It

Addressing—and Eliminating—Barriers at Molson

As a classic example of making decisions to overcome a problem, consider how Canadian brewer Molson handled a barrier to success: a free-trade agreement that threatened to open Canadian borders to U.S. beer. Although the borders were not due to open for another five years, Molson decided to deal immediately with the impending threat of increased beer competition from the United States by increasing production and sales of its other product line: specialty chemical products. Within four years, Molson's chemical sales exceeded its beer sales. Essentially, the company identified its problem—the threat of increased U.S. competition for beer sales—and dealt with it by emphasizing sales in a different division.[16] ■

Chester Barnard has stated that organizational problems are brought to the attention of managers mainly by the following means:[17]

1. Orders issued by managers' supervisors
2. Situations relayed to managers by their subordinates
3. The normal activity of the managers themselves

Listing Alternative Solutions

Once a problem has been identified, managers should list the various possible solutions. Few organizational problems are solvable in only one way. Managers must search out the numerous available alternative solutions to most organizational problems.

Before searching for solutions, however, managers should be aware of five limitations on the number of problem-solving alternatives available:[18]

1. **Authority factors** (e.g., a manager's superior may have told the manager that a certain alternative is not feasible)
2. **Biological or human factors** (e.g., human factors within the organization may be inappropriate for implementing certain alternatives)
3. **Physical factors** (e.g., the physical facilities of the organization may be inappropriate for certain alternatives)
4. **Technological factors** (e.g., the level of organizational technology may be inadequate for certain alternatives)
5. **Economic factors** (e.g., certain alternatives may be too costly for the organization)

Figure 8.4 presents additional factors that can limit a manager's decision alternatives. This diagram uses the term *discretionary area* to depict all the feasible alternatives available to managers. Factors that limit or rule out alternatives outside this area are legal restrictions, moral and ethical norms, formal policies and rules, and unofficial social norms.[19]

Finally, managers should be aware of the negative effects of generating too many alternatives. Intuitively, generating more alternatives would seemingly lead to more effective decision making. Research suggests, however, that having too many alternatives may actually demotivate decision makers, which harms decision making; this is known as the **paradox of choice**.[20]

Selecting the Most Beneficial Alternative

Decision makers can select the most beneficial solution only after they have evaluated each alternative carefully. This evaluation should consist of three steps. First, decision makers should list, as accurately as possible, the potential effects of each alternative as if the alternative had already been chosen and implemented. Second, they should assign a probability factor to each of the potential effects; that is, indicate how probable the occurrence of the effect would be if the alternative were implemented. Third, keeping organizational goals in mind, decision makers should compare each alternative's expected effects and the respective probabilities of those effects.[21] After these steps have been completed, managers will know which alternative seems most advantageous to the organization.

FIGURE 8.4
Additional factors that limit a manager's number of acceptable alternatives

Scholastic, Inc., the U.S. publisher of the Harry Potter series of books, decided to honor the request of author J. K. Rowling that no one be allowed to see a copy of any new book before its publication date. Implementing that decision required gaining the cooperation of booksellers all over the country. Here an Amazon.com employee prepares copies of *Harry Potter and the Order of the Phoenix* for shipping.

class discussion highlight

MODERN RESEARCH AND DECISION-MAKING SKILL

The Influence of Information Speed on Decision Making

One key to effective decision making is gathering as much useful information as possible. Recent advances in technology allow individuals to receive information much faster than they could even a few years ago. A recent study by Professors Luri and Swaminathan examined the extent to which timely information improves decision making.[22]

In their study, the authors conducted a computer-based experiment with undergraduate students in France. In this experiment, the students were told they were retailers trying to sell "wodgets" over 30 rounds. In each round, the students could purchase wodgets for 3 francs and sell them for 12 francs. If customer demand (reported by the experimenters to the students) exceeded the number of wodgets a student ordered, then the student received profits on all of the sales but ran out of inventory. In contrast, if customer demand

was less than the number of wodgets ordered, then the students lost the money associated with the remaining inventory (think of unsold wodgets as spoiled inventory). The students were told that the goal of the experiment was to maximize profits.

To examine the effects of timely information on decision making, the authors of the study placed students into one of three categories: subjects received information about consumer demand and were allowed to purchase wodgets every round, every three rounds, or every six rounds. In other words, the first group received information very quickly (every round), and the last group received information very slowly (every six rounds). Based on these differences in information flow, which students do you think made the best decisions? Why or why not?

Source: This highlight was based on Nicholas H. Lurie and Jayashankar M. Swaminathan, "Is timely information always better? The effect of feedback frequency on decision making," *Organizational Behavior and Human Decision Processes* 108, (2009): 315–329.

Implementing the Chosen Alternative

The next step is to put the chosen alternative into action. Decisions must be supported by appropriate action if they are to have a chance of success.

Gathering Problem-Related Feedback

After the chosen alternative has been implemented, decision makers must gather feedback to determine the effect of the implemented alternative on the identified problem. If the identified problem is not being solved, managers need to seek out and implement some other alternative.

BOUNDED RATIONALITY

In the previous section, we described the rational decision-making process. Herbert Simon, however, questioned the ability of managers to make rational decisions. In his opinion, managers are not able to make perfectly rational decisions. Instead, Simon put forth the idea that managers deal with **bounded rationality**, which refers to the fact that managers are bounded in terms of time, computational power, and knowledge when making decisions.[23] In other words, managers do not always have access to the resources required to make rational decisions. As a result of bounded rationality, Simon suggests that managers **satisfice**, which occurs when an individual makes a decision that is not optimal but is "good enough." For example, a manager may hire the first employee who is acceptable according to the hiring criteria without interviewing the remaining candidates. In this example, a better candidate may exist, but the manager has satisficed by selecting the first "acceptable" candidate.

DECISION MAKING AND INTUITION

As already discussed, the rational decision-making process includes a sequence of five steps. We also noted, however, that researchers have highlighted the potential influence of bounded rationality on this process. More recently, research suggests that individuals may also rely on additional processes when making decisions. In fact, Stanovich and West suggest that individuals use two different processes when making decisions.[24] According to their framework, the rational decision-making process discussed in the previous section is known as "System 2."

Complementing this formal system of decision making, Stanovich and West suggest that individuals also rely on a less formal process based on intuition to make decisions; they refer to this process as "System 1." Consistent with their framework, System 2 is a process described as being slow, comprehensive, and deliberate, while System 1 is described as being fast, automatic, and intuitive. **Intuition**, in fact, refers to an individual's inborn ability to synthesize information quickly and effectively.[25] Taken together, some researchers suggest that individuals employ the more sophisticated System 2 process to monitor or override the more automatic System 1 process. Often, however, System 2 does not monitor effectively; in such cases intuition drives decision making.

Decision-Making Heuristics and Biases

Daniel Kahneman and Amos Tversky were awarded the Nobel Prize for further examining the role of intuition in decision making. In particular, their ground-breaking research examined how individuals use **heuristics**, or simple rules of thumb, to make decisions. In addition, Kahneman and Tversky examined how these heuristics introduce bias in decision-making processes. **Bias** refers to departures from rational theory that produce suboptimal decisions. In other words, when managers rely on rules of thumb when making decisions, these decisions are often flawed. Kahneman and Tversky's work spurred a great deal of interest in the discovery and examination of a number of decision-making biases. Researchers have discovered many other decision-making biases; Table 8.2 summarizes some of the more prominent biases examined by decision-making researchers.

Decision-Making Conditions: Risk and Uncertainty

In most instances, it is impossible for decision makers to know exactly what the future consequences of an implemented alternative will be. The word *future* is the key in discussing decision-making conditions. Because organizations and their environments are constantly changing, future

TABLE 8.2	Common Decision-Making Biases
Name of Bias	**Brief Description**
Bandwagon Effect	The tendency to believe certain outcomes (i.e., the stock market will increase) because others believe the same
Confirmation Bias	The tendency to search for information that supports one's preconceived beliefs and to ignore information that contradicts those beliefs
Loss Aversion	Characteristic of individuals who tend to more strongly prefer avoiding losses rather than acquiring gains
Overconfidence	When assessing our ability to predict future events, the tendency to believe that our forecasts are better than they truly are
Unrealistic Optimism	Individuals' tendency to believe that they are less susceptible to risky events (i.e., earthquakes, disease transmission, etc.) than others

Source: For a complete review of research involving heuristics and biases, see T. Gilovich, D. Griffin, and D. Kahneman, *Heuristics and Biases: The Psychology of Intuitive Judgment* (Cambridge: Cambridge University Press, 2002).

consequences of implemented decisions are not perfectly predictable. In general, the two different conditions under which decisions are made are risk and uncertainty. Although many managers use them interchangeably, these two terms are in fact different.

Frank Knight distinguished between risk and uncertainty almost a century ago.[26] According to his framework, **risk** refers to situations in which statistical probabilities can be attributed to alternative potential outcomes. For example, the probabilities associated with the potential outcomes of roulette are known to individuals in advance. In contrast, **uncertainty** refers to situations where the probability that a particular outcome will occur is not known in advance. A manager, for instance, may be unable to articulate the probability that building a new manufacturing facility will increase a firm's sales in five years.[27]

Despite this distinction between risk and uncertainty, it is important to note that objective standards are not always available when examining a situation with alternative potential outcomes. Specifically, two managers may attribute differing levels of uncertainty or risk to the same or similar decisions. For example, suppose that the managers of two competing firms—Alpha Inc. and Beta Inc.—are each considering opening new manufacturing facilities in China but are unsure whether the new plants will improve profitability. Suppose, however, that the manager of Alpha Inc. has previously opened 12 new facilities in China, but the manager of Beta Inc. has no experience opening such facilities. As such, the manager of Alpha Inc. has more information about opening these plants and might be able to better estimate the risk probabilities associated with profitability versus failure as compared to the manager of Beta Inc. In fact, the manager of Beta Inc. might not be able to estimate any risk probabilities and instead view this plant with complete uncertainty.

Now that we have distinguished between risk and uncertainty, the question remains: Why do we need to distinguish between these two terms? Research suggests that individuals dislike uncertainty even more than they dislike risk.[28] Vague or unknown probabilities of success are more likely to discourage managers from undertaking actions. This negative influence of uncertainty has implications for all sorts of decisions such as hiring new employees, introducing new products, or acquiring other firms.

DECISION-MAKING TOOLS

Most managers develop an intuition about what decisions to make—a largely subjective feeling, based on years of experience in a particular organization or industry, which gives them insights into decision making for that industry or organization.[29] Although intuition is often an important factor in making a decision, managers generally emphasize more objective decision-making tools. The two most widely used such tools are probability theory and decision trees.[30]

Probability Theory

Probability theory is a decision-making tool used in risk situations—situations in which decision makers are not completely sure of the outcome of an implemented alternative.[31] Probability refers to the likelihood that an event or outcome will actually occur. It is estimated by calculating an expected value for each alternative considered. Specifically, the **expected value (EV)** for an alternative is the income (*I*) that alternative would produce, multiplied by its probability of producing that income (*P*). In formula form, EV = I × P. Decision makers generally choose and implement the alternative with the highest expected value.[32]

An example will clarify the relationship of probability, income, and expected value. A manager is trying to decide where to open a store that specializes in renting surfboards. She is considering three possible locations (A, B, and C), all of which seem feasible. For the first year of operation, the manager has projected that, under ideal conditions, her company would earn $90,000 in Location A, $75,000 in Location B, and $60,000 in Location C. After studying historical weather patterns, however, she has determined that there is only a 20 percent chance—or a .2 probability—of ideal conditions occurring during the first year of operation in Location A. Locations B and C have a .4 and a .8 probability, respectively, for ideal conditions during the first year of operations. Expected values for each of these locations are as follows: Location A—$18,000; Location B—$30,000; Location C—$48,000. Figure 8.5 shows the situation this decision maker faces. According to her probability analysis, she should open a store in Location C, the alternative with the highest expected value.

Decision Trees

In the previous section, probability theory was applied to a relatively simple decision situation. Some decisions, however, are more complicated and involve a series of steps. These steps are interdependent; that is, each step is influenced by the step that precedes it. A **decision tree** is a graphic decision-making tool typically used to evaluate decisions involving a series of steps.[33]

John F. Magee developed a classic illustration that outlines how decision trees can be applied to a production decision.[34] In his illustration (see Figure 8.6), the Stygian Chemical Company must decide whether to build a small or a large plant to manufacture a new product with an expected life of 10 years (Decision Point 1 in Figure 8.6). If the choice is to build a large plant, the company could face high or low average product demand, or high initial and then low demand. If, however, the choice is to build a small plant, the company could face either initially high or initially low product demand. If the small plant is built and product demand is high during an initial two-year period, management could then choose whether to expand the plant (Decision Point 2). Whether the decision is made to expand or not to expand, management could then face either high or low product demand.

FIGURE 8.5
Expected values from locating surfboard rental store in each of three possible locations

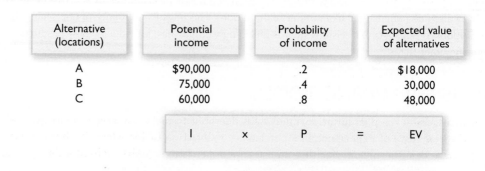

Alternative (locations)	Potential income	Probability of income	Expected value of alternatives
A	$90,000	.2	$18,000
B	75,000	.4	30,000
C	60,000	.8	48,000

I	x	P	=	EV

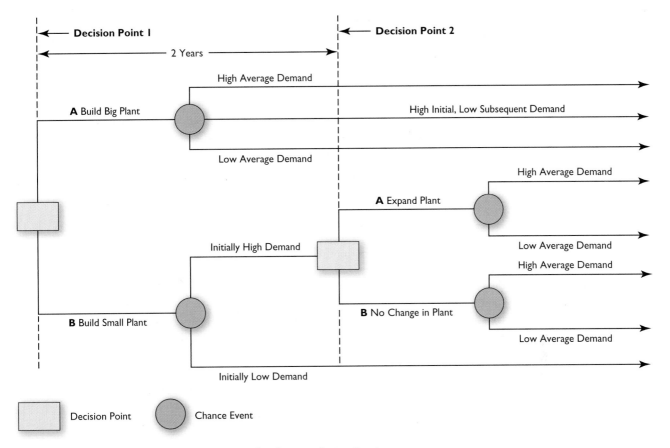

FIGURE 8.6   A basic decision tree illustrating the decision facing Stygian management

Now that various possible alternatives related to this decision have been outlined, the financial consequence of each different course of action must be compared. To adequately compare these consequences, management must do the following:

1. Study estimates of investment amounts necessary for building a large plant, for building a small plant, and for expanding a small plant.
2. Weigh the probabilities of facing different product demand levels for various decision alternatives.
3. Consider projected income yields for each decision alternative.

Analysis of the expected values and net expected gain for each decision alternative helps management decide on an appropriate choice.[35] *Net expected gain* is defined in this situation as the expected value of an alternative minus the investment cost. For example, if building a large plant yields the highest net expected gain, Stygian management should decide to build the large plant.[36]

GROUP DECISION MAKING

Earlier in this chapter, decision makers were defined as individuals or groups that actually make a decision—that is, choose a decision alternative from those available. This section focuses on groups as decision makers. The two key topics discussed here are the advantages and disadvantages of using groups to make decisions, and the best processes for making group decisions.

Advantages and Disadvantages of Using Groups to Make Decisions

Groups commonly make decisions in organizations.[37] For example, groups are often asked to decide what new product should be offered to customers, how policies for promotion should be improved, and how the organization should reach higher production goals. Groups are so often asked to make organizational decisions because certain advantages come with having a group of people rather than an individual manager make a decision. One is that a group can generally come up with more and better decision alternatives than an individual can: A group can draw on collective, diverse organizational experiences as the foundation for decision making, while the individual manager has only the limited experiences of one person to draw on.[38] Another advantage is that when a group makes a decision, the members of that group tend to support the implementation of the decision more fervently than they would if the decision had been made by an individual. This support can be of significant help to a manager in successfully implementing a decision. A third advantage of using a group rather than an individual to make a decision is that group members tend to perceive the decision as their own, and this ownership perception makes it more likely that they will strive to implement the decision successfully rather than prematurely giving in to failure.

Having groups rather than individual managers make organizational decisions may also involve some disadvantages. Perhaps the one most often discussed disadvantage is that it takes longer to make a group decision because groups must take the time to present and discuss all the members' views. Another disadvantage is that group decisions cost the organization more than individual decisions do simply because they take up the time of more people in the organization. Finally, group decisions can be of lower quality than individual decisions if they become contaminated by the group members' efforts to maintain friendly relationships among themselves. This phenomenon of compromising the quality of a decision to maintain relationships within a group is referred to as *groupthink* and is discussed more fully in Chapter 18, "Groups and Teams."[39]

Managers must weigh all these advantages and disadvantages of group decision making carefully, factoring in unique organizational situations, and give a group authority to make a decision only when the advantages of doing so clearly outweigh the disadvantages.

Processes for Making Group Decisions

Making a sound group decision regarding complex organizational circumstances is a formidable challenge. Fortunately, several useful processes have been developed to assist groups in meeting this challenge. The following sections discuss three such processes: brainstorming, nominal group technique, and Delphi technique.

Brainstorming **Brainstorming** is a group decision-making process in which negative feedback on any suggested alternative by any group member is forbidden until all members have presented alternatives that they perceive as valuable.[40] Figure 8.7 shows this process. Brainstorming is carefully designed to encourage all group members to contribute as many viable decision alternatives as they can think of. Its premise is that if the evaluation of alternatives starts before all possible alternatives have been offered, valuable alternatives may be overlooked. During brainstorming, group members are encouraged to state their ideas, no matter how wild they may seem, while an appointed group member records all ideas for discussion.[41]

FIGURE 8.7
The brainstorming process

Armstrong International's David Armstrong discovered an intriguing method for discouraging the premature evaluation of ideas during a brainstorming session. He allows only one negative comment per group member. Before discussion begins, he hands every member one piece of M&M's candy. Once a member makes a negative comment, he or she must eat the piece of candy. Because a group member is required to have an uneaten piece of candy to make a negative comment, members use their sole opportunity to be negative very carefully.[42] Once everyone's ideas have been presented, the group evaluates them and chooses the one that holds the most promise.

Nominal Group Technique

Nominal Group Technique The **nominal group technique** is another useful process for helping groups make decisions. This process is designed to ensure that each group member has equal participation in making the group decision.[43] It involves the following steps:

STEP 1 Each group member writes down individual ideas on the decision or problem being discussed.
STEP 2 Each member presents individual ideas orally. The ideas are usually written on a board for all other members to see and refer to.
STEP 3 After all members present their ideas, the entire group discusses these ideas simultaneously. Discussion tends to be unstructured and spontaneous.
STEP 4 When discussion is completed, a secret ballot is taken to allow members to support their favorite ideas without fear. The idea receiving the most votes is adopted and implemented.

Delphi Technique

Delphi Technique The **Delphi technique** is a third useful process for helping groups make decisions. The Delphi technique involves circulating questionnaires on a specific problem among group members, sharing the questionnaire results with them, and then continuing to recirculate and refine individual responses until a consensus regarding the problem is reached.[44] In contrast to the nominal group technique or brainstorming, the Delphi technique does not have group members meet face to face. The formal steps followed in the Delphi technique are the following:

STEP 1 A problem is identified.
STEP 2 Group members are asked to offer solutions to the problem by providing anonymous responses to a carefully designed questionnaire.
STEP 3 Responses of all group members are compiled and sent out to all group members.
STEP 4 Individual group members are asked to generate a new individual solution to the problem after they have studied the individual responses of all other group members compiled in Step 3.
STEP 4 Steps 3 and 4 are repeated until a consensus problem solution is reached.

Evaluating Group Decision-Making Processes

All three of the processes presented here for assisting groups in reaching decisions have both advantages and disadvantages. Brainstorming offers the advantage of encouraging the expression of as many useful ideas as possible, but the disadvantage of wasting the group's time on ideas that are wildly impractical. The nominal group technique, with its secret ballot, offers a structure in which individuals can support or reject an idea without fear of recrimination. Its disadvantage is group members have no way of knowing why individuals voted the way they did. The advantage of the Delphi technique is ideas can be gathered from group members who are too geographically separated or busy to meet face to face. Its disadvantage is members are unable to ask questions of one another.

As with any other management tool, managers must carefully weigh the advantages and disadvantages of these three group decision-making tools and adopt the one—or some combination of the three—that best suits their unique organizational circumstances.

CHALLENGE CASE SUMMARY

When evaluating the issue of how to reorganize late-night programming, management at NBC Universal definitely faced a formal decision situation, a situation requiring a choice of a number of alternatives. NBC management scrutinized this decision carefully because of its significance to the organization as a whole and to the careers of the NBC managers actually making the decision. Technically, this decision would be nonprogrammed in nature and therefore would be characterized more by judgment than by simple quantitative data.

NBC chief executive Jeff Zucker probably had the ultimate responsibility for making such a broad decision. This responsibility does not mean, however, that Zucker made the decision by himself. He most likely asked for advice from other NBC leaders and perhaps even appointed a group of leaders to arrive at a consensus on which decision alternative should be implemented.

As management at NBC evaluated its decision about late-night programming, they were most likely aware of all the elements in the decision situation. Both the internal and external environments of NBC would be one focus of the analysis. For example, internally, does NBC have the financial resources and expertise to support the programming changes? Externally, will viewers respond by watching Leno at the new hour and then subsequently watching Conan on "The Tonight Show"? Reason and sound judgment would need to characterize management's orientation in making this decision. Also, management would have had to keep the NBC organizational objectives in mind and formulated relevant alternatives for additional changes besides the reshuffled programming slots. For example, NBC could have chosen to stick with more costly drama programming for the 10 pm Eastern/9 pm Central time slot or encouraged Jay Leno to begin a phased-in retirement, with increased use of guest hosts until Leno was ready to turn the reins over to O'Brien. Management probably listed such relevant alternatives in some order of desirability before choosing an alternative to implement.

To further explore the decision-making process, assume that NBC management is facing a decision to increase ratings. Management would first need to identify the problem. For example, management must find out whether low ratings are the result of less-appealing guests on "The Tonight Show," funnier sketches on David Letterman's show, or growing competition from cable programming. Once the problem is identified, management would have to list all possible problem solutions—for example: Can the quality of the guests be improved? Does Jay need better writers? Should we also advertise on cable channels?

After eliminating infeasible solutions, NBC management would have to evaluate all remaining solutions, select one, and implement it. If poor ratings resulted from viewers thinking David Letterman was funnier, the best alternative might be to hire new writers. Additional feedback would be extremely important once changes were made. Zucker would need to find out whether the changes led to improved ratings. If not, he would need to decide what additional action should be taken.

NBC must also face a decision regarding how to handle competition from other programs in the late-night time slots. The decision-making process contains a great deal of uncertainty. NBC management could decide, for example, to introduce new talent to fight off the competition, but management has no guarantee that such measures would produce the desired results. Management *does* know, however, what has worked in the past to stop competitors, and thus is not dealing with a complete unknown. Therefore, NBC management could perhaps determine the outcome probability for each proposed alternative and base its decision on the alternative that looked most advantageous.

As discussed earlier, leaders at NBC have two tools they can use to make better decisions. First, they can use probability theory to obtain an expected value for various decision alternatives and then implement the alternative with the highest expected value. For example, in determining a tactic for handling competition, NBC management may need to decide whether to devote more of the company's resources to improving programming or initiating more effective advertising. This decision would depend on the projected value of each alternative once implemented.

Second, with decisions that involve a series of steps related to each of several alternatives, NBC management could use a decision tree to assist in picturing and evaluating each alternative. For example, to handle competition from other networks, management could choose to create new programming or devote more resources to improving existing programming. Each of these alternatives would lead to different decision-making steps.

NBC management must remember, however, that business judgment is an essential adjunct to the effective use of any decision-making tool. The purpose of the tool is to improve the quality of the judgment, not to replace it. In other words, NBC management must not only choose alternatives based on probability theory and decision trees, but must also use good judgment in deciding what is best for the network.

NBC management also had to decide which individuals would be involved in making the decision to revise late-night programming. First, a decision of this magnitude should probably be made by a group of top leaders drawn from many different organizational areas. A group decision would almost certainly be better than an individual decision in this case, because a group would have a broader view of NBC and the market than any one person in the company would. Therefore, the group would be more likely to make an appropriate decision.

Perhaps the group decision-making process used in this case should be a combination of the three processes discussed in the text. Brainstorming sessions would ensure that all thoughts and ideas related to this crucial decision surface, while the nominal group technique would focus group members on the urgency of making the decision by requiring them to vote on whether to make the change. The Delphi technique could be used to obtain important input on the decision from experts around the country by asking them to present their written views through a specially designed questionnaire.

Unquestionably, using a group to make this decision would be time-consuming and expensive. Once the decision is made, however, group members would be committed to it, perceive it as their own, and do all in their power to ensure that they are successful—even if the decision were *not* to make changes in the late-night time slots.

MANAGEMENT SKILL ACTIVITIES

This section is specially designed to help you develop decision-making skill. An individual's management skill is based on an understanding of management concepts and the ability to apply those concepts in management situations. As a result, the following activities are designed both to heighten your understanding of decision-making concepts and to help you gain facility in applying these concepts in various management situations.

UNDERSTANDING DECISION-MAKING CONCEPTS

To check your understanding and to practice using the concepts in this chapter, go to www.mymanagementlab.com and explore the material associated with Chapter 8.

Know Key Terms

Understanding the following key terms is critical to your understanding of chapter material. Define each of these terms. Refer to the page(s) referenced after a term to check your definition or to gain further insight regarding the term.

decision **182**
programmed decision **182**
nonprogrammed decision **182**
scope of the decision **183**
consensus **184**
relevant alternative **186**
rational decision-making process **186**

paradox of choice **188**
bounded rationality **190**
satisfice **190**
intuition **190**
heuristics **190**
bias **190**
risk **191**

uncertainty **191**
probability theory **192**
expected value (EV) **192**
decision tree **192**
brainstorming **194**
nominal group technique **195**
Delphi technique **195**

Know How Management Concepts Relate

This section is comprised of activities that will further sharpen your understanding of management concepts. Answer essay questions as completely as possible. Also, remember that many additional true/false and multiple choice questions appear online at MyManagementLab.com to help you further refine your understanding of management concepts.

1. Distinguish between programmed versus nonprogrammed decisions. Use examples to support your response.

2. Describe the primary steps involved in the rational decision-making process.
3. What is the relationship between bounded rationality and satisficing?
4. Describe the relationship between "System 1" and "System 2" decision-making processes.
5. Compare the advantages and disadvantages associated with group decision making.

DEVELOPING MANAGEMENT SKILLS

Learning activities in this section are aimed at helping you to develop your decision-making skill. Learning activities include Exploring Your Management Skill: Parts 1 & 2, Experiential Exercises, Cases, and a VideoNet Exercise.

Exploring Your Management Skill: Part 1

Before studying this chapter, respond to the following questions regarding the type of advice you would give to NBC CEO Jeff Zucker, referenced in the Challenge Case. Then address the concerning decision-making challenges that he presently faces within the company. You are not expected to be a decision-making expert at this point. Answering the questions now can help you focus on important points when you study the chapter. Also, answering the questions again after you study the chapter will give you an idea of how much you have learned.

Record your answers here or go to MyManagementLab.com. Recording your answers in MyManagementLab will allow you to get immediate results and see how your score compares to your classmates. If you answer the questions in the book, look up answers in the Exploring Your Management Skill section at the end of the book.

FOR EACH STATEMENT CIRCLE:
• "Y" if you would give the advice to Jeff Zucker.
• "N" if you would NOT give the advice to Jeff Zucker.
• "NI" if you have no idea whether you would give the advice to Jeff Zucker.

Mr. Zucker, in meeting your decision-making challenges at NBC, you should . . .

Before   After
Study   Study

1. realize that nonprogrammed decisions typically take less time to make than programmed decisions.
   Y, N, NI

2. understand that as decisions at NBC affect more levels of the total management system, the scope of the decision increases.
   Y, N, NI

3. recognize that at NBC, decision makers with exploitative orientations are more likely to ask others for advice as compared to decision makers with receptive orientations.
   Y, N, NI

4. understand that all employees at NBC will employ the rational decision-making process when making decisions.
   Y, N, NI

5. teach other employees at NBC that the rational decision-making process ends when an alternative has been chosen.
   Y, N, NI

6. understand that *risk* and *uncertainty* represent two terms that have the same meaning.
   Y, N, NI

7. realize that managers often operate in a state of bounded rationality, which suggests that managers often make decisions without all of the necessary information.
   Y, N, NI

8. understand that decision makers at NBC will always satisfice, which means that employees will always choose the best available alternative.
   Y, N, NI

9. understand that decision makers at NBC will often rely on heuristics, or rules of thumb, when making decisions.
   Y, N, NI

10. teach others that decisions will not be biased if decision makers are respectful of individuals with diverse backgrounds.
    Y, N, NI

11. be prepared to use probability theory to make important decisions at NBC.
    Y, N, NI

12. realize that decisions made by groups are always better than decisions made by individuals.
    Y, N, NI

13. teach others to use both brainstorming and barnstorming techniques to improve group decision-making processes.
    Y, N, NI

14. realize that *risk* is a subjective term, and different managers at NBC may associate different levels of risk with a particular decision.
    Y, N, NI

15. communicate to NBC managers that they are responsible for identifying organizational problems, and lower-level employees are not qualified to identify problems.
    Y, N, NI

Exploring Your Management Skill: Part 2

As you recall, you completed Exploring Your Management Skill before you started to study this chapter. Your responses gave you an idea of how much you initially knew about decision making and helped you focus on important points as you studied the chapter. Answer the Exploring Your Management Skill questions again now and compare your score to the first time you took it. This comparison will give you an idea of how much you have learned from your studying this chapter and

pinpoint areas for further clarification before you start studying the next chapter. Record your answers within the text or go to MyManagementLab.com. Recording your answers in MyManagementLab will allow you to get immediate results and see how your score compares to your classmates. If you complete the test in the book, look up answers in the Exploring Your Management Skill section at the end of the book.

Your Management Skills Portfolio

Your Management Learning Portfolio is a collection of activities especially designed to demonstrate your management knowledge and skill. By completing these activities at MyManagementLab.com, you will be able to print, complete with cover sheet, as many activities as you choose. Be sure to save your work. Taking your printed portfolio to an employment interview could be helpful in obtaining a job.

The portfolio activity for this chapter is Making a Decision at Microsoft. Study the following information and complete the exercises that that follow.[45]
Robbie Bach, president of Microsoft's entertainment and devices division, recently contacted you in reference to a situation that is developing at Microsoft. Specifically, Microsoft is receiving reports that its gaming system, the Xbox 360, is having

problems. Users from around the world are contacting the company to complain that their systems, which sell for as much as $500 at some retail locations, are not working after only one year or so of use. It seems that systems with this problem will display three red lights, and then the systems stop working. Although this problem is not affecting every Xbox 360 owner, it is clear that the problem is somewhat widespread.

Robbie Bach has contacted you for your advice in handling this situation. The Xbox 360 is important to Microsoft, as it looks to find new entertainment products and services to sell to customers around the globe. He feels as if he is under a spotlight, as customers around the globe are watching to see how Microsoft deals with customers. Your mission is to walk Bach through the various steps in the decision-making process:

1. Identify the existing problem.

2. List possible alternatives for solving the problem.

3. Select the most beneficial of these alternatives.

4. Implement the selected alternative.

5. Gather feedback to find out whether the implemented alternative is solving identified problem.

Experiential Exercises

1 Decision Making as a Group

Directions. Read the following scenario and then perform the listed activities. Your instructor may want you to perform the activities as an individual or within groups. Follow all of your instructor's directions carefully.

A representative of McDonald's has contacted your group to help make an important decision. Due to the increasing hostility of the press regarding the unhealthy nature of some of the company's products, top management is concerned about the company's future. In response, some members of McDonald's management team would like the company to diversify into other markets/industries that have nothing to do with food products. Use the nominal group technique, which is discussed in the chapter, to address this important issue for McDonald's.

At the end of this exercise, you should have at least one recommendation for McDonald's top management team. When you have finished this exercise, list the primary advantages and disadvantages of this technique. Be prepared to share your conclusions with the rest of your class.

2 You and Your Career

Earlier in the chapter, we discussed the importance of decision making and described a number of factors that influence decision making. Describe a scenario in which poor decision-making skills could hinder your career as a manager. What are some strategies you might employ to improve your decision-making skill? Explain. Describe two examples from your life that help you communicate your decision-making skill to potential employers.

VideoNet Exercise

Decision Making at Insomnia Cookies

Video Highlights

Insomnia Cookies recently decided that its business model would be composed of 50 percent retail sales and 50 percent delivery sales in any given geography. Previously, the retail component was not a given. The COO explains the thinking behind this decision and talks about how Insomnia Cookies approaches the decision-making process as it relates to opening new stores/operations in new locations/geographies. The CEO and director of marketing also chime in.

Discussion Questions

1. Who makes the decisions at Insomnia Cookies? Is this effective?
2. What is the most likely decision-making condition when Insomnia Cookies is trying to determine whether to enter a new market? Explain.
3. Which group decision process best describes the decision-making method at Insomnia Cookies?

Internet Activity

Go to Insomnia Cookies' home page at www.insomniacookies.com. How many locations are currently under operation? How will the decision-making process change as this organization continues to grow?

CASES

1 NBC CHIEF MAKES TOUGH DECISIONS

"Making Difficult Decisions at NBC Universal" was written to help you better understand the management concepts contained in this chapter. Answer the following discussion questions about the Challenge Case to better understand how decision-making concepts can be applied in a company such as NBC.

1. List three alternatives that NBC management might consider in handling competition from other television networks *before* making a decision to remodel the company's programming schedule.
2. What information would management need to evaluate these three alternatives?
3. Do you think you would enjoy making the decision about whether to remodel NBC's programming schedule? Explain.

2 GATEWAY CHIEF MAKES DARING DECISIONS

Read the case and answer the questions that follow. Studying this case will help you better understand how decision-making concepts can be applied in a company such as Gateway.

Bill Gates, Michael Dell, and…Ted Waitt? Like Gates and Dell, Waitt left college to form a computer company, Gateway. He and Mike Hammond, now senior vice president of manufacturing, started the firm in a farmhouse with a loan secured by a $10,000 CD owned by Waitt's grandmother. Initially, they sold hardware peripherals and software to owners of PCs made by Texas Instruments; later they expanded into designing and assembling their own fully configured PC systems for direct sale to consumers and businesses.

As his company grew, Waitt used his Midwestern roots to differentiate the South Dakota–based company from competitors such as Dell and Hewlett-Packard. For example, he used eye-catching cow spots to establish a brand image, which can be quite difficult in the standardized computer industry. Every Gateway computer came packed inside a white box with cow-like black spots, and the company served cow-shaped cookies at its annual shareholder meetings. By 1998, the company was reporting net income of $346 million on $7.5 billion in annual revenues.

However, to sustain the company's extraordinary growth during the coming years, Waitt realized that changes were needed. First, he decided to relocate the top management team to new administrative headquarters in San Diego. Not only would this help Gateway attract top talent, it would bring the office closer to Silicon Valley partners and suppliers. Waitt also decided to reduce the company's reliance on the cow motif as he courted business customers, who might not see a clear connection between high-quality computers and cows. Gateway's growth

roared on and by 2000, the company had a workforce of 20,000, mainly concentrated in its U.S. manufacturing facilities.

Next, Waitt made an even more expensive change. Instead of taking orders only by phone or via the Web, as rival Dell does, Waitt plunged into retailing. He opened hundreds of Gateway Country stores in the United States, Europe, and Japan so customers could see the different computer models and get advice from knowledgeable sales staff. When much of the world fell into economic recession during 2001, demand for computers dropped off and Gateway's market share, revenues, and profits started to decline as well. Now the founder faced more challenges. Rather than continue operating the entire retail chain, he ordered some stores closed and had the remaining outlets remodeled to better showcase new merchandise. Another big decision Waitt made was to diversify into popular consumer electronics products such as flat-panel televisions. This put Gateway into direct competition with Sony and other well-known firms—even as it was struggling to hold its own in the computer industry.

By 2004, the company had experienced three years of losses, both financially and in PC market share. It was time to reverse some of the earlier decisions. Waitt cut costs by outsourcing much of the company's production activities and laying off thousands of employees. He closed all the Gateway Country stores and arranged for the Best Buy chain to purchase the consumer electronics for resale. And the founder made yet another bold decision: He acquired the computer maker eMachines and its CEO, Wayne Inouye, became Gateway's CEO (Waitt became board chair).

Inouye quickly announced that the company would narrow its product line to make the most of the Gateway brand's appeal to computer buyers: "The fact is, we were not making a lot of money on the consumer electronics side at all," he said. "Our route to profitability is to fix our core business, and that's PCs and PC-related products." He also made major changes to the distribution strategy by selling PCs under the eMachines and Gateway brands in Best Buy stores, even as he sought shelf space in other national retail chains. Coupled with additional layoffs, these decisions helped Gateway increase its revenues and narrow its losses. Still, some observers wonder whether Inouye and Waitt will be able to complete the turnaround and restore Gateway's growth and financial success.

QUESTIONS

1. Knowing that growth is one of Gateway's long-term objectives, do you agree with Inouye's decision to reduce the product line and refocus on PCs? Explain.

2. What kind of programmed decisions might have arisen from some of the nonprogrammed decisions made by Ted Waitt and Wayne Inouye during the past few years?

3. Looking at Gateway's recent history, what would you identify as the top two or three problems that Waitt and Inouye must address today?

Endnotes

1. "What Marketers Can Learn from NBC's Tonight Show Meltdown," *ResearchPlan.com,* January 25, 2010, http://www.researchplan.com; Katia McGlynn, "Everything You Need to Know about the Conan/Leno Drama in One Easy Post," *Huffington Post,* January 22, 2010, http://www.huffingtonpost.com, Susan Todd, "NBC Debacle Is a Good Example of Bad Decision-Making," *Star-Ledger,* January 22, 2010, http://www.blog.nj.com; "NBC's Zucker: It's Just Business," *Marquee,* January 19, 2010, http://marquee.blogs.cnn.com.

2. For an excellent discussion of various decisions that managers make, see Michael Verespej, "Gutsy Decisions of 1991," *Industry Week,* February 17, 1992, 21–31. For an interesting discussion of decision making in government agencies, see Burton Gummer, "Decision Making under Conditions of Risk, Ambiguity, and Uncertainty: Recent Perspectives," *Administration in Social Work* 2 (1998): 75–93.

3. Abraham Zaleznik, "What Makes a Leader?" *Success* (June 1989): 42–45; Daphne Main and Joyce C. Lambert, "Improving Your Decision Making," *Business and Economic Review* 44, no. 3 (April/June 1998): 9–12.

4. Mervin Kohn, *Dynamic Managing: Principles, Process, Practice* (Menlo Park, CA: Cummings, 1977), 38–62.

5. William H. Miller, "Tough Decisions on the Forgotten Continent," *Industry Week,* June 6, 1994, 40–44.

6. Walt Nett, "Family-Run Recycling Company Faces Big Decisions As It Grows," *Lubbock Avalanche-Journal,* April 18, 2010, http://www.lubbockonline.com.

7. Gary Hamel, "Moon Shots for Management," *Harvard Business Review,* February 2009, http://hbr.org.

8. Marcia V. Wilkof, "Organizational Culture and Decision Making: A Case of Consensus Management," *R&D Management* (April 1989): 185–199.

9. Charles Wilson and Marcus Alexis, "Basic Frameworks for Decision," *Academy of Management Journal* 5 (August 1962): 151–164. To better understand the role of ethics in decision making, see Roselie McDevitt, Catherine Giapponi, and Cheryl Tromley, "A Model of Ethical Decision Making: The Integration of Process and Content," *Journal of Business Ethics* 73, no. 2 (2007): 219–229.

10. For a discussion of the importance of understanding decision makers in organizations, see Walter D. Barndt Jr., "Profiling Rival Decision Makers," *Journal of Business Strategy* (January/February 1991): 8–11; see also Bard Kuvaas and Geir Kaufmann, "Impact of Mood, Framing, and Need for Cognition on Decision Makers' Recall and Confidence," *Journal of Behavioral Decision Making* 17 (2004): 59.

11. For an analysis of several flawed decisions made by executives as well as recommendations for avoiding decision-making pitfalls, see Sydney Finkelstein, Jo Whitehead, and Andrew Campbell, "Think Again: Why Good Leaders Make Bad Decisions," *Business Strategy Review* 20, no. 2 (Summer 2009): 62–69.

12. Maria Panaritis, "Putting Trust Where Others Don't Dare," *Philadelphia Inquirer,* March 21, 2010, http://www.philly.com.

13. "New OCC Guidelines for Appraising Management," *Issues in Bank Regulation* (Fall 1989): 20–22. For an interesting discussion of decision-making processes used in the United States versus those used in the United Kingdom, see Mark Andrew Mitchell, Ronald D. Taylor, and Faruk Tanyel, "Product Elimination Decisions: A Comparison of American and British Manufacturing Firms," *International Journal of Commerce & Management* 8, no. 1 (1998): 8–27.

14. For an extended discussion of this model, see William B. Werther Jr., "Productivity Through People: The Decision-Making Process," *Management Decisions* (1988): 37–41.

15. These assumptions are adapted from James G. March and Herbert A. Simon, *Organizations* (New York: Wiley, 1958), 137–138.

16. William C. Symonds, "There's More Than Beer in Molson's Mug," *Business Week,* February 10, 1992, 108.

17. Chester I. Barnard, *The Function of the Executive* (Cambridge, MA: Harvard University Press, 1938).

18. For further elaboration on these factors, see Robert Tannenbaum, Irving R. Weschle, and Fred Massarik, *Leadership and Organization: A Behavioral Science Approach* (New York: McGraw-Hill, 1961), 277–278.

19. For more discussion of these factors, see F. A. Shull Jr., A. I. Delbecq, and L. L. Cummings, *Organizational Decision Making* (New York: McGraw-Hill, 1970).

20. Thomas Kidaa; Kimberly K. Morenob; James F. Smitha, "Investment Decision Making: Do Experienced Decision Makers Fall Prey to the Paradox of Choice?" *Journal of Behavioral Finance* 11, no. 1 (2010): 21–30. See also, B. Scheibehenne, Rainer Greifendeder, and Peter M. Tood, "Can There Ever Be Too Many Options? A Meta-Analytic Review of Choice Overload," *Journal of Consumer Research,* 2010, 37.

21. For a worthwhile discussion of forecasting and evaluating the outcomes of alternatives, see J. R. C. Wensley, "Effective Decision Aids in Marketing," *European Journal of Marketing* (1989): 70–79.

22. This discussion was based on Nicholas H. Lurie and Jayashankar M. Swaminathan, "Is timely information always better? The effect of feedback frequency on decision making," *Organizational Behavior and Human Decision Processes* 108 (2009): 315–329.

23. H. A. Simon, *Models of Man: Social and Rational* (New York: Wiley, 1957).

24. K. E. Stanovich and R. F. West, "Individual differences in reasoning: Implications for the rationality debate," in T. Gilovich, D. Griffin, and D. Kahneman (Eds.), *Heuristics and Biases: The Psychology of Intuitive Judgment* (Cambridge: Cambridge University Press, 2002); Daniel Kahneman, "A Perspective on Judgment and Choice," *American Psychologist* 58, no. 9: 697–720. See also Jonathan St. B. T. Evans, 2008, "Dual-Processing Accounts of Reasoning, Judgment, and Social Cognition," *Annual Review of Psychology,* 59: 255–278.

25. Erik Dane and Michael G. Pratt, "Exploring Intuition and Its Role in Managerial Decision Making," *Academy of Management Review* 32 (2007): 33–54.

26. Frank Knight, *Risk, Uncertainty, and Profit* (Boston: Houghton Mifflin, 1921).

27. Many chief executives resort to reorganization in an attempt to improve their company's performance, but research suggests most reorganizations fail because they don't improve the quality of decision making. See Marcia W. Blenko, Michael C. Mankins, and Paul Rogers, "The Decision-Driven Organization," *Harvard Business Review,* June 2010, http://hbr.org.

28. Truman F. Bewley, "Knightian Decision Theory, Part I," *Decisions in Economics and Finance* 25, no. 2 (2002): 79–110.

29. Steven C. Harper, "What Separates Executives from Managers," *Business Horizons* (September/October 1988): 13–19; to better understand the negative influence of poor decision making, see Joseph L. Bower and Clark G. Gilbert, "How Managers' Everyday Decisions Create or Destroy Your Company's Strategy," *Harvard Business Review* 85, no. 2 (2007): 72–79. For a different viewpoint on the value of intuition in decision making, see Andrew McAfee, "The Future of Decision Making: Less Intuition, More Evidence," *Harvard Business Review,* January 7, 2010, http://blogs.hbr.org.

30. The scope of this text does not permit elaboration on these three decision-making tools. However, for an excellent discussion on how they are used in decision making, see Richard M. Hodgetts, *Management: Theory, Process and Practice* (Philadelphia: Saunders, 1975), 234–266.

31. For more information on probability theory and decisions, see Johannes Honekopp, "Precision of Probability Information and Prominence of Outcomes: A Description and Evaluation of Decisions Under Uncertainty," *Organizational Behavior and Human Decision Processes* 90 (2003): 124.

32. Richard C. Mosier, "Expected Value: Applying Research to Uncertainty," *Appraisal Journal* (July 1989): 293–296. See also Amartya Sen, "The Formulation of Rational Choice," *American Economic Review* 84 (May 1994): 385–390. For an illustration of how probability theory can be applied to solve personal problems, see Jeff D. Opdyke, "'Will My Nest Egg Last?'—Probability Theory, an Old Math Technique, Is Providing New—and Better—Answers to That Question," *Wall Street Journal,* June 5, 2000, 7.

33. For an example of how financial analysts use decision trees to reduce risk, see Joseph J. Mezrich, "When Is a Tree a Hedge?" *Financial Analysts Journal* 50, no. 6 (November/December 1994): 75–81.

34. John F. Magee, "Decision Trees for Decision Making," *Harvard Business Review* (July/August 1964). To better understand the relationships among decision trees, firm strategy, and financial analysis, see Michael Brydon, "Evaluating Strategic Options Using Decision-Theoretic Planning," *Information and Technology Management* 7, no. 1 (2006): 35–49.

35. Rakesh Sarin and Peter Wakker, "Folding Back in Decision Tree Analysis," *Management Science* 40 (May 1994): 625–628; Eric H. Sorensen, Keith L. Miller, and Chee K. Ooi, "The Decision Tree Approach to Stock Selection," *Journal of Portfolio Management* 27, no. 1 (Fall 2000): 42–52.

36. For a different view of how organizations can incorporate a scientific approach in their decision-making process, see "Putting the Science in Management Science?" *MIT Sloan Management Review,* March 2010, http://sloanreview.mit.edu.

37. This section is based on Samuel C. Certo, *Supervision: Quality and Diversity Through Leadership* (Homewood, IL: Austen Press/Irwin, 1994), 198–202. See also Norbert L. Kerr and R. Scott Tindale, "Group Performance and Decision Making," *Annual Review of Psychology* 55 (2004): 623–655. See also, George P. Huber and Kyle Lewis, "Cross-Understanding: Implications for Group Cognition and Performance," *Academy of Management Review* 35, no.1 (2010): 6–26.

38. Clark Wigley, "Working Smart on Tough Business Problems," *Supervisory Management* (February 1992): 1.

39. Ferda Erdem, "Optimal Trust and Teamwork: From Groupthink to Teamthink," *Work Study* 52 (2003): 229.

40. Joseph Alan Redman, "Nine Creative Brainstorming Techniques," *Quality Digest* (August 1992): 50–51.

41. For more information on idea generation, see Merry Baskin, "Idea Generation," *Brand Strategy* 172 (2003): 35.

42. David M. Armstrong, "Management by Storytelling," *Executive Female* (May/June 1992): 38–41.

43. Philip L. Roth, L. F. Lydia, and Fred S. Switzer, "Nominal Group Technique—An Aid for Implementing TQM," *CPA Journal* (May 1995): 68–69; Karen L. Dowling, "Asynchronous Implementation of the Nominal Group Technique: Is It effective?" *Decision Support Systems* 29, no. 3 (October 2000): 229–248.

44. N. Delkey, *The Delphi Method: An Experimental Study of Group Opinion* (Santa Monica, CA: Rand Corporation, 1969); Gene Rowe and George Wright, "The Delphi Technique as a Forecasting Tool: Issues and Analysis," *International Journal of Forecasting* 15, no. 4 (October 1999).

45. This case was based on Nick Wingfield, "Microsoft's Videogame Efforts Take a Costly Hit," *Wall Street Journal,* July 6, 2007, A3.

chapter 9

Strategic Planning

STRATEGIES, TACTICS, AND COMPETITIVE DYNAMICS

Target Skill

strategic planning skill: the ability to engage in long-range planning that focuses on the organization as a whole

objectives

To help build my *strategic planning skill,* when studying this chapter, I will attempt to acquire:

1. Definitions of both *strategic planning* and *strategy*

2. An understanding of the strategic management process

3. A knowledge of the impact of environmental analysis on strategy formulation

4. Insights into how to use critical question analysis and SWOT analysis to formulate strategy

5. An understanding of how to use business portfolio analysis and industry analysis to formulate strategy

6. Insights into what tactical planning is and how strategic and tactical planning should be coordinated

7. An awareness of how competitive dynamics can influence an organization's financial performance

CHALLENGE CASE

SAMSUNG PLANS FOR THE FUTURE

SAMSUNG ELECTRONICS STORY PROVIDES a "rags-to-riches" narrative grounded firmly in the importance of strategic planning. Founded in 1969 as Samsung Electric, by the mid-1990s the South Korean company had established its reputation as a second-tier manufacturer of low-priced small appliances crafted apparently with little thought to design or quality control. During that time, for example, consumers would be unlikely to name Samsung as a manufacturer of high-quality televisions.

But a turning point came in 1997, when the Asian currency crisis forced many companies, including Samsung, to retrench. Samsung was forced to lay off one-fourth of its workforce and sell or dissolve 100 business units. At the same time, however, the downturn created an opportunity for Samsung. While another company might have reacted by cutting costs and conducting business as usual, Samsung used the downturn to rethink its mission. The outcome of that self-assessment: a transformed company, with a new focus on quality.

Samsung's new strategic plan yielded almost immediate results. The company's market share grew dramatically in several product categories, landing it close to the leader in televisions, cell phones, and computer displays. The company's new image also made it a sought-after partner for many organizations.

Samsung's internal transformation resulted in financial success. The company's significantly improved financial performance came through self-improvement—not, for example, by outsourcing the work to other firms. Today, Samsung operates 167 subsidiaries in a variety of industries ranging from consumer electronics to construction, chemicals, securities, and even sugar. The company's more than 161,000 employees work in nearly 200 cities. Today, Samsung is the world's largest manufacturer of LCD televisions and computer chips; in the mobile phone industry Samsung is second only to Nokia.

Recognizing its responsibility in the world economy, Samsung has outlined an ambitious strategic plan regarding carbon reduction. The company pledges to reduce greenhouse gas emissions from its operations and from the use of its products by 50 percent by 2013. A similar initiative started in 2001 cut greenhouse gas emissions by 45 percent over eight years.

Under the terms of its latest plan, Samsung allocated $21.6 billion to research and development that will enable it to expand into such green markets as solar and wind power, energy efficiency, and LED technology. Samsung will leverage its know-how in some industries to enhance its research in others—for example, it will apply its knowledge in LCD televisions to research in solar panels. Samsung's goal: to be number one in solar energy by 2015.[1]

■ *Samsung's improved product quality has made it the world's largest electronics company, selling hundreds of product lines, such as LCD television sets and home theaters.*

EXPLORING YOUR MANAGEMENT SKILL

You can explore your level of strategic planning skill before studying the chapter by completing the exercise "Exploring Your Management Skill: Part 1" on page 221 and after studying this chapter by completing the exercise "Exploring Your Management Skill: Part 2" on page 221.

THE STRATEGIC PLANNING CHALLENGE

The Challenge Case highlights the competitive course recently taken by Samsung. Developing a new course of this sort is actually part of Samsung's strategic planning process. The material in this chapter explains how developing a competitive strategy fits into strategic planning and discusses the strategic planning process as a whole. Major topics included in this chapter are (1) strategic planning, (2) tactical planning, (3) comparing and coordinating strategic and tactical planning, and (4) competitive dynamics.

STRATEGIC PLANNING

If managers are to be successful strategic planners, they must understand the fundamentals of strategic planning and how to formulate strategic plans.[2]

Fundamentals of Strategic Planning

This section presents the basic principles of strategic planning. In doing so, it discusses definitions of both *strategic planning* and *strategy* in detail.

Defining Strategic Planning **Strategic planning** is long-range planning that focuses on the organization as a whole.[3] In doing strategic planning, managers consider the organization as a total unit and ask themselves what must be done in the long term to attain organizational goals.[4] *Long range* is usually defined as a period of time extending about three to five years into the future. Hence, in strategic planning, managers try to determine what their organization should do to be successful three to five years from now. The most successful managers tend to be those who take a comprehensive approach to strategic planning and are careful not to "cut corners" during the process, all while encouraging innovative strategic thinking within their organization.[5]

Managers may have a problem trying to decide exactly how far into the future they should extend their strategic planning. As a general rule, they should follow the **commitment principle**, which states that managers should commit funds for planning only if they can anticipate, in the foreseeable future, a return on planning expenses as a result of long-range planning analysis. Realistically, planning costs are an investment and therefore should not be incurred unless a reasonable return on that investment is anticipated.

Defining Strategy **Strategy** is defined as a broad and general plan developed to reach long-term objectives. Organizational strategy can, and generally does, focus on many different organizational areas, such as marketing, finance, production, research and development, and public relations. It gives broad direction to the organization.[6]

Strategy is actually the end result of strategic planning. Although larger organizations tend to be more precise in developing organizational strategy than smaller organizations are, every organization should have a strategy of some sort.[7] For a strategy to be worthwhile, though, it must be consistent with organizational objectives, which, in turn, must be consistent with organizational purpose. Table 9.1 illustrates this relationship between organizational objectives and strategy by presenting sample organizational objectives and strategies for three well-known business organizations.

TABLE 9.1	Examples of Organizational Objectives and Related Strategies for Three Organizations in Different Business Areas		
Company	**Type of Business**	**Sample Organizational Objectives**	**Strategy to Accomplish Objectives**
Ford Motor Company	Automobile manufacturing	1. Regain market share recently lost to Toyota 2. Regain quality reputation that was damaged because of Pinto gas tank explosions	1. Resize and downsize present models 2. Continue to produce subintermediate, standard, and luxury cars 3. Emphasize use of programmed combustion engines instead of diesel engines
Burger King	Fast food	1. Increase productivity	1. Increase people efficiency 2. Increase machine efficiency
CP Railroad	Transportation	1. Continue company growth 2. Continue company profits	1. Modernize 2. Develop valuable real estate holdings 3. Complete an appropriate railroad merger

Strategic Management

Strategic management is the process of ensuring that an organization possesses and benefits from the use of an appropriate organizational strategy. In this definition, an appropriate strategy is one best suited to the needs of an organization at a particular time.

The strategic management process is generally thought to consist of five sequential and continuing steps:[8]

1. Environmental analysis
2. Establishment of an organizational direction
3. Strategy formulation
4. Strategy implementation
5. Strategic control

The relationships among these steps are illustrated in Figure 9.1.

Environmental Analysis   The first step of the strategic management process is environmental analysis. Chapter 2 presented organizations as open management systems that are continually interacting with their environments. In essence, an organization can be successful only if it is appropriately matched to its environment. **Environmental analysis** is the study of the organizational environment to pinpoint environmental factors that can significantly influence organizational operations. Managers commonly perform environmental analyses to help them understand what is happening both inside and outside their organizations and to increase the probability that the organizational strategies they develop will appropriately reflect the organizational environment.

FIGURE 9.1   Steps of the strategic management process

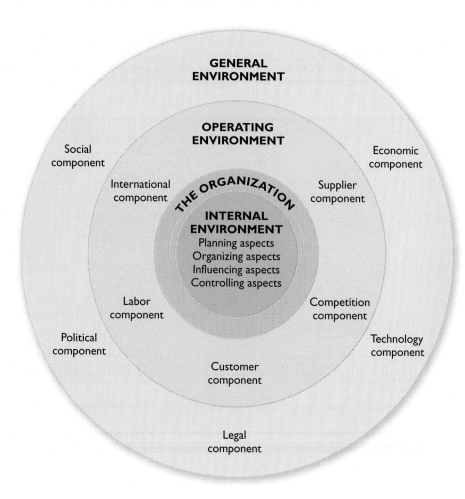

FIGURE 9.2
The organization, the levels of its environment, and the components of those levels

To perform an environmental analysis efficiently and effectively, a manager must thoroughly understand how organizational environments are structured. For purposes of environmental analysis, the environment of an organization is generally divided into three distinct levels: general environment, operating environment, and internal environment.[9] Figure 9.2 illustrates the positions of these levels relative to one another and to the organization; it also shows the important components of each level. Managers must be well aware of these three environmental levels, understand how each level affects organizational performance, and then formulate organizational strategies in response to this understanding.

THE GENERAL ENVIRONMENT The level of an organization's external environment that contains components having broad long-term implications for managing the organization is the **general environment**. The components normally considered part of the general environment are economic, social, political, legal, technological, and international.

The economic component The economic component is that part of the general environment that indicates how resources are being distributed and used within the environment. This component is based on **economics**, the science that focuses on understanding how people of a particular community or nation produce, distribute, and use various goods and services. Important issues to be considered in an economic analysis of an environment are generally the wages paid to labor, inflation, the taxes paid by labor and businesses, the cost of materials used in the production process, and the prices at which produced goods and services are sold to customers.

These economic issues can significantly influence the environment in which a company operates, and the ease or difficulty the organization experiences in attempting to reach its objectives. For example, it should be somewhat easier for an organization to sell its products at higher prices if potential consumers in the environment are earning relatively high wages and paying relatively low taxes than if these same potential customers are earning relatively low wages and have significantly fewer after-tax dollars to spend.

Organizational strategy should reflect the economic issues in the organization's environment. To build on the preceding example, if the total amount of after-tax income that potential customers earn has significantly declined, an appropriate organizational strategy might be to lower the price of goods or services to make them more affordable. Such a strategy should be evaluated carefully; however, because it could have a serious impact on organizational profits.

The social component The social component is part of the general environment that describes the characteristics of the society in which the organization exists. Two important features of a society commonly studied during environmental analysis are demographics and social values.[10]

Demographics are the statistical characteristics of a population. These characteristics include changes in numbers of people and income distribution among various population segments. Such changes can influence the reception of goods and services within the organization's environment and thus should be reflected in organizational strategy.

For example, the demand for retirement housing would probably increase dramatically if both the number and the income of retirees in a particular market area doubled.[11] Effective organizational strategy would include a mechanism for dealing with such a probable increase in demand within the organization's environment.

An understanding of demographics is also helpful for developing a strategy aimed at recruiting new employees to fill certain positions within an organization. Knowing that only a small number of people have a certain type of educational background, for example, would tell an organization that it should compete more intensely to attract these people. To formulate a recruitment strategy, managers need a clear understanding of the demographics of the groups from which employees eventually will be hired. The practice known as strategic workforce planning, or SWP, helps organizations identify the workforce they need to achieve their strategic goals. Some early adopters of SWP, such as 3M, are not only able to track their workforce spending and determine how it impacts revenues but also compare their data to those of competitors. The recent global economic downturn has stalled the growth of SWP, however. In attempting to "ride out" the recession, many employers have adopted a "wait and see" attitude toward workforce planning until business stabilizes.[12]

Social values are the relative degrees of worth that society places on the ways in which it exists and functions. Over time, social values can change dramatically, causing significant changes in how people live. These changes alter the organizational environment and, as a result, have an impact on organizational strategy. It is important for managers to remember that although changes in the values of a particular society may come either slowly or quickly, they are inevitable.

The political component The political component is that part of the general environment related to government affairs. Examples include the type of government in existence, government's attitude toward various industries, lobbying efforts by interest groups, progress on the passage of laws, and political party platforms and candidates. The reunification of Germany and the shift from a Marxist-Socialist government in the Soviet Union in the 1980s illustrate how the political component of an organization's general environment can change at the international level.

The legal component The legal component is that part of the general environment that contains passed legislation. This component comprises the rules or laws that society's members must follow. Some examples of legislation specifically aimed at the operation of organizations are the Clean Air Act, which focuses on minimizing air pollution; the Occupational Safety and Health Act, which aims at ensuring a safe workplace; the Comprehensive Environmental Response, Compensation, and Liability Act, which emphasizes controlling hazardous waste sites; and the Consumer Products Safety Act, which upholds the notion that businesses must provide safe products for consumers. Over time, new laws are passed and some old ones are amended or eliminated.

The technology component The technology component is that part of the general environment that includes new approaches to producing goods and services. These approaches can be new procedures as well as new equipment. The trend toward exploiting robots to improve productivity is an example of the technology component. The increasing use of robots in the next decade should vastly improve the efficiency of U.S. industry.

Consumer tastes and preferences are among the factors that firms consider in their environmental analysis. For instance, will this fragrance from Singapore appeal to Western customers? Its manufacturer will try to answer that question in planning its export strategy.

TABLE 9.2   Important Aspects of the International Component of the Organization's Operating Environment

Legal Environment	Cultural Environment
Legal tradition	Customs, norms, values, beliefs
Effectiveness of legal system	Language
Treaties with foreign nations	Attitudes
Patent and trademark laws	Motivations
Laws affecting business firms	Social institutions
	Status symbols
Economic Environment	Religious beliefs
Level of economic development	
Population	**Political System**
Gross national product	Form of government
Per capita income	Political ideology
Literacy level	Stability of government
Social infrastructure	Strength of opposition parties and groups
Natural resources	Social unrest
Climate	Political strife and insurgency
Membership in regional economic blocs (EEC, LAFTA, etc.)	Government attitude toward foreign firms
	Foreign policy
Monetary and fiscal policies	
Nature of competition	
Currency convertibility	
Inflation	
Taxation system	
Interest rates	
Wage and salary levels	

The international component The international component is the operating environment segment that is composed of all the factors relating to the international implications of organizational operations. Although not all organizations must deal with international issues, the number that have to do so is increasing dramatically and continually in the early twenty-first century. Factors in the international component include other countries' laws, culture, economics, and politics.[13] Important variables within each of these four categories are presented in Table 9.2.

how managers do it

Achieving Global Efficiencies at Kraft

U.S.-based Kraft's recent acquisition of British candy maker Cadbury provides an example illustrating the importance of the company's international component. According to industry observers, the acquisition triples Kraft's market share of chocolate and candy sales worldwide, and Cadbury was expected to add $4 billion in value to the company. Another benefit of the acquisition: a significant streamlining of the two companies' IT capabilities. Kraft chairman Irene Rosenfeld also asserted that combining the two companies would result in substantial tax advantages that would increase the company's profitability.[14] ■

THE INDUSTRY ENVIRONMENT The level of an organization's external environment that contains components normally having relatively specific and immediate implications for managing the organization is the **industry environment**. The **Five Forces Model**, perhaps the best-known tool for industry analysis, was developed by internationally acclaimed strategic management expert Michael E. Porter.[15] Essentially, Porter's Model outlines the primary forces that determine competitiveness within an industry and illustrates how those forces are related.

Porter's Model is presented in Figure 9.3. According to the model, the attractiveness of an industry is determined by five alternative forces. First, the **threat of new entrants** refers to the ability of new firms to enter an industry; as the threat of new entrants increases, the attractiveness of an industry decreases. Second, **buyer power** refers to the power that customers have over the firms operating in an industry; as buyer power increases, the attractiveness of an industry decreases. Third, **supplier power** denotes the power that suppliers have over the firms operating in an industry. As supplier power increases, industry attractiveness decreases. Fourth, the **threat of substitute products** refers to the extent to which customers may use products or services from another industry instead of the focal industry. As the threat of substitutes increases, which implies that customers have more choices, the attractiveness of an industry decreases. Finally, **intensity of rivalry** refers to the intensity of competition among the organizations in an industry. As the intensity of rivalry increases, the attractiveness of an industry decreases.

THE INTERNAL ENVIRONMENT The level of an organization's environment that exists inside the organization and normally has immediate and specific implications for managing the organization is the **internal environment.** In broad terms, the internal environment includes marketing, finance, and accounting. From a more specific management viewpoint, it includes planning, organizing, influencing, and controlling within the organization.

Establishing Organizational Direction The second step of the strategic management process is establishing organizational direction. Through an interpretation of information gathered

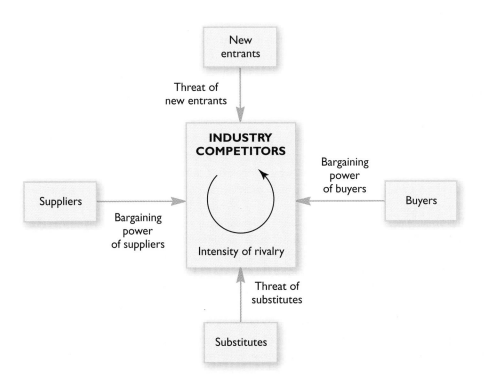

FIGURE 9.3
Porter's Model of Factors that determine competitiveness within an industry

class discussion highlight

MODERN RESEARCH AND PLANNING SKILL

The Influence of the Industry Environment

Researchers in strategic management have devoted a great deal of attention to examining the influence of the industry environment on a firm's performance. Specifically, does the performance of a firm depend on the industry in which it operates? In other words, does a rising tide lift all boats?

To examine this question, Professor Misangyi and colleagues examined more than 1,500 U.S.–based corporations operating in approximately 75 industries over a 16-year time frame. Using a sophisticated statistical technique known as multilevel modeling, the authors were able to examine the influence of industry on firm profitability. According to their findings, what percentage of firm profitability is explained by industry membership? Explain how you arrived at your answer. Do you think that this percentage will remain constant across different countries?

Source: This research highlight is based on Vilmos Misangyi, Heather Elms, Thomas Grekhamer, and Jeffrey Lepine, "A New Perspective on a Fundamental Debate: A Multilevel Approach to Industry, Corporate, and Business Unit Effects," *Strategic Management Journal* 27, 571–590.

during environmental analysis, managers can determine the direction in which an organization should move. Two important ingredients of organizational direction are organizational mission and organizational objectives.

Determining Organizational Mission The most common initial act in establishing organizational direction is determining an organizational mission. **Organizational mission** is the purpose for which—the reason why—an organization exists. In general, the firm's organizational mission reflects such information as what types of products or services it produces, who its customers tend to be, and what important values it holds. Organizational mission is a broad statement of organizational direction and is based on a thorough analysis of information generated through environmental analysis.[16]

Developing a Mission Statement A **mission statement** is a written document developed by management, normally based on input by managers as well as nonmanagers, which describes and explains what the mission of an organization actually is.[17] The mission is expressed in writing to ensure that all organization members will have easy access to it and thoroughly understand exactly what the organization is trying to accomplish.

The Importance of Organizational Mission An organizational mission is important to an organization because it helps management increase the probability that the organization will be successful. There are several reasons why it does this. First, the existence of an organizational mission helps management focus human effort in a common direction. The mission makes explicit the major targets the organization is trying to reach and helps managers keep these targets in mind as they make decisions. Second, an organizational mission serves as a sound rationale for allocating resources. A properly developed mission statement gives managers general, but useful, guidelines about how resources should be used to best accomplish organizational purpose. Third, a mission statement helps management define broad but important job areas within an organization and therefore critical jobs that must be accomplished.[18]

The Relationship Between Mission and Objectives Organizational objectives were defined in Chapter 7 as the targets toward which the open management system is directed. Sound organizational objectives reflect and flow naturally from the purpose of the organization. The organization's purpose is expressed in its mission statement. As a result, useful organizational objectives must reflect and flow naturally from an organizational mission that, in turn, was designed to reflect and flow naturally from the results of an environmental analysis.[19]

Strategy Formulation: Tools After managers involved in the strategic management process have analyzed the environment and determined organizational direction through the development of a mission statement and organizational objectives, they are ready to formulate strategy. **Strategy formulation** is the process of determining appropriate courses of action for achieving organizational objectives and thereby accomplishing organizational purpose.

Managers formulate strategies that reflect environmental analysis, lead to fulfillment of organizational mission, and result in reaching organizational objectives. Special tools they can use to assist them in formulating strategies include the following:

1. Critical question analysis
2. SWOT analysis
3. Business portfolio analysis

These three strategy development tools are related but distinct. Managers should use the tool or combination of tools that seems most appropriate for them and their organizations.

CRITICAL QUESTION ANALYSIS A synthesis of the ideas of several contemporary management writers suggests that formulating appropriate organizational strategy is a process of **critical question analysis**—answering the following four basic questions:[20]

- **What are the purposes and objectives of the organization?** The answer to this question will tell management where the organization should be going. As indicated earlier, appropriate strategy reflects both organizational purpose and objectives. By answering this question during the strategy formulation process, managers are likely to remember this important point and thereby minimize inconsistencies among the organization's purposes, objectives, and strategies.

- **Where is the organization presently going?** The answer to this question can tell managers whether the organization is achieving its goals and, if it is, whether the level of progress is satisfactory. Whereas the first question focuses on where the organization should be going, this one focuses on where the organization is actually going.

- **In what kind of environment does the organization now exist?** Both internal and external environments—factors inside and outside the organization—are covered in this question. For example, assume that a poorly trained middle-management team and a sudden influx of competitors in a market are respective factors in the internal and external environments of an organization. Any strategy formulated, if it is to be appropriate, must deal with these factors.

- **What can be done to better achieve organizational objectives in the future?** It is the answer to this question that results in the strategy of the organization. The question should be answered, however, only *after* managers have had an adequate opportunity to reflect on the answers to the previous three questions. Managers cannot develop an appropriate organizational strategy unless they have a clear understanding of where the organization wants to go, where it is going, and in what environment it exists. This understanding is typically achieved through discussion, negotiation, and compromise.[21]

SWOT ANALYSIS **SWOT analysis** is a strategic development tool that matches internal organizational strengths and weaknesses with external opportunities and threats. (SWOT is an acronym for a firm's **S**trengths and **W**eaknesses and its environmental **O**pportunities and **T**hreats.) It is important to note that when using SWOT analysis, strengths and weaknesses refer to the manager's firm, and opportunities and threats refer to the firm's external environment. SWOT analysis is based on the assumption that if managers carefully review such strengths, weaknesses, opportunities, and threats, a useful strategy for ensuring organizational success will become evident to them.[22]

Because it must be set at the highest level of the firm, the company's direction is the responsibility of the CEO. Xerox CEO Ursula Burns has overseen the company's successful return to profitability by shifting its focus from being a photocopier company to being a supplier of document-management tools and services.

BUSINESS PORTFOLIO ANALYSIS Business portfolio analysis is another strategy development tool that has gained wide acceptance. **Business portfolio analysis** is an organizational strategy formulation technique that is based on the philosophy that organizations should develop strategy much as they handle investment portfolios. Just as sound financial investments should be supported and unsound ones discarded, sound organizational activities should be emphasized and unsound ones deemphasized. Two business portfolio tools are the BCG Growth-Share Matrix and the GE Multifactor Portfolio Matrix.

The BCG Growth-Share Matrix The Boston Consulting Group (BCG), a leading manufacturing consulting firm, developed and popularized a portfolio analysis tool that helps managers develop organizational strategy based on market share of businesses and the growth of markets in which businesses exist.

The first step in using the BCG Growth-Share Matrix is identifying the organization's strategic business units (SBUs). A **strategic business unit** is a significant organization segment that is analyzed to develop organizational strategy aimed at generating future business or revenue. Exactly what constitutes an SBU varies from organization to organization. In larger organizations, an SBU could be a company division, a single product, or a complete product line. In smaller organizations, it might be the entire company. Although SBUs vary drastically in form, each has the following four characteristics:[23]

1. It is a single business or collection of related businesses.
2. It has its own competitors.
3. It has a manager who is accountable for its operation.
4. It is an area that can be independently planned for within the organization.

After SBUs have been identified for a particular organization, the next step in using the BCG Matrix is to categorize each SBU within one of the following four matrix quadrants (see Figure 9.4):

*   **Star**—An SBU that is a "star" has a high share of a high-growth market and typically needs large amounts of cash to support rapid and significant growth. Stars also generate large amounts of cash for the organization and are usually segments in which management can make additional investments and earn attractive returns.

*   **Cash Cow**—An SBU that is a cash cow has a large share of a market that is growing only slightly. Naturally, these SBUs provide the organization with large amounts of cash, but because their market is not growing significantly, the cash is generally used to meet the financial demands of the organization in other areas, such as the expansion of a star SBU.

FIGURE 9.4
The BCG Growth-Share Matrix

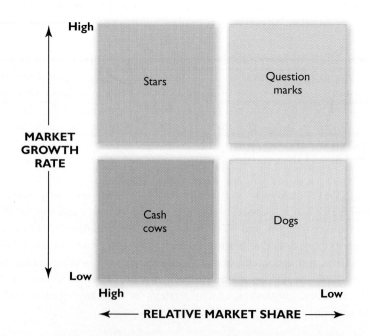

- **Question Mark**—An SBU that is a question mark has a small share of a high-growth market. They are dubbed "question marks" because it is uncertain whether management should invest more cash in them to gain a larger share of the market or deemphasize or eliminate them. Management will choose the first option when it believes it can turn the question mark into a star, and the second when it thinks further investment would be fruitless.

- **Dog**—An SBU that is a dog has a relatively small share of a low-growth market. They may barely support themselves; in some cases, they actually drain off cash resources generated by other SBUs. Examples of dogs are SBUs that produce typewriters or cash registers.

Companies such as Westinghouse and Shell Oil have successfully used the BCG Matrix in their strategic management processes. This technique, however, has some potential pitfalls. For one thing, the matrix does not consider such factors as (1) various types of risk associated with product development, (2) threats that inflation and other economic conditions can create in the future, and (3) social, political, and ecological pressures. These pitfalls may be the reason for recent research results indicating that the BCG Matrix does not always help managers make better strategic decisions.[24] Managers must remember to weigh such factors carefully when designing organizational strategy based on the BCG Matrix.

The GE Multifactor Portfolio Matrix With the help of McKinsey and Company, a leading consulting firm, the General Electric Company (GE) developed another popular portfolio analysis tool. Called the GE Multifactor Portfolio Matrix, this tool helps managers develop organizational strategy that is based primarily on market attractiveness and business strengths. The GE Multifactor Portfolio Matrix was deliberately designed to be more complete than the BCG Growth-Share Matrix.

Its basic use is illustrated in Figure 9.5. Each of the organization's businesses or SBUs is plotted on a matrix in two dimensions: industry attractiveness and business strength. Each of these two dimensions is actually a composite of a variety of factors that each firm must determine for itself, given its own unique situation. As examples, industry attractiveness might be determined by such factors as the number of competitors in an industry, the rate of industry growth, and the weakness of competitors within an industry; while business strengths might be determined by

I – Invest/grow
S – Selective investment
H – Harvest/divest

FIGURE 9.5
GE's Multifactor Portfolio Matrix

Wal-Mart has adopted a consistent and tough-to-beat low-price strategy, as these signs in a San Antonio, TX, Wal-Mart store show.

such factors as a company's financially solid position, its good bargaining position over suppliers, and its high level of technology use.

Several circles appear on Figure 9.5, each representing a company line of business or SBU. Circle size indicates the relative market size for each line of business. The shaded portion of a circle represents the proportion of the total SBU market that a company has captured.

Specific strategies for a company are implied by where their businesses (represented by circles) fall on the matrix. Businesses falling in the cells that form a diagonal from lower left to upper right are medium-strength businesses that should be invested in only selectively. Businesses above and to the left of this diagonal are the strongest and the ones that the company should invest in and help to grow. Businesses in the cells below and to the right of the diagonal are low in overall strength and are serious candidates for divestiture.

Portfolio models are graphic frameworks for analyzing relationships among the businesses of an organization, and they can provide useful strategy recommendations. However, no such model yet devised gives managers a universally accepted approach for dealing with these issues. Portfolio models, then, should never be applied in a mechanistic fashion, and any conclusions they suggest must be carefully considered in light of sound managerial judgment and experience.

STRATEGY FORMULATION: TYPES Understanding the forces that determine competitiveness within an industry should help managers develop strategies that will make their companies more competitive within the industry. Porter has developed three generic strategies to illustrate the kind of strategies managers might develop to make their organizations more competitive.[25]

Differentiation **Differentiation**, the first of Porter's strategies, focuses on making an organization more competitive by developing a product or products that customers perceive as being different from products offered by competitors. Differentiation includes uniqueness in such areas as product quality, design, and level of after-sales service. Examples of products that customers commonly purchase because they perceive them as being different are Nike's Air Jordan shoes (because of their high-technology "air" construction) and Honda automobiles (because of their high reliability).

Cost leadership **Cost leadership** is a strategy that focuses on making an organization more competitive by producing products more cheaply than competitors can. According to the logic behind this strategy, by producing products more cheaply than its competitors, an organization will be able to offer products to customers at lower prices than competitors can, and thereby increase its market share. Examples of tactics managers might use to gain cost leadership are obtaining lower prices for product parts purchased from suppliers and using technology such as robots to increase organizational productivity.

Focus **Focus** is a strategy that emphasizes making an organization more competitive by targeting a particular customer. Magazine publishers commonly use a focus strategy in offering their products to specific customers. *Working Woman* and *Ebony* are examples of magazines that are aimed, respectively, at the target markets of employed women and African Americans.

SAMPLE ORGANIZATIONAL STRATEGIES Analyzing the organizational environment and applying one or more of the strategy tools—critical question analysis, SWOT analysis, business portfolio analysis, and Porter's Model—will give managers a foundation on which to formulate an organizational strategy. The four common organizational strategies that evolve this way are growth, stability, retrenchment, and divestiture. The following discussion of these organizational strategies features business portfolio analysis as the tool used to arrive at the strategy, although the same strategies could result from critical question analysis, SWOT analysis, or Porter's Model.

Growth **Growth** is a strategy adopted by management to increase the amount of business that an SBU is currently generating. The growth strategy is generally applied to star SBUs or question mark SBUs that have the potential to become stars. Management generally invests substantial amounts of money to implement this strategy and may even sacrifice short-term profit to build long-term gain.[26]

Managers can also pursue a growth strategy by purchasing an SBU from another organization.

---

how managers do it

Pursuing Growth by Acquisition at Black & Decker

Black & Decker held the leadership position in power tools for many years, but the company wanted to extend its reach beyond that product line. Rather than attempt to develop its own line of power tools, Black & Decker purchased General Electric's small-appliance business. Through this purchase, Black & Decker hoped that the amount of business it did would grow significantly over the long term. Similarly, President Enterprises, the largest food company in Taiwan, recently bought the American Famous Amos brand of chocolate chip cookies. Despite a downturn in the U.S. cookie market, management at President saw the purchase as important for company growth because it gave the company a nationally recognized product line in the United States.[27] ■

Stability **Stability** is a strategy adopted by management to maintain or slightly improve the amount of business that an SBU is generating. This strategy is generally applied to cash cows, because these SBUs are already in an advantageous position. Management must be careful, however, that in its pursuit of stability it does not turn cash cows into dogs.

Retrenchment In this section, *retrench* is used in the military sense: to defend or fortify. Through **retrenchment** strategy, management attempts to strengthen or protect the amount of business an SBU is generating. This strategy is generally applied to cash cows or stars that are beginning to lose market share.

Divestiture **Divestiture** is a strategy adopted to eliminate an SBU that is not generating a satisfactory amount of business and that has little hope of doing so in the near future. In essence, the organization sells or closes down the SBU in question. This strategy is usually applied to SBUs that are dogs or question marks that have failed to increase market share but still require significant amounts of cash.

Strategy Implementation

Strategy implementation, the fourth step of the strategic management process, is putting formulated strategies into action.[28] Without successive implementation, valuable strategies developed by managers are virtually worthless.[29]

The successful implementation of strategy requires four basic skills:[30]

1. **Interacting skill** is the ability to manage people during implementation. Managers who are able to understand the fears and frustrations others feel during the implementation of a new strategy tend to be the best implementers. These managers empathize with organization members and bargain for the best way to put a strategy into action.
2. **Allocating skill** is the ability to provide the organizational resources necessary to implement a strategy. Successful implementers are talented at scheduling jobs, budgeting time and money, and allocating other resources that are critical for implementation.

3. **Monitoring skill** is the ability to use information to determine whether a problem has arisen that is blocking implementation. Good strategy implementers set up feedback systems that continually tell them about the status of strategy implementation.

4. **Organizing skill** is the ability to create throughout the organization a network of people who can help solve implementation problems as they occur. Good implementers customize this network to include individuals who can handle the special types of problems anticipated in the implementation of a particular strategy.

Overall, then, the successful implementation of a strategy requires handling people appropriately, allocating resources necessary for implementation, monitoring implementation progress, and solving implementation problems as they occur. Perhaps the most important requirements are knowing which people can solve specific implementation problems and being able to involve them when those problems arise.

Strategic Control   **Strategic control**, the last step of the strategic management process, consists of monitoring and evaluating the strategic management process as a whole to ensure that it is operating properly. Strategic control focuses on the activities involved in environmental analysis, organizational direction, strategy formulation, strategy implementation, and strategic control itself—checking that all steps of the strategic management process are appropriate, compatible, and functioning properly.[31] Strategic control is a special type of organizational control, a topic that is featured in Chapters 21 and 22.

TACTICAL PLANNING

Tactical planning is short-range planning that emphasizes the current operations of various parts of the organization. *Short range* is defined as a period of time extending about one year or less into the future. Managers use tactical planning to outline what the various parts of the organization must do for the organization to be successful at some point one year or less into the future.[32] Tactical plans are usually developed in the areas of production, marketing, personnel, finance, and plant facilities.

Comparing and Coordinating Strategic and Tactical Planning

In striving to implement successful planning systems within organizations, managers must remember several basic differences between strategic planning and tactical planning:

1. Because upper-level managers generally have a better understanding of the organization as a whole than lower-level managers do, and because lower-level managers generally have a better understanding of the day-to-day organizational operations than upper-level managers do, strategic plans are usually developed by upper-level management and tactical plans by lower-level management.

2. Because strategic planning emphasizes analyzing the future and tactical planning emphasizes analyzing the everyday functioning of the organization, facts on which to base strategic plans are usually more difficult to gather than are facts on which to base tactical plans.

3. Because strategic plans are based primarily on a prediction of the future and tactical plans on known circumstances that exist within the organization, strategic plans are generally less detailed than tactical plans.

4. Because strategic planning focuses on the long term and tactical planning on the short term, strategic plans cover a relatively long period of time whereas tactical plans cover a relatively short period of time.

These major differences between strategic and tactical planning are summarized in Table 9.3. Despite their differences, tactical planning and strategic planning are integrally related. As Russell L. Ackoff states, "We can look at them separately, even discuss them separately, but we cannot separate them in fact."[33] In other words, managers need both tactical and strategic planning programs, and these programs must be closely related to be successful. Tactical planning

TABLE 9.3	Major Differences Between Strategic and Tactical Planning	
Area of Difference	Strategic Planning	Tactical Planning
Individuals involved	Developed mainly by upper-level management	Developed mainly by lower-level management
Facts on which to base planning	Facts are relatively difficult to gather	Facts are relatively easy to gather
Amount of detail in plans	Plans contain relatively little detail	Plans contain substantial amounts of detail
Length of time plans cover	Plans cover long periods of time	Plans cover short periods of time

should focus on what to do in the short term to help the organization achieve the long-term objectives determined by strategic planning.

COMPETITIVE DYNAMICS

In the previous sections, we examined the first two components of strategic planning: strategic and tactical actions. In this section, we discuss the final component of strategic planning that is gaining more attention from both researchers and practitioners: competitive dynamics. **Competitive dynamics** refers to the process by which firms undertake strategic and tactical actions and how competitors respond to these actions. While the previous sections distinguish between and classify different types of strategic and tactical actions, the study of competitive dynamics is important in order to understand *why* managers undertake such actions. Inevitably, it is these actions and reactions that influence a firm's ultimate financial performance.

An example of competitive dynamics in strategic planning involves HP and Microsoft. HP recently announced plans to acquire Palm, the manufacturer of numerous PDAs as well as the WebOS smartphone. Not only would the acquisition give HP an automatic boost in the smartphone business—consumers gave HP's own product, the iPaq, a lukewarm reception—it also affords a platform for HP to extend the WebOS architecture to other products. The proposed transaction raises a red flag for Microsoft, as HP had earlier agreed to work with the organization on its Windows Phone 7 product line. Industry observers predict massive change on the horizon.[34] ■

how managers do it

Competing for Smartphone "Bandwidth" at HP

Many studies of strategic planning and competition involve the analysis of industries. In contrast, research in competitive dynamics focuses on competitive dyads, which are groups of two companies competing vigorously within a particular industry.[35] By focusing on only two firms, researchers are able isolate the factors that affect the competitive actions of both the attacker—the first firm to make a strategic or tactical action—and the defender—the second firm, which must choose whether or not to respond to the attacker.[36]

This example may help illustrate the influence of competitive dynamics in strategic planning. On a recent Monday morning, Barnes & Noble reduced the price of its ebook reader—the Nook—by 23 percent. This decision resulted after careful deliberation by the top managers at Barnes & Noble. Hours later, Amazon.com announced through a press release that it would reduce the price of its ebook reader—the Kindle—by an even wider margin, 27 percent.[37] The price war between Barnes & Noble and Amazon.com illustrates the intense rivalry between the two companies as they compete in the market for ebook readers as well as in the market for

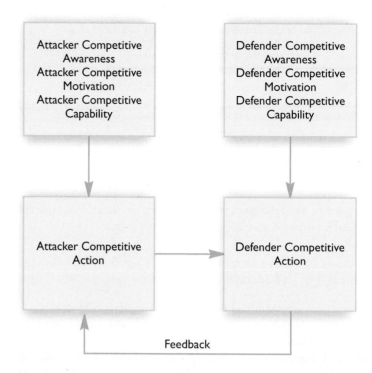

FIGURE 9.6
Competitive Dynamics

ebook sales. In this example, Barnes & Noble represents the attacker, and Amazon.com represents the defender.

Research suggests that three primary factors influence a firm's action or reaction: awareness, motivation, and capability.[38] These factors are illustrated in Figure 9.6. **Competitor awareness** refers to how mindful a company is of its competitor's actions. In the example above, Amazon.com was clearly aware of Barnes & Noble's price cuts, which garnered a great deal of media attention. This media coverage is expected, as larger firms typically receive higher levels of media attention.[39] In addition to media coverage, companies may learn more about competitive actions by taking note of a competitor's press releases. Alternatively, companies may learn more about their competitors' actions by seeking information from common customers or suppliers or from employees who previously worked for the competitor.

Competitor motivation refers to the incentives that an organization has to take action. Extending this example, Amazon.com was highly motivated to respond to Barnes & Noble's price cuts. If Amazon.com did not respond to these price cuts, many customers may have opted to purchase a Nook instead of a Kindle. This buyer decision becomes important, as sales of ebook readers also lead to subsequent ebook sales. A customer purchase of a Nook, for instance, is also likely to multiply ebook purchases from Barnes & Noble. Considering such future sales highlights just how motivated both companies are in the market for ebook readers. In addition, managers' incentives (e.g., pay packages) may also influence their motivation to engage in particular competitive actions.

Finally, **competitor capability** refers to a firm's ability to undertake an action. Often, capability refers to the resources that a firm has to take an action. For instance, a firm's competitor capability includes items such as available cash or the experience of the firm's management team. Once again extending the previous example, Amazon.com does not necessarily need cash to implement a price reduction for its Kindle. Nonetheless, Amazon.com does have to consider the long-term, financial effects stemming from selling Kindles at a reduced price. While tactical actions may not require substantial resources, more strategic actions may require larger investments and thus, higher levels of resources.

Effective strategic planning requires an understanding of competitors' competitive actions. The competitor awareness, motivation, and capability framework provides a useful tool that managers may use to aid in forecasting competitor actions and reactions. To the degree that managers can measure their organization's activities (and those of its competitors) in an extremely "granular" manner, they will be able to gain insights about organizational performance and enhance their growth strategies.[40]

CHALLENGE CASE SUMMARY

In developing a plan to compete in its industry, management at Samsung would normally begin by thinking strategically. That is, management should try to determine what can be done to ensure that Samsung will continue to be successful at some point three to five years in the future. For example, developing a loyalty program that best suits the marketplace is part of this thinking. Samsung management must be careful, however, to spend funds on strategic planning only if they can anticipate a return on these expenses in the foreseeable future.

The end result of Samsung's overall strategic planning will be a strategy—a broad plan that outlines what must be done to reach long-range objectives and carry out the organizational purpose of the company. This strategy will focus on many organizational areas, one of which will be competing with other companies that develop strategies in the same industries as Samsung. Once the strategy has been formulated using the results of an environmental analysis, Samsung management must conscientiously carry out the remaining steps of the strategic management process: strategy implementation and strategic control.

As part of the strategy development process, Samsung management should spend time analyzing the environment in which the organization exists. Naturally, they should focus on Samsung's general, operating, and internal environments. Environmental factors that probably would be important to consider as it pursues strategic planning include the number of companies with which Samsung competes and knowing whether this number will be increasing or decreasing, strengths and weaknesses of its products when compared to those of competitors, the technologies that consumers want in electronics, and even the methods competitors such as Amazon.com are using to promote electronics to their customers. Obtaining information about environmental issues such as these will increase the probability that any strategy developed for Samsung will be appropriate for the environment in which the company operates and that the company will be successful in the long term.

Based on the previous information, after Samsung has performed its environmental analysis, it must determine the direction in which the organization will move regarding its competitive position. Issues such as entering green markets will naturally surface. Developing a mission statement with related objectives would be clear signals to all Samsung employees about the role of green markets in the organization's future. Samsung management has several tools available to assist them in formulating strategy. If they are to be effective in this area, however, they must use the tools in conjunction with environmental analysis. One of the tools, critical question analysis, would require management to analyze the purpose of Samsung, the direction in which the company is going, the environment in which it exists, and how the goals might be better achieved.

SWOT analysis, another strategy development tool, would require management to generate information regarding the internal strengths and weaknesses of Samsung as well as the opportunities and threats that exist within the company's environment. Management probably would classify the technological innovations from online competitors such as Amazon.com as threats and significant factors to be considered in the strategy development process.

One approach to business portfolio analysis would suggest that Samsung management classify each major product line (SBU) within the company as a star, cash cow, question mark, or dog, depending on the growth rate of the market and the market share the Samsung product line possesses. Management could decide, for example, to consider the green market and each of its major businesses—solar, wind, and so forth—as a unit for SBU analysis and categorize them according to the four classifications. As a result of this categorization process, they could develop, perhaps for each different product line that they offer, growth, stability, retrenchment, or divestiture strategies. Samsung management should use whichever strategy development tools they think would be most useful. Their objective in this case, of course, is to develop an appropriate strategy for the development of Samsung's product lines.

To be successful at using the strategy that they develop, management at Samsung must apply its interacting skill, allocating skill, monitoring skill, and organizing skill. In addition, management must be able to improve the strategic management process when necessary.

In addition to developing strategic plans for its organization, Samsung management should consider tactical, or short-range, plans that would complement its strategic plans. Tactical plans for Samsung should emphasize what can be done within approximately the next year to reach the organization's three- to five-year objectives and to steal competition from its competitors. For example, Samsung could devote more resources to aggressive, short-range research and development, or increase sales by aggressively reducing the introductory prices of mobile phones or LCD televisions.

In addition, Samsung management must closely coordinate strategic and tactical planning within the company. They must keep in mind that strategic planning and tactical planning are different types of activities that may involve different people within the organization and result in plans with different degrees of detail. Yet they must also remember that these two types of plans are interrelated. While lower-level managers would be mostly responsible for developing tactical plans, upper-level managers would mainly spend time on long-range planning and developing strategic plans that reflect company goals.

MANAGEMENT SKILL ACTIVITIES

This section is specially designed to help you develop strategic planning skill. An individual's management skill is based on an understanding of management concepts and the ability to apply those concepts in management situations. As a result, the following activities are designed both to heighten your understanding of strategic planning concepts and to help you gain facility in applying these concepts in various management situations.

UNDERSTANDING STRATEGIC PLANNING CONCEPTS

 To check your understanding and to practice using the concepts in this chapter, go to www.mymanagementlab.com and explore the material associated with Chapter 9.

Know Key Terms

Understanding the following key terms is critical to your understanding of chapter material. Define each of these terms. Refer to the page(s) referenced after a term to check your definition or to gain further insight regarding the term.

strategic planning **204**
commitment principle **204**
strategy **204**
strategic management **205**
environmental analysis **205**
general environment **206**
economics **206**
demographics **207**
social values **207**
industry environment **209**
Five Forces Model **209**
threat of new entrants **209**
buyer power **209**
supplier power **209**
threat of substitute products **209**
intensity of rivalry **209**

internal environment **209**
organizational mission **210**
mission statement **210**
strategy formulation **211**
critical question analysis **211**
SWOT analysis **211**
business portfolio analysis **212**
strategic business unit **212**
star **212**
cash cow **212**
question mark **213**
dog **213**
differentiation **214**
cost leadership **214**
focus **214**
growth **215**

stability **215**
retrenchment **215**
divestiture **215**
strategy implementation **215**
interacting skill **215**
allocating skill **215**
monitoring skill **216**
organizing skill **216**
strategic control **216**
tactical planning **216**
competitive dynamics **217**
competitor awareness **218**
competitor motivation **218**
competitor capability **218**

Know How Management Concepts Relate

This section is comprised of activities that will further sharpen your understanding of management concepts. Answer essay questions as completely as possible. Also, remember that many additional true/false and multiple choice questions appear online at MyManagementLab.com to help you further refine your understanding of management concepts.

1. Describe the five steps involved with the strategic management process. In your opinion, which step is most important?

2. Compare and contrast the different strategy formulation tools. In your opinion, which tool is best suited for large organizations? Explain.

3. Describe how an organization might use the BCG Growth-Share Matrix to evaluate its different strategic business

units. Now, explain how an organization might use the GE Multifactor Portfolio Matrix to evaluate its strategic business units.

4. Describe Porter's generic business strategies and provide an example of each strategy.

5. Describe Porter's Five Forces model. Why do organizations use Porter's Five Forces?

6. From your local newspaper or a national publication like *BusinessWeek* or *Wall Street Journal*, choose a company featured in the news. Then, analyze the company's actions. In your opinion, how did competitive dynamics play a role in the company's recent behavior?

DEVELOPING MANAGEMENT SKILLS

Learning activities in this section are aimed at helping you develop your strategic planning skill. Learning activities include Exploring Your Management Skill: Parts 1 and 2, Experiential Exercises, Cases, and a VideoNet Exercise.

Exploring Your Management Skill: Part 1

Before studying this chapter, respond to the following questions regarding the type of advice you would give to Samsung's vice-chairman Lee Yoon-woo. Then address the concerning planning challenges that he presently faces within the company. You are not expected to be a strategic planning expert at this point. Answering the questions now can help you focus on important points when you study the chapter. Also, answering the questions again after you study the chapter will give you an idea of how much you have learned.

Record your answers here or online at MyManagementLab.com. Completing the questions at MyManagementLab.com will allow you to get feedback about your answers automatically. If you answer the questions in the book, look up answers in the Exploring Your Management Skill section at the end of the book.

FOR EACH STATEMENT CIRCLE:
- "Y" if you would give the advice to Lee Yoon-woo.
- "N" if you would NOT give the advice to Lee Yoon-woo.
- "NI" if you have no idea whether you would give the advice to Lee Yoon-woo.

Mr. Yoon-woo, in meeting your strategic planning challenges at Samsung, you should . . .

Before   After
Study   Study

1. ensure that Samsung's top executives engage in the strategic planning process once per year.
   Y, N, NI

2. implement Samsung's strategy prior to establishing the firm's organizational direction.
   Y, N, NI

3. make sure that strategic controls are in place to assess the strategic management process.
   Y, N, NI

4. focus primarily on the economic component when analyzing Samsung's general environment.
   Y, N, NI

5. understand that Samsung's general environment will exert a larger influence on its performance than its industry environment.
   Y, N, NI

6. use Porter's Five Forces model to better understand the attractiveness of the consumer electronics industry.
   Y, N, NI

7. establish an effective mission statement to effectively guide the overall direction of Samsung.
   Y, N, NI

8. review the firm's mission statement when determining how to allocate resources such as capital and employees.
   Y, N, NI

9. allocate resources equally among Samsung's different strategic business units (SBUs).
   Y, N, NI

10. consult both the BCG Growth-Share Matrix and the GE Multifactor Portfolio Matrix when evaluating the performance of Samsung's SBUs.
    Y, N, NI

11. understand that differentiation strategies lead to better firm performance than cost leadership strategies.
    Y, N, NI

12. oversee Samsung's tactical planning and delegate strategic planning to lower-level employees.
    Y, N, NI

13. understand that strategic planning is long term, and tactical planning is more focused on the short term.
    Y, N, NI

14. take steps to stay aware of your competitors' actions and be motivated to respond to them.
    Y, N, NI

15. decide whether, in its interactions in the marketplace, Samsung should assume the role of attacker or defender.
    Y, N, NI

Exploring Your Management Skill: Part 2

As you recall, you completed Exploring Your Management Skill before you started to study this chapter. Your responses gave you an idea of how much you initially knew about strategic planning and helped you focus on important points as you studied the chapter. Answer the Exploring Your Management Skill questions again now and compare your score to the first time you took it. This comparison will give you an idea of how much you have learned from studying this chapter and pinpoint areas for further clarification before you start studying the next chapter. Record your answers within the text or online at MyManagementLab.com. Completing the survey at MyManagementLab.com will allow you to grade and compare your test scores automatically. If you complete the test in the book, look up answers in the Exploring Your Management Skill section at the end of the book.

Your Management Skills Portfolio

Your Management Learning Portfolio is a collection of activities especially designed to demonstrate your management knowledge and skill. By completing these activities online at MyManagementLab.com, you will be able to print, complete with cover sheet, as many activities as you choose. Be sure to save your work. Taking your printed portfolio to an employment interview could be helpful in obtaining a job.

The portfolio activity for this chapter is Strategic Planning at the Washington Post. Study the information and complete the exercises that follow.[41]

The Washington Post Company is one of the most respected news and educational organizations in the world. Although known primarily for the *Washington Post* newspaper,

the company is also involved in additional markets such as television, cable, education, and magazine publishing.

Despite the popularity and prestige associated with the *Washington Post* newspaper, the company's CEO, Donald Graham, is facing a difficult operating environment. Specifically, the emergence of the Internet and forms of digital news threaten the existence of the traditional newspaper industry. As a result, the Washington Post is generating lower levels of circulation; this decrease in circulation has also caused a dip in advertising. In sum, the profitability of the newspaper industry is decreasing.

Donald Graham has contacted you to help the company develop a new strategic plan. The following sections will help you apply the strategic planning process to a real scenario.

1. Perform an environmental analysis for the Washington Post Company. Which segment of the environment is causing the company's problem(s)?

2. Based on this analysis, develop a mission statement for the company. Also develop three objectives that will help the company fulfill its mission.

3. Review Porter's generic strategies. Which one of these strategies would you recommend for the Washington Post Company? Explain.

4. Which of the four strategy implementation skills do you think will be most important for the company as it moves forward? Why?

Experiential Exercises

1 Applying Porter's Model to Dell Inc.

Directions. Read the following scenario and then perform the listed activities. Your instructor may want you to perform the activities as an individual or within groups. Follow all of your instructor's directions carefully.

Michael Dell, the CEO of Dell Inc., has contacted your group for consulting purposes. In particular, Dell is concerned about the current state of the personal computer industry. He would like your group to use Porter's Model for Industry Analysis to analyze the personal computer industry. What are the most important factors affecting each of the five forces in Porter's Model? After performing this analysis, describe the most important threat. In addition, describe whether your group finds the personal computer industry attractive.

2 You and Your Career

SWOT analysis represents an important tool for your strategic planning skill. Using SWOT analysis, top executives can better understand the strengths and weaknesses of their organization as well as the opportunities and threats in the external environment. Suppose you are interviewing for a position in an organization. How might SWOT analysis help you prepare for an interview? Now suppose you have just started working at an organization. How might SWOT analysis help you better understand your position and role in the organization?

VideoNet Exercise

Strategic Planning: Nom Nom

Video Highlights

Nom Nom is a food truck that sells banh mi, Vietnamese sandwiches, in the Los Angeles area. Prior to the actual launch of the business, Nom Nom's owners created a Web site and other electronic links to the venture, creating buzz with photos and descriptions of their as-yet non-existent products. Response for Nom Nom was so great that the truck sold out completely within 30 minutes of its first day of operation. Nom Nom has never looked back. It has become a key player in the cultural lives of many local Angelenos, with movie companies, reality shows, TV and newspaper reporters all clamoring to jump on the Nom Nom bandwagon. Currently Nom Nom owners plan to expand to "brick and mortar" restaurants, and are looking into franchising their business. The film is done mainly in interview form, with co-owners David Stankulas and Jennifer Green talking about their venture.

Discussion Questions

1. Do the special advantages of having a restaurant on a truck outweigh the disadvantages for the owners of Nom Nom? Explain.

2. What was the strategy of Stankunas and the other owners of Nom Nom when they began the venture? How has this strategy changed or evolved?

3. How does owner David Stankunas feel about planning a business? What advice does he give for would-be entrepreneurs?

Internet Activity

Visit Nom Nom's Web site at nomnomtruck.com. Browse the menu, check out the photos, read the Twitter! Check out the "About" link. How did the company get its unique name? The Web site states that *Locations & hours are subject to change without notice. For our most up-to-date hours please follow us on Twitter!* What do you think of this unique business strategy? List some of the pros and cons of this strategy.

CASES

1 SAMSUNG PLANS FOR THE FUTURE

"Samsung Plans for the Future" (p. 203) and its related Challenge Case Summary sections were written to help you better understand the management concepts contained in this chapter. Answer the following discussion questions about the Challenge Case to better understand how strategic planning concepts can be applied in a company such as Samsung.

1. For Samsung's management, is adding a solar and wind power unit a strategic management issue? Explain.

2. Give three factors in Samsung's internal environment that management should be assessing in determining the company's organizational direction. Why are these factors important?

3. Using the business portfolio matrix, categorize the new solar and wind power unit as a dog, question mark, star, or cash cow. From a strategic planning viewpoint, what do you recommend Samsung management do as a result of this categorization? Why?

2 UNILEVER REVITALIZES ITS MISSION AND STRATEGY

Read the case and answer the questions that follow. Studying this case will help you better understand how strategic planning concepts can be applied in a company such as Unilever.

It's not every day that a corporate giant changes its mission statement. Then again, Unilever is not an everyday company. Formed from the 1930 merger of the British soap manufacturer Lever Brothers and the Dutch margarine firm Margarine Unie, Unilever still maintains headquarters in both countries. It operates in 150 nations and sells 150 million items every day, ranging from Dove soaps and Calvin Klein perfumes to Slim-Fast diet foods and Ben & Jerry's ice cream. With $53 billion in annual revenues and 234,000 employees, Unilever's size, scope, and skills provide strength for ongoing competition with Procter & Gamble, Colgate-Palmolive, Danone, Reckitt Benckiser, Nestlé, and other major manufacturers of food, household, and personal care products.

Niall FitzGerald, Unilever's former chairperson, changed the mission as the company neared the end of its 2000–2005 "Path to Growth" strategy, which called for annual revenue growth of 5 to 6 percent and significant improvement in profit margins. When the strategy was first implemented, FitzGerald arranged the $24 billion acquisition of Bestfoods to bring in such blockbuster product lines as Hellmann's mayonnaise and Knorr soups. At the same time, he began the process of selling off 140 business units representing more than 1,000 brands (including Mentadent, Pond's, and Elizabeth Arden) so he could focus Unilever's organizational resources on a core portfolio of 400 brands capable of maintaining lucrative, market-leading performance for the long term. As an example, he authorized higher advertising budgets for the top brands and larger investments to develop new fragrances and other high-margin products.

By the time FitzGerald was ready to retire in 2004, the strategy was showing some success. Where Unilever had just four $1 billion-a-year brands in 1999, it now had 12 such brands; moreover, its profit margins had doubled within the past four years. However, revenue growth was stalled well below the targeted 5–6 percent level and some brands were having difficulty coping with critical environmental elements. For instance, Slimfast's managers were slow to recognize the threat posed by growing consumer interest in low-carbohydrate diets. By the time they introduced products with lower carbohydrate content, Slimfast's sales had fallen 22 percent. Also, sales of Unilever's prestigious fragrance products, including Calvin Klein perfumes, were lower than expected due to weak economic conditions and fewer travelers passing through airports worldwide, where the fragrances enjoy good distribution.

To guide development of a new strategy for 2005–2010, FitzGerald decided to revamp the corporate mission statement. After analyzing important trends, such as increased urbanization in many countries, the aging population, and increased consumer interest in healthy living, the Fitzgerald and Unilever's managers crafted a statement declaring that "Unilever's new mission is to add vitality to life. We meet everyday needs for nutrition, hygiene, and personal care with products that help people feel good, look good, and get more out of life." This broad statement helps managers and employees connect their work activities with the well-being of the customers and communities they serve. It also suggests how Unilever will differentiate itself from rivals within the pressured global marketplace.

Now FitzGerald's successor, Patrick Cescau, has taken over the process of implementing the "Unilever 2010" strategy. He's giving the corporate name more prominence by ensuring that it appears on all company products, communications, and promotional materials. Instead of publicly explaining the corporation's growth goals in detail, he's talking more generally about a range of assumptions for sales, profits, costs, and debt. He's continuing the former CEO's policy of benchmarking shareholder return against a peer group of 20 competitors to check its performance. On the competitive front, Cescau has to deal with Reckitt Benckiser's strength in product innovation, Procter & Gamble's marketing power, and Nestlé's brand-building abilities. And he must keep Unilever's brands at the top of their categories to retain prime shelf space in Wal-Mart and other big retail chains.

QUESTIONS

1. How effectively do you think Unilever's mission statement establishes the company's direction and important values? What changes, if any, would you recommend, and why?

2. Identify one or more of Unilever's strengths, weaknesses, opportunities, and threats. How might Cescau use the strengths to counteract the threats?

3. Where on the BCG Matrix would you place Unilever's 400 remaining brands? Where would you place any newly developed products being introduced? Explain.

Endnotes

1. Company Web site, http://www.samsung.com, accessed July 4, 2010; "Samsung Raises 2010 Investment Plan to Record 26 Trillion Won," *Business Wire,* May 17, 2010, http://www.businesswire.com; "Samsung to Invest $20.6 Billion in Green Technology," *Greentech Media,* May 11, 2010, http://www.solarfeeds.com; Kim Yoo-chul, "Samsung Stresses Sustainable Management," *Korea Times,* December 17, 2009, http://www.koreatimes.co.kr; Michael Kanellos, "Will Samsung Be the Next Green Giant?" *GreentechMedia,* September 24, 2009, http://www.greentechmedia.com.

2. For a model of learning to think strategically, see Andrea J. Casey and Ellen F. Goldman, "Enhancing the Ability to Think Strategically: A Learning Model," *Management Learning* 41, no. 2 (April 2010): 167–185.

3. To better understand the different dimensions of strategic planning, see Peter Brews and Devavrat Purohit, "Strategic Planning in Unstable Environments," *Long Range Planning* 40 (2007): 64–83.

4. For an article on the importance of strategic planning, see Sarah Kaplan and Eric Beinhocker, "The Real Value of Strategic Planning," *MIT Sloan Management Review* 44 (2003): 71. To better understand the influence of strategic planning in developing countries, see Jose Santos, "Strategy Lessons from Left Field," *Harvard Business Review* (2007): 20–21.

5. Ed Barrows, "Four Fatal Flaws of Strategic Planning," *Harvard Business Review,* March 13, 2009, http://blogs.hbr.org. For reasons why strategic thinking matters more to managers now than ever before, see Keith H. Hammonds, "Michael Porter's Big Ideas," *Fast Company* (March 2001): 150–156. For an interesting discussion of strategic planning in the context of service firms, see Povl Larsen, Richard Tonge, and Alan Lewis, "Strategic Planning and Design in the Service Sector," *Management Decision* 45, no. 2 (2007): 180–195.

6. Dyan Machan, "The Strategy Thing," *Forbes,* May 23, 1994, 113–114. For an example of a successful business strategy, see Laura Haller, "Target Reiterates Stable Strategy," *DSN Retailing Today,* June 4, 2001, 6.

7. For a detailed discussion of strategy formulation in small family-owned businesses, see Nancy Drozdow and Vincent P. Carroll, "Tools for Strategy Development in Family Firms," *Sloan Management Review* 39, no. 1 (Fall 1997): 75–88; see also Michael Beer and Russell Eisenstat, "How to Have an Honest Conversation about Your Business Strategy," *Harvard Business Review* 82 (2004): 82.

8. This section is based on Samuel C. Certo and J. Paul Peter, *Strategic Management: Concepts and Applications* (Chicago: Austen Press/Irwin, 1995), 3–27.

9. Samuel C. Certo and J. Paul Peter, *The Strategic Management Process,* 4th ed. (Chicago: Austen Press/Irwin, 1995), 32; William Drohan, "Principles of Strategic Planning," *Association Management* 49, no. 1 (January 1997): 85–87. For a recent study examining the interaction between organizations and environment, see Max Boisot and John Child, "Organizations as Adaptive Systems in Complex Environments: The Case of China," *Organization Science* 10, no. 3 (May/June 1999): 237–252.

10. This section is based on William F. Glueck and Lawrence R. Jauch, *Business Policy and Strategic Management* (New York: McGraw-Hill, 1984), 99–110.

11. John F. Watkins, "Retirees as a New Growth Industry? Assessing the Demographic and Social Impact," *Review of Business* (Spring 1994): 9–14.

12. Patrick J. Kiger, "Serious Progress in Strategic Workforce Planning," *Workforce Management,* July 2010, http://www.workforce.com.

13. Inga S. Baird, Marjorie A. Lyles, and J. B. Orris, "The Choice of International Strategies by Small Businesses," *Journal of Small Business Management* 32, no. 1 (January 1994): 48–60.

14. "When Kraft Gains 25%, Thank Cadbury," *Forbes,* July 1, 2010, http://blogs.forbes.com; Ian Grant, "Kraft Keeps Systems Integrators Waiting over Cadbury," *ComputerWeekly.com,* January 19, 2010, http://www.computerweekly.com.

15. This discussion of Porter's model is based on Chapters 1 and 2 of Porter's *Competitive Strategy* (New York: The Free Press, 1980); and Chapter 1 of Porter's *Competitive Advantage: Creating and Sustaining Superior Performance* (New York: The Free Press, 1985). For an application of Porter's concepts, see William P. Munk and Barry Shane, "Using Competitive Analysis Models to Set Strategy in the Northwest Hardboard Industry," *Forest Products Journal* (July/August 1994): 11–18.

16. M. Klemm, S. Sanderson, and G. Luffman, "Mission Statements: Selling Corporate Values to Employees," *Long-Range Planning* (June 1991): 73–78. For a recent review of effective mission statements, see Shirleen Holt, "Mission Possible," *BusinessWeek,* August 16, 1999, F12.

17. Forest David and Fred Davis, "It's Time to Redraft Your Mission Statement," *Journal of Business Strategy* 24 (2003): 11.

18. Colin Coulson-Thomas, "Strategic Vision or Strategic Cons: Rhetoric or Reality," *Long-Range Planning* (February 1992): 81–89; Rhymer Rigby, "Mission Statements," *Management Today*

(March 1998): 56–58; Jeffrey Abrahams, *101 Mission Statements from Top Companies* (Berkeley, CA: Ten Speed Press, 2007).

19. For an interesting discussion of holding leaders accountable for attaining the objective of developing organizational integrity as a strategic asset, see Joseph A. Petrick and John F. Quinn, "The Challenge of Leadership Accountability for Integrity Capacity as a Strategic Asset," *Journal of Business Ethics* 34 (2001): 331–343.

20. This section is based primarily on Thomas H. Naylor and Kristin Neva, "Design of a Strategic Planning Process," *Managerial Planning* (January/February 1980): 2–7; Donald W. Mitchell, "Pursuing Strategic Potential," *Managerial Planning* (May/June 1980): 6–10; Benton E. Gup, "Begin Strategic Planning by Asking Three Questions," *Managerial Planning* (November/December 1979): 28–31, 35; Rainer Feurer and Kazem Chaharbaghi, "Dynamic Strategy Formulation and Alignment," *Journal of General Management* 20, no. 3 (Spring 1995): 76–91.

21. Paula Jarzabkowski and Julia Balogun, "The Practice and Process of Delivering Integration through Strategic Planning," *Journal of Management Studies* 46, no. 8 (July 6, 2009): 1255–1288.

22. For a practical example of SWOT applied in the business world, see Robert H. Woods, "Strategic Planning: A Look at Ruby Tuesday," *Cornell Hotel & Restaurant Administration Quarterly* (June 1994): 41–49; for a review of the advantages of SWOT analysis, see George Panagiotou, "Bringing SWOT into Focus," *Business Strategy Review* 14 (2003): 8.

23. Philip Kotler, *Marketing Management Analysis, Planning and Control,* 7th ed. (Upper Saddle River, NJ: Prentice Hall, 1991), 39–41.

24. See also J. Scott Armstrong and Roderick J. Brodie, "Effects of Portfolio Planning Methods on Decision Making: Experimental Results," *International Journal of Research in Marketing* (January 1994): 73–84; For an interesting description of how firms alter their product portfolios over time, see Chris Zook, "Finding Your Next CORE Business," *Harvard Business Review* 85, no. 4 (2007): 66–75.

25. For an interesting summary of the research examining Porter's generic strategies, see John A. Parnell, "Generic Strategies After Two Decades: A Reconceptualization of Competitive Strategy," *Management Decision* 44, no. 8 (2006): 1139–1154.

26. Ian C. MacMillan, Donald C. Hambrick, and Diana L. Day, "The Product Portfolio and Profitability—A PIMS-Based Analysis of Industrial-Product Businesses," *Academy of Management Journal* (December 1982): 733–755. For more information on establishing growth businesses, see Jeffrey G. Covin and Morgan P. Miles, "Strategic Use of Corporate Venturing," *Entrepreneurship Theory and Practice* 31, no. 2 (2007): 183–207.

27. Walecia Konrad and Bruce Einhorn, "Famous Amos Gets a Chinese Accent," *BusinessWeek,* September 28, 1992, 76.

28. For a practical discussion of strategy implementation, see Brooke Dobni, "Creating a Strategy Implementation Environment," *Business Horizons* 46 (2003): 43.

29. William Sandy, "Avoid the Breakdowns Between Planning and Implementation," *Journal of Business Strategy* (September/October 1991): 30–33.

30. Thomas V. Bonoma, "Making Your Marketing Strategy Work," *Harvard Business Review* (March/April 1984): 69–76. For an article illustrating the importance of strategy implementation, see Loizos Heracleous, "The Role of Strategy Implementation in Organization Development," *Organization Development Journal* 18, no. 3 (Fall 2000): 75–86.

31. For other useful articles on strategic control, see William B. Carper and Terry A. Bresnick, "Strategic Planning Conferences," *Business Horizons* (September/October 1989): 34–40; Stephen Bungay and Michael Goold, "Creating a Strategic Control System," *Long-Range Planning* (June 1991): 32–39; for a useful article on strategic control, see Pierre Kunsch, Alain Chevalier, and Jean-Pierre Brans, "A Framework for Strategic Control and Planning in Corporate Organizations," *Central European Journal of Operations Research* 10 (2002): 45.

32. For a detailed discussion of the characteristics of strategic and tactical planning, see George A. Steiner, *Top Management Planning* (Toronto, Canada: Collier-Macmillan, 1969), 37–39.

33. Russell L. Ackoff, *A Concept of Corporate Planning* (New York: Wiley, 1970), 4.

34. Tom Krazit, "New Competition for Mobile with HP and WebOS," *CNET News,* April 28, 2010, http://news.cnet.com.

35. M. J. Chen, "Competitive Dynamics Research: An Insider's Odyssey," *Asia Pacific Journal of Management* 26 (2009): 5–25.

36. M. J. Chen, K. H. Su, and W. Tsai, "Competitive Tension: The Awareness-Motivation-Capability Perspective," *Academy of Management Journal* 50 (2007): 101–118.

37. Geoffrey A. Fowler, "Price Cuts Electrify E-Reader Market," *The Wall Street Journal,* June 21, 2010, http://online.wsj.com.

38. See K. G. Smith, W. J. Ferrier, and H. Ndofor, "Competitive Dynamics Research: Critique and Future Directions," in M. Hitt, R. E. Freeman, and J. Harrison (Eds.), *Handbook of Strategic Management* (London: Blackwell, 2001).

39. For further information on the relationship between firm size and media coverage, see L. Fang and J. Peress, "Media Coverage and the Cross-Section of Stock Returns," *Journal of Finance* 64, no. 5 (2009): 2023–2052.

40. Mehrdad Baghai, Sven Smit, and Patrick Viguerie, "Is Your Growth Strategy Flying Blind?" *Harvard Business Review,* May 2009, http://hbr.org.

41. This exercise was based in part on Marc Gunther, "Hard News," *Fortune,* August 6, 2007, 80–85.

chapter 10

Plans and Planning Tools

Target Skill

planning tools skill: the ability to employ the qualitative and quantitative techniques necessary to help develop plans

objectives

To help build my *planning tools skill*, when studying this chapter, I will attempt to acquire:

1. A complete definition of a plan

2. Insights regarding various dimensions of plans

3. An understanding of various types of plans

4. Insights into why plans fail

5. A definition of forecasting

6. An ability to see the advantages and disadvantages of various methods of sales forecasting

7. A definition of scheduling

8. An understanding of Gantt charts and PERT

CHALLENGE CASE

MICROSOFT PLANS FOR SMALL BUSINESSES

FOUNDED IN 1975, MICROSOFT is the worldwide leader in computer software and consumer electronics. Thanks to ambitious planning, Microsoft became a household word, with the vast majority of computer users running some version of Microsoft software on a Windows operating system.

While Microsoft provides a common denominator for the global business world, the company has enjoyed less success with selling products and services to small-business owners.

But that is about to change, promises Microsoft VP Birger Steen, who leads the multinational giant's sales effort for small and mid-sized businesses. Under his direction, Microsoft plans to entice this segment with its newest product, Windows 7, and a cloud named Azure.

Steen recognizes that historically, entrepreneurs and owners of small businesses have been forced to make large capital investments in technology upfront—when they can least afford it. Now, Microsoft plans to make products for this market segment available on Azure, its cloud-based operating system. According to Steen, cloud computing provides an effective way for Microsoft to serve this segment because small-business owners need not make the upfront cash outlay. Instead, they can pay as they go.

What makes this latest Microsoft plan even more interesting is the fact that while the company will continue to offer "on-premise" software licensing to customers, it also intends to deliver *all* of its software on the cloud. Industry observers say Azure could provide the perfect solution for smaller businesses because it will provide access to the software and technology they need, without undue expense.

Heralded by a massive ad campaign, the recent introduction of Windows 7 is attracting the attention of small-business owners. While many businesses—small and otherwise—largely ignored its predecessor Windows Vista, industry observers see stronger interest in Windows 7, as signaled by retailers' orders for computers installed with Windows 7 Professional and Ultimate, the business versions of the company's popular operating systems.

While the quest for the hearts and minds of small-business owners may be an uphill climb, it's one that Steen is prepared to make. This time, he says, the company examined more carefully the needs of small-business owners, and planned its strategy accordingly.[1]

■ *Microsoft Corporation promises the small-business owner that Windows 7 will provide faster start-up and shutdown, less demanding hardware reuirements, and more security.*

EXPLORING YOUR MANAGEMENT SKILL

You can explore your level of planning tools skills **before** studying the chapter by completing the exercise "Exploring Your Management Skill: Part 1" on page 243 and **after** studying this chapter by completing the exercise "Exploring Your Management Skill: Part 2" on page 244.

THE CHALLENGE OF USING PLANNING TOOLS

The Challenge Case ends with the notion that management at Microsoft has been planning to improve its performance. This chapter emphasizes several fundamental issues about plans that should be useful to managers such as those at Microsoft who are involved in such planning. This chapter describes what plans are and discusses several valuable tools that can be used in actually developing plans.

To manange its planned expansion abroad, such as this new store in Beijing, Carrefour Hypermarkets, the French supermarket giant, prepares a master plan that is both deep and broad.

PLANS: A DEFINITION

A **plan** is a specific action proposed to help the organization achieve its objectives. A critical part of the management of any organization is developing logical plans and then taking the steps necessary to put the plans into action.[2] Regardless of how important experience-related intuition may be to managers, successful management actions and strategies typically are based on reason.[3] Rational managers are crucial to the development of an organizational plan.

Dimensions of Plans

Kast and Rosenzweig identify a plan's four major dimensions as follows:[4]

1. Repetitiveness
2. Time
3. Scope
4. Level

Each dimension is an independent characteristic of a plan and should be considered during plan development.

Repetitiveness The **repetitiveness dimension** of a plan is the extent to which the plan is used over and over again. Some plans are specially designed for one situation that is relatively short term in nature. Plans of this sort are essentially nonrepetitive. Other plans, however, are designed to be used time after time for long-term recurring situations. These plans are basically repetitive in nature.

Time The **time dimension** of a plan is the length of time the plan covers. In Chapter 9, strategic planning was defined as long term in nature, while tactical planning was defined as short term. It follows, then, that strategic plans cover relatively long periods of time and tactical plans cover relatively short periods of time.

how managers do it

Planning for Expansion at
Nationwide Children's Hospital

Take, for example, the multi-year expansion program launched by Columbus, Ohio–based Nationwide Children's Hospital. The plan, introduced in 2005, unfolded in phases, with the construction of new clinical and research facilities, a parking garage, an eco-friendly energy plant, and more. Completion of the plan is expected in late 2012.[5] ■

Scope The **scope dimension** of a plan is the portion of the total management system at which the plan is aimed. Some plans are designed to cover the entire open management system: the organizational environment, inputs, process, and outputs. Such a plan is often referred to as a *master plan*. Other plans are developed to cover only a portion of the management system. An example of the latter would be a plan that covers the recruitment of new workers—a portion of the organizational input segment of the management system. The greater the portion of the management system that a plan covers, the broader the plan's scope is said to be.

Level The **level dimension** of a plan is the level of the organization at which the plan is aimed. Top-level plans are those designed for the organization's top management, whereas middle- and lower-level plans are designed for middle and lower management, respectively. Because all parts of the management system are interdependent, however, plans designed for any level of the organization have some effect on all other levels.

Figure 10.1 illustrates the four dimensions of an organizational plan. This figure indicates that when managers develop a plan, they should consider the degree to which it will be used over and over again, the period of time it will cover, the parts of the management system on which it focuses, and the organizational level at which it is aimed.

Types of Plans

With the repetitiveness dimension as a guide, organizational plans are usually divided into two types: standing and single-use. A **standing plan** is used over and over again because it focuses on organizational situations that occur repeatedly. A **single-use plan** is used only once—or, at most, a few times—because it focuses on unique or rare situations within the organization. As Figure 10.2 illustrates, standing plans can be subdivided into policies, procedures, and rules and single-use plans into programs and budgets.

Standing Plans: Policies, Procedures, and Rules
A **policy** is a standing plan that furnishes broad guidelines for taking action consistent with reaching organizational objectives. For example, an organizational policy relating to personnel might be worded as follows: "Our organization will strive to recruit only the most talented employees." This policy statement is broad, giving managers only a general idea of what to do in the area of recruitment. The policy is intended to emphasize the extreme importance management attaches to hiring competent employees and to guide managers' actions accordingly.

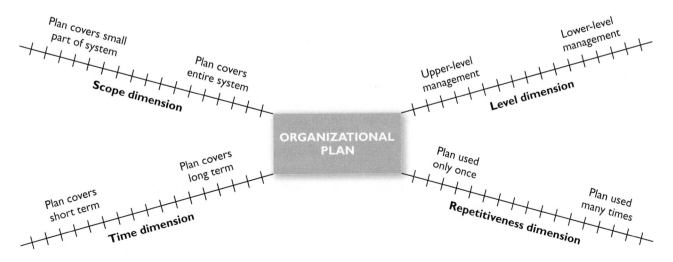

FIGURE 10.1 Four major dimensions to consider when developing a plan

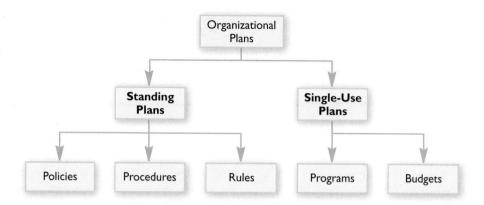

FIGURE 10.2
Standing plans and single-use plans

As another example of an organizational policy, consider companies' responses to studies showing that one out of every four workers in the United States was attacked, threatened, or harassed on the job during a recent 12-month operating period. To deal with this problem, many managers are developing weapons policies. A sample policy could be: "Management strongly discourages any employee from bringing a weapon to work." This policy would encourage managers to deal forcefully and punitively with employees who bring weapons into the workplace.[6]

how managers do it

Creating Sustainability
Policy at H&M

As mentioned in a previous chapter, many organizations today adopt sustainability policies. For example, consider H&M, a discount retailer of men's, women's, and children's fashion apparel. H&M's sustainability policy is closely linked to its business objective, which is to offer fashion and quality at the best price. That means H&M aims to sell only merchandise that has been produced using methods that are environmentally and socially sustainable. In addition, H&M commits to "clean and efficient" transportation as well as environmentally friendly production protocols throughout its global supply chain.[7] ■

A **procedure** is a standing plan that outlines a series of related actions that must be taken to accomplish a particular task. In general, procedures outline more specific actions than policies do. Organizations usually have many different sets of procedures covering the various tasks to be accomplished. Managers must carefully apply the appropriate organizational procedures for the situations they face and apply them properly.[8]

As an example, Apple changed its manufacturing procedures to integrate green principles into its operations. To eliminate lead in its computer displays, Apple eliminated cathode-ray tubes from its designs. Through innovation, the company also managed to eliminate two other deadly chemicals, arsenic and mercury, from its products.[9]

A **rule** is a standing plan that designates specific required action. In essence, a rule indicates what an organization member should or should not do and allows no room for interpretation. An example of a rule that many companies are now establishing is no smoking. The concept of rules may become clearer if one thinks about the purpose and nature of rules in such games as Scrabble and Monopoly.

Although policies, procedures, and rules are all standing plans, they are different from one another and have different purposes within the organization. As Figure 10.3 illustrates, however,

class discussion highlight

MODERN RESEARCH AND PLANNING SKILL

Policies, Procedures, and Corporate Crime

White-collar crime is an important issue in management. When employees commit illegal acts, the company loses resources. How can companies reduce white-collar crime? Karen Schnatterly tried to answer this question by examining the extent to which company policies and procedures can help reduce white-collar crime. According to her logic, clear policies and procedures help communicate to employees the "rules of the game." In contrast, policies and procedures that are vague may encourage employees to engage in criminal activity.

To address this question, Professor Schnatterly examined documents available to the public—such as annual reports and proxy statements—and assessed whether these documents referred to the firm's policies and procedures. Documents that referred to such policies and procedures were given high scores, and documents that made no mention of these policies and procedures were given low scores. She then investigated the influence of these policies and procedures on corporate crimes.

Do you think she found a relationship between policies and procedures and corporate crime? If so, what type of association (i.e., positive or negative) would you expect between policies and procedure and corporate crime? Explain.

Source: This highlight was based on Karen Schnatterly, "Increasing Firm Value through Detection and Prevention of White-Collar Crime," *Strategic Management Journal* 24 (2003): 587–614. For more information on white-collar crime, see Gerhard Blickle, Alexander Schlegel, Pantaleon Fassbender, and Uwe Klein, "Some Personality Correlates of Business White-Collar Crime," *Applied Psychology* 55, no. 2 (2006): 220–233.

for the standing plans of an organization to be effective, policies, procedures, and rules must be consistent and mutually supportive.

Single-Use Plans: Programs and Budgets
A **program** is a single-use plan designed to carry out a special project within an organization. The project itself is not intended to remain in existence over the entire life of the organization. Rather, it exists to achieve some purpose that, if accomplished, will contribute to the organization's long-term success.

A common example is the management development program found in many organizations. This program exists to raise the skill levels of managers in one or more of the areas mentioned in

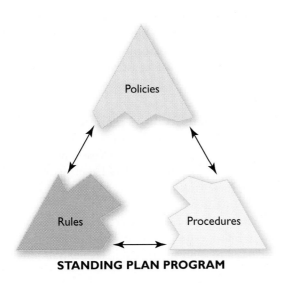

STANDING PLAN PROGRAM

FIGURE 10.3
A successful standing plan program with mutually supportive policies, procedures, and rules

One-time events require multiple layers of single-use plans. The 2012 Summer Olympics, for instance, will be held in London. The Games will challenge the U.K. to prepare, adapt, and even build new athletic and housing facilities to acccommodate hundreds of unique competitions, each with its own set of physical and environmental requirements, and all without disrupting the normal life and commerce of the city.

Chapter 1: technical, conceptual, or human relations skills. Increasing managerial skills, however, is not an end in itself. The end or purpose of the program is to produce competent managers who are equipped to help the organization be successful over the long term. In fact, once managerial skills have been raised to a desired level, the management development program can be deemphasized. Activities on which modern management development programs commonly focus include understanding and using the computer as a management tool, handling international competition, and planning for a major labor shortage.[10]

A **budget** is a single-use financial plan that covers a specified length of time. It details how funds will be spent on labor, raw materials, capital goods, information systems, marketing, and so on, as well as how the funds will be obtained.[11] Although budgets are planning devices, they are also strategies for organizational control. They are discussed in more detail in Chapter 22.

Why Plans Fail

If managers know why plans fail, they can take steps to eliminate the factors that cause failure and thereby increase the probability that their plans will be successful. A study by K. A. Ringbakk determined that plans fail when:[12]

1. Corporate planning is not integrated into the total management system.
2. There is a lack of understanding of the different steps of the planning process.
3. Managers at different levels in the organization have not properly engaged in or contributed to planning activities.
4. Responsibility for planning is wrongly vested solely in the planning department.
5. Management expects that plans developed will be realized with little effort.
6. In starting formal planning, too much is attempted at once.
7. Management fails to operate by the plan.
8. Financial projections are confused with planning.
9. Inadequate inputs are used in planning.
10. Management fails to grasp the overall planning process.

It is important to note that failed plans do not always lead to permanent business failures. In some instances, a failing plan can be salvaged through some adjustment or a bit of fine-tuning. In such cases, "Plan B" may provide just the right fit.[13]

Planning Areas: Input Planning

As discussed earlier, organizational inputs, process, outputs, and environment are major factors in determining how successful a management system will be. Naturally, a comprehensive organizational plan should focus on each of these factors. The following two sections cover planning in two areas normally associated with the input factor: plant facilities planning and human resource planning. Planning in these areas is called **input planning**—the development of proposed action that will furnish sufficient and appropriate organizational resources for reaching established organizational objectives.

Plant Facilities Planning
Plant facilities planning involves determining the type of buildings and equipment an organization needs to reach its objectives. A major part of this determination is called **site selection**—deciding where a plant facility should be located. Table 10.1 lays out several major areas to be considered in plant-site selection and gives sample questions that can be asked as these areas are being explored. The specifics of site selection will vary from organization to organization.[14]

One factor that significantly influences site selection is foreign location. Management in a foreign country planning to select a site must deal with such issues as differences among foreign governments in time taken to approve site purchases and political pressures that may slow

TABLE 10.1	Major Areas of Consideration When Selecting a Plant Site and Sample Exploratory Questions to Be Asked
Major Areas of Consideration in Site Selection	**Sample Questions to be Asked**
Profit	
Market location	Where are our customers in relation to the site?
Competition	What competitive situation exists at the site?
Operating costs	
Suppliers	Are materials available near the site at reasonable cost?
Utilities	What are utility rates at the site? Are utilities available in sufficient amounts?
Wages	What wage rates are paid by comparable organizations near the site?
Taxes	What are tax rates on income, sales, property, and so on for the site?
Investment costs	
Land/development	How expensive are land and construction at the site?
Others	
Transportation	Are airlines, railroads, highways, and so on accessible from the site?
Laws	What laws related to zoning, pollution, and so on will influence operations if the site is chosen?
Labor	Does an adequate labor supply exist around the site?
Unionization	What is the degree of unionization in the site area?
Living conditions	Are housing, schools, and so on around the site appropriate?
Community relations	Does the community support the organization's moving into the area?

down or prevent the purchase of a site. For example, Japanese investors who locate businesses in the United States tend to select those states that have low unionization rates, low employment rates, relatively impoverished populations, and the highest possible educational levels under those conditions. Japanese managers believe that these factors enhance the chances of success of Japanese business in the United States.[15]

Many organizations use a weighting process to compare site differences among foreign countries. Basically, this process involves the following steps:

1. Deciding on a set of variables critical to obtaining an appropriate site
2. Assigning each of these variables a weight reflecting its relative importance
3. Ranking alternative sites according to how they reflect these different variables

Table 10.2 shows the results of such a weighting process for seven site variables in six countries. In this table, "living conditions" are worth 100 points and are the most important variable; "effect on company reputation" is worth 35 points and is the least important variable. The six countries are given a number of points for each variable, depending on the importance of the

| TABLE 10.2 | Results of Weighting Seven Site Variables for Six Countries | | | | | | | |

Criteria	Maximum Value Assigned	Sites					
		Japan	Chile	Jamaica	Australia	Mexico	France
Living conditions	100	70	40	45	50	60	60
Accessibility	75	55	35	20	60	70	70
Industrialization	60	40	50	55	35	35	30
Labor availability	35	30	10	10	30	35	35
Economics	35	15	15	15	15	25	25
Community capability and attitude	30	25	20	10	15	25	15
Effect on company reputation	35	25	20	10	15	25	15
Total	370	260	190	165	220	275	250

variable and how well it is reflected within the country. The table shows that, using this particular set of weighted criteria, Japan, Mexico, and France are more desirable sites than Chile, Jamaica, and Australia.

Human Resource Planning Human resources are another area of concern to input planners. Organizational objectives cannot be attained without appropriate personnel. Future needs for human resources are influenced mainly by employee turnover, the nature of the present workforce, and the rate of growth of the organization.[16] Issues external to the organization—such as the recent global economic downturn, can also influence an organization's human resource planning.[17]

The following are representative of the kinds of questions personnel planners should try to answer:

1. What types of people does the organization need to reach its objectives?
2. How many of each type are needed?
3. What steps should the organization take to recruit and select such people?
4. Can present employees be further trained to fill future needed positions?
5. At what rate are employees being lost to other organizations?

Figure 10.4 shows the human resource planning process developed by Bruce Coleman. According to his model, **human resource planning** involves reflecting on organizational objectives to determine overall human resource needs; comparing these needs to the existing human resource inventory to determine net human resource needs; and, finally, seeking appropriate organization members to meet the net human resource needs.[18]

how managers do it

Overcoming Cultural Obstacles in HR Planning at Raba

Ferenc Vissi, the head of human resources for Hungary–based truck manufacturer Raba, explains the difficulties his country's culture presents for human resource planning.[19] According to Vissi, "The lack of labor mobility is a fact. It's part of the culture of the Hungarian population that they don't like to move." This lack of qualified labor presents a problem for the company, as human resource planners such as Vissi are forced to find foreign workers to work in the company's newest facilities. ∎

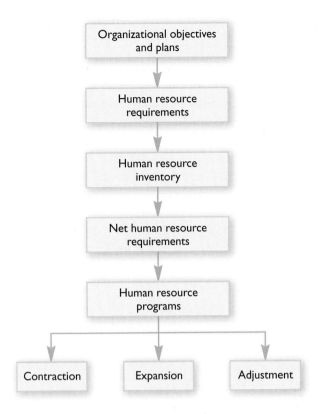

FIGURE 10.4
The human resource planning process

PLANNING TOOLS

Planning tools are techniques managers can use to help develop plans. The remainder of this chapter discusses forecasting and scheduling, two of the most important of these tools.

Forecasting

Forecasting is the process of predicting future environmental happenings that will influence the operation of the organization. Although sophisticated forecasting techniques have been developed rather recently, the concept of forecasting can be traced at least as far back in the management literature as Fayol. The importance of forecasting lies in its ability to help managers understand the future makeup of the organizational environment, which, in turn, helps them formulate more effective plans.[20] Despite the importance of forecasting, a recent survey of manufacturers suggests that forecasting is an imprecise science.[21] According to this survey, on average, sales forecasts are off by approximately 20 percent. As such, managers continue to search for more accurate forecasting tools. In the following sections, we describe the forecasting process, and then we list a number of tools managers might use to improve forecasts.

How Forecasting Works William C. House, in describing the Insect Control Services Company, developed an excellent illustration of how forecasting works. In general, Insect Control Services forecasts by attempting to do the following:[22]

1. Establish relationships between industry sales and national economic and social indicators.[23]
2. Determine the impact government restrictions on the use of chemical pesticides will have on the growth of chemical, biological, and electromagnetic energy pest-control markets.

Forecasting is essential but never easy. Here, PepsiCo president and CEO Indra Nooyi addresses her first-ever press conference in India. Her position requires her to constantly make and revise predictions about the company's future, not only to assist in planning PepsiCo's strategy but also to inform the company's many stakeholders and the public about its position.

3. Evaluate sales growth potential, profitability, resources required, and risks involved in each of its market areas (commercial, industrial, institutional, governmental, and residential).
4. Evaluate the potential for expansion of marketing efforts in geographical areas of the United States as well as in foreign countries.
5. Determine the likelihood of technological breakthroughs that would make existing product lines obsolete.

Types of Forecasts In addition to the general type of organizational forecasting done by Insect Control Services, specialized types of forecasting, such as economic, technological, social trends, and sales forecasting, are available. Although a complete organizational forecasting process should, and usually does, include all these types of forecasting, sales forecasting is considered the key organizational forecast. A *sales forecast* is a prediction of how high or low sales of the organization's products or services will be over the period of time under consideration. It is the key forecast for organizations because it serves as the fundamental guideline for planning. Only after the sales forecast has been completed can managers decide, for example, whether more salespeople should be hired, whether more money for plant expansion must be borrowed, or whether layoffs and cutbacks in certain areas are necessary. Managers must continually monitor forecasting methods to improve them and to reformulate plans based on inaccurate forecasts.[24]

Methods of Sales Forecasting Modern managers have several different methods available for forecasting sales. The two broad types of sales forecasting methods are qualitative and quantitative. In the following sections, we highlight popular qualitative (i.e., jury of executive opinion, salesforce estimation) and quantitative (i.e., moving average, regression, product stages) forecasting methods.

QUALITATIVE METHODS

Jury of executive opinion method The **jury of executive opinion method** of sales forecasting is straightforward. Appropriate managers within the organization assemble to discuss their opinions on what will happen to sales in the future. Because these discussion sessions usually revolve around hunches or experienced guesses, the resulting forecast is a blend of informed opinions.[25]

A similar, more recently developed forecasting method, called the *Delphi method,* also gathers, evaluates, and summarizes expert opinions as the basis for a forecast, but the procedure is more formal than that for the jury of executive opinion method.[26] The basic Delphi method employs the following steps:

STEP 1 Various experts are asked to answer, independently and in writing, a series of questions about the future of sales or whatever other area is being forecasted.

STEP 2 A summary of all the answers is then prepared. No expert knows how any other expert answered the questions.

STEP 3 Copies of the summary are given to the individual experts with the request that they modify their original answers if they think it necessary.

STEP 4 Another summary is made of these modifications, and copies again are distributed to the experts. This time, however, expert opinions that deviate significantly from the norm must be justified in writing.

STEP 5 A third summary is made of the opinions and justifications, and copies are once again distributed to the experts. Justification in writing for *all* answers is now required.

STEP 6 The forecast is generated from all of the opinions and justifications that arise from step 5.

Salesforce estimation method The **salesforce estimation method** is a sales forecasting technique that predicts future sales by analyzing the opinions of salespeople as a group. Salespeople continually interact with customers, and from this interaction they usually develop a knack for predicting future sales. As with the jury of executive opinion method, the resulting forecast normally is a blend of the informed views of the group.

The salesforce estimation method is considered to be a valuable management tool and is commonly used in business and industry throughout the world. Although the accuracy of this method is generally good, managers have found that it can be improved by taking such simple steps as providing salespeople with sufficient time to forecast and offering incentives for accurate forecasts. Some companies help their salespeople become better forecasters by training them to better interpret their interactions with customers.[27]

Quantitative Methods

Moving average The **moving average method** utilizes historical data to predict future sales levels. Specifically, forecasters compute average sales levels for *x* historical time periods; forecasters are able to choose the number of time periods that best fit their situations. Suppose, for example, that forecasters at Toyota are using a five-year moving average to predict future automobile sales. In 2009, they would select the five most recent years—2004 to 2008—and compute average automobile sales during that period. In 2010, they would rely on sales data from 2005 to 2009, and in 2011 they would rely on sales data from 2006 to 2010. Because the five-year time period changes each year to reflect the five most recent years, this method is referred to as a "moving" average.

Regression The **regression method** predicts future sales by analyzing the historical relationship between sales and time.[28] Using this information, analysts can use regression to forecast future sales. Specifically, regression provides forecasters with a trend-line that best explains the historical relationship between sales and time. Forecasters can use this trend-line, then, to predict future sales. Figure 10.5 illustrates an example of a trend-line that can be used to forecast future sales. Managers often use statistical programs such as SPSS or SAS to conduct regression analysis.

Although the actual number of time periods included in regression will vary from company to company, as a general rule, managers should include as many time periods as necessary to ensure that important sales trends do not go undetected. For example, at the Coca-Cola Company, management believes that to validly predict the annual sales of any one year, it must chart annual sales in each of the 10 previous years.[29]

FIGURE 10.5
Regression analysis method

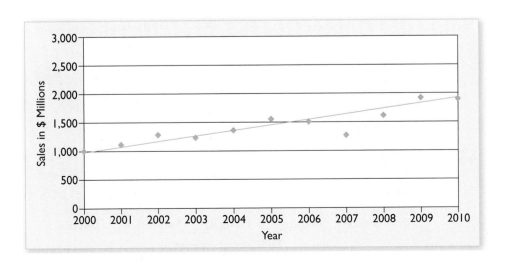

Product stages The data in Figure 10.5 indicate steadily increasing sales for B. J.'s Men's Clothing over time. However, because in the long term products generally go through what is called a product life cycle, the predicted increase based on the last decade of sales should probably be considered overly optimistic. A **product life cycle** is the five stages through which most products and services pass. These stages are introduction, growth, maturity, saturation, and decline.[30] The **product stages method** predicts future sales by using the product life cycle to better understand the history and future of the product.

Figure 10.6 shows how the five stages of the product life cycle are related to sales volume for seven products over a period of time. In the introduction stage, when a product is brand new, sales are just beginning to build (Web-capable cell phones). In the growth stage, the product has been in the marketplace for some time and is becoming more accepted, so product sales continue to climb (e.g., cellular phones and MP3 players). During the maturity stage, competitors enter the market, and although sales are still climbing, they are climbing at a slower rate than they did in the growth stage (e.g., personal computers). After the maturity stage comes the saturation stage, when nearly everyone who wanted the product has it (e.g., refrigerators and microwaves). Sales during the saturation stage typically are due to the need to replace a worn-out product or to population growth. The last product life cycle stage—decline—finds the product being replaced by a competing product (e.g., conventional, or not high-definition, televisions).

Managers may be able to prevent some products from entering the decline stage by improving product quality or by adding innovations. Other products, such as scissors, may never reach this last stage of the product life cycle because there are no competing products to replace them.

Evaluating Sales Forecasting Methods The sales forecasting methods just described are not the only ones available to managers. Other, more complex methods include the statistical correlation method and the computer simulation method.[31] The methods just discussed, however, do provide a basic foundation for understanding sales forecasting.

In practice, managers find that each sales forecasting method has distinct advantages and disadvantages. Before deciding to use a particular sales forecasting method, a manager must carefully weigh these advantages and disadvantages as they relate to the manager's organization. The best decision may be to use a combination of methods to forecast sales rather than just one. Whatever method or methods are finally adopted, the manager should be certain the framework is logical, fits the needs of the organization, and can be adapted to changes in the environment.

FIGURE 10.6
Stages of the product life cycle

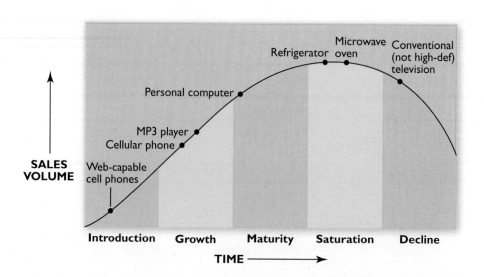

TABLE 10.3	Familiarity with Forecasting Methods		
	1980s	**1990s**	**2000s**
Qualitative Methods			
Jury of Executive Opinion	87%	82%	74%
Salesforce Estimation	84	85	83
Quantitative Methods			
Moving Average	92%	98%	100%
Regression	80	88	97

Note: The numbers in this table reflect the percentage of respondents who were "familiar" or "somewhat familiar" with the corresponding forecasting method.

A recent study surveyed forecasters to gauge their familiarity with using these forecasting methods.[32] The authors of the study then compared these familiarity statistics with two similar studies conducted in the 1980s and 1990s. The results of the study, which are displayed in Table 10.3, revealed some interesting trends. First, these results suggest the increasing popularity of quantitative forecasting methods; in fact, 100 percent of forecasters polled in the 2000s were familiar with the moving average method. In contrast, familiarity with qualitative methods—especially the jury of executive opinion method—has decreased over time.

Scheduling

Scheduling is the process of formulating a detailed listing of activities that must be accomplished to attain an objective, allocating the resources necessary to attain the objective, and setting up and following timetables for completing the objective. Scheduling is an integral part of every organizational plan. Two popular scheduling techniques are Gantt charts and the program evaluation and review technique (PERT).

Gantt Charts The **Gantt chart**, a scheduling device developed by Henry L. Gantt, is essentially a bar graph with time on the horizontal axis and the resource to be scheduled on the vertical axis. It is used for scheduling resources, including management system inputs such as human resources and machines.

Scheduling is an important type of forecasting and is accomplished in many ways. These X-ray technicians in a Santa Monica, CA hospital rely on the scheduling board behind them to coordinated their work with a steady stream of patients undergoing tests of many different types.

FIGURE 10.7
Completed Gantt chart

Figure 10.7 shows a completed Gantt chart for a work period entitled "Workweek 28." The resources scheduled over the five workdays on this chart were the human resources Wendy Reese and Peter Thomas. During this workweek, both Reese and Thomas were supposed to produce 10 units a day. Note, however, that actual production deviated from planned production. There were days when each of the two workers produced more than 10 units, as well as days when each produced fewer than 10 units. Cumulative actual production for workweek 28 shows that Reese produced 40 units and Thomas 45 units over the five days.

FEATURES Although simple in concept and appearance, the Gantt chart has many valuable managerial uses.[33] First, managers can use it as a summary overview of how organizational resources are being employed. From this summary, they can detect such facts as which resources are consistently contributing to productivity and which are hindering it. Second, managers can use the Gantt chart to help coordinate organizational resources. The chart can show which resources are not being used during specific periods, thereby allowing managers to schedule those resources for work on other production efforts. Third, the chart can be used to establish realistic worker output standards. For example, if scheduled work is being completed too quickly, output standards should be raised so that workers are scheduled for more work per time period.

Program Evaluation and Review Technique (PERT)

The main weakness of the Gantt chart is that it does not contain any information about the interrelationship of tasks to be performed. Although all tasks to be performed are listed on the chart, it is not possible to tell whether one task must be performed before another can be started. The **program evaluation and review technique (PERT),** a technique that evolved partly from the Gantt chart, is a scheduling tool that does emphasize the interrelationship of tasks.

DEFINING PERT PERT is a network of project activities showing both the estimates of time necessary to complete each activity and the sequence of activities that must be followed to complete the project. This scheduling tool was developed in 1958 for designing and building the Polaris submarine weapon system. The people who were managing this project found Gantt charts and other existing scheduling tools of little use because of the complicated nature of the Polaris project and the interdependence of the tasks to be performed.[34]

The PERT network contains two primary elements: activities and events. An **activity** is a specified set of behavior within a project, and an **event** is the completion of major project tasks. Within the PERT network, each event is assigned corresponding activities that must be performed before the event can materialize.[35]

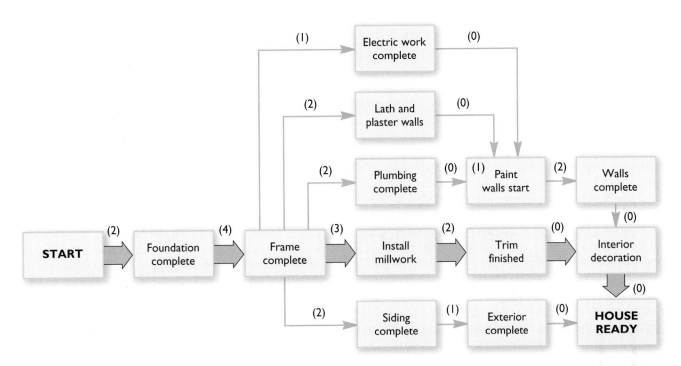

FIGURE 10.8   PERT network designed for building a house

FEATURES A sample PERT network designed for building a house is presented in Figure 10.8. Events are symbolized by boxes and activities by arrows. To illustrate, the figure indicates that after the event "Foundation Complete" (represented by a box) has materialized, certain activities (represented by an arrow) must be performed before the event "Frame Complete" (represented by another box) can materialize.

Two other features of the network shown in Figure 10.8 should be emphasized. First, the left-to-right presentation of events shows how the events interrelate or the sequence in which they should be performed. Second, the numbers in parentheses above each arrow indicate the units of time necessary to complete each activity. These two features help managers ensure that only necessary work is being done on a project and that no project activities are taking too long.[36]

CRITICAL PATH Managers need to pay close attention to the **critical path** of a PERT network—the sequence of events and activities requiring the longest period of time to complete. This path is called *critical* because a delay in completing this sequence results in a delay in completing the entire project. The critical path in Figure 10.8 is indicated by thick arrows; all other paths are indicated by thin arrows. Managers try to control a project by keeping it within the time designated by the critical path. The critical path helps them predict which features of a schedule are becoming unrealistic and provides insights into how those features might be eliminated or modified.[37]

STEPS IN DESIGNING A PERT NETWORK When designing a PERT network, managers should follow four primary steps:[38]

STEP 1 List all the activities/events that must be accomplished for the project and the sequence in which these activities/events should be performed.

STEP 2 Determine how much time will be needed to complete each activity/event.

STEP 3 Design a PERT network that reflects all of the information contained in steps 1 and 2.

STEP 4 Identify the critical path.

CHALLENGE CASE SUMMARY

In developing plans in a company like Microsoft, management is actually developing recommendations for future actions. As such, plans should be action oriented; they should state precisely what management is going to do to achieve its goals.

In developing plans, managers such as those at Microsoft should consider how often the plans will be used and the length of time they will cover. Will a plan be implemented only once or be used on a long-term basis to handle an ongoing issue, such as maintaining a product line? A plan similar to Microsoft's plan to serve a different market might not be used by other companies and would be designed to cover a specific amount of time.

In addition, managers should consider what part of the organization the plans they develop will be aimed at and on what level the plans will focus. For instance, a plan to cut costs may encompass all of Microsoft's internal operations, whereas a plan to improve product quality may affect only one part of the company, such as its product development function. Similarly, a plan to cut costs may be aimed at top-level management, whereas a product-quality plan may be aimed toward lower-level management and the programmers themselves. Managers such as those at Microsoft must realize that management systems are interdependent, which means that any plans they implement will affect the system as a whole.

Managers would normally use both standing plans and single-use plans in a company. Standing plans include policies, procedures, and rules and should be developed for situations that occur repeatedly. For example, one policy Microsoft management could develop might focus on the level of product quality they want to emphasize with employees.

Single-use plans include programs and budgets and should be developed to help manage less repetitive situations. In developing such plans, managers should thoroughly understand the reasons that plans fail and take steps to avoid those pitfalls.

Plant facilities planning and human resource planning are two types of planning that managers commonly pursue. In the case of Microsoft, plant facilities planning would entail developing the types of worksites the company needs to reach its objectives. Such planning addresses questions such as where a new facility should be located, how to expand and remodel an existing worksite, and how to lay out a plant to best facilitate the effective and efficient production of software.

Human resource planning involves obtaining or developing the personnel an organization needs to reach its objectives. In this area, for example, Microsoft management might discuss the types of engineers needed to improve existing products or design new products that meet specified requirements. Discussion would inevitably focus on issues such as how many new employees, if any, Microsoft will need as economic conditions vary; in what areas they will be needed; when these employees would be needed; how they will be obtained; and how they will be appropriately trained.

One of the planning tools available to Microsoft management is forecasting, which involves predicting future environmental events that could influence the operation of the company. Although various specific types of forecasting—such as economic, technological, and social trends forecasting—are available to them, Microsoft management would probably use sales forecasting as its key, because it will predict how high or low sales will be during the time period they are considering.

To forecast sales, Microsoft management could also ask its retailers (salesforce) for opinions on predicted sales. Although the opinions of such individuals may not be completely reliable, these people are closest to the market and must ultimately make the sales. Microsoft might also follow the jury of executive opinion method by having Microsoft executives discuss their opinions of future sales. This method would be quick and easy to use and, assuming that Microsoft executives have a good feel for product demand, might be as valid as any other method the company might use.

Finally, Microsoft management could use the regression analysis method by analyzing the relationship between sales and time. Although this method takes into account the cyclical patterns and past history of sales, it also assumes the continuation of these patterns in the future without considering outside influences such as economic downturns, which could cause the patterns to change.

Because each sales forecasting method has advantages and disadvantages, managers at Microsoft should carefully analyze them before deciding which method or combination of methods should be used.

Scheduling is another planning tool available to Microsoft management. It involves the detailed listing of activities that must be accomplished to reach an objective. For example, if Microsoft's goal is to have all of its employees working proficiently on updated equipment within two years, management needs to schedule activities such as installing the equipment, training the employees, and establishing new output standards.

MANAGEMENT SKILL ACTIVITIES

This section is specially designed to help you develop planning tools skill. An individual's management skill is based on an understanding of management concepts and the ability to apply those concepts in management situations. As a result, the following activities are designed both to heighten your understanding of planning tools concepts and to help you gain facility in applying these concepts in various management situations.

UNDERSTANDING PLANNING TOOLS CONCEPTS

 To check your understanding and to practice using the concepts in this chapter, go to www.mymanagementlab.com and explore the material associated with Chapter 10

Know Key Terms

Understanding the following key terms is critical to your understanding of chapter material. Define each of these terms. Refer to the page(s) referenced after a term to check your definition or to gain further insight regarding the term.

plan **228**	budget **232**	product life cycle **238**
repetitiveness dimension **228**	input planning **232**	product stages method **238**
time dimension **228**	plant facilities planning **232**	scheduling **239**
scope dimension **229**	site selection **232**	Gantt chart **239**
level dimension **229**	human resource planning **234**	program evaluation and review
standing plan **229**	planning tools **235**	technique (PERT) **240**
single-use plan **229**	forecasting **235**	activity **240**
policy **229**	jury of executive opinion method **236**	event **240**
procedure **230**	salesforce estimation method **237**	critical path **241**
rule **230**	moving average method **237**	
program **231**	regression method **237**	

Know How Management Concepts Relate

This section is comprised of activities that will further sharpen your understanding of management concepts. Answer essay questions as completely as possible. Also, remember that many additional true/false and multiple choice questions appear on-line at MyManagementLab.com to help you further refine your understanding of management concepts.

1. Describe the four dimensions of plans.
2. Describe the differences between policies, rules, and procedures. Provide examples of each.
3. Compare and contrast qualitative versus quantitative sales forecasting methods.
4. Describe the differences between Gantt charts and PERT. In your opinion, which one is better for organizations? Explain.
5. Explain five of the primary reasons why plans fail. In your opinion, which one of these reasons is most important? Why?

DEVELOPING MANAGEMENT SKILLS

Learning activities in this section are aimed at helping you develop your plans and planning tools skill. Learning activities include Exploring Your Management Skill: Part 2, Experiential Exercises, Cases, and a VideoNet Exercise.

Exploring Your Management Skill: Part 1

Before studying this chapter, respond to the following questions regarding the type of advice that you would give to Microsoft VP Birger Steen, referenced in the Challenge Case. Then address the concerning planning challenges that he presently faces within the company. You are not expected to be a planning tools expert at this point. Answering the questions now can help you focus on important points when you study the chapter. Also, answering the questions again after you study the chapter will give you an idea of how much you have learned.

Record your answers here or go to MyManagement Lab.com. Recording your answers in MyManagementLab will allow you to get immediate results and see how your score compares to your classmates. If you answer the questions in the book, the answers are located in the Exploring Your Management Skill Appendix at the end of the book.

FOR EACH STATEMENT CIRCLE:
- "Y" if you would give the advice to Birger Steen.
- "N" if you would NOT give the advice to Birger Steen.
- "NI" if you have no idea whether you would give the advice to Birger Steen.

Mr. Steen, in meeting your planning tools challenges at Microsoft, you should . . .

| Before Study | After Study |

1. understand that plans at Microsoft will vary in terms of repetitiveness, time, scope, and level.
   Y, N, NI

2. recognize that *policy*, *procedure*, and *rule* are different words that describe the same concept.
   Y, N, NI

3. communicate to Microsoft employees that large companies such as Microsoft only establish standing plans and avoid single-use plans.
   Y, N, NI

4. delegate responsibility for planning solely to the planning department.
   Y, N, NI

5. recognize that in addition to forming your own plans, it is important to operate by plans established by managers.
   Y, N, NI

6. communicate to employees that when forming plans for future locations, "living conditions" is always the most important variable to consider.
   Y, N, NI

7. understand that Microsoft's human resource planning depends primarily on three factors: employee turnover within Microsoft, the nature of the present workforce, and the growth rate of the organization.
   Y, N, NI

8. require Microsoft employees to rely solely on the jury of executive opinion method for sales forecasts.
   Y, N, NI

9. realize that of all of the different forecasting methods, forecasters on average are most familiar with the moving average method.
   Y, N, NI

10. understand that qualitative and quantitative forecasts will always produce the same results in the software industry.
    Y, N, NI

11. require Microsoft employees to favor quantitative rather than qualitative forecasting methods when forecasting future software sales.
    Y, N, NI

12. realize that scheduling is often more important than forecasting.
    Y, N, NI

13. communicate to Microsoft's employees that Gantt charts have no real weaknesses.
    Y, N, NI

14. encourage Microsoft's employees to use both Gantt charts and PERT to prepare long-term sales forecasts.
    Y, N, NI

15. stress the importance of both activities and events when using PERT for scheduling purposes.
    Y, N, NI

Exploring Your Management Skill: Part 2

As you recall, you completed Exploring Your Management Skill before you started to study this chapter. Your responses gave you an idea of how much you initially knew about plans and planning tools and helped you focus on important points as you studied the chapter. Answer the Exploring Your Management Skill questions again now and compare your score to the first time you took it. This comparison will give you an idea of how much you have learned from studying this chapter and pinpoint areas for further clarification before you start studying the next chapter. Record your answers within the text or online at MyManagementLab.com. Completing the survey at MyManagementLab.com will allow you grade and compare your test scores automatically. If you complete the test in the book, look up answers in the Exploring Your Management Skill section at the end of the book.

Your Management Skills Portfolio

Your Management Learning Portfolio is a collection of activities especially designed to demonstrate your management knowledge and skill. By completing these activities online at My ManagementLab.com, you will be able to print, complete with cover sheet, as many activities as you choose. Be sure to save your work. Taking your printed portfolio to an employment interview could be helpful in obtaining a job.

The portfolio activity for this chapter is Forecasting Sales at Best Buy. Study the following information and complete the exercises that that follow.[39]

Best Buy is a retailer that specializes in consumer electronics, entertainment software, appliances, and home office products. In addition, Best Buy has established a number of services, such as its popular Geek Squad, to help consumers install, use, and troubleshoot the products they purchase in Best Buy stores. The company competes with other electronics retailers as well as larger and more general retailers such as Wal-Mart and Target.

Best Buy sells a number of different products and services, but personal computers (PCs) represent a substantial source of the company's sales each year. Because of the importance of PCs for Best Buy's performance, Robert Willett, Best Buy's chief information officer, has contacted you. Mr. Willett would like you to forecast Best Buy's PC sales for next year.

Explain how you would apply the five forecasting methods described in the chapter to help Mr. Willett better understand future personal computer sales. Assume that Mr. Willett has provided you with information that details Best Buy's PC sales over the past 10 years. You do not need to perform the actual calculations, but explain how you would use that information with the following methods. Keep in mind that some of these methods may not require the use of such information.

1. Jury of Executive Opinion Method

2. Salesforce Estimation Method

3. Moving Average Method

4. Regression Method

5. Product Stages Method

Experiential Exercises

1 Solving a Customer Service Issues

Directions. Read the following scenario and then perform the listed activities. Your instructor may want you to perform the activities as an individual or within groups. Follow all of your instructor's directions carefully.

Jeff Fettig is the CEO of Whirlpool Corporation, a manufacturer of home appliances such as refrigerators, dishwashers, washers and dryers, microwaves, and stoves. Recently, a customer called and reported that the interior walls of his new Whirlpool refrigerator were cracking, such that the cracks looked like spider webs. Fettig is concerned that this problem may appear in other refrigerators around the world. As such, Fettig has contacted your group to form a procedure to handle similar customer calls in the future. Specifically, your group should develop a procedure that details the steps a customer service agent should utilize when fielding such calls. Steps in the procedure, for example, might include taking digital pictures, sending service agents to the location, and so on. The final steps in the procedure should outline potential solutions, which may include doing nothing, fixing the cracks with tape, or replacing the refrigerator. For each step in the procedure, identify the associated major costs.

2 You and Your Career

Earlier, the chapter describes the importance of scheduling tools such as Gantt charts and PERT. How might your skills with Gantt charts and PERT help your career? In particular, imagine a job that you would like to obtain after school, and think of a scenario in which you might employ one of these scheduling tools. Can you think of an example from your life (e.g., previous jobs, previous appointments with organizations on campus, etc.) that might have benefited from using either Gantt charts or PERT?

Videonet Exercise

Planning Tools: Triple Rock Brewing

Video Highlights

In this video, three managers at Triple Rock Brewing describe the operation of their brewery and restaurant. The managers aspire to a relaxed and calm organizational culture. But general manager Jesse Sariñana also focuses on the importance of control through enforcement of standards. Do these two organizational elements conflict? General manager Jesse Sariñana's comments in the introduction about wanting to perpetuate a laid-back, relaxed atmosphere. (He mentions some form of the word *relax* three times!) In the Planning segment, Chef Jim Humberd said that good planning leads to more confident and relaxed employees.

Discussion Questions

1. Why do the managers of Triple Rock Brewing desire a relaxed and calm organizational culture?
2. Do the Triple Rock Brewing managers value planning? Why or why not?
3. Describe Jesse's and Jim's methods of control. Are a relaxed organizational culture and managerial control mutually exclusive?

Internet Activity

Browse the Triple Rock Brewery site at www.triplerock.com. Click around the site. Check out the brewing processes. Now, visit the "pub" link and read about the history of the brewery and its owners. The Web site reflects the organizational culture of a relaxed, laid-back atmosphere. Contrast the desired organizational culture with the discussion in the Controlling segment of the video about standards and efficiency. Jesse said, "Everybody has to be doing the same, exact thing." Are a relaxed culture and control mutually exclusive? Can a manager achieve both?

CASES

1 MICROSOFT PLANS FOR SMALL BUSINESSES

"Microsoft Plans for Small Businesses" (p. 227) and its related Challenge Case Summary were written to help you better understand the management concepts contained in this chapter. Answer the following discussion questions about the Challenge Case to better understand how concepts relating to plans and planning tools can be applied in a company such as Microsoft.

1. Should Microsoft's plan to improve the company's performance be related to its human resource planning? Explain.

2. Explain this statement: "The quality of Microsoft's decision about how to improve the company's performance is largely determined by product improvement planning."

3. Do you think that Microsoft management should use forecasted sales as a component of product improvement planning? Explain.

2 PLANNING FOR FAST FASHION AT ZARA

Read the case and answer the questions that follow. Studying this case will help you better understand how concepts relating to plans and planning tools can be applied in a company such as Zara.

Today's styles can become history overnight in the fast-paced world of women's fashion, as managers of the Zara retail company know all too well. Owned by Spain's Industria de Diseno Textil (Inditex), Zara was founded 30 years ago by Amancio Ortega Gaona, who remains chairman. From one small store selling popularly priced women's clothing in La Coruña, Spain, Zara has now blossomed into a powerful 600-store chain with a presence in more than 40 nations.

Staying on top of ever-changing and unpredictable fashion trends requires careful planning and forecasting. When a celebrity brings a certain style into the spotlight or a designer makes a splash with an innovative look, Zara competitors such as the U.S. retailer Gap and the Swedish retailer Hennes & Mauritz might need as long as six months to order the right fabric, design the garment and accessories, have everything manufactured, and ship the merchandise to their stores. In contrast, Zara follows a "fast fashion" strategy and can create, produce, and deliver an entirely new product line to store shelves in a matter of weeks.

"We don't want to miss out on the latest trend, which means a fast response to the demands of our customers and the market," explains Raul Estravera, one of Zara's communication managers. "Having our own factories allows us this flexibility—15 days from product decision to delivery and twice-weekly shipments of fresh merchandise—and there is less chance of error." To keep costs down and avoid holding mountains of merchandise that might suddenly turn into yesterday's fashions, Zara manufactures only what each store needs, based on forecasting. Yet because the company makes most of the clothing it sells, its managers can more tightly control crucial planning details such as production schedules, staffing, and budgets.

Zara's planners prepare store-by-store sales forecasts and tailor each store's assortment of merchandise to local tastes and trends, not an easy task for a company offering 12,000 styles every year. However, these initial forecasts are simply starting points. If a garment's early sales point to a big hit or store employees report unusually positive customer reaction to a particular style, the planners reforecast short-term sales, reorder immediately, and send shipments to stores where demand is highest.

Moving merchandise quickly is Zara's strength: Its state-of-the-art distribution center in Zaragoza, Spain, can handle 80,000 garments every *hour*, and management insists that stores receive deliveries no more than 35 hours after shipments leave the center. The company trucks merchandise to stores within one day's drive of Zaragoza and ships by air to more distant stores. As efficient as this system may be for the European stores, it could limit Zara's expansion in the United States, where the company now has 10 stores. Inditex's CEO notes that sending a cargo jet filled with merchandise to New York twice a week would enable Zara to stock up to 50 U.S. stores.

Meanwhile, Zara's managers continue to scout locations for new stores, analyzing local demographics and shopping patterns, examining the competition, estimating leasing and renovation or construction costs, and assessing local legal and regulatory issues. However, they can't always find the kind of facilities they want. For instance, Zara is seeking to expand in Ireland, but Mike Shearwood, that territory's executive, can't easily locate sufficiently large stores at affordable rents in good shopping districts.

Once he selects a site, Shearwood has a renovation budget of about $2 million and will make the most of the space by allocating about 85 percent for retail purposes, leaving just 15 percent for back-office operations. He also has to plan for the grand opening, not knowing exactly how things will go. When Shearwood opened a new store in Dublin, customer reaction was so enthusiastic that, he says, "We almost sold out and had to arrange a special delivery to be shipped in to ensure we had sufficient stock for the weekend."

QUESTIONS

1. Which of the three sales forecasting methods would you recommend Zara's planners use for projecting sales item by item? Why?

2. What kinds of procedures, policies, and rules would Zara's management be likely to establish to guide planning for the grand opening of a new store?

3. If you were designing a PERT network for a Zara store opening, what type of activities would you consider part of the critical path? Explain.

Endnotes

1. Company Web site, http://www.microsoft.com, accessed June 3, 2010; Ina Fried, "Microsoft's Latest Small-Business Plan," *CNET News,* March 31, 2010, http://news.cnet.com; Ina Fried, "Microsoft: Small Businesses Start to Eye Windows 7," *CNET News,* March 2, 2010, http://news.cnet.com; Paul Krill, "Microsoft and Intuit Forge Small-Business Web Apps Partnership," *InfoWorld,* January 20, 2010, http://www.infoworld.com; Tony Bradley, "Microsoft Ups Cloud Computing Ante with Azure and 'Dallas,'" *PC World,* November 17, 2009, http://www.pcworld.com; Peter Bright, "Microsoft: Azure to Go Live in January, for Pay in February," *Ars Technica,* November 17, 2009, http://arstechnica.com.

2. Charles B. Ames, "Straight Talk from the New CEO," *Harvard Business Review* (November/December 1989): 132–138.

3. Scholars hold different perspectives on the importance of business planning. For three examples, see Peter Bregman, "Why Not Having a Plan Can Be the Best Plan of All," *Harvard Business Review,* April 28, 2010, http://blogs.hbr.org; Jan Brinckmann, Dietmar Grichnik, and Diana Kapsa, "Should Entrepreneurs Plan or Just Storm the Castle? A Meta-Analysis on Contextual Factors Impacting the Business Planning–Performance Relationship in Small Firms," *Journal of Business Venturing* 25, no. 1 (January 2010): 24–40; and Thomas C. Powell, "Untangling the Relationship between Strategic planning and performance: The Role of Contingency Factors," *Canadian Journal of Administrative Sciences* 11, no. 1 (April 2009): 125–138.

4. Fremont E. Kast and James E. Rosenzweig, *Organization and Management: A Systems Approach* (New York: McGraw-Hill, 1970), 443–449. For a classic discussion on expanding this list of characteristics to 13, see P. LeBreton and D. A. Henning, *Planning Theory* (Upper Saddle River, NJ: Prentice Hall, 1961), 320–344. These authors list the dimensions of a plan as (1) complexity, (2) significance, (3) comprehensiveness, (4) time, (5) specificity, (6) completeness, (7) flexibility, (8) frequency, (9) formality, (10) confidential nature, (11) authorization, (12) ease of implementation, and (13) ease of control.

5. Organization Web site, "Nationwide Children's Hospital to Break Ground in 2010 for Third Research Facility as Final Piece to Expansion Plan," January 8, 2010, http://www.nationwidechildrens.org.

6. Jennifer A. Knight, "Loss Control Solution to Limiting Costs of Workplace Violence," *Corporate Cashflow* (July 1994): 16–17. For an interesting study that explores the emotional conflicts and confusion around corporate success and failure, see Mikita Brottman, "The Company Man: A Case on White-Collar Crime," *American Journal of Psychoanalysis* 69, no. 2 (2009): 121–135.

7. Company Web site, http://www.hm.com, accessed May 4, 2010.

8. Kirkland Wilcox and Richard Discenza, "The TQM Advantage," *CA Magazine* (May 1994): 37–41.

9. Company Web site, "A Greener Apple," http://www.apple.com, accessed May 21, 2010.

10. From "Seize the Future—Make Top Trends Pay Off Now," *Success* (March 1990): 39–45.

11. For an interesting article outlining the ethical and cultural challenges involved with budgeting, see Patricia Casey Douglas and Benson Wier, "Cultural and Ethical Effects in Budgeting Systems: A Comparison of U.S. and Chinese Managers," *Journal of Business Ethics* 60, no. 2 (2005): 159–174.

12. Kjell A. Ringbakk, "Why Planning Fails," *European Business* (July 1970). See also William G. Gang, "Strategic Planning and Competition: A Survival Guide for Electric Utilities," *Fortnightly,* February 1, 1994, 20–23.

13. Alden M. Hayashi, "Do You Have a 'Plan B'?" *MIT Sloan Management Review,* October 1, 2009, http://sloanreview.mit.edu.

14. For information that ranks U.S. cities on the possible site selection criterion of growth, see John Case, "Where the Growth Is," *Inc.* (June 1991): 66–79. See also Walt Yesberg, "Get a Grip on Building Costs," *ABA Banking Journal* 82 (March 1990): 90, 92.

15. Douglas P. Woodward, "Locational Determinants of Japanese Manufacturing Start-Ups in the United States," *Southern Economic Journal* (January 1992): 690–708.

16. Greg Nakanishi, "Building Business Through Partnerships," *HR Magazine* (June 1991): 108–112. For an interesting description of a company that performs human resource planning for other companies, see Eryn Brown, "PeopleSoft: Tech's Latest Publicly Traded Cult," *Fortune,* May 25, 1998, 155–156. For a study assessing the importance of human resource planning, see Senga Briggs and William Keogh, "Integrating Human Resource Strategy and Strategic Planning to Achieve Business Excellence," *Total Quality Management* 10, no. 4/5 (July 1999): S447–453.

17. Fay Hansen, "Strategic Workforce Planning in an Uncertain World," *Workforce Management,* July 2009, http://www.workforce.com.

18. For further ideas on the implementation of human resources planning, see Nen-Chen Hwang and Konstantin Kogan, "Dynamic Approach to Human Resources Planning for Major Professional Companies with a Peak-Wise Demand," *International Journal of Production Research* 41 (2003): 1255.

19. Jan Cienski and Christopher Condon, "Eastern Europe Hit by Shortage of Workers," *Financial Times,* June 5, 2007, 10.

20. Charles F. Kettering, "A Glimpse at the Future," *IndustryWeek* (July 1, 1991): 34.

21. Joanne Tokle and Dennis Krumwiede, "An Overview of Forecasting Error Among International Manufacturers," *Journal of International Business Research* 5, no. 2 (2006): 97–105.

22. William C. House, "Environmental Analysis: Key to More Effective Dynamic Planning," *Managerial Planning* (January/February 1977): 25–29. The basic components of this forecasting method, as well as of other methods, are discussed in Chaman L. Jain, "How to Determine the Approach to Forecasting," *Journal of Business Forecasting Methods & Systems* (Summer 1995): 2, 28. For information about software applications designed to help companies in their planning and forecasting, see Anonymous, "Planning and Forecasting," *Financial Executive* 17, no. 3 (May 2001): 14–15.

23. For an excellent discussion of the influence of industry dynamics on forecasting, see Hao Tan and John A. Mathews, "Identification and analysis of industry cycles," *Journal of Business Research* 63, no. 5 (2010): 454–462.

24. Marshall L. Fisher et al., "Making Supply Meet Demand in an Uncertain World," *Harvard Business Review* (May/June 1994): 83–89; Tony Dear, "Fast and Slow Approaches to Sales Forecasting," *Logistics Focus* 6, no. 4 (May 1998): 24–25.

25. For a new product sales forecast model based on an Analytic Network Process framework, see Dimitra Voulgaridou, Dimitra, Konstantinos Kirytopoulos and Vrassidas Leopoulos, "An analytic network process approach to sales forecasting," *Operational Research* 9, no. 1 (2009): 35–53.

26. Olfa Hemler, "The Uses of Delphi Techniques in Problems of Educational Innovations," no. 8499, RAND Corporation, December 1966. For an interesting article employing the Delphi method to analyze international trends, see Michael R. Czinkota and Ilkka A. Ronkainen, "International Business and Trade in the Next Decade: Report from a Delphi Study," *Journal of International Business Studies* 28, no. 4 (Fourth Quarter 1997): 827–844.

27. James E. Cox Jr., "Approaches for Improving Salespersons' Forecasts," *Industrial Marketing Management* 18 (November 1989): 307–311; Jack Stack, "A Passion for Forecasting," *Inc.* (November 1997): 37–38. For more information on forecasting, see Nassim N. Taleb, *The Black Swan: The Impact of the Highly Improbable* (New York: Random House, 2007).

28. For an application of time series analysis, see Lester Hunt and Yasushi Ninomiya, "Unraveling Trends and Seasonality: A Structural Time Series Analysis of Transport Oil Demand in the UK and Japan," *Energy Journal* 24 (2003): 63.

29. N. Carroll Mohn, "Forecasting Sales with Trend Models—Coca-Cola's Experience," *Journal of Business Forecasting* 8 (Fall 1989): 6–8. For an interesting article that describes the use of time series analysis in predicting the alcohol consumption of Europeans, see David E. Smith and Hans S. Solgaard, "Global Trends in European Alcoholic Drinks Consumption," *Marketing and Research Today* 26, no. 2 (May 1998): 80–85. For a historical perspective of time series analysis, see D. S. G. Pollock, "Statistical Visions in Time: A History of Time Series Analysis, 1662–1938," *Economica* 67, no. 267 (August 2000): 459–461.

30. For information on product life cycles, see George S. Day, "The Product Life Cycle: Analysis and Applications Issues," *Journal of Marketing* 45, no. 4 (1981): 60–67; David Rink and Harold Fox, "Using the Product Life Cycle Concept to Formulate Actionable Purchasing Strategies," *Singapore Management Review* 25 (2003): 73; see also Kuang-Jung Tseng, "Application of Thermodynamics on Product Life Cycle," *Journal of American Academy of Business* 4 (2004): 464.

31. For elaboration on these methods, see George A. Steiner, *Top Management Planning* (London: Collier-Macmillan, 1969), 223–227.

32. This discussion and accompanying table is based on Teresa M. McCarthy, Donna F. Davis, Susan L. Golicic, and John T. Mentzer, "The Evolution of Sales Forecasting Management: A 20-Year Longitudinal Study of Forecasting Practices," *Journal of Forecasting* 25 (2006): 303–324. For an alternative view of several case studies related to worst business forecasting practices of companies and their solutions, see Lad A. Dilgard "Worst Forecasting Practices in Corporate America and Their Solutions-Case Studies," *Journal of Business Forecasting* 28, no. 2 (2009): 4–13.

33. James Wilson, "Gantt Charts: A Centenary Appreciation," *European Journal of Operational Research* 149 (2003): 430. To better understand the sensitivity of Gantt charts, see S. A. Oke and O. E. Charles-Owaba, "A sensitivity analysis of an optimal Gantt charting maintenance scheduling model," *The International Journal of Quality & Reliability Management* 23, no. 2/3 (2006): 197–229.

34. Willard Fazar, "The Origin of PERT," *The Controller* (December 1962). For a discussion of software packages that draw preliminary PERT and Gantt charts, see Pat Sweet, "A Planner's Best Friend?" *Accountancy* (February 1994): 56, 58. Also see Curtis F. Franklin Jr., "Project Managers Toolbox," *CIO* 11, no. 2 (October 15, 1997): 64–70. For an extension of the Gantt chart, see Harvey Maylor, "Beyond the Gantt Chart: Project Management Moving On," *European Management Journal* 19, no. 1 (February 2001): 92–100.

35. See also H. M. Soroush, "The Most Critical Path in a PERT Network," *Journal of the Operational Research Society* 45 (March 1994): 287–300.

36. For insights about using PERT, see Jose Perez, Salvador Rambaud, and Jose Velasco, "Some Indications to Correctly Use Estimations of an Expert in the PERT Methodology," *Central European Journal of Operations Research* 11 (2003): 183. To better understand the dynamics involved with PERT, see Amir Azaron and Reza Tavakkoli-Moghaddam, "Multi-objective time-cost trade-off in dynamic PERT networks using an interactive approach," *European Journal of Operational Research* 180, no. 3 (2007): 1186–1200.

37. Avraham Shrub, "The Integration of CPM and Material Management in Project Management," *Construction Management and Economics* 6 (Winter 1988): 261–272; Michael A. Hatfield and James Noel, "The Case for Critical Path," *Cost Engineering* 40, no. 3 (March 1998): 17–18.

38. For extended discussion of these steps, see Edward K. Shelmerdine, "Planning for Project Management," *Journal of Systems Management* 40 (January 1989): 16–20.

39. This exercise was based on Nick Wingfield, "Microsoft's Videogame Efforts Take a Costly Hit," *Wall Street Journal,* July 6, 2007, A3.

Fundamentals of Organizing

Target Skill

organizing skill: the ability to establish orderly uses for resources within the management system

objectives

To help build my *organizing skill,* when studying this chapter, I will attempt to acquire:

1. An understanding of the organizing function

2. An appreciation for the complexities of determining appropriate organizational structure

3. An understanding of the distinction between vertical and horizontal dimensioning

4. Insights into the advantages and disadvantages of division of labor

5. A working knowledge of the relationship between division of labor and coordination

6. An appreciation for the advantages and disadvantages associated with the different types of departmentalization

7. An understanding of span of management and the factors that influence its appropriateness

8. An understanding of scalar relationships

CHALLENGE CASE

SONY ORGANIZES FOR SUCCESS

SONY CORPORATION DESIGNS, MANUFACTURES, AND SELLS electronic equipment and devices to both consumers and companies. Although the electronics division accounts for a majority of its sales, Sony also develops, manufactures, and sells other entertainment products such as film, music, and videogame hardware and software. In addition, Sony also has a financial services division, which accounts for a majority of its income. Given the broad array of products and services Sony offers, Sony's executives have faced some difficulties in determining the company's optimal organizational structure, which has resulted in some financial problems that jeopardize the company's operations.

Sir Howard Stringer, Sony's chief executive officer, has implemented several organizational structure changes to address the problem. One of the main causes for Sony's recent lackluster performance is the company's electronics division. In the past, Sony has relied on this division to produce new, innovative products such as the Sony Walkman. Recently, however, Sony has faced more difficulties in producing innovative products.

To face these challenges in the electronics division, Stringer has promised to change elements of the division's structure. In particular, he has vowed to restructure the electronics division to allow more communication. Hopefully, increased communication will lead to more innovations and, consequently, new Sony products. This increased communication will also improve coordination between the different units. At one point, for example, three different divisions within Sony were developing their own digital music players.[1]

Sony has also restructured its music business, which ranks third in U.S. market share, to improve the company's overall performance. Specifically, the company has reduced a large number of support positions in sales, manufacturing, and distribution.

According to Sony, many employees in these positions were performing similar activities. By eliminating some of this overlap, Sony can redirect money to develop new artists, which is a crucial activity in the music business.

Finally, Sony will continue to search for new ways to combine its music, film, and electronics businesses

■ *Sony has implemented changes in its organizational structure to reduce financial problems that threatened to jeopardize its operations.*

249

with its videogame business. Sony's videogame business, which develops and sells its PlayStation 3 (PS3) gaming system, represents Sony's largest profit driver. By developing linkages among Sony's businesses, the company may be better able to leverage its success in the videogame market. For example, when Sony first released its 3D update for its PS3, it timed the introduction with its launch of 3D capable televisions.

Some questions remain as to whether Sony can rebound from its current downturn. According to Stringer, Sony's ability to restructure represents a key determinant of the company's future success. What organizing challenges do you see in Stringer's future?

EXPLORING YOUR MANAGEMENT SKILL

You can explore your level of organizing skill **before** studying the chapter by completing the exercise "Exploring Your Management Skill: Part 1" on page 266 and **after** studying this chapter by completing the exercise "Exploring Your Management Skill: Part 2" on page 267.

THE ORGANIZING CHALLENGE

The Challenge Case illustrates many different organizing challenges that Stringer, the CEO, will have to meet if Sony is to be successful. The remaining material in this chapter explains organizing concepts and helps develop the corresponding organizing skill that you will need to meet organizing challenges throughout your career. After studying chapter concepts, read the Challenge Case Summary at the end of the chapter to help you relate chapter content to meeting organizing challenges at Sony.

DEFINITIONS OF ORGANIZING AND ORGANIZING SKILL

Organizing is the process of establishing orderly uses for resources within the management system. Correspondingly, **organizing skill** is the ability to establish orderly uses for resources within the management system. This chapter focuses on organizing and helping you develop the target skill for this chapter, organizing skill.

Orderly uses of resources emphasize the attainment of management system objectives and assist managers not only in making objectives apparent but in clarifying which resources will be used to attain them.[2] A primary focus of organizing is determining what individual employees will do in an organization and how their individual efforts should best be combined to advance the attainment of organizational objectives.[3] *Organization* refers to the result of the organizing process. Fayol presents a number of guidelines for effective organizations; these guidelines are displayed in Figure 11.1.

The Importance of Organizing

The organizing function is extremely important to the management system because it is the primary mechanism managers use to activate plans.[4] Organizing creates and maintains relationships between all organizational resources by indicating which resources are to be used for specified activities and when, where, and how they are to be used. A thorough organizing effort helps managers minimize costly weaknesses, such as duplication of effort and idle organizational resources.

Some management theorists consider the organizing function so important that they advocate the creation of an organizing department within the management system. Typical responsibilities of this department would include three primary responsibilities.[5] First, the department should periodically formulate reorganization plans that make the management system more effective and efficient. Companies, for example, typically restructure to devote more resources to profitable divisions and fewer resources to divisions losing money. Second, the department should foster and support an advantageous organizational climate within the management system. Finally, the department should develop plans to improve managerial skills to fit current management system needs.

In essence, each organizational resource represents an investment from which the management system must get a return. Appropriate organization of these resources increases the efficiency and effectiveness of their use. Henri Fayol developed 16 general guidelines for organizing resources:

1. Judiciously prepare and execute the operating plan.
2. Organize the human and material facets so that they are consistent with objectives, resources, and requirements of the concern.
3. Establish a single competent, energetic guiding authority (formal management structure).
4. Coordinate all activities and efforts.
5. Formulate clear, distinct, and precise decisions.
6. Arrange for efficient selection so that each department is headed by a competent, energetic manager, and all employees are placed where they can render the greatest service.
7. Define duties.
8. Encourage initiative and responsibility.
9. Offer fair and suitable rewards for services rendered.
10. Make use of sanctions against faults and errors.
11. Maintain discipline.
12. Ensure that individual interests are consistent with the general interests of the organization.
13. Recognize the unity of command.
14. Promote both material and human coordination.
15. Institute and effect controls.
16. Avoid regulations, red tape, and paperwork.

FIGURE 11.1
Organization: Fayol's guidelines

how managers do it

Developing Managers at General Electric

General Electric (GE) is known the world over for its ability to develop managerial talent. Although GE is famous for its products and services ranging from light bulbs to NBC television, many suggest that the key to GE's success is due primarily to the company's ability to identify and develop managers.[6] ■

The Organizing Process

The five main steps of the organizing process are presented in Figure 11.2: reflect on plans and objectives, establish major tasks, divide major tasks into subtasks, allocate resources and directives for subtasks, and evaluate the results of implemented organizing strategy.[7] As the figure implies, managers should continually repeat these steps. Through repetition, they obtain feedback that will help them improve the existing organization.[8]

The management of a restaurant can serve as an illustration of how the organizing process works. The first step the restaurant manager would take to initiate the organizing process would be to reflect on the restaurant's plans and objectives. Because planning involves determining how the restaurant will attain its objectives, and organizing involves determining how the restaurant's resources will be used to activate plans, the restaurant manager must start to organize by understanding planning.

The second and third steps of the organizing process focus on tasks to be performed within the management system. The manager must designate major tasks or jobs to be done within the restaurant. Two such tasks are serving customers and cooking food. Then the tasks must be divided into subtasks. For example, the manager might decide that serving customers includes the subtasks of taking orders and clearing tables.

FIGURE 11.2
The five main steps of the organizing process

The fourth organizing step is determining who will take orders, who will clear the tables, and what the details of the relationship between these individuals will be. The size of tables and how they are to be set are other factors to be considered at this point.

In the fifth step, evaluating the results of the implemented organizing strategy, the manager gathers feedback on how well the strategy is working. This feedback should furnish information that can be used to improve the existing organization. For example, the manager may find that a particular type of table is not large enough and that larger ones must be purchased if the restaurant is to attain its goals.

CLASSICAL ORGANIZING THEORY

Classical organizing theory comprises the cumulative insights of early management writers on how organizational resources can best be used to enhance goal attainment. The following sections discuss three major components of classical organizing theory: Weber's bureaucratic model, division of labor, and structure.

To organize any large project, like this study of the effect of chemicals on plant growth at Limburger Hof research station, managers must establish objectives (or in this case a hypothesis) and major tasks. Then they break tasks into smaller sub-tasks, allocate resources to each task, and finally evaluate the results.

Weber's Bureaucratic Model

The writer who probably had the most profound influence on classical organizing theory was Max Weber. Most agree that Weber's most notable contribution to classical organizing theory was his concept of bureaucracy.[9] Specifically, Weber used the term **bureaucracy** to label the management system that includes three primary components: detailed procedures and rules, a clearly outlined organizational hierarchy, and impersonal relationships among organization members.

Although he firmly believed in the bureaucratic approach to organizing, he was concerned that managers were inclined to overemphasize the merits of a bureaucracy. He cautioned that a bureaucracy is not an end in itself, but rather a means to the end of management system goal attainment. The main criticism of Weber's bureaucracy model, as well as the concepts of other classical organizing theorists, is that they give short shrift to the human variable within organizations. In fact, it is recognized today that the bureaucratic approach without an appropriate emphasis on the human variable is almost certainly a formula for organizational failure.[10]

how managers do it

Eliminating Bureaucracy at General Motors

Another criticism of bureaucracy is that it may negatively influence organizational effectiveness.[11] For an example of bureaucracy negatively influencing organizational effectiveness, consider General Motors (GM). For years, GM was not only one of the world's largest companies but also a huge bureaucracy. Although over the years various GM chief executives tried to cut layers of management, the company continued to post losses and, by 2009, faced bankruptcy. Before the U.S. government would provide further aid, GM was ordered to make significant and deep organizational cuts. With a slimmed-down GM emerging from bankruptcy, company vice chairman Bob Lutz pledged that GM will maintain its focus on eliminating bureaucracy, saying "If you tell yourself you're done [cutting costs], that probably means you're complacent."[12] Even though appropriate organization can improve efficiency and effectiveness, this example illustrates the potential problems associated with inappropriate organization. ∎

Division of Labor

A primary consideration of any organizing effort is how to divide labor. **Division of labor** is the assignment of various portions of a particular task among a number of organization members.[13] Rather than one individual doing the entire job, several individuals perform different parts of it. Production is divided into a number of steps, with the responsibility for completing various steps assigned to specific individuals. The essence of division of labor is that individuals specialize in doing part of a task rather than the entire task.[14]

A commonly used illustration of division of labor is the automobile production line. Rather than one person assembling an entire car, specific portions of the car are assembled by various workers. Although most associate division of labor with automobiles, division of labor plays an important role in a variety of businesses. For example, division of labor plays an important role in the manufacturing of art in China. At some manufacturing facilities, several artists help to paint copies of the same picture. When individuals finish painting their particular sections, they pass the painting on to other members to finish their own sections.[15] This approach allows Chinese galleries such as the JiYiYuang Gallery to sell paintings for lower prices. It is clear, then, that the division of labor influences a variety of organizations. The following sections discuss the advantages and disadvantages of division of labor, the relationship between division of labor and coordination, and Mary Parker Follett's coordination guidelines.

Advantages and Disadvantages of Division of Labor Even the peerless physicist Albert Einstein, famous for his independent theorizing, believed that division of labor could be advantageous in many undertakings.[16] Several explanations have been offered for the usefulness of division of labor. First, when workers specialize in a particular task, their skill at performing that task tends to increase. Second, workers who have one job and one place in which to do it do not lose valuable time changing tools or locations. Third, when workers concentrate on performing only one job, they naturally try to make the job easier and more efficient. Lastly, division of labor creates a situation in which workers need only to know how to perform their part of the work task rather than the entire process for producing the end product. The task of understanding their work, therefore, does not become too burdensome.

Arguments have also been presented against the use of an extreme division of labor.[17] Essentially, these arguments contend that division of labor focuses solely on efficiency and economic benefit and overlooks the human variable in organizations. Work that is extremely specialized tends to be boring and therefore will eventually cause production rates to go down as workers become resentful of being treated like machines. Clearly, managers need to find a reasonable balance between specialization and human motivation. Finding this balance is an ongoing challenge for organizations and an area of continued study.[18]

Division of Labor and Coordination In a division-of-labor situation, the importance of effective coordination of the different individuals doing portions of the task is obvious. Mooney has defined **coordination** as "the orderly arrangement of group effort to provide unity of action in the pursuit of a common purpose." In essence, coordination is a means for achieving any and all organizational objectives.[19] It involves encouraging the completion of individual portions of a task in a synchronized order that is appropriate for the overall task. Groups cannot maintain their productivity without coordination.[20] Part of the synchronized order of assembling an automobile, for example, is that seats are installed only after the floor has been installed; adhering to this order of installation is an example of coordination.

Establishing and maintaining coordination may require close supervision of employees, though managers should try to break away from the idea that coordination can only be achieved this way.[21] They can, instead, establish and maintain coordination through bargaining, formulating a common purpose for the group, or improving on specific problem solutions so the group will know what to do when it encounters those problems. Each of these efforts is considered a specific management tool.

Follett's Guidelines on Coordination Mary Parker Follett provided valuable advice on how managers can establish and maintain coordination within the organization. First, Follett said that coordination can be attained with the least difficulty through direct horizontal relationships and personal communications. In other words, when a coordination problem arises, peer discussion may be the best way to resolve it. Second, Follett suggested that coordination be a discussion topic throughout the planning process. In essence, managers should plan for coordination. Third, maintaining coordination is a continuing process and should be treated as such. Managers cannot assume that because their management system shows coordination today it will show coordination tomorrow.

Follett also noted that coordination can be achieved only through purposeful management action—it cannot be left to chance. Finally, she stressed the importance of the human element and advised that the communication process is an essential consideration in any attempt to encourage coordination. Primary considerations include employee skill levels, employee motivation levels, and the effectiveness of the human communication process used during coordination activities.[22]

Structure

In any organizing effort, managers must choose an appropriate structure. **Structure** refers to the designated relationships among resources of the management system. Its purpose is to facilitate the use of each resource, individually and collectively, as the management system attempts to attain its objectives.[23] The two basic types of structure within management systems are formal and informal structures. **Formal structure** is defined as the relationships among organizational resources as outlined by management; formal structure is represented primarily by the organization chart. In contrast, **informal structure** is defined as the patterns of relationships that develop because of the informal activities of organization members. It evolves naturally and tends to be molded by individual norms and values and social relationships. Essentially, an organization's informal structure is the system or network of interpersonal relationships that exists within, but is not usually identical to, the organization's formal structure.[24]

Organization structure is represented primarily by means of a graphic illustration called an **organization chart**. Traditionally, an organization chart is constructed in pyramid form, with individuals toward the top of the pyramid having more authority and responsibility than those toward the bottom.[25] The relative positioning of individuals within boxes on the chart indicates broad working relationships, and lines between boxes designate formal lines of communication between individuals. In addition to specifying formal relationships within the firm, an organization chart can also communicate to outsiders the complexity of the organization. Structure involves two primary dimensions: the vertical dimension and the horizontal dimension. The following sections discuss each dimension in detail.[26]

Vertical Dimensioning
Vertical dimensioning refers to the extent to which an organization uses vertical levels to separate job responsibilities. Vertical dimensioning is directly related to the concept of the **scalar relationship**—that is, the chain of command. Every organization is built on the premise that the individual at the top possesses the most authority and that other individuals' authority is scaled downward according to their relative position on the organization chart. The lower a person's position on the organization chart, then, the less authority that person possesses.[27]

The scalar relationship, or chain of command, is related to the unity of command. **Unity of command** is the management principle that recommends that an individual have only one boss. If too many bosses give orders, the result will probably be confusion, contradiction, and frustration—a sure recipe for ineffectiveness and inefficiency in an organization. Although the unity-of-command principle made its first appearance in management literature well over 75 years ago, it is still discussed today as a critical ingredient of successful organizations.[28]

SPAN OF MANAGEMENT   When examining the vertical dimensioning of an organization chart, it is important for managers to consider the influence of **span of management**—the number of individuals a manager supervises. The more individuals a manager supervises, the greater the span of management. Conversely, the fewer individuals a manager supervises, the smaller the span of management. The span of management has a significant effect on how well managers carry out their responsibilities. Span of management is also called *span of control, span of authority, span of supervision,* and *span of responsibility.*[29]

The central concern of span of management is to determine how many individuals a manager can supervise effectively.[30] To use the organization's human resources effectively, managers should supervise as many individuals as they can best guide toward production quotas. If they are supervising too few people, however, they are wasting a portion of their productive capacity. If they are supervising too many, they are losing part of their effectiveness.

DESIGNING SPAN OF MANAGEMENT: A CONTINGENCY VIEWPOINT   As reported by Harold Koontz, several important situational factors influence the appropriateness of the size of an individual's span of management:[31]

- **Similarity of functions**—the degree to which activities performed by supervised individuals are similar or dissimilar. As the similarity of subordinates' activities increases, the span of management appropriate for the situation widens. The converse is also generally true.

- **Geographic continuity**—the degree to which subordinates are physically separated. In general, the closer subordinates are physically, the more of them managers can supervise effectively.

These employees at a Bangalore, India call center all perform essentially the same customer-service function, which means the span of management for their department can be relatively wide.

- **Complexity of functions**—the degree to which workers' activities are difficult and involved. The more difficult and involved the activities are, the more difficult it is to manage a large number of individuals effectively. This is particularly true for research and development departments, which typically include numbers of engineers and scientists.[32]

- **Coordination**—the amount of time managers must spend synchronizing the activities of their subordinates with the activities of other workers. The greater the amount of time that must be spent on such coordination, the smaller the span of management should be.

- **Planning**—the amount of time managers must spend developing management system objectives and plans and integrating them with the activities of their subordinates. The more time managers must spend on planning activities—whether those activities are repetitive and routine or infrequent but complex—the fewer individuals they can manage effectively.[33]

Table 11.1 summarizes the factors that tend to increase and decrease the span of management.

GRAICUNAS AND SPAN OF MANAGEMENT Perhaps the best-known contribution to span-of-management literature was made by the management consultant V. A. Graicunas.[34] He developed a formula for determining the number of *possible* relationships between a manager and subordinates when the number of subordinates is known. **Graicunas's formula** is as follows:

$$C = n\left(\frac{2^n}{2} + n - 1\right)$$

TABLE 11.1 Major Factors That Influence the Span of Management		
Factor	**Factor Has Tendency to Increase Span of Management When—**	**Factor Has Tendency to Decrease Span of Management When—**
1. Similarity of functions	1. Subordinates have similar functions	1. Subordinates have different functions
2. Geographic contiguity	2. Subordinates are physically close	2. Subordinates are physically distant
3. Complexity of functions	3. Subordinates have simple tasks	3. Subordinates have complex tasks
4. Coordination	4. Work of subordinates needs little coordination	4. Work of subordinates needs much coordination
5. Planning	5. Manager spends little time planning	5. Manager spends much time planning

C is the total number of possible relationships between manager and subordinates, and *n* is the known number of subordinates. As the number of subordinates increases arithmetically, the number of possible relationships between the manager and those subordinates increases geometrically.

A number of criticisms have been leveled at Graicunas's work. Some have argued that he failed to take into account a manager's relationships outside the organization and that he considered only *potential* relationships rather than *actual* relationships. These criticisms have some validity, but the real significance of Graicunas's work lies outside them. His main contribution involved pointing out that span of management is an important consideration that can have a far-reaching impact on the organization.[35]

HEIGHT OF ORGANIZATION CHART   Span of management directly influences the height of an organization chart. Normally, the greater the height of the organization chart, the smaller the span of management, and the lower the height of the chart, the greater the span of management.[36] Organization charts with little height are usually referred to as *flat*, while those with much height are usually referred to as *tall*.[37]

Figure 11.3 is a simple example of the relationship between organization chart height and span of management. Organization chart A has a span of management of six, and organization chart B has a span of management of two. As a result, chart A is flatter than chart B. Note that both charts have the same number of individuals at the lowest level. The larger span of management in A is reduced in B merely by adding a level to B's organization chart.

An organization's structure should be built from top to bottom to ensure that appropriate spans of management are achieved at all levels. Increasing spans of management merely to eliminate certain management positions and thereby reduce salary expenses may prove to be a shortsighted move. Increasing spans of management to achieve such objectives as speeding up organizational decision making and building a more flexible organization is more likely to help the organization achieve success in the long run.[38] A survey of organization charts of the 1990s reveals that top managers were creating flatter organizational structures than top managers used in the 1980s. Overall, managers seem to be using flatter organizational structures now than in the past.

One company that has derived benefits from a flatter organizational structure is steel manufacturer Nucor Corporation. In recent years, Nucor increased its layers of management, which resulted in increased employee costs. In an effort to decrease these costs and improve efficiencies, the company drastically reduced its layers of management. Although some of its competitors had as many as 30 layers of management, Nucor reduced its structure to only four. This reduction in layers of management reduced costs, but has also increased satisfaction among employees at lower levels now that they are less removed from the top layer of the organization.[39]

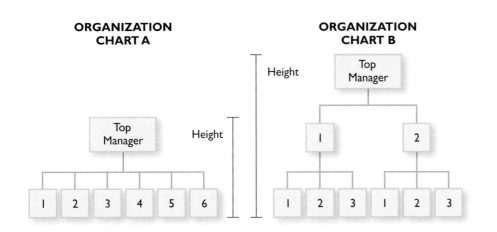

ORGANIZATION CHART A

ORGANIZATION CHART B

FIGURE 11.3
Relationship between organization chart height and span of management

Horizontal Dimensioning The **horizontal dimensioning** of an organization refers to the extent to which firms use lateral subdivisions or specialties within an organization. Overall, to build organizations horizontally, organizations establish departments. A **department** is a unique group of resources established by management to perform some organizational task. **Departmentalizing** is the process of establishing departments within the management system. Typically, these departments are based on, or contingent on, such situational factors as the work functions being performed, the product or service being offered, the territory being covered, and the customer being targeted.

The following sections highlight several different ways in which managers may departmentalize their organizations. In particular, the following illustrate how Sony, the company highlighted in the Challenge Case, might employ the various departmental structures discussed. Table 11.2 summarizes the major advantages and disadvantages associated with each type of departmentalization.

DEPARTMENTS BASED ON FUNCTION Perhaps the most widely used basis for establishing departments within the formal structure is the type of *work functions* (activities) being performed within the management system.[40] Functions are typically divided into the major categories of marketing, production, and finance. Figure 11.4 is an organization chart showing structure based primarily on function for Sony.

TABLE 11.2 Advantages and Disadvantages of Departmentalization Modes

Departmentalization	Advantages	Disadvantages
Functional	• Power of functional heads promotes consistency (i.e., consistent marketing messages) • Relatively easy to assign blame or credit for the performance of a function (i.e., the performance of the company's marketing program)	• May prove difficult to coordinate between various functions • Difficult to assign credit or blame when a product performs well or poorly
Product	• Allows managers to focus on the products sold by the company • Relatively easy to assign credit or blame on the performance of a product	• Focus on product may force managers to miss differences in customers or geographic regions • May be difficult to coordinate across products
Geographic	• Managers can focus on the various regions (and their differences) served by the company • Allows firms to develop human resources by rotating managers across different regions	• May prove difficult to coordinate between various regions • May prove difficult to assign credit or blame based on the performance of a particular product
Customer	• Allows managers to focus on and cater to the most important customers • Relatively easy to assign blame or credit regarding customer relationships	• May prove difficult to coordinate across various customers • May introduce complexities as customers span different products and geographic areas
Matrix	• Allows firm to pool human resources for both short-term and long-term projects • Allows firm to maintain flexibility over time	• Difficult for employees to understand power structure within the firm • Difficult for employees to prioritize responsibilities based on multiple authority figures

FIGURE 11.4
Departments by function at Sony

Functional departmentalizing brings with it both advantages and disadvantages. Perhaps the primary advantage of functional departmentalizing is the control conferred to the various functional heads. The vice president of marketing for Sony, for example, is able to control and coordinate the marketing plan for all of the organization's products, geographic regions, and customers. This structure allows for consistent marketing messages throughout the company. At the same time, however, the marketing plan emanating from such a structure may not be differentiated enough to suit the needs of Sony's diverse products, geographic regions, and customers. In other words, this structure may implicitly impose functional standardization that may not optimize the needs of the organization's various products and services.

DEPARTMENTS BASED ON PRODUCT OR SERVICE Organization structure based primarily on *product or service* departmentalizes resources according to the products or services being offered. As more and more products are offered by a company, it becomes increasingly difficult for management to coordinate activities across the organization. Organizing according to product or service permits the logical grouping of resources necessary to produce and market each product or service. Figure 11.5 is an organization chart for Sony showing structure based primarily on product.

Product or service departmentalizing also has both advantages and disadvantages. One of the primary advantages is the ability to focus the organization's efforts on each of the firm's products or services. With this structure, for example, the vice president of electronics for Sony has the power and authority to control all aspects of the electronics business. Moreover, this type of structure directly associates responsibility for each of the firm's products. If the electronics

FIGURE 11.5
Departments by product at Sony

Most hospitals are organized into departments based on the services they provide, such as radiology, surgery, or obstetrics. This doctor at Coney Island Hospital in New York works in the emergency room, a critical department in most medical facilities.

division does not perform well, for example, it is relatively easy for Sony's CEO to determine responsibility for the poor performance.

One of the primary disadvantages of this structure, though, is that the different units may result in some duplication of efforts, which may lead to higher costs. Continuing the example of Sony, the managers of the electronics division and the music division may both request more capital for marketing expenditures. Moreover, they may both create marketing positions within their units to aid in the marketing efforts. Taken together, these types of requests may strain the organization's resources.

DEPARTMENTS BASED ON GEOGRAPHY Structure based primarily on *territory* departmentalizes according to the places where the work is being done or the geographic markets on which the management system is focusing. The physical distances can range from quite short (between two points in the same city) to quite long (between two points in the same state, in different states, or even in different countries).[41] As market areas and work locations expand, the physical distances between places can make the management task extremely cumbersome. To minimize this problem, resources can be departmentalized according to territory. Figure 11.6 is an organization chart for Sony based primarily on territory.

Several advantages and disadvantages are associated with geographic departmentalizing. One of the primary advantages of this structure is that it helps the organization focus equally on the

FIGURE 11.6
Departments by geography at Sony

FIGURE 11.7
Departments by customer at Sony

organization's various geographic locations. For a company such as Sony, for example, the vice president of North America is in charge of operations in North America, and the vice president of Asia is in charge of operations in Asia. The organization defines clearly the individuals responsible for these various regions.

At the same time, however, this type of departmentalizing also brings with it disadvantages. One of the main disadvantages, for example, is the lack of focus on products and services. In this example, the vice president for North America is responsible for selling movies, electronics, and music in North America. At the same time, the vice president of Asia is responsible for selling these same products in Asia; no single manager is responsible for the performance of movies, electronics, or music. Instead, the responsibility is shared among various divisional vice presidents; this dispersion of responsibility may produce coordination problems.

DEPARTMENTS BASED ON CUSTOMER Structure based primarily on the *customer* establishes departments in response to the organization's major customers. This structure, of course, assumes that major customers can be identified and divided into logical categories. Figure 11.7 is an organization chart for Sony based primarily on customers. Sony obviously can clearly identify its customers and divide them into logical categories.

onsider the new organizational structure created at Salt Lake City–based Energy*Solutions*, a firm in the nuclear energy industry. Formerly, the company consisted of four operating groups, organized by function and reporting to a Chief Operating Officer (COO). Reorganizing as three customer-focused groups has permitted the company to better integrate its service offerings for customers—and eliminate the role of COO.[42] ∎

how managers do it

Restructuring at
Energy*Solutions*

Like the previously discussed organizational structures, customer departmentalization has both advantages and disadvantages. One of the primary advantages of customer departmentalization is that the firm focuses explicitly on its customers. Sony, for example, could follow this structure and include a vice president for each of its largest customers. This structure increases the likelihood that Sony will maintain its focus on its most important sources of sales. At the same time, however, this structure may also create some redundancies and increased costs. For example, the vice presidents may require their own marketing departments, which increases the likelihood for duplicated efforts.

DEPARTMENTS BY MATRIX The previous sections discussed several different types of departmentalizing; the potential advantages and disadvantages associated with each type were highlighted. These potential disadvantages have in part driven research examining "postbureaucratic" forms of organization.[43] These various organizational forms have arisen as a way to circumvent the possible disadvantages of the previously mentioned types of departmentalizing.

One of the most popular examples of postbureaucratic organizational forms is a matrix structure. The matrix structure is best understood by first visualizing a more traditional form of organization structure. Figure 11.4, for example, shows a more traditional organizational form for Sony departmentalized by function. Figure 11.8 adds a series of projects (PlayStation 3, Spider-Man 3, and Portable Digital Music Player) and a manager for each project to the original organization structure to form a matrix organization for Sony. Essentially, a matrix organization is one in which a project manager(s) borrows workers from various parts of the

FIGURE 11.8

Matrix departments at Sony

organization to complete some specific project.[44] For this reason, matrix organizations are also called *project organizations*. The project itself may be either long term or short term, and once finished, the employees borrowed to complete it return to their original jobs. Within a matrix structure, the workers are responsible for their original activities along with project activities. Because of the importance of matrix structure projects, project managers generally report directly to the company CEO.

As with other types of departmentalizing, departmentalizing by matrix has both advantages and disadvantages. Perhaps the chief advantage of the matrix structure is that it allows the organization to focus on various projects simultaneously. For example, the matrix structure in Figure 11.8 allows Sony to focus on PlayStation 3, Spider-Man 3, and the Portable Digital Music Player at the same time.

As with any organization structure, the matrix structure also has disadvantages. For example, the matrix structure can be confusing, and employees may not be able to effectively cope with two bosses. In the Sony example, assume that the PlayStation 3 project manager and the vice president of marketing both ask the same employee to complete different tasks. Which task should the employee complete first? Issues such as these can make matrix structure confusing.

Forces Influencing Formal Structure According to Shetty and Carlisle, the formal structure of a management system is continually evolving. Four primary forces influence this evolution: forces in the manager, forces in the task, forces in the environment, and forces in the

class discussion highlight

RESEARCH FOR DEVELOPING ORGANIZING SKILL

Does Structure Help Firms Satisfy Customers?

The preceding information focused on formally establishing organization structure. Scholars have long debated whether formal organizational structures always lead to better firm performance. To examine this issue, researchers distinguish between mechanistic and organic organizational structures. A **mechanistic structure** is a formal organizational structure such as those discussed in this chapter, and an **organic structure** is less formal and represents loosely coupled networks of workers. Some researchers suggest that mechanistic structures are better suited for some organizations, but organic structures are better for other organizations.

A study by Huang, Kristal, and Schroeder examined this issue in detail by investigating how organizational structures help firms compete. Specifically, these researchers examined which

type of organizational structure is best suited for firms engaging in mass customization, which is the ability to create customized products in an efficient manner. Dell, for example, mass customizes its products by allowing customers to alter the specifications of computers that they order from the company.

Mass customization is notoriously difficult to implement. The authors studied 238 mid- to large-sized manufacturing plants in eight countries to better understand how mass customization strategies succeed. Which type of organizational structure do you think is best for firms producing mass customized products: a more formal mechanistic structure or a less formal organic structure? Why?

Source: This feature is based on: Xiaowen Huang, Mehment Kristal, and Roger Schroeder. "The impact of organizational structure on mass customization capability: A contingency view." Production and Operations Management, in press.

subordinates.[45] The evolution of a particular organization is actually the result of a complex and dynamic interaction among these forces.

Forces in the manager are the unique way in which a manager perceives organizational problems.[46] Naturally, background, knowledge, experience, and values influence the manager's perception of what the organization's formal structure should be or how it should be changed. In the same way, similar forces influence the employee and play a key role in how he or she views work.[47]

Forces in the task include the degree of technology involved in performing the task and the task's complexity. As task activities change, a force is created to change the existing organization. Forces in the environment include the customers and suppliers of the management system, along with existing political and social structures. Forces in the subordinates include the needs and skill levels of subordinates. Obviously, as the environment and subordinates change, forces are created simultaneously to change the organization.

Fayol's Advice on Using Formal Structure The preceding discussion emphasized how to establish organization structure and related chain of command. Should a manager always adhere to established organization structure and related chain of command? Fayol has indicated that strict adherence to a particular chain of command is not always advisable.[48] Figure 11.9 explains his rationale. If individual F needs information from individual G and follows the concept of chain of command, F has to go through individuals D, B, A, C, and E before reaching G. The information would get back to F only by going from G through E, C, A, B, and D. Obviously, this long, involved process can be time consuming and therefore expensive for the organization.

To avoid this lengthy process, Fayol recommended that in some situations a bridge, or gangplank, be used to allow F to go directly to G for information. This bridge is represented in Figure 11.9 by the dotted line connecting F and G. Managers should be careful in allowing the use of these organizational bridges, however, because although F might get the information from G more quickly and cheaply that way, individuals D, B, A, C, and E would be excluded from the communication channel, and their ignorance might prove more costly to the organization in the long run than would following the established chain of command. When managers allow the use of an organizational bridge, they must be extremely careful to inform all other appropriate individuals within the organization of any information received that way.

FIGURE 11.9
Sample organization chart showing that adhering to the chain of command is not advisable

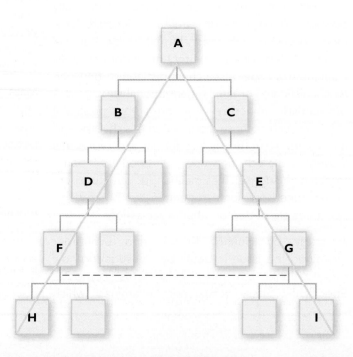

CHALLENGE CASE SUMMARY

The Challenge Case at the beginning of the chapter generally describes how Sony is being organized to be more competitive. Concepts in this chapter would be useful to a manager such as Sir Howard Stringer, Sony's CEO, in meeting organizing challenges similar to those discussed in the case.

In contemplating how Sony should be organized, a manager such as Stringer can focus on answering several important questions. These questions should be aimed at establishing an orderly use of Sony's organizational resources. Because these resources represent an investment on which he must get a return, Stringer's questions should be geared toward gaining information that will be used to maximize this return. Overall, such questions should focus on determining the use of Sony's resources that will best accomplish its goals.

Some preliminary questions could be as follows:

1. What organizational objectives exist at Sony? For example, does Sony want to focus more on international markets or focus its attention on Japanese consumers? Does Sony want to grow or maintain its present size?
2. What plans does Sony have to accomplish these objectives? Is Sony going to open more offices in international locations? Are additional training programs being added to enable employees to understand how to best work in international locations?
3. What are the major tasks Sony must go through to establish profitable linkages between its different divisions? For example, how many steps are involved in developing a videogame based on one of its current movies?
4. What resources does Sony have to run its operations? Answers to this question focus on issues such as the number of employees, financial resources available, equipment being used, and so on.

To develop a sound organizing effort, a manager should take classical organizing theory into consideration. Stringer, for example, should examine Sony's structure and how it influences working relationships among all Sony employees. To develop an effective organizational structure, Stringer must analyze situational factors in the company, such as functions, products, geographic locations, customers, and processes involved in offering its products to customers.

Within the case there is information indicating that Stringer's organization structure for Sony is based primarily on products or services being offered. For example, two of the main areas at Sony are "music" and "videogames." In essence, Sony is arranging its resources to focus on its main product/service areas. A manager typically uses an organization chart to represent organization structure. Such a chart would not only allow Stringer

to see the lines of authority and responsibility at Sony but also to understand the broad working relationships among his employees.

In developing the most appropriate way to organize Sony employees, a manager can reflect on another major element in classical organizing theory—division of labor. Stringer could decide, for example, that instead of having one person do all the work involved in servicing a retail outlet such as Best Buy or Circuit City, the labor could be divided so that for each business customer one person would make the initial contact, another would assess the communication needs of the organization, and a third would explore the alternative ways that Sony could offer to meet those needs. In this way, employees could work more quickly and can specialize in one area of business customer relations, such as business needs assessment or meeting business customer needs.

In considering the appropriateness of division of labor at Sony, a manager could also consider creating a mechanism for enhancing coordination. In order to develop such a mechanism, Stringer must have a thorough understanding of how various Sony business processes occur so he can divide various tasks and maintain coordination within the various Sony divisions. In addition, a manager like Stringer must stress communication as a prerequisite for coordination. Without Sony employees continually communicating with one another, coordination will be virtually impossible. In taking action aimed at enhancing organizational coordination, Stringer must also continually plan for and take action toward maintaining such coordination.

The last two major elements in classical organizing theory that a manager could reflect on are span of management and scalar relationships. Span of management focuses on the number of subordinates that managers in various roles at Sony can successfully supervise. In thinking about span of management, Stringer might explore several important situational factors, such as similarities among various Sony activities, the extent to which Sony workers being managed are physically separated, and the complexity of various Sony work activities.

For example, Stringer should consider that distributing CDs to consumer outlets can be fairly simple and that developing new videogames can be much more involved and complicated. Therefore, the span of management for workers doing the former job should generally be larger than the span of management for workers doing the latter job. Other important factors Stringer should consider in determining spans of management for various Sony managers are the amount of time managers must spend coordinating workers' activities and the amount of time managers spend planning. With all this information, Stringer should be quite capable of determining appropriate spans of management for his managers.

MANAGEMENT SKILL ACTIVITIES

This section is specially designed to help you develop organizing skill. An individual's organizing skill is based on an understanding of organizing concepts and the ability to apply those concepts in management situations. The following activities are designed both to heighten your understanding of organizing fundamentals and to develop your ability to apply those concepts in various management situations.

UNDERSTANDING ORGANIZING CONCEPTS

 To check your understanding and to practice using the concepts in this chapter, go to www.mymanagementlab.com and explore the material associated with Chapter 11.

Know Key Terms

Understanding the following key terms is critical to your understanding of chapter material. Define each of these terms. Refer to the page(s) referenced after a term to check your definition or to gain further insight regarding the term.

organizing **250**	informal structure **255**	horizontal dimensioning **258**
organizing skill **250**	organization chart **255**	department **258**
bureaucracy **253**	vertical dimensioning **255**	departmentalizing **258**
division of labor **253**	scalar relationship **255**	mechanistic structure **263**
coordination **254**	unity of command **255**	organic structure **263**
structure **254**	span of management **255**	
formal structure **255**	Graicunas's formula **256**	

Know How Management Concepts Relate

This section is comprised of activities that will further sharpen your understanding of management concepts. Answer essay questions as completely as possible. Also, remember that many additional true/false and multiple choice questions appear on-line at MyManagementLab.com to help you further refine your understanding of management concepts.

1. Describe the fundamental components of the organizing process. In your opinion, which of these components is most important? Which is least important? Explain.

2. Discuss the roles of vertical and horizontal differentiation as they relate to organizational structure. In your opinion, which of these concepts is most important for an effective organizational structure?

3. Compare and contrast the various types of departmentalization. In your opinion, which type of departmentalization is best?

4. Assume that you are the manager for Green Furniture, a company operating a number of furniture stores operating throughout the United States. Illustrate how the various types of departmentalization might apply to this company. In other words, discuss the various advantages and disadvantages of these types of departmentalization as they apply to Green Furniture.

5. Discuss the advantages and disadvantages associated with the concept of division of labor. How is the concept of span of management related to division of labor?

DEVELOPING MANAGEMENT SKILLS

Learning activities in this section are aimed at helping you develop your organizing skill. Learning activities include Exploring Your Management Skill: Parts 1 & 2, Experiential Exercise, Cases, and a VideoNet Exercise.

Exploring Your Management Skill: Part 1

Before studying this chapter, respond to the following questions regarding the type of advice that you would give to Sir Howard Stringer, Sony's CEO discussed in the Challenge Case. Then address the concerning organizing challenges that he presently faces within the company. You are not expected to

be an organizing expert at this point. Answering the questions now can help you focus on important points when you study the chapter. Also, answering the questions again after you study the chapter will give you an idea of how much you have learned.

Record your answers here or go to MyManagementLab.com. Recording your answers in MyManagementLab will allow you to get immediate results and see how your score compares to your classmates. If you answer the questions in the book, the answers are located in the Exploring Your Management Skill Appendix at the end of the book.

FOR EACH STATEMENT CIRCLE:
- "Y" if you would give the advice to Stringer.
- "N" if you would NOT give the advice to Stringer.
- "NI" if you have no idea whether you would give the advice to Stringer.

Mr. Stringer, in meeting your organizing challenges at Sony, you should . . .

Before After
Study Study

1. design organizing activities to be more closely related to controlling activities than planning activities.
   Y, N, NI

2. concentrate more on clearly outlining an organization chart and less on how characteristics of people will affect the success of the chart.
   Y, N, NI

3. design an organization chart to reflect authority, responsibility, and informal communication patterns.
   Y, N, NI

4. know subordinates well because their makeup should influence the type of organization to be established.
   Y, N, NI

5. create more and more specialization within jobs to make jobs more interesting, and thereby make workers more productive.
   Y, N, NI

6. make sure that managers at lower levels of the organization have more individuals to supervise than those at upper levels of the organization.
   Y, N, NI

7. decide to manage more organization members if the members are performing complex jobs than if performing simple jobs.
   Y, N, NI

8. increase the height of an organization chart to help managers manage people performing jobs of high complexity.
   Y, N, NI

9. emphasize organizing as a means of putting controls into action.
   Y, N, NI

10. commonly establish situations in which organizations have more than one boss.
    Y, N, NI

11. ensure that authority is properly scaled within the organization chart.
    Y, N, NI

12. establish division of labor to increase worker efficiency and worker interest level in jobs.
    Y, N, NI

13. focus on using primary organizational inputs such as money, people, raw materials, and plans.
    Y, N, NI

14. encourage peer-level members of different departments to communicate directly with one another without going through their managers to enhance organizational efficiency.
    Y, N, NI

15. use division of labor to minimize time wasted by organization members moving from location to location to perform different jobs.
    Y, N, NI

Exploring Your Management Skill: Part 2

As you recall, you completed Exploring Your Management Skill before you started to study this chapter. Your responses gave you an idea of how much you initially knew about organizing and helped you focus on important points as you studied the chapter. Answer the Exploring Your Management Skill questions again now and compare your score to the first time you took it. This comparison will give you an idea of how much you have learned from studying this chapter and pinpoint areas for further clarification before you start studying the next chapter. Record your answers within the text or online at MyManagementLab.com. Completing the survey at MyManagementLab.com will allow you to grade and compare your test scores automatically. If you complete the test in the book, look up answers in the Exploring Your Management Skill section at the end of the book.

Your Management Skills Portfolio

Your Management Skills Portfolio is a collection of activities especially designed to demonstrate your management knowledge and skill. By completing these activities at MyManagementLab.com, you will be able to print, complete with cover sheet, as many activities as you choose. Be sure to save your work. Taking your printed portfolio to an employment interview could be helpful in obtaining a job.

The portfolio activity for this chapter is Organizing Skill: Examining Organization Charts. Examine the organization chart shown and then answer the questions that follow.

1. Is the organization chart of the Department of Health and Human Services based mainly on function, product, geography, or customer? Argue why this basis might be appropriate for its tasks.

2. Does this organization chart reflect a division of labor emphasis? Explain.

3. Give an illustration of how coordination is important to the success of the Department of Health and Human Services.

4. Present an argument discussing why the span of management for the Secretary is appropriate or inappropriate.

Experiential Exercises

1 Frogs of the World

Directions. Read the following scenario and then perform the listed activities. Your instructor may ask you to perform the activities as an individual or within groups. Follow all of your instructor's directions carefully.

Your company, Frogs of the World, has been manufacturing and selling plastic toy frogs for more than 15 years. Overall, the company has been successful and has become a market leader in the toy industry. Exploring the introduction of a new product, top management has just decided to begin manufacturing and selling a paper frog that hops. Mr. Hopper is the name of the new product. Your instructor will distribute design specifications for producing Mr. Hopper.

Top management has informed your group that it will immediately begin manufacturing Mr. Hopper. The department will only include people in your group. At some point, your instructor will appoint a leader for your group, give each member

the raw materials needed to produce Mr. Hopper, and instruct you to actually begin the production process.

Your team will be judged by the number and quality of the Mr. Hoppers that you produce.

2 You and Your Career

The preceding section discusses vertical dimensioning, an important aspect of organizing skill. Assume that you are interviewing with a company for a potential job. Given your major, the classes you have taken so far, and your general interests, how might the vertical characteristics of the organization with which you are interviewing influence your career prospects and projected overall job satisfaction if working within the organization? Should you find out the vertical characteristics of organization structure of a potential employer before you start working for the company? Why?

VideoNet Exercise

Organizational Structure and Design at Insomnia Cookies

Video Highlights

How does a small, quickly growing company develop and plan for a new structure that can expand with the company? Currently, the Insomnia Cookies headquarters consists of three to four people who oversee operations on 14 different college campuses. Each campus has its own manager and staff. Within the next year, Insomnia plans to open retail and delivery operations on six more campuses or locations. The

following year, they will continue to launch in new locations. More people will have to be added to the senior management team to accommodate this level of growth, but Insomnia Cookies is grappling with how and when to bring on new people to help run the company. CEO Seth Berkowitz is determined to keep the company from becoming top-heavy. Learn from the top management team at Insomnia as they take their own crash course on organizational structure and design.

Discussion Questions

1. What do you think the current organization chart at Insomnia Cookies looks like? Is this structure appropriate for its needs? Explain.
2. What forces have most influenced the structure of Insomnia Cookies?
3. Describe CEO and founder Seth Berkowitz's span of management.

Internet Activity

Go to the Insomnia Cookies Web site at www.insomniacookies.com. In reviewing the site, list three organizational issues top management must monitor to be successful in the future. How important will this be to company success? Why?

CASES

1 SONY ORGANIZES FOR SUCCESS

"Sony Organizes for Success" (p. 249) was written to help you better understand the organizing concepts contained in this chapter. Answer the following discussion questions about the Challenge Case to better understand how basic organization principles can be applied in a company such as Sony.

1. Does it seem reasonable that Stringer is attempting to better organize Sony to remain more competitive? Explain.
2. List five questions that Stringer should ask himself in exploring how best to organize Sony.
3. Explain why it would be important for Stringer to ask each of the questions you listed.

2 HOW 3M IS DEPARTMENTALIZED

Read the case and answer the questions that follow. Studying this case will help you better understand how concepts relating to organizational structure can be applied in a company such as 3M.

When the company known as 3M (a shorter way of saying Minnesota Mining and Manufacturing Company) began in 1902, the goal of the firm was to mine a heavy abrasive for grinding wheels. However, it discovered that the mine in Minnesota simply wasn't going to provide the firm with the necessary materials. After well over a decade, 3M did however finally succeed in producing sandpaper for the rapidly growing auto industry. By 1925, 3M was on its way to diversification with the invention of masking tape. And the rest is innovation history for this fast-paced company.[49]

Today 3M operates in more than 65 countries, and the product offerings of 3M include widely held retail consumer items as well as other less popular products. For example, the average consumer has probably heard of Post-It Notes and Scotch Tape. But one may not be aware of FireDam Spray 200, 3M Oil Quality Monitoring System, Vikuiti Anti-Reflection Films, or Safe-tique Floor Matting. Its products cover consumer to aerospace and from manufacturing to drive-through restaurant technologies.

To make all this happen, 3M has about 75,000 employees throughout the world—fewer than half that number are in the United States. Additionally, of those 75,000 employees, almost 7,000 are in the roles of researchers. This keeps 3M at the forefront of new product development. According to

George W. Buckley, president and CEO of 3M, the company has strategically positioned itself in a very difficult economy. "3M," he said, "is a much stronger and more innovative enterprise than it was even a year ago."[50] Innovation is the cornerstone of 3M's success. To ensure 3M remains above the competition when it comes to new product development, it has invested heavily in research and development. Buckley stated that in 2009, 3M "maintained investments of more than a billion dollars in R&D at a time when many companies were forced to dramatically cut back."[51]

So how does a multibillion dollar, international company that is heavily diversified organize its businesses? Keeping in mind that operations are geographically dispersed and 35 companies exist under the 3M umbrella, it might appear to be a daunting task. However, 3M has taken a straightforward product departmentalization approach to the company.

All 35 business units are grouped together in six larger business segments based on the kinds of products manufactured. The six segments are consumer & office, display & graphics, electro & communications, health care, industrial & transportation, and safety, security, & protection services.

As an example, the brands most people are familiar with (Post-It, Scotch, Scotch-Brite, Command, Nexcare, and Filtrete) are in the consumer and office segment. However, those in the health care industry could readily identify 3M's full line of products related to oral care, drug delivery, and health information systems.

By grouping similar types of businesses by the products they manufacture, 3M is attempting to utilize resources carefully and strategically. In other words, researchers in the industrial and transportation business segment at 3M can focus their efforts on those innovations related to abrasives, adhesives, and filtration systems without having their attention diverted by developing products that are more consumer-focused. With this approach, concentrated research and development can take place within each of the six business segments.

Additionally, some resources can be shared. Functions like marketing and human resources cut across each business segment. As one might suspect, marketing a Post-It Note is completely different than marketing an industrial-grade abrasive. The ultimate buyer is different in both cases and the methods of promotion are unrelated. Whereas Post-It Notes might be advertised on TV, marketing a heavy abrasive to a manufacturing company may require an in-person sales call.

For Buckley, appropriate departmentalization is important, but he realizes that is just one facet of 3M's strategy. The company must also foster innovation while maintaining profits. As Buckley pointed out, "There is no question that we at 3M are optimistic about our creative capabilities, confident in our operational strength, and reassured by our strong balance sheet."[52]

QUESTIONS

1. Do you feel that a product departmentalization structure is best for 3M? Why or why not?

2. What challenges do you envision for Buckley in attempting to maintain his current organizational structure?

3. Based on 3M's departmentalization, do you think it has a very tall organizational chart or a very short organizational chart? Why?

Endnotes

1. Marc Gunther, "The Welshman, the Walkman, and the Salarymen," *Fortune,* June 12, 2006, 70–83. Matt Peckham, "3D For PlayStation 3 Games (But Not Blu-ray) Dropping Tomorrow," *PCWorld* (http://www.pcworld.com), accessed June 14, 2010.

2. A. Tacket, "Organizing and Organizations: An Introduction," *The Journal of the Operational Research Society* 53 (2002): 1401.

3. Douglas S. Sherwin, "Management of Objectives," *Harvard Business Review* (May/June 1976): 149–160. See also Lloyd Sandelands and Robert Drazin, "On the Language of Organization Theory," *Organizational Studies* 10 (1989): 457–77.

4. Tim Peakman, "Organizing the Organization," *Drug Discovery Today* 8 (2003): 673.

5. For a discussion emphasizing the importance of continually adapting organization structure, see Michael A. Vercspej, "When Change Becomes the Norm," *Industry Week,* March 16, 1992, 35–36.

6. Betsy Morris, "The GE Mystique," *Fortune,* March 6, 2006, 98–102. For an interesting analysis of General Electric's management development process, see Derek Lehmberg, W. Glenn Rowe, Roderick E. White, and John R. Phillips, "The GE Paradox: Competitive Advantage through Fungible Non-Firm-Specific Investment," *Journal of Management* 35, no. 5 (October 1, 2009): 1129–1153.

7. Saul W. Gellerman, "In Organizations, as in Architecture, Form Follows Function," *Organizational Dynamics* 18 (Winter 1990): 57–68.

8. For an example of how organizing principles can be applied to the educational arena, see A. Georges Romme, "Organizing Education by Drawing on Organization Studies," *Organization Studies* 24 (2003): 697.

9. Max Weber, *Theory of Social and Economic Organization,* trans. and ed. A. M. Henderson and Talcott Parsons (London: Oxford University Press, 1947); Thomas A. Stewart, "Get with the New Power Game," *Fortune,* January 13, 1997, 58–62.

10. Sandra T. Gray, "Fostering Leadership for the New Millennium," *Association Management* (January 1995): L78–L82.

11. David Courpasson and Stewart Clegg, "Dissolving the Iron Cages? Tocqueville, Michels, Bureaucracy and the Perpetuation of Elite Power," *Organization* 13 (2006): 319–343.

12. "GM Timeline," *MSNBC.com,* http://www.msnbc.com, accessed June 3, 2010; Ryan Chilcote and Steve Rothwell, "GM to Focus on Cutting Spending, Reducing Bureaucracy," *Bloomberg.com,* March 2, 2010, http://www.bloomberg.com.

13. For a review focusing on division of labor, see "Division of Labor Welcomed," *Business Insurance* 34, no. 10 (March 6, 2000): 8.

14. Jeff Lewis and Walter Knott, "Division of Labor: To Gain the Benefits of a Team, Each Member Can't Do Everything," *OnWall Street,* August 1, 2003, 1.

15. Example based on "Painting by Numbers: China's Art Business," *The Economist,* June 10, 2006, 77.

16. Carol Ann Dorn, "Einstein: Still No Equal," *Journal of Business Strategy* (November/December 1994): 20–23.

17. C. R. Walker and R. H. Guest, *The Man on the Assembly Line* (Cambridge, MA: Harvard University Press, 1952). For an excellent example of how technology can affect division of labor, see John P. Walsh, "Technological Change and the Division of Labor: The Case of Retail Meatcutters," *Work and Occupations* 16 (May 1989): 165–183.

18. For an interesting analysis of how such structural organizational factors as specialization influence organizational memory, see Marina Fiedler and Isabell Welpe, "How Do Organizations Remember? The Influence of Organizational Structure on Organizational Memory," *Organization Studies* 31, no. 4 (2010), 381–407.

19. J. Mooney, "The Principles of Organization," in *Ideas and Issues in Public Administration,* ed. D. Waldo (New York: McGraw-Hill, 1953), 86. See also Peter Jackson, "Speed versus Heed," *CA Magazine* (November 1994): 56–57. For an application of the coordination principle, see Gail Karet and Tim Studt, "Managing Biotech Requires Cross-Functional Coordination," *Research & Development* 43, no. 3 (March 2001): 12–17; see also Jody Gittell and Leigh Weiss, "Coordination Networks Within and Across Organizations: A Multi-Level Framework," *The Journal of Management Studies* 41 (2004): 127.

20. Bruce D. Sanders, "Making Work Groups Work," *Computerworld* 24, March 5, 1990, 85–89.

21. George D. Greenberg, "The Coordinating Roles of Management," *Midwest Review of Public Administration* 10 (1976): 66–76; Stephen Ackroyd, "How Organizations Act Together: Interorganizational Coordination in Theory and Practice," *Administrative Science Quarterly* 43, no. 1 (March 1998): 217–221.

22. Henry C. Metcalf and Lyndall F. Urwick, eds., *Dynamic Administration: The Collected Papers of Mary Parker Follett* (New York: Harper & Bros., 1942), 297–299; James F. Wolf, "The Legacy of Mary Parker Follett," *Bureaucrat Winter* (1988–1989): 53–57. For a recent discussion of the work of Mary Parker Follett, see David M. Boje and Grace Ann Rosile, "Where's the Power in Empowerment? Answers from Follett and Clegg," *Journal of Applied Behavioral Science* 37, no. 1 (March 2001): 90–117.

23. Lyndall Urwick, *Notes on the Theory of Organization* (New York: American Management Association, 1952). For a recent look at the implications of organizational structure on misbehavior, see Granville King III, "The Implications of an Organization's Structure on Whistleblowing," *Journal of Business Ethics* 20, no. 4 (July 1999): 315–326.

24. David Stamps, "Off the Charts," *Training* 34, no. 10 (October 1997): 77–83.

25. For an interesting discussion of a nontraditional organization structure, see David M. Lehmann, "Integrated Enterprise Management: A Look at the Functions, the Enterprise, and the Environment—Can You See the Difference?" *Hospital Material Management Quarterly* 19, no. 4 (May 1998): 22–26.

26. Eric J. Walton, "The Persistence of Bureaucracy: A Meta-Analysis of Weber's Model of Bureaucratic Control," *Organization Studies* 26, no. 4: 569–600.

27. S. R. Maheshwari, "Hierarchy: Key Principle of Organization," *Employment News* 21, no. 49 (March 8–14, 1997): 1–2.

28. Cass Bettinger, "The Nine Principles of War," *Bank Marketing* 21 (December 1989): 32–34; Donald C. Hambrick, "Corporate Coherence and the Top Management Team," *Strategy & Leadership* 25, no. 5 (September/October 1997): 24–29.

29. Leon McKenzie, "Supervision: Learning from Experience," *Health Care Supervisor* 8 (January 1990): 1–11. For a recent discussion of span of control, see "Span of Control vs. Span of Support," *Journal for Quality and Participation* 23, no. 4 (Fall 2000): 4.

30. For a look at the concept of span of management in public organizations, see Kenneth Meier and John Bohte, "Span of Control and Public Organizations: Implementing Gulick's Research Design," *Public Administration Review* 63 (2003): 61.

31. Harold Koontz, "Making Theory Operational: The Span of Management," *Journal of Management Studies* (October 1966): 229–43; see also John S. McClenahen, "Managing More People in the '90s," *Industry Week* 238 (March 1989): 30–38.

32. For an account of how Corning Inc. organized its knowledge workers into an effective research and development department that exists to this day, see W. Bernard Carlson and Stuart K. Sammis, "Revolution or Evolution? The Role of Knowledge and Organization in the Establishment and Growth of R & D at Corning," *Management & Organizational History* 4, no. 1 (2009): 37–65.

33. The U.S. space program offers an interesting study of the forms of work organization—both simple and complex—required to ultimately succeed in putting an astronaut on the moon. See Martin Parker, "Space Age Management," *Management & Organizational History* 4, no. 3 (2009): 317–332.

34. V. A. Graicunas, "Relationships in Organization," *Bulletin of International Management Institute* (March 1933): 183–187; L. F. Urwick, "V. A. Graicunas and the Span of Control," *Academy of Management Journal* 17 (June 1974): 349–354; Luther Gulick, Lyndall Urwick, James D. Mooney, Henri Fayol, et al. "Papers on the Science of Administration," *International Journal of Public Administration* 21, no. 2–4 (1998): 441–641.

35. For discussion about why managers should increase spans of management see Stephen R. Covey, "The Marketing Revolution," *Executive Excellence* 14, no. 3 (March 1997): 3–4.

36. John R. Brandt, "Middle Management: 'Where the Action Will Be,' " *Industry Week* (May 2, 1994): 30–36.

37. For a discussion of the benefits of tall structures, see Harold J. Leavitt, "Why Hierarchies Thrive," *Harvard Business Review* 81, no. 3 (2006): 96–102.

38. Philip R. Nienstedt, "Effectively Downsizing Management Structures," *Human Resources Planning* 12 (1989): 155–165.

39. Paul Glader, "It's Not Easy Being Lean," *Wall Street Journal,* June 19, 2006, B1.

40. Geary A. Rummler and Alan P. Brache, "Managing the White Space on the Organization Chart," *Supervision* (May 1991): 6–12.

41. Roderick E. White and Thomas A. Poynter, "Organizing for Worldwide Advantage," *Business Quarterly* 54 (Summer 1989): 84–89.

42. "EnergySolutions Announces New Organizational Structure," *Marketwire,* March 30, 2010, http://www.marketwire.com.

43. M. Lindgren and J. Packendorff, "What's New in New Forms of Organizing? On the Construction of Gender in Project-Based Work," *Journal of Management Studies* 43, no. 4 (2006): 841–866.

44. C. J. Middleton, "How to Set Up a Project Organization," *Harvard Business Review* (March/April 1967): 73. See also George J. Chambers, "The Individual in a Matrix Organization," *Project Management Journal* 20 (December 1989): 37–42, 50.

45. Y. K. Shetty and Howard M. Carlisle, "A Contingency Model of Organization Design," *California Management Review* 15 (1972): 38–45. For additional discussion of factors influencing formal structure, see Paul Dwyer, "Tearing Up Today's Organization Chart," *BusinessWeek,* November 18, 1994, 80–90.

46. For insights on how Ralph Larsen, CEO of Johnson & Johnson, views problems and how his view might influence the formal structure of his organization, see Brian Dumaine, "Is Big Still Good?" *Fortune,* April 30, 1992, 50–60.

47. An employee's *locus of control*—that is, those aspects that an individual perceives to be within his or her own ability to modify—figures strongly in work outcomes. For a study of the influences on work outcomes, see Steven M. Elias, "Restrictive Versus Promotive Control and Employee Work Outcomes: The Moderating Role of Locus of Control," *Journal of Management* 35, no. 2 (March 1, 2009): 369–392. Elias also provides another interesting study of employee perceptions during the restructuring of their organization's design. See "Employee Commitment in Times of Change: Assessing the Importance of Attitudes toward Organizational Change," *Journal of Management* 35, no. 1 (February 1, 2009): 37–55.

48. Henri Fayol, *General and Industrial Administration* (Belmont, CA: Pitman, 1949).

49. www.3M.com

50. 3M. (2009) *Annual Report.*

51. Ibid.

52. Ibid.

chapter 12

Responsibility, Authority, and Delegation

Target Skill

responsibility and delegation skill: the ability to understand one's obligation to perform assigned activities and to enlist the help of others to complete those activities

objectives

To help build my *responsibility and delegation skill*, when studying this chapter, I will attempt to acquire:

1. An understanding of the relationship of responsibility, authority, and delegation

2. Information on how to divide and clarify the job activities of individuals working within an organization

3. Knowledge of the differences among line authority, staff authority, and functional authority

4. An appreciation for the issues that can cause conflict in line and staff relationships

5. Insights into the value of accountability to the organization

6. An understanding of how to delegate

CHALLENGE CASE

TOYOTA TO DELEGATE AUTHORITY

JAPANESE AUTOMAKER TOYOTA MOTOR CORP. has long been known for its lean production system, a protocol replicated by its competitors as well as by manufacturers in other industries. Toyota also became famous for its effective supply chain, streamlining it to focus on strong relationships and the pursuit of quality—another practice emulated by competitors.

But somewhere on the road to worldwide industry dominance, Toyota evidently took its eye off the goal. Its world began to unravel in 2010 with the widespread news of problems in Toyota and Lexus models. Before long, the company was forced to issue a series of product recalls, involving as many as 8 million cars sold since 2000. At least 34 deaths and numerous injuries have been reported from Toyotas that accelerated out of control without warning.

As consumer fears deepened, the U.S. Congress launched an investigation of Toyota vehicles, calling company executives to come forward and explain how the automaker was addressing the problems. What eventually was revealed was nearly as shocking as the many deaths and injuries arising from the accidents: Toyota's American executives wielded little or no authority in the company's operations. Because of this insufficient authority, the American executives were unable to issue a safety recall even when confronted with evidence of a serious problem. Precious time elapsed while word of a possible design defect made its way from the United States to Japan and a Japanese executive gave approval for a recall.

Known for its attention to detail and a passion for perfection, how could Toyota have gone so far astray? Industry insiders say in its quest to fulfill the 1998 directive of its former chairman—to double

global market share by 2010—Toyota lost sight of its fundamental values.

Going forward, some industry observers suggest that Toyota must delegate authority to non-Japanese leaders and trust them to use their knowledge and experience to act wisely. In addition, Toyota must decentralize its decision-making function.

Company executives have indicated that such changes are afoot. Before a Senate subcommittee, Toyota executive vice president Shinichi Sasaki asserted that U.S. managers will have a greater role in decisions regarding recalls and other safety matters. Toyota U.S.A. president James Lentz, the firm's highest-ranking American, had testified earlier that Toyota's Japanese headquarters exerted total authority over U.S. matters, including recalls. Meanwhile, with talk of class action law suits swirling, the automaker is striving to recapture its customers' trust.[1]

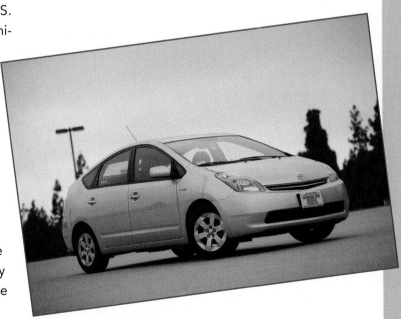

■ *The Toyota Prius, shown here, was recalled due to a problem in the anti-lock brake system (ABS) software, causing slow reaction time on rough or slick road surfaces.*

EXPLORING YOUR MANAGEMENT SKILL

You can explore your level of responsibility and delegation skill **before** studying the chapter by completing the exercise "Exploring Your Management Skill: Part 1" on page 288 and **after** studying this chapter by completing the exercise "Exploring Your Management Skill: Part 2" on page 289.

THE RESPONSIBILITY AND DELEGATION CHALLENGE

The Challenge Case describes Toyota's efforts to grow and expand. As a company grows, its management must constantly focus on organizing resources appropriately so that goals can be attained. To create such organization, Toyota executives must answer such questions as: How should responsibility be established across the organization? How should authority be distributed within the organization? Information in this chapter should be of great value to a manager in answering such questions.

RESPONSIBILITY

Perhaps the most fundamental method of channeling the activity of individuals within an organization, **responsibility** is the obligation to perform assigned activities. It is the self-assumed commitment to handle a job to the best of one's ability. The source of responsibility lies within the individual. A person who accepts a job agrees to carry out a series of duties or activities or to see that someone else carries them out.[2] The act of accepting the job means that the person is obligated to a superior to see that job activities are successfully completed. Even though a manager may delegate a task to another employee, the manager still remains responsible for the completion of the task. In other words, responsibility is, in a sense, shared by both the manager and the employee.

Nonetheless, responsibility is often difficult to identify.

how managers do it

Accepting Responsibility for Actions at Goldman Sachs

Some believe that the actions of investment firm Goldman Sachs helped fuel the nation's recent financial meltdown. Goldman Sachs executives defended their practice of selling an investment to a client—while "betting" on the investment to falter and making a profit when it declined in value—saying the practice was common in the investment industry. Only after a six-hour grilling by a Senate investigation panel did an executive acknowledge that his company may have had a share of responsibility in the economic crisis. In this example, although the firm's executive officers bear some responsibility for the company's actions, the Goldman Sachs employees who processed these transactions for investors also bear some responsibility.[3] ■

The Job Description

An individual's job activities within an organization are usually summarized in a formal statement called a **job description**—a list of specific activities that must be performed by whoever holds the position. Unclear job descriptions can confuse employees and may cause them to lose interest in their jobs. On the other hand, a clear job description can help employees to become successful by focusing their efforts on the issues that are important for their position. When properly designed, job descriptions communicate job content to employees, establish performance levels that employees must maintain, and act as a guide that employees should follow to help the organization reach its objectives.[4]

Job activities are delegated by management to enhance the accomplishment of management system objectives. Management analyzes its objectives and assigns specific duties that will lead to reaching those objectives. A sound organizing strategy delineates specific job activities for every individual in the organization. Note, however, that as objectives and other conditions within the management system change, so will individual job activities.

The three areas related to responsibility include dividing job activities, clarifying the job activities of managers, and being responsible. Each of these topics is discussed in the sections that follow.

Dividing Job Activities

Obviously, one person cannot be responsible for performing all of the activities that take place within an organization. Because so many people work in a given management system, organizing necessarily involves dividing job activities among a number of individuals. Some method of distributing these job activities is essential.

The Functional Similarity Method The **functional similarity method** is, according to many management theorists, the most basic method of dividing job activities. Simply stated, the method suggests that management should take four basic interrelated steps to divide job activities in the following sequence:

1. Examine management system objectives
2. Designate appropriate activities that must be performed to reach those objectives
3. Design specific jobs by grouping similar activities
4. Make specific individuals responsible for performing those jobs

Figure 12.1 illustrates this sequence of activities.

Functional Similarity and Responsibility At least three additional guides can be used to supplement the functional similarity method.[5] The first of these supplemental guides suggests that overlapping responsibility should be avoided when making job activity divisions. **Overlapping responsibility** refers to a situation in which more than one individual is responsible for the same activity. Generally speaking, only one person should be responsible for completing any one activity. When two or more employees are unclear about who should do a job because of overlapping responsibility, it usually leads to conflict and poor working relationships.[6] Often the job does not get done because each employee assumes the other will do it.

The second supplemental guide suggests that responsibility gaps should be avoided. A **responsibility gap** exists when certain tasks are not included in the responsibility area of any individual organization member. In this situation, nobody within the organization is obligated to perform certain necessary activities.[7]

The third supplemental guide suggests that management should avoid creating job activities for accomplishing tasks that do not enhance goal attainment. Organization members should be obligated to perform *only* those activities that lead to goal attainment.

The absence of clear, goal-related, nonoverlapping responsibilities undermines organizational efficiency and effectiveness.[8]

When job responsibilities are distributed inappropriately, the organization will have both responsibility gaps and overlapping responsibilities.

Each member of a train crew performs separate tasks, eliminating the possibility of overlapping responsibilities.

FIGURE 12.1
Sequence of activities for the functional similarity method of dividing job activities

The effects of responsibility gaps on product quality are obvious, but overlapping responsibilities also impair product quality. When two (or more) employees are uncertain as to who is responsible for a task, four outcomes are possible:

1. One of the two may perform the job. The other may either forget to or choose not to do the job—and neither of these is a desirable outcome for product quality control.
2. Both employees may perform the job. At the least, this situation results in duplicated effort, which dampens employee morale. At worst, one employee may diminish the value of the other employee's work, resulting in a decrement in product quality.
3. Neither employee may perform the job because each assumed the other would do it.
4. The employees may spend valuable time negotiating each aspect and phase of the job to carefully mesh their job responsibilities, thus minimizing both duplication of effort and responsibility gaps. Though time-consuming, this is actually the most desirable option in terms of product quality.

Note that each of these outcomes negatively affects both product quality and overall productivity.

Clarifying Job Activities of Managers

Clarifying the job activities of managers is even more important than dividing the job activities of nonmanagers because managers affect greater portions of resources within the management system. Responsibility gaps, for instance, usually have a more significant impact on the management system when they relate to managers than when they relate to nonmanagers.

One process used to clarify management job activities "enables each manager to actively participate with his or her superiors, peers, and subordinates in systematically describing the managerial job to be done and then clarifying the role each manager plays in relationship to his or her work group and to the organization."[9] The purpose of this interaction is to eliminate overlaps or gaps in perceived management responsibilities and to ensure that managers are performing only those activities that lead to the attainment of management system objectives. Although this process is typically used to clarify the responsibilities of managers, it can also be effective in clarifying the responsibilities of nonmanagers.

Management Responsibility Guide A specific tool developed to implement this interaction process is the **management responsibility guide,** some version of which is used in most organizations. This guide helps management to describe the various responsibility relationships that exist in the organization and to summarize how the responsibilities of various managers relate to one another.

The seven main organizational responsibility relationships covered by the management responsibility guide are listed in Table 12.1. Once it is decided which of these relationships exist within the organization, the relationships between these responsibilities can be defined.

TABLE 12.1 Seven Responsibility Relationships Among Managers, as Used in the Management Responsibility Guide

1. General Responsibility—The individual who guides and directs the execution of the function through the person accepting operating responsibility

2. Operating Responsibility—The individual who is directly responsible for the execution of the function

3. Specific Responsibility—The individual who is responsible for executing a specific or limited portion of the function

4. Must Be Consulted—The individual whose area is affected by a decision and must be called on to render advice or relate information before any decision is made or approval is granted (This individual does not, however, make the decision or grant approval.)

5. May Be Consulted—The individual who may be called on to relate information, render advice, or make recommendations before the action is taken

6. Must Be Notified—The individual who must be notified of any action that has been taken

7. Must Approve—The individual (other than persons holding general and operating responsibility) who must approve or disapprove the decision

TABLE 12.2	Four Key Dimensions of Responsible Management Behavior		
Attitude Toward and Conduct with Subordinates	**Behavior with Upper Management**	**Behavior with Other Groups**	**Personal Attitudes and Values**
Responsible managers—	Responsible managers—	Responsible managers—	Responsible managers—
1. Take complete charge of their work groups	1. Accept criticism for mistakes and buffer their groups from excessive criticism	1. Make sure that any gaps between their areas and those of other managers are securely filled	1. Identify with the group
2. Pass praise and credit along to subordinates	2. Ensure that their groups meet management expectations and objectives		2. Put organizational goals ahead of personal desires or activities
3. Stay close to problems and activities			3. Perform tasks that offer no immediate reward but help subordinates, the company, or both
4. Take actions to maintain productivity and are willing to terminate poor performers if necessary			4. Conserve corporate resources as if the resources were their own

Responsible Managers Managers can be described as responsible if they perform the activities they are obligated to perform.[10] Because managers have more impact on an organization than nonmanagers, responsible managers are a prerequisite for management system success. Several studies have shown that responsible management behavior is highly valued by top executives because the responsible manager guides many other individuals within the organization in performing their duties appropriately.

The degree of responsibility that a manager possesses can be determined by appraising the manager on the following four dimensions:

1. Attitude toward and conduct with subordinates
2. Behavior with upper management
3. Behavior with other groups
4. Personal attitudes and values

Table 12.2 summarizes what each of these dimensions entails.

AUTHORITY

Individuals are assigned job activities to channel their behavior within the organization appropriately. Once they have been given specific assignments, they must be given a commensurate amount of authority to perform those assignments satisfactorily.

Authority is the right to perform or command. It allows its holder to act in certain designated ways and to directly influence the actions of others through orders. It also allows its holder to allocate the organization's resources to achieve organizational objectives.[11]

Authority on the Job

The following example illustrates the relationship between job activities and authority. Two primary tasks for which a particular service station manager is responsible are pumping gasoline and repairing automobiles. The manager has the authority necessary to perform both of these tasks, or he or she may choose to delegate automobile repair to the assistant manager. Along with the activity of repairing, the assistant should also be delegated the authority to order parts, to command certain attendants to help, and to do anything else necessary to perform repair jobs. Without this authority, the assistant manager may find it impossible to complete the delegated job activities.

Practically speaking, authority merely increases the probability that a specific command will be obeyed.[12] The following excerpt emphasizes that authority does not always exact obedience:[13]

People who have never exercised power have all kinds of curious ideas about it. The popular notion of top leadership is a fantasy of capricious power: the top man [or woman] presses a button and something remarkable happens; he [or she] gives an order as the whim strikes him [or her], and it is obeyed. Actually, the capricious use of power is relatively rare except in some large dictatorships and some small family firms. Most leaders are hedged around by constraints—tradition, constitutional limitations, the realities of the external situation, rights and privileges of followers, the requirements of teamwork, and most of all, the inexorable demands of large-scale organization, which does not operate on capriciousness. In short, most power is wielded circumspectly.

Acceptance of Authority

As Chapter 11 showed, the positioning of individuals on an organization chart indicates their relative amount of authority. Those positioned toward the top of the chart possess more authority than those positioned toward the bottom. Chester Barnard writes, however, that the exercise of authority is determined less by formal organizational decree than by acceptance among those under the authority. According to Barnard, authority exacts obedience only when it is accepted.

In line with this rationale, Barnard defines *authority* as the character of communication by which an order is accepted by an individual as governing the actions that individual takes within the system. Barnard maintains that authority will be accepted only under the following conditions:

1. The individual can understand the order being communicated.
2. The individual believes the order is consistent with the purpose of the organization.
3. The individual sees the order as compatible with his or her personal interests.
4. The individual is mentally and physically able to comply with the order.

The fewer of these four conditions that are present, the lower the probability that authority will be accepted and obedience be exacted.

Barnard offers some guidance on what managers can do to raise the odds that their commands will be accepted and obeyed. He maintains that more and more of a manager's commands will be accepted over the long term if:[14]

1. The manager uses formal channels of communication and these are familiar to all organization members.
2. Each organization member has an assigned formal communication channel through which orders are received.
3. The line of communication between manager and subordinate is as direct as possible.
4. The complete chain of command is used to issue orders.
5. The manager possesses adequate communication skills.
6. The manager uses formal communication lines only for organizational business.
7. A command is authenticated as coming from a manager.

Types of Authority

Three main types of authority can exist within an organization: line authority, staff authority, and functional authority. Each type exists only to enable individuals to carry out the different types of responsibilities with which they have been charged.[15]

Line and Staff Authority **Line authority**, the most fundamental authority within an organization, reflects existing superior–subordinate relationships. It consists of the right to make decisions and to give orders concerning the production-, sales-, or finance-related behavior of subordinates. In general, line authority pertains to matters directly involving management system production, sales, and finance and, as a result, the attainment of objectives. People directly responsible for these areas within the organization are delegated line authority to assist them in performing their obligatory activities.[16]

Whereas line authority involves giving orders concerning production activities, **staff authority** consists of the right to advise or assist those who possess line authority as well as other staff personnel. Staff authority enables those responsible for improving the effectiveness of line personnel to perform their required tasks. Examples of organization members with staff authority are people working in the accounting and human resource departments. Obviously, line and staff personnel must work together closely to maintain the efficiency and effectiveness of the organization. To ensure that line and staff personnel do work together productively, management must make sure both groups understand the organizational mission, have specific objectives, and realize that they are partners in helping the organization reach its objectives.[17]

Size is perhaps the most significant factor in determining whether an organization will have staff personnel. Generally speaking, the larger the organization, the greater the need and ability to employ staff personnel. As an organization expands, it usually needs employees with expertise in diversified areas. Although small organizations may also require this kind of diverse expertise, they often find it more practical to hire part-time consultants to provide it as needed than to hire full-time staff personnel, who may not always be kept busy.

Line authority, such as this sewing factory supervisor holds, defines the superior–subordinate relationship.

Line–Staff Relationships Figure 12.2 shows how line–staff relationships can be presented on an organization chart. The plant manager on this chart has line authority over each immediate subordinate—the human resource manager, the production manager, and the sales manager. However, the human resource manager has staff authority in relation to the plant manager, meaning the human resource manager possesses the right to advise the plant manager on human resource matters. Still, final decisions concerning human resource matters are in the hands of the plant manager, the person holding line authority. Similar relationships exist between the sales manager and the sales research specialist, as well as between the production manager and the quality control manager.

Roles of Staff Personnel Harold Stieglitz has pinpointed three roles that staff personnel typically perform to assist line personnel:[18]

1. **The advisory or counseling role**—In this role, staff personnel use their professional expertise to solve organizational problems. The staff personnel are, in effect, internal consultants whose relationship with line personnel is similar to that of a professional and

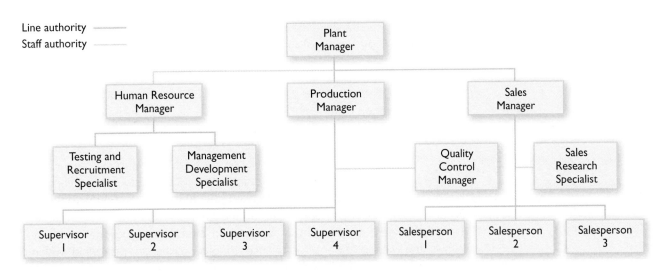

FIGURE 12.2 Possible line–staff relationships in selected organizational areas

a client. For example, the staff quality control manager might advise the line production manager on possible technical modifications to the production process that will enhance the quality of the organization's products.

2. **The service role**—Staff personnel in this role provide services that can more efficiently and effectively be provided by a single centralized staff group than by many individuals scattered throughout the organization. This role can probably best be understood if staff personnel are viewed as suppliers and line personnel as customers. For example, members of a human resource department recruit, employ, and train workers for all organizational departments. In essence, they are the suppliers of workers, and the various organizational departments needing workers are their customers.

3. **The control role**—In this role, staff personnel help establish a mechanism for evaluating the effectiveness of organizational plans. Staff personnel exercising this role are representatives, or agents, of top management.

These three are not the only roles performed by staff personnel, but they are the major ones. In the final analysis, the roles of staff personnel in any organization should be specially designed to best meet the needs of that organization. In some organizations, the same staff people must perform all three major roles.

Conflict in Line–Staff Relationships Most management practitioners readily admit that a noticeable amount of organizational conflict centers around line–staff relationships.[19] From the viewpoint of line personnel, conflict is created because staff personnel tend to assume line authority, do not give sound advice, steal credit for success, fail to keep line personnel informed of their activities, and do not see the whole picture. From the viewpoint of staff personnel, conflict is created because line personnel do not make proper use of staff personnel, resist new ideas, and refuse to give staff personnel enough authority to do their jobs. In some organizations, the distribution and use of authority is a matter requiring careful negotiation.[20]

Staff personnel can often avert line–staff conflicts if they strive to emphasize the objectives of the organization as a whole, encourage and educate line personnel in the appropriate use of staff personnel, obtain any necessary skills they do not already possess, and deal intelligently with resistance to change rather than view it as an immovable barrier. Line personnel can do their part to minimize line–staff conflict by using staff personnel wherever possible, making proper use of the staff abilities, and keeping staff personnel appropriately informed.[21]

Functional Authority **Functional authority** consists of the right to give orders within a segment of the organization in which this right is normally nonexistent. This authority is usually assigned to individuals to complement the line or staff authority they already possess. Functional authority generally covers only specific task areas and is operational only for designated amounts of time. Typically, it is given to individuals who, in order to meet responsibilities in their own areas, must be able to exercise some control over organization members in other areas. Wise leaders know how to delegate functional authority properly to ensure optimal productivity.[22]

how managers do it

Exercising Functional Authority at Kroger Company

Michael Schlotman serves as chief financial officer of national supermarket chain Kroger Company. Schlotman's role as CFO includes functional authority, with his primary responsibility involves the monitoring of responsibility in Kroger's financial system. To do so requires having appropriate financial information continually flowing in from various segments of the organization. The vice president for finance, therefore, is usually delegated the functional authority to order various departments to furnish the kinds and amounts of information he or she needs to perform an analysis. In effect, this functional authority allows the vice president for finance to give orders to personnel within departments in which he or she normally cannot give orders. ■

PROPOSED LARGE HOSPITAL ORGANIZATION
AUTHORITY AND RELATIONSHIPS

FIGURE 12.3   Proposed design for incorporating three types of authority in a hospital

From this discussion of line authority, staff authority, and functional authority, it is logical to conclude that although authority can exist within an organization in various forms, these forms should be used in a combination that will best enable individuals to carry out their assigned responsibilities and thereby best help the management system accomplish its objectives. When trying to decide on an optimal authority combination for a particular organization, managers should be aware that each type of authority has both advantages and disadvantages. The organization chart illustrated in Figure 12.3 shows how the three types of authority could be combined for the overall benefit of a hospital management system.[23]

Accountability

Accountability refers to the management philosophy whereby individuals are held liable, or accountable, for how well they use their authority and live up to their responsibility of performing predetermined activities.[24] The concept of accountability implies that if an individual does not perform predetermined activities, some type of penalty, or punishment, is justifiable.[25] The punishment theme of accountability has been summed up by one company executive: "Individuals who do not perform well simply will not be around too long."[26] The accountability concept also implies that some kind of reward will follow if predetermined activities are performed well. Accountability is especially important for successful knowledge management in an organization.[27]

DELEGATION

So far in this chapter we have discussed responsibility and authority as complementary factors that channel activity within the organization. **Delegation** is the actual process of assigning job activities and corresponding authority to specific individuals within the organization.[28] This section focuses on the steps in the delegation process, obstacles to the delegation process, elimination of obstacles to the delegation process, and centralization and decentralization.

Steps in the Delegation Process

According to Newman and Warren, the delegation process consists of three steps, all of which may be either observable or implied.[29] The first step is assigning specific duties to the individual. In all cases, the manager must be sure that the subordinate assigned to specific duties has a clear

TABLE 12.3   Guidelines for Making Delegation Effective

- Give employees freedom to pursue tasks in their own way.
- Establish mutually agreed-upon results and performance standards for delegated tasks.
- Encourage employees to take an active role in defining, implementing, and communicating progress on tasks.
- Entrust employees with completion of whole projects or tasks whenever possible.
- Explain the relevance of delegated tasks to larger projects or to department or organization goals.
- Give employees the authority necessary to accomplish tasks.
- Allow employees access to all information, people, and departments necessary to perform delegated tasks.
- Provide training and guidance necessary for employees to complete delegated tasks satisfactorily.
- When possible, delegate tasks on the basis of employee interests.

understanding of what these duties entail. Whenever possible, the activities should be stated in operational terms so the subordinate knows exactly what action must be taken to perform the assigned duties. The second step of the delegation process involves granting appropriate authority to the subordinate—that is, the subordinate must be given the right and power within the organization to accomplish the duties assigned. The last step involves creating the obligation for the subordinate to perform the duties assigned. The subordinate must be aware of the responsibility to complete the duties assigned and must accept that responsibility. Table 12.3 offers several guidelines managers can follow to ensure the success of the delegation process.

Obstacles to the Delegation Process

Obstacles that can make delegation within an organization difficult or even impossible can be classified into three general categories: (1) obstacles related to the supervisor, (2) obstacles related to subordinates, and (3) obstacles related to organizations.

An example of the first category is the supervisor who resists delegating his authority to subordinates because he cannot bear to part with any authority. Two other supervisor-related obstacles are the fear that subordinates will not do a job well and the suspicion that surrendering some authority may be seen as a sign of weakness. Moreover, if supervisors are insecure in their jobs or believe certain activities are extremely important to their personal success, they may find it hard to put the performance of these activities into the hands of others.

Supervisors who do wish to delegate to subordinates may encounter several subordinate-related roadblocks. First, subordinates may be reluctant to accept delegated authority because they are afraid of failing, lack self-confidence, or feel the supervisor doesn't have confidence in them.[30] These obstacles will be especially apparent in subordinates who have never before used delegated authority. Other subordinate-related obstacles are the fear that the supervisor will be unavailable for guidance when needed and the reluctance to exercise authority that may complicate comfortable working relationships.[31]

Characteristics of the organization itself may also make delegation difficult. For example, a very small organization may present the supervisor with only a minimal number of activities to be delegated. In organizations where few job activities and little authority have been delegated in the past, an attempt to initiate the delegation process may make employees reluctant and apprehensive, for the supervisor would be introducing a significant change in procedure and change is often strongly resisted.[32]

Eliminating Obstacles to the Delegation Process

Because delegation has significant advantages for the organization, eliminating obstacles to the delegation process is important to managers. Among the advantages of delegation are enhanced employee confidence, improved subordinate involvement and interest, more free time for the supervisor to accomplish tasks, and, as the organization gets larger, assistance from subordinates in completing tasks the manager simply wouldn't have time for otherwise. True, there are potential disadvantages to delegation—such as the possibility that the manager will lose track of the progress of a delegated task—but the potential advantages of some degree of delegation generally outweigh the potential disadvantages.[33]

What can managers do to eliminate obstacles to the delegation process? First of all, they must continually strive to uncover any obstacles to delegation. Then they should approach taking action to eliminate these obstacles with the understanding that they may be deeply ingrained and therefore require much time and effort to overcome. Among the most effective managerial actions that can be taken to eliminate obstacles to delegation are building subordinate confidence in the use of delegated authority, minimizing the impact of delegated authority on established working relationships, and helping delegatees cope with problems whenever necessary.[34]

Koontz, O'Donnell, and Weihrich believe that overcoming the obstacles to delegation requires certain critical characteristics in managers. These characteristics include the willingness to consider the ideas of others seriously, the insight to allow subordinates the free rein necessary to carry out their responsibilities, trust in the abilities of subordinates, and the wisdom to allow people to learn from their mistakes without suffering unreasonable penalties for making them. Frequently, the lack of such personal attributes in a manager spells the difference between a productive, cohesive team and one that is perennially dysfunctional.[35]

Centralization and Decentralization

Noticeable differences can be found from organization to organization in the relative number of job activities and the relative amount of authority delegated to subordinates. These differences are seldom a case of delegation existing in one organization and not existing in another. Rather, the differences come from degree of delegation.[36]

The terms **centralization** and **decentralization** describe the general degree to which delegation exists within an organization. They can be visualized as opposite ends of the delegation continuum depicted in Figure 12.4. It is apparent from this figure that centralization implies that a minimal number of job activities and a minimal amount of authority have been delegated to subordinates by management, whereas decentralization implies the opposite.

class discussion highlight

MODERN RESEARCH AND RESPONSIBILITY AND DELEGATION SKILL

Authority and Trust

Can you trust your manager? This important question has many implications for an employee's behavior. When employees trust their managers, they are likely to act in ways consistent with the desires of their managers. Conversely, when employees do not trust their managers, they may be less likely to engage in positive behaviors and more likely to engage in negative behaviors.

To examine the issue of trust in authority, David De Cremer and Tom Tyler ran a series of experiments examining how trust influences individuals' intentions to cooperate. Specifically, the authors asked subjects (i.e., students and employees) to rate their willingness to cooperate with a team led by a fictional leader. In one condition, the team leader could not be trusted, and in another condition the team leader could be trusted.

What do you think the authors found? Do you think that trust influenced subjects' intentions to cooperate with the leader? Why or why not? How might trust influence a manager's ability to delegate?

Source: This highlight was based on David De Cremer and Tom R. Tyler, "The effects of trust in authority and procedural fairness on cooperation," *Journal of Applied Psychology* 92, no. 3 (2007): 639–649.

FIGURE 12.4 Centralized and decentralized organizations on delegation continuum

The issues practicing managers usually face are determining whether to further decentralize an organization and, if that course of action is advisable, deciding how to decentralize.[37] The section that follows presents practical suggestions on both issues.

Decentralizing an Organization: A Contingency Viewpoint The appropriate degree of decentralization for an organization depends on the unique situation of that organization. Some specific questions managers can use to determine the amount of decentralization appropriate for a situation are as follows:

1. **What is the present size of the organization?** As noted earlier, the larger the organization, the greater the likelihood that decentralization will be advantageous. As an organization increases in size, managers have to assume more and more responsibility and different types of tasks. Delegation is typically an effective means of helping them manage this increased workload.

   In some cases, however, top management will conclude that the organization is actually too large and decentralized. One signal that an organization is too large is labor costs that are high relative to other organizational expenses. In this instance, increased centralization of certain organizational activities could reduce the need for some workers and thereby lower labor costs to a more acceptable level.[38]

2. **Where are the organization's customers located?** As a general rule, the more physically separated the organization's customers are, the more viable a significant amount of decentralization is. Decentralization places appropriate management resources close to customers and thereby makes quick customer service possible. For example, by decentralizing its purchasing activities, JCPenney gives its managers authority to buy merchandise best suited to the customers of its individual stores.[39]

3. **How homogeneous is the organization's product line?** Generally, as the product line becomes more heterogeneous, or diversified, the appropriateness of decentralization increases. Different kinds of decisions, talents, and resources are needed to manufacture different products.

how managers do it

Reaping the Benefits of Decentralization at Johnson & Johnson

Johnson & Johnson, the world's largest health care company, consists of more than 250 companies in 57 countries. With such a comprehensive array of products and services, the decision to decentralize authority enables Johnson & Johnson to recruit high-performing individuals whose leadership and expertise drive their business.[40] Decentralization usually minimizes the confusion that can result from diversification by separating organizational resources by product and keeping pertinent decision making close to the manufacturing process.[41] ∎

4. **Where are organizational suppliers?** The location of raw materials needed to manufacture the organization's products is another important consideration. Time loss and high transportation costs associated with shipping raw materials over great distances from supplier to manufacturer could signal the need to decentralize certain functions.

    For example, the wood necessary to manufacture a certain type of bedroom set may be available only from tree growers in certain northern states. If the bedroom set in question is an important product line for a furniture company, and if the costs of transporting the lumber are substantial, a decision to decentralize may be a sound one. The effect of this decision would probably be building a plant that produces only bedroom sets in a northern state, close to where the necessary wood is readily available. The advantages of such a costly decision, of course, would accrue to the organization only over the long term.

5. **Are quick decisions needed in the organization?** If speedy decision making is essential, a considerable amount of decentralization is probably in order. Decentralization cuts red tape and allows the subordinate to whom authority has been delegated to make on-the-spot decisions when necessary. It goes without saying that this delegation is advisable only if the potential delegatees have the ability to make sound decisions. If they don't, faster decision making results in no advantage for the organization. Quite the contrary, the organization may find itself saddled with the effects of unsound decisions.

6. **Is creativity a desirable feature of the organization?** If creativity is desirable, then some decentralization is advisable, for decentralization allows delegatees the freedom to find better ways of doing things. The mere existence of this freedom encourages the incorporation of new and more creative techniques within the task process.[42]

Decentralization at Massey-Ferguson: A Classic Example from the World of Management

Positive decentralization is decentralization that is advantageous for the organization in which it is being implemented; negative decentralization is disadvantageous for the organization. To see how an organization should be decentralized, it is worthwhile to study a classic example of an organization that achieved positive decentralization: Massey-Ferguson.[43]

GUIDELINES FOR DECENTRALIZATION Massey-Ferguson is a worldwide farm equipment manufacturer that has enjoyed noticeable success with decentralization over the past several years. The company has three guidelines for determining the degree of decentralization of decision making that is appropriate for a situation:

1. The competence to make decisions must be possessed by the person to whom authority is delegated. A derivative of this principle is that the superior must have confidence in the subordinate to whom authority is delegated.

If an organization faces high costs associated with transporting raw materials over great distances, decentralization that puts facilities closer to resources might be an appropriate and cost-saving organization structure.

2. Adequate and reliable information pertinent to the decision is required by the person making the decision. Decision-making authority therefore cannot be pushed below the point at which all information bearing on the decision is available.

3. If a decision affects more than one unit of the enterprise, the authority to make the decision must rest with the manager accountable for the most units affected by the decision.

DELEGATION AS A FRAME OF MIND Massey-Ferguson also encourages a definite attitude toward decentralization in its managers. The company's organization manual indicates that delegation is not delegation in name only but a frame of mind that includes both what a supervisor says to subordinates and the way the supervisor acts toward them. Managers at Massey-Ferguson are prodded to allow subordinates to make a reasonable number of mistakes and to help them learn from these mistakes.

COMPLEMENTING CENTRALIZATION Another feature of the positive decentralization at Massey-Ferguson is that decentralization is complemented by centralization:

> The organization plan that best serves our total requirements is a blend of centralized and decentralized elements. Marketing and manufacturing responsibilities, together with supporting service functions, are located as close as possible to local markets. Activities that determine the long-range character of the company, such as the planning and control of the product line; the planning and control of facilities and money; and the planning of the strategy to react to changes in the patterns of international trade, are highly centralized.

Thus, Massey-Ferguson management recognizes that decentralization is not necessarily an either/or decision and uses the strengths of both centralization and decentralization to its advantage.

MANAGEMENT RESPONSIBILITIES Not all activities at Massey-Ferguson are eligible for decentralization. Only management is allowed to follow through on the following responsibilities:

1. Responsibility for determining the overall objectives of the enterprise
2. Responsibility for formulating the policies that guide the enterprise
3. Final responsibility for control of the business within the total range of the objectives and policies, including control over any changes in the nature of the business
4. Responsibility for product design where a product decision affects more than one area of accountability
5. Responsibility for planning for achievement of overall objectives and for measuring actual performance against those plans
6. Final approval of corporate plans or budgets
7. Decisions pertaining to availability and application of general company funds
8. Responsibility for capital investment plans

CHALLENGE CASE SUMMARY

Toyota executives have been faced with the challenge of organizing the activities of their expanding firm. For example, they must decide how to organize the activities of the company's salesforce—the tremendous growth means that the company has more customers. Organizing the sales department should help to ensure success if the activities directly reflect company objectives. Management's specific steps to organize should include the analysis of company sales objectives, the outlining of specific sales activities that must be performed to reach these objectives, the designing of sales jobs by the grouping of similar activities, and the assigning of these sales jobs to company personnel. To supplement these steps, Toyota must be careful not to create overlapping responsibilities, responsibility gaps, or responsibilities for sales activities that do not lead directly to the attainment of Toyota's goals.

In organizing the activities of employees in a growing organization like Toyota, leadership must recognize, for example, that a manager's activities within the company, as well as those of subordinates, are a major factor in company success. Because the activity of a department manager can affect all personnel within that department, the activities of the department manager must be well defined. From the viewpoint of company divisions, one department manager's activities should be coordinated with those of other departments: For example, the activities in the sales department should be coordinated with activities in the company's marketing department.

Overall, for managers at Toyota to be responsible, they must perform the activities they are obligated to perform. Managers in the sales department, for example, are obligated to monitor the performance of all salespeople and to provide unbiased assessments. What's more, executives in Toyota's other geographic divisions, such as North America and the United States, must be permitted to use their knowledge and expertise to provide leadership and add value to the company's operations.

Toyota leadership must be sure that any individuals within the company who are delegated job activities are given a commensurate amount of authority to give orders and carry out those activities. Managers throughout the company must recognize, however, that authority must be accepted if obedience is to be exacted. To increase the probability of acceptance, care should be taken to ensure that individuals understand internal orders and see orders as being consistent with the objectives of the department they work in and the company. Employees should perceive the orders they receive as being compatible with their individual interests, and they should see themselves as being mentally and physically able to follow those orders. Management must be careful to delegate jobs only to those organization members who are mentally and physically able to carry them out.

Assuming that one of Toyota's main objectives is to produce and sell the highest quality automobiles possible, company personnel who are directly responsible for achieving this objective should possess line authority to perform their responsibilities. For example, individuals responsible for manufacturing cars must be given the right to do everything necessary to produce the highest-quality vehicles possible.

As in all organizations, the potential for conflict between Toyota line and staff personnel could be significant. Management should be aware of this potential and encourage both line and staff personnel to minimize it.

Functional authority and accountability are two additional factors that Toyota must consider when organizing employee activities. Some employees may have to be delegated functional authority to supplement the line or staff authority they already have. A Toyota human resource manager (staff person), for example, may need to gather information from the company's sales department in order to understand whether the company needs to hire additional salespeople. Functional authority would enable staff individuals to command that this information be channeled to them.

In organizing employee activity, Toyota should also stress the concept of accountability—that living up to assigned responsibilities brings rewards and not living up to them brings negative consequence.

To delegate activities effectively, Toyota must assign specific duties to individuals, grant corresponding authority to these individuals, and make sure these individuals are aware that they are obligated to perform these activities.

In encouraging the use of delegation, Toyota must be aware that obstacles to delegation may exist on the part of company managers, their subordinates, or the departments in which they work. Leadership must be sure that managers can meet the delegation challenge by discovering which obstacles exist in their work environments and taking steps to eliminate them. If Toyota managers are to be successful delegators, they also must be willing to consider the ideas of subordinates, allow them the free rein necessary to perform their assigned tasks, trust them, and help them learn from their mistakes without suffering unreasonable penalties.

Centralization implies that few job activities and little authority have been delegated to subordinates; decentralization implies that many job activities and much authority have been delegated. Toyota leadership will have to determine the best degree of delegation for subordinates regarding all job activities. For guidelines, they can rely on certain rules of thumb to determine that greater degrees of delegation will be appropriate for the company (1) as departments become larger, (2) as manufacturing facilities become more geographically dispersed and diversified, and (3) as the needs for quick decision making and creativity increase.

The Massey-Ferguson decentralization situation could provide Toyota with many valuable insights on what characteristics the decentralization process within the company should assume. First, managers should use definite guidelines to decide whether their situation warrants added decentralization. In general, additional delegation probably is warranted within the company as the competence of subordinates increases, as managers' confidence in their subordinates increases, and as more adequate and reliable decision-making information within the company becomes available to subordinates. For delegation to be advantageous for Toyota, company managers must help subordinates learn from their mistakes. Depending on their situations, individual managers may want to consider supplementing decentralization with centralization.

MANAGEMENT SKILL ACTIVITIES

This section is specially designed to help you develop responsibility and delegation skill. An individual's management skill is based on an understanding of management concepts and the ability to apply those concepts in management situations. As a result, the following activities are designed both to heighten your understanding of responsibility and delegation concepts and to help you gain facility in applying these concepts in various management situations.

UNDERSTANDING RESPONSIBILITY AND DELEGATION CONCEPTS

 To check your understanding and to practice using the concepts in this chapter, go to www.mymanagementlab.com and explore the material associated with Chapter 12.

Know Key Terms

Understanding the following key terms is critical to your understanding of chapter material. Define each of these terms. Refer to the page(s) referenced after a term to check your definition or to gain further insight regarding the term.

responsibility **274**
job description **274**
functional similarity method **275**
overlapping responsibility **275**
responsibility gap **275**

management responsibility guide **276**
authority **277**
line authority **278**
staff authority **279**
functional authority **280**

accountability **281**
delegation **281**
centralization **283**
decentralization **283**

Know How Management Concepts Relate

This section is comprised of activities that will further sharpen your understanding of management concepts. Answer essay questions as completely as possible. Also, remember that many additional true/false and multiple choice questions appear online at MyManagementLab.com to help you further refine your understanding of management concepts.

1. Distinguish between responsibility and authority, and provide examples to support your distinctions.

2. Describe the three main types of authority that can exist within an organization.
3. Explain the three major steps in the delegation process.
4. Compare and contrast centralization versus decentralization. In your opinion, which is best for organizations?
5. What is acceptance of authority, and under which conditions will employees accept authority?

DEVELOPING MANAGEMENT SKILLS

Learning activities in this section are aimed at helping you to develop your responsibility and delegation skill. Learning activities include Exploring Your Management Skill: Parts 1 and 2, Experiential Exercises, Cases, and a VideoNet Exercise.

Exploring Your Management Skill: Part 1

Before studying this chapter, respond to the following questions regarding the type of advice that you would give to Toyota's executive vice president Shinichi Sasaki, referenced in the Challenge Case. Then address the concerning human resource management challenges that he presently faces within the company. You are not expected to be a responsibility and delegation expert at this point. Answering the questions now can help

you focus on important points when you study the chapter. Also, answering the questions again after you study the chapter will give you an idea of how much you have learned.

Record your answers here or go to MyManagementLab.com. Recording your answers in MyManagementLab will allow you to get immediate results and see how your score compares to your classmates. If you answer the questions in the book, the answers are located in the Exploring Your Management Skill Appendix at the end of the book.

FOR EACH STATEMENT CIRCLE:
- "Y" if you would give the advice to Shinichi Sasaki.
- "N" if you would NOT give the advice to Shinichi Sasaki.
- "NI" if you have no idea whether you would give the advice to Shinichi Sasaki.

Sasaki-san, in meeting your responsibility and delegation challenges at Toyota, you should...

Before   After
Study   Study

1. clarify the responsibilities of each employee at Toyota.

2. make sure that one person is responsible for performing all of the activities that take place in Toyota.
   Y, N, NI

3. eliminate responsibility gaps when dividing job activities.
   Y, N, NI

4. communicate to employees that *responsibility* and *authority* are essentially interchangeable terms that have the same meaning.
   Y, N, NI

5. understand that throughout Toyota, authority does not necessarily imply that employees will follow the instructions of managers.
   Y, N, NI

6. realize that several factors—such as ability, communication, and consistency—will determine whether employees accept a manager's authority.
   Y, N, NI

7. focus primarily on line authority and don't worry about the staff authority at Toyota.
   Y, N, NI

8. hold employees accountable for their job responsibilities in some circumstances, but understand that accountability often backfires as a management approach.
   Y, N, NI

9. hesitate to delegate responsibilities, because delegation will often reduce quality at Toyota.
   Y, N, NI

10. give employees freedom to pursue tasks in their own way when delegating at Toyota.
    Y, N, NI

11. recognize that neither centralization nor decentralization always works and instead take into account the context of Toyota when considering these two organizing alternatives.
    Y, N, NI

12. recognize that as Toyota's products become more diverse, centralization becomes more effective.
    Y, N, NI

13. understand that as Toyota grows, decentralization becomes more effective.
    Y, N, NI

14. realize that as Toyota's customers become more diverse (in terms of tastes, geographic location, etc.), centralization becomes more effective.
    Y, N, NI

15. understand that in different circumstances, either supervisors or subordinates may provide obstacles in the delegation process.
    Y, N, NI

Exploring Your Management Skill: Part 2

As you recall, you completed Exploring Your Management Skill before you started to study this chapter. Your responses gave you an idea of how much you initially knew about responsibility and delegation and helped you focus on important points as you studied the chapter. Answer the Exploring Your Management Skill questions again now and compare your score to the first time you took it. This comparison will give you an idea of how much you have

learned from studying this chapter and pinpoint areas for further clarification before you start studying the next chapter. Record your answers within the text or online at MymanagementLab.com. Completing the survey at MyManagementLab.com will allow you to grade and compare your test scores automatically. If you complete the test in the book, look up answers in the Exploring Your Management Skill section at the end of the book.

Your Management Skills Portfolio

Your Management Learning Portfolio is a collection of activities especially designed to demonstrate your management knowledge and skill. By completing these activities online at MyManagementLab.com, you will be able to print, complete with cover sheet, as many activities as you choose. Be sure to save your work. Taking your printed portfolio to an employment interview could be helpful in obtaining a job.

The portfolio activity for this chapter is Delegating Basketball Duties at Texas A&M. Study the following information and complete the exercises that that follow.[43]
Athletics programs are big business for universities, and the influence of athletics is no different at Texas A&M University. Recently, Texas A&M hired Mark Turgeon as the new men's basketball coach. Turgeon, who coached at Wichita State before

joining Texas A&M, has a great deal of work to complete. Some of Turgeon's responsibilities as the new head basketball coach include recruiting new players, designing offensive plays, designing defensive plays, and others.

As the new head coach at Texas A&M, Turgeon has asked you to help him perform his job both efficiently and

effectively. Specifically, Turgeon believes that he needs to delegate effectively, but needs help in this process. In the following exercise, answer the questions related to the delegation process.

1. This exercise identified some of Turgeon's responsibilities as the new head basketball coach at Texas A&M University. List some of Turgeon's other responsibilities.

2. The first step in the delegation process is to assign specific duties to individuals. What do you think are Turgeon's primary duties, and to whom can he assign these duties? How would you state these duties in operational terms such that the employees understand them?

3. The second step in the delegation process involves granting authority to subordinates. How would Turgeon grant authority to others? How would he make sure that others accepted this new authority?

4. The third step in the delegation process entails making sure the subordinate accepts responsibility for the delegated tasks. How would Turgeon ensure that subordinates accept responsibility?

5. Finally, many obstacles could damage the effectiveness of Turgeon's delegation efforts. List the primary obstacles that Turgeon must overcome.

Experiential Exercises

1 Debating Centralization at Pottery Barn

Directions. Read the following scenario and then perform the listed activities. Your instructor may want you to perform the activities as an individual or within groups. Follow all of your instructor's directions carefully.

As discussed in the chapter, scholars have long debated the advantages and disadvantages of centralization and decentralization. Executives at Pottery Barn have contacted your group to help them better understand whether the company should be either more centralized or more decentralized. Visit Pottery Barn's Web site, and take note of the firm's size, locations, product line, and so on. After studying the company, revisit the discussion of centralization and decentralization in the chapter. How centralized or decentralized should Pottery Barn be? Use the guidelines presented in the text to frame and support your arguments.

2 You and Your Career

Earlier discussions in the chapter highlight the role of responsibility in management. To manage other people, individuals must accept responsibility. Think about, for example, the various responsibilities of managers of your favorite retail store or the responsibilities of the chief executive officer of a large company. Given the role of responsibility in management, can you think of some examples that demonstrate your ability to accept responsibility? How has accepting responsibility helped your career? How might you integrate these examples into interview discussions? If you are currently employed, think of your responsibilities with your current employer. How might these responsibilities help you to advance in the company?

VideoNet Exercise

Foundations of Behavior at TerraCycle

Video Highlights

What do you need to know about human behavior when many of the people you hire are right out of college or previously unemployed? How can you tell if someone has the right attitude and personality for the company? How can you tell if someone has the right aptitude to do the job? Then, once you've made the hire, how do you ensure people are satisfied and will stick around? Small companies like TerraCycle move quickly and cannot afford to make bad hires or experience high turnover. So how do the managers at TerraCycle ensure their company continues to thrive by picking and retaining the right people?

Discussion Questions

1. Is there division of duties at TerraCycle? If so, how are they divided? Explain.
2. Which staff role does Milton, assistant production manager, describe in the video?
3. What are some of the possible obstacles to the delegation process faced by top management at TerraCycle? Explain.

Internet Activity

Go to TerraCycle's Web site at www.TerraCycle.net. Combining what you view on TerraCycle's history, story, and CEO with the information provided on the video clip, list three tasks that the chief executive officer might delegate to other top managers. To which managers would the tasks be delegated? Why?

CASES

1 TOYOTA TO DELEGATE AUTHORITY

"Toyota to Delegate Authority" (p. 273) and its related Challenge Case Summary were written to help you better understand the management concepts contained in this chapter. Answer the following discussion questions about the Challenge Case to better understand how concepts relating to plans and planning tools can be applied in a company such as Toyota.

1. Discuss the roles of responsibility, authority, and accountability in organizing the activities of individuals at Toyota.
2. Describe how cultural differences between the U.S. and Japan may have played a role in Toyota's quality problems.
3. Do you think Toyota managers in Japan will face any personal difficulties when delegating responsibilities to Toyota managers in the U.S.?

2 GETTING THE JOB DONE AT HOME DEPOT

Read the case shown below and answer the questions that follow. Studying this case will help you better see how your understanding of responsibility, authority, and delegation can be applied in a company like Home Depot.

For two decades, do-it-yourself management was the accepted practice at each store of the home improvement retailing chain Home Depot. "Every store was a separate fiefdom, and corporate headquarters was called the store support center," explained Robert L. Nardelli, a former CEO of Home Depot. "The company's co-founders used to tell store managers to ignore messages from headquarters and do what they each thought best." Tom Taylor, who joined the company in its second year, agrees that store managers were aggressive and independent, pushing hard to build sales by giving local customers what they wanted. "We were a little bit rebellious, a little bit dangerous," he says.

Today, with $70 billion in annual sales and 2,200 stores, Home Depot is getting the management job done in a new way. Gone are the days when store managers could buy whatever merchandise they thought would sell well or decide when and where to put up displays. Facing intense competition from long-time rival Lowe's, Nardelli moved to standardize products and processes in all stores across the chain.

For example, he took purchasing authority away from store managers and gave it to headquarters staff, which allows the company much more power when negotiating with suppliers for larger orders. Also, he centralized control of merchandise displays for more consistent presentation from store to store. Learning that the company lacked the technology for the CEO to e-mail store managers—let alone enable store managers to e-mail each other—Nardelli installed an updated electronic communication system. Now store managers share ideas and advice via e-mail, spreading best practices and encouraging collaboration throughout the chain. As a result, all Home Depots benefit when one store discovers the most efficient method of accomplishing something, such as keeping garden center plants properly watered.

In the past, store managers were allowed considerable leeway in responding to local needs and trends. Nardelli wanted to continue this successful tradition of catering to customers at the store level while keeping management focused on both higher performance and accountability. To this end, he introduced a series of reports and controls that helped store managers identify and analyze problems; maintain sufficient inventory to satisfy customers without exceeding cost targets; and better manage personnel matters such as hiring, scheduling, and evaluation.

Some managers were less than enthusiastic about Nardelli's changes. "It was time to infuse some different thinking in the company, but his 'do it my way' style undercut the sense of ownership [that] employees had," says a manager who ultimately went to work at another firm. "It was revolution, not evolution." For his part, Nardelli noted that "being an outsider, I had the advantage of not having to stick with the past." Thanks to his changes, Home Depot capitalized on its strengths to sell more high-profit products, increased the average sale size, and expanded into new markets and new services.

Looking beyond financial goals, Home Depot is in a unique position to help preserve the world's rainforests. In 2000, under pressure from environmental activists, the company added an environmental global project manager to its corporate staff and implemented a policy of not buying lumber from endangered forests. In addition, this manager has facilitated meetings of lumber executives and environmentalists to broker agreements about preserving forest land in

Chile, a model that Home Depot plans to apply in Indonesia and other areas.

Although Home Depot is showing positive results, it must prove itself day in and day out to customers, employees, investors, and other stakeholders. That's why the CEO made time to visit as many Home Depot stores as he can. "I can walk through a store and know within five minutes if it is operating successfully," Nardelli said. "It's all about whether store associates look you in the eye and say hello, whether they have an energy in their step, whether the shelves are full, the lights are bright, the place is clean."

QUESTIONS

1. Describe the state of line-staff relationships before and after Nardelli became CEO. How do you think this change has affected Home Depot?

2. Are store managers being responsible if they devote more time to customer sales and satisfaction than to corporate reporting?

3. Under what circumstances would you recommend that Home Depot move toward a higher degree of decentralization?

Endnotes

1. Mark Huffman, "Problems Fixed in Three Million Recalled Vehicles, Toyota Says," *ConsumerAffairs.com*, May 5, 2010, http://www.consumeraffairs.com; Greg Gardner, "Dysfunction in Toyota Culture Exposed by Recall Crisis," *Wichita Eagle*, March 14, 2010, http://www.kansas.com; "Learning from Toyota's Mistakes," *Business Management*, March 9, 2010, http://www.busmanagement.com; Alex Taylor III, "Toyota Starts the Long Road Back," *CNNMoney.com*, March 9, 2010, http://money.cnn.com; Neil Roland, "Toyota's North America Unit to Get More Authority over U.S. Results," *Automotive News*, March 2, 2010, http://www.automotivenews.com.

2. Andre Nelson, "Have I the Right Stuff to Be a Supervisor?" *Supervision* 51 (January 1990): 10–12. For a recent responsibility-related trend, see "Office Professionals' Responsibilities Set to Soar," *British Journal of Administrative Management* (May/June 2001): 6.

3. "Goldman Sachs: Key Executive Accepts Some Responsibility for Meltdown," *Los Angeles Times*, April 27, 2010, http://www.latimes.com.

4. J. E. Osborne, "Job Descriptions Do More Than Describe Duties," *Supervisory Management* (February 1992): 8. Charlene Marmer Solomon, "Repatriation Planning Checklist," *Personnel Journal* (January 1995): 32; Peggy Anderson and Marcia Pulich, "Making Performance Appraisals Work More Effectively," *The Health Care Supervisor* 16, no. 4 (June 1998): 20–27.

5. Robert J. Theirauf, Robert C. Klekamp, and Daniel W. Geeding, *Management Principles and Practices: A Contingency and Questionnaire Approach* (New York: Wiley, 1977), 334.

6. Deborah S. Kezsbom, "Managing the Chaos: Conflict Among Project Teams," *AACE Transactions* (1989): A4.1–A4.8. For an example of how overlapping responsibilities can impact a political organization, see Carolyn Ban and Norma Riccucci, "New York State Civil Service Reform in a Complex Political Environment," *Review of Public Personnel Administration* 14, no. 2 (Spring 1994): 28–40.

7. Richard Korman, "A Responsibility Gap Crashes at Location C3," *ENR* 250 (2003): 12.

8. Chuck Douros, "Clear Division of Responsibility Defeats Inefficiency," *Nation's Restaurant News* (February 21, 1994): 20.

9. Robert D. Melcher, "Roles and Relationships: Clarifying the Manager's Job," *Personnel* 44 (May/June 1967): 34–41.

10. This section is based primarily on John H. Zenger, "Responsible Behavior: Stamp of the Effective Manager," *Supervisory Management* (July 1976): 18–24.

11. Stephen Bushardt, David Duhon, and Aubrey Fowler, "Management Delegation Myths and the Paradox of Task Assignment," *Business Horizons* (March/April 1991): 37–43.

12. Max Weber, "The Three Types of Legitimate Rule," trans. Hans Gerth, *Berkeley Journal of Sociology* 4 (1953): 1–11. For a current illustration of this concept, see Gail DeGeorge, "Yo, Ho, Ho, and a Battle for Bacardi," *BusinessWeek*, (April 16, 1990): 47–48.

13. John Gardner, "The Anti-Leadership Vaccine," *Carnegie Foundation Annual Report* (1965).

14. Chester I. Barnard, *The Functions of the Executive* (Cambridge, MA: Harvard University Press, 1938).

15. To better understand the interplay between incentives and authority, see Jan Bouwens and Laurence Van Lent, "Assessing the performance of business unit managers," *Journal of Accounting Research* 45, no. 4 (2007): 667–697.

16. For an illustration of how line authority issues can impact the operation of the IRS, see "TEI Recommends Changes in IRS Appeals Large Case Program," *Tax Executive* 48, no. 4 (July/August 1996): 265.

17. Patti Wolf, Gerald Grimes, and John Dayani, "Getting the Most Out of Staff Functions," *Small Business Reports* 14 (October 1989): 68–70.

18. Harold Stieglitz, "On Concepts of Corporate Structure," *Conference Board Record* 11 (February 1974): 7–13.

19. Wendell L. French, *The Personnel Management Process: Human Resource Administration and Development* (Boston: Houghton Mifflin, 1987), 66–68.

20. For a discussion of the complex negotiations that attend the distribution of authority in some organizations, see Chantal Benoit-Barne and Francois Cooran, "The Accomplishment of Authority through Presentification," *Management Communication Quarterly* 23, no. 1 (2009): 5–31.

21. Derek Sheane, "When and How to Intervene in Conflict," *Personnel Management* (November 1979): 32–36.

22. For a discussion of how giving up authority can be good for the organization, see A. D. Amar, Carsten Hentrich, and Vlatka Hlupic, "To Be a Better Leader, Give Up Authority," *Harvard Business Review*, December 2009, http://hbr.org.

23. Researchers have devised an interesting way to map the distribution of authority within an organization. For a description of this technique, see Michael Segalla, "Find the Real Power in Your Organization," *Harvard Business Review* (May 2010): 34–35.

24. Robert Albanese, *Management* (Cincinnati: South-Western Publishing, 1988), 313; Michael T. McCue and John Gress, "Accountability: A New Commandment," *Managed Healthcare Executive* 11, no. 6 (June 2001): 14.

25. Anthony Buono, "Accountability: Freedom and Responsibility Without Control," *Personnel Psychology* 56 (2003): 546.

26. "How Ylvisaker Makes 'Produce or Else' Work," *BusinessWeek*, (October 27, 1973): 112. For an interesting discussion of the importance of establishing an environment of accountability in a small women's specialty retail store, see Nan Napier, "Change Is Big Even for a Little Guy," *Business Quarterly* (Winter 1994): 21–27.

27. See Chris Rivinus, "Ignorance Management," *Business Information Review* 27, no. 1 (2010): 33–38.

28. For a practical discussion related to the delegation process, see Kenneth Corts and Darwin Neher, "Credible Delegation," *European Economic Review* 47 (2003): 395; see also Massimo Colombo and Marco Delmastro, "Delegation of Authority in Business Organizations: An Empirical Test," *The Journal of Industrial Economics* 52 (2004): 53.

29. William H. Newman and E. Kirby Warren, *The Process of Management: Concepts, Behavior, and Practice*, 4th ed. (Upper Saddle River, NJ: Prentice Hall, 1977), 39–40; Dave Wiggins, "Stop Doing It All

Yourself! Some Keys to Effective Delegation," *Journal of Environmental Health* 60, no. 9 (May 1998): 29–30. See also Kristin Gilpatrick, "Step Up to Delegation," *Credit Union Management* 24, no. 4 (April 2001): 18.

30. R. S. Drever, "The Ultimate Frustration," *Supervision* (May 1991): 22–23.

31. To better understand the intricacies of delegation in international contexts, see Zhen Xiong Chen and Samuel Aryee, "Delegation and employee work outcomes: An examination of the cultural context of mediating processes in China," *Academy of Management Journal* 50, no. 1 (2007): 226–238.

32. For more recommendations regarding delegation, see Joni Youngworth, "Delegation dilemmas," *Journal of Financial Planning* 20 (September 2007): 10–12.

33. Ted Pollock, "Secrets of Successful Delegation," *Production* (December 1994): 10–11; Robert B. Nelson, "Mastering Delegation," *Executive Excellence* 7 (January 1990): 13–14.

34. Roz Ayres-Williams, "Mastering the Fine Art of Delegation," *Black Enterprise* (April 1992): 91–93.

35. Harold Koontz, Cyril O'Donnell, and Heinz Weihrich, *Essentials of Management,* 8th ed. (New York: McGraw-Hill, 1986), 231–233. See also Robert I. Sutton, "Some Bosses Live in a Fool's Paradise," *Harvard Business Review,* June 3, 2010, http://blogs.hbr.org; Andrew O'Connell, "Why Controlling Bosses Have Unproductive Employees," *Harvard Business Review,* May 25, 2010, http://blogs.hbr.org.

36   For a practical look at the process of centralization, see "Pros and Cons of Centralization," *Nature* 423 (2003): 787; see also Marco Adria and Shamsud Chowdhury, "Centralization as a Design Consideration for the Management of Call Centers," *Information and Mnagement* 41 (2004): 497

37. For an interesting discussion of whether to centralize the marketing function, see Richard Kitaeff, "The Great Debate: Centralized vs. Decentralized Marketing Research Function," *Marketing Research: A Magazine of Management & Applications* (Winter 1994): 59; Charlotte Sibley, "The Pros and Cons of Centralization and Decentralization," *Medical Marketing and Media* 32, no. 5 (May 1997): 72–76; Christine Tierney and Katherine Schmidt, "Schrempp, the Survivor? To Tighten His Grip, He Will Centralize Decision-Making," *BusinessWeek,* (March 5, 2001): 54.

38. Steve Weinstein, "A Look at Fleming's New Look," *Progressive Grocer* 74 (1995): 47–49. To understand the effects of globalization on decentralization, see Francesca Sanna-Randaccio and Reinhilde Veugelers, "Multinational knowledge spillovers with decentralized R&D: A game-theoretic approach," *Journal of International Business Studies* 38, no. 1 (2007): 47–63.

39. H. Gilman, "J.C. Penney Decentralizes Its Purchasing," *Wall Street Journal,* (May 8, 1986): 6.

40. Jack Neff, 'What's Ailing J&J—and Why Isn't Its Rep Hurting?' *Advertising Age,* May 10, 2010, http://www.adage.com.

41. To better understand how decentralization influences innovation and new products, see Nicolaj Siggelkow and Jan Rivken, "When exploration backfires: Unintended consequences of multi-level organizational search," *Academy of Management Journal* 49, no. 4 (2006): 779–795.

42. Donald O. Harper, "Project Management as a Conrol and Planning Tool in the Decentralized Company," *Management Accounting* (November 1968): 29–33.

43. Information for this section is mainly from John G. Staiger, "What Cannot Be Decentralized," *Management Record* 25 (January 1963): 19–21. At the time the article was written, Staiger was vice president of administration, North American Operations, Massey-Ferguson, Limited.

44. This exercise was based on the company's Web site as well as Jena McGregor, "Room & Board Plays Impossible to Get," *BusinessWeek,* (October 1, 2007): 80.

Human Resource Management

Target Skill

human resource management skill: the ability to take actions that increase the contributions of individuals within the organization

objectives

To help build my *human resource management skill,* when studying this chapter, I will attempt to acquire:

1. An overall understanding of how appropriate human resources can be provided for the organization

2. An appreciation for the relationship among recruitment efforts, an open position, sources of human resources, and the law

3. Insights into the use of tests and assessment centers in employee selection

4. An understanding of how the training process operates

5. A concept of what performance appraisals are and how they can best be conducted

CHALLENGE CASE

CISCO RECRUITS THE BEST MINDS IN CHINA

JOHN CHAMBERS IS THE CEO OF CISCO SYSTEMS, a company that manufactures and sells networking communications equipment to a wide array of customers in both the private and public sectors. In recent years, Cisco's success has been evidenced by its tremendous financial performance. Cisco's sales have been known to grow more than 50 percent annually over five-year periods—an astronomical rate for any corporation, especially for a company as large as Cisco.

To a large extent, Cisco's success has been the result of its human resource strategy. Often, Cisco has acquired other companies mainly to gain their bright engineers. As employees of acquired companies, people normally became Cisco's new employees. During a recent two-year period, Cisco averaged an acquisition every other week and doubled its employee base to 44,000 workers.

Complementing its acquisition strategy, Cisco used other tactics to recruit new employees during the technology boom in the late 1990s. For example, Cisco used focus groups to learn what type of movies and Web sites the best and brightest potential employees favored. Then, Cisco programmed its Web site to recognize visitors from its chief rival 3Com and greeted these visitors with a special screen stating, "Welcome to Cisco; would you like a job?" Cisco figured that competitors bold enough to visit its Web site were just the type of employees it needed.

More recently, Cisco increased its focus on hiring employees in other countries. Specifically, Cisco concentrated intensely on recruiting and retaining employees in China. However, Cisco is not the only multinational company to recognize the importance of China's supply of human resources—Cisco competes with other companies such as Intel and IBM for these potential employees.

Despite China's enormous population, only a limited supply of qualified engineers there also speak English. As such, the competition for recruiting these employees remains fierce. In fact, Cisco has instituted several new tactics in hiring new employees. The company, for example, offers private shuttle buses from subways to the company's office. In addition, the company offers management development seminars to help the employees, who are young and focus largely on technology, improve their management skills. Relying on practices such as these has helped Cisco hire some of the most talented engineers in Shanghai.

In short, Cisco is applying the human resource management practices perfected in the United States to other global markets. As market conditions change, though, John Chambers knows that Cisco's human resource strategy will also need to change its focus internationally if it wants to recruit and retain the best and brightest minds in the technology sector.[1]

■ *Cisco's human resources managers adapt their strategies to ensure the company recruits and retains the right people to meet its goals.*

EXPLORING YOUR MANAGEMENT SKILL

You can explore your level of human resource management skill **before** studying the chapter by completing the exercise "Exploring Your Management Skill: Part 1" on page 312 and **after** studying this chapter by completing the exercise "Exploring Your Management Skill: Part 2" on page 313.

THE HUMAN RESOURCE MANAGEMENT CHALLENGE

The Challenge Case discusses tactics that management at Cisco Systems has used to hire and retain its brightest employees in China. The task of hiring and retaining not just people, but the *right* people—particularly top performers at senior levels in the organization—is part of managing human resources in any organization.[2] This chapter outlines the process of managing human resources within an organization and emphasizes how hiring and retaining the right people is part of this process for managers at a company such as Cisco. This chapter discusses this process by first defining appropriate human resources and then examining the steps to be followed in providing them.

DEFINING APPROPRIATE HUMAN RESOURCES

The phrase **appropriate human resources** refers to the individuals within the organization who make a valuable contribution to management system goal attainment. This contribution results from their productivity in the positions they hold. The phrase *inappropriate human resources* refers to organization members who do not make a valuable contribution to the attainment of management system objectives. For one reason or another, these individuals are ineffective in their jobs.

Productivity in all organizations is determined by how human resources interact and combine to use all other management system resources. Such factors as background, age, job-related experience, and level of formal education all play a role in determining how appropriate the individual is for the organization. Although the process of providing appropriate human resources for the organization is involved and somewhat subjective, the following section offers insights on how to increase the success of this process.

STEPS IN PROVIDING HUMAN RESOURCES

To provide appropriate human resources to fill both managerial and nonmanagerial openings, managers follow four sequential steps.[3]

1. Recruitment
2. Selection
3. Training
4. Performance appraisal

Figure 13.1 illustrates these steps.

Recruitment

Recruitment is the initial attraction and screening of the supply of prospective human resources available to fill a position. Its purpose is to narrow a large field of prospective employees to a relatively small group of individuals from which someone eventually will be hired. To be effective, recruiters must know the job they are trying to fill, where potential human resources can be located, and how the law influences recruiting efforts. What's more, with advances in technology, recruiting continues to evolve and change. To maintain appropriate human resources, today's managers must keep abreast of the trends.[4]

FIGURE 13.1

Four steps to providing appropriate human resources for an organization

Knowing the Job Recruitment activities must begin with a thorough understanding of the position to be filled so the broad range of potential employees can be narrowed intelligently. The technique commonly used to gain that understanding is known as **job analysis**. Basically, job analysis is aimed at determining a job description (the activities a job entails)—which was discussed in the previous chapter—and a **job specification** (the characteristics of the individual who should be hired for the job).[5] Figure 13.2 shows the relationship of job analysis to job description and job specification.[6]

The U.S. Civil Service Commission has developed a procedure for performing a job analysis. As with all job analysis procedures, the Civil Service procedure uses information gathering as the primary means of determining what workers do and how and why they do it. Naturally, the quality of the job analysis depends on the accuracy of information gathered. This information is used to develop both a job description and a job specification.[7]

Knowing Sources of Human Resources Besides a thorough knowledge of the position the organization is trying to fill, recruiters must be able to pinpoint sources of human resources. The supply of individuals from which to recruit is continually changing, which means that at times, finding appropriate human resources will be much harder than at other times. Human resources specialists in organizations continually monitor the labor market so they will know where to recruit suitable people and what kind of strategies and tactics to use to attract job applicants in a competitive marketplace.[8]

Sources of human resources available to fill a position can be generally categorized in two ways: sources inside the organization and sources outside the organization.

Sources Inside the Organization The pool of employees within the organization is one source of human resources. Some individuals who already work for the organization may be well qualified for an open position. Although existing personnel are sometimes moved laterally within an organization, most internal movements are promotions. Promotion from within has the advantages of building employee morale, encouraging employees to work harder in hopes of being promoted, and enticing employees to stay with the organization because of the possibility of future promotions. Companies such as Exxon and General Electric find it especially rewarding to train their managers for advancement within the organization.[9]

HUMAN RESOURCE INVENTORY A **human resource inventory** consists of information about the characteristics of organization members. The focus is on past performance and future

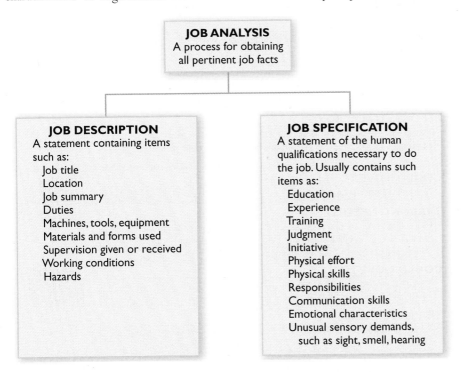

FIGURE 13.2
Relationship of job analysis, job description, and job specification

potential, and the objective is to keep management up to date about the possibilities for filling a position from within. This inventory should indicate which individuals in the organization would be appropriate for filling a position if it became available. In a classic article, Walter S. Wikstrom proposed that organizations keep three types of records that can be combined to maintain a useful human resource inventory.[10] Although Wikstrom focused on filling managerial positions, slight modifications to his inventory forms would make his records equally useful for filling nonmanagerial positions. Many organizations computerize records like the ones Wikstrom suggests to make their human resource inventory system more efficient and effective.

- The first of Wikstrom's three types of records for a human resource inventory is the **management inventory card**. The management inventory card in Figure 13.3 has been completed for a fictional manager named Mel Murray. It indicates Murray's age, year of employment, present position and the length of time he has held it, performance ratings, strengths and weaknesses, the positions to which he might move, when he would be ready to assume these positions, and additional training he would need to fill the positions. In short, this card contains an organizational history of Murray and an indication of how he might be used in the future. Note that Figures 13.3, 13.4, and 13.5 depict a computerized version of Wikstrom's human resource inventory system.

- Figure 13.4 shows Wikstrom's second type of human resource inventory record—the **position replacement form**. This record focuses on position-centered information rather than the people-centered information maintained on the management inventory card. Note that the form in Figure 13.4 indicates little about Murray, but much about two individuals who could replace him. The position replacement form is helpful in determining what would happen to Murray's present position if Murray were selected to be moved within the organization or if he decided to leave the organization.

- Wikstrom's third human resource inventory record is the **management manpower replacement chart** (see Figure 13.5). This chart presents a composite view of the individuals

FIGURE 13.3
Management inventory card

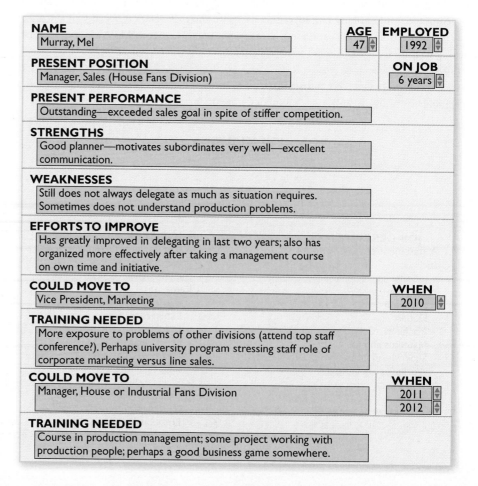

NAME		AGE	EMPLOYED
Murray, Mel		47	1992

PRESENT POSITION		ON JOB
Manager, Sales (House Fans Division)		6 years

PRESENT PERFORMANCE
Outstanding—exceeded sales goal in spite of stiffer competition.

STRENGTHS
Good planner—motivates subordinates very well—excellent communication.

WEAKNESSES
Still does not always delegate as much as situation requires. Sometimes does not understand production problems.

EFFORTS TO IMPROVE
Has greatly improved in delegating in last two years; also has organized more effectively after taking a management course on own time and initiative.

COULD MOVE TO	WHEN
Vice President, Marketing	2010

TRAINING NEEDED
More exposure to problems of other divisions (attend top staff conference?). Perhaps university program stressing staff role of corporate marketing versus line sales.

COULD MOVE TO	WHEN
Manager, House or Industrial Fans Division	2011 / 2012

TRAINING NEEDED
Course in production management; some project working with production people; perhaps a good business game somewhere.

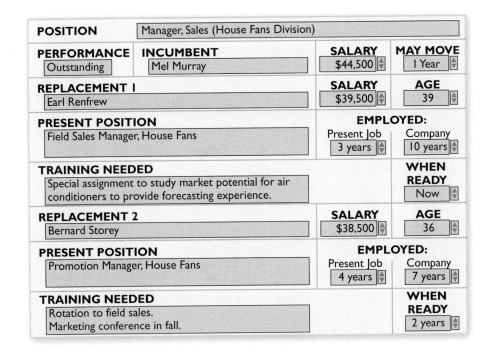

FIGURE 13.4
Position replacement form

FIGURE 13.5 Management manpower replacement chart

management considers significant for human resource planning. Note in Figure 13.5 how Murray's performance rating and promotion potential can easily be compared with those of other employees when the company is trying to determine which individual would most appropriately fill a particular position.

The management inventory card, the position replacement form, and the management manpower replacement chart are three separate record-keeping devices for a human resource inventory. Each form furnishes different data on which to base a hiring-from-within decision. These forms help management answer the following questions:

1. What is the organizational history of an individual, and what potential does that person possess (management inventory card)?
2. If a position becomes vacant, who might be eligible to fill it (position replacement form)?
3. What are the merits of one individual being considered for a position compared to those of another individual under consideration (management manpower replacement chart)?

Overall, Wikstrom's human resource inventory system can serve as the foundation for succession planning in organizations. **Succession planning** is the process of outlining who will follow whom in various organizational positions. Studies show that it will be among the top five challenges executives face in the future.[11] Michael Eisner, the chief executive officer at Walt Disney Company, has been strongly criticized for not developing a plan for who would succeed him. In 1994, moments before he underwent heart bypass surgery, Eisner summoned his wife and two sons to his hospital gurney. Eisner told them that if it becomes an issue, he thought that either Barry Diller or Michael Orvitz should succeed him. Criticism of Eisner several years later indicated that he still did not have a plan for who would succeed him. Conscientiously keeping a human resource inventory can help a manager such as Eisner to determine a plan not only for who would succeed him, but all other managers at Disney.[12] Computer software is available to aid managers in keeping track of the organization's complex human resource inventories and in making better decisions about how employees can best be deployed and developed.[13]

Sources Outside the Organization

If a position cannot be filled by someone currently employed by the organization, management has available numerous sources of human resources outside the organization. These sources include the following:

1. **Competitors**—One often-tapped external source of human resources is competing organizations. Because of several advantages in luring human resources away from competitors, this type of piracy has become a common practice. Among the advantages are the following:
   * The individual knows the business.
   * The competitor will have paid for the individual's training up to the time of hire.
   * The competing organization will probably be weakened somewhat by the loss of the individual.
   * Once hired, the individual will be a valuable source of information about how to best compete with the other organization.
2. **Employment agencies**—Employment agencies help people find jobs and help organizations find job applicants. Such agencies can be either public or private. Public employment agencies do not charge fees, whereas private ones collect a fee from either the person hired or the organization doing the hiring, once the hire has been finalized.
3. **Readers of certain publications**—Perhaps the most widely used external source of human resources is the readership of certain publications. To tap this source, recruiters simply place an advertisement in a suitable publication. The advertisement describes the open position in detail and announces that the organization is accepting applications from qualified individuals. The type of position to be filled determines the type of publication in which the advertisement is placed. The objective is to advertise in a publication whose readers are likely to be interested in filling the position. An opening for a top-level executive might be advertised

Job applicants, like this woman, are an important source of human resources that companies can also attract through various recruitment strategies like job fairs.

in the *Wall Street Journal*, a training director opening might be advertised in the *Journal of Training and Development*, and an educational opening might be advertised in the *Chronicle of Higher Education*.

4.   **Educational institutions**—Many recruiters go directly to schools to interview students close to graduation time. Liberal arts schools, business schools, engineering schools, junior colleges, and community colleges all have somewhat different human resources to offer. Recruiting efforts should focus on the schools with the highest probability of providing human resources appropriate for the open position.

To increase hiring at educational institutions, Intel Corp. and 24 venture capital firms have created a $3.5 billion strategic alliance called "Invest in America." The alliance has enlisted 18 technology firms, including Cisco Systems, eBay, Google, and Yahoo!, who have committed to increase their hiring of college grads. Offering more opportunity to recent grads is one way U.S. business can help support the recovering economy.[14] ■

how managers do it

Recruiting at the "Invest in America" Alliance

Knowing the Law   Legislation has had a major impact on modern organizational recruitment practices. Managers need to be aware of the laws that govern recruitment efforts. The Civil Rights Act, passed in 1964 and amended in 1972, created the **Equal Employment Opportunity Commission (EEOC)** to enforce federal laws prohibiting discrimination on the basis of race, color, religion, sex, and national origin in recruitment, hiring, firing, layoffs, and all other employment practices. Such laws include the Pregnancy Discrimination Act,[15] requiring the treatment of pregnancy as a medical disability; the Age Discrimination in Employment Act, prohibiting the arbitrary setting of age limits for job holders; and the Americans with Disabilities Act, prohibiting discrimination against individuals with mental or physical disabilities in the area of employment.

   Equal opportunity legislation protects the right of a citizen to work and obtain a fair wage based primarily on merit and performance. The EEOC seeks to uphold this right by overseeing the employment practices of labor unions, private employers, educational institutions, and government bodies.

Affirmative Action In response to equal opportunity legislation, many organizations have established an **affirmative action program**.[16] Translated literally, *affirmative action* means positive movement: "In the area of equal employment opportunity, the basic purpose of positive movement or affirmative action is to eliminate barriers and increase opportunities for the purpose of increasing the utilization of underutilized and/or disadvantaged individuals."[17] An organization can judge how much progress it is making toward eliminating such barriers by taking the following steps:

1. Determining how many minority and disadvantaged individuals it presently employs
2. Determining how many minority and disadvantaged individuals it should be employing according to EEOC guidelines
3. Comparing the numbers obtained in steps 1 and 2

If the two numbers obtained in step 3 are nearly the same, the organization's employment practices probably should be maintained; if they are not nearly the same, the organization should modify its employment practices accordingly.

Modern management writers recommend that managers follow the guidelines of affirmative action, not merely because they are mandated by law, but because of the characteristics of today's labor supply.[18] According to these writers, more than half of the U.S. workforce now consists of minorities, immigrants, and women. Because the overall workforce is so diverse, it follows that employees in today's organizations will also be more diverse than in the past. Thus today's managers face the challenge of forging a productive workforce out of an increasingly diverse labor pool, and this task is more formidable than simply complying with affirmative action laws.

Diversity also suggests diversity in age, and with the aging of America's baby boom generation, recruiting managers are increasingly paying attention to real and perceived differences in work values among younger generations of workers.[19]

Selection

The second major step involved in providing human resources for the organization is **selection**—choosing an individual to hire from all those who have been recruited. Selection, obviously, is dependent on the first step, recruitment.

Selection is represented as a series of stages through which job applicants must pass to be hired.[20] Each stage reduces the total group of prospective employees until, finally, one individual is hired. Figure 13.6 lists the specific stages of the selection process, indicates reasons for eliminating applicants at each stage, and illustrates how the group of potential employees is narrowed to the individual who ultimately is hired. Two tools often used in the selection process are testing and assessment centers.

STAGES OF THE SELECTION PROCESS	REASONS FOR ELIMINATION	
Preliminary screening from records, data sheets, etc.	Lack of adequate educational and performance record	
Preliminary interview	Obvious misfit from outward appearance and conduct	
Intelligence tests	Failure to meet minimum standards	
Aptitude tests	Failure to have minimum necessary aptitude	
Personality tests	Negative aspects of personality	
Performance references	Unfavorable or negative reports on past performance	
Diagnostic interview	Lack of necessary innate ability, ambition, or other qualities	
Physical examination	Physically unfit for job	
Personal judgment	Remaining candidate placed in available position	

FIGURE 13.6 Summary of major factors in the selection process

Testing **Testing** is examining human resources for qualities relevant to performing available jobs. Although many different kinds of tests are available for organizational use, they generally can be divided into the following four categories.[21]

1. **Aptitude tests**—Tests of aptitude measure the potential of an individual to perform a task. Some aptitude tests measure general intelligence, while others measure special abilities, such as mechanical, clerical, or visual skills.[22]
2. **Achievement tests**—Tests that measure the level of skill or knowledge an individual possesses in a certain area are called achievement tests. This skill or knowledge may have been acquired through various training activities or through experience in the area. Examples of skill tests are typing and keyboarding tests.
3. **Vocational interest tests**—Tests of vocational interest attempt to measure an individual's interest in performing various kinds of jobs. They are administered on the assumption that certain people perform jobs well because they find the job activities stimulating. The basic purpose of this type of test is to select for an open position the individual who finds most aspects of that position interesting.
4. **Personality tests**—Personality tests attempt to describe an individual's personality dimensions in such areas as emotional maturity, subjectivity, honesty, and objectivity. These tests can be used advantageously if the personality characteristics needed to do well in a particular job are well defined and if individuals possessing those characteristics can be identified and selected. Managers must be careful, however, not to expose themselves to legal prosecution by basing employment decisions on personality tests that are invalid and unreliable.[23]

Testing Guidelines Several guidelines should be observed when tests are used as part of the selection process. First, care must be taken to ensure that the test being used is both valid and reliable. A test is *valid* if it measures what it is designed to measure and *reliable* if it measures similarly time after time.[24] Second, test results should not be used as the sole determinant of a hiring decision. People change over time, and someone who doesn't score well on a particular test might still develop into a productive employee. Such factors as potential and desire to obtain a position should be assessed subjectively and used along with test scores in the final selection decision. Third, care should be taken to ensure that tests are nondiscriminatory; many tests contain language or cultural biases that may discriminate against minorities, and the EEOC has the authority to prosecute organizations that use discriminatory testing practices. Finally, employers should acknowledge that such tests may increase employee anxiety, as they worry about the potential effects of such testing.[25]

Assessment Centers Another tool often used in employee selection is the assessment center. Although the assessment center concept is discussed in this chapter primarily as an aid to selection, it is also used in such areas as human resource training and organization development. The first industrial use of the assessment center is usually credited to AT&T. Since AT&T's initial efforts, the assessment center concept has expanded greatly, and today it is used not only as a means for identifying individuals to be hired from outside an organization, but also for identifying individuals from inside the organization who should be promoted. Corporations that have used assessment centers extensively include JCPenney, Standard Oil of Ohio, and IBM.[26]

An **assessment center** is a program (not a place) in which participants engage in a number of individual and group exercises constructed to simulate important activities at the organizational levels to which they aspire.[27] These exercises can include such activities as participating in leaderless discussions, giving oral presentations, and leading a group in solving some assigned problem.[28] The individuals performing the activities are observed by managers or trained observers who evaluate their ability and their potential. In general, participants are assessed according to job-related criteria such as oral communication, conflict resolution, leadership, persuasion, and problem solving.[29]

TABLE 13.1	Management Training Topics for Police Within the Alabama Department of Public Safety
-Organization Theory	-Effective Communication
-Leadership	-Hiring Practices
-Organizational Goals	-Training Process
-Media Relations	-Measuring Productivity
-Problem Solving	-Employee Evaluations
-Decision Making	-Discipline
-Time Management	-Legal Aspects of Discipline and Termination
-Stress Management	-Motivation
-Ethics and Integrity	-Contingency Planning

Training

After recruitment and selection, the next step in providing appropriate human resources for the organization is training. **Training** is the process of developing qualities in human resources that will enable them to be more productive and thus contribute more to organizational goal attainment. The purpose of training is to increase the productivity of employees by influencing their behavior. Table 13.1 provides an overview of the types and popularity of training being offered by organizations today.

The training of individuals is essentially a four-step process:

1. Determining training needs
2. Designing the training program
3. Administering the training program
4. Evaluating the training program

These steps are presented in Figure 13.7 and are described in the sections that follow.

Determining Training Needs The first step of the training process is determining the organization's training needs.[30] **Training needs** are the information or skill areas of an individual or group that require further development to increase the productivity of that individual or group. Only if training focuses on these needs can it be productive for the organization.

FIGURE 13.7
Steps of the training process

The training of organization members is typically a continuing activity. Even employees who have been with the organization for some time and who have undergone initial orientation and skills training need continued training to improve their skills.

DETERMINING NEEDED SKILLS Several methods are available for determining on which skills to focus with established human resources. One method calls for evaluating the production process within the organization. Such factors as excessive rejected products, unmet deadlines, and high labor costs are clues to deficiencies in production-related expertise. Another method for determining training needs calls for getting direct feedback from employees on what they believe are the organization's training needs. Organization members are often able to verbalize clearly and accurately exactly what types of training they require to do a better job. A third way of determining training needs involves looking into the future. If the manufacture of new products or the use of newly purchased equipment is foreseen, some type of corresponding training almost certainly will be needed.

how managers do It

Investing in Training Programs at South Coast Health System

For example, South Coast Health System in New Bedford, Mass., recently adopted a new paperless system shortly after a recent round of layoffs. For the remaining IT employees to be able to support the new system, management at South Coast recognized they would need additional training. As a result, the company made a significant investment in outside training programs.[31] ■

Designing the Training Program Once training needs have been determined, a training program aimed at meeting those needs must be designed. Basically, designing a program entails assembling various types of facts and activities that will meet the established training needs. Obviously, as training needs vary, so will the facts and activities designed to meet those needs.

Administering the Training Program The next step in the training process is administering the training program—that is, actually training the individuals selected to participate in the program. Various techniques exist for both transmitting necessary information and developing needed skills in training programs, and several of these techniques are discussed in the sections that follow.

TECHNIQUES FOR TRANSMITTING INFORMATION Two techniques for transmitting information in training programs are lectures and programmed learning. Although it could be argued that these techniques develop some skills in individuals as well as transmit information to them, they are primarily devices for the dissemination of information.

1. **Lectures**—Perhaps the most widely used technique for transmitting information in training programs is the lecture. The **lecture** is primarily a one-way communication situation in which an instructor orally presents information to a group of listeners. The instructor typically does most of the talking, and trainees participate primarily through listening and note taking.

   An advantage of the lecture is that it allows the instructor to expose trainees to a maximum amount of information within a given time period. The lecture, however, has some serious disadvantages:[32]

   The lecture generally consists of a one-way communication: The instructor presents information to the group of passive listeners. Thus, little or no

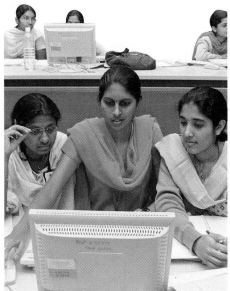

In the offices of Wipro in Bangalore, India, employees receive a great deal of specialized training in order to provide software support services to the company's international clients.

opportunity exists to clarify meanings, to check on whether trainees really understand the lecture material, or to handle the wide diversity of ability, attitude, and interest that may prevail among the trainees. Also, this format permits little or no opportunity for practice, reinforcement, knowledge of results, or overlearning. Ideally, the competent lecturer should make the material meaningful and intrinsically motivating to his or her listeners. However, whether most lectures achieve this goal is a moot question. These limitations, in turn, impose further limitations on the lecture's actual content. A skillful lecturer may be fairly successful in transmitting conceptual knowledge to a group of trainees who are ready to receive it; however, all the evidence available indicates that the nature of the lecture situation makes it of minimal value in promoting attitudinal or behavioral change.

2. **Programmed learning**—Another commonly used technique for transmitting information in training programs is called programmed learning. **Programmed learning** is a technique for instructing without the presence or intervention of a human instructor.[33] Small parts of information that require related responses are presented to individual trainees. The trainees can determine from checking their responses against provided answers whether their understanding of the information is accurate. The types of responses required of trainees vary from situation to situation but usually are multiple-choice, true-false, or fill-in-the-blank.

    With advances in technology, some training professionals are developing new forms of programmed learning. Selected employers, for example, are incorporating the use of virtual-world programs like Second Life into their training programs.[34]

    Like the lecture method, programmed learning has both advantages and disadvantages. Among the advantages are that it can be computerized and students can learn at their own pace, know immediately whether they are right or wrong, and participate actively in the leaning process. The primary disadvantage of this method is that no one is present to answer a confused learner's questions.

TECHNIQUES FOR DEVELOPING SKILLS Techniques for developing skills in training programs can be divided into two broad categories: on-the-job and classroom. Techniques for developing skills on the job, referred to as **on-the-job training**, reflect a blend of job-related knowledge and experience. They include coaching, position rotation, and special project committees. *Coaching* is direct critiquing of how well an individual is performing a job.[35] *Position rotation* involves moving an individual from job to job to enable the person to gain an understanding of the organization as a whole. *Special project committees* are vehicles for assigning a particular task to an individual to furnish him or her with experience in a designated area.[36]

Classroom techniques for developing skills also reflect a blend of job-related knowledge and experience. The skills addressed through these techniques can range from technical, such as computer programming skills, to interpersonal, such as leadership skills. Specific classroom techniques aimed at developing skills include various types of management games and role-playing activities. The most common format for *management games* requires small groups of trainees to make and then evaluate various management decisions. The *role-playing format* typically involves acting out and then reflecting on some people-oriented problem that must be solved in the organization.

In contrast to the typical one-way communication of the lecturer, the skills instructor in the classroom encourages high levels of discussion and interaction among trainees, develops a climate in which trainees learn new behavior from carrying out various activities, clarifies related information, and facilitates learning by eliciting trainees' job-related knowledge and experience in applying that knowledge. The difference between the instructional role in information dissemination and the instructional role in skill development is dramatic.[37]

Evaluating the Training Program After the training program has been completed, management should evaluate its effectiveness.[38] Because training programs represent an investment—costs include materials, trainer time, and production loss while employees are being trained rather than doing their jobs—a reasonable return is essential.

Basically, management should evaluate the training program to determine whether it meets the needs for which it was designed. Answers to questions such as the following help determine training program effectiveness:

1. Has the excessive reject rate of products declined?
2. Are deadlines being met more regularly?
3. Are labor costs per unit produced decreasing?

If the answer to such questions is yes, the training program can be judged as at least somewhat successful, though perhaps its effectiveness could be enhanced through certain selective changes. If the answer is no, significant modification to the training program is warranted.

In a noteworthy survey of businesspeople, 50 percent of respondents thought their sales per year would be unaffected if training programs for experienced salespeople were halted.[39] Management needs to seek and scrutinize this kind of feedback to see whether present training programs should be discontinued, slightly modified, or drastically altered to make them more valuable to the organization. The results of the survey just mentioned indicate a need to make significant changes in sales training programs at the companies covered by the survey.

Performance Appraisal

Even after individuals have been recruited, selected, and trained, the task of making them maximally productive within the organization is not finished. The fourth step in the process of providing appropriate human resources for the organization is **performance appraisal**—the process of reviewing individuals' past productive activity to evaluate the contribution they have made toward attaining management system objectives. Like training, performance appraisal—which is also called *performance review* and *performance evaluation*—is a continuing activity that focuses on both established human resources within the organization and newcomers. Its main purpose is to furnish feedback to organization members about how they can become more productive and useful to the organization in its quest for quality.[40] Table 13.2 describes several methods of performance appraisal.

Why Use Performance Appraisals? Most U.S. firms engage in some type of performance appraisal. Douglas McGregor has suggested the following three reasons for using performance appraisals:[41]

1. They provide systematic judgments to support salary increases, promotions, transfers, and sometimes demotions or terminations.

TABLE 13.2 Descriptions of Several Methods of Performance Appraisal

Appraisal Method	Description
Rating scale	Individuals appraising performance use a form containing several employee qualities and characteristics to be evaluated (e.g., dependability, initiative, leadership). Each evaluated factor is rated on a continuum or scale ranging, for example, from 1 to 7.
Employee comparisons	Appraisers rank employees according to such factors as job performance and value to organization. Only one employee can occupy a particular ranking. This method is also known as a "forced distribution" or "forced ranking" system.[42]
Free-form essay	Appraisers simply write down their impressions of employees in paragraph form.
Critical-form essay	Appraisers write down particularly good or bad events involving employees as these events occur. Records of all documented events for any one employee are used to evaluate that person's performance.

Performance appraisals provide feedback to organization members that can help them become more productive in their jobs. Managers who rely on day-to-day observation of employees, as this manager does, can accumulate needed evidence to back up their appraisals.

2. They are a means of telling subordinates how they are doing and of suggesting needed changes in behavior, attitudes, skills, or job knowledge; they let subordinates know where they stand with the boss.

3. They furnish a useful basis for the coaching and counseling of individuals by superiors.

class discussion highlight

MODERN RESEARCH AND HUMAN RESOURCES SKILL

The Timing of Job Offers

Receiving a job offer is always an exciting event for an individual. At the same time, extending a job offer is an important commitment from an organization. While many students worry about receiving job offers, very few consider job offers from the organization's perspective. When an organization extends an offer, human resource managers want to do everything they can to ensure the individual accepts their offer. A very important issue for organizations and organizational researchers, then, involves understanding how to increase the likelihood that individuals accept job offers.

To better understand this issue, Professors Becker, Connolly, and Slaughter examined how the timing of an offer (i.e., how long after the candidate's interview) influenced an individual's likelihood of accepting the job offer. To answer this question, the researchers analyzed more than 3,000 job offers made by one large organization over time. The sample of job offers included both those made to students as well as those extended to more experienced candidates. Do you think that the timing of an offer (e.g., offers made quickly after an interview versus those made long after an interview) influenced the likelihood of an individual accepting the offer? Do you think this differed among the two sets of individuals (e.g., students vs. experienced workers)? Why or why not?

Source: William Becker, Terry Connolly, and Jerel Slaughter, "The Effect of Job Offer Timing on Offer Acceptance, Performance, and Turnover," *Personnel Psychology*, 63 (2010): 223–241.

Handling Performance Appraisals If performance appraisals are not handled well, their benefits to the organization will be minimal.[43] Several guidelines can assist management in increasing the appropriateness with which appraisals are conducted. The first guideline is that performance appraisals should stress performance in the position the individual holds and the success with which the individual is attaining organizational objectives. Although conceptually separate, performance and objectives should be inseparable topics of discussion during performance appraisals. The second guideline is that appraisals should emphasize how well the individual is doing the job, not the evaluator's impression of the individual's work habits. In other words, the goal is an objective analysis of performance rather than a subjective evaluation of habits.

The third guideline is the appraisal should be acceptable to both the evaluator and the subject—that is, both should agree that it has benefit for the organization and the worker. The fourth, and last, guideline is performance appraisals should provide a base for improving individuals' productivity within the organization by making them better equipped to produce.[44]

Potential Weaknesses of Performance Appraisals To maximize the payoff of performance appraisals to the organization, managers must avoid several potential weaknesses of the appraisal process, including the following pitfalls:[45]

1. Performance appraisals focus employees on short-term rewards rather than on issues that are important to the long-run success of the organization.
2. Individuals involved in performance appraisals view them as a reward–punishment situation.
3. The emphasis of performance appraisal is on completing paperwork rather than on critiquing individual performance.
4. Individuals being evaluated view the process as unfair or biased.
5. Subordinates react negatively when evaluators offer unfavorable comments.

To avoid these potential weaknesses, supervisors and employees should look on the performance appraisal process as an opportunity to increase the worth of the employee through constructive feedback, not as a means of rewarding or punishing the employee through positive or negative comments. Paperwork should be viewed only as an aid in providing this feedback, not as an end in itself. Also, care should be taken to make appraisal feedback as tactful and objective as possible to minimize negative reactions.

---

how managers do it

Using a New Performance Appraisal System at Aetna

In the spirit of continuous improvement, executives at Aetna recently changed the company's performance appraisal system. The former system, which was paper-based, required a great deal of time to complete; as such, many managers did not have the time needed to appraise their employees. Aetna's new system, however, uses technology that constantly allows managers to assess their employees. At any time, managers can access a dashboard that allows them to assess employee skills, evaluate career growth, and suggest training needs. The new plan seems to work. In a recent poll, 83 percent of Aetna's employees reported that they understood how they contribute to the company's goals. Just a few years earlier, less than 60 percent of the company's employees understood their contributions.[46] ■

CHALLENGE CASE SUMMARY

After training needs at Cisco have been determined and programs have been designed to meet those needs, the programs must be administered. Administering training programs at Cisco might involve the lecture technique as well as the programmed learning technique for transmitting information to trainees. For actually developing skills in trainees, Cisco could use on-the-job training methods, such as coaching, position rotation, or special project committees. For developing skills in a classroom setting, Cisco could use instructional techniques, such as role-playing activities. For example, salespeople could be asked to handle customers with various kinds of needs and budgets. These situations then could be analyzed from the viewpoint of how to improve salespeople–customer relationships.

Once a Cisco training program has been completed, it must be evaluated to determine whether it met the training need for which it was designed. Training programs aimed at specific skills such as computer programming would be much easier to evaluate than would training programs aimed at interpersonal skills such as developing customer relations. The evaluation of any training program at Cisco of course, should emphasize how to improve the program the next time it is implemented.

In hiring new employees for an operation like Cisco, management must be careful to emphasize not just hiring workers, but hiring the right workers. For Cisco, appropriate human resources are those people who will make a valuable contribution to the attainment of the company's organizational objectives. In hiring engineers, managers, salespeople, and administrative assistants, for example, management should consider hiring only those people who will best help the organization become successful. In finding appropriate human resources, management at Cisco has to follow four basic steps: (1) recruitment, (2) selection, (3) training, and (4) performance appraisal.

Basically, recruitment would entail the initial screening of individuals available to fill open positions at Cisco. For recruitment efforts to be successful, recruiters have to know the jobs they are trying to fill, where potential human resources can be located, and how the law influences recruiting efforts.

Recruiters could acquire an understanding of open positions at a company such as Cisco by performing a job analysis. The job analysis would force them to determine the job description of the open position—the activities of an engineer, programmer, salesperson, for example—and the job specification of the position, including the type of individual who should be hired to fill that position.

A successful recruitment effort at Cisco would require recruiters to know where to locate the available human resources to fill open positions at Cisco. These sources may be both within Cisco and outside it.

To ensure that Cisco maintains its position as one of the best technology companies in the world, management must plan for obtaining needed appropriate human resources along with other resources like equipment and real estate. To do this, management can keep current on the possibilities of filling positions from within by maintaining some type of human resource inventory. This inventory can help management organize information about the organizational histories and potential of various Cisco employees as well as the relative abilities of various Cisco employees to fill the necessary openings. Some of the sources of potential human resources outside Cisco that management could be aware of are competitors, public and private employment agencies, the reader of industry-related publications, and various types of educational institutions. As mentioned in the case, Cisco went to great lengths to attract employees from 3Com, one of its main competitors.

Cisco management must also be aware of how the law influences its recruitment efforts. Basically, the law says that Cisco recruitment practices cannot discriminate on the basis of race, color, religion, sex, or national origin. If recruitment practices at Cisco are found to be discriminatory, the company is subject to prosecution by the Equal Employment Opportunity Commission.

After the initial screening of potential human resources, Cisco will be faced with the task of selecting the individuals to be hired from those who have been screened. Two tools that Cisco could use to help in this selection process are testing and assessment centers.

For example, after screening potential employees for positions at Cisco, management could use aptitude tests, achievement tests, vocational interest tests, or personality tests to see whether any of the individuals screened had the qualities necessary to work a specific job. In using these tests, however, management must make sure the tests are both valid and reliable, that they are not the sole basis on which a selection decision is made, and that they are nondiscriminatory.

Cisco can also use assessment centers to simulate the tasks necessary to perform jobs that workers will be performing. Individuals who performed well on these tasks would probably be more appropriate for the positions than would those who did poorly. The use of assessment centers might be particularly appropriate in evaluating applicants for sales positions. Simulating this job would probably give management an excellent idea of how prospective salespeople would actually interact with customers during sales presentations.

After hiring, Cisco must train new employees, including those simply transferred to new locations within the company, to be productive organization members. To train effectively, Cisco must determine training needs, design a corresponding training program, and administer and evaluate the training program.

Designing a training program requires that Cisco assemble facts and activities that address specific company training needs. These needs are information or skill areas that must be further developed in Cisco employees to make them more productive. Over the long term, training at Cisco should focus on more established employees, employees transferred within the company, and employees hired outside the company.

As mentioned in the case, Cisco historically has used acquisitions to gain new employees. In these situations, management should probably try to learn as much as possible about the training programs employees went through at the acquired companies. Knowing the strengths and weakness of training programs at such companies would probably help management at Cisco understand what further training, if any, these employees need to work effectively.

The last step in providing appropriate human resources at Cisco is performance appraisal through which the contributions Cisco employees make toward

the attainment of management system objectives must be evaluated. Because of Cisco's rapid expansion, employees will have various levels of experience at Cisco. As such, the performance appraisal process at Cisco should focus on newer as well as more established employees.

It would be difficult to visualize a Cisco employee who could not benefit from a properly conducted performance appraisal. Such an appraisal would stress activities on the job and effectiveness in accomplishing job objectives. An objective appraisal would provide Cisco employees with tactful, constructive criticism that should help increase their productivity. Handled properly, Cisco's appraisals would not be a reward or a punishment in themselves, but an opportunity to increase value to the company. Objective analysis of performance in a company such as Cisco should help employees become more productive over time rather than being without guidance and perhaps moving toward the inevitable outcome of being fired. Overall, if these performance appraisal issues are addressed at Cisco, as well as issues related to recruitment, selection, and training, management should be successful in providing appropriate human resources for the company.

MANAGEMENT SKILL ACTIVITIES

This section is specially designed to help you develop human resource management skill. An individual's management skill is based on an understanding of management concepts and the ability to apply those concepts in management situations. As a result, the following activities are designed both to heighten your understanding of human resource management concepts and to help you gain facility in applying these concepts in various management situations.

UNDERSTANDING HUMAN RESOURCE MANAGEMENT CONCEPTS

 To check your understanding and to practice using the concepts in this chapter, go to www.mymanagementlab.com and explore the material associated with Chapter 13.

Know Key Terms

Understanding the following key terms is critical to your understanding of chapter material. Define each of these terms. Refer to the page(s) referenced after a term to check your definition or to gain further insight regarding the term.

Know How Management Concepts Relate

This section is comprised of activities that will further sharpen your understanding of management concepts. Answer essay questions as completely as possible. Also, remember that many additional true/false and multiple choice questions appear online at MyManagementLab.com to help you further refine your understanding of management concepts.

1. Describe the four steps in the human resource management process. In your opinion, which step is most important? Explain.

2. Compare and contrast the three types of records used to record an organization's human resource inventory.

3. Review and describe the different types of tests organizations might use in the selection process.

4. Describe the four main steps in the training process. In your view, how important is the training process for organizations?

5. What are performance appraisals, and why are they important? Use an example from your life to illustrate either an effective or ineffective performance appraisal.

DEVELOPING MANAGEMENT SKILLS

Learning activities in this section are aimed at helping you develop your human resource management skill. Learning activities include Exploring Your Management Skill: Parts 1 and 2, Experiential Exercises, Cases, and a VideoNet Exercise.

Exploring Your Management Skill: Part 1

Before studying this chapter, respond to the following questions regarding the type of advice you would give to Cisco's John Chambers referenced in the Challenge Case. Then address the concerning human resource management challenges that he presently faces within the company. You are not expected to be a human resource management expert at this point. Answering the questions now can help you focus on important points when you study the chapter. Also, answering the questions again after you study the chapter will give you an idea of how much you have learned.

Record your answers here or go to MyManagementLab.com. Recording your answers in MyManagementLab will allow you to get immediate results and see how your score compares to your classmates. If you answer the questions in the book, the answers are located in the Exploring Your Management Skill Appendix at the end of the book.

FOR EACH STATEMENT CIRCLE:

- "Y" if you would give the advice to John Chambers.
- "N" if you would NOT give the advice to John Chambers.
- "NI" if you have no idea whether you would give the advice to John Chambers.

Mr. Chambers, in meeting your human resource management challenges at Cisco, you should...

Before   After
Study   Study

1. focus on hiring and retaining both appropriate and inappropriate human resources.
   Y, N, NI

2. recognize the three steps in the human resource management process: recruitment, selection, and training.
   Y, N, NI

3. focus primarily on hiring employees first and then work with the newly hired employees to define their jobs.
   Y, N, NI

4. understand that job openings may be filled by individuals who work within Cisco as well as other individuals who do not work at Cisco.
   Y, N, NI

5. rely on human resource inventory techniques such as the management inventory card, position replacement form, and management manpower replacement chart to monitor Cisco's human resources.
   Y, N, NI

6. understand that Cisco can choose potential employees based on race, color, religion, and gender for hiring, firing, and layoff policies.
   Y, N, NI

7. rely exclusively on personality tests—and not aptitude or achievement tests—in the selection process.
   Y, N, NI

8. focus on valid tests in the selection process and not worry as much about test reliability.
   Y, N, NI

9. understand that training is typically an ongoing activity, whereby individuals are trained multiple times throughout their careers at Cisco.
   Y, N, NI

10. employ both lectures and programmed learning as techniques for training Cisco employees.
    Y, N, NI

11. evaluate Cisco's training program periodically to assess its effectiveness.
    Y, N, NI

12. use performance appraisals to support salary increases but rely on other techniques for promotions, demotions, and terminations.
    Y, N, NI

13. performance appraisals should focus primarily on the evaluator's impression of the employee's performance and not on objective measures of the employee's performance.
    Y, N, NI

14. performance appraisals should focus on both short-term and long-term measures of the employee's performance.
    Y, N, NI

15. individuals involved with the performance appraisal process should view the process as a punishment-reward situation.
    Y, N, NI

Exploring Your Management Skill: Part 2

As you recall, you completed Exploring Your Management Skill before you started to study this chapter. Your responses gave you an idea of how much you initially knew about human resource management and helped you focus on important points as you studied the chapter. Answer the Exploring Your Management Skill questions again now and compare your score to the first time you took it. This comparison will give you an idea of how much you learned from studying this chapter and pinpoint areas for further clarification before you start studying the next chapter. Record your answers within the text or go to MyManagementLab.com. Recording your answers in MyManagementLab will allow you to get immediate results and see how your score compares to your classmates. If you answer the questions in the book, the answers are located in the Exploring Your Management Skill Appendix at the end of the book.

Your Management Skills Portfolio

Your Management Learning Portfolio is a collection of activities especially designed to demonstrate your management knowledge and skill. By completing these activities online at MyManagementLab.com, you will be able to print, complete with cover sheet, as many activities as you choose. Be sure to save your work. Taking your printed portfolio to an employment interview could be helpful in obtaining a job.

The portfolio activity for this chapter is Designing a Human Resource Management Program at Room & Board. Study the information and complete the exercises that follow.[47]

Room & Board is a furniture retailer based in Minneapolis. Although the company operates only a limited number of locations, customers have flocked to Room & Board stores to purchase sleek furniture. Resulting from customer demand, the company recently introduced an annual "cata-zine" and also introduced a Web site to fulfill online orders. As a result of its success, a number of investors are encouraging Room & Board's founder, John Gabbert, to expand its locations quickly.

Despite Room & Board's success, Gabbert is somewhat concerned that a rapid expansion of the company will damage the company's human resources policies and procedures. Currently, the organization's culture is positive, and the relatively flat organizational structure provides employees with high levels of authority and responsibility, which most find important. Moreover, the company encourages employees to work smarter—not harder—and encourages employees to only work 40 hours per week.

Gabbert has asked you to provide an analysis of the human resources policies at Room & Board. In particular, he is interested in learning more about how growth will influence a small company's human resource function. To help him better understand the situation, use the knowledge you have developed through this chapter to answer the questions.

1. How will growth influence a Room & Board's *recruitment* polices?

2. How will growth influence Room & Board's *selection* policies?

3. How will growth influence Room & Board's *training* policies?

4. How will growth influence Room & Board's *performance appraisal* system?

5. Write a job description for a sales associate position at Room & Board.

Experiential Exercises

1 Determining Training Needs at Wal-Mart

Directions. Read the following scenario and then perform the listed activities. Your instructor may want you to perform the activities as an individual or within groups. Follow all of your instructor's directions carefully.

Wal-Mart and Dell recently reached an agreement to sell Dell computers to customers in Wal-Mart stores. However, top executives at Wal-Mart and Dell are somewhat concerned, because most of Wal-Mart's sales associates do not have any experience selling computers.

As such, Wal-Mart has contacted your group to help design the training program that will be used in all Wal-Mart locations. Specifically, the executives want you to determine the training needs, which is the first step in the training process. Your group should describe the process you would use to determine these training needs. Assume that Wal-Mart

and Dell will give you the resources necessary to implement your process (i.e., access to employees, managers, etc.). Also, rely on your own experiences with purchasing and using personal computers to describe some of the training needs from a customer's perspective.

2 You and Your Career

The beginning of the chapter distinguished between appropriate and inappropriate human resources and implied that employees should focus on demonstrating how they contribute to the organization's goals. The previous section suggests that training can help employees improve their job skills. How might training influence whether your employer (or future employer) considers you an "appropriate" human resource? How might your view of the training process affect your performance as an employee?

VideoNet Exercise

Human Resources at KPMG

Video Highlights

Employees stick around when they see a bright future ahead of them. To amp up the perceived wattage for employees looking down the road, KPMG designed interactive software called Employee Career Architecture (ECA). Using this tool, someone in accounting who is beginning to doubt his or her passion for number-crunching can explore new functions and jobs within the company and choose to participate in a rotation, which allows him or her to sample options firsthand. People can see where different tracks lead in terms of their earning potential, and they can see what kinds of skills they'll need to develop to continue moving upward.

Discussion Questions

1. What are some of the challenges faced by KPMG in trying to recruit employees from outside the organization? How do these impact the external recruiting sources?

2. How does the Employee Career Architecture program used by KPMG differ from a more traditional performance appraisal system?

3. How does KPMG use its career program to help determine training needs?

Internet Activity

Go to the KPMG Web site at www.kpmg.com. How does KPMG use its company Web site as a recruiting tool? Which of the external recruiting sources would most likely be attracted to the information provided on the site?

CASES

1 CISCO RECRUITS THE BEST MINDS IN CHINA

"Cisco Recruits the Best Minds in China" (p. 295) and its related Challenge Case Summary were written to help you better understand the management concepts contained in this chapter. Answer the following discussion questions about the Challenge Case to better see how your understanding of managing human resources can be applied in a company such as Cisco.

1. How important is the training of employees to an organization such as Cisco? Explain.

2. What actions besides training must an organization such as Cisco take to make employees as productive as possible?

3. Based on information in the case, what do you think will be the biggest challenge for Cisco management in successfully providing appropriate human resources for the organization? Explain.

2 HOW RAISING CANE'S USES SOCIAL MEDIA TO ATTRACT CANDIDATES

Read the case and answer the questions that follow. Studying this case will help you better understand how concepts relating to recruiting can be applied in a company such as Raising Cane's.

Recruiting new employees in the restaurant industry has certainly changed in the last five to ten years. Very recently, a restaurant manager could simply put a "help wanted" sign on the door and it was sufficient to garner candidates for everything from server and busboy to cook and general manager.

But recruiting opportunities are more challenging now and one restaurant chain that has embraced the latest forms of recruiting is Raising Cane's Chicken Fingers. Founded by Todd Graves, the Louisiana-based company is named after Graves' pet dog.

Graves' story is that of the driven entrepreneur. His vision of a restaurant devoted to chicken fingers was met with disdain—even his college professor said it was a terrible idea and gave his business plan the worst grade in the class. Graves, though, held on to his vision. Attempting to garner enough money to start his first restaurant, he took jobs as a boilermaker in a refinery and even took on 20-hour workdays for a commercial fishery off the coast of Alaska. Finally, he had enough money and a business plan to convince a lender to front him the funds to open Raising Cane's Chicken Fingers.

Today, the chain has nearly 100 stores. Keeping all those locations fully staffed is an ongoing endeavor, and as more locations are added to the chain, the recruiting effort becomes even greater.

Graves believes strongly in the type of employee he is seeking. He wants individuals who have fun while getting their jobs done. "The people who work behind the register and in the kitchen are a little crazy," Graves acknowledged. "They love what they do for a living. They work hard and play hard. They take pride in what they do."[48]

So how does a successful and growing restaurant chain recruit the best employees it can find? It uses many tactics, but its use of social media is among the strongest in the industry. Utilizing Facebook, Twitter, and YouTube, the chain attempts to reach candidates through the venues they use most often.

On Raising Cane's Facebook page, individuals can readily discover what job opportunities are available. This is an especially important means of connecting with job candidates because most likely, they would not be visiting Raising Cane's Facebook page if they were not already a loyal fan of the chain. "It goes without saying," said Graves, "that I get very excited as more and more people want to know about Raising Cane's. I love seeing my dream and the dream of our crew, become a reality everyday. It's wonderful bringing great people together to grow something truly great."[49]

Also, photos of employees and store locations can be found on the Facebook page. Caniacs—the very loyal fans of the restaurant—make comments on Facebook, with praises for good food and great service. All this serves to blend both marketing and recruiting in a seamless fashion. The idea is that if customers really enjoy the restaurant, they may also find a career there.

The chain posts videos on YouTube to showcase not only the menu offerings, but opportunities to work at the restaurant as well. One such video is over a minute and a half long and gives a straightforward description of what it is like to work at Raising Cane's. A casual dress code permitting jeans is emphasized, but so is the opportunity to earn a solid income. Also, the video highlights career path opportunities, including how one can start as a cashier or server and work one's way to a general manager position. Overall, the YouTube video features the relaxed and fun working environment of Raising Cane's and it gives specific instructions on how to apply for a variety of jobs with the chain.

Successful restaurateurs like Graves have realized the importance of social media, whether it be for marketing or recruiting talent. Attracting the right candidates for jobs is critical, especially at a firm that relies so heavily on positive customer contact. Fortunately, Grave's enthusiasm permeates everything the company does—opening new locations, overseeing the marketing of the chain, or making certain the best candidates are hired. "This isn't my job," said Graves. "It's my passion."[50]

QUESTIONS

1. How important is social media such as Facebook, Twitter, and YouTube in attracting qualified candidates for jobs? Explain.

2. If a company were to rely exclusively on social media as a recruiting tool, what challenges would it encounter? What would you recommend to overcome these challenges?

3. Based on what you just read, is Raising Cane's the kind of organization for which you would enjoy working? Why or why not?

Endnotes

1. This case was based on Bruce Einhorn, "The Shanghai Scramble," *BusinessWeek*, August 20, 2007, 53; and Bruce Einhorn, "Selling Cisco to China's Tech Talent Pool," *BusinessWeek Online*, September 18, 2007, 23. A recent study of successful mid- and senior-level executives in China provides additional insight into developing high-performing leaders for emerging markets. See Jean Lee, "Emerging Need," *MIT Sloan Management Review*, May 24, 2010, http://sloanreview.mit.edu.

2. For an interesting discussion on how organizations can retain their best executives, see Elizabeth Craig, John R. Kimberly, and Peter Cheese, "How to Keep Your Best Executives," *MIT Sloan Management Review*, October 22, 2009, http://sloanreview. mit.edu.

3. To see how the performance of these steps can be shared in an organization, see Brenda Paik Sunoo, "Growing without an HR Department" *Workforce* 77, no. 1 (January 1998): 16–17. For a review of effective recruitment techniques, see Daniel Bates, "Do You Have Great People?: Roadshow Recruitment," *SBN Pittsburgh* 7, no. 10 (February 1, 2001): 32.

4. Jamie Minier, "Here Today, Gone Tomorrow: Keeping up with the Current State of Recruiting," *Workplace Management*, July 2009, http://www.workforce.com.

5. For a look at job descriptions, see Jeff Archer, "New Job Description?" *Education Week* 22 (2003): 18. For another view, see Man-Ki Yoon, Chang-Gun Lee, and Junghee Han, "Migrating from Per-Job Analysis to Per-Resource Analysis for Tighter Bounds of End-to-End Response Times," *IEEE Transactions on Computers* 59, no. 7 (July 2010): 933–942.

6. Bruce Shawkey, "Job Descriptions," *Credit Union Executive* 29 (Winter 1989–1990): 20–23; Howard D. Feldman, "Why Are Similar Managerial Jobs So Different?" *Review of Business* 11 (Winter 1989): 15–22.

7. "Job Analysis," *Bureau of Intergovernmental Personnel Programs*, December 1973, 135–152; Gundars E. Kaupins, "Lies, Damn Lies, and Job Evaluations," *Personnel* 66 (November 1989): 62–65; Jim Meade, "Identifying Criteria for Success Helps in Making Effective Hiring Decisions," *HR Magazine* 43, no. 5 (April 1998): 49–50.

8. James H. Martin and Elizabeth B. Franz, "Attracting Applicants from a Changing Labor Market: A Strategic Marketing Framework," *Journal of Managerial Issues* (Spring 1994): 33–53.

9. Fred K. Foulkes, "How Top Nonunion Companies Manage Employees," *Harvard Business Review* (September/October 1981): 90.

10. Walter S. Wikstrom, "Developing Managerial Competence: Concepts, Emerging Practices," *Studies in Personnel Policy*, no. 189, National Industrial Conference Board (1964): 95–105.

11. Robert Kleinsorge, "Expanding the Role of Succession Planning," *T+D* 64, vol. 4 (April 2010): 66–69.

12. Richard Verrier and James Bates, "Eisner's Heir Far from Apparent at Disney," *Orlando Sentinel*, December 8, 2003: A1, A10.

13. Patricia Panchak, "Resourceful Software Boosts HR Efficiency," *Modern Office Technology* 35 (April 1990): 76–80.

14. James Temple, "Alliance to Boost Startups, Hire More Grads," *SFGate.com*, February 24, 2010, http://articles.sfgate.com.

15. For discussion of recent EEOC guidelines on discrimination, see Diane Hatch, James Hall and Mark Kobata, "New EEOC Guidance on National-Origin Discrimination," *Workforce* 82 (2003): 76.

16. For issues regarding affirmative action, see Glenn Cook, "A Victory for Affirmative Action," *American School Board Journal* 190 (2003): 7. For more information regarding the potential legal issues associated with discrimination, see Richard A. Posthuma, Mark V. Roehling, and Michael A. Campion. "Applying U.S. employment discrimination laws to international employers: Advice for scientists and practitioners." *Personnel Psychology* 59, no. 3 (2006): 705–739. For a history of employment discrimination, including affirmative action, see Walter Vertreace, "Equal Employment Opportunity: Mission Accomplished, or Dream Deferred?" *Black Collegian* 40, no. 2 (January 2010): 57–60.

17. Ray H. Hodges, "Developing an Effective Affirmative Action Program," *Journal of Intergroup Relations* 5 (November 1976): 13. For a discussion of EEOC operations, see Ellen Rettig, "EEOC Gets Tough with Employers," *Indianapolis Business Journal* 20, no. 46 (January 24, 2000): 1.

18. R. Roosevelt Thomas, Jr., "From Affirmative Action to Affirming Diversity," *Harvard Business Review* 68 (March/April 1990): 107–117. For a recent article supporting the notion of affirmative action, see Albert R. Hunt, "A Persuasive Case for Affirmative Action," *Wall Street Journal*, February 1, 2001, A23.

19. For a different view of generational differences among those entering the workforce, Jean M. Twenge, Stacy M. Campbell, Brian J. Hoffman, and Charles E. Lance, "Generational Differences in Work Values: Leisure and Extrinsic Values Increasing, Social and Intrinsic Values Decreasing," *Journal of Management*, March 1, 2010, http://jom.sagepub.com.

20. For more discussion of the stages of the selection process, see David J. Cherrington, *Personnel Management: The Management of Human Resources* (Dubuque, IA: Wm. C. Brown, 1987), 186–231. For an interesting study examining the perceived fairness of selection processes, see Deidra J. Schleicher, Vijaya Venkataramani, Frederick P. Morgeson, and Michael A. Campion. "So you didn't get the job…Now what do you think? Examining opportunity-to-perform fairness perceptions," *Personnel Psychology* 59, no. 3 (2006): 559–590.

21. This section is based on Andrew F. Sikula, *Personnel Administration and Human Resource Management* (New York: Wiley, 1976), 188–190. For an overview of the potential errors involved with selection, see Herman Aguinis and Marlene A. Smith, "Understanding the impact of test validity and bias on selection errors and adverse impact in human resource selection," *Personnel Psychology* 60, no. 1 (2007): 165–199.

22. For an example of an aptitude test for accident proneness, see Hiroshi Matsuoka, "Development of a Short Test for Accident Proneness," *Perceptual and Motor Skills* 85, no. 3 (December 1997): 903–906.

23. Daniel P. O'Meara, "Personality Tests Raise Questions of Legality and Effectiveness," *HR Magazine*, January 1994, 97–100. See also Joyce Hogan, Paul Barrett, and Robert Hogan, "Personality Measurement, Faking, and Employment Selection," *Journal of Applied Psychology* 92, no. 5 (2007): 1270–1285. For a study on the value of personality test norms, see Robert Tett, Jenna Fitzke, Patrick Wadlington, Scott Davies, Michael Anderson, and Jeff Foster, "The use of personality test norms in work settings: Effects of sample size and relevance," *Journal of Occupational & Organizational Psychology* 82, no. 3 (September 2009): 639–659.

24. Clive Fletcher, "Testing the Accuracy of Psychometric Measures," *People Management* 3, no. 21 (October 23, 1997): 64–66. For a discussion of EEOC guidelines concerning appropriate pre-employment testing for Americans with disabilities, see Melanie K. St. Clair and David W. Arnold, "Preemployment Screening: No More Test Stress," *Security Management* (February 1995): 73.

25. Julie McCarthy, Coreen Hrabluik, and R. Blake Jelley, "Progression Through the Ranks: Assessing Employee Reactions to High-Stakes Employment Testing." *Personnel Psychology*, 62 (2009): 793–832.

26. David Littlefield, "Menu for Change at Novotel," *People Management* (January 26, 1995): 34–36; Susan O. Hendricks and Susan E. Ogborn, "Supervisory and Managerial Assessment Centers in Health Care," *Health Care Supervisor* 8 (April 1990): 65–75.

27. Barry M. Cohen, "Assessment Centers," *Supervisory Management* (June 1975): 30. See also Paul Taylor, "Seven Staff Selection Myths," *Management* 45, no. 4 (May 1998): 61–65.

28. To examine the possible impact of assessment centers for inmates, see Ralph Fretz, "New Jersey's Assessment Centers Helping Inmates Take the Final Step Toward Release," *Corrections Today* 64 (2002): 78.

29. A. M. Gibbons and D. E. Rupp, "Dimension Consistency as an Individual Difference: A New (Old) Perspective on the Assessment Center Construct Validity Debate." *Journal of Management*, 35 (2009): 1154–1180.

30. William Umiker and Thomas Conlin, "Assessing the Need for Supervisory Training: Use of Performance Appraisals," *Health Care Supervisor* 8 (January 1990): 40–45. For a look at innovative training techniques, see Rob Eure, "E-Commerce (A Special Report): The Classroom—On the Job: Corporate E-Learning Makes Training Available Anytime, Anywhere," *Wall Street Journal*, March 12, 2001, R33.

31. Jim Schakenbach, "Employee Training Programs Show Signs of Improvement," *Mass High Tech*, January 6, 2010, http://www.masshightech.com.

32. Bass and Vaughn, *Training in Industry*. For discussion on using technology to improve lecture effectiveness, see "Switches Offer Classroom Control," *Computer Dealer News* 14, no. 17 (May 4, 1998): 58.

33. David Sutton, "Further Thoughts on Action Learning," *Journal of European Industrial Training* 13 (1989): 32–35. For further information regarding the relationship between training and learning, see Andrew Neal, Stuart T. Godley, Terry Kirkpatrick, and Graham Dewsnap, "An Examination of Learning Processes During Critical Incident Training: Implications for the Development of Adaptable Trainees," *Journal of Applied Psychology* 91, no. 6 (2007): 1276–1291.

34. Garry Kranz, "It's 'Game On' for Training in Virtual Worlds," *Workforce Management*, May 2010, 4.

35. Anne Fisher, "Don't Blow Your New Job," *Fortune*, June 22, 1998: 159–162.

36. For an example of how training improves the effectiveness of consultants, see F. Lievens and J. I. Sanchez, "Can training improve the quality of inferences made by raters in competency modeling? A quasi-experiment," *Journal of Applied Psychology* 92, no. 3 (2007): 812–819.

37. Samuel C. Certo, "The Experiential Exercise Situation: A Comment on Instructional Role and Pedagogy Evaluation," *Academy of Management Review* (July 1976): 113–116. For a worthwhile discussion of the advantages of facilitation over lecturing for overcoming trainee resistance to learning, see Margaret Kaeter, "Coping with Resistant Trainees," *Training* 31 (1994): 110–114.

38. "Training Program's Results Measured in Unique Way," *Supervision* (February 1992): 18–19.

39. William Keenan Jr., "Are You Overspending on Training?" *Sales and Marketing Management* 142 (January 1990): 56–60.

40. For a review of the literature linking performance appraisal and training needs, see Glenn Herbert and Dennis Doverspike, "Performance Appraisal in the Training Needs Analysis Process: A Review and Critique," *Public Personnel Management* (Fall 1990): 253–270. See also Mike Deblieux, "Performance Reviews Support the Quest for Quality," *HR Focus* (November 1991): 3–4. For a discussion on how performance appraisals can cause undesirable consequences, see Anne Jefferson, "Performance Appraisal Applied to Leadership," *Educational Studies* 36, no. 1 (February 2010): 111–114.

41. This highlight was based on Charlotte Fritz and Sabine Sonnentag. "Recovery, well-being, and performance-related outcomes: The role of workload and vacation experiences," *Journal of Applied Psychology* 91, no. 4 (2006): 936–945.

42. A "forced distribution" or "forced ranking" rating system was put in place at General Electric years ago, and its value has been the subject of some debate ever since. For the findings of a study of employees' reactions to this methodology, see Deidra J. Schleicher, "Rater Reactions

to Forced Distribution Rating Systems," *Journal of Management* 35, no. 4 (August 1, 2009): 899–927.

43. For information regarding the role of documentation in handling performance appraisals, see Brian Crawford, "Performance Appraisals: The Importance of Documentation," *Fire Engineering* 156 (2003): 100; see also Audrey Bland, "Motivate and Reward: Performance Appraisal and Incentive Systems for Business Success," *Human Resource Management Journal* 14 (2004): 99–100.

44. Linda J. Segall, "KISS Appraisal Woes Goodbye," *Supervisory Management* 34 (December 1989): 23–28. To see an example of how appraisal systems work for not-for-profits (in this case, a police department), see Victor M Catano, Wendy Darr, and Catherine A. Campbell, "Performance Appraisal of Behavior-Based Competencies: A Reliable and Valid Procedure," *Personnel Psychology* 60, no. 1 (2006): 201–230.

45. Robert M. Gerst, "Assessing Organizational Performance," *Quality Progress* (February 1995): 85–88. See also George A. Rider, "Performance Review: A Mixed Bag," *Harvard Business Review* (July/August 1973): 61–67; Robert Loo, "Quality Performance Appraisals," *Canadian Manager* 14 (December 1989): 24–26.

46. Michael Myser, "Bosses Get a Helping Hand," *Business 2.0* 8, no. 6 (July 2007): 31.

47. This exercise was based on the company's Web site as well as Jena McGregor, "Room & Board Plays Impossible to Get," *BusinessWeek*, October 1, 2007, 80.

48. www.raisingcane.com

49. Ibid.

50. King, Paul. "Raising Cane's Chicken Fingers Seeing the Big Picture by Implementing a Vision." *Nation's Restaurant News* 37, no. 19 (2003): 56.

chapter 14

Organizational Change

STRESS, CONFLICT, AND VIRTUALITY

Target Skill

organizational change skill: the ability to modify an organization in order to enhance its contribution to reaching company goals

objectives

To help build my *organizational change skill,* when studying this chapter, I will attempt to acquire:

1. A working definition of *changing an organization*

2. An understanding of the relative importance of change and stability to an organization

3. Some ability to recognize what kinds of changes should be made within an organization

4. An appreciation for why the people affected by a change

should be considered when the change is being made

5. Some facility at evaluating change

6. An understanding of how organizational change and stress are related

7. Insights concerning how to handle conflict as a factor related to organizational change

8. Knowledge about virtuality as a vehicle for organizational change

CHALLENGE CASE

WRIGLEY CONTINUES TO CHANGE

The WILLIAM WRIGLEY JR. COMPANY manufactures and markets chewing gum and other confectionary products to more than 150 countries and territories. The Wrigley Company's primary business involves chewing gum and other similar products. Wrigley Company began in 1891 as a soap and baking soda manufacturer that gave away chewing gum as a promotion.

In time, the company became publicly traded, but the Wrigley family has continued to own a large portion of the company's shares. In essence, then, the family has maintained tight control over the company since its inception. Over the years, the Wrigley Company and the Wrigley family have developed reputations as being both financially and strategically conservative.

In 1999, William Wrigley Jr. succeeded his father Bill Sr. as CEO of the Wrigley Company. After his arrival, Wrigley made a number of changes in the company that turned the conservative organization into more of a risk-taking company. One of his first moves involved changing the flavor formulations of the company's core brands such as Juicy Fruit, Spearmint, Doublemint, and Winter Fresh. To publicize these new formulations, he also reintroduced the brands with edgier marketing campaigns.

Wrigley also focused more of the company's resources on attacking the sugar-free chewing gum market. When he became CEO in 1999, the company offered only one sugar-free gum in the United States, Extra, and controlled only about 30 percent of the sugar-free market. Since then, the Wrigley Cmpany has introduced popular sugar-free gums such as Eclipse and Orbit—today the Wrigley Company controls more than 50 percent of the sugar-free gum market.

Not all of Wrigley's changes have provided such positive results. For example, he created a subsidiary devoted to developing chewing gums that released medication. One year later, the subsidiary released its first chewing gum, Surpass, which was formulated to fight antacid. Unfortunately, consumers did not respond well to Surpass, and Wrigley decided to stop its production.

At one of the Wrigley Company's recent annual meetings, Wrigley used a John F. Kennedy quote to demonstrate his position to shareholders: "There are risks and costs to any program of action, but they are far less than the long-range risks and costs of comfortable inaction." It seems as though Wrigley Company is committed to continual change to improve operations and solve problems on the horizon. Recent examples of this change include improving organization structure and dealing with impending competition. Such change will normally cause uneasiness among many of the company's employees and shareholders. However, such change over time will undoubtedly be necessary if Wrigley Company is to survive.[1]

■ *Pictured are some of the popular products sold by Wrigley Company.*

EXPLORING YOUR MANAGEMENT SKILL

You can explore your level of organizational change skill **before** studying the chapter by completing the exercise "Exploring Your Management Skill: Part 1" on page 338 and **after** studying this chapter by completing the exercise "Exploring Your Management Skill: Part 2" on page 339.

THE ORGANIZATIONAL CHANGE CHALLENGE

The Challenge Case illustrates organizational change challenges that William Wrigley Jr., the CEO of Wrigley Company, must meet. Wrigley must constantly assess the nature of his organization and make appropriate organizational changes that enhance goal attainment. Recent changes at the Wrigley Company have focused on adding new products. Wrigley knows, however, that the company will need to institute other types of change in the future to maintain the company's competitiveness. Managers such as Wrigley, who are faced with meeting organizational change challenges, would find the major topics in this chapter useful and practical. These topics are (1) fundamentals of changing an organization, (2) factors to consider when changing the organization, (3) change and stress, (4) change and conflict, and (5) virtuality.

FUNDAMENTALS OF CHANGING AN ORGANIZATION

Thus far, discussion in this "Organizing" section of the text has centered on the fundamentals of organizing, furnishing appropriate human resources for the organization, authority, delegation, and responsibility. This chapter focuses on changing the organization.

Defining Changing an Organization

Changing an organization is the process of modifying an existing organization to increase organizational effectiveness—that is, the extent to which an organization accomplishes its objectives. These modifications can involve virtually any organizational segment, but typically affect the lines of organizational authority, the levels of responsibility held by various organization members, and the established lines of organizational communication. Driven by new technology, expanding global opportunities, and the trend toward organizational streamlining, almost all modern organizations are changing in some way.[2]

The Importance of Change Most managers agree that if an organization is to thrive, it must change continually in response to significant developments in the environment, such as changing customer needs, technological breakthroughs, and new government regulations. The study of organizational change is extremely important because managers at all organizational levels are faced throughout their careers with the task of changing their organization. Managers who can determine appropriate changes and then implement such changes successfully enable their organizations to be more flexible and innovative.[3] Because change is such a fundamental part of organizational existence, such managers are valuable to organizations of all kinds.[4]

Many managers consider change to be so critical to organizational success that they encourage employees to continually search for areas in which beneficial changes can be made. To take a classic example, General Motors has traditionally provided employees with a "think list" to encourage them to develop ideas for organizational change and to remind them that change is vital to the continued success of GM. The think list contains the following questions:[5]

1. Can a machine be used to do a better or faster job?
2. Can the fixture now in use be improved?
3. Can handling of materials for the machine be improved?
4. Can a special tool be used to combine the operations?
5. Can the quality of the part being produced be improved by changing the sequence of the operation?

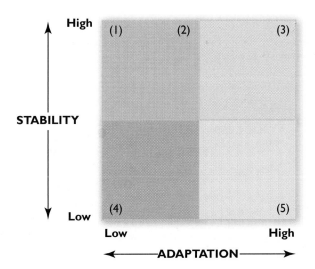

(1) High death probability (slow)
(2) High survival probability
(3) High survival and growth probability
(4) Certainty of death (quick)
(5) Certainty of death (quick)

FIGURE 14.1
Adaptation, stability, and organizational survival

6. Can the material used be cut or trimmed differently for greater economy or efficiency?
7. Can the operation be made safer?
8. Can paperwork regarding this job be eliminated?
9. Can established procedures be simplified?

The recent changes at GM—brought about by its financial collapse, bankruptcy filing, and subsequent bailout by the U.S. government—demonstrate that organizations sometimes need to take radical steps to restructure, or "reengineer," their operations in order to stay in business.[6]

Change Versus Stability

In addition to organizational change, some degree of stability is a prerequisite for long-term organizational success. Figure 14.1 presents a model developed by Hellriegel and Slocum that shows the relative importance of change and stability to organizational survival. Although these authors use the word *adaptation* in their model rather than *change,* the two terms are essentially synonymous.

The model stresses that organizational survival and growth are most probable when both stability and adaptation are high within the organization (number 3 on the model depicted in Figure 14.1). The organization without enough stability to complement change is at a definite disadvantage. When stability is low, the probability of organizational survival and growth declines. Change after change without regard for the essential role of stability typically results in confusion and employee stress.[7]

FACTORS TO CONSIDER WHEN CHANGING AN ORGANIZATION

How managers deal with the major factors that need to be considered when an organizational change is being made will largely determine how successful that change will be. The following factors should be considered whenever change is being contemplated: (1) the change agent, (2) determining what should be changed, (3) the kind of change to make, (4) individuals affected by the change, and (5) evaluation of the change.

Although the following sections discuss each of these factors individually, Figure 14.2 makes the point that it is a collective influence that ultimately determines the success of a change.[8]

FIGURE 14.2
The collective influence of five
major factors on the success of
changing an organization

The Change Agent

Perhaps the most important factor managers need to consider when changing an organization is
who will be the **change agent**—the individual inside or outside the organization who tries to
modify the existing organizational situation.[9] The change agent might be a self-designated manager
within the organization, or an outside consultant hired because of a special expertise in a particular
area. This individual might be responsible for making broad changes, such as altering the culture of
the whole organization; or more narrow ones, such as designing and implementing a new safety
program or a new quality program.[10] Although in some circumstances the change agent will not be
a manager, the terms *manager* and *change agent* are used synonymously throughout this chapter.

Special skills are necessary for success as a change agent. Among them are the ability to determine how a change should be made, the skill to solve change-related problems, and facility in using behavioral science tools to influence people appropriately during the change process.[11]
Perhaps the most overlooked skill of successful change agents, however, is the ability to determine
how much change employees can withstand.[12]

Overall, managers should choose change agents who have the most expertise in all these areas. A potentially beneficial change might not result in any advantages for the organization if a person without expertise in these areas is designated as change agent.

Determining What Should Be Changed

Another major factor managers need to consider is exactly what should be changed within the organization. In general, managers should make only those changes that will increase organizational
effectiveness.

It has been generally accepted for many years that organizational effectiveness depends primarily on activities centering around three classes of factors:

1. People
2. Structure
3. Technology

People factors are attitudes, leadership skills, communication skills, and all other characteristics of the human resources within the organization; **structural factors** are organizational controls, such as policies and procedures; and **technological factors** are any types of
equipment or processes that assist organization members in the performance of their jobs.

For an organization to maximize its effectiveness, appropriate people must be matched with appropriate technology and appropriate structure. Thus, people factors, technological factors, and structural factors are not independent determinants of organizational effectiveness. Instead, as Figure 14.3
shows, organizational effectiveness is determined by the relationship among these three factors.

FIGURE 14.3
Determination of organizational effectiveness by the relationship among people, technological, and structural factors

how managers do it

As an example of technological change, consider the situation faced by University Health System in San Antonio, Texas. The organization needed a data technology system that would allow clinical staff to operate more efficiently. Previously, staff at its University Hospital and 20 off-site clinics had to manually input critical temperature data for refrigerated medications. With 172 cold-storage facilities in the hospital alone, this hourly recording was not only subject to human error but took valuable time away from patient care. By upgrading the organization's technology with special health care software, University Health System was able to automate this process and many others, streamlining staff operations.[13] ■

how managers do it

Making Technological Change at University Health System

The Kind of Change to Make

The kind of change to make is the third major factor that managers need to consider when they set out to change an organization. Most changes can be categorized as technological, structural, or people. Note that these three kinds of change correspond to the three main determinants of organizational effectiveness—each change is named for the determinant it emphasizes.

For example, **technological change** emphasizes modifying the level of technology in the management system. Because this kind of change so often involves outside experts and highly technical language, it is more profitable to discuss structural change and people change in detail in this text.

Structural Change Structural change emphasizes increasing organizational effectiveness by changing controls that influence organization members during the performance of their jobs. The following section further describes this approach and provides managers with insights regarding how to deal with structural change issues.

Describing Structural Change **Structural change** is change aimed at increasing organizational effectiveness through modifications to the existing organizational structure. These modifications can take several forms:

1. Clarifying and defining jobs
2. Modifying organizational structure to fit the communication needs of the organization

3. Decentralizing the organization to reduce the cost of coordination, increase the controllability of subunits, increase motivation, and gain greater flexibility

Although structural change must take account of people and technology to be successful, its primary focus is obviously on changing organizational structure. In general, managers choose to make structural changes within an organization if information they have gathered indicates the present structure is the main cause of organizational ineffectiveness. The precise structural changes they choose to make will vary from situation to situation, of course. After changes to organizational structure have been made, management should conduct periodic reviews to make sure the changes are accomplishing their intended purposes.[14]

People Change Although successfully changing people factors necessarily involves some consideration of structure and technology, the primary emphasis is on people. The following sections discuss people change and examine grid organization development, one commonly used means of changing organization members.

Describing People Change: Organization Development (OD) People

change emphasizes increasing organizational effectiveness by changing certain aspects of organization members. The focus of this kind of change is on such factors as employees' attitudes and leadership skills. In general, managers should attempt to make this kind of change when human resources are shown to be the main cause of organizational ineffectiveness.

The process of people change can be referred to as **organization development (OD)**. Although OD focuses mainly on changing certain aspects of people, these changes are based on an overview of structure, technology, and all other organizational ingredients.

Fiat's CEO Sergio Marchionne has high hopes that the redesigned Fiat 500 will revive the automaker's fortunes. The plan to develop the new model was the result of many earlier decisions about what kind of changes the company needed to make in order to turn itself around.

how managers do it

Implementing People Change at Caterpillar, Inc.

Peoria, Illinois–based Caterpillar, Inc. provides a good example of an organization focused on people change. A leading manufacturer of heavy equipment related to construction and mining, Caterpillar recently committed to improving management attitudes and capabilities related to evaluating and improving employee performance. To bring about change, Caterpillar held performance management training workshops for more than 20,000 managers. The workshop emphasized how managers were to improve the performance of their people and how employees were to take responsibility for their own development. The workshop also presented a new performance evaluation process that managers were expected to use and focused on building related management skills in the areas of coaching, goal setting, feedback, and communication. Management believes that the program successful in changing people in areas like getting employees to be better team players, to be more focused on company goals, and to be more consistent in rating the performance of others.[15] ∎

Grid OD One traditionally used OD technique for changing people in organizations is called **grid organization development**, or **grid OD**.[16] The **managerial grid**, a basic model describing various managerial styles, is used as the foundation for grid OD. The managerial grid is based on the premise that various managerial styles can be described by means of two primary attitudes of the manager: concern for people and concern for production. Within this model, each attitude is placed on an axis, which is scaled 1 through 9 and is used to generate five managerial styles. Figure 14.4 shows the managerial grid, its five managerial styles, and the factors that characterize each of these styles.

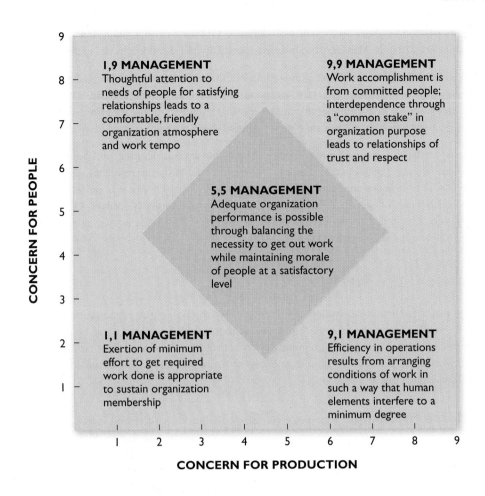

FIGURE 14.4
The managerial grid

THE IDEAL STYLE The central theme of this managerial grid is that 9,9 management (as shown on the grid in Figure 14.4) is the ideal managerial style. Managers using this style have a high concern for both people and production. Managers using any other style have lesser degrees of concern for people or production, and are thought to reduce organizational success accordingly. The purpose of grid OD is to change organization managers so they will use the 9,9 management style.

MAIN TRAINING PHASES How is a grid OD program conducted? The program has six main training phases that are used with all managers within the organization. The first two phases focus on acquainting managers with the managerial grid concept and assisting them in determining which managerial style they most commonly use. The last four phases of the grid OD program concentrate on encouraging managers to adopt the 9,9 management style and showing them how to use this style within their specific job situation. Emphasis throughout the program is on developing teamwork within the organization.

Some evidence suggests that grid OD is effective in enhancing profit, positively changing managerial behavior, and positively influencing managerial attitudes and values.[17] Grid OD will have to undergo more rigorous testing for an extended period of time, however, before conclusive statements can be made about it.

The Status of Organization Development

If the entire OD area is taken into consideration, changes that emphasize both people and the organization as a whole seem to have inherent strength. However, several commonly voiced weaknesses in OD efforts include the following:[18]

1. The effectiveness of an OD program is difficult to evaluate.
2. OD programs are generally too time-consuming.
3. OD objectives are commonly too vague.
4. The total costs of an OD program are difficult to gauge at the time the program starts.
5. OD programs are generally too expensive.

These weaknesses, however, should not eliminate OD from consideration, but should indicate areas to perfect within it. Managers can improve the quality of OD efforts by doing the following:[19]

1. Systematically tailoring OD programs to meet the specific needs of the organization
2. Continually demonstrating exactly how people should change their behavior
3. Conscientiously changing organizational reward systems so organization members who change their behavior in ways suggested by the OD program are rewarded

Managers have been employing OD techniques for several decades, and broad and useful applications of these techniques continue to be documented in the more recent management literature.[20] OD techniques are currently being applied not only to business organizations, but also to many other types of organizations, such as religious organizations. Moreover, OD applications are being documented throughout the world, with increasing use being reported in countries such as Hungary, Poland, and the United Kingdom.[21]

Individuals Affected By the Change

A fourth major factor to be considered by managers when changing an organization is the people who will be affected by the change. A good assessment of what to change and how to make the change will be wasted if organization members do not support the change. To increase the chances of employee support, managers should be aware of the usual employee resistance to change and how this resistance can be reduced.

Resistance to Change   Resistance to change within an organization is as common as the need for change. After managers decide to make some organizational change, they typically meet with employee resistance aimed at preventing that change from occurring.[22] Behind this resistance by organization members lies the fear of some personal loss, such as a reduction in personal prestige, a disturbance of established social and working relationships, and personal failure because of inability to carry out new job responsibilities.[23]

Reducing Resistance to Change   To ensure the success of needed modifications, managers must be able to reduce the effects of the resistance that typically accompanies proposed change.[24] Resistance can usually be lowered by following these guidelines:[25]

1. **Avoid surprises**—People need time to evaluate a proposed change before management implements it. Unless they are given time to evaluate and absorb how the change will affect them, employees are likely to be automatically opposed to it. Whenever possible, therefore, individuals who will be affected by a change should be informed of the kind of change being considered and the probability that it will be adopted.
2. **Promote real understanding**—When fear of personal loss related to a proposed change is reduced, opposition to the change is also reduced. Most managers find ensuring that organization members thoroughly understand a proposed change is a major step in reducing this fear. Understanding may even generate enthusiastic support for the change if it focuses employees on individual gains that could materialize as a result of it. People should be given information that will help them answer the following change-related questions they invariably will have:
   * Will I lose my job?
   * Will my old skills become obsolete?
   * Am I capable of producing effectively under the new system?
   * Will my power and prestige decline?
   * Will I be given more responsibility than I care to assume?
   * Will I have to work longer hours?
   * Will it force me to betray or desert my good friends?
3. **Set the stage for change**—Perhaps the most powerful tool for reducing resistance to change is management's positive attitude toward the change. This attitude should be displayed openly by top and middle management as well as by lower management. In essence,

management should convey that change is one of the basic prerequisites for a successful organization. Management should also strive to encourage change for increasing organizational effectiveness, rather than for the sake of trying something new.

Storytelling—the sharing of anecdotes or personal narratives to build emotional connections among work groups—is a useful communication technique that can help set the stage for organizational change. By breaking down barriers and resistance to change, storytelling enables management to also honor the organizational traditions of the past and helps employees accept new ways of doing things.[26]

To reinforce a positive attitude toward change, some portion of organizational rewards should be earmarked for those organization members who are most instrumental in implementing constructive change.

4. **Make tentative change**—Resistance to change can also be reduced if the changes are made on a tentative basis. This approach establishes a trial period during which organization members spend some time working under a proposed change before voicing support or nonsupport of it. Tentative change is based on the assumption that a trial period during which organization members live under a change is the best way of reducing feared personal loss. Judson has summarized the benefits of using the tentative approach:

- Employees affected by the change are able to test their reactions to the new situation before committing themselves irrevocably to it.
- Those who will live under the change are able to acquire more facts on which to base their attitudes and behavior toward the change.
- Those who had strong preconceptions about the change are in a better position to assess it with objectivity. Consequently, they may review and modify some of their preconceptions.
- Those involved are less likely to regard the change as a threat.
- Management is better able to evaluate the method of change and make any necessary modifications before carrying it out more fully.

class discussion highlight

MODERN RESEARCH AND ORGANIZATIONAL CHANGE SKILL

Employee Attitudes toward Change in a Large Public Hospital

Individuals can be affected by organizational change in various ways. This highlight focuses on a research study that explores the relationship between employee attitudes about change and various organizational levels at which the employees worked. Overall, the research tried to discover whether employee attitudes about change might be more positive for employees who worked at upper organizational levels than employees who worked at lower organizational levels.

The study was conducted in a large public hospital where employees were experiencing extensive organizational change. Changes focused on the downsizing of staff and the establishment of new multidisciplinary work teams. All hospital staff was mailed an anonymous survey focusing on their thoughts about organizational changes currently in progress and a postage-paid envelope for returning the survey once completed. A total of 1,500 surveys were sent to employees with 779 being returned for analysis. Of the surveys returned, 70 percent were women and 30 percent were men. Also, 62 percent were 20 to 40 years of age and 38 percent were 41 and over. The group of responding employees was representative of the composition of the organization's total workforce.

The purpose of the study was to test the prediction that upper-level staff would be more positive in their appraisals of change than lower-level staff. Do you think that results of the study were consistent with the prediction? Why? Why not?

Source: Angela J. Martin, Elizabeth S. Jones, and Victor J. Callan, "Status Differences in Employee Adjustment During Organizational Change," *Journal of Managerial Psychology* 21, no. 1–2 (2006): 145–162.

The effects of change in an organization can be profound, as many autoworkers have found in recent years while the industry has suffered steadily declining sales and job losses.

Evaluation of the Change

As with all other managerial actions, managers should spend some time evaluating the changes they make. The purpose of this evaluation is not only to gain insight into how the change itself might be modified to further increase its organizational effectiveness, but to determine whether the steps taken to make the change should be modified to increase organizational effectiveness the next time they are used.

According to Margulies and Wallace, making this evaluation may be difficult because the data from individual change programs may be unreliable.[27] Nevertheless, managers must do their best to evaluate change to increase the organizational benefits from the change.[28]

Evaluation of change often involves watching for symptoms that indicate further change is necessary. For example, if organization members continue to be oriented more to the past than the future, if they recognize the obligations of rituals more readily than they do the challenges of current problems, or if they pay greater allegiance to departmental goals than to overall company objectives, the probability is high that further change is necessary.

A word of caution is needed at this point. Although symptoms such as those listed in the preceding paragraph generally indicate that further change is warranted, the decision to make additional changes should not be made solely on that basis. More objective information should be considered. In general, additional change is justified if it will accomplish any of the following goals:[29]

1. Further improve the means for satisfying someone's economic wants
2. Increase profitability
3. Promote human work for human beings
4. Contribute to individual satisfaction and social well-being

CHANGE AND STRESS

Whenever managers implement changes, they should be concerned about the stress they may be creating. If the stress is significant enough, it may well cancel out the improvement that was anticipated from the change. In fact, stress could result in the organization being *less* effective than it was before the change was attempted. This section defines stress and discusses the importance of studying and managing it.

Defining Stress

The bodily strain that an individual experiences as a result of coping with some environmental factor is **stress**.[30] Hans Selye, an early authority on this subject, said stress constitutes the factors affecting wear and tear on the body. In organizations, this wear and tear is caused primarily by the body's unconscious mobilization of energy when an individual is confronted with organizational or work demands.[31]

The Importance of Studying Stress

The study of stress is important for several reasons:[32]

- Stress can have damaging psychological and physiological effects on employees' health and on their contributions to organizational effectiveness. It can cause heart disease, and it can prevent employees from concentrating or making decisions. Increased levels of stress have also been associated with adverse effects on family relationships,[33] decreased productivity in the workplace, and increased psychiatric symptoms.[34]

- Stress is a major cause of employee absenteeism and turnover. Certainly, such factors severely limit the potential success of an organization.

- A stressed employee can affect the safety of other workers or even the public.

- Stress represents a significant cost to organizations. Some estimates put the cost of stress-related problems in the U.S. economy at $150 billion a year. As examples of these costs, many modern organizations spend a great deal of money treating stress-related employee problems through medical programs, and they must absorb expensive legal fees when handling stress-related lawsuits.

Managing Stress in Organizations

Because stress is felt by virtually all employees in all organizations, insights about managing stress are valuable to all managers. This section is built on the assumption that to appropriately manage stress in organizations, managers must understand how stress influences worker performance, identify where unhealthy stress exists in organizations, and help employees handle stress.

Understanding How Stress Influences Worker Performance To deal with stress among employees, managers must understand the relationship between the amount of stress felt by a worker and the worker's performance. This relationship is shown in Figure 14.5. Note that

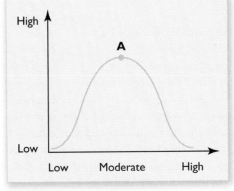

FIGURE 14.5
The relationship between worker stress and the level of worker performance

extremely high and extremely low levels of stress tend to have negative effects on production. Additionally, while increasing stress tends to bolster performance up to some point (Point A in the figure), when the level of stress increases beyond this point, performance will begin to deteriorate.

In sum, a certain amount of stress among employees is generally considered to be advantageous for the organization because it tends to increase production. However, when employees experience too much or too little stress, it is generally disadvantageous for the organization because it tends to decrease production.

Identifying Unhealthy Stress in Organizations Once managers understand the impact of stress on performance, they must identify where stress exists within the organization.[35] After areas of stress have been pinpointed, managers must then determine whether the stress is at an appropriate level or is too high or too low. Because most stress-related organizational problems involve too much stress rather than too little, the remainder of this section focuses on how to relieve undesirably high levels of stress.

Managers often find it difficult to identify the people in the organization who are experiencing detrimentally high levels of stress. Part of this difficulty is that people respond to high stress in different ways, and part is that physiological reactions to stress are hard, if not impossible, for managers to observe and monitor. Such reactions include high blood pressure, pounding heart, and gastrointestinal disorders.

Nevertheless, managers can learn to recognize several observable symptoms of undesirably high stress levels:[36]

- Constant fatigue
- Low energy
- Moodiness
- Increased aggression
- Excessive use of alcohol
- Temper outbursts
- Compulsive eating
- High levels of anxiety
- Chronic worrying

A manager who observes one or more of these symptoms in employees should investigate to determine whether those exhibiting the symptoms are indeed under too much stress. If so, the manager should try to help those employees handle their stress or should attempt to reduce stressors in the organization.[37]

Helping Employees Handle Stress A **stressor** is an environmental demand that causes people to feel stress. Stressors are common in situations where individuals are confronted by circumstances for which their usual behaviors are inappropriate or insufficient and where negative consequences are associated with failure to deal properly with the situation. Organizational change characterized by continual layoffs or firings is an obvious stressor, but many other factors related to organizational policies, structure, physical conditions, and processes can also act as stressors.[38]

A recent study identified workplace bullying as a stressor in the work lives of doctors in India and Malaysia. **Workplace bullying** refers to individuals being isolated or excluded socially and having work efforts devalued. According to study results, workplace bullying is frequently experienced by junior doctors and leads to reduced job satisfaction, depression and anxiety, sickness, and absence. This stressor may lead to positive outcomes such as doctors feeling challenged and thereby increasing their productivity. On the other hand, this stressor might lead to undesirable consequences like doctors showing low morale and poorer work performance that can negatively affect patient care. Because workplace bullying is generally seen as a negative factor on doctors, countries such as England, Sweden, Norway, and Finland have implemented programs to eliminate workplace bullying.

Stress is seldom significantly reduced until the stressors causing it have been coped with satisfactorily or withdrawn from the environment. For example, if too much organizational change is causing undesirably high levels of stress, management may be able to reduce that stress by improving organizational training that is aimed at preparing workers to deal with job demands resulting from the change. Management might also choose to reduce such stress by refraining from making further organizational changes for a while.[39]

Management can also adopt several strategies to help prevent the initial development of unwanted stressors in organizations. Four such strategies follow:[40]

1. **Create an organizational climate that is supportive of individuals**—Organizations commonly evolve into large bureaucracies with formal, inflexible, impersonal climates. This setup leads to considerable job stress. Making the organizational environment less formal and more supportive of employee needs will help prevent the development of unwanted organizational stressors.

2. **The implementation of stress management courses**—Recent research has demonstrated that employees who participated in a stress management course were less depressed than employees who did not participate in a stress management course.[41] The stress management course involved a group session in which educational materials about coping strategies and stress prevention were presented. An additional part of the stress management course involved teaching employees about the benefits of relaxation. Those employees who participated in the stress management course demonstrated significant improvement in their depressive symptoms. Clearly, the implementation of a stress management course could be beneficial for the workplace.

3. **Make jobs interesting**—Routine jobs that do not allow employees some degree of freedom often result in undesirable employee stress. A management focus on making jobs as interesting as possible should help prevent the development of stressors related to routine, boring jobs.

4. **Design and operate career counseling programs**—Employees often experience considerable stress when they do not know what their next career step might be or when they might take it. If management can show employees that next step and when it can realistically be achieved, it will discourage unwanted organizational stressors in this area.

IBM is an example of a company that for many years has focused on career planning for its employees as a vehicle for reducing employee stress.[42] IBM has a corporation-wide program to encourage supervisors to annually conduct voluntary career planning sessions with employees that result in one-page career action plans. Thus, IBM employees have a clear idea of where their careers are headed.

CHANGE AND CONFLICT[43]

Defining Conflict

Managers often encounter conflict as a result of planning and making organizational changes. As used here, **conflict** is defined as a struggle that results from opposing needs or feelings between two or more people. In the case of organizational change, conflict generally results from managers making changes that threaten others or create competing views between others and managers concerning when, how, or if particular organizational change should be made. Conflict sometimes results in positive impact for the organization. For example, a manager in conflict with a subordinate regarding how a subordinate's job will change might get good suggestions from the subordinate as a result of the conflict regarding how to improve the planned change. On the other hand, conflict sometimes results in negative impact on the organization. For example, the situation just discussed regarding conflict between manager and subordinate could result in the two of them destroying their work relationship and frustrating the employee to the point where he or she, in order to get back at the manager, finds ways to sabotage the success of the planned change.

Conflict can have either negative or positive effects, depending on how the parties handle their disagreement.

Strategies for Settling Conflict

Fortunately for managers, several useful techniques are available for handling conflict. These techniques, depicted in Figure 14.6, include *compromising, avoiding, forcing,* and *resolving.* Each of these techniques is discussed in the following sections.

Compromising   One conflict management strategy a manager can use is to **compromise**, which means the parties to the conflict settle on a solution that gives both of them *part* of what they wanted. Neither the manager nor employees get exactly what they initially wanted. All parties agree to an organizational change that they presumably can accept.

Managers who choose to compromise generally feel that a solution completely acceptable to everyone would be difficult to reach and they would rather not force someone to accept a completely disagreeable choice. Compromise is generally appropriate to adopt as a conflict management technique if a planned change is relatively minor and the time to make an organizational change is somewhat limited.

Avoiding   Some managers adopt the avoiding technique as means to manage conflict. **Avoiding** is a conflict management technique whereby managers simply ignore the conflict. For example, if a sales manager finds that individuals in the human resources department are a continual source of conflict because they are inflexible and resist proposed change, the manager can avoid dealing with the department. The manager can opt to propose and implement desirable change by dealing with others in the organization as opposed to human resource personnel.

This strategy makes sense if you assume that all conflict is bad. If you successfully avoid all conflicts, the work environment could seem positive on the surface. However, managers do often disagree with others in organizations, and sometimes people with opposing viewpoints have important ideas to share through conflict. Managers should be selective in avoiding conflict. The avoiding technique is perhaps generally appropriate when the potential conflict faced will not limit organizational goal attainment.

The avoiding technique should also be assessed in relation to the high level of workforce diversity that exists in most modern organizations. An employee's point of view can often seem puzzling, irritating, or completely incorrect to a manager if the employee is of another race, age, or sex. Managers must work hard to understand people who are different. Managers must give equal attention to the views of all employees, not only those the manager easily understands.

FIGURE 14.6
Techniques for handling conflict

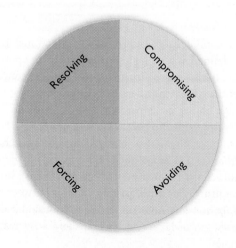

Pretending that everyone views a situation the same way is inaccurate and may give some employees the belief is discriminating against them.

Managers must keep in mind that people in many non-Western cultures believe it is best to avoid conflicts, placing a higher value on harmony than on confrontation. Employees with such values are less likely, than employees from Western cultures, to become involved in conflict with a manager regarding an organizational change that is being implemented. To make sure that organizational change is designed and implemented most effectively and efficiently, a manager must ensure that employees know the manager wants to be aware of any thoughts employees might have about how to improve organizational change.

Forcing Rather than avoiding conflict, a manager may want to try a more direct approach to managing conflict. **Forcing** is a technique for managing conflict in which managers use authority to declare that conflict is ended. In essence, managers declare that conflict is ended because they have the authority to do so. For example, assume that a worker complains to a manager that a recently changed and implemented procedure is unfair because the procedure does not allow the worker a fair share of overtime hours. Managers can force a behavior simply by declaring that "I make the assignments, and your job is to do what you're told."

Considering the management of work teams also illustrates how managers can force an end to conflict. For example, assume that a manager is leading his employees in a project to reduce the time needed to deliver a product and, because of conflict within the team regarding what change should be made and how it should be made, the team is virtually deadlocked in determining what to do. In such situations, managers may simply force or dictate what organizational change needs to be made and how it should be made.

Forcing a solution is a relatively fast way to manage a conflict, and it may be the best approach in an emergency. However, forcing a solution can frustrate employees. In addition, this frustration can be the cause of future management–employee conflict.

Resolving Perhaps the most direct—and sometimes the most difficult—way to manage conflict is to work out the difference(s) between managers and employees. This conflict management strategy is called **resolving**. The manager initiates this technique by pinpointing differences related to organizational change that exists between managers and employees. Pinpointing these differences requires that managers and employees listen to the viewpoints of others in an honest effort to understand rather than to argue. Next, managers and employees should identify the issues about change on which they agree and the ways they can both benefit from implementing change that reflects the ideas on which they agree. Both management and employees should examine their own thoughts honestly and carefully to reach a mutually agreed-upon, change-related strategy.

Resolving is based on an assumption about the conflict that is somewhat different from other strategies for conflict management. The other techniques tend to assume managers and employees are in a *win–lose conflict*. In other words, the outcome of the conflict will be that one side wins (achieves a desired outcome) and the other side loses (does not achieve a desired outcome). In contrast, *resolving* assumes that many conflicts are *win–win conflicts,* in which the resolution can leave both management and employees achieving desirable outcomes and correspondingly, helping the organization maximize organizational success.

VIRTUALITY

One specific, commonplace type of organizational change being made in modern organizations throughout the world is the trend toward "virtuality." Because this trend is indeed significant and expected to grow even more in the future, this section emphasizes it by defining a virtual organization, discussing degrees of virtuality in organizations, and describing the virtual office.[44]

Defining a Virtual Organization

Overall, a **virtual organization** has the essence of a traditional organization, but without some aspect of traditional boundaries and structure.[45] Virtual organizations are also referred to as *network organizations* or *modular corporations.*[46] In essence, managers go beyond traditional boundaries and structure for the good of the organization by using recent developments in information technology. Perhaps the most prominent of these developments are the Internet and hardware and software tools enabling managers to use these two more easily.[47] Both large and small organizations can have virtual aspects.[48]

Degrees of Virtuality

Organizations can vary drastically in terms of their degree of virtuality. Perhaps the company exhibiting the most extensive degree is known as the **virtual corporation**, an organization that goes significantly beyond the boundaries and structure of a traditional organization by comprehensively "tying together" a company's stakeholders—employees, suppliers, and customers—via an elaborate system of e-mail and other Internet-related vehicles such as videoconferencing. This tying together allows all stakeholders to communicate and participate in helping the organization become more successful.

On the other hand, some organizations have much lesser degrees of virtuality. For example, some organizations limit their virtuality to **virtual teams**, groups of employees formed by managers that go beyond the boundaries and structure of traditional teams by having members in geographically dispersed locations meeting via real-time messaging on an intranet or the Internet to discuss special or unanticipated organizational problems.[49] As another example, organizations may limit their virtuality to **virtual training**, a training process that goes beyond the boundaries and structure of traditional training. Such training can go beyond traditional training limits by, for example, instructing employees via Internet-assisted learning materials.[50] The following sections discuss virtual offices, a popular type of virtuality being introduced into many organizations.

The Virtual Office

An exciting component of the organization virtuality is the virtual office.[51] The following sections discuss the definition of the term, various reasons for establishing a virtual office, and challenges to managing a virtual office.

Defining a Virtual Office A **virtual office** is a work arrangement that extends beyond the structure and boundaries of the traditional office arrangement. Specifics of the arrangements vary from organization to organization but can be conceptualized using the alternative work arrangements continuum shown in Figure 14.7. This continuum is based on the degree of worker mobility reflected within a particular virtual office, moving from "occasional telecommuting" to "fully mobile." The definitions of the alternative work arrangements shown on the continuum follow.

OCCASIONAL TELECOMMUTING Workers have fixed, traditional offices and work schedules but occasionally work at home. In this situation, most are traditional workers in traditional office situations.

HOTELING Workers come into the traditional office frequently, but because they are not always physically present, they are not allocated permanent office space. Instead, workers can reserve a room or cubicle in advance of their arrival, sometimes called a "hotel room," where they can receive and return telephone calls and link into a computer network.

FIGURE 14.7 Continuum of alternative work arrangements

TETHERED IN OFFICE "Tethered" workers have some mobility but are expected to report to the office on a regular basis. As an example, some tethered workers are expected to appear at the office in the morning to receive a cellular phone and portable computer. The equipment is returned to the office in the afternoon, sometimes accompanied by a meeting or progress report for the workday.

HOME-BASED, SOME MOBILITY A home-based worker has no traditional office. The workspace of this type of worker could be a kitchen table or a bedroom desk. A home-based worker may visit customers or go outside the home occasionally, but his or her work is mainly done via the telephone or computer inside the home. Some companies support home-based workers through activities such as leasing office furniture, providing computers, and procuring high-speed phone lines.

os Angeles–based OnSite Consulting is an example of a virtual office. CEO James Sinclair says the system works because the company's management includes team leaders, each responsible for five or six employees working remotely. Team leaders define project goals clearly and ensure that their direct reports adhere to daily and weekly tasks.[52] ■

how managers do it

Managing a Virtual Office
at OnSite Consulting

FULLY MOBILE A worker who is fully mobile works out of a car. In essence, the car is an office containing equipment such as a cellular phone, portable computer, and fax machine. This type of worker is expected to be on the road or at work areas such as customer locations during the entire workday, and they are typically field sales representatives or customer service specialists.

Reasons for Establishing a Virtual Office Managers design and implement virtual offices for many different reasons. Cost reduction is the most commonly cited reason, and real estate or rental costs are the most commonly cited costs to be reduced. Traditional office space needed for an organization can be reduced by more than 50 percent by using virtual offices. Managers also use virtual offices to increase productivity. History in some organizations shows that people work faster and are interrupted less when working at home. Third, firms also establish virtual offices as part of redesigning jobs to make employees more effective and efficient. For example, some organizations need to reduce the amount of time taken to address customer problems. Some managers meet this need by establishing fully mobile customer service employees. According to the rationale, fully mobile customer service employees have a better chance of arriving at customer locations quickly than customer service employees in traditional offices, and thereby have a better chance of solving problems quickly.

Challenges to Managing a Virtual Office Undoubtedly, managers face many new and different challenges when using the virtual office concept. For example, virtual offices make it more difficult to build desired corporate culture. For employees, traditional offices represent a place to become familiar with fellow workers and socialize into a purposefully designed corporate culture. Due simply to their lack of proximity, employees working in virtual offices are more difficult for managers to integrate into the fabric of organizational culture. Another management challenge to using virtual offices is that such offices make it more difficult for managers to control workers. An individual's presence in a traditional office can give a manager constant feedback throughout the day concerning worker commitment and performance, whereas in a virtual office situation, it is not as easy. Last, virtual offices make communication more difficult. Planned or unplanned face-to-face communication that takes place in a traditional office is essentially nonexistent in a virtual office. As a result, management may experience more difficulty in gathering information relevant to employee attitudes and work concerns.

CHALLENGE CASE SUMMARY

The previous information furnishes several insights about how Bill Wrigley should make decisions such as whether to recommend a particular type of change in the company. Wrigley should evaluate such change in relation to the degree that it better enables the company to accomplish its objectives. Wrigley should understand that making such change is extremely important. If the company is to have continued success over the long run, such changes will probably have to be made a number of times. In fact, appropriate change is so important to a company that Wrigley might want to consider initiating some type of program that would encourage employees to submit their ideas on a continuing basis regarding new ideas that could increase company effectiveness. When considering possible changes, however, Wrigley must keep in mind that some level of stability is also necessary if his company is to survive and grow over the long term. To illustrate such stability, Wrigley Company has been manufacturing and selling Spearmint and Juicy Fruit for more than 100 years.

In the Challenge Case, it is clear that Wrigley is a change agent. Given his role as top management, he is probably the individual in the company best suited to evaluate the overall advantages and disadvantages of making changes such as offering one type of chewing gum as opposed to another or one type of candy as opposed to another. Because Wrigley has been involved with this business most of his life, he has the perspective necessary to evaluate such advantages and disadvantages. However, he would probably not be the person in the company best suited to change the training program for newly hired line workers.

In general, change agents such as Wrigley must have the ability to use behavioral science tools to influence organization members during the implementation of planned change. As examples, Wrigley must determine how much organizational change the company's employees can withstand and implement this change, perhaps gradually, so employees will not be overwhelmed. Changing the Wrigley Company's product line too dramatically, for example, would require Wrigley to transfer a large number of employees to different divisions, which may diminish employee morale. Overall, the ability to use behavioral science tools will help the change agent be successful in implementing needed work situation changes at the company.

Wrigley can make many different types of changes. The preceding information indicates that change agents can change technological factors, people factors, and structural factors to increase organizational effectiveness. Wrigley's product line decisions discussed in the Challenge Case likely include change regarding all of these factors. For example, product line changes would likely precipitate changes to structural factors. That is, new departments might be created while others might be eliminated. In addition, the product line changes would probably include technological change. For example, the company might need new technology to develop new and better tasting sugar-free gums. Lastly, product line changes would probably include a focus on people and will be facilitated through action such as communicating with employees about product lines as well as motivating workers to achieve the objectives toward which product line change is aimed.

Technically, modifying the product line at the Wrigley Company would not be classified as people change. It is clear, however, that such modification changes will precipitate the need for people change. Wrigley is attempting to radically change the company's strategic position, and he will need to develop employees who will be able to help him make these modifications. As a result, he may find it useful to implement organization development (OD) to spur the people change that will be required to support his strategy. Alternatively, Wrigley may find it necessary to use grid OD to modify management styles. Of course, Wrigley may use both of these techniques to develop the managers that he will need to ensure his organizational change succeeds.

Wrigley must realize that even though he may formulate structural change that would be beneficial to the company, any attempt to implement this change could prove unsuccessful if it does not appropriately consider the people affected by the change. For example, if the company introduces a new departmental structure, employees working under the old structure may fear this change will diminish their opportunities for promotion within the company. As a result, they may subtly resist the change.

To overcome such resistance, Wrigley could use strategies such as giving employees enough time to fully evaluate and understand the change, presenting a positive attitude about the change, and, if resistance is strong, suggesting that the proposed change will be tentative until it is fully evaluated.

All changes at the Wrigley Company need to be evaluated after implementation to discover whether further organizational change is necessary and whether the change process used might be improved for future use. For example, concerning the establishment of a new departmental structure at the company, the evaluation process would include monitoring department activities to determine whether departments are functioning according to plan. If not, further changes to the departmental structure might be necessary.

Wrigley should be careful not to create too much stress on other organization members as a result of planned change. Such stress could be significant enough to eliminate any planned improvement at the company and eventually result in physical symptoms and the inability to make sound decisions.

Although some additional stress on organization members as a result of changes might improve the company's effectiveness, too much stress could have a negative impact on production. Signs to look for include constant fatigue, increased aggression, temper outbursts, and chronic worrying.

If Wrigley determines that undesirably high levels of stress have resulted from changes related to the company's new product line, he should try to reduce the stress. Wrigley may be able to do so through training programs aimed at better equipping organization members to execute new job demands resulting from the change. Alternatively, Wrigley may want simply to slow the rate of planned change.

It would probably be wise for Wrigley to take action that would prevent unwanted stressors from developing as a result of planned work-situation change. In this regard, he could ensure that the organizational climate at the Wrigley Company is supportive of individual needs and that jobs resulting from the planned change are as interesting as possible.

Wrigley should also keep in mind that conflict is a usual by-product of planning and implementing organizational changes. In handling this conflict, Wrigley can *compromise* (settle on a modified problem solution that reflects a change in the ideas of all conflicting parties, but which all parties find acceptable), *avoid* (pretend that no conflict exists), *force* (demand that a change be made), or *resolve* (confront the problem(s) causing the conflict and solve it).

Although Wrigley has focused on changes that improve the company's sales, he might also consider changes that improve the firm's cost structure. For example,

he could consider establishing a virtual focus within the company. Such organizational change probably would not be as drastic as establishing the William Wrigley Jr. Company as a virtual corporation, but recommending some degree of virtuality that might begin by establishing virtual teams.

Wrigley could choose among various options that help give the company a virtual dimension. For example, he could establish a virtual office that had workers in its market research group telecommute. Other options available for establishing a virtual office at the company could include workers "hoteling," tethered in the office, home-based with some mobility, or fully mobile. Wrigley's rationale for establishing this type of virtual office at the company probably should include cost savings due to rent savings and enhanced worker productivity. With such a virtual structure, the company would enable its market researchers to spend less time at work and more time on the road visiting with focus groups.

As with any type of change, establishing a virtual dimension at Wrigley Company will include a number of important challenges that must be met for newly established virtual components to be successful. Perhaps the most significant of these challenges is appropriately integrating virtual workers into the Wrigley Company's corporate culture. Building good communication among Wrigley's managers and virtual workers is an important step for integrating these workers into the culture and maintaining their continued presence. To build this communication, Wrigley's managers could take steps that include establishing regular communication times with virtual workers, publishing an online newsletter aimed at helping virtual workers deal with their unique problems, and having regular social events where virtual workers could meet and interact with other virtual workers as well as the company's employees in traditional work settings.

MANAGEMENT SKILL ACTIVITIES

This section is specially designed to help you develop organizational change skill. An individual's organizational change skill is based on an understanding of organizational change concepts and the ability to apply those concepts in management situations. The following activities are designed both to heighten your understanding of organizational change fundamentals and to develop your ability to apply those concepts in various management situations.

UNDERSTANDING ORGANIZATIONAL CHANGE CONCEPTS

To check your understanding and to practice using the concepts in this chapter, go to www.mymanagementlab.com and explore the material associated with Chapter 14.

Know Key Terms

Understanding the following key terms is critical to your understanding of chapter material. Define each of these terms. Refer to the page(s) referenced after a term to check your definition or to gain further insight regarding the term.

changing an organization **320**
change agent **322**
people factors **322**
structural factors **322**
technological factors **322**
technological change **323**
structural change **323**
people change **324**
organization development (OD) **324**

grid organization development
(grid OD) **324**
managerial grid **324**
stress **329**
stressor **330**
workplace bullying **330**
conflict **331**
compromise **332**
avoiding **332**

forcing **333**
resolving **333**
virtual organization **334**
virtual corporation **334**
virtual teams **334**
virtual training **334**
virtual office **334**

Know How Management Concepts Relate

This section is comprised of activities that will further sharpen your understanding of management concepts. Answer essay questions as completely as possible. Also, remember that many additional true/false and multiple choice questions appear online at MyManagementLab.com to help you further refine your understanding of management concepts.

1. List and explain five reasons why organizations should undergo change.

2. What role should "organizational stability" play in the organizational change process?

3. Discuss an example of how you might use "freezing, unfreezing, and refreezing" in making a specific organizational change.

4. Discuss grid OD as a technique for changing people in organizations.

5. Why is handling conflict an important part of making organizational change?

DEVELOPING MANAGEMENT SKILLS

Learning activities in this section are aimed at helping you develop organizational change skill. Learning activities include Exploring Your Management Skill: Parts 1 & 2, Experiential Exercise, Cases, and a VideoNet Exercise.

Exploring Your Management Skill: Part 1

Before studying this chapter, respond to the following questions regarding the type of advice that you would give to William Wrigley, Jr., the CEO referenced in the Case. Then address the concerning organizational change challenges that he faces within the company. You are not expected to be an organizational change expert at this point. Answering the questions now can help you focus on important points when you study the chapter. Also, answering the questions again after you study the chapter will give you an idea of how much you have learned.

Record your answers here or go to MyManagementLab.com. Recording your answers in MyManagementLab will allow you to get immediate results and see how your score compares to your classmates. If you answer the questions in the book, the answers are located in the Exploring Your Management Skill Appendix at the end of the book.

FOR EACH STATEMENT CIRCLE:
• "Y" if you would give the advice to Wrigley.
• "N" if you would NOT give the advice to Wrigley.
• "NI" if you have no idea whether you would give the advice to Wrigley.

Mr. Wrigley, in meeting your organizational change challenges at Wm Wrigley Jr. Company, you should…

Before After
Study Study

1. remember that most of the time, changes should be aimed at helping the organization better achieve its goals.
Y, N, NI

2. also consider maintaining a desirable level of stability within the company.
Y, N, NI

3. normally appoint yourself as change agent.
Y, N, NI

4. generally focus more on structural change within the company rather than people or technology change.
Y, N, NI

5. sometimes consider structural change from the viewpoint of decentralizing the organization to reduce the costs of coordination.
Y, N, NI

6. normally view OD at Wrigley Company as a process for improving technology effectiveness.
   Y, N, NI

7. focus on avoiding surprises with employees as a tool for reducing resistance to changes to be made within Wrigley Company.
   Y, N, NI

8. keep in mind that a change being considered for implementation should probably be implemented if it creates more human work for Wrigley employees.
   Y, N, NI

9. evaluate potential change at Wrigley independent of the stress that the change might create for Wrigley employees.
   Y, N, NI

10. keep in mind that adverse effects of Wrigley employee stress will normally be evidenced in employee family life, but generally not employee work life because employees will not want to lose their jobs.
    Y, N, NI

11. be alert for continual employee fatigue because such fatigue could be a signal that change at Wrigley is causing too much employee stress.
    Y, N, NI

12. as a change agent, bully employees slightly to accept organizational change because small amounts of such bullying by change agents have been shown to speed employee acceptance of organizational changes.
    Y, N, NI

13. consider establishing virtual offices as a means of improving organizational effectiveness and efficiency.
    Y, N, NI

14. consider *hoteling* Wrigley employees as a program for establishing fully mobile Wrigley employees.
    Y, N, NI

15. probably establish some units at Wrigley Company as virtual work units because making such change normally lowers labor costs and generally does cause new or different change-related challenges.
    Y, N, NI

Exploring Your Management Skill: Part 2

As you recall, you completed Exploring Your Management Skill before you started to study this chapter. Your responses gave you an idea of how much you initially knew about organizational change and helped you focus on important points as you studied the chapter. Answer the Exploring Your Management Skill questions again now and compare your score to the first time you took it. This comparison will give you an idea of how much you have learned from studying this chapter and pinpoint areas for further clarification before you start studying the next chapter. Record your answers within the text or go to MyManagementLab.com. Recording your answers in MyManagementLab will allow you to get immediate results and see how your score compares to your classmates. If you answer the questions in the book, the answers are located in the Exploring Your Management Skill section at the end of the book.

Your Management Skills Portfolio

Your Management Learning Portfolio is a collection of activities especially designed to demonstrate your management knowledge and skill. By completing these activities online at MyManagementLab.com, you will be able to print, complete with cover sheet, as many activities as you choose. Be sure to save your work. Taking your printed portfolio to an employment interview could be helpful in obtaining a job.

The portfolio activity for this chapter is *Managing Change-Related Stress. Read the highlight about the Ericson Manufacturing Company and answer the questions that follow.*[53]

For more than 80 years, the Ericson Manufacturing Company has been an industry leader in the manufacturing of temporary electrical power products. The company has built a reputation of manufacturing safe, high-quality products. Products the company manufactures are varied and include electrical plugs, extension cords, and hand lamps.

For most of its nearly nine decades in business, management saw no need for extensive sales forecasting. Recently, however, Ericson's business world began to change. Rising costs of domestic materials used to make its products began to rise sharply. As a result of this price increase, the company began buying materials and parts from overseas vendors. Naturally, parts and materials purchased from overseas vendors took longer to arrive than the same goods purchased from domestic vendors. This delay in the delivery of materials and parts significantly disrupted Ericson's traditional production process and related work scheduling of employees. Manufacturing began to be delayed and customer complaints began to rise significantly. Management began to find that as predicted delivery times from overseas vendors became more unreliable, warehouse managers began to order more parts than necessary to keep extra on hand when needed. Too much money was being tied up in inventory and the company was becoming less profitable.

Assume that you are the president of Ericson Electric Company. You know that you must make some changes within the company and that you'll need a well-reasoned strategy for making the changes and minimizing the negative effects of employee stress related to the changes. Answering the following questions will help you develop this strategy.

What are four organizational changes you would like to make at Ericson?

1. _____
2. _____
3. _____
4. _____

Why would you like to make each change?

1. _____
2. _____
3. _____
4. _____

What is a stressor inherent in each of your proposed changes that could affect worker productivity at Ericson?

1. _____
2. _____
3. _____
4. _____

What will you do to try to eliminate the negative impact of each stressor?

1. _____
2. _____
3. _____
4. _____

Experiential Exercises

1 Managing Florida's Quarterback[54]

Directions. Read the following scenario and then perform the listed activities. Your instructor may want you to perform the activities as an individual or within groups. Follow all of your instructor's directions carefully.

Recently, the University of Florida football team defended its national championship title. Urban Meyer, the head coach at Florida, along with every Gator football fan, fully expected sophomore quarterback Tim Tebow to have an important role in this title defense. Tebow was a high school All American who proved that he can both throw and run the football.

Observing pre-season workouts, Meyer started to worry about Tebow. Tebow's arm was often sore, which prohibited him from throwing the football or forced him to sit out at practice. Meyer believed that Tebow's baseball style of throwing the football was causing this soreness. Meyer decided that he'd like for Tebow to change his passing style from his historical baseball passing style to a traditional shorter, more compact football throwing style.

Questions

Your instructor will divide the class into small groups. Groups should answer the following questions.

1. Should Meyer attempt to change Tebow's throwing style? Why?
2. List three reasons why Tebow might not want to change his style.
3. List three reasons why Meyer might want to change Tebow's style.
4. Assuming that Meyer's attempts to change Tebow result in conflict between Meyer and Tebow, which technique(s) for handling conflict discussed in the chapter would you advise Meyer to adopt? Why?

Role Play

Think about answers to the preceding questions and assume that Tebow is adamant about not wanting to change his style. Half of the groups assigned by the instructor should be prepared to play the role of Tebow and the other half prepared to play the role of Meyer. In the role-play situation, Meyer is having a meeting with Tebow to introduce the idea of Tebow changing his passing style. Meyer definitely wants Tebow to change, Tebow definitely does not want to change. Meyer has invited Tebow to his office and starts the conversation. The conversation might be videotaped by the instructor for instructional replay.

2 You and Your Career

For the past 10 years, you have been working as a mid-level manager at Microsoft Corporation, a company that provides software products for various computing devices worldwide.[55] Your career has been progressing nicely given the company's traditional posture toward developing new, revolutionary software products. However, Microsoft's competition has now become much more formidable and you just heard that to continue its success, the company must now focus on developing software product groups, products that interact and work well together, rather than simply developing independent software products. You have also heard that such a strategy will demand that the company place higher value on managers with internal collaboration and customer services skills. The company is planning to reorganize by establishing departments aimed at developing the new product groups. The new departments will be held accountable for both developing and selling the new product groups via department profit and loss statements. The next upward move for your career would be to manage one of the newly formed departments in about two years. Would you modify your personal career plan given the recent plans for change at Microsoft? If not, why? If so, how?

VideoNet Exercise

Organizational Change: Homestarrunner.com

Video Highlights

HomestarRunner.com is a small company that creates the Internet-based cartoon, "Homestar Runner." It is run primarily by two brothers, Matt and Mike Chapman, with help from friends and other family members. Both men are interviewed in the video and provide insight into the company's beginnings and the internal processes of the business.

Discussion Questions

1. How did HomestarRunner.com get started in the Internet cartoon business?
2. Describe how HomestarRunner.com uses technology in its business. How does it incorporate technological updates into work?

3. How do the Chapman brothers measure job performance?

Internet Activity

Browse the Homestarrunner site at www.homestarrunner.com. Click around the site. Check out the cartoons, games and characters. The Web site uses technology to reach out to its subscribers and revise its content to better meet user needs. One of the major challenges facing business in the twenty-first century is the rapid pace of changing technology. How would these challenges directly impact a company like Homestarrunner? Can you think of any ways this company might be indirectly impacted by changing technology? Describe these. What are some things Homestarrunner might do to successfully manage these changes?

CASES

1 WRIGLEY CONTINUES TO CHANGE

"Wrigley Continues to Change" (p. 319) and its related Challenge Case Summary sections were written to help you better understand the management concepts contained in this chapter. Answer the following discussion questions about the Challenge Case to better understand how concepts relating to organizational change and stress can be applied in a company such as Wrigley.

1. How complicated would it be for other change agents who are not members of the Wrigley family to implement the product line changes in the company? Explain.
2. Do you think that certain employees at the Wrigley Company would subtly resist this change? Why or why not?
3. What elements of this change could cause organization members to experience stress, and what might the change agent do to help alleviate this stress? Be specific.

2 P&G CHANGES THE GAME

Read the case and answer the questions that follow. Studying this case will help you better understand how concepts relating to organizational change can be applied in a company such as Procter & Gamble.

Sometimes organizational change occurs gradually—a slow process that may take months or even years to fully materialize. But occasionally, change may be swift and sudden, resulting in significant alterations to the status quo. In 2010, Procter & Gamble Company (P&G) instituted a bold move that will continue to reverberate throughout the manufacturing and retail sectors in the coming years.

Historically, large manufacturers of consumer products have sold their goods to retailers who in turn, sell to consumers. If a consumer wants a box of Tide laundry detergent, for example, that consumer visits a nearby retail store to make that purchase. But, that has changed with P&G's new "eStore." Now consumers can go directly to the manufacturer of Tide and buy the product—bypassing the retailer. From toilet paper to batteries and from air fresheners to cold medicine, P&G is changing how consumers buy products.

Kirk Perry, vice president of P&G North America, said, "the eStore is an exciting initiative that we feel will help us listen, learn, and collaborate with online shoppers to find new opportunities to serve consumers' household, beauty, and grooming needs" (*Mass Market Retailer, 2010*). The Web site's launch is designed to garner customer feedback on P&G's various consumer products such as Gillette, Swiffer, Cover Girl, Pampers, and other brands. Visitors to the eStore can even become part of the eStore community by posting comments. Able to be viewed by others visiting the Web site, the comments include praise for certain products, frustrations about out-of-stock items, or new ideas about uses for P&G products.

The ultimate goal Perry said "is to test concepts and progress that can be reapplied with all of our online retail partners" (*Women's Wear Daily*, 2010).[57] Still, this does present a major change in how manufacturers conduct business. Selling directly to the consumer is a departure from the norm and has the potential to change the e-commerce arena for other consumer products manufacturers.

On P&G's eStore site, a consumer can buy shaving gel, refills for a razor, and aftershave lotion. No matter how much is purchased, there is a flat shipping rate of only $5. And of course, the customer has the convenience of shopping from home without having to wait in long check-out lines or deal with crowded parking lots. Products are categorized such as "Health," "Pets," and "Home Care." But, site visitors can also search based on brand name, new products, or any special offers currently available. The special offers include coupons that the consumer can immediately submit upon checkout.

P&G does not expect eStore to impact the bottom line any time soon. It sees the majority of revenue continuing to come from traditional business relationships with retailers. Instead, the Web site is being presented as a data gathering opportunity for the company. Perry said, "We envision that the eStore will help deliver new tools, service, and features that can ultimately be shared with retailers in order to provide a real convenience and value for shoppers, while also delivering innovation for the industry and more specifically for our product categories" (*Mass Market Retailer, 2010*).[58]

Whether as marketing research or simply a new way for a manufacturer to directly reach the consumer, P&G's eStore is sure to impact the retailing industry. This is especially true if national retail chains begin to sense that they have been cut out of the supply chain. Retailers have enjoyed a direct connection to the consumer, while manufacturers have relied on retailers to sell the products they make. P&G has turned the consumer relationship with products on end by enabling the consumer to come directly to the manufacturer. Of course, some very small or regional manufacturers have taken similar steps, but P&G is the largest U.S. manufacturer to make such a move. With eStore, P&G has truly changed the consumer products environment.

QUESTIONS

1. The chapter discusses three classes of factors (people, structure, and technology) in determining what should be changed. With P&G's eStore, how have each of these factors been affected?

2. Because P&G must continue to maintain strong relationships with traditional retailers, what would you recommend P&G do to help retailers adjust to the change the eStore presents?

3. What changes do you envision for online retailing of consumer products in the next five years?

Endnotes

1. "Wm. Wrigley Jr. Company Realigns Commercial Operations Structure," *PR Newswire,* February 26, 2007; "Wrigley Is in a Sticky Spot; Firepower May Be Lacking to Counter the Big Threat of a Cadbury–Hershey Tie," *Wall Street Journal,* April 4, 2007, C.12.

2. John H. Zimmerman, "The Principles of Managing Change," *HR Focus* (February 1995): 15–16.

3. For an in-depth analysis of effective change in the workplace, see Angela Mansell, Paula Brough, and Kevin Cole, "Stable Predictors of Job Satisfaction, Psychological Strain, and Employee Retention: An Evaluation of Organizational Change Within the New Zealand Customs Service," *International Journal of Stress Management,* 13 (2006): 84–107.

4. Rosabeth Moss Kanter, "The New Managerial Work," *Harvard Business Review* (November/December 1989): 85–92. For a review of planned change models as related to a nursing environment, see Constance Rimmer Tiffany *et al.*, "Planned Change Theory: Survey of Nursing Periodical Literature," *Nursing Management* (July 1994): 54–59; see also William Kahn, "Facilitating and Undermining Organizational Change: A Case Study," *The Journal of Applied Behavioral Science* 40 (2004): 7.

5. John S. Morgan, *Managing Change: The Strategies of Making Change Work for You* (New York: McGraw-Hill, 1972), 99.

6. Jeremy Smerd, "General Motors Shakes up HR Leadership," *Workforce Management,* July 30, 2009, http://www.workforce.com. For additional information on radical change, see Mark Hughes, "Reengineering Works: Don't Report, Exhort," *Management & Organizational History* 4, no. 1 (2009): 105–122.

7. Bart Nooteboom, "Paradox, Identity, and Change in Management," *Human Systems Management* 8 (1989): 291–300.

8. For discussion of the importance of change see Freek Vermeulen, Phanish Puranam, and Ranjay Gulati, "Change for Change's Sake," *Harvard Business Review,* June 2010, http://www.hbr.org.

9. For a different perspective on the behaviors required for change agents, see Sharon K. Parker and Catherine G. Collins, "Taking Stock: Integrating and Differentiating Multiple Proactive Behaviors," *Journal of Management* 36, no. 3 (May 2010): 633–662.

10. For a discussion of the value of outside change agents, see John H. Sheridan, "Careers on the Line," *Fortune,* September 16, 1991, 29–30. See also John H. Zimmerman, "The Deming Approach to Construction Safety Management," *Professional Safety* (December 1994): 35–37.

11. For a recent article on being an effective change agent, see Shelley Cohen, "Change Agents Bolster New Practices in the Workplace," *Nursing Management* 37 (2006): 16–17.

12. Myron Tribus, "Changing the Corporate Culture—A Roadmap for the Change Agent," *Human Systems Management* 8 (1989): 11–22. For a review of the effects of structural change within an organization, see Shawn Young, "Structural Changes Pay Off in Profits for Top U.S. Long-Distance Carriers," *Wall Street Journal,* January 19, 1999.

13. "University Health System Modernizes Operations with Technology Upgrades," *San Antonio Business Journal,* April 20, 2010, http://www.bizjournals.com.

14. For an interesting case illustrating the changing nature of organization structure at Procter & Gamble, see Aelita G. B. Martinsons and Maris G. Martinsons, "In Search of Structural Excellence," *Leadership & Organization Development Journal* 15 (1994): 24–28. See also Saul W. Gellerman, "In Organizations, as in Architecture, Form Follows Function," *Organizational Dynamics* 18 (Winter 1990): 57–68.

15. Frederick A. Goh and Merrill C Anderson, "Driving Business Value from Performance Management at Caterpillar," *Organization Development Journal* 25, no. 2 (Summer 2007): 219–226.

16. This section is based primarily on R. Blake, J. Mouton, and L. Greiner, "Breakthrough in Organization Development," *Harvard Business Review* (November/December 1964): 133–155.

17. Blake, Mouton, and Greiner, "Breakthrough in Organization Development."

18. W. J. Heisler, "Patterns of OD in Practice," *Business Horizons* (February 1975): 77–84.

19. Martin G. Evans, "Failures in OD Programs—What Went Wrong," *Business Horizons* (April 1974): 18–22.

20. For one such article on organization development, see Jeana Wirtenberg, David Lipsky, Lilian Abrams, Malcolm Conway, and Joan Slepian, "The Future of Organizational Development: Enabling Sustainable Business Performance Through People," *Organization Development* 25 (Summer 2007): 11–22.

21. David Coghlan, "OD Interventions in Catholic Religious Orders," *Journal of Managerial Psychology* 4 (1989): 4–6. See also Paul A. Iles and Thomas Johnston, "Searching for Excellence in Second-Hand Clothes?: A Note," *Personnel Review* 18 (1989): 32–35; Ewa Maslyk-Musial, "Organization Development in Poland: Stages of Growth," *Public Administration Quarterly* 13 (Summer 1989): 196–214.

22. For an interesting discussion of resistance to change from inherited staff, see Margaret Russell, "Records Management Program-Directing: Inherited Staff," *ARMA Records Management Quarterly* 24 (January 1990): 18–22.

23. For a recent article on resistance to change in the workplace, see David Stanley, John Meyer, and Laryssa Topolnytsky, "Employee Cynicism and Resistance to Organizational Change," *Journal of Business and Psychology* 19 (2005): 429–459.

24. For more information about internal resistance to change, see Robert Sevier, "Overcoming Internal Resistance to Change," *University Business* 6 (2003): 23.

25. This strategy for minimizing resistance to change is based on "How Companies Overcome Resistance to Change," *Management Review* (November 1972): 17–25. See also Hank Williams, "Learning to Manage Change," *Industrial and Commercial Training* 21 (May/June 1989): 17–20.

26. For discussions on how storytelling can facilitate change and help an organization's workforce through transitions, see Andrew D. Brown, Yiannis Gabriel, and Silvia Gherardi, "Storytelling and Change: An Unfolding Story," *Organization* 16, no. 3 (2009): 323–333; and Michaela Driver, "From Loss to Lack: Stories of Organizational Change as Encounters with Failed Fantasies of Self, Work and Organization," *Organization* 16, no. 3 (2009): 353–369.

27. Newton Margulies and John Wallace, *Organizational Change: Techniques and Applications* (Chicago: Scott, Foresman, 1973), 14.

28. For a recent article on evaluating change within a pharmaceutical organization, see Bill Cowley, "Why Change Succeeds: An Organizational Self-Assessment," *Organization Development Journal* 25 (2007): 25–30.

29. Edgar C. Williams, "Changing Systems and Behavior: People's Perspectives on Prospective Changes," *Business Horizons* (August 1969): 53.

30. For an article on recent developments concerning stress in the workplace, see "Employers See Rise in Stress at Work," *Occupational Health* 55 (2003): 5; see also Patricia Sikora, David Beaty, and John Forward, "Updating Theory on Organizational Stress: The Asynchronous Multiple Overlapping Change (AMOC) Model of Workplace Stress," *Human Resource Development Review* 3 (2004): 3.

31. Hans Selye, *The Stress of Life* (New York: McGraw-Hill, 1956). See also James C. Quick and Jonathan D. Quick, *Organizational Stress and Preventive Management* (New York: McGraw-Hill, 1984).

32. James D. Bodzinski, Robert F. Scherer, and Karen A. Gover, "Workplace Stress," *Personnel Administrator* 34 (July 1989): 76–80.

33. For an article regarding the role of stress in the overall quality of life of employees, see Cary Cooper, "The Challenges of Managing the Changing Nature of Workplace Stress," *Journal of Public Mental Health* 5 (2005): 6–9.

34. For an article that describes the relationship between workplace stress and psychiatric disorders, see Carolyn Dewa, Elizabeth Lin, Mieke Kooehoorn, and Elliot Goldner, "Association of Chronic Work Stress, Psychiatric Disorders, and Chronic Physical Conditions with Disability Among Workers," *Psychiatric Services* 58 (2007): 652–658.

35. Corinne M. Smereka, "Outwitting, Controlling Stress for a Healthier Lifestyle," *Healthcare Financial Management* 44 (March 1990): 70–75.

36. J. Clifton Williams, *Human Behavior in Organizations* (Cincinnati: South-Western, 1982), 212–213; Thomas L. Brown, "Are You Living in 'Quiet Desperation'?" *Industry Week,* March 16, 1992, 17.

37. For more information about the relationship between stress, burnout, and depression, see A. Iacovides, K. Fountoulakis, S. Kaprinis, and G. Kaprinis, "The Relationship Between Job Stress, Burnout and Clinical Depression," *Journal of Affective Disorders* 75 (2003): 209.

38. Stewart L. Stokes Jr., "Life after Rightsizing," *Information Systems Management* (Fall 1994): 69–71. For a discussion of other stressors, see "Workplace Stress," *HR Magazine* (August 1991): 75–76.

39. For an interesting article addressing how managers can handle their own stress, see Thomas Brown, "Are You Stressed Out?" *Industry Week,* September 16, 1991, 21.

40. Fred Luthans, *Organizational Behavior* (New York: McGraw-Hill, 1985), 146–148. For one successful method of reducing workplace stress, see J. Michael Krivyanski, "Employer-Sponsored Programs Try to Keep Workplace Stress in Check," *Business Times Journal* 20, no. 38 (April 6, 2001): 34.

41. For an article outlining the advantages of workplace stress management classes, see Yoshio Mino, Akira Babazono, Toshihide Tsuda, and Nobufumi Yasuda, "Can Stress Management at the Workplace Prevent Depression? A Randomized Controlled Trial," *Psychotherapy and Psychosomatics* 75 (2006): 177–182.

42. Donald B. Miller, "Career Planning and Management in Organizations," *S.A.M. Advanced Management Journal* 43 (Spring 1978): 33–43.

43. This section is based on Samuel C. Certo, *Supervision: Concepts and Skill-Building* (Burr Ridge, IL: McGraw-Hill Irwin, 2008), 376–381.

44. William H. Davidow and Michael S. Malone, *The Virtual Corporation* (New York: HarperCollins, 1992).

45. P. Maria Joseph Christie and Reuven R. Levary, "Virtual Corporations: Recipe for Success," *Industrial Management* (July/August 1998): 7–11.

46. Charles C. Snow, Raymond E. Miles, and Henry J. Coleman Jr., "Managing 21st Century Network Organizations," *Organizational Dynamics* (Winter, 1992): 5–20.

47. Judith R. Gordon, *Organizational Behavior: A Diagnostic Approach* (Upper Saddle River, NJ: Prentice Hall, 1999), 385.

48. Christopher Barnatt, "Virtual Organizations in the Small Business Sector: The Case of Cavendish Management Resources," *International Small Business Journal* 15, no. 4 (July/September 1997): 36–47.

49. Anthony M. Townsend, Samuel M. DeMarie, and Anthony R. Hendrickson, "Virtual Teams: Technology and the Workplace of the Future," *Academy of Management Executive* 12, no. 3 (August 1998): 17–29. For a recent article that examines the role of culture in the virtual workplace, see John Symons and Claudia Stenzel, "Virtually Borderless: An Examination of Culture in Virtual Teaming," *Journal of General Management* 32 (2007): 1–17.

50. For other examples of types of virtuality in organizations, see Daniel E. O'Leary, Daniel Kuokka, and Robert Plant, "Artificial Intelligence and Virtual Organizations," *Communication of the Ach* 40, no. 1 (January 1997): 52–59.

51. This section draws heavily from Thomas H. Davenport and Keri Pearlson, "Two Cheers for the Virtual Office," *Sloan Management Review* (Summer 1998): 51–65. For a further look at the advantages of a virtual office, see Stephen Roth, "Consultants Use a Virtual Office to Make New Services a Reality," *The Business Journal* 19, no. 20 (January 26, 2001): 8.

52. Diana Ransom, "Six Ways to Manage a Virtual Work Force," *Entrepreneur,* April 19, 2010, http://www.entrepreneur.com.

53. This exercise is based on Jay Ericson, "Radical Change for a Small Business—To Remain Competitive, Ericson Manufacturing Needed to Do a Better Job of Business Forecasting," *Optimize* 5, no. 8 (August 2006): 55.

54. This exercise is based on Dave Curtis, "Tebow, Retooled," *Orlando Sentinel*, August 20, 2007, C1.

55. Carrie Olsen, David White, and Iris Lemmer, "Career Models and Culture Change at Microsoft," *Organization Development Journal* Summer 25, no. 2 (2007): 31–35, 236.

57. "P&G Enters E-Commerce Arena," *WWD: Women's Wear Daily* 199, no. 13 (January 20, 2010): 5–1.

58. "P&G, PFSweb Team Up On Internet Shopping Site," *Mass Market Retailer* 27, no. 9 (June 14, 2010): 155.

Influencing and Communication

Target Skill

communication skill: the ability to share information with other individuals

objectives

To help build my *communication skill,* when studying this chapter, I will attempt to acquire:

1. An understanding of the relationship between influencing and emotional intelligence

2. An understanding of interpersonal communication

3. A knowledge of how to use feedback

4. An appreciation for the importance of nonverbal communication

5. Insights into formal organizational communication

6. An appreciation for the importance of the grapevine

7. Some hints on how to encourage organizational communication

CHALLENGE CASE

JETSTAR AIRWAYS SOARS ON COMMUNICATION

FOUNDED IN 2004, Jetstar Airways offers low fares to Australia and Singapore. Although owned by Qantas, Jetstar is managed and operated separately. Headed by CEO Bruce Buchanan, the airline has made a name for itself through its emphasis on operational excellence—including its attention to communication.

From the outset, Jetstar management worked to create an organizational culture that would be focused on providing excellent customer service. Managers knew that such a culture could exist only if the company's employees enjoyed their work and their affiliation with their employer. As a result, Jetstar leadership has been committed to creating the kind of organization employees are proud to be part of.

In model organizations, good communication dictates that employees never "read about their company in the media." In other words, all important news about an organization should come to employees from management, not from learning about it in a newspaper or on TV. To that end, Jetstar invested substantially in communication strategies that would ensure optimal communication. The airline's user-friendly company intranet, known as "dashboard," can be accessed remotely. An intranet that allowed remote access was key because, by the very nature of their work, airline employees are geographically dispersed. For example, Jetstar estimates that, on any given day, two-thirds of its 3,000 employees are working outside an office. That Jetstar's dashboard can be accessed remotely ensures that employees, regardless of their location, can obtain information where and when they need it.

Another feature of Jetstar's communication strategy is what management calls "the weekly wrap," a brief voicemail summary of the company's week delivered from Buchanan or other member of senior leadership. Transmitted to Jetstar's employees via their cell phones, the weekly wrap ensures that news is communicated in a timely fashion, even to those whose jobs don't routinely involve computer use.

In fact, Jetstar's emphasis on connectivity extends beyond its workforce. The airline recently announced that it would offer iPad handsets on selected flights, giving passengers the ability to access music, movies, TV shows, games, and books enroute to their destination. If the trial program is successfully, says Buchanan, Jetstar will extend iPad connectivity to all flights.[1]

■ *The Jetstar A320, pictured here, provides comfortable leather seating and can carry 177 passengers within Australia and New Zealand.*

EXPLORING YOUR MANAGEMENT SKILL

You can explore your level of communication skill **before** studying the chapter by completing the exercise "Exploring Your Management Skill: Part 1" on page 363 and **after** studying this chapter by completing the exercise "Exploring Your Management Skill: Part 2" on page 364.

THE COMMUNICATION CHALLENGE

As described in the Challenge Case, Jetstar CEO Bruce Buchanan understands the importance of information flow within the organization. According to the case, Buchanan wants to build Jetstar into a high-performing organization that processes information efficiently. This chapter emphasizes the challenge of improving communication within organizations such as Jetstar and offers some insight into how this challenge can be accomplished. The chapter is divided into two main parts: fundamentals of influencing and communication.

FUNDAMENTALS OF INFLUENCING

The four basic managerial functions—planning, organizing, influencing, and controlling—were introduced in Chapter 1. *Planning* and *organizing* have already been discussed; *influencing* is the third of these basic functions covered in this text. A definition of *influencing* and a discussion of the influencing subsystem follow.

Defining Influencing

Influencing is the process of guiding the activities of organization members in appropriate directions. *Appropriate directions,* of course, are those that lead to the attainment of management system objectives. Influencing involves focusing on organization members as people and dealing with such issues as morale, arbitration of conflicts, and the development of good working relationships.[2] It is a critical part of a manager's job. In fact, the ability to influence others is a primary determinant of how successful a manager will be.[3]

The Influencing Subsystem

Like the planning and organizing functions, the influencing function can be viewed as a subsystem within the overall management system (see Figure 15.1). The primary purpose of the influencing subsystem, as already stated, is to enhance the attainment of management system objectives by guiding the activities of organization members in appropriate directions.[4]

FIGURE 15.1

Relationship between overall management system and influencing subsystem

Figure 15.2 shows the constituents of the influencing subsystem. The input of this subsystem is composed of a portion of the total resources of the overall management system, and its output is appropriate organization member behavior. The process of the influencing subsystem involves the performance of six primary management activities:

1. Leading
2. Motivating
3. Considering groups
4. Communicating
5. Encouraging creativity and innovation
6. Building corporate culture

Managers transform a portion of organizational resources into appropriate organization member behavior mainly by performing these activities.

As Figure 15.2 shows, leading, motivating, considering groups, building corporate culture, communicating, and encouraging creativity and innovation are interrelated. Managers accomplish each of these influencing activities, to some extent, by communicating with organization members.

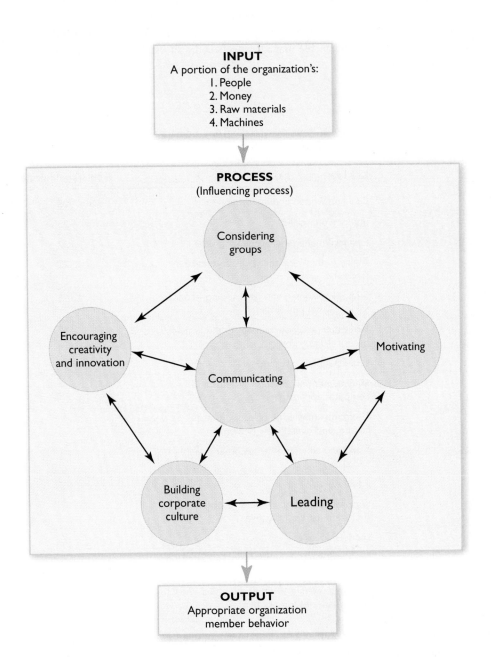

FIGURE 15.2
The influencing subsystem

For example, managers can only decide what kind of leader they need to be after they analyze the characteristics of the various groups with which they will interact and determine how those groups can best be motivated. Then, regardless of the leadership strategy they adopt, their leading, motivating, and working with groups, for example, will be accomplished—at least partly—through communication with other organization members.

In fact, all management activities are accomplished at least partly through communication or communication-related endeavors. Because communication is used repeatedly by managers, the ability to communicate is often referred to as the fundamental management skill.

A recent survey of chief executives supports this notion that communication is the fundamental management skill. The results, which appear in Table 15.1, show that CEOs ranked oral and written communication skills first (along with interpersonal skills) among those that should be taught to management students.

Emotional Intelligence

Earlier sections defined influencing and the influencing system. Overall, this influencing function of management focuses on guiding people to accomplish goals. Emotional intelligence, a concept developed by Daniel Goleman, is growing in popularity and prominence among both managers and management scholars. Overall, Goleman's concept enriches a discussion of influencing by focusing on specific skills that enable managers to become successful in guiding people toward goal accomplishment.[5]

TABLE 15.1	Chief Executives' Ranking of Skills They Believe Should Be Taught to Management Students	
Rank*	**Key Learning Area**	**Frequency Indicated**
1	Oral and written communication skills	25
1	Interpersonal skills	25
3	Financial/managerial accounting skills	22
4	Ability to think, be analytical, and make decisions	20
5	Strategic planning and goal setting—concern for long-term performance	13
6	Motivation and commitment to the firm—giving 110 percent	12
7	Understanding of economics	11
8	Management information systems and computer applications	9
8	Thorough knowledge of your business, culture, and overall environment	9
8	Marketing concept (the customer is king) and skills	9
11	Integrity	7
11	Knowledge of yourself: setting long- and short-term career objectives	7
13	Leadership skills	6
13	Understanding of the functional areas of the business	6
15	Time management: setting priorities—how to work smart, not long or hard	1

*1 is most important.

Emotional intelligence is the capacity of people to recognize their own feelings and the feelings of others, to motivate themselves, and to manage their own emotions as well as the emotions in relationships with others. Overall, an individual's emotional intelligence is characterized by self-awareness, self-motivation, self-regulation, empathy for others, and adeptness in building relationships.

Studies indicate many interesting points regarding emotional intelligence. Some research indicates that managers with higher levels of emotional intelligence are likely to be successful because they are likely to build organization culture characterized by trust, learning, information-sharing, and desirable risk taking. Other studies reveal that managers with higher levels of emotional intelligence are more interpersonally effective when compared to managers with lower levels of emotional intelligence.[6] Studies have also shown that managers with higher levels of emotional intelligence are likely to be more satisfied in their jobs than other managers, and employees who work for managers with higher levels of emotional intelligence are more satisfied with their jobs than employees who work for managers with lower levels of emotional intelligence. Ongoing studies reveal that a steady, five-year rise in emotional intelligence seems to be leveling off, perhaps implying that more training in this area needs to take place.[7]

In some ways, research in the area of emotional intelligence has produced somewhat puzzling results. On one hand, emotional intelligence research traditionally seems to indicate that managers with lower levels of emotional intelligence are likely to be relatively unsuccessful because they are less likely to produce a positive work culture.[8] On the other hand, another study suggests that the farther an individual goes up the corporate ladder, the lower his or her emotional intelligence because some organizations promote employees based on their financial performance rather than people skills.[9]

At first glance, the close relationship between the traditional influencing function of management and Goleman's emotional intelligence may be hard to recognize. Upon inspecting the skills that Goleman outlines as being necessary to being an emotionally intelligent manager, however, the relationship becomes clearer. Figure 15.3 lists several of the skills of the emotionally intelligent manager. As you can see by inspecting Figure 15.3, the influencing section of this book and the concept of emotional intelligence both emphasize critical management concepts and skills in areas of motivation, communication, leadership, teamwork, creativity, and innovation—all important attributes in building positive psychological capital in an organization.[10]

Communication is discussed further in the rest of this chapter. Leading, motivating, and considering groups and teams, corporate culture, and creativity and innovation are discussed in Chapters 16, 17, 18, 19, and 20, respectively.

Emotionally intelligent managers:

1. Motivate others
2. Focus on personal and organizational achievement
3. Understand others
4. Communicate efficiently and effectively
5. Lead others
6. Build successful teams
7. Handle conflict appropriately
8. Change organizations appropriately
9. Manage diversity
10. Manage creativity and innovation

FIGURE 15.3
Ten Skills possessed by emotionally intelligent managers

COMMUNICATION

Communication is the way we share thoughts and ideas with others.

Communication is the process of sharing information with other individuals. Information, as used here, is any thought or idea that managers want to share with others. In general, communication involves the process of one person projecting a message to one or more other people, which results in everyone arriving at a common understanding of the message. Because communication is a commonly used management skill and ability and is often cited as the skill most responsible for a manager's success, prospective managers must learn how to communicate.[11] To help managers become better interpersonal communicators, new training techniques are constantly being developed and evaluated.[12]

The communication activities of managers generally involve interpersonal communication—sharing information with other organization members.[13] The following sections feature both the general topic of interpersonal communication and the more specific topic of interpersonal communication in organizations.

Interpersonal Communication

To be a successful interpersonal communicator, a manager must understand the following:

1. How interpersonal communication works
2. The relationship between feedback and interpersonal communication
3. The importance of verbal versus nonverbal interpersonal communication

How Interpersonal Communication Works Interpersonal communication is the process of transmitting information to others.[14] To be complete, the process must have the following three basic elements:[15]

1. **The source/encoder**—The **source/encoder** is the person in the interpersonal communication situation who originates and encodes information to be shared with others. Encoding is putting information into a form that can be received and understood by another individual. Putting one's thoughts into a letter is an example of encoding. Until information is encoded, it cannot be shared with others. (From here on, the *source/encoder* will be referred to simply as the *source.*)
2. **The signal**—Encoded information that the source intends to share constitutes a **message**. A message that has been transmitted from one person to another is called a **signal**.
3. **The decoder/destination**—The **decoder/destination** is the person or persons with whom the source is attempting to share information. This person receives the signal and decodes, or interprets, the message to determine its meaning. Decoding is the process of converting messages back into information. In all interpersonal communication situations, message meaning is a result of decoding. (From here on, the *decoder/destination* will be referred to simply as the *destination.*)

The classic work of Wilbur Schramm clarifies the role played by each of the three elements of the interpersonal communication process. As implied in Figure 15.4, the source determines what information to share, encodes this information in the form of a message, and then transmits the message as a signal to the destination. The destination decodes the transmitted message to determine its meaning and then responds accordingly.

FIGURE 15.4
Role of the source, signal, and destination in the communication process

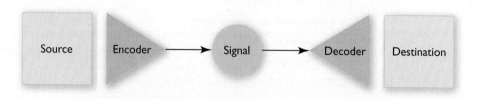

A manager who desires to assign the performance of a certain task to a subordinate would use the communication process in the following way: First, the manager would determine exactly what task he or she wanted the subordinate to perform. Then the manager would encode and transmit a message to the subordinate that would accurately reflect this assignment. The message transmission itself could be as simple as the manager telling the subordinate what the new responsibilities include. Next, the subordinate would decode the message transmitted by the manager to ascertain its meaning and then respond to it appropriately.

Successful and Unsuccessful Interpersonal Communication **Successful communication** refers to an interpersonal communication situation in which the information the source intends to share with the destination and the meaning the destination derives from the transmitted message are the same. Conversely, **unsuccessful communication** is an interpersonal communication situation in which the information the source intends to share with the destination and the meaning the destination derives from the transmitted message are different.

To increase the probability that communication will be successful, the message must be encoded so the source's experience of the way a signal should be decoded is equivalent to the destination's experience of the way it should be decoded. If these experiences match up, the probability is high that the destination will interpret the signal as intended by the source. Figure 15.5 illustrates these overlapping fields of experience that ensure successful communication.

Barriers to Successful Interpersonal Communication Factors that decrease the probability that communication will be successful are called *communication barriers*. A clear understanding of these barriers will help managers maximize their communication success. The following sections discuss both communication macrobarriers and communication microbarriers.

MACROBARRIERS **Communication macrobarriers** are factors that hinder successful communication in a general communication situation.[16] These factors relate primarily to the communication environment and the larger world in which communication takes place. Some common macrobarriers are the following:[17]

1. **The increasing need for information**—Because society is changing constantly and rapidly, individuals have a greater and greater need for information. This growing need tends to overload communication networks, thereby distorting communication. To minimize the effects of this barrier, managers should take steps to ensure that organization members are not overloaded with information. Only information critical to the performance of their jobs should be transmitted to them.

The White House is an example of an organization that regularly faces increasing needs for information from a variety of audiences, including the American public. After an evaluation of President Barack Obama's first year in office, the White House staff decided to retool elements of its communication strategy to better meet increasing needs for information that others might have. As a result of this evaluation, the White House staff decided to take specific steps aimed at better meeting such increasing needs—for example, staffers will be more aggressive in taking initiative in sending out information before it's requested. In addition, they will provide speedier, more exact responses to information requests and help the President to be more efficient when communicating with others.[18] ∎

how managers do it

Dealing with Increasing
Needs for Information
at the White House

2. **The need for increasingly complex information**—Because of today's rapid technological advances, most people are confronted with complex communication situations in their everyday lives. If managers take steps to emphasize simplicity in communication, the effects of this barrier can be lessened. Furnishing organization members with adequate training to deal with more technical areas is another strategy for overcoming this barrier.

FIGURE 15.5
Overlapping fields of experience that ensure successful communication

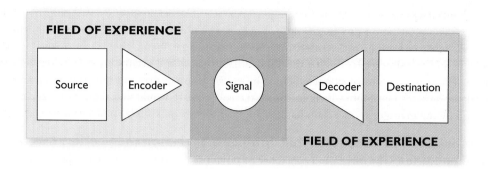

3. **The reality that people in the United States are increasingly coming into contact with people who use languages other than English**—As U.S. business becomes more international in scope, and as organization members travel more frequently, the need to know languages other than English increases. The potential communication barrier of this multilanguage situation is obvious. Moreover, people who deal with foreigners need to be familiar not only with their languages, but also with their cultures. Formal knowledge of a foreign language is of little value unless the individual knows which words, phrases, and actions are culturally acceptable.[19]

4. **The constant need to learn new concepts cuts down on the time available for communication**—Many managers feel pressured to learn new and important concepts that they did not have to know in the past. Learning about the intricacies of international business or computer usage, for example, takes up significant amounts of managerial time. Many managers also find that the increased demands that training employees makes on their time leaves them with less time for communicating with other organization members.

MICROBARRIERS A **communication microbarrier** is a factor that hinders successful communication in a specific communication situation.[20] These factors relate directly to such variables as the communication message, the source, and the destination. Among the microbarriers are the following:[21]

1. **The source's view of the destination**—The source in any communication situation has a tendency to view the destination in a specific way, and this view influences the messages sent. For example, individuals usually speak differently to people they think are informed about a subject than to those they believe are uninformed. The destination can sense the source's attitudes, which often block successful communication. Managers should keep an open mind about the people with whom they communicate and be careful not to imply negative attitudes through their communication behaviors. Figure 15.6 lists several examples of negative attitudes or stereotypes that managers in our modern society might possess regarding various types of employees. If managers possess such negative feelings about employees, the feelings will inevitably negatively impact the manner in which managers communicate to those employees and ultimately limit organizational success. Such negative attitudes or stereotypes have no place in the world of modern management.

2. **Message interference**—Stimuli that compete with the communication message for the attention of the destination are called **message interference**, or noise. An instance of message interference is a manager talking to an office worker while the worker is trying to input

FIGURE 15.6
Examples of managers' potentially negative attitudes toward employees

Employee Type	Possible Negative Attitude Held
Women	Women have weak math ability
Senior citizens	Older people have bad memory
Gay men	Gay men are dangerous to young children
Whites	Whites are racists
Men	Men are less capable than women in dealing with emotional issues
Black men	Black men are more coordinated than white men

Source: This figure is based on Loriann Roberson and Carol T. Kulik, "Stereotype Threat at Work," *Academy of Management Perspectives* 21, no. 2 (May 2007); 28–29.

data into a computer. The inputting of data is message interference here because it is competing with the manager's communication message. Managers should attempt to communicate only when they have the total attention of the individuals with whom they wish to share information.

3. **The destination's view of the source**—Certain attitudes of the destination toward the source can also hinder successful communication. If, for example, a destination believes the source has little credibility in the area about which the source is communicating, the destination may filter out much of the source's message and pay only slight attention to that part of the message actually received. Managers should attempt to consider the worth of messages transmitted to them independently of their personal attitudes toward the source. Many valuable ideas will escape them if they allow their personal feelings toward others to influence which messages they attend to.

4. **Perception**—**Perception** is an individual's interpretation of a message. Different individuals may perceive the same message in different ways. The two primary factors that influence how a stimulus is perceived are the destination's education level and the destination's amount of experience. To minimize the negative effects of this perceptual factor on interpersonal communication, managers should try to send messages with precise meanings. Ambiguous words generally tend to magnify negative perceptions. What's more, trite or insincere messages are easy for employees to recognize.[22]

5. **Multimeaning words**—Because many words in the English language have several meanings, a destination may have difficulty deciding which meaning should be attached to the words of a message. A manager should not assume that a word means the same thing to all the people who use it.

   A classic study by Lydia Strong substantiates this point. Strong concluded that for the 500 most common words in our language, there are 4,070 different dictionary definitions. On the average, each of these words has more than eight usages. The word *run* is an example:[23]

   Babe Ruth scored a run.
   Did you ever see Jesse Owens run?
   I have a run *in my stocking.*
   There is a fine run *of salmon this year.*
   Are you going to run *this company or am I?*
   You have the run *of the place.*
   What headline do you want to run?
   There was a run *on the bank today.*
   Did he run *the ship aground?*
   I have to run *(drive the car) downtown.*
   Who will run *for president this year?*
   Joe flies the New York–Chicago run *twice a week.*
   You know the kind of people they run *around with.*
   The apples run *large this year.*
   Please run *my bathwater.*

When encoding information, managers should be careful to define the terms they are using whenever possible, never use obscure meanings for words when designing messages, and strive to use words in the same way their destination uses them.

Feedback and Interpersonal Communication
Feedback is the destination's reaction to a message. Feedback can be used by the source to ensure successful communication. For example, if the destination's message reaction is inappropriate, the source can conclude that communication was unsuccessful and that another message should be transmitted. If the destination's message reaction is appropriate, the source can conclude that communication was successful (assuming, of course, that the appropriate reaction did not happen merely by chance). Because of its potentially high value, managers should encourage feedback whenever possible and evaluate it carefully.[24]

Gathering and Using Feedback
Feedback can be either verbal or nonverbal.[25] To gather verbal feedback, the source can simply ask the destination pertinent message-related questions; the destination's answers should indicate whether the message was perceived as intended. To gather

nonverbal feedback, the source can observe the destination's nonverbal response to a message.[26] Say a manager has transmitted a message to a subordinate specifying new steps that must be taken in the normal performance of the subordinate's job. The subordinate's failure to follow the steps accurately constitutes nonverbal feedback telling the manager that the initial message needs to be clarified.

If managers discover their communication effectiveness is relatively low over an extended period of time, they should assess the situation to determine how to improve their communication skills. It may be that their vocabulary is confusing to their destinations. For example, a study conducted by Group Attitudes Corporation found that when managers used certain words repeatedly in communicating with steelworkers, the steelworkers usually became confused.[27] Among the words causing confusion were *accrue, contemplate, designate, detriment, magnitude,* and *subsequently.*

Achieving Communication Effectiveness In general, managers can sharpen their communication skills by adhering to the following "10 commandments of good communication" as closely as possible:[28]

1. **Seek to clarify your ideas before communicating**—The more systematically you analyze the problem or idea to be communicated, the clearer it becomes. This is the first step toward effective communication. Many communications fail because of inadequate planning. Good planning must consider the goals and attitudes of those who will receive the communication and those who will be affected by it.

2. **Examine the true purpose of each communication**—Before you communicate, ask yourself what you really want to accomplish with your message—obtain information, initiate action, change another person's attitude? Identify your most important goal and then adapt your language, tone, and total approach to serve that specific objective. Don't try to accomplish too much with each communication. The sharper the focus of your message, the greater its chances of success.

3. **Consider the total physical and human setting whenever you communicate**—Meaning and intent are conveyed by more than words alone. Many other factors influence the overall impact of a communication, and managers must be sensitive to the total setting in which they communicate. Consider, for example, your sense of timing, or the circumstances under which you make an announcement or render a decision; the physical setting; whether you communicate in private or otherwise, for example, the social climate that pervades work relationships within your company or department and sets the tone of its communications; and custom and practice, or the degree to which your communication conforms to, or departs from, the expectations of your audience. Be constantly aware of the total setting in which you communicate. Like all living things, communication must be capable of adapting to its environment.

4. **Consult with others, when appropriate, in planning communications**—Frequently, it is desirable or necessary to seek the participation of others in planning a communication or in developing the facts on which to base the communication. Such consultation often lends additional insight and objectivity to your message. Moreover, those who have helped you plan your communication will give it their active support.

5. **Be mindful of the overtones while you communicate rather than merely the basic content of your message**—Your tone of voice, your expression, your apparent receptiveness to the responses of others—all have a significant effect on those you wish to reach. Frequently overlooked, these subtleties of communication often affect a listener's reaction to a message even more than its basic content. Similarly, your choice of language—particularly your awareness of the fine shades of meaning and emotion in the words you use—predetermines, in large part, the reactions of your listeners.

6. **Take the opportunity, when it arises, to convey something of help or value to the receiver**—Consideration of the other person's interests and needs—trying to look at things from the other person's point of view—frequently points out opportunities to convey something of immediate benefit or long-range value to the other person. Subordinates are most responsive to managers whose messages take the subordinates' interests into account.

7. **Follow up your communication**—Your best efforts at communication may be wasted, and you may never know whether you have succeeded in expressing your true meaning and intent, if you do not follow up and evaluate how well your message was received. You can do this by asking questions, by

encouraging the receiver to express his or her reactions, by following up on contacts, and by subsequently reviewing performance. Make certain that you get feedback for every important communication so that complete understanding and appropriate action result.

8. **Communicate for tomorrow as well as today**—Even though communications may be aimed primarily at meeting the demands of an immediate situation, they must be planned with the past in mind if they are to be viewed as consistent by the receiver. Most importantly, however, communications must be consistent with long-range interests and goals. For example, it is not easy to communicate frankly on such matters as poor performance or the shortcomings of a loyal subordinate, but postponing disagreeable communications makes these matters more difficult in the long run and is actually unfair to your subordinates and your company.

Nonverbal communication uses gestures, tone, and facial expression to convey information. What do you think Donald Trump is communicating?

9. **Be sure your actions support your communications**—In the final analysis, the most persuasive kind of communication is not what you say, but what you do. When your actions or attitudes contradict your words, others tend to discount what you have said. For every manager, good supervisory practices—such as clear assignment of responsibility and authority, fair rewards for effort, and sound policy enforcement—communicate more than all the gifts of oratory.

10. **Last, but by no means least, seek not only to be understood, but also to understand—be a good listener**—When you start talking, you often cease to listen, or at least to be attuned to the other person's unspoken reactions and attitudes. Even more serious is the occasional inattentiveness you may be guilty of when others are attempting to communicate with you. Listening is one of the most important, most difficult, and most neglected skills in communication. It demands that you concentrate, not only on the explicit meanings another person is expressing, but also on the implicit meanings, unspoken words, and undertones that may be far more significant.

Verbal and Nonverbal Interpersonal Communication

Interpersonal communication is generally divided into two types: verbal and nonverbal. Up to this point, the chapter has emphasized **verbal communication**—communication that uses either spoken or written words to share information with others.

Nonverbal communication is the sharing of information without using words to encode thoughts. Factors commonly used to encode thoughts in nonverbal communication are gestures, vocal tones, and facial expressions.[29] In most interpersonal communication, verbal and nonverbal communications are not mutually exclusive. Instead, the destination's interpretation of a message is generally based both on the words contained in the message and on such nonverbal factors as the source's gestures and facial expressions.

The Importance of Nonverbal Communication

In an interpersonal communication situation in which both verbal and nonverbal factors are present, nonverbal factors may have more influence on the total effect of the message.[30] Over two decades ago, Albert Mehrabian developed the following formula to show the relative contributions of verbal and nonverbal factors to the total effect of a message: Total message impact = .07 words + .38 vocal tones + .55 facial expressions. Other nonverbal factors besides vocal tones that can influence the effect of a verbal message are facial expressions, gestures, gender, and dress. Managers who are aware of this great potential influence of nonverbal factors on the effect of their communications will use nonverbal message ingredients to complement their verbal message ingredients whenever possible.[31]

Nonverbal messages can also be used to add content to verbal messages. For instance, a head might be nodded or a voice toned to show either agreement or disagreement.

Managers must be especially careful when they are communicating that verbal and nonverbal factors do not present contradictory messages. For example, if the words of a message express approval while the nonverbal factors express disapproval, the result will be message ambiguity that leaves the destination frustrated.

Managers who are able to communicate successfully through a blend of verbal and nonverbal communication are critical to the success of virtually every organization. In fact, a recent survey of corporate recruiters across the United States, commissioned by the Darden Graduate School

ABInBev

Announcement of a company's financial performance to employees by a CEO is an example of downward organizational communication. Here Anheuser-Busch InBev Chief Executive Carlos Brito presents the company's financial results.

of Business at the University of Virginia, revealed that the skill organizations most seek in prospective employees is facility at verbal and nonverbal communication.

Interpersonal Communication in Organizations

To be effective communicators, managers must understand not only general interpersonal communication concepts, but also the characteristics of interpersonal communication within organizations, or **organizational communication**. Organizational communication directly relates to the goals, functions, and structure of human organizations.[32] To a major extent, organizational success is determined by the effectiveness of organizational communication.[33]

Although organizational communication was frequently referred to by early management writers, the topic did not receive systematic study and attention until after World War II. From World War II through the 1950s, the discipline of organizational communication made significant advances in such areas as mathematical communication theory and behavioral communication theory, and the emphasis on organizational communication has grown stronger in colleges of business throughout the nation since the 1970s.[34] The following sections focus on three fundamental organizational communication topics: (1) formal organizational communication, (2) informal organizational communication, and (3) the encouragement of formal organizational communication.

Formal Organizational Communication In general, organizational communication that follows the lines of the organization chart is called **formal organizational communication**.[35] As discussed in Chapter 11, the organization chart depicts relationships of people and jobs and shows the formal channels of communication among them.

Types of Formal Organizational Communication The three basic types of formal organizational communication are downward, upward, and lateral.

1. **Downward organizational communication** is communication that flows from any point on an organization chart downward to another point on the organization chart. This type of formal organizational communication relates primarily to the direction and control of employees. Job-related information that focuses on what activities are required, when they should be performed, and how they should be coordinated with other activities within the organization must be transmitted to employees. This downward communication typically includes a statement of organizational philosophy, management system objectives, position descriptions, and other written information relating to the importance, rationale, and interrelationships of various departments.

how managers do it

Podcasts Enhance
Downward Communication
at Ericsson

Downward communication can refer to the messages that management delivers to employees. Such communication can have a significant impact on an organization's productivity and, hence, its profitability. Thanks to technological advances, many organizations are able to leverage technology to enhance the communication that flows from management to the workforce. Consider, for example, Ericsson, a leading manufacturer of telecommunication equipment and a service provider. With a geographically dispersed workforce, Ericsson leadership sought an efficient way to communicate company news quickly and uniformly throughout the organization. Ericsson turned to audio podcasting as a solution to delivering up-to-the-minute information to its over 75,000 employees in the field. Podcasts have helped the company boost the effectiveness of its salesforce.[36] ∎

2. **Upward organizational communication** is communication that flows from any point on an organization chart upward to another point on the organization chart.[37] This type of organizational communication contains primarily the information managers need to evaluate

the organizational area for which they are responsible and to determine whether something is going wrong within it. Techniques that managers commonly use to encourage upward organizational communication are informal discussions with employees, attitude surveys, the development and use of grievance procedures, suggestion systems, and an "open door" policy that invites employees to come in whenever they would like to talk to management.[38] Organizational modifications based on the feedback provided by upward organizational communication will enable a company to be more successful in the future.

3. **Lateral organizational communication** is communication that flows from any point on an organization chart horizontally to another point on the organization chart. Communication that flows across the organization usually focuses on coordinating the activities of various departments and developing new plans for future operating periods. Within the organization, all departments are related to all other departments. Only through lateral communication can these departmental relationships be coordinated well enough to enhance the attainment of management system objectives.

Patterns of Formal Organizational Communication By its very nature, organizational communication creates patterns of communication among organization members. These patterns evolve from the repeated occurrence of various serial transmissions of information. According to Haney, a **serial transmission** involves passing information from one individual to another in a series. It occurs under the following circumstances:[39]

> A communicates a message to B; B then communicates A's message (or rather his or her interpretation of A's message) to C; C then communicates his or her interpretation of B's interpretation of A's message to D; and so on. The originator and the ultimate recipient of the message are separated by middle people.

One obvious weakness of a serial transmission is that messages tend to become distorted as the length of the series increases. Research has shown that message details may be omitted, altered, or added in a serial transmission.

The potential inaccuracy of transmitted messages is not the only weakness of serial transmissions. A classic article by Alex Bavelas and Dermot Barrett[40] makes the case that serial transmissions can also influence morale, the emergence of a leader, the degree to which individuals involved in the transmissions are organized, and their efficiency. Three basic organizational communication patterns and the corresponding effects on the variables just mentioned are shown in Figure 15.7.

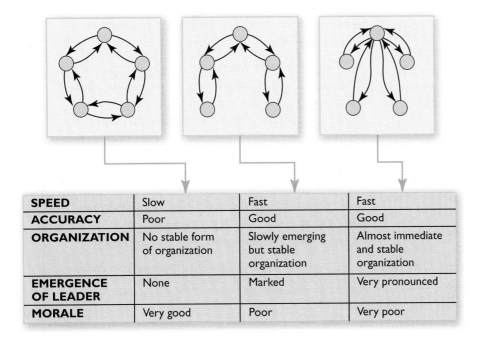

FIGURE 15.7
Comparison of three patterns of organizational communication based on the variables of speed, accuracy, organization, emergence of leader, and morale

SPEED	Slow	Fast	Fast
ACCURACY	Poor	Good	Good
ORGANIZATION	No stable form of organization	Slowly emerging but stable organization	Almost immediate and stable organization
EMERGENCE OF LEADER	None	Marked	Very pronounced
MORALE	Very good	Poor	Very poor

Informal Organizational Communication **Informal organizational communication** is organizational communication that does not follow the lines of the organization chart.[41] Instead, this type of communication typically follows the pattern of personal relationships among organization members: One friend communicates with another friend, regardless of their relative positions on the organization chart. Informal organizational communication networks generally exist because organization members have a desire for information that is not furnished through formal organizational communication.[42] In times of economic downturn, informal communication tends to increase because organization members are scavenging for information from almost anyone regarding how well the organization is doing and if job cutbacks seem eminent.[43]

To manage informal organizational communication appropriately, managers must strive to understand how this informal network operates in their organizations. For example, at Steelcase in Grand Rapids, Michigan, management conducted a study to better understand the informal communication that went on within the company. The study yielded valuable information: for instance, at Steelcase the days of standing around the water cooler to exchange the latest organizational gossip or company news may be over. Only 1 percent of Steelcase employees go to the cooler for more than water. At Steelcase, informal communication conversations are more likely to take place in the office kitchen, at a co-worker's desk, or through e-mail.[44]

Patterns of Informal Organizational Communication The informal organizational communication network, or **grapevine**, has three main characteristics:

1. It springs up and is used irregularly within the organization.
2. It is not controlled by top executives, who may not even be able to influence it.
3. It exists largely to serve the self-interests of the people within it.

class discussion highlight

MODERN RESEARCH AND COMMUNICATION SKILL

The Impact of Diversity on Organizational Communication in Foreign Subsidiaries

Various attributes of people can affect the interpersonal communication process in organizations. This highlight focuses on a research study by Vesa Peltokorpi that explores the relationship between employee diversity and interpersonal communication in organizations.

The study focused on nine different sales subsidiaries in Japan owned by different Nordic companies. Nordic refers to the northwestern European countries of Norway, Sweden, Denmark, Iceland, and Finland. For the study, a survey was specially designed to see whether individuals from diverse cultural backgrounds within a company were reluctant to communicate with one another. Employees in all subsidiaries, including Nordic expatriates, were analyzed together. Overall, 110 employees from the nine subsidiaries participated in the study. All subjects were engaged in sales activities, but the industries in which they operated varied.

The researchers wanted to see whether diversity variables—such as differences in employee ages, gender, race, education, and work values—would encourage or discourage communication among the employees in organizations. The researcher predicted that differences in characteristics would actually discourage people from communicating with one another. Do you think results of the study were consistent with the prediction? Why? Why not? How would you use your expected findings to increase your communication skill as a manager?

Source: Vesa Peltokorpi, "The Impact of Relational Diversity and Socio-Cultural Context on Interpersonal Communication: Nordic Subsidiaries in Japan," *Asian Business & Management* 5, no. 3 (September 2006): 333–356.

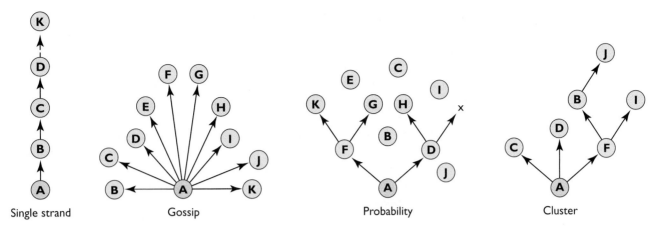

FIGURE 15.8 Four types of organizational grapevines

Understanding the grapevine is a prerequisite for a complete understanding of organizational communication. It has been estimated that 70 percent of all communication in organizations flows along the organizational grapevine. Not only do grapevines carry great amounts of communication, but they carry it at rapid speeds. Employees commonly cite the company grapevine as the most reliable and credible source of information about company events.[45]

Like formal organizational communication, informal organizational communication uses serial transmissions. The difference is that it is more difficult for managers to identify organization members involved in these transmissions than members of the formal communication network. A classic article by Keith Davis that appeared in the *Harvard Business Review* has been a significant help to managers in understanding how organizational grapevines spring up and operate. Figure 15.8 sketches the four most common grapevine patterns as outlined by Davis. They are as follows:[46]

1. **The single-strand grapevine**—*A* tells *B*, who tells *C*, who tells *D*, and so on. This type of grapevine tends to distort messages more than any other.
2. **The gossip grapevine**—*A* informs everyone else on the grapevine.
3. **The probability grapevine**—*A* communicates randomly—for example, to *F* and *D*. *F* and *D* then continue to inform other grapevine members in the same way.
4. **The cluster grapevine**—*A* selects and tells *C, D,* and *F. F* selects and tells *I* and *B,* and *B* selects and tells *J*. Information in this grapevine travels only to selected individuals.

DEALING WITH GRAPEVINES Clearly, grapevines are a factor managers must deal with because they can, and often do, generate rumors that are detrimental to organizational success. Exactly how individual managers should deal with the grapevine, of course, depends on the specific organizational situation in which they find themselves. Managers can use grapevines advantageously to maximize information flow to employees. When employees have what they view as sufficient organizational information, it seems to build their sense of belonging to the organization and their level of productivity. Some writers even argue that managers should encourage the development of grapevines and strive to become grapevine members to gain feedback that could be valuable in improving the organization.[47]

Encouraging Formal Organizational Communication
Because the organization acts only in the way its organizational communication directs it to act, organizational communication is often called the nervous system of the organization. Formal organizational communication is generally the more important type of communication within an organization, so managers should encourage its free flow.

One strategy for promoting formal organizational communication is to listen attentively to messages that come through formal channels. Listening shows organization members that the manager is interested in what subordinates have to say and encourages them to use formal communication channels in subsequent situations. Table 15.2 presents some general guidelines for listening well.

TABLE 15.2   Ten Commandments for Good Listening

1. *Stop talking!*

   You cannot listen if you are talking.

   Polonius (*Hamlet*): "Give every man thine ear, but few thy voice."

2. *Put the talker at ease.*

   Help the talker feel free to talk.

   This is often called establishing a permissive environment.

3. *Show the talker that you want to listen.*

   Look and act interested. Do not read your mail while he or she talks.

   Listen to understand rather than to oppose.

4. *Remove distractions.*

   Do not doodle, tap, or shuffle papers.

   Will it be quieter if you shut the door?

5. *Empathize with the talker.*

   Try to put yourself in the talker's place so that you can see his or her point of view.

6. *Be patient.*

   Allow plenty of time. Do not interrupt the talker.

   Do not start for the door to walk away.

7. *Hold your temper.*

   An angry person gets the wrong meaning from words.

8. *Go easy on argument and criticism.*

   This puts the talker on the defensive. He or she may "clam up" or get angry.

   Do not argue: even if you win, you *lose*.

9. *Ask questions.*

   This encourages the talker and shows you are listening.

   It helps to develop points further.

10. *Stop talking!*

   This is the first and last commandment, because all other commandments depend on it. You just can't do a good listening job while you are talking. Nature gave us two ears but only one tongue, which is a gentle hint that we should listen more than we talk.

how managers do it

Increasing Listening at McDonald's

The United Kingdom segment of McDonald's offers a useful example on how to increase listening within a company. When faced with meeting a number of daunting organizational challenges, U.K. CEO Peter Beresford instituted a program called *Listening Campaign*. Under the program, Beresford and his staff had face-to-face meetings with various stakeholder groups including staff, customers, and investors. The purpose: to listen to stakeholders and gather input regarding the challenges Beresford faced. According to Beresford, the success of *Listening Campaign* was undeniable. Through listening, he achieved numerous benefits, including building more effective work teams, identifying organizational problems and their solutions, and implementing sound problem solutions.[48] ■

Some other strategies to encourage the flow of formal organizational communication are as follows:

- Support the flow of clear and concise statements through formal communication channels. Receiving an ambiguous message through a formal organizational communication channel can discourage employees from using that channel again.

- Take care to ensure all organization members have free access to formal communication channels. Obviously, organization members cannot communicate formally within the organization if they don't have access to the formal communication network.

- Assign specific communication responsibilities to staff personnel who could be of enormous help to line personnel in spreading important information throughout the organization.

- Make sure leaders sending messages are trusted by the workforce. Interestingly, a recent study reported than less than 40 percent of employees have trust or confidence in their senior leadership.[49]

CHALLENGE CASE SUMMARY

One of Jetstar CEO Bruce Buchanan's primary responsibilities is *influencing*—guiding the activities of Jetstar employees to enhance the accomplishment of organizational objectives. Buchanan could perform this function by *leading* such individuals as division managers or perhaps corporate market research staff, by *motivating* them to do better jobs, by working well with various *groups* of employees, *encouraging creativity and innovation*, and by *communicating* successfully with employees.

Of all of these influencing activities, however, communication should be especially important to Buchanan. Communication is the main tool through which Buchanan and his leadership team should, at least to some extent, accomplish their duties. As an example in the Challenge Case, through the weekly wrap voicemail communications Buchanan and his team spread the message that Jetstar needs to focus on customer needs when delivering service. Almost any impact Buchanan plans to exert on Jetstar (planning, organizing, or controlling) will require him to communicate with other Jetstar employees. In essence, Buchanan must be a good communicator if he is to be a successful manager at Jetstar.

In discussing Bruce Buchanan's ability to communicate, we are actually discussing his ability to share ideas with other Jetstar employees. For Buchanan to be a successful communicator, he must concentrate on the three essential elements of the communication process. The first element is the source—the individual who wishes to share information with another. In this case, the source is Buchanan. The second element is the signal—the message transmitted by Buchanan. The third element is the destination—the Jetstar employee with whom Buchanan wishes to share information. Buchanan should communicate with Jetstar employees by determining what information he wants to share, encoding the information, and then transmitting the message. The subordinates would then interpret the message and respond accordingly. Buchanan's communication would be successful if subordinates interpreted messages as he intended.

If Buchanan is to be a successful communicator, he must minimize the impact of numerous communication barriers. These barriers include:

1. Jetstar employees need to have more information and more complex information to do their jobs
2. Message interference
3. Buchanan's view of the destination as well as the destination's view of Buchanan
4. The perceptual process of the people involved in the communication attempt
5. Multimeaning words

The employees' reactions to Buchanan's messages can provide Buchanan with perhaps his most useful tool in making communication successful—feedback. When feedback does not seem appropriate, Buchanan should transmit another message to clarify the meaning of his first message. He must be alert to both verbal and nonverbal feedback. Over time, if feedback indicates that Buchanan is a relatively unsuccessful communicator, he should analyze his situation carefully to improve his communication effectiveness. He might find, for instance, that he is using vocabulary that is generally inappropriate for certain employees or that he is not following one or more of the 10 commandments of good communication.

In addition, Buchanan must remember that he can communicate to others without using words. His facial expressions, gestures, and even the tone of his voice say things to people. Most of Buchanan's communication situations involve both verbal and nonverbal messages to Jetstar employees. Because the impact of a message may be generated mostly by its nonverbal components, Buchanan must be certain that his nonverbal messages complement his verbal messages. By delivering the weekly wrap mentioned in the Challenge Case to all employees' cell phones, for example, Buchanan nonverbally conveyed the importance of delivering timely communication to all of Jetstar's employees, regardless of their location.

As chairman at Jetstar, Bruce Buchanan must strive to understand the intricacies of organizational communication—interpersonal communication as it takes place within the organization. The success of organizational communication at Jetstar is an important factor in determining the company's level of success. Buchanan can communicate with his people in two basic ways: formally and informally.

In general, Buchanan's formal communication should follow the lines on the organization chart. Buchanan can communicate downward to, for example, divisional managers or upward to, for example, Jetstar's board of directors. Buchanan's downward communication will commonly focus on the activities subordinates are performing. His upward communication will usually illustrate how the company is performing. Because Buchanan is CEO and has no one at the same level within the organization, he would not communicate laterally. He should, however, take steps to ensure that lateral communication does occur at other organizational levels to enhance planning and coordination at Jetstar.

It is certain that an extensive grapevine exists at Jetstar. Although the company grapevine must be dealt with, Buchanan may not be able to influence it significantly. Jetstar employees, like employees at any company, typically are involved in grapevines for self-interest and because the formal organization has not furnished them with the information they believe they need.

By developing various social relationships, Buchanan could conceivably become part of the grapevine and obtain valuable feedback from it. Also, because grapevines generate rumors that could have a detrimental effect on Jetstar's success, Buchanan should try to ensure that personnel are given all the information they need to do their jobs well through formal organizational communication, thereby reducing the need for a grapevine.

Because formal organizational communication is vitally important to Jetstar, Buchanan should try to encourage its flow as much as possible. By listening intently to messages that come to him over formal channels, supporting the flow of clear messages, and making sure that all Jetstar employees have access to these channels, Buchanan can make sure Jetstar's communication is the best it can be.

MANAGEMENT SKILL ACTIVITIES

This section is specially designed to help you develop communication skill. An individual's communication skill is based on an understanding of communication concepts and the ability to apply those concepts in management situations. The following activities are designed both to heighten your understanding of communication fundamentals and to develop your ability to apply those concepts in various management situations.

UNDERSTANDING COMMUNICATION CONCEPTS

 To check your understanding and to practice using the concepts in this chapter, go to www.mymanagementlab.com and explore the material associated with Chapter 15.

Know Key Terms

Understanding the following key terms is critical to your understanding of chapter material. Define each of these terms. Refer to the page(s) referenced after a term to check your definition or to gain further insight regarding the term.

influencing **346**
emotional intelligence **349**
communication **350**
source/encoder **350**
message **350**
signal **350**
decoder/destination **350**
successful communication **351**

unsuccessful communication **351**
communication macrobarrier **351**
communication microbarrier **352**
message interference **352**
perception **353**
feedback **353**
verbal communication **355**
nonverbal communication **355**

organizational communication **356**
formal organizational
    communication **356**
serial transmission **357**
informal organizational
    communication **358**
grapevine **358**

Know How Management Concepts Relate

This section is comprised of activities that will sharpen your understanding of communication concepts. Answer essay questions as completely as possible. Also, remember that additional true/false and multiple choice questions appear online at MyManagementLab.com to help you further refine your understanding of communication.

1. Discuss the significance of "field of experience" in communication.

2. What is feedback and how should managers use it when communicating?

3. How can managers encourage the flow of formal communication in organizations?

4. What is "emotional intelligence" and how does it relate to influencing people in organizations?

5. Draw three types of organizational grapevines and explain how communication effectiveness might be impacted by each type.

DEVELOPING MANAGEMENT SKILLS

Learning activities in this section are aimed at helping you to develop communication skill. Learning activities include Exploring Your Management Skill: Parts 1 & 2, Experiential Exercises, Cases, and a VideoNet Exercise.

Exploring Your Management Skill: Part 1

Before studying this chapter, respond to the following questions regarding the type of advice you would give to Bruce Buchanan, the CEO referenced in the Challenge Case. Then address the concerning communication challenges that he faces within Jetstar. You are not expected to be a communication expert at this point. Answering the questions now can help you focus on important points when you study the chapter. Also, answering the questions again after you study the chapter will give you an idea of how much you have learned.

Record your answers here or go to MyManagement Lab.com. Recording your answers in MyManagementLab will allow you to get immediate results and see how your score compares to your classmates. If you answer the questions in the book, the answers are located in the Exploring Your Management Skill Appendix at the end of the book.

FOR EACH STATEMENT CIRCLE:
• "Y" if you would give the advice to Buchanan.
• "N" if you would NOT give the advice to Buchanan.
• "NI" if you have no idea whether you would give the advice to Buchanan.

Mr. Buchanan, in meeting your communication challenges at Jetstar, you should…

Before   After
Study   Study

1. communicate as well as lead and plan to exercise the influencing management functions.
   Y, N, NI

2. be aware of your own emotions as well as the emotions of others in trying to influence people.
   Y, N, NI

3. keep in mind that sometimes the primary goal of your communication is simply to share information with other employees.
   Y, N, NI

4. decode a message and then send it to Jetstar employees.
   Y, N, NI

5. think of yourself as a source/encoder who projects a message signal to a decoder destination.
   Y, N, NI

6. be careful not to overload Jetstar employees with information that's too complex.
   Y, N, NI

7. ensure that you don't use words in your messages that have too many meanings.
   Y, N, NI

8. consider field of experience in attempting to communicate successfully.
   Y, N, NI

9. not be concerned that your view of the Jetstar employee with whom you're communicating can affect your messages to that individual.
   Y, N, NI

10. keep in mind that interpersonal communication is essentially the same as organizational communication.
    Y, N, NI

11. use serial transmissions to avoid communication breakdowns.
    Y, N, NI

12. focus on eliminating the grapevine.
    Y, N, NI

13. construct communication networks to influence issues such as morale and accuracy of communication.
    Y, N, NI

14. remember that your communication effectiveness will probably be affected by your listening ability.
    Y, N, NI

15. keep in mind that your informal communication will usually be a detriment to attaining company goals.
    Y, N, NI

Exploring Your Management Skill: Part 2

As you recall, you completed Exploring Your Management Skill before you started to study this chapter. Your responses gave you an idea of how much you initially knew about communication and helped you focus on important points as you studied the chapter. Answer the Exploring Your Management Skill questions again now and compare your score to the first time you took it. This comparison will give you an idea of how much you have learned from studying this chapter and pinpoint areas for further clarification before you start studying the next chapter. Record your answers within the text or go to MyManagementLab.com. Recording your answers in MyManagementLab will allow you to get immediate results and see how your score compares to your classmates. If you answer the questions in the book, the answers are located in the Exploring Your Management Skill section at the end of the book.

Your Management Skills Portfolio

Your Management Learning Portfolio is a collection of activities especially designed to demonstrate your management knowledge and skill. By completing these activities online at MyManagementLab.com, you will be able to print, complete with cover sheet, as many activities as you choose. Be sure to save your work. Taking your printed portfolio to an employment interview could be helpful in obtaining a job.

The portfolio activity for this chapter is Developing a New Communication Environment.[50] Read the highlight about Ericsson and answer the questions that follow.

Ericsson, headquartered in Stockholm, Sweden, is a world-leading provider of telecommunications equipment with more than 1,000 networks in 140 countries. Forty percent of all mobile calls are made through Ericsson's systems. Ericsson has about 63,000 employees and is one of a few companies that offer worldwide solutions for all major mobile communication networks. A recent joint venture with Sony enabled Ericsson to offer a wide range of mobile devices, including cell phones and related equipment. The company's portfolio containing more than 20,000 patents is evidence of successful research efforts and its goal to be on the cutting edge of technology.

Over the years, Ericsson has invested heavily in maintaining its internal communication. Traditionally, the majority of this investment has been in the area of print and electronic publishing devices. Recently, management indicated that this historical investment approach for maintaining internal communications is no longer appropriate because it no longer meets Ericsson's ambitions for global best practice in all areas of the business. As part of rebuilding internal communications, all the publishing activities were outsourced to an external agency. A new area for significant investment in management's program was to improve internal communications by improving managers' interpersonal communication skills. Further, management wants the company's communication environment to change from an environment where internal communication was more focused on news flow, to an environment where the communication focuses on helping management achieve organizational goals.

Assuming you have the primary responsibility at Ericsson for building this new communication environment, answer the following questions.

What four goals would you set for building the new communication environment at Ericsson?

1. _____
2. _____
3. _____
4. _____

Explain what each goal contributes toward establishing the new environment that supports reaching organizational goals.

1. _____
2. _____
3. _____
4. _____

List a primary step you would take in trying to achieve each goal.

1. _____
2. _____
3. _____
4. _____

How long do you think it would take to establish the new communication environment at Ericsson? Why? Explain fully.

1. _____
2. _____
3. _____
4. _____

Experiential Exercises

1 Developing Nonverbal Communication Skills

Directions. Read the following scenario and then perform the listed activities. Your instructor may want you to perform the activities as an individual or within groups. Follow all of your instructor's directions carefully.

The purpose of this exercise is to help you develop your nonverbal communication skills. Apply yourself as much as possible. The more you focus on the exercise, the greater your chance of developing your skill.

Procedure

1. Your instructor will divide the class into groups of approximately four members.
2. Each group will have about 10 minutes to complete the following task through a group discussion:

   List as many advantages and disadvantages as you can to allowing illegal aliens or undocumented workers to remain in the United States.

3. Before discussion begins, each group will be given approximately five minutes so that *members can work individually* to (a) list two feelings they would like to project during the group discussion, and (b) list corresponding nonverbal actions they will use to express those feelings. For example, one feeling might be anger and the related nonverbal action could be yelling words. Individual should *NOT* share their work with other group members.
4. Once members have finished their individual work in number 3, the instructor will signal for group discussion to begin.

5. After the discussion, the instructor will allow each group about five minutes so that individuals can tell what feelings they think other individuals were trying to communicate. All should keep track of how many times their nonverbal messages were successful in communicating their target feelings.
6. The instructor will open discussion about the exercise by asking questions such as the following:

   a. Were you successful in communicating nonverbally? Why?
   b. Is it easy for you to communicate nonverbally? Why?
   c. What did *you* learn from this exercise about increasing your managerial skill to communicate nonverbally?

2 You and Your Career[51]

John Black is a production supervisor in a low-tech toy company that produces wooden cars and boats for children 2–4 years of age. John supervises 25 employees and has been performing well in this same job for five years. In personal reflection, John wants to be promoted, but doesn't think he'll be offered a promotion in the foreseeable future. John doesn't really understand why, however. John has 24/7 e-mail access and is "always on" via his wireless technology. In fact, John is somewhat of a legend at the company for always being on his BlackBerry. John not only has conversations through his BlackBerry, but does quite a bit of message texting. John has always believed that because of the efficiency involved, electronic means of communication are better than face-to-face communication.

Can John's personal philosophy about communication affect his career? If yes, why? If no, why not? If you were John, what personal philosophy about communication would you have to maximize not only your job success, but also the success of your career?

VideoNet Exercise

Communication: Zifty.com

Video Highlights

Zifty.com is a pick-up and delivery service in Atlanta, Georgia. Customers place orders via the Zifty.com Web site for food from local restaurants and for DVDs, personal care products, medicines, and so on, stored in the company warehouse. The video features company managers and a delivery driver who discuss Zifty's management and communication styles. The video provides an excellent discussion of organizational communication. Zifty.com has a very informal communication system, which encourages internal information to flow upward as well as downward. The

company also demonstrates a program of excellent customer service based on frequent communication with its customer base.

Discussion Questions

1. Describe the many roles of Zifty.com managers as discussed by Sarah Bellamy and Dylan Kight in the video.
2. How do employees at Zifty.com communicate with each other? Is communication formal or informal? Does information flow only from the top down—from owners to managers to drivers—or does it flow upward as well?
3. Give some examples of how Zifty.com has adapted to customer requests.

Internet Activity

Browse the Zifty.com site at www.zifty.com. Look at the services offered. Browse the delivery or pick-up section of the site. Check out the FAQs. What do you think of the Zifty.com business model? Is this a service that will attract new customers? Managers at Zifty.com believe they still have growth potential in the Atlanta market. They feel people in that area are willing to pay a premium price for delivery because, after enduring the long commute home, customers prefer having items delivered instead of venturing out again themselves. What do you think of Zifty.com's outlook for growth and for the future?

CASES

1 JETSTAR AIRWAYS SOARS ON COMMUNICATION

"Jetstar Airways Soars on Communication" (p. 345) and its related Challenge Case Summary were written to help you better understand the management concepts contained in this chapter. Answer the following discussion questions about the Challenge Case to better see how your understanding of influencing and communication can be applied in a company like Jetstar.

1. List three problems that could be caused at Jetstar if Buchanan happened to be a poor communicator.
2. Explain *how* the problems you listed in number 1 can be caused by Buchanan's inability to communicate.
3. Assuming that Buchanan is a good communicator, discuss three ways he is positively affecting Jetstar as a result of this communication expertise.

2 HOW EBAY STAYS CONNECTED TO ITS COMMUNITY

Read the case and answer the questions that follow. Studying this case will help you better see how your understanding of influencing and communication can be applied in a company such as eBay.

Staying in touch with a worldwide community of 114 million buyers and sellers is all in a day's work for eBay CEO Meg Whitman. When she joined eBay in 1998, it employed fewer than 100 people; today, the San Jose–based company employs 6,300 people and auctions $24 billion worth of merchandise annually. From clothing to cars to computers, eBay auctions a diverse mix of 29 million items daily on its sites in the Americas, Europe, and Asia. In this fast-paced environment, far-flung employees, managers, buyers, and sellers routinely communicate using their keyboards rather than by talking things over in person.

Fresh from management jobs at Walt Disney, Hasbro, Stride-Rite, and other big corporations, Whitman was both amazed and impressed by the reaction of eBay users she met soon after becoming CEO. "Their passion for eBay [good and bad] was nothing I'd ever seen in 20 years of business," she remembers. This vivid introduction to the eBay community helped shape her approach to influencing and communication.

First, Whitman listens carefully and respectfully before responding. Each morning, she chats with staff members in the cubicles surrounding her own before she logs on to read and then answer e-mail from traders. Every few hours, she checks eBay's message boards to get a sense of what's going on in the community. And after auctioning furniture and other possessions on her company's site, she insists that other eBay executives auction items to gain firsthand knowledge of the experience and learn to appreciate the user's perspective.

Second, the CEO and her colleagues pay close attention to feedback. For example, only after surveying 50,000 users and finding that 80 percent approved did management move ahead with a proposed change to the customizable features of its My eBay page. Although sellers in particular are quick to criticize changes that might impair auction activity or confuse buyers, "most of these sellers know more about eBay than most [eBay] employees," acknowledges Whitman. "They use it every single day. They're the experts." Still, she and her team can't always predict how a particular change will strike the community. Not long ago, Whitman heard from thousands of users complaining about a new enhancement to the eBay site. "That week, I probably got a total of 3,000 or 4,000 e-mails from pottery and glass sellers saying, 'My business is down. You've done the wrong thing,'" she says. Her response? "We fixed it. We rolled back the changes."

Third, Whitman proves through her actions that she understands what eBay really means to its users. In 1999, when technical glitches crashed the site for 22 hours and then caused intermittent problems for several weeks afterward, the CEO drove to the office at 4 A.M. on the first morning trouble erupted. She knew little about hardware and software, yet she stayed and brainstormed solutions day and night with employees and vendors. Whitman explains: "I did the only thing I knew how to do—be there. If I was there, then the best people from the vendors would be there." Looking back, the CEO of Sun Microsystems (which supplies eBay with servers) observed that Whitman "has an amazing velvet-glove touch. Instead of making me angry, she made me want to do just about anything we could to solve her problem. And that's what we did."

Once this crisis was resolved, the CEO shuffled tech management and set tough new standards to prevent similar problems in the future. Now eBay is known around the world for the reliability of its operations, with the site unavailable for just a few seconds during an average month. Small wonder that Whitman receives loud applause when she appears at the company's annual member conference. "I have one of the best jobs in corporate America," she says. "It's this unique blend of commerce and community. The community of users is endlessly interesting and endlessly surprising. That's what I love the most."

QUESTIONS

1. What macrobarriers and microbarriers might hinder successful communication between Meg Whitman and eBay users? What do you suggest she do to address these potential barriers?
2. Do you think the channels of communication in an online business such as eBay differ from those in a traditional business? Explain.
3. How would you recommend new managers at eBay establish rapport with buyers and sellers?

Endnotes

1. Company Web site, http://www.jetstar.com, accessed June 20, 2010; Kevin May, "Jetstar Airline to Trial iPad Hire with Passengers," *Tnooz.com*, June 1, 2010, http://www.tnooz.com "Come Together: Intranets Are Re-Emerging As a Way to Connect Dislocated Employees," *HR Monthly*, April 12, 2010, http://www.intranetdashboard.com Sarah O'Carroll, "Jetstar Tackles Communication Challenges," *Lawyers Weekly*, August 30, 2009, http://www.lawyersweekly.com.

2. For a recent article describing why some managers prefer certain influence tactics, see H. Steensma, "Why managers prefer some influence tactics to other tactics: A net utility explanation," *Journal of Occupational and Organizational Psychology* 80 (2007): 355.

3. Derek Torrington and Jane Weightman, "Middle Management Work," *Journal of General Management* 13 (Winter 1987): 74–89. For a useful discussion of how to influence people, see Martin Wilding, "Win Friends and Influence People by Being Sincere," *Marketing*, February 23, 1995, 16; Esther Bogin, "From Staff to Dream Team," *Financial Executive*, January/February 1995, 54–56.

4. For a recent article describing the most effective influencing tactics, see Joyce Leong, Michael Bond, and Ping Ping Fu, "Perceived Effectiveness of Influence Strategies Among Hong Kong Managers," *Asia Pacific Journal of Management* 24 (2007): 75–97.

5. Daniel Goleman, "Leadership that Gets Results," *Harvard Business Review* (March–April 2000): 78–90; Daniel Goleman, *Emotional Intelligence* (New York: Bantam Books, 1995); Daniel Goleman, *Working with Emotional Intelligence* (New York: Bantam Books, 1998).

6. Joseph Rode et al., "Emotional Intelligence and Individual Performance: Evidence of Direct and Moderated Effects," *Journal of Organizational Behavior* 28 (2007): 399–421.

7. Nick Tasler and Travis Bradberry, "Emotional Intelligence: Skills Worth Learning," *Bloomberg Businessweek*, March 27, 2009, http://www.businessweek.com.

8. "Why Emotional Intelligence Matters at Work," *Work & Family Life* 17, no. 4 (April 2003): 4.

9. Kristi Casey Sanders, "What's Your EQ?" *PlanYourMeetings.com*, August 23, 2009, http://www.planyourmeetings.com.

10. For more on positive psychological capital, see James B. Avey, Fred Luthans, and Carolyn M. Youssef, "The Additive Value of Positive Psychological Capital in Predicting Work Attitudes and Behaviors," *Journal of Management* 36, no. 2 (March 2010): 430–452.

11. For discussion of the importance of communication, see Terrence Coan, "Communication: The Key to Success," *Information Management Journal* (May/June 2002): 1.

12. Bernard Reilly and Joseph DiAngelo Jr., "Communication: A Cultural System of Meaning and Value," *Human Relations* 43 (February 1990): 29–40. Christine Clements, Richard J. Wagner, and Christopher Roland, "The Ins and Outs of Experimental Training," *Training & Development* (February 1995): 52–56. For a discussion of communication techniques, see "The Elements of Effective Communication," *Agency Sales* 30, no. 12 (December 2000): 45–46.

13. For a recent article describing the most important aspects of effective communication, see Donald English, Edgar Manton, and Janet Walker, "Human Resource Managers' Perception of Selected Communication Competencies," *Education* 127 (2007): 410–419.

14. This section is based on the following classic article on interpersonal communication: Wilbur Schramm, "How Communication Works," *The Process and Effects of Mass Communication*, ed. Wilbur Schramm (Urbana, IL: University of Illinois Press, 1954), 3–10. For an innovative assignment on communication, see Karl L. Smart and Richard Featheringham, "Developing Effective Interpersonal Communication and Discussion Skills," *Business Communication Quarterly* 69 (2006): 276–283.

15. For more information regarding the elements of interpersonal communication, see Phyl Johnson, "Handbook of Interpersonal Communication," *Organization Studies* 24 (2003): 989.

16. David S. Brown, "Barriers to Successful Communication: Part I, Macrobarriers," *Management Review* (December 1975): 24–29. For a discussion of successful communication, see Jeanelle Barrett, "Successful Communication for Business and Management," *Business Communication Quarterly* 63, no. 4 (December 2000): 102.

17. James K. Weekly and Raj Aggarwal, *International Business: Operating in the Global Economy* (New York: Dryden Press, 1987).

18. Michael D. Shear, "White House Revamps Communication Strategy," *Washington Post*, February 15, 2010, http://www.washingtonpost.com.

19. For an interesting case study describing communication skills within the global arena, see Sabine Jaccaud and Bill Quirke, "Structuring Global Communication to Improve Efficiency," *Strategic Communication Management* 10 (2006): 18–21.

20. Davis S. Brown, "Barriers to Successful Communication: Part II, Microbarriers," *Management Review* (January 1976): 15–21. For study results having implications for e-mail as a communication microbarrier, see Norman Frohlich and Joe Oppenheimer, "Some Consequences of E-mail vs. Face-to-Face Communication in Experiment," *Journal of Economic Behavior & Organization* 35, no. 3 (April 15, 1998): 389–403.

21. Sally Bulkley Pancrazio and James J. Pancrazio, "Better Communication for Managers," *Supervisory Management* (June 1981): 31–37. See also John S. Fielden, "Why Can't Managers Communicate?" *Business* 39 (January/February/March 1989): 41–44.

22. Kris Dunn, "The Five Biggest Lies in HR," *Workforce Management*, March 2010, http://www.workforce.com.

23. Lydia Strong, "Do You Know How to Listen?" In *Effective Communications on the Job*, ed. M. Joseph Dooher and Vivienne Marquis (New York: American Management Association, 1956), 28.

24. Robert E. Callahan, C. Patrick Fleenor, and Harry R. Knudson, *Understanding Organizational Behavior: A Managerial Viewpoint* (Columbus, OH: Charles E. Merrill, 1986). For a discussion of the process of generating feedback, see Elizabeth Wolfe Morrison and Robert J. Bies, "Impression Management in the Feedback-Seeking Process: Literature Review and Research Agenda," *Academy of Management Review* (July 1991): 522–541.

25. For more on nonverbal issues, see J. T. Sheppard, "Silent Signals," *Supervisory Management* (March 1986): 31–33.

26. For a recent study demonstrating the importance of feedback format, see L. Atwater and J. Brett, "Feedback format: Does it influence manager's reactions to feedback?" *Journal of Occupational and Organizational Psychology* 79 (2006): 517.

27. Verne Burnett, "Management's Tower of Babel," *Management Review* (June 1961): 4–11.

28. Reprinted by permission of the publisher from "Ten Commandments of Good Communication," by American Management Association AMA-COM et al., from *Management Review* (October 1955). © 1955 American Management Association, Inc. All rights reserved. See also Robb Ware, "Communication Problems," *Journal of Systems Management* (September 1991): 20; "Communicating: Face-to-Face," *Agency Sales Magazine*, January 1994, 22–23.

29. Ted Pollock, "Mind Your Own Business," *Supervision*, May 1994, 24–26; Joseph R. Bainbridge, "Joint Communication: Verbal and Nonverbal," *Army Logistician* 30, no. 4 (July/August): 40–42.

30. Paul Preston, "Nonverbal Communication: Do You Really Say What You Mean?" *Journal of Healthcare Management* 50 (2005): 83–86.

31. For a practical article emphasizing the role of gestures in communication, see S. D. Gladis, "Notes Are Not Enough," *Training and Development Journal* (August 1985): 35–38. See also Nicole Steckler and Robert Rosenthal, "Sex Differences in Nonverbal and Verbal Communication with Bosses, Peers, and Subordinates," *Journal of Applied Psychology* (February 1985): 157–163; W. Alan Randolph, *Understanding and Managing Organizational Behavior* (Homewood, IL: Richard D. Irwin, 1985), 349–350; Karen O. Down and Jeanne Liedtka, "What Corporations Seek in MBA Hires: A Survey," *Selections* (Winter 1994): 34–39.

32. Gerald M. Goldhaber, *Organizational Communication* (Dubuque, IA: Wm. C. Brown, 1983). For a discussion on the important role of organizational communication within a corporation, see Bauke Visser, "Organizational Communication Structure and Performance," *Journal of Economic Behavior & Organization* 42, no. 2 (June 2000): 231–252.

33. For an article that describes how employees perceive different types of organizational communication, see Zinta S. Byrne and Elaine LeMay, "Different Media for Organizational Communication: Perceptions of Quality and Satisfaction," *Journal of Business and Psychology* 21 (2006): 149–173.

34. Kenneth R. Van Voorhis, "Organizational Communication: Advances Made During the Period from World War II Through the 1950s," *Journal of Business Communication* 11 (1974): 11–18.

35. Paul Preston, "The Critical 'Mix' in Managerial Communications," *Industrial Management* (March/April 1976): 5–9. For a discussion of implementing organizational communication reflecting a worldwide structure, see "Iridium Delays Full Start of Global System," *New York Times*, September 10, 1998, C6.

36. Company Web site, "Boost Sales Effectiveness via Internet Podcasting," http://www.mobilecastmedia.com, accessed May 19, 2010.

37. For a discussion of how to communicate failures upward in an organization, see Jay T. Knippen, Thad B. Green, and Kurt Sutton, "How to Communicate Failures to Your Boss," *Supervisory Management* (September 1991): 10.

38. For an article stressing the importance of upward and downward communication for managers, see W. H. Weiss, "Communications: Key to Successful Supervision," *Supervision* 59, no. 9 (September 1998): 12–14.

39. William V. Haney, "Serial Communication of Information in Organizations," in *Concepts and Issues in Administrative Behavior*, ed. Sidney Mailick and Edward H. Van Ness (Englewood Cliffs, NJ: Prentice Hall, 1962), 150. For a discussion involving implications of off-site patterns of communication, see Robert M. Egan, Wendy Miles, John R. Birstler, and Margaret Klayton-Mi, "Can the Rift Between Allison and Penny Be Mended?" *Harvard Business Review* 76, no. 4 (July/August 1998): 28–35.

40. Alex Bavelas and Dermot Barrett, "An Experimental Approach to Organizational Communication," *Personnel* 27 (1951): 366–371.

41. Polly LaBarre, "The Other Network," *Industry Week* (September 19, 1994): 33–36.

42. For an article describing how to assess the existence of informal organizational communication, see R. Guimera, L. Danon, A. Diaz-Guilera, F. Giralt, and A. Arenas, "The Real Communication Network Behind the Formal Chart: Community Structure in Organizations," *Journal of Economic Behavior and Organization* 61 (2006): 653–667.

43. "Recession Ripening the Office Grapevine? Three Communication Tips to Keep Employees on Track," *Business Management Daily*, August 13, 2009, http://www.businessmanagementdaily.com.

44. "Steelcase Workplace Index Survey Examines 'Water Cooler' Conversations at Work: Study Confirms Gossip Is Here to Stay, Which May Benefit Employers," *PR Newswire*, August 9, 2007.

45. George de Mare, "Communicating: The Key to Establishing Good Working Relationships," *Price Waterhouse Review* 33 (1989): 30–37; Stanley J. Modic, "Grapevine Rated Most Believable," *Industry Week* (May 15, 1989): 11, 14.

46. Keith Davis, "Management Communication and the Grapevine," *Harvard Business Review* (January/February 1953): 43–49.

47. Linda McCallister, "The Interpersonal Side of Internal Communications," *Public Relations Journal* (February 1981): 20–23. See also Joseph M. Putti, Samuel Aryee, and Joseph Phua, "Communication Relationship Satisfaction and Organizational Commitment," *Group and Organizational Studies* 15 (March 1990): 44–52.

48. Ali Carruthers, "Listening to Company Stakeholders at McDonald's Restaurants," *The Business Communicator* 6, no. 4 (September 2005): 8–9.

49. D. Keith Denton, "Creating Trust," *Organization Development Journal*, December 1, 2009, http://findarticles.com.

50. This skills portfolio exercise draws from www.ericcson.com; Per Zetterquist and Bill Quirke, "Transforming Internal Communication at Ericsson," *Strategic Communication Management* 11, no. 1 (December 2006/January, 2007): 18–21.

51. This highlight is based on Jane Read, "Are We Losing the Personal Touch?" *British Journal of Administrative Management* (April/May 2007): 22–23.

chapter 16

Leadership

Target Skill

leadership skill: the ability to direct the behavior of others toward the accomplishment of objectives

objectives

To help build my *leadership skill,* when studying this chapter, I will attempt to acquire:

1. A working definition of *leadership*

2. An understanding of the relationship between leading and managing

3. An appreciation for the trait and situational approaches to leadership

4. Insights into using leadership theories that emphasize decision-making situations

5. Insights into using leadership theories that emphasize more general organizational situations

6. An understanding of alternatives to leader flexibility

7. An appreciation of emerging leadership styles and leadership issues of today

CHALLENGE CASE

IWATA FACES MANY DIFFERENT ISSUES AT NINTENDO

HIS BUSINESS CARD may say "President," but if you ask Nintendo's Satoru Iwata where his loyalties lie, he will tell you this: in his mind he's a game developer—and in his heart, he's still a gamer.

Iwata taught himself how to program while in high school, designing games and playing them with his friends. In college, he landed a part-time job designing games at HAL Laboratory, a firm that developed computer peripherals. (The company was named after the mythic "HAL" in the film *2001*.) After graduation, Iwata joined HAL full-time and rose through the ranks.

However, HAL filed for bankruptcy in 1992, only to be rescued by a client for whom it had designed many video games—Nintendo. As part of the restructuring plan, the 33-year-old Iwata became HAL's president. In the next seven years, Iwata turned his company around.

Iwata joined Nintendo in 2000 and became president in 2002. Rather than compete directly with companies like Sony and Microsoft, Iwata made the decision to broaden the video game market to attract people who did not already play video games. Iwata implemented that strategy with the introduction of the Wii console, a product with broad-based family appeal and dozens of applications. Not only did Wii create new opportunities for Nintendo and generate unprecedented growth, it sold a record 7.8 million units in Year One. Another Nintendo product, the DS handheld game machine, contributed to the company's revenues.

Even then, however, Iwata was concerned. It would be easy, he said, for complacency to set in. He wanted to keep the company hungry and humble.

Iwata's concerns may have been prophetic. With declining sales of the DS and a price cut on the Wii, in 2009 Nintendo posted a 41 percent decline in profits—its first in four years. Despite its performance, however, *BusinessWeek* named Nintendo the world's best company for 2009, calling the Wii "the true disrupter of the entertainment industry" and citing Nintendo's commitment to innovation even in the face of declining sales and consumer confidence.

Some industry observers say Nintendo was unable to keep pace with its revenue growth, leading to overworked developers. Since then, rather than hire additional employees, Nintendo has addressed the staffing issues by outsourcing some of its less important software projects.

■ *President of Nintendo Satoru Iwata holds Nintendo's 3DS portable console gaming device.*

Its latest innovation, the 3-DS handheld game, delivers 3-D imagery without special glasses. The 3-DS will compete with Sony's PlayStation Portable and Apple's iPad in the portable game player market.[1]

As a leader, Iwata has faced many different issues over the years—turning around an organization, moving from one company to another, sparking innovation, handling company growth, creating humility within a corporate culture, and handling declining profits. Iwata made handling these issues look easy. It was not.

EXPLORE YOUR MANAGEMENT SKILL

You can explore your level of leadership skill before studying the chapter by completing the exercise "Exploring Your Management Skill: Part 1" on page 391 and **after** studying this chapter by completing the exercise" Exploring Your Management Skill: Part 2" on page 392.

THE LEADERSHIP CHALLENGE

The Challenge Case reviews how Satoru Iwata turned around a bankrupt company before becoming president of Nintendo, then presided over record growth at Nintendo before its most recent financial decline. The information in the chapter would be helpful to an individual such as Iwata as the basis for developing a useful leadership strategy to achieve success in such circumstances. Often, leaders can learn as much, if not more, from their mistakes as from their successes. The chapter discusses (1) how to define leadership, (2) the difference between a leader and a manager, (3) the trait approach to leadership, (4) the situational approach to leadership, (5) leadership today, and (6) current topics in leadership.

DEFINING LEADERSHIP

Leadership is the process of directing the behavior of others toward the accomplishment of some objective. Directing, in this sense, means causing individuals to act in a certain way or to follow a particular course. Ideally, this course is perfectly consistent with such factors as established organizational policies, procedures, and job descriptions. The central theme of leadership is getting things accomplished through people.[2]

As indicated in Chapter 15, leadership is one of the four main interdependent activities of the influencing subsystem and is accomplished, at least to some extent, by communicating with others. It is extremely important that managers have a thorough understanding of what leadership entails. Leadership has always been considered a prerequisite for organizational success. Today, given the increased capability afforded by enhanced communication technology and the rise of international business, leadership is more important than ever before.[3]

Leader Versus Manager

Leading is not the same as managing. Many executives fail to grasp the difference between the two and therefore labor under a misapprehension about how to carry out their organizational duties. Although some managers are leaders and some leaders are managers, leading and managing are not identical activities.[4] According to Theodore Levitt, management consists of

> the rational assessment of a situation and the systematic selection of goals and purposes (what is to be done); the systematic development of strategies to achieve these goals; the marshalling of the required resources; the rational design, organization, direction, and control of the activities required to attain the selected purposes; and, finally, the motivating and rewarding of people to do the work.[5]

Leadership, as one of the four primary activities of the influencing function, is a subset of management. Managing is much broader in scope than leading and focuses on nonbehavioral as well as behavioral issues. Leading emphasizes mainly behavioral issues. Figure 16.1 makes the point that although not all managers are leaders, the most effective managers over the long term are leaders.

Merely possessing management skills is no longer sufficient for success as an executive in the business world. Modern executives need to understand the difference between managing and leading and know how to combine the two roles to achieve organizational success. A manager makes sure that a job gets done, and a leader cares about and focuses on the people who do the job. To combine management and leadership, therefore, requires demonstrating a calculated and logical focus on organizational processes (management) along with a genuine concern for workers as people (leadership).[6]

THE TRAIT APPROACH TO LEADERSHIP

The **trait approach to leadership** is based on early leadership research that assumed a good leader is born, not made. The mainstream of this research attempted to describe successful leaders as precisely as possible. The reasoning was that if a complete profile of the traits of a successful leader could be drawn, it would be fairly easy to identify the individuals who should and should not be placed in leadership positions.[7]

Many of the early studies that attempted to summarize the traits of successful leaders were documented. One of these summaries concludes that successful leaders tend to possess the following characteristics:[8]

1. Intelligence, including judgment and verbal ability
2. Past achievement in scholarship and athletics
3. Emotional maturity and stability
4. Dependability, persistence, and a drive for continuing achievement
5. The skill to participate socially and adapt to various groups
6. A desire for status and socioeconomic position

Evaluations of these trait studies, however, have concluded that their findings are inconsistent. One researcher says that 50 years of study have failed to produce one personality trait or set of qualities that can be used consistently to differentiate leaders from nonleaders.[9] Still, researchers continue to examine the issue. A recent study by Frank Walter and Helka Bruch analyzes the phenomenon of the charismatic leader and identifies some traits inherent in such leaders.[10] Thus far, however, research has failed to definitively articulate a trait or combination of traits that indicate an individual will be a successful leader. Leadership is apparently a much more complex issue.

Contemporary management writers and practitioners generally agree that leadership ability cannot be explained by an individual's traits or inherited characteristics. They believe, rather, that individuals can be trained to be good leaders. In other words, leaders are made, not born.[11] That is why thousands of employees each year are sent through leadership training programs.[12]

Traits that mark the leadership style of Bill Gates, CEO of Microsoft, include high intelligence and a strong drive to succeed.

Companies are finding the benefits of building leadership talent include not only enhancing company success, but also gaining an advantage in attracting the best college graduates as new hires.

THE SITUATIONAL APPROACH TO LEADERSHIP: A FOCUS ON LEADER BEHAVIOR

Leadership studies have shifted emphasis from the trait approach to the situational approach, which suggests that leadership style must be appropriately matched to the situation the leader faces. The more modern **situational approach to leadership** is based on the assumption that each instance of leadership is different and therefore requires a unique combination of leaders, followers, and leadership situations.[13]

This interaction is commonly expressed in formula form: $SL = f(L,F,S)$, where SL is *successful leadership*; f stands for *function of*; and L, F, and S are, respectively, the *leader*, the *follower*, and the *situation*.[14] Translated, this formula says that successful leadership is a function of a leader, follower, and situation that are appropriate for one another.

Leadership Situations and Decisions

The Tannenbaum and Schmidt Leadership Continuum Because one of the most important tasks of a leader is making sound decisions, all practical and legitimate leadership thinking emphasizes decision making. Tannenbaum and Schmidt, who wrote one of the first and perhaps most often quoted articles on the situational approach to leadership, stress situations in which a leader makes decisions.[15] Figure 16.2 presents their model of leadership behavior.

This model is actually a continuum, or range, of leadership behavior available to managers when they are making decisions. Note that each type of decision-making behavior depicted in the figure has both a corresponding degree of authority used by the manager and a related amount of freedom available to subordinates. Management behavior, at the extreme left of the model, characterizes the leader who makes decisions by maintaining high control and allowing subordinates little freedom. Behavior at the extreme right characterizes the leader who makes decisions by exercising little control and allowing subordinates much freedom and self-direction. Behavior in between the extremes reflects graduations in leadership from autocratic to democratic.

Managers displaying leadership behavior toward the right of the model are more democratic, and are called *subordinate-centered* leaders. Those displaying leadership behavior toward the left of the model are more autocratic, and are called *boss-centered* leaders.

BOSS-CENTERED LEADERSHIP   **SUBORDINATE-CENTERED LEADERSHIP**

Use of authority by the manager

Area of freedom for subordinates

| Manager makes decision and announces it | Manager "sells" decision | Manager presents ideas and invites questions | Manager presents tentative decision subject to change | Manager presents problem, gets suggestions, makes decision | Manager defines limits; asks group to make decision | Manager permits subordinates to function within limits defined by superior |

FIGURE 16.2 Continuum of leadership behavior that emphasizes decision making

Each type of leadership behavior in this model is explained in more detail in the following list:

1. **The manager makes the decision and announces it**—This behavior is characterized by the manager (a) identifying a problem, (b) analyzing various alternatives available to solve it, (c) choosing the alternative that will be used to solve it, and (d) requiring followers to implement the chosen alternative. The manager may or may not use coercion, but the followers have no opportunity to participate directly in the decision-making process.

2. **The manager "sells" the decision**—The manager identifies the problem and independently arrives at a decision. Rather than announce the decision to subordinates for implementation, however, the manager tries to persuade subordinates to accept the decision.

3. **The manager presents ideas and invites questions**—Here, the manager makes the decision and attempts to gain acceptance through persuasion. One additional step is taken, however: Subordinates are invited to ask questions about the decision.

4. **The manager presents a tentative decision that is subject to change**—The manager allows subordinates to have some part in the decision-making process but retains the responsibility for identifying and diagnosing the problem. The manager then arrives at a tentative decision that is subject to change on the basis of subordinate input. The final decision is made by the manager.

5. **The manager presents the problem, gets suggestions, and then makes the decision**—This leadership activity is the first of those described thus far that allows subordinates the opportunity to offer problem solutions before the manager does. The manager, however, is still the one who identifies the problem.

6. **The manager defines the limits and asks the group to make a decision**—In this type of leadership behavior, the manager first defines the problem and sets the boundaries within which a decision must be made. The manager then enters into partnership with subordinates to arrive at an appropriate decision. The danger here is that if the group of subordinates does not perceive that the manager genuinely desires a serious group decision-making effort, it will tend to arrive at conclusions that reflect what it thinks the manager wants rather than what the group actually wants and believes is feasible.

7. **The manager permits the group to make decisions within prescribed limits**—Here, the manager becomes an equal member of a problem-solving group. The entire group identifies and assesses the problem, develops possible solutions, and chooses an alternative to be implemented. Everyone within the group understands the group's decision will be implemented.

Determining How to Make Decisions as a Leader
The true value of the model developed by Tannenbaum and Schmidt lies in its use of making practical and desirable decisions.

The degree to which managers allow subordinates freedom and seek their input to decision making is what differentiates boss-centered and subordinate-centered leadership. Which type of leadership do you think is being used in this case?

According to these authors, the three primary factors, or forces, that influence a manager's determination of which leadership behavior to use in making decisions are as follows:

1. **Forces in the Manager**—Managers should be aware of four forces within themselves that influence their determination of how to make decisions as a leader. The first force is the manager's values, such as the relative importance to the manager of organizational efficiency, personal growth, the growth of subordinates, and company profits. For example, a manager who values subordinate growth highly will probably want to give group members the valuable experience of making a decision, even though he or she could make the decision much more quickly and efficiently alone.

    The second influencing force is level of confidence in subordinates. In general, the more confidence a manager has in his or her subordinates, the more likely it is that the manager's decision-making style will be democratic, or subordinate-centered. The reverse is also true: The less confidence a manager has in subordinates, the more likely it is the manager's decision-making style will be autocratic, or boss-centered.

    The third influencing force within the manager is personal leadership strengths. Some managers are more effective issuing orders than leading group discussions, and vice versa. Managers must be able to recognize their own leadership strengths and capitalize on them.

    The fourth influencing force within the manager is tolerance for ambiguity. The move from a boss-centered style to a subordinate-centered style means some loss of certainty about how problems should be solved. A manager who is disturbed by this loss of certainty will find it extremely difficult to be successful as a subordinate-centered leader.

2. **Forces in Subordinates**—A manager also should be aware of forces within subordinates that influence the manager's determination of how to make decisions as a leader.[16] To lead successfully, the manager needs to keep in mind that subordinates are both somewhat different and somewhat alike and that any cookbook approach to leading all subordinates is therefore impossible. Generally speaking, however, managers can increase their leadership success by allowing subordinates more freedom in making decisions when:

    * The subordinates have a relatively high need for independence (people differ greatly in the amount of direction they desire).
    * They have a readiness to assume responsibility for decision making (some see additional responsibility as a tribute to their ability; others see it as someone above them "passing the buck").
    * They have a relatively high tolerance for ambiguity (some employees prefer to be given clear-cut directives; others crave a greater degree of freedom).
    * They are interested in the problem and believe it is important to solve it.
    * They understand and identify with the organization's goals.
    * They have the necessary knowledge and experience to deal with the problem.
    * They have learned to expect to share in decision making (people who have come to expect strong leadership and then are suddenly told to participate more fully in decision making are often upset by this new experience; conversely, people who have enjoyed a considerable amount of freedom usually resent the boss who assumes full decision-making powers).

    If subordinates do not have these characteristics, the manager should probably assume a more autocratic, or boss-centered, approach to making decisions.

3. **Forces in the Situation**—The last group of forces that influence a manager's determination of how to make decisions as a leader are forces in the leadership situation. The first such situational force is the type of organization in which the leader works. Organizational factors, including the size of working groups and their geographic distribution, are especially important influences on leadership style. Extremely large work groups or wide geographic separations of work groups, for example, could make a subordinate-centered leadership style impractical.

    The second situational force is the effectiveness of a group. To gauge this force, managers should evaluate such issues as the experience of group members in working together and the degree of confidence they have in their ability to solve problems as a group. As a general rule, managers should assign decision-making responsibilities only to effective work groups.

The third situational force is the problem to be solved. Before deciding to act as a subordinate-centered leader, a manager should be sure the group has the expertise necessary to make a decision about the problem in question. If it does not, the manager should move toward more boss-centered leadership.

The fourth situational force is the time available to make a decision. As a general guideline, the less time available, the more impractical it is to assign decision making to a group because a group typically takes more time than an individual to reach a decision.

As the situational approach to leadership implies, managers will be successful decision makers only if the method they use to make decisions appropriately reflects the leader, the followers, and the situation.

Determining How to Make Decisions as a Leader: An Update Tannenbaum and Schmidt's 1957 article on leadership decision making was so widely accepted that the two authors were invited by *Harvard Business Review* to update their original work in the 1970s.[17] In this update, they warned that in modern organizations, the relationship among forces within the manager, subordinates, and situation had become more complex and more interrelated since the 1950s, which obviously made it harder for managers to determine how to lead.

The update also pointed out that new organizational environments had to be considered in determining how to lead. For example, such factors as affirmative action and pollution control—which hardly figured in the decision making of managers in the 1950s—have become significant influences on the decision making of leaders since the 1970s.

The Vroom–Yetton–Jago Model Another major decision-focused theory of leadership that has gained widespread attention was first developed in 1973 and refined and expanded in 1988.[18] This theory, which we will call the **Vroom–Yetton–Jago (VYJ) model of leadership** after its three major contributors, focuses on how much participation to allow subordinates in the decision-making process. The VYJ model is built on two important premises:

1. Organizational decisions should be of high quality (should have a beneficial impact on performance).
2. Subordinates should accept and be committed to organizational decisions that are made.

Decision Styles The VYJ model suggests five different decision styles or ways that leaders make decisions. These styles range from autocratic (the leader makes the decision) to consultative (the leader makes the decision after interacting with the followers) to group-focused (the manager meets with the group, and the group makes the decision). All five decision styles within the VYJ model are described in Figure 16.3.

DECISION STYLE	DEFINITION
AI	Manager makes the decision alone.
AII	Manager asks for information from subordinates but makes the decision alone. Subordinates may or may not be informed about what the situation is.
CI	Manager shares the situation with individual subordinates and asks for information and evaluation. Subordinates do not meet as a group, and the manager alone makes the decision.
CII	Manager and subordinates meet as a group to discuss the situation, but the manager makes the decision.
GII	Manager and subordinates meet as a group to discuss the situation, and the group makes the decision.
A = autocratic; C = consultative; G = group	

FIGURE 16.3
The five decision styles available to a leader according to the Vroom–Yetton–Jago Model

Using the Model The VYJ model, presented in Figure 16.4, is a method for determining when a leader should use which decision style. As you can see, the model is a type of decision tree. To determine which decision style to use in a particular situation, the leader starts at the left of the decision tree by stating the organizational problem being addressed. Then the leader asks a series of questions about the problem as determined by the structure of the decision tree until he or she arrives at a decision style appropriate for the situation at the far right side of the model.

Consider, for example, the bottom path of the decision tree. After stating an organizational problem, the leader determines that a decision related to that problem has a low quality requirement, that it is important subordinates be committed to the decision, and it is uncertain whether a decision made solely by the leader will be committed to by subordinates. In this situation, the model suggests the leader use the GII decision—that is, the leader should meet with the group to discuss the situation, and then allow the group to make the decision.

The VYJ model seems promising. Research on an earlier version of this model yielded some evidence that managerial decisions consistent with the model are more successful than are managerial decisions inconsistent with the model.[19] The model is rather complex, however, and therefore difficult for practicing managers to apply.[20]

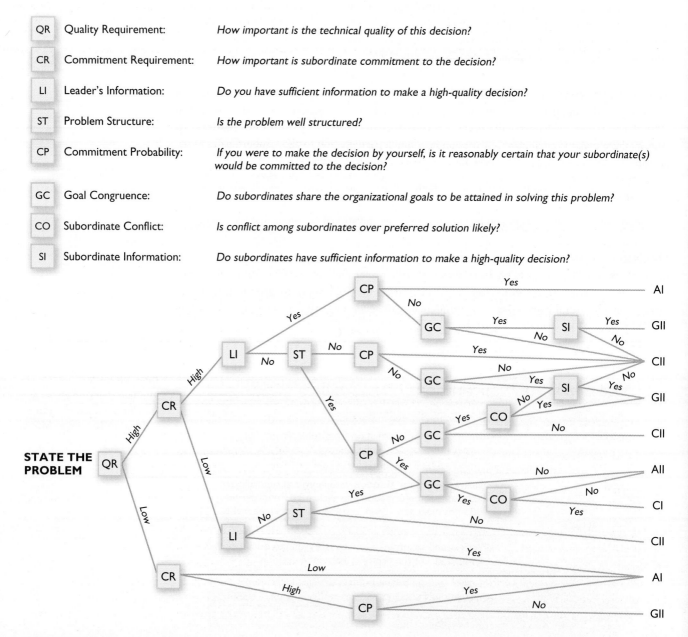

QR	Quality Requirement:	*How important is the technical quality of this decision?*
CR	Commitment Requirement:	*How important is subordinate commitment to the decision?*
LI	Leader's Information:	*Do you have sufficient information to make a high-quality decision?*
ST	Problem Structure:	*Is the problem well structured?*
CP	Commitment Probability:	*If you were to make the decision by yourself, is it reasonably certain that your subordinate(s) would be committed to the decision?*
GC	Goal Congruence:	*Do subordinates share the organizational goals to be attained in solving this problem?*
CO	Subordinate Conflict:	*Is conflict among subordinates over preferred solution likely?*
SI	Subordinate Information:	*Do subordinates have sufficient information to make a high-quality decision?*

FIGURE 16.4 The Vroom–Yetton–Jago model

class discussion highlight

MODERN RESEARCH AND LEADERSHIP SKILL

How important is transformational leadership? That is a question that continues to drive researchers. In a recent study, researchers examined how transformational leaders helped the performance of small groups. To better understand this effect, the authors examined over time the performance of 62 research and development (R&D) groups in a large pharmaceutical company. One of the objectives of the study was to understand whether transformational leaders led to better group performance.

In addition, the authors examined whether transformational leadership influenced the relationship between the group's diversity and group performance. In a previous chapter, we reviewed the benefits of diversity. The authors measured the diversity (in terms of age, nationality, and educational background) of the groups and studied if transformational leadership improved the benefits of diversity. In other words, they studied whether the positive aspects of diversity depend on whether or not the team had a transformative leader. What do you think? Why or why not?

Source: Kearney, E. and Gebert, D. "Managing Diversity and Enhancing Team Outcomes: The Promise of Transformational Leadership," *Journal Applied Psychology* 94, no. 1 (2009): 77–89.

Leadership Behaviors

The failure to identify predictive leadership traits led researchers in this area to turn to other variables to explain leadership success. Rather than looking at traits leaders should possess, the behavioral approach looked at what good leaders do. Are they concerned with getting a task done, for instance, or do they concentrate on keeping their followers happy and maintaining high morale?

Two major studies were conducted to identify leadership behavior, one by the Bureau of Business Research at Ohio State University (referred to as the OSU studies), and another by the University of Michigan (referred to as the Michigan studies).

The OSU Studies The OSU studies concluded that leaders exhibit two main types of behavior:

- **Structure behavior** is any leadership activity that delineates the relationship between the leader and the leader's followers or establishes well-defined procedures followers should adhere to in performing their jobs. Overall, structure behavior limits the self-guidance of followers in the performance of their tasks, but while it can be relatively firm, it is never rude or malicious.

  Structure behavior can be useful to leaders as a means of minimizing follower activity that does not significantly contribute to organizational goal attainment. Leaders must be careful, however, not to go overboard and discourage follower activity that *will* contribute to organizational goal attainment.

- **Consideration behavior** is leadership behavior that reflects friendship, mutual trust, respect, and warmth in the relationship between leader and followers. This type of behavior generally aims to develop and maintain a good human relationship between the leader and the followers.

Recent research by consulting firm Lore International Institute reveals that, to succeed in the workplace, it's important for leaders to demonstrate trustworthiness, honesty, and an ability to collaborate. According to the findings, leaders can "kill" trust between themselves and workers by being (1) *credit hogs* who take credit for the good ideas of others, (2) *lone rangers* who work mostly by themselves and not closely with other workers, (3) *egomaniacs* who believe that success will only come through the efforts of management as opposed to workers, or (4) *mules* who are stubborn and inflexible.[21]

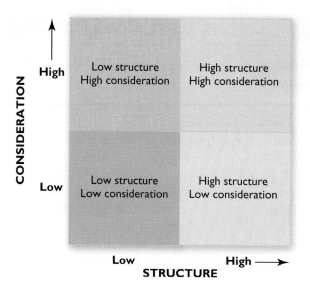

FIGURE 16.5
Four fundamental leadership styles based on structure behavior and consideration behavior

Leadership Style The OSU studies resulted in a model that depicts four fundamental leadership styles. A **leadership style** is the behavior a leader exhibits while guiding organization members in appropriate directions.[22] Each of the four leadership styles depicted in Figure 16.5 is a different combination of structure behavior and consideration behavior. For example, the high structure/low consideration leadership style emphasizes structure behavior and deemphasizes consideration behavior.

The OSU studies made a significant contribution to our understanding of leadership, and the central ideas generated by these studies still serve as the basis for modern leadership thought and research.[23]

The Michigan Studies About the same time the OSU leadership studies were being carried out, researchers at the University of Michigan, led by Rensis Likert, were also conducting a series of historically significant leadership studies.[24] After analyzing information based on interviews with leaders and followers (managers and subordinates), the Michigan studies pinpointed two basic types of leader behavior: job-centered behavior and employee-centered behavior.

JOB-CENTERED BEHAVIOR **Job-centered behavior** is leader behavior that focuses primarily on the work a subordinate is doing. The job-centered leader is interested in the job the subordinate is doing and in how well the subordinate is performing that job.

EMPLOYEE-CENTERED BEHAVIOR **Employee-centered behavior** is leader behavior that focuses primarily on subordinates as people. The employee-centered leader is attentive to the personal needs of subordinates and is interested in building cooperative work teams that are satisfying to subordinates and advantageous for the organization. Considerable research has been focused on this relationship and its outcomes, sometimes referred to as the *Pygmalion effect*, a phenomenon in which the more leaders believe their subordinates can achieve, the more they *do* achieve.[25]

The results of the OSU studies and the Michigan studies are similar. Both research efforts indicated two primary dimensions of leader behavior: a work dimension (structure behavior/job-centered behavior) and a people dimension (consideration behavior/employee-centered behavior). The following section focuses on determining which of these two primary dimensions of leader behavior is more advisable for a manager to adopt.

Effectiveness of Various Leadership Styles An early investigation of high school superintendents concluded that desirable leadership behavior is associated with high leader emphasis on both structure and consideration and that undesirable leadership behavior is associated with low leader emphasis on both dimensions. Similarly, the managerial grid described in Chapter 14 implies that the most effective leadership style is characterized by high consideration and high structure. Results of a more recent study indicate that high consideration is always preferred by subordinates.[26]

Comparing Styles One should be cautious, however, about concluding any single leadership style is more effective than any other. Leadership situations are so varied pronouncing one leadership style as the most effective is an oversimplification. In fact, a successful leadership style for managers in one situation may prove ineffective in another situation. Recognizing the need to link leadership styles to appropriate situations, A. K. Korman notes, in a classic article, that a worthwhile contribution to leadership literature would be a rationale for systematically linking appropriate styles with various situations so as to ensure effective leadership.[27] The life cycle theory of leadership, which is covered in the next section, provides such a rationale.

The Hersey–Blanchard Life Cycle Theory of Leadership The **life cycle theory of leadership** is a rationale for linking leadership styles with various situations to ensure effective leadership. This theory posits essentially the same two types of leadership behavior as the OSU leadership studies, but it calls them "task" and "relationships" rather than "structure" and "consideration."

Maturity The life cycle theory is based on the relationship among follower maturity, leader task behavior, and leader relationship behavior. In general terms, according to this theory, leadership style should reflect the maturity level of the followers. Maturity is defined as the ability of followers to perform their job independently, to assume additional responsibility, and to desire to achieve success. The more of each of these characteristics followers possess, the more mature they are said to be. (Maturity here is not necessarily linked to chronological age.)

The Life Cycle Model Figure 16.6 illustrates the life cycle theory of leadership model. The curved line indicates the maturity level of the followers: Maturity level increases as the maturity curve runs from right to left. In more specific terms, the theory indicates that effective leadership behavior should shift as follows:[28] (1) high-task/low-relationships behavior to (2) high-task/high-relationships behavior to (3) high-relationships/low-task behavior to (4) low-task/low-relationships behavior, as one's followers progress from immaturity to maturity. In sum, a manager's leadership style will be effective only if it is appropriate for the maturity level of the followers.

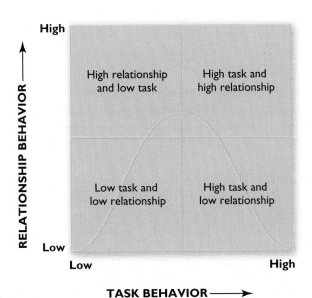

FIGURE 16.6
The life cycle theory of leadership model

Exceptions to the Model Some exceptions apply to the general philosophy of the life cycle theory. For example, if there is a short-term deadline to meet, a leader may find it necessary to accelerate production through a high-task/low-relationships style rather than use a low-task/low-relationships style, even if the followers are mature. A high-task/low-relationships leadership style carried out over the long term with such followers, though, would typically result in a poor working relationship between leader and subordinates.

Applying Life Cycle Theory Following is an example of how the life cycle theory applies to a leadership situation:

- A man has just been hired as a salesperson in a men's clothing store. At first, this individual is extremely immature—that is, unable to solve task-related problems independently. According to the life cycle theory, the appropriate style for leading this salesperson at his level of maturity is high-task/low-relationships—that is, the leader should tell the salesperson exactly what should be done and how to do it. The salesperson should be shown how to make cash and charge sales and how to handle merchandise returns. The leader should also begin laying the groundwork for developing a personal relationship with the salesperson. Too much relationship behavior at this point, however, should be avoided, because it can easily be misinterpreted as permissiveness.

- As time passes and the salesperson gains somewhat in job-related maturity, the appropriate style for leading him would be high-task/high-relationships. Although the salesperson's maturity has increased somewhat, the leader still needs to watch him closely because he requires guidance and direction at times. The main difference between this leadership style and the first one is the amount of relationship behavior displayed by the leader. Building on the groundwork laid during the period of the first leadership style, the leader can now start to encourage an atmosphere of mutual trust, respect, and friendliness between her and the salesperson.

- As more time passes and the salesperson's maturity level increases still further, the appropriate style for leading this individual will become high-relationships/low-task. The leader can now deemphasize task behavior because the salesperson is of above-average maturity in his job and is capable of independently solving most job-related problems. The leader would continue to develop a human relationship with her follower.

- Once the salesperson's maturity level reaches its maximum, the appropriate style for leading him is low-task/low-relationships. Again, the leader deemphasizes task behavior because the follower is thoroughly familiar with the job. Now, however, the leader can also deemphasize relationship behavior because she has fully established a good working relationship with the follower. At this point, task behavior is seldom needed, and relationship behavior is used primarily to nurture the good working rapport that has developed between the leader and the follower. The salesperson, then, is left to do his job without close supervision, knowing that he has a positive working relationship with a leader who can be approached for guidance whenever necessary.

The life cycle approach more than likely owes its acceptance to its intuitive appeal. Although at first glance it appears to be a useful leadership concept, managers should bear in mind that little scientific investigation has been conducted to verify its worth, and therefore it should be applied with caution.[29]

Fiedler's Contingency Theory Situational theories of leadership such as the life cycle theory are based on the concept of **leader flexibility**—the idea that successful leaders must change their leadership styles as they encounter different situations. Can any leader be so flexible as to span all major leadership styles? The answer to this question is that some leaders can be that flexible, and some cannot.

Unfortunately, numerous obstacles get in the way of leader flexibility. One is a leadership style is sometimes so ingrained in a leader it takes years to even approach flexibility. Another is some leaders have experienced such success in a basically static situation they believe developing a flexible style is unnecessary. Yet another obstacle is the widely held notion that, for leaders to be considered successful in a new role, they need to generate "quick wins." This concentration on making a significant contribution to the organization soon after assuming the leadership role actually impedes a leader's ability to be flexible and exhibit his or her true style. [30]

Changing the Organization to Fit the Leader One strategy, proposed by Fred Fiedler, for overcoming these obstacles is changing the organizational situation to fit the leader's style, rather than changing the leader's style to fit the organizational situation. [31] Applying this idea to the life cycle theory of leadership, an organization may find it easier to shift leaders to situations appropriate for their leadership styles than to expect those leaders to change styles as situations change. After all, it would probably take three to five years to train a manager to use a concept such as life cycle theory effectively, while changing the situation that the leader faces can be done quickly simply by exercising organizational authority.

According to Fiedler's **contingency theory of leadership**, leader–member relations, [32] task structure, and the position power of the leader are the three primary factors that should be considered when moving leaders into situations appropriate for their leadership styles:

- **Leader–member relations** is the degree to which the leader feels accepted by the followers.

- **Task structure** is the degree to which the goals—the work to be done—and other situational factors are outlined clearly.

- **Position power** is determined by the extent to which the leader has control over the rewards and punishments followers receive.

How these three factors can be arranged in eight different combinations, called *octants,* is presented in Table 16.1.

Figure 16.7 shows how effective leadership varies among the eight octants. From an organizational viewpoint, this figure implies management should attempt to match permissive, passive, and considerate leaders with situations reflecting the middle of the continuum containing the octants. It also implies management should try to match controlling, active, and structuring leaders with the extremes of this continuum.

Fiedler suggests some actions that can be taken to modify the leadership situation. They are as follows: [33]

1. In some organizations, we can change the individual's task assignment. We may assign to one leader the structured tasks that have implicit or explicit instructions telling him what to do and how to do it, and we may assign to another the tasks that are nebulous and vague. The former are the typical production tasks; the latter are exemplified by committee work, by the development of policy, and by tasks that require creativity.

TABLE 16.1 Eight Combinations, or Octants, of Three Factors: Leader–Member Relations, Task Structure, and Leader Position Power

Octant	Leader–Member Relations	Task Structure	Leader Position Power
I	Good	High	Strong
II	Good	High	Weak
III	Good	Weak	Strong
IV	Good	Weak	Weak
V	Moderately poor	High	Strong
VI	Moderately poor	High	Weak
VII	Moderately poor	Weak	Strong
VIII	Moderately poor	Weak	Weak

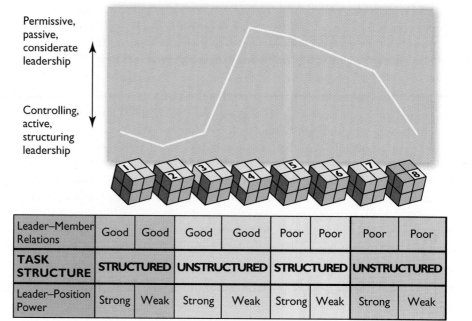

Leader–Member Relations	Good	Good	Good	Good	Poor	Poor	Poor	Poor
TASK STRUCTURE	**STRUCTURED**		**UNSTRUCTURED**		**STRUCTURED**		**UNSTRUCTURED**	
Leader–Position Power	Strong	Weak	Strong	Weak	Strong	Weak	Strong	Weak

FIGURE 16.7
How effective leadership style varies with Fiedler's eight octants

2. We can change the leader's position power. We not only can give him a higher rank and corresponding recognition, we also can modify his position power by giving him subordinates who are equal to him in rank and prestige or subordinates who are two or three ranks below him. We can give him subordinates who are experts in their specialties or subordinates who depend on the leader for guidance and instruction. We can give the leader the final say in all decisions affecting his group, or we can require that he make decisions in consultation with his subordinates, or even that he obtain their concurrence. We can channel all directives, communications, and information about organizational plans through the leader alone, giving him expert power, or we can provide these communications concurrently to all his subordinates.

3. We can change the leader–member relations in this group. We can have the leader work with groups whose members are very similar to him in attitude, opinion, technical background, race, and cultural background, or we can assign him subordinates with whom he differs in any one or several of these important aspects. Finally, we can assign the leader to a group in which the members have a tradition of getting along well with their supervisors or to a group that has a history and tradition of conflict.

Fiedler's work certainly helps destroy the myths about one best leadership style and that leaders are born, not made. Further, his work supports the theory that almost every manager in an organization can be a successful leader if placed in a situation appropriate to that person's leadership style. This matching of leadership style to the situation, of course, assumes that someone in the organization has the ability to assess the characteristics of the organization's leaders and other important organizational variables and then to bring the two together accordingly.

Fiedler's model, like all theoretical models, has its limitations; even though it may not provide concrete answers, it does emphasize the importance of situational variables in determining leadership effectiveness. As said earlier, it may actually be easier to change the leadership situation or move the leader to a more favorable situation than to try to change a leader's style.[34]

The Path–Goal Theory of Leadership The **path–goal theory of leadership** suggests that the primary activities of a leader are to make desirable and achievable rewards available to organization members who attain organizational goals and to clarify the kinds of behavior that must be performed to earn those rewards.[35] The leader outlines the goals that followers should aim for and clarifies the path that followers should take to achieve those goals and earn the rewards contingent on doing so.[36] Overall, the path–goal theory maintains that managers can facilitate job performance by showing employees how their performance directly affects their reception of desired rewards.

Although it isn't appropriate for every management situation, directive leadership—in which the leader tells followers exactly what to do—is highly appropriate for emergencies like this one, where quick decisions and unambiguous actions are critical.

Leadership Behavior According to the path–goal theory of leadership, leaders exhibit four primary types of behavior:

1. **Directive behavior**—Directive behavior is aimed at telling followers what to do and how to do it. The leader indicates what performance goals exist and precisely what must be done to achieve them.
2. **Supportive behavior**—Supportive behavior is aimed at being friendly with followers and showing interest in them as human beings. Through supportive behavior, the leader demonstrates sensitivity to the personal needs of followers.
3. **Participative behavior**—Participative behavior is aimed at seeking suggestions from followers regarding business operations to the extent that followers are involved in making important organizational decisions. Followers often help determine the rewards that will be available to them in organizations and what they must do to earn those rewards.
4. **Achievement behavior**—Achievement behavior is aimed at setting challenging goals for followers to reach and expressing and demonstrating confidence that they will measure up to the challenge. This leader behavior focuses on making goals difficult enough that employees will find achieving them challenging, but not so difficult that they will view them as impossible and give up trying to achieve them.

Adapting Behavior to Situations As with other situational theories of leadership, the path–goal theory proposes that leaders will be successful if they appropriately match these four types of behavior to situations that they face. For example, if inexperienced followers do not have a thorough understanding of a job, a manager may appropriately use more directive behavior to develop this understanding and ensure that serious job-related problems are avoided. For more experienced followers, who have a more complete understanding of a job, directive behavior would probably be inappropriate and might create interpersonal problems between leader and followers.

If jobs are highly structured, with little room for employee interpretation of how the work should be done, directive behavior is less appropriate than when much room is provided for employees to determine how the work gets done. When followers are deriving much personal satisfaction and encouragement from work and enjoy the support of other members of their work group, supportive behavior by the leader is not as important as when followers are gaining little or no satisfaction from their work or from personal relationships in the work group.

The primary focus of the path–goal theory of leadership is on how leaders can increase employee effort and productivity by clarifying performance goals and the path to be taken to achieve those goals. This theory of leadership has gained increasing acceptance in recent years. In fact, research suggests that the path–goal theory is highly promising for enhancing employee commitment to achieving organizational goals and thereby increasing the probability that organizations

	LEADER	MANAGER
	SOUL	**MIND**
	Visionary	Rational
	Passionate	Consultative
	Creative	Persistent
	Flexible	Problem-solving
	Inspirational	Tough-minded
	Innovative	Analytical
	Courageous	Structured
	Imaginative	Deliberate
	Experimental	Authoritative
	Independent	Stabilizing

FIGURE 16.8

Characteristics of the emerging leader versus characteristics of the manager

will be successful. It should be pointed out, however, the research done on this model has been conducted mostly on its parts rather than on the complete model.[37]

LEADERSHIP TODAY

Leaders in modern organizations have been confronting many situations rarely encountered by organizational leaders of the past.[38] Today's leaders are often called upon to make massive personnel cuts to eliminate unnecessary levels of organizations and thereby lower labor expenses, to introduce work teams to enhance organizational decision making and workflow, to reengineer work so organization members will be more efficient and effective, and to initiate programs designed to improve the overall quality of organizational functioning.

In reaction to these new situations, organizations are emphasizing leadership styles that concentrate on getting employees involved in the organization and giving them the freedom to use their abilities as they think best. This type of leadership is dramatically different from that known in organizations of the past, which largely concentrated on controlling people and work processes and depends, to a great degree, on a high level of trust between managers and employees.[39] Figure 16.8 contrasts the "soul" of the new leader with the "mind" of the manager.

The information in this section of the text points out the trend among today's leaders to get employees involved in their organizations and to give them the freedom to make and carry out decisions.

Five leadership styles have emerged in recent years to suit these new situations: transformational leadership, coaching, "superleadership," servant leadership, and entrepreneurial leadership.[40] Each of these new styles is discussed in the following sections.

Transformational Leadership

Transformational leadership is leadership that inspires organizational success by profoundly affecting followers' beliefs in what an organization should be, as well as their values, such as justice and integrity.[41] This style of leadership creates a sense of duty within an organization, encourages new ways of handling problems, and promotes learning for all organization members.[42] Transformational leadership is closely related to concepts such as charismatic leadership and inspirational leadership.

how managers do it

Ben & Jerry's as Transformational Leaders

Bennett Cohen and Jerry Greenfield, co-founders of the iconic Ben & Jerry's ice cream brand, are an example of transformational leaders. From the outset, profitability was only one of their goals. They were equally interested in creating an enterprise that operated in environmentally responsible ways and gave back to the communities in which they did business. According to Greenfield, "We measured our success not just by how much money we made, but by how much we contributed to the community."[43] ■

Perhaps transformational leadership is receiving more attention nowadays because of the dramatic changes many organizations are going through and the critical importance of transformational leadership in successfully "transforming" or changing organizations. In fact, recent studies have found evidence that links certain traits—hope, optimism, and resiliency—to the success of transformational leaders.[44]

The Tasks of Transformational Leaders Transformational leaders perform several important tasks. First, they raise followers' awareness of organizational issues and their consequences. Organization members must understand an organization's high-priority issues and what will happen if these issues are not successfully resolved. Second, transformational leaders create a vision of what the organization should be, build commitment to that vision throughout the organization, and facilitate organizational changes that support the vision. In sum, transformational leadership is consistent with strategy developed through an organization's strategic management process.[45]

Managers of the future will continue to face the challenge of significantly changing their organizations, primarily because of the accelerating trend to position organizations to be more competitive in a global business environment. Therefore, transformational leadership will probably get increasing attention in the leadership literature. Although the practical appeal and interest in this style of leadership are high, more research is needed to develop insights into how managers can become successful transformational leaders.

Coaching

Coaching is leadership that instructs followers on how to meet the special organizational challenges they face.[46] Operating like an athletic coach, the coaching leader identifies inappropriate behavior in followers and suggests how they might correct that behavior.[47] The increasing use of teams has elevated the importance of coaching in today's organizations, and recent research has begun to identify the leader's role in fostering a team's success.[48] Characteristics of an effective coach are presented in Table 16.2.

Coaching Behavior A successful coaching leader is characterized by many different kinds of behavior. Among these behaviors are the following:

- **Listens closely**—The coaching leader tries to gather the facts in what is said and the feelings and emotions behind what is said. Such a leader is careful to really listen and not fall into the trap of immediately rebutting statements made by followers.

- **Gives emotional support**—The coaching leader gives followers personal encouragement.[49] Such encouragement should constantly be aimed at motivating them to do their best to meet the high demands of successful organizations.

- **Shows by example what constitutes appropriate behavior**—The coaching leader shows followers, for instance, how to handle an employee problem or a production glitch. By demonstrating expertise, the coaching leader builds the trust and respect of followers.

Superleadership

Superleadership is leading by showing others how to lead themselves. If superleaders are successful, they develop followers who are productive, work independently, and need only minimal attention from the superleader.

In essence, superleaders teach followers how to think on their own and act constructively and independently.[50] They encourage people to eliminate negative thoughts and beliefs about the company and co-workers and to replace them with more positive and constructive beliefs. An important aspect of superleadership is building the self-confidence of followers by convincing them they are competent, have a significant reservoir of potential, and are capable of meeting the difficult challenges of the work situation.

TABLE 16.2   Characteristics of an Effective Coach

Trait, Attitude, or Behavior	Action Plan for Improvement
1. Empathy (putting self in other person's shoes)	*Sample:* Will listen and understand person's point of view.
	Your own:
2. Listening skill	*Sample:* Will concentrate extra hard on listening.
	Your own:
3. Insight into people (ability to size them up)	*Sample:* Will jot down observations about people on first meeting, then verify in the future.
	Your own:
4. Diplomacy and tact	*Sample:* Will study book of etiquette.
	Your own:
5. Patience toward people	*Sample:* Will practice staying calm when someone makes a mistake.
	Your own:
6. Concern for welfare of people	*Sample:* When interacting with another person, will ask myself, "How can this person's interests best be served?"
	Your own:
7. Minimum hostility toward people	*Sample:* Will often ask myself, "Why am I angry at this person?"
	Your own:
8. Self-confidence and emotional stability	*Sample:* Will attempt to have at least one personal success each week.
	Your own:
9. Noncompetitiveness with team members	*Sample:* Will keep reminding myself that all boats rise with the same tide.
	Your own:
10. Enthusiasm for people	*Sample:* Will search for the good in each person.
	Your own:

A manager who uses the coaching style demonstrates many characteristics of an athletic coach, including to followers, showing by example, and offering emotional support to members of the team.

The objective of superleaders is to develop followers who require very little leadership. This objective is important in the typical organization of today, where structure is flatter than that of organizations of the past and therefore has fewer leader–managers. Organizations cannot be successful in such a situation unless their members become proficient at leading themselves.

Servant Leadership

Servant leadership is an approach to leading in which leaders view their primary role as helping followers in their quests to satisfy personal needs, aspirations, and interests.[51] Servant leaders see pursuit of their own personal needs, aspirations, and interests as secondary to the followers' pursuit of these factors.[52] Overall, servant leaders place high value on service to others over self-interests[53] and see their main responsibility as the care of human resources of the organizations.[54] Servant leaders maintain that human resources are the most valuable resources in organizations and constantly strive to transform their followers into wiser and more autonomous individuals. Logically, the result of wiser and more autonomous followers is more successful organizations.

Some industry observers would characterize Tony Hsieh as a servant leader because his focus on building organizations emphasizes helping followers to be more effective in fulfilling their personal needs, aspirations, and interests. Hsieh, the CEO of Zappos.com, a leading online retailer, believes a healthy work environment is the most important attribute of a successful business. Early in his career, Hsieh built a successful company, but as it grew, he found it increasingly difficult to enjoy his work. The problem, he determined, was that employees were not engaged or truly interested in their work. As a result, Hsieh became progressively more dissatisfied with his own company. In his *next* company, Zappos.com, Hsieh focused on building a work environment that made employees feel so good about their career and their daily contribution that they were delighted to come to work.[55] ■

how managers do it

Servant Leadership at Zappos.com

Servant leaders possess several distinctive characteristics which, when taken together, better enable servant leaders to help followers pursue their needs, aspirations, and interests.[56] As a few of the more notable of these characteristics, servant leaders are[57]

. . . **good listeners.** Listening is a critical characteristic of servant leaders. The ability to listen carefully to follower comments, for example, helps the servant leader more accurately define the critical factors of follower needs, aspirations, and interests and thereby more effectively assist followers in their quest to achieve them. Without such accurate definition, the servant leader's task of helping followers achieve these factors would virtually be hopeless. Overall, listening provides servant leaders with feedback they can use to better serve their followers.

. . . **persuasive.** Seldom do servant leaders use authority to mandate action to be taken by followers. Instead, servant leaders focus on convincing followers of activity that should be performed. Such persuasive ability enables servant leaders to ensure that followers act appropriately without creating the resentment between leader and followers that typically appears when a leader mandates activity without follower input.

. . . **aware of their surroundings.** Servant leaders are keenly aware of organizational surroundings. As such, servant leaders know what factors might create barriers to followers in their quest to pursue needs, interests, and aspirations and take action to eliminate those barriers. Servant leaders help followers handle such barriers by furnishing followers with critical ideas and information regarding formidable organizational challenges.[58]

. . . **empathetic. Empathy** is the intellectual identification with the feelings, thoughts, or attitudes of another. Being empathetic helps servant leaders to better relate to followers in helping them solve problems. Servant leaders appreciate the situations in which followers find themselves and are thereby better equipped to assist them in their pursuit of interests, aspirations, and needs.

. . . stewards. A **steward** is defined as an individual who is entrusted with managing the affairs of another. Overall, servant leaders see themselves as being entrusted with managing the human assets of an organization and are responsible for helping organization members maximize their potential. Servant leaders are committed to building human assets that are more instrumental in achieving organizational success.

Undeniably, servant leadership has gained increasing and significant popularity in recent decades. The notion of servant leadership, however, is not new. Servant leadership was first introduced by Christianity's founder, Jesus Christ, and has been practiced by ancient monarchs for more than 1,000 years.[59] Some of the growing popularity of the servant leadership concept is probably attributable to the intuitive attractiveness of the concept.[60] For example, some management theorists believe that servant leadership's focus on empowerment, sense of community, and sharing of authority suggest that servant leadership is likely a theory with significant potential for enhancing organizational success.[61]

Recent research has analyzed the relationship between servant leadership and personality characteristics.[62] For example, one study assessed whether[63] a relationship between one's ability to be a servant leader and personality traits such as agreeableness could be identified. Agreeableness has been defined in this context to describe someone who is altruistic, generous, and eager to help others. The results of this study indicated that managers who were rated by their employees as servant leaders were also highly agreeable people. Also, servant leaders demonstrated high values of empathy, integrity, and competence. Although some research has been done in this area, additional research aimed at more precisely defining the worth of servant leadership theory to practicing managers is advisable.

Entrepreneurial Leadership

Entrepreneurial leadership is leadership that is based on the attitude that the leader is self-employed.[64] Leaders of this type act as if they are playing a critical role in the organization rather than a mostly unimportant one. In addition, they behave as if they are taking the risk of losing money but will receive the profit if one is made. They approach each mistake as if it were a significant error rather than a smaller error that will be neutralized by the normal functioning of the organization.[65]

Each of these contemporary leadership styles has received notable attention in recent management literature. Managers should realize that these five styles are not mutually exclusive; they can be combined in various ways to generate a unique style. For example, a leader can assume both a coaching and an entrepreneurial role. Figure 16.9 shows the various combinations of these five leadership styles that a leader can adopt. The shaded portion of the figure represents a leader whose style comprises all five.

how managers do it

Developing Entrepreneurial Leaders at Disney

The Walt Disney Company recently instituted an *action learning* program aimed at developing skills of entrepreneurial leaders. Action learning is defined as a means of developing people by having involving them in solving real, complex business issues. The program had about five teams of six to eight people working as groups solve a real and complex business problem. The problem that participants focused on was to create a new business opportunity for Disney that actually could be launched within six months after the program ended. To be a valid problem solution, the proposed opportunity had to be able to positively affect Disney's level of profitability. According to managers who designed this action learning program, program activities helped to hone systems thinking of participants, a fundamental skill of an entrepreneurial leader.[66]

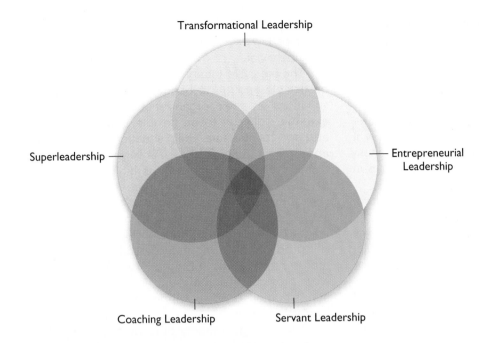

FIGURE 16.9
Various combinations of transformational, coaching, superleader, servant, and entrepreneurial leadership styles.

CHALLENGE CASE SUMMARY

As noted in the preceding material, managers such as Satoru Iwata, president of Nintendo in the Challenge Case, should understand that leadership activities involve directing the behavior of organization members so the company will achieve its success. Managers also should understand that leading and managing are not the same thing. Managing involves planning, organizing, influencing, and controlling, while leading is performing an activity that is part of the influencing function of management. To maximize long-term success, managers should strive to be both a manager and a leader.

In assessing leadership, managers such as Iwata should not fall into the trap of trying to increase leadership success by changing personal traits or attitudes to mirror those of successful leaders they might know. Studies based on the trait approach to leadership indicate to managers that merely changing their characteristics will not guarantee leadership success.

The situational approach to leadership affords more insights on how managers can help their companies achieve success than does the trait approach. The situational approach suggests that successful leadership is determined by the appropriateness of a combination of three factors: (1) the manager as a leader, (2) the manager's employees as followers, and (3) the situation(s) within the company the manager faces. Each of these factors plays a significant role in determining whether managers are successful leaders.

One of the most important activities managers perform as leaders is making decisions. They can make decisions in any number of ways, ranging from authoritarian to democratic. As described in the Challenge Case, Iwata made the decision not to compete directly with Microsoft and Sony in the existing marketplace. Instead, he attacked by introducing an innovative product, the Wii, whose introduction arguably transformed the nature of video entertainment. Iwata could have authoritatively made the decision to compete via the Wii without consulting any employees. Alternatively, Iwata could have used a subordinate-centered style by defining broad competition limits within which Nintendo could compete and then allow employees to make the final decision on how to compete within those limits. Most likely, Iwata was less extreme in his decision making, in that his leadership behavior probably fell in the middle of the continuum. For example, he most likely suggested to the appropriate Nintendo personnel the type of competitive tactics Nintendo needed and asked them to develop ideas accordingly. Next, Iwata probably made his decision about how the company should compete by reflecting on his ideas and the ideas of other organization members.

In trying to decide exactly how to make decisions as leaders, managers should consider forces in themselves as managers, forces in the manager's subordinates, and forces in the specific organizational situations they face. Forces within managers include their own ideas about how to lead and their level of confidence in the employees they are leading. If managers believe that they are more knowledgeable about achieving acquisition success, for example, than their staff is, they will likely make boss-centered decisions about what steps to take to create acquisition success. Forces within subordinates, such as the need for independence, the readiness to assume responsibility, and the knowledge of and interest in the issues to be decided, also affect managers' decisions as leaders. If a manager's staff is relatively independent and responsible and its members feel strongly about acquisition success, and how it should be achieved, then a manager should be more inclined to allow his or her employees more freedom in deciding how to achieve that acquisition success.

Forces within the company include the number of people making decisions and the problem to be solved. For example, if the manager's staff is small, he or she will be more likely to use a democratic decision-making style, allowing his or her employees to become involved in such decisions as how to best achieve acquisition success. Managers will also be likely to use a subordinate-centered leadership style if their employees are knowledgeable about what makes a company successful. The VYJ model suggests that managers should try to make decisions in such a fashion that the quality of decisions is enhanced and followers are committed to the decisions. Managers can try to ensure such decisions are made by matching their decision style (autocratic, consultative, or group) to the particular situation they face.

The OSU leadership studies should furnish a manager with insights on leadership behavior in general situations. According to these studies, managers can exhibit two general types of leadership behavior: structure and consideration. Managers will be using structure behavior if they tell personnel what to do—for example, exactly how to design new ink-jet cartridges for HP printers. In contrast, they will be using consideration behavior if they attempt to develop a more human rapport with their employees by discussing their concerns and developing friendships with them.

Of course, depending on how managers emphasize these two behaviors, their leadership styles can reflect a combination of structure and consideration ranging from high structure/low consideration to low structure/high consideration. For example, if managers stress giving orders to employees and deemphasize developing relationships, they will be exhibiting high structure/low consideration. If they emphasize a good rapport with their employees and allow their members to function mostly independently, their leadership styles will be termed low structure/high consideration.

Although no single leadership style is more effective than any other in all situations, the life cycle theory of leadership provides managers with a strategy for using various styles in various situations. According to the theory, managers should make their style consistent primarily with the maturity level of the organization members they are leading. As followers progress from immaturity to maturity, managers' leadership style should shift systematically from (1) high task/low relationships behavior to (2) high task/high relationships behavior to (3) high relationships/low task behavior to (4) low task/low relationships behavior.

The life cycle theory suggests that managers should be flexible enough to behave as required according to situations at their organizations. If managers find it extremely difficult to be flexible, however, they should attempt to structure their situation so as to make it appropriate for their style. As suggested by Fiedler, if a manager's leadership style is high task in nature, he or she generally will be a more successful leader in situations best described by octants 1, 2, 3, and 8 in Table 16.1 and Figure 16.7. If, however, a manager's leadership style is more relationship oriented, he or she will probably be a more successful leader in situations representative of octants 4, 5, 6, and 7. Overall, Fiedler's work provides managers with insights on how to engineer situations so they will be appropriate for their own leadership styles.

The path–goal theory of leadership suggests that in leading, managers should emphasize clarifying what rewards are available to followers in the organization, how those rewards can be earned, and eliminating barriers that could prohibit followers from earning the rewards. Managers can use directive behavior, supportive behavior, participative behavior, and achievement behavior in implementing the path–goal theory.

Based on the preceding information, perhaps Iwata could be characterized as a transformational leader, one who inspires followers to seriously focus on achieving organizational objectives. As a transformational leader, Iwata would have encouraged new ideas, created a sense of duty, and encouraged employees to learn and grow. As Nintendo experienced significant growth, the importance of its leader being a transformational leader increased.

Three other popular leadership styles also offer managers such as Iwata insights about how to lead. As coaching leaders, managers can focus on instructing followers to meet special challenges they face such as expansion through global acquisition. In the role of coaching leaders, they would listen closely, give emotional support, and show by example what should be done. As superleaders, managers would teach followers how to think on their own and act constructively and independently. As entrepreneurial leaders, managers would act much like a self-employed owner of the company. They would act, for example, like an individual personally incurring the risk of acquiring another computer company, but also benefiting from the profit if it is made.

Overall, managers must keep in mind that these leadership styles are aimed at getting people involved in an organization and giving them the freedom to use their abilities as they think best. Such leaders must always keep in mind that regardless of the type of leader they may be, they must earn and maintain the trust of their followers if they are to be successful in the long run.

MANAGEMENT SKILL ACTIVITIES

This section is specially designed to help you develop leadership skill. An individual's leadership skill is based on an understanding of leadership concepts and the ability to apply those concepts in management situations. The following activities are designed both to heighten your understanding of leadership fundamentals and to develop your ability to apply those concepts in various management situations.

UNDERSTANDING LEADERSHIP CONCEPTS

 To check your understanding and to practice using the concepts in this chapter, go to www.mymanagementlab.com and explore the material associated with Chapter 16.

Know Key Terms

Understanding the following key terms is critical to your understanding of chapter material. Define each of these terms. Refer to the page(s) referenced after a term to check your definition or to gain further insight regarding the term.

leadership **370**
trait approach to leadership **371**
situational approach to leadership **372**
Vroom–Yetton–Jago (VYJ) model
    of leadership **375**
structure behavior **377**
consideration behavior **377**
leadership style **378**
job-centered behavior **378**

employee-centered behavior **378**
life cycle theory of leadership **379**
leader flexibility **380**
contingency theory of leadership **381**
leader–member relations **381**
task structure **381**
position power **381**
path–goal theory of leadership **382**
directive behavior **383**

supportive behavior **383**
participative behavior **383**
achievement behavior **383**
transformational leadership **384**
coaching **385**
superleadership **385**
servant leadership **387**
entrepreneurial leadership **388**

Know How Management Concepts Relate

This section is comprised of activities that will further sharpen your understanding of management concepts. Answer essay questions as completely as possible. Also, remember that many additional true/false and multiple choice questions appear online at MyManagementLab.com to help you further refine your understanding of management concepts.

1. Is it important for you as a manager to understand the difference between leadership and management? Explain fully.

2. What is the difference between the "situational approach" and the "trait approach" to leadership? Which approach seems to have more relevance to you as a manager? Explain.

3. Draw and explain the life cycle model of leadership. Would this model be useful to you as a manager? Why?

4. Would it be easy for you to be a "servant leader"? Why?

5. Given all that you've learned in this chapter, what kind of leader will you try to be as a manager? Explain.

DEVELOPING MANAGEMENT SKILLS

Learning activities in this section are aimed at helping you to develop leadership skill. Learning activities include Exploring Your Management Skill: Parts 1 and 2, Experiential Exercises, Cases, and a VideoNet Exercise.

Exploring Your Management Skill: Part 1

Before studying this chapter, respond to the following questions regarding the type of advice you would give to Satoru Iwata, the president of Nintendo referenced in the Challenge Case. You are not expected to be a leadership expert at this point. Answering the questions now can help you focus on important points when you study the chapter. Also, answering the questions again after you study the chapter will give you an idea of how much you have learned.

    Record your answers here or go to MyManagement Lab.com. Recording your answers in MyManagementLab will allow you to get immediate results and see how your score compares to your classmates. If you answer the questions in the

book, the answers are located in the Exploring Your Management Skill Appendix at the end of the book.

FOR EACH STATEMENT CIRCLE:
• "Y" if you would give the advice to Iwata.
• "N" if you would NOT give the advice to Iwata.
• "NI" if you have no idea whether you would give the advice to Iwata.

Iwata-san, in meeting your leadership challenges, you should . . .
    Before After
    Study Study

1. remember that managing and leading are synonyms.
   Y, N, NI

2. realize that you'll be successful as a leader because, given your traits, it's obvious that you were born to be a leader.
   Y, N, NI

3. use subordinate-centered leadership to make and announce your decisions to your subordinates.
   Y, N, NI

4. understand that the profitability of your organization is a force influencing your leadership decisions.
   Y, N, NI

5. make decisions alone even if your subordinates are capable of helping you to make those decisions.
   Y, N, NI

6. work to constantly improve your leadership style, your view of what you should be as a leader.
   Y, N, NI

7. focus on matching your low task and low relationship leadership style with followers who are of average job maturity.
   Y, N, NI

8. use chronological follower maturity as the main factor to determine your leadership style.
   Y, N, NI

9. use position power to influence follower behavior.
   Y, N, NI

10. use the path–goal theory of leadership as your rationale to clarify follower behavior necessary to earn organizational rewards.
    Y, N, NI

11. be flexible, changing leadership style as dictated by circumstances.
    Y, N, NI

12. always tell followers what they must do in their jobs.
    Y, N, NI

13. sometimes act entrepreneurially, functioning as if you're self-employed.
    Y, N, NI

14. probably sometimes think of yourself as a steward, following the concept of servant leadership.
    Y, N, NI

15. think about integrating concepts from theories such as transformational leadership, servant leadership, and superleadership to develop the best leadership style for you personally.
    Y, N, NI

Exploring Your Management Skill: Part 2

As you recall, you completed Exploring Your Management Skill before you started to study this chapter. Your responses gave you an idea of how much you initially knew about leadership and helped you focus on important points as you studied the chapter. Answer the Exploring Your Management Skill questions again now and compare your score to the first time you took it. This comparison will give you an idea of how much you have learned from studying this chapter and pinpoint areas for further clarification before you start studying the next chapter. Record your answers within the text or go to MyManagementLab.com. Recording your answers in MyManagementLab will allow you to get immediate results and see how your score compares to your classmates. If you answer the questions in the book, the answers are located in the Exploring Your Management Skill Appendix at the end of the book.

Your Management Skills Portfolio

Your Management Learning Portfolio is a collection of activities especially designed to demonstrate your management knowledge and skill. By completing these activities online at MyManagementLab.com, you will be able to print, complete with cover sheet, as many activities as you choose. Be sure to save your work. Taking your printed portfolio to an employment interview could be helpful in obtaining a job.

The portfolio activity for this chapter is Leadership Skill in a Special Situation.[67] Read the highlight about Martha Stewart and answer the questions that follow.

Homemaking icon Martha Stewart strolled outdoors with her dog and fed her horses, hours after returning from prison to the multimillion-dollar estate. Stewart's release came one day shy of the one-year anniversary of her conviction in New York on charges stemming from her 2001 sale of nearly 4,000 shares of the biotechnology company ImClone Systems Inc. She was convicted of obstructing justice and lying to the government.

For the next five months, Stewart must wear an electronic anklet so authorities can track her every move. But she is allowed to receive her $900,000 salary again and can leave home for up to 48 hours a week to work, shop, or run other approved errands.

Leaving the women's prison in Alderson, West Virginia, shortly after midnight Friday, Stewart flew in a private jet to Westchester County airport and then was driven to the 61-hectare (153-acre) estate in Katonah, 65 kilometers (40 miles) north of midtown Manhattan.

Stewart hopes to turn around the fortunes of her company, Martha Stewart Living, which produces everything from television shows and magazines to bed sheets and bakeware. In 2004, the company suffered a loss and its revenues sagged, but the stock price rose considerably during her prison stint as investors bet on a Stewart comeback. Stewart's contract with her company says her salary, which was suspended while she was behind bars, will be reinstated during home detention. While in home confinement, Stewart will be free to entertain colleagues, neighbors, friends, and relatives as long as they're not criminals. Convicted felons aren't allowed to consort with other convicted felons.

Activity 1

Circle the option that best reflects your opinion about Martha Stewart's leadership situation at Martha Stewart Living:
Martha Stewart's background as a convicted felon will present special leadership challenges that Martha will have to overcome.

1. Definitely
2. Probably Will
3. Maybe
4. Probably Won't
5. Definitely Not

Activity 2

Now that you have expressed your opinion about Martha Stewart's possible new leadership challenges, in the following space explain this opinion in 50 words or less.

Activity 3

In the first few months after returning as top manager at Martha Stewart Living, should Stewart portray a leadership style that focuses more on low task/low relationships, low task/high relationships, high task/high relationships, or low relationships/high task? Why?

Activity 4

Using the life cycle theory of leadership's four main leadership styles, how should Stewart change her leadership style over time, if at all? Explain fully.

Experiential Exercises

1 Make a Decision at Wendy's[68]

Directions. Read the following scenario and then perform the listed activities. Your instructor may want you to perform the activities as an individual or within groups. Follow all of your instructor's directions carefully.

According to Jack Schuessler, Wendy's CEO, management is considering whether to begin offering a breakfast menu that was discontinued about 20 years ago. Schuessler did indicate, however, that if offered, Wendy's breakfast menu would need to be significantly different from the sausage-and-biscuits or egg-on-an-English-muffin approach offered by competitors.

Some individuals support Schuessler's new breakfast menu idea. Some believe that the best opportunity for Wendy's to improve profitability is to introduce breakfast. In addition, Wendy's owns Tim Horton's, a chain dominant in Canada but small in the United States, that knows the breakfast business. Wendy's should be able to use the knowledge and experience at Tim Horton's as help in introducing a new successful breakfast menu.

The competition in the fast-food breakfast segment is heavy. McDonald's, the nation's largest restaurant chain, began offering breakfast in the 1970s and is the market leader of the morning sales period. Burger King reportedly is testing new breakfast sandwiches and platters. In addition, California-based Carl's Jr. recently introduced a breakfast burger topped with a fried egg at its 1,000 restaurants.

Although offering breakfast at Wendy's could improve sales by making use of the store during hours it is empty, the company has found that breakfast can be disastrous if not done correctly. According to Schuessler, when Wendy's offered breakfast between 1983 and 1985, it operated inappropriately and as a result breakfast was not a profitable activity. The breakfast offered was expensive, it wasn't portable, service was too slow, and offering breakfast took away some of the focus on the company's burger business.

Learning Activity

Your instructor will divide the class into small groups and ask each group to arrive at a consensus in answering the following questions.

1. Assume you are Jack Schuessler. As a leader at Wendy's, how would you make the decision regarding whether to introduce breakfast?
   a. Simply make the decision and announce it.
   b. Make the decision but try to convince others it's best.
   c. Present a tentative decision subject to change based on input.
   d. Present the dilemma and ask for input before making the decision.
   e. Allow a group to make the decision.

2. Explain your answer to question 1. Be sure to focus on why you chose the option you did as well as why you did not choose other options.

3. As a leader, would you find making this decision at Wendy's challenging? Why?

2 You and Your Career[69]

You have just graduated from college and are interested in a career in government. In looking for your first job, you found out that the city manager's office of the City of Sacramento, California, has recently begun to recognize the significant retirement projections among its baby-boomer employees. According to the city manager, to deal with the impending retirements, Sacramento's city government will start designing and offering leadership development programs to its employees. According to the city manager, the programs will focus on helping younger leaders understand how various parts of city government operate as well as helping them develop a broad network of relationships within city government as a whole.

Would this information you've found out about Sacramento's city government raise or lower your interest in working there? Explain. How would you find out if other potential employers offer similar programs? Name another topic you would like to see covered in Sacramento's leadership development program and explain its significance.

VideoNet Exercise

Leadership at Kluster

Video Highlight

What kind of leader demotes himself? Ben Kaufman, that's who. His parents re-mortgaged their house so he could start a company focused on creating innovative iPod accessories. After launching some great products, Ben's plan is to now revolutionize the way consumer products are developed via his latest entrepreneurial venture, Kluster (formerly known as the Illuminator Project). He's fearless, charismatic, and prone to having visions. Will he rock the world the same way the founders of YouTube, Facebook, and Google have? Hear the 20-year-old's thoughts on leadership and find out if his colleagues think he's the real thing.

Discussion Questions

1. Is there evidence in the video clip that Kaufman is both a leader and a manager? Explain.
2. Describe Kaufman using the trait approach to leadership.
3. Using the Vroom–Yetton–Jago model, explain how Kaufman makes decisions for Kluster.

Internet Activity

Go to the Kluster home page at www.kluster.com. Watch the video presented under the link "What Happened Here." Based on Ben Kaufman's dialogue, which leadership style do you think best applies to his way of doing business? Explain.

CASES

1 IWATA FACES MANY DIFFERENT ISSUES AT NINTENDO

"Iwata Faces Many Different Issues at Nintendo" (p. 369) and its related Challenge Case Summary were written to help you better understand the management concepts contained in this chapter. Answer the following discussion questions about the Challenge Case to further enrich your understanding of chapter content.

1. List and define five activities that Iwata might have performed as a manager while fostering Nintendo's growth as outlined in the Challenge Case.
2. Do you feel that Iwata should use more of a boss-centered or subordinate-centered leadership style in leading at Nintendo? Why?
3. If you were Iwata, would understanding the transformational and the entrepreneurial leadership styles be valuable to you in leading Nintendo employees? Explain fully.

2 OPRAH LEADS AN EMPIRE

Read the case and answer the questions that follow. Studying this case will help you better understand how concepts relating to leadership can be applied in a company such as Harpo, Inc.

Her distinctive name, solid following among television and radio audiences, and strong business sense have catapulted Oprah Winfrey to the top of the media world. It is difficult to *not* see or hear her name on television, satellite radio, print media, and the Internet. Initially, she gained national recognition through her television show, but her presence has evolved to a worldwide scale. She adeptly combines a humble approach to life with a shrewd eye for business.

Under the umbrella of Harpo, Inc. (Oprah spelled in reverse), the world of Oprah Winfrey is vast. So powerful is her persona, that she has been named the most influential woman in the world,[70] and her personal net worth is estimated to be more than $2.3 billion.[71] There is, of course, her television program,

The Oprah Winfrey Show. But also there are films, magazines, numerous radio and television shows, a book club, and philanthropy.[72] All this started in her early 20's when she developed a television talk show in Chicago. Soon, it became a nationwide phenomenon, surpassing similar talk shows that had been around for years.

Since that time, she continued building businesses—expanding her reach into other media. With well over $340 million in sales, Harpo, Inc. has grown exponentially and is so much more than just a television show. Few individuals have been able to take a single business and develop it to a successful conglomerate in such a short a period of time. Despite this growth of the business, Oprah is probably best known for giving cars and other gifts to show audiences, or for building a girl's academy in South Africa, than she is for building her own wealth.[73] "I haven't planned one thing—ever," she said. "I have just been led by a strong instinct, and I have made choices based on what was right for me at the time."[74] Along the way, her strategy has been to maintain control of every facet of her business—name, creativity, content, and branding. "I don't care about money," she added. "It throws people off all the time in business meetings."

She admits that business has been a learning process for her. As new elements such as *O* magazine developed under the Harpo umbrella, her knowledge of managing a business increased. "I'm just now getting to the point of understanding how strategic planning, creating an infrastructure, and having a vision can be very helpful," she said. "And as I move forward in creating other companies, I'm operating more as a businesswoman."[75]

Harpo, Inc. is nestled among the tall buildings of the Chicago skyline—it's actually in several buildings. More than 400 employees work in offices and studios, while an in-house café, spa, and gym provide a diversion from day-to-day tasks. Employees receive the usual benefits one expects—medical, dental, vision, and so on—but they also get four weeks of vacation.[76] In addition, to celebrate *The Oprah Winfrey Show's* 20th anniversary, she chartered planes and took Harpo employees and their families to Hawaii for a vacation—more than 1,000 individuals were part of this event.

Oprah is cognizant of how people prefer to be managed while working in an organization. She is not the type of boss who ridicules employees or belittles them. And she certainly doesn't create a ruthless, oppressive working environment. "I don't yell at people," she said. "I don't mistreat people." Her goal is to create a climate where employees are comfortable, yet productive. "Treating people with respect," she continued, "is the most important thing to me. It's not just talk."[77]

As *The Oprah Winfrey Show* ends its 25-year run in 2010, Oprah is on to her next big thing—OWN, a 24-hour cable station that will provide programming centered on self-discovery. Focusing on health, relationships, and home, the network is expected to attract a huge audience, appealing to a variety of viewers. "Fifteen years ago," she said, "I wrote in my journal that one day I would create a television network, as I always felt my show was just the beginning of what the future could hold. For me, the launch of OWN is the evolution of the work I've been doing on television all these years and a natural extension of my show."[78]

QUESTIONS

1. Which theory of leadership do you think is most applicable in describing Oprah Winfrey? Explain.
2. Compare and contrast your leadership style with Oprah's.
3. Do you think Oprah Winfrey is a better leader or a better manager? Explain.

Endnotes

1. Osamu Inoue, "Iwata and Miyamoto: Business Ascetics—An Excerpt from Nintendo Magic," *Gamasutra*, May 14, 2010, http://www.gamasutra.com; "Nintendo Teams Had Difficulty Coping with Explosive Growth," *Silicon Era*, April 11, 2010, http://www.siliconera.com; Dean Takahashi, "Nintendo Isn't Worried about Apple, and You Won't See Mario on Facebook," *VentureBeat*, March 2, 2010, http://games.venturebeat.com; "Overview of Nintendo's Latest Financial Report," *Silicon Era*, January 28, 2010, http://www.siliconera.com; "Nintendo Nine-Month Profit down 41 Percent, Keeps Outlook," *Reuters*, January 28, 2010, http://www.reuters.com; Leo Chan, "Nintendo Ranked World's Best Company for 2009," *Neoseeker*, October 6, 2009, http://www.neoseeker.com.

2. Elise Goldman, "The Significance of Leadership Style," *Educational Leadership* 55, no. 7 (April 1998): 20–22. For a worthwhile look at the importance of instilling leadership in all members of a corporation, see Scott Payne, "Corporate Training Trend: Building Leadership," *Grand Rapids Business Journal*, November 13, 2000, B2; see also Dusya Vera and Mary Crossan, "Strategic Leadership and Organizational Learning," *Academy of Management Review* 29 (2004): 222.

3. David Nadler and Michael L. Tushman, "Beyond the Charismatic Leader: Leadership and Organizational Change," *California Management Review* 32 (Winter 1990): 77–97; Peter R. Scholtes, *The Leader's Handbook: A Guide to Inspiring Your People and Managing the Daily Workflow* (New York: McGraw-Hill, 1998).

4. Abraham Zaleznik, "Executives and Organizations: Real Work," *Harvard Business Review* (January/February 1989): 57–64.

5. Theodore Levitt, "Management and the Post-Industrial Society," *Public Interest* (Summer 1976): 73.

6. Patrick L. Townsend and Joan E. Gebhardt, "We Have Lots of Managers ... We Need Leaders," *Journal for Quality and Participation* (September 1989): 18–20; Craig Hickman, "The Winning Mix: Mind of a Manager, Soul of a Leader," *Canadian Business* 63 (February 1990): 69–72. For discussion of how successful executives place more importance and emphasis on leadership than management, see Michael E. McGrath, "The Eight Qualities of Success," *Electronic Business* 24, no. 4 (April 1998): 9–10.

7. For a recent study assessing the validity of traits theory, see Dean Gehring, "Applying traits theory of leadership to project management," *Project Management Journal* 38 (2007): 44–55.

8. Ralph M. Stogdill, "Personal Factors Associated with Leadership: A Survey of the Literature," *Journal of Psychology* 25 (January 1948): 35–64.

9. Cecil A. Gibb, "Leadership," in Gardner Lindzey (Ed.), *Handbook of Social Psychology* (Reading, MA: Addison-Wesley, 1954).

10. Frank Walter and Helka Bruch, "An Affective Events Model of Charismatic Leadership Behavior: A Review, Theoretical Integration, and Research Agenda," *Journal of Management* 35, no. 6 (December 2009): 1428–1452.

11. Valerie Sessa, "Creating Leaderful Organizations: How to Bring Out Leadership in Everyone," *Personnel Psychology* 56 (2003): 762.

12. J. Oliver Crom, "What's New in Leadership?" *Executive Excellence* 7 (January 1990): 15–16.

13. For an interesting application of the situational leadership model, see R. Vecchko, R. Bullie, and D. Brazil, "The utility of situational leadership theory: A replication in a military setting," *Small Group Research* 37 (2006): 407.

14. For a discussion of a leader in a military situation, see Sherrill Tapsell, "Managing for Peace," *Management* 45, no. 5 (June 1998): 32–37.

15. Robert Tannenbaum and Warren H. Schmidt, "How to Choose a Leadership Pattern," *Harvard Business Review* (March/April 1957): 95–101.

16. William E. Zierden, "Leading Through the Follower's Point of View," *Organizational Dynamics* (Spring 1980): 27–46. See also Tannenbaum and Schmidt, "How to Choose a Leadership Pattern."

17. Robert Tannenbaum and Warren H. Schmidt, "How to Choose a Leadership Pattern," *Harvard Business Review* (May/June 1973): 162–180.

18. Victor H. Vroom and Arthur G. Jago, *The New Leadership* (Upper Saddle River, NJ: Prentice Hall, 1988).

19. Gary A. Yukl, *Leadership in Organizations*, 2d ed. (Upper Saddle River, NJ: Prentice Hall, 1989).

20. For a recent application of the Vroom-Yetton model, see "The behaviour of managers in Austria and the Czech Republic: An intercultural comparison based on the Vroom/Yetton Model of leadership and decision making," *Journal of East European Management Studies* 9 (2004): 411–430.

21. Charles S. Lauer, "In Each Other We Trust," *Modern Healthcare* 37, no. 37 (September 17, 2007): 20.

22. For an interesting discussion on the relationship between leadership and employee retention, see Pamela Ribelin, "Retention Reflects Leadership Style," *Nursing Management* 34 (2003): 18.

23. Vishwanath V. Baba and Merle E. Ace, "Serendipity in Leadership: Initiating Structure and Consideration in the Classroom," *Human Relations* 42 (June 1989): 509–525. For a further discussion of leadership style, see Maria Guzzo, "People to Watch: Mike Parton—Classic Leadership Style," *Pittsburgh Business Times Journal*, June 23, 2000, 14.

24. Rensis Likert, *New Patterns of Management* (New York: McGraw-Hill, 1961).

25. Xander M. Bezuijen, Peter T. van den Berg, Karen van Dam, and Hank Thierry, "Pygmalion and Employee Learning: The Role of Leader Behaviors," *Journal of Management* 35, no. 5 (October 2009): 1248–1267.

26. Harvey A. Hornstein, Madeline E. Heilman, Edward Mone, and Ross Tartell, "Responding to Contingent Leadership Behavior," *Organizational Dynamics* 15 (Spring 1987): 56–65.

27. A. K. Korman, "'Consideration,' 'Initiating Structure,' and Organizational Criteria—A Review," *Personnel Psychology* 19 (Winter 1966): 349–361. See also Rick Roskin, "Management Style and Achievement: A Model Synthesis," *Management Decision* 27 (1989): 17–22.

28. P. Hersey and K. H. Blanchard, "Life Cycle Theory of Leadership," *Training and Development Journal* (May 1969): 26–34.

29. Mary J. Keenan, Joseph B. Hurst, Robert S. Dennis, and Glenna Frey, "Situational Leadership for Collaboration in Health Care Settings," *Health Care Supervisor* 8 (April 1990): 19–25. See also Jane R. Goodson, Gail W. McGee, and James F. Cashman, "Situational Leadership Theory: A Test of Leadership Prescriptions," *Group and Organizational Studies* 14 (December 1989): 446–461.

30. Mark E. Van Buren and Todd Safferstone, "The Quick Wins Paradox," *Harvard Business Review*, January 2009, http://hbr.org.

31. Fred E. Fiedler, "Engineer the Job to Fit the Manager," *Harvard Business Review* (September/October 1965): 115–122.

32. For an interesting look at how different types of leaders and followers perform at different types of tasks, see R. Miller, J. Butler and C. Cosentino, "Followership effectiveness: An extension of Fiedler's contingency model," *Leadership and Organization Development* 25 (2004): 362.

33. F. E. Fiedler, *A Theory of Leadership Effectiveness* (New York: McGraw-Hill, 1967), 255–256. © 1967 by McGraw-Hill, Inc. Used with permission of McGraw-Hill Company.

34. L. H. Peters, D. D. Harike, and J. T. Pohlmann, "Fiedler's Contingency Theory of Leadership: An Application of the Meta-Analysis Procedures of Schmidt and Hunter," *Psychological Bulletin* 97 (1985): 224–285.

35. Robert J. House and Terence R. Mitchell, "Path–Goal Theory of Leadership," *Journal of Contemporary Business* (Autumn 1974): 81–98; Gary A. Yukl, *Leadership in Organizations*.

36. For a recent article on the path–goal theory, see C. Schriesheim, S. Castro, X. Zhou and L. DeChurch, "An investigation of path–goal and transformational leadership theory predications at the individual level of analysis, *Leadership Quarterly* 17 (2006): 21.

37. For a worthwhile review of the path–goal theory of leadership, see Gary A. Yukl, *Leadership in Organizations*.

38. To learn how some managers are reacting to modern challenges, see Jaclyn Fierman, "Winning Ideas from Maverick Managers," *Fortune*, February 6, 1995, 66–80. For a fresh approach to

leadership that modern managers are taking, see George Fraser, "The Slight Edge: Valuing and Managing Diversity," *Vital Speeches of the Day* 64, no. 8 (February 1, 1998): 235–240.

39. Holly H. Brower, Scott W. Lester, M. Audrey Korsgaard, and Brian R. Dineen, "A Closer Look at Trust between Managers and Subordinates: Understanding the Effects of Both Trusting and Being Trusted on Subordinate Outcomes," *Journal of Management* 35, no. 2 (March 2009): 327–347.

40. Andrew J. DuBrin, *Reengineering Survival Guide* (Cincinnati, OH: Thomson Executive Press, 1996), 115–129.

41. Karl W. Kuhnert and Philip Lewis, "Transactional and Transformational Leadership: A Constructive/Developmental Analysis," *Academy of Management Review* (October 1987): 648–657; Shirley M. Ross and Lynn R. Offermann, "Transformational Leaders: Measurement of Personality Attributes," *Personality and Social Psychology Bulletin,* October 1997, 1078–1086.

42. For a recent article describing the effects of this type of leadership, see J. Schaubroeck, S. Lam, and S. Cha, "Embracing transformational leadership: Team values and the impact of leader behavior on team performance," *Journal of Applied Psychology* 92 (2007): 1020.

43. Lauren Folino, "The Great Leaders Series: Ben Cohen and Jerry Greenfield, Co-Founders of Ben & Jerry's Homemade," *Inc.,* February 18, 2010, http://www.inc.com.

44. Suzanne J. Peterson, Fred O. Walumbwa, Kristin Byron, and Jason Myrowitz, "CEO Positive Psychological Traits, Transformational Leadership, and Firm Performance in High-Technology Start-up and Established Firms," *Journal of Management* 35, no. 2 (March 2009): 348–368.

45. Bernard M. Bass, *Leadership and Performance Beyond Expectations* (New York: Free Press, 1985).

46. For an in-depth look at the positive effects of coaching on employee productivity, see Bill Blades, "Great Coaching Can Increase Revenue," *Arizona Business Gazette,* January 18, 2001, 5.

47. For practical tips on developing this style of leadership, see M. Wakefield, "New Views on Leadership Coaching," *The Journal for Quality and Participation* 29 (2006): 9–14.

48. Frederick P. Morgeson, D. Scott DeRue, and Elizabeth P. Karam, "Leadership in Teams: A Functional Approach to Understanding Leadership Structures and Processes," *Journal of Management* 36, no. 1 (January 2010): 5–39.

49. For more information on empathy and leadership, see William G. Pagonis, "The Work of the Leader," *Harvard Business Review* (November/December 1992): 118–126.

50. Charles C. Manz, "Helping Yourself and Others to Master Self-Leadership," *Supervisory Management* (November 1991): 19–38; C. Manz and Henry P. Sims Jr., "SuperLeadership: Beyond the Myth of Heroic Leadership," *Organizational Dynamics* (Spring 1991): 28–40.

51. Robert K. Greenleaf, *Servant Leadership: A Journey into the Nature of Legitimate Power and Greatness* (Mahwah, New Jersey: Paulist Press, 1977).

52. To learn about how servant leadership is associated with trust, E. Joseph and B. Winston, "A correlation of servant leadership, leader trust, and organizational trust," *Leadership and Organization Development Journal* 26 (2005): 6–23.

53. Max E. Douglas, "Servant Leadership: An Emerging Supervisory Model," *SuperVision* 64, no. 2 (February 2003): 6–9.

54. Sen Sendjaya and James C. Sarros, "Servant Leadership: Its Origin, Development, and Application in Organizations," *Journal of Leadership and Organizational Studies* 9, no. 2 (Fall 2002): 57–64.

55. "On a Scale of 1 to 10, How Weird Are You?" *New York Times,* January 10, 2010, http://www.nytimes.com.

56. For a look at the personality characteristics of servant leaders, see R. Washington, C. Sutton, and H. Field, "Individual differences in servant leadership: The roles of values and personality," *Leadership and Organization Development Journal* 27 (2006): 700–716.

57. Ron Rowe, "Leaders as Servants," *New Zealand Management* 50, no. 1 (February 2003): 24–25.

58. Reylito A. H. Elbo, "In the Workplace," *BusinessWorld,* September 4, 2002, 1.

59. Keshavan Nair, *A Higher Standard of Leadership: Lessons from the Life of Gandhi* (San Francisco, California: Berrett-Koehler, 1994).

60. Robert F. Russell and A. Gregory Stone, "A Review of Servant Leadership Attributes: Developing a Practical Model," *Leadership and Organization Development Journal* 23, no. 3: 145–157.

61. Bernard M. Bass, "The Future of Leadership in Learning Organizations," *Journal of Leadership Studies* 7, no. 3 (2000): 18–40.

62. See R. Washington, C. Sutton, and H. Field, "Individual differences in servant leadership: The roles of values and personality," *Leadership and Organization Development Journal* 27 (2006): 700–716.

63. See R. Washington, C. Sutton, and H. Field, "Individual differences in servant leadership: The roles of values and personality," *Leadership and Organization Development Journal* 27 (2006): 700.

64. For a detailed review of entrepreneurial leadership, see L. W. Fernald, G. T. Solomon, and A. Tarabishy, "A new paradigm: Entrepreneurial leadership," *Southern Business Review* 30, no. 1 (2005): 1-10.

65. A profile of a successful female entrepreneurial leader in a multicultural situation is contained in Daniel J. McCarthy, Sheila M. Puffer, and Alexander I. Naumov, "Case Study–Olga Kirova: A Russian Entrepreneur's Quality Leadership," *International Journal of Organizational Analysis* 5, no. 3 (July 1997): 267–290.

66. Jane Horan, "Business Driven Action Learning: A Powerful Tool for Building World-Class Entrepreneurial Business Leaders" *Organization Development Journal* 25, no. 3 (Fall 2007): 75–80.

67. This material based on James Fitzgerald, "Martha Stewart Arrives Home After Five-Month Prison Term to Begin Detention for Lying about Stock Sale," *Financial Times Information Ltd.,* March 5, 2005.

68. Barnet D. Wolf, "Breakfast Could Make a Return to Wendy's," *The Columbus Dispatch,* March 5, 2005.

69. Brian W. T. Moffitt, "City Management Institute: A Blueprint for Leadership Succession," *Government Finance Review* 23, no. 4 (August 2007): 55–59.

70. Tamny, John (2007) "Embrace the Wealth Gap," *American Spectator.* http://spectator.org/archives/2007/05/08/embrace-the-wealth-gap.

71. www.forbes.com (2009) "Oprah Winfrey–The Forbes 400 Richest Americans 2009."

72. www.oprah.com

73. Graves Jr., Earl G. "Recognizing True Leadership." *Black Enterprise*, June 14–15, 2008.

74. Alleyne, Sonia. "Oprah Means Business," *Black Enterprise* 38, no. 11 (2008): 116–128.

75. Ibid.

76. Ibid.

77. Ibid.

78. See note 72 above.

chapter 17

Motivation

Target Skill

motivation skill: the ability to create organizational situations in which individuals performing organizational activities are simultaneously satisfying personal needs and helping the organization attain its goals

objectives

To help build my *motivation skill,* when studying this chapter, I will attempt to acquire:

1. A basic understanding of human motivation

2. Insights into various human needs

3. An appreciation for the importance of motivating organization members

4. An understanding of various motivation strategies

CHALLENGE CASE

MOTIVATION SAVVY MANAGEMENT AT BRISTOL-MYERS SQUIBB ENSURES CUTTING-EDGE INTERNET PRESENCE

BRISTOL-MYERS SQUIBB is a world-renowned manufacturer of personal care products and over-the-counter pharmaceuticals; it produces and markets popular household brands such as Bufferin, Excedrin, and Nuprin. The company's annual sales exceed $18 billion. With its international infrastructure, ever-changing marketplace, and competitive industry, Bristol-Myers has a lot to consider in formulating and refining its Internet strategy.

Formulating the strategy is only the beginning. After the strategy is formulated, it must be implemented. Jack Cooper, a top Bristol-Myers manager, champions many of the company's activities aimed at implementing Internet strategy. Cooper coordinates implementation activities with a firm grasp of the organization's business priorities. According to Cooper, implementing Internet strategy can be tricky. It is challenging because it requires implementing multiple project phases concurrently. To be successful in implementing Internet strategy, managers need to know how to commit resources, set deadlines, and control implementation costs.

In addition to the technical issues involved in implementing Internet strategy, people issues are also involved. Managers implementing Internet strategy in organizations must be sound leaders. Motivating people involved in implementing Internet strategy is key. According to Cooper, it is easy for people to see reasons why Internet strategy implementation will not work. Managers must help people see beyond those reasons if Internet strategy implementation is to be successful. Managers must emphasize the desire to win and to create solutions in the face of adversity.

A recent version of the company's Web site is extensive and complex. Sections focusing on company news, products offered, research and development projects, investor information, business alliances, corporate responsibility, and career information all reflect highly motivated workers dedicated to implementing Internet strategy.[1]

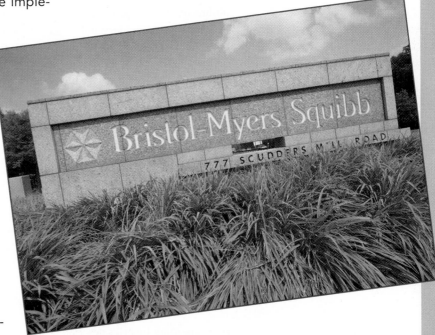

■ *Bristol-Myers Squibb relied on motivation to overcome internal objections while building its Internet strategy.*

EXPLORING YOUR MANAGEMENT SKILL

You can explore your level of motivation skill **before** studying the chapter by completing the exercise "Exploring Your Management Skill: Part 1" on page 417 and **after** studying this chapter by completing the exercise "Exploring Your Management Skill: Part 2" on page 418.

THE MOTIVATION CHALLENGE

Jack Cooper, a member of top management at Bristol-Myers Squibb in the Challenge Case, focuses on implementing Internet strategy within the company. According to the case, in implementing Internet strategy, Cooper concentrates on more technical issues such as properly committing resources, setting deadlines, and controlling related costs. Cooper knows that if he is to be successful in implementing Internet strategy; however, he must focus on related people issues in addition to such technical issues. The material in this chapter discusses insights into why managers such as Cooper should focus on motivating workers in such situations and how this might be accomplished. Major topics in this chapter are (1) the motivation process, and (2) motivating organization members.

THE MOTIVATION PROCESS

To be successful in working with subordinates, managers need to acquire a thorough understanding of the motivation process. To this end, the definition of motivation, various motivation models, and theories of people's needs are the main discussion topics in this section of the chapter.

Defining Motivation

Motivation is the inner state that causes an individual to behave in a way that ensures the accomplishment of some goal.[2] In other words, motivation explains why people act as they do.[3] The better a manager understands organization members' behavior, the more able that manager will be to influence subordinates' behavior to make it more consistent with the accomplishment of organizational objectives. Because productivity is a result of the behavior of organization members, motivating organization members is the key to reaching organizational goals.[4]

Several motivation theories have been proposed over the years. Most of these theories can be categorized into two basic types: process theories and content theories. A **process theory of motivation** is an explanation of motivation that emphasizes how individuals are motivated. Process theories focus, essentially, on the steps that occur when an individual is motivated. A **content theory of motivation** is an explanation of motivation that emphasizes people's internal characteristics. Content theories focus on understanding what needs people have and how these needs can be satisfied. For years, industrial and organizational (I/O) psychologists have worked to integrate the many theories of motivation and identify where each has an effect in the motivation process.[5]

The following sections discuss important process and content theories of motivation and establish a relationship between them that should prove useful to managers in motivating organization members.

Process Theories of Motivation

Four important theories describe how motivation occurs:

1. Needs-goal theory
2. Vroom expectancy theory
3. Equity theory
4. Porter–Lawler theory

These theories build on one another to furnish a description of the motivation process that begins at a relatively simple and easily understood level and culminates at a somewhat more intricate and realistic level.

The Needs-Goal Theory of Motivation The **needs-goal theory** of motivation, diagrammed in Figure 17.1, is the most fundamental of the motivation theories discussed in this

FIGURE 17.1
The needs-goal theory
of motivation

chapter. As the figure indicates, motivation begins with an individual feeling a need. This need is then transformed into behavior directed at supporting, or allowing, the performance of goal behavior to reduce the felt need. Theoretically, goal-supportive behavior and goal behavior itself continue until the felt need has been significantly reduced.

When an individual feels hunger, for example, this need is typically transformed first into behavior directed at supporting the performance of the goal behavior of eating. This supportive behavior could include such activities as buying, cooking, and serving the food to be eaten. The goal-supportive behaviors and the goal behavior itself—eating—generally continue until the individual's hunger substantially subsides. When the individual experiences hunger again, however, the entire cycle is repeated.

Washington Nationals pitcher Ron Villone provides an example of the needs-goal theory of motivation. When Villone was with the New York Yankees, he heard an interesting statistic: if his team made the playoffs that year, they would be the only team to reach the postseason both that year and the preceding year. Instead of relishing the glory, Villone immediately started thinking about the playoff team he would face, the strengths and weaknesses of its hitters, and how he might pitch to each one's weakness. Villone was demonstrating a high need to perform well as a pitcher. Because of his need, he started performing goal-supportive activities that included planning how to pitch to each hitter. Once in a game situation, Villone's goal behavior—that is, how players would hit his pitches—would be the feedback that determined whether he satisfied his felt need.

class discussion highlight

MODERN RESEARCH AND MOTIVATION SKILL

Goal setting can play a prominent role in influencing motivation. For more than 30 years, researchers have provided evidence suggesting that individuals who set goals have an easier time focusing on activities relevant to those goals and avoiding distractions that prevent them from reaching those goals.

A team of researchers examined the role of goal setting while studying the performance of undergraduate students struggling with their grades. This is an important context to study, as almost 25 percent of students who start undergraduate programs never graduate. The researchers recruited 85 students who were struggling with their grades. Over the course of a semester, half of those students went through a

goal-setting program, which helped them identify personal goals and derive strategies for reaching those goals. The other students were placed in a control group and did not participate in this program (these students were instead asked to complete a number of tasks that were unrelated to goal setting).

After approximately 16 weeks, the researchers examined the performance of the students in both groups. Do you think that there was a difference between the two groups of students? Why or why not?

Source: Morisano, D., Hirsch, J. B., Peterson, J. B., Pihl, R. O., and Shore, B. M. "Setting, Elaborating, and Reflecting on Personal Goals Improves Academic Performance," *Journal of Applied Psychology* 95, no. 2 (2010): 255–264.

The Role of Individual Needs If managers are to have any success in motivating employees, they must understand the personal needs of those employees. When managers offer rewards that are not relevant to employees' personal needs, the employees will not be motivated. For example, if a top executive is already extremely well paid, more money is not likely to be an effective motivator. What is required is a more meaningful incentive—perhaps a higher-level title or an offer of partnership in the firm. Managers must be familiar with needs their employees have and offer them rewards that can satisfy these needs.[6]

The Vroom Expectancy Theory of Motivation In reality, the motivation process is more complex than supposed by the needs-goal theory. The **Vroom expectancy theory** of motivation encompasses some of these complexities.[7] Like the needs-goal theory, the Vroom expectancy theory is based on the premise that felt needs cause human behavior. However, the Vroom theory also addresses the issue of **motivation strength**—an individual's degree of desire to perform a behavior. As this desire increases or decreases, motivation strength fluctuates correspondingly.

Motivation and Perceptions Vroom's expectancy theory is shown in equation form in Figure 17.2. According to this theory, motivation strength is determined by the perceived value of the result of performing a behavior and the perceived probability that the behavior performed will cause the result to materialize. As both of these factors increase, so does motivation strength, or the desire to perform the behavior. People tend to perform the behaviors that maximize their personal rewards over the long term.

To see how Vroom's theory applies to human behavior, suppose a college student has been offered a summer job painting three houses at the rate of $200 per house. Assuming the student needs money, her motivation strength, or desire, to paint the houses will be determined by two major factors: her perception of the value of $600 and her perception of the probability that she can actually paint the houses satisfactorily and receive the $600. As the student's perceived value of the $600 reward and perceived probability that she can paint the houses increase, the student's motivation strength to paint the houses will also increase.

Equity Theory of Motivation **Equity theory**, the work of J. Stacy Adams, looks at an individual's perceived fairness of an employment situation and finds that perceived inequities can lead to changes in behavior. Adams found that when individuals believe they have been treated unfairly in comparison with their co-workers, they will react in one of the following ways to try to right the inequity:[8]

1. Some will change their work outputs to better match the rewards they are receiving. If they believe they are being paid too little, they will decrease their work outputs; if they believe they are being paid more than their co-workers, they will increase their work outputs to match their rewards.
2. Some will try to change the compensation they receive for their work by asking for a raise or by taking legal action.
3. If attempts to change the actual inequality are unsuccessful, some will try to change their own perception of the inequality. They may do this by distorting the status of their jobs or by rationalizing away the inequity.
4. Some will leave the situation rather than try to change it. People who feel they are being treated unfairly on the job may decide to quit that job rather than endure the inequity.

Perceptions of inequities can arise in any number of management situations—among them, work assignments, promotions, ratings reports, and office assignments—but they occur most often in the

FIGURE 17.2
Vroom's expectancy theory of motivation in equation form

$$\text{Motivation strength} = \text{Perceived value of result of performing behavior} \times \text{Perceived probability that result will materialize}$$

area of pay. All of these issues are emotionally charged, however, because they pertain to people's feelings of self-worth. What is a minor inequity in the mind of a manager can loom as extremely important in the mind of an employee. Effective managers strive to deal with equity issues because the steps workers are prone to take to balance the scales are often far from good for the organization.

For example, after American Airlines employees and union workers took pay cuts and made other concessions worth more than $1.6 million, they learned that American had awarded bonuses totaling $21 million to company executives. Representatives of the Transport Workers Union soon presented American Airlines chief executive Gerard J. Arpey with a petition bearing 17,000 signatures protesting the company's executive compensation practices. The perceived inequity between concessions made by nonmanagers and the bonuses awarded to managers is the kind of issue that can lead to business disruptions like work slowdowns and strikes.[9] ■

The Porter–Lawler Theory of Motivation Porter and Lawler developed a motivation theory that provides a more complete description of the motivation process than either the needs-goal theory or the Vroom expectancy theory.[10] Still, the **Porter–Lawler theory** of motivation (see Figure 17.3) is consistent with those two theories in that it accepts the premises that felt needs cause human behavior and that effort expended to accomplish a task is determined by the perceived value of rewards that will result from finishing the task and the probability that those rewards will materialize.

The Motivation Process In addition, the Porter–Lawler motivation theory stresses three other characteristics of the motivation process:

1. The perceived value of a reward is determined by both intrinsic and extrinsic rewards that result in need satisfaction when a task is accomplished. An **intrinsic reward** comes directly from performing the task, while an **extrinsic reward** is extraneous to the task.[11] For example, when a manager counsels a subordinate about a personal problem, the manager may get some intrinsic reward in the form of personal satisfaction at helping another individual. In addition to this intrinsic reward, however, the manager also receives an extrinsic reward in the form of the overall salary the manager is paid.[12]

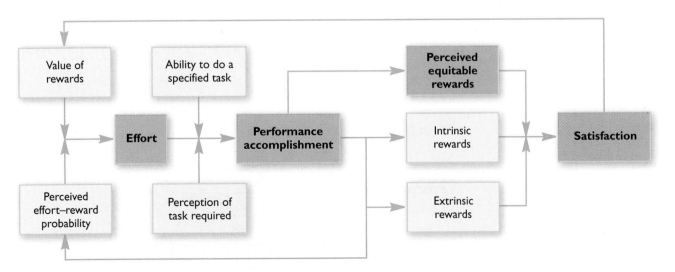

FIGURE 17.3 The Porter–Lawler theory of motivation

2. The extent to which an individual effectively accomplishes a task is determined primarily by two variables: the individual's perception of what is required to perform the task and the individual's ability to perform the task. Effectiveness at accomplishing a task increases as the perception of what is required to perform the task becomes more accurate and the ability to perform the task increases.

3. The perceived fairness of rewards influences the amount of satisfaction produced by those rewards. The more equitable an individual perceives the rewards to be, the greater the satisfaction that individual will experience as a result of receiving them.

Content Theories of Motivation: Human Needs

The motivation theories discussed thus far imply that an understanding of motivation is based on an understanding of human needs. Some evidence indicates that most people have strong needs for self-respect, respect from others, promotion, and psychological growth.[13] Although identifying all human needs is impossible, several theories have been developed to help managers better understand these needs:

1. Maslow's hierarchy of needs
2. Alderfer's ERG theory
3. Argyris's maturity-immaturity continuum
4. McClelland's acquired needs theory

Maslow's Hierarchy of Needs   Perhaps the most widely accepted description of human needs is the hierarchy of needs concept developed by Abraham Maslow.[14] Maslow states that human beings possess the five basic needs described here and theorizes that these five basic needs can be arranged in a hierarchy of importance—the order in which individuals generally strive to satisfy them.[15] The needs and their relative positions in the hierarchy of importance are shown in Figure 17.4.

- A **physiological need** relates to the normal functioning of the body. Physiological needs include the needs for water, food, rest, sex, and air. Until these needs are met, a significant portion of an individual's behavior will be aimed at satisfying them. Once the needs are satisfied, however, behavior is aimed at satisfying the needs on the next level of Maslow's hierarchy.

- A **security** or **safety need** relates to the individual's desire to be free from harm, including both bodily and economic disaster.

  Traditionally, management has best helped employees satisfy their physiological and security needs through adequate wages or salaries, which employees use to purchase such things as food and housing.

- A **social need** includes the desire for love, companionship, and friendship. Social needs reflect a person's desire to be accepted by others. As they are satisfied, behavior shifts to satisfying esteem needs.

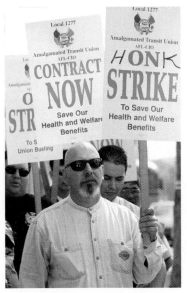

Members of the AFL-CIO Amalgamated Transit Union striking in Los Angeles. An employee strike usually indicates unmet human needs.

FIGURE 17.4
Maslow's hierarchy of needs

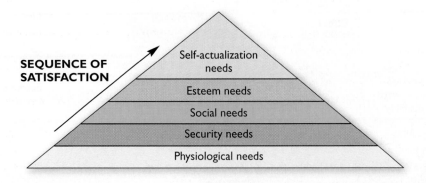

- An **esteem need** is concerned with the desire for respect. Esteem needs are generally divided into two categories: self-respect and respect from others. Once esteem needs are satisfied, the individual moves to the pinnacle of the hierarchy and emphasizes satisfying self-actualization needs.

- A **self-actualization need** refers to the desire to maximize whatever potential an individual possesses. For example, in the nonprofit public setting of a high school, a principal who seeks to satisfy self-actualization needs would strive to become the best principal possible. Self-actualization needs occupy the highest level of Maslow's hierarchy.[16]

The traditional concerns about Maslow's hierarchy are that it has no research base, that it may not accurately pinpoint basic human needs, and that it is questionable whether human needs can be neatly arranged in such a hierarchy. Nevertheless, Maslow's hierarchy is probably the most popular conceptualization of human needs to date, and it continues to be positively discussed in management literature.[17] Still, the concerns expressed about it should remind managers to look upon Maslow's hierarchy more as a subjective statement than an objective description of human needs.[18]

Alderfer's ERG Theory

Clayton Alderfer responded to some of the criticisms of Maslow's work by conducting his own study of human needs.[19] He identified three basic categories of needs:

1. **Existence need**—the need for physical well-being
2. **Relatedness need**—the need for satisfying interpersonal relationships
3. **Growth need**—the need for continuing personal growth and development

The first letters of these needs form the acronym ERG, by which the theory is now known. **Alderfer's ERG theory** is similar to Maslow's theory except in three major respects. First, Alderfer identified only three orders of human needs, compared to Maslow's five orders. Second, in contrast to Maslow, Alderfer found that people sometimes activate their higher-level needs before they have completely satisfied all of their lower-level needs. Third, Alderfer concluded that movement in his hierarchy of human needs is not always upward. For instance—and this is reflected in his frustration-regression principle—he found that a worker frustrated by his failure to satisfy an upper-level need might regress by trying to fulfill an already satisfied lower-level need.

Alderfer's work, in conjunction with Maslow's, has implications for management. Employees frustrated by work that fails to provide opportunities for growth or development on the job might concentrate their energy on trying to make more money, thus regressing to a lower level of needs. To counteract such regression, management might use job enrichment strategies designed to help people meet their higher-order needs.

Argyris's Maturity-Immaturity Continuum

Argyris's maturity-immaturity continuum also furnishes insights into human needs.[20] This continuum concept focuses on the personal and natural development of people to explain human needs. According to Argyris, as people naturally progress from immaturity to maturity, they move:

1. From a state of passivity as an infant to a state of increasing activity as an adult
2. From a state of dependence on others as an infant to a state of relative independence as an adult
3. From being capable of behaving only in a few ways as an infant to being capable of behaving in many different ways as an adult
4. From having erratic, casual, shallow, and quickly dropped interests as an infant to having deeper, more lasting interests as an adult
5. From having a short time perspective as an infant to having a much longer time perspective as an adult
6. From being in a subordinate position as an infant to aspiring to occupy an equal or superordinate position as an adult
7. From a lack of self-awareness as an infant to awareness and control over self as an adult

According to Argyris's continuum, then, as individuals mature, they have increasing needs for more activity, enjoy a state of relative independence, behave in many different ways, have deeper and more lasting interests, are capable of considering a relatively long time perspective, occupy an equal position vis-à-vis other mature individuals, and have more awareness of themselves and control over their own destiny. Note that, unlike Maslow's needs, Argyris's needs are not arranged in a hierarchy. Like Maslow's hierarchy, however, Argyris's continuum is a primarily subjective explanation of human needs.

McClelland's Acquired Needs Theory Another theory about human needs, called **McClelland's acquired needs theory**, focuses on the needs that people acquire through their life experiences. This theory, formulated by David C. McClelland in the 1960s, emphasizes three of the many needs human beings develop in their lifetimes:

1. **Need for achievement (nAch)**—the desire to do something better or more efficiently than it has ever been done before
2. **Need for power (nPower)**—the desire to control, influence, or be responsible for others
3. **Need for affiliation (nAff)**—the desire to maintain close, friendly, personal relationships

The individual's early life experiences determine which of these needs will be highly developed and therefore dominate the personality.

how managers do it

Achievement Motivation at C. Crane

Bob Crane, the entrepreneurial founder of C. Crane, is an example of an individual motivated by the need for achievement. Crane's dream is to save the world energy, and he works to achieve that vision by inventing energy-saving devices that are better and more efficient than any before. His latest product, the GeoBulb, is an LED light bulb that uses half the energy of a fluorescent bulb, contains no lead or mercury, and will last 30,000 hours or up to 10 years. Bob's not in it for the money. As he puts it, "It's 100% altruistic, and we hope that we'll get paid in time." Although the company hasn't made Crane a wealthy man, he says working toward his goal makes him happy."[21] ∎

McClelland's studies of these three acquired human needs have significant implications for management.

NEED FOR ACHIEVEMENT McClelland claims that in some businesspeople, the need to achieve is so strong that it is more motivating than the quest for profits. To maximize their satisfaction, individuals with high achievement needs set goals for themselves that are challenging, yet achievable. Although such people are willing to assume risk, they assess it carefully because they do not want to fail. Therefore, they will avoid tasks that involve too much risk. People with a low need for achievement, on the other hand, generally avoid challenges, responsibilities, and risk.

NEED FOR POWER People with a high need for power are greatly motivated to influence others and to assume responsibility for subordinates' behavior. They are likely to seek advancement and to take on increasingly responsible work activities to earn that advancement. Power-oriented managers are comfortable in competitive situations and enjoy their decision-making role.

NEED FOR AFFILIATION Managers with a high need for affiliation have a cooperative, team-centered managerial style. They prefer to influence subordinates to complete tasks through

Generous company benefits and a congenial work environment that encourages employees to pursue their love of the outdoors are among the motivating strategies employed by Patagonia's founder and CEO, Yvon Chouinard.

team efforts. The danger is that managers with a high need for affiliation can lose their effectiveness if their need for social approval and friendship interferes with their willingness to make managerial decisions.[22]

MOTIVATING ORGANIZATION MEMBERS

People are motivated to perform behavior that satisfies their personal needs. Therefore, from a managerial viewpoint, motivation is the process of furnishing organization members with the opportunity to satisfy their needs by performing productive behavior within the organization. In reality, managers do not motivate people. Rather, they create environments in which organization members motivate themselves.[23]

As discussed in Chapter 15, motivation is one of the four primary interrelated activities of the influencing function performed by managers to guide the behavior of organization members toward the attainment of organizational objectives. The following sections discuss the importance of motivating organization members and present some strategies for doing so.

The Importance of Motivating Organization Members

Figure 17.5 makes the point that unsatisfied needs can lead organization members to perform either appropriate or inappropriate behavior. Successful managers minimize inappropriate behavior and maximize appropriate behavior among subordinates, thus raising the probability that productivity will increase and lowering the probability that it will decrease.

Strategies for Motivating Organization Members

Managers have various strategies at their disposal for motivating organization members. Each strategy is aimed at satisfying subordinates' needs (consistent with the descriptions of human needs in Maslow's hierarchy, Alderfer's ERG theory, Argyris's maturity-immaturity continuum, and McClelland's acquired needs theory) through appropriate organizational behavior. These managerial motivation strategies are as follows:

1. Managerial communication
2. Theory X–Theory Y
3. Job design
4. Behavior modification
5. Likert's management systems
6. Monetary incentives
7. Nonmonetary incentives

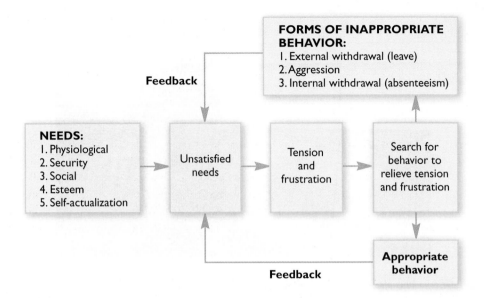

FIGURE 17.5
Unsatisfied needs of organization members resulting in either appropriate or inappropriate behavior

The strategies are discussed in the sections that follow.

Throughout the discussion, it is important to remember that no single strategy will always be more effective for a manager than any other. Most managers find that some combination of these strategies is most effective in the organization setting.

Managerial Communication   Perhaps the most basic motivation strategy for managers is to communicate well with organization members. Effective manager–subordinate communication can satisfy such basic human needs as recognition, a sense of belonging, and security. For example, such a simple managerial action as attempting to become better acquainted with subordinates can contribute substantially to the satisfaction of each of these three needs. For another example, a message praising a subordinate for a job well done can help satisfy the subordinate's recognition and security needs.

As a general rule, managers should strive to communicate often with other organization members, not only because communication is the primary means of conducting organizational activities, but also because it is a basic tool for satisfying the human needs of organization members.[24]

Theory X–Theory Y   Another motivation strategy involves managers' assumptions about human nature. Douglas McGregor identified two sets of assumptions: **Theory X** involves negative assumptions about people that McGregor believes managers often use as the basis for dealing with their subordinates (e.g., the average person has an inherent dislike of work and will avoid it whenever he or she can). **Theory Y** represents positive assumptions about people that McGregor believes managers should strive to use (e.g., people will exercise self-direction and self-control in meeting their objectives).[25]

The Theory X/Theory Y debate resonates for managers across many work settings.[26] McGregor implies that managers who use Theory X assumptions are "bad" and that those who use Theory Y assumptions are "good."[27] Reddin, however, argues that production might be increased by using *either* Theory X or Theory Y assumptions, depending on the situation the manager faces: "Is there not a strong argument for the position that any theory may have desirable outcomes if appropriately used?" The difficulty is that McGregor considered only the ineffective application of Theory X and the effective application of Theory Y. Reddin proposes a **Theory Z**—an effectiveness dimension that implies managers who use either Theory X or Theory Y assumptions when dealing with people can be successful, depending on their situation.[28]

The basic rationale for using Theory Y rather than Theory X in most situations is that managerial activities that reflect Theory Y assumptions generally are more successful in satisfying the human needs of most organization members than are managerial activities that reflect Theory X assumptions. Therefore, activities based on Theory Y assumptions are more apt to motivate organization members than are activities based on Theory X assumptions.[29]

Job Design

A third strategy managers can use to motivate organization members involves designing jobs that organization members perform. The following two sections discuss earlier and more recent job design strategies.

Earlier Job Design Strategies

A movement has long existed in American business to make jobs simpler and more specialized to increase worker productivity. The idea behind this movement is to make workers more productive by enabling them to be more efficient. Perhaps the best example of a job design inspired by this movement is the automobile assembly line. The negative result of work simplification and specialization, however, is job boredom. As jobs become simpler and more specialized, they typically become more boring and less satisfying to workers, and, consequently, productivity suffers.

JOB ROTATION The first major attempt to overcome job boredom was **job rotation**—moving workers from job to job rather than requiring them to perform only one simple and specialized job over the long term.[30] For example, a gardener would do more than just mow lawns; he might also trim bushes, rake grass, and sweep sidewalks.

Although job rotation programs have been known to increase organizational profitability, most of them are ineffective as motivation strategies because, over time, people become bored with all the jobs they are rotated into.[31] Job rotation programs, however, are often effective for achieving other organizational objectives, such as training, because they give individuals an overview of how the various units of the organization function. Job rotation can also be an effective intervention for reducing absenteeism—a significant problem in some organizations.[32]

JOB ENLARGEMENT Another strategy developed to overcome the boredom of doing very simple and specialized jobs is **job enlargement**, or increasing the number of operations an individual performs to enhance the individual's satisfaction in work. According to the job enlargement concept, the gardener's job would become more satisfying as such activities as trimming bushes, raking grass, and sweeping sidewalks were added to his initial activity of mowing grass. Some research supports the contention that job enlargement does make jobs more satisfying, and some does not.[33] Still, job enlargement programs are more successful at increasing job satisfaction than job rotation programs.

A number of other job design strategies have evolved since the development of job rotation and job enlargement programs. Two of these more recent strategies are job enrichment and flextime.

Job Enrichment

Frederick Herzberg concluded from his research that the degrees of satisfaction and dissatisfaction organization members feel as a result of performing a job are two different variables determined by two different sets of items.[34] The items that influence the degree of job dissatisfaction are called **hygiene** or **maintenance factors**, while those that influence the degree of job satisfaction are called **motivating factors (motivators)**. Hygiene factors relate to the work environment, and motivating factors to the work itself. The items that make up Herzberg's hygiene and motivating factors are presented in Table 17.1.

Herzberg believes that when the hygiene factors of a particular job situation are undesirable, organization members will become dissatisfied. Making these factors more desirable—for example, by increasing salary—will rarely motivate people to do a better job, but it will keep them from becoming dissatisfied. In contrast, when the motivating factors of a particular job situation are high, employees usually are motivated to do a better job. People tend to be more motivated and productive as more motivators are built into their job situation. During periods of economic recession or high unemployment, many workers are dissatisfied, either because they are doing the work of several people as the result of layoffs in their organization or they feel "trapped" by a boring job they cannot afford to leave due to the difficulty of finding a new one.[35]

TABLE 17.1 Herzberg's Hygiene Factors and Motivators

Dissatisfaction: Hygiene or Maintenance Factors	Satisfaction: Motivating Factors
1. Company policy and administration	1. Opportunity for achievement
2. Supervision	2. Opportunity for recognition
3. Relationship with supervisor	3. Work itself
4. Relationship with peers	4. Responsibility
5. Working conditions	5. Working conditions
6. Salary	6. Personal growth
7. Relationship with subordinates	

The process of incorporating motivators into a job situation is called **job enrichment**.[36] Early reports indicated that companies such as Texas Instruments and Volvo had notable success in motivating organization members through job enrichment programs. More recent reports, even though they continue to support the value of job enrichment, indicate that for a job enrichment program to be successful, it must be carefully designed and administered.[37]

Many management theorists espouse views that seem consistent with Herzberg's hygiene factor-motivator concept. David Pink, for example, believes that pay in itself is not a motivator. Instead, Pink claims that motivation comes from three different sources: autonomy (the ability to direct one's own life), mastery (continuous improvement at something an individual regards as important), and purpose (to contribute to something larger than one's self).[38]

JOB ENRICHMENT AND PRODUCTIVITY Herzberg's overall conclusions are that the most productive organization members are those involved in work situations that have both desirable hygiene and motivating factors. The needs in Maslow's hierarchy that desirable hygiene factors and motivating factors generally satisfy are shown in Figure 17.6. Esteem needs can be satisfied by both types of factors. An example of esteem needs satisfied by a hygiene factor is a private parking space—a status symbol and a working condition evidencing the employee's importance to the organization. An example of esteem needs satisfied by a motivating factor is an award given for outstanding performance—a public recognition of a job well done that displays the employee's value to the organization.

Flextime Another more recent job design strategy for motivating organization members is based on a concept called *flextime*.[39] Perhaps the most common traditional characteristic of work in the United States is that jobs are performed within a fixed eight-hour workday. This tradition has been challenged. Faced with motivation problems and excessive absenteeism, many managers have turned to scheduling innovations as a possible solution.[40]

FIGURE 17.6
Needs in Maslow's hierarchy of needs that desirable hygiene and motivating factors generally satisfy

Flextime can be highly motivating to some workers, giving them greater control over their work day and often leading to higher productivity and job satisfaction. If flextime allowed you to avoid rush hour, for instance, would you become more productive?

The main purpose of these scheduling innovations is not to reduce the total number of work hours, but rather to give workers greater flexibility in scheduling their work hours. The main thrust of **flextime**, or a flexible working hours program, is that it allows workers to complete their jobs within a workweek of a normal number of hours that they arrange themselves.[41] The choices of starting and finishing times can be as flexible as the organizational situation allows. To ensure that flexibility does not become counterproductive within the organization, however, many flextime programs stipulate a core period during which all employees must be on the job.

ADVANTAGES OF FLEXTIME Various kinds of organizational studies have indicated that flextime programs have some positive organizational effects. Douglas Fleuter, for example, reported that flextime contributes to greater job satisfaction, which typically results in greater productivity. Other researchers conclude that flextime programs can result in higher motivation levels of workers. Because organization members generally consider flextime programs desirable, organizations that have such programs can usually better compete with other organizations in recruiting qualified new employees. (A listing of the advantages and disadvantages of flextime programs appears in Table 17.2.) Although many well-known companies, such as Scott Paper, Sun

TABLE 17.2 Advantages and Disadvantages of Using Flextime Programs

Advantages	Disadvantages
Improved employee attitude and morale	Lack of supervision during some hours of work
Accommodation of working parents	Key people unavailable at certain times
Decreased tardiness	Understaffing at times
Fewer commuting problems—workers can avoid congested streets and highways	Problem of accommodating employees whose output is the input for other employees
Accommodation of those who wish to arrive at work before normal workday interruptions begin	Employee abuse of flextime program
Increased production	Difficulty in planning work schedules
Facilitation of employees scheduling of medical, dental, and other types of appointments	Problem of keeping track of hours worked or accumulated
Accommodation of leisure-time activities of employees	Inability to schedule meetings at convenient times
Decreased absenteeism	Inability to coordinate projects
Decreased turnover	

Oil, and Samsonite, have adopted flextime programs,[42] more research is needed before flextime's true worth can be conclusively assessed.

Behavior Modification A fourth strategy that managers can use to motivate organization members is based on a concept known as behavior modification. As stated by B. F. Skinner, the Harvard psychologist considered by many to be the father of behavioral psychology, **behavior modification** focuses on encouraging appropriate behavior by controlling the consequences of that behavior.[43] According to the law of effect, behavior that is rewarded tends to be repeated, while that which is punished tends to be eliminated.

Although behavior modification programs typically involve the administration of both rewards and punishments, it is rewards that are generally emphasized because they are more effective than punishments in influencing behavior. Obviously, the main theme of behavior modification is not new.

REINFORCEMENT Behavior modification theory asserts that if managers want to modify subordinates' behavior, they must ensure that appropriate consequences occur as a result of that behavior. **Positive reinforcement** is a reward that consists of a desirable consequence of behavior, and **negative reinforcement** is a reward that consists of the elimination of an undesirable consequence of behavior.[44]

If arriving at work on time is positively reinforced, or rewarded, the probability increases that a worker will arrive on time more often.[45] If arriving late for work causes a worker to experience some undesirable outcome, such as a verbal reprimand, that worker will be negatively reinforced when this outcome is eliminated by on-time arrival. According to behavior modification theory, positive reinforcement and negative reinforcement are both rewards that increase the likelihood that a behavior will continue.

PUNISHMENT **Punishment** is the presentation of an undesirable behavior consequence or the removal of a desirable behavior consequence that decreases the likelihood the behavior will continue. To use our earlier example, a manager could punish employees for arriving late for work by exposing them to some undesirable consequence, such as verbal reprimand, or by removing a desirable consequence, such as their wages for the amount of time they are late.[46] Although punishment would probably quickly convince most workers to come to work on time, it might have undesirable side effects, such as high absenteeism and turnover, if it is emphasized over the long term.[47]

Applying Behavior Modification Behavior modification programs have been applied both successfully and unsuccessfully in a number of organizations. Management at Emery Worldwide, for example, found that an effective feedback system is crucial to making a behavior modification program successful.[48] This feedback system should be aimed at keeping employees informed of the relationship between various behaviors and their consequences.

Other ingredients of successful behavior modification programs are the following:[49]

1. Giving different levels of rewards to different workers according to the quality of their performances
2. Telling workers what they are doing wrong
3. Punishing workers privately to avoid embarrassing them in front of others
4. Always giving out rewards and punishments that are earned to emphasize that management is serious about its behavior modification efforts.

The behavior modification concept is also being applied to cost control in organizations, with the objective of encouraging employees to be more cost conscious. Under this type of behavior modification program, employees are compensated in a manner that rewards cost control and cost reduction and penalizes cost acceleration.[50]

Recently, managers have added another component to the behavior modification process that identifies the role of cognitions in workplace behavior.[51] More specifically, when tackling problems such as inappropriate corporate culture, managers may recognize a need to change the way employees think about corporate culture in addition to the way they behave. Cognitive behavior modification programs are best implemented by an expert outside consultant who can identify negative cognitive and behavioral processes. Even though these programs have demonstrated much promise, further empirical analysis is necessary to solidify their place in the corporate environment.

Likert's Management Systems Another strategy that managers can use to motivate organization members is based on the work of Rensis Likert, a noted management scholar.[52] After studying several types and sizes of organizations, Likert concluded that management styles in organizations can be categorized into the following systems:

- **System 1**—This style of management is characterized by a lack of confidence or trust in subordinates. Subordinates do not feel free to discuss their jobs with superiors and are motivated by fear, threats, punishments, and occasional rewards. Information flow in the organization is directed primarily downward; upward communication is viewed with great suspicion. The bulk of all decision making is done at the top of the organization.

- **System 2**—This style of management is characterized by a condescending master-to-servant–style confidence and trust in subordinates. Subordinates do not feel free to discuss their jobs with superiors and are motivated by rewards and actual or potential punishments. Information flows mostly downward; upward communication may or may not be viewed with suspicion. Although policies are made primarily at the top of the organization, decisions within a prescribed framework are made at lower levels.

- **System 3**—This style of management is characterized by substantial, though not complete, confidence in subordinates. Subordinates feel fairly free to discuss their jobs with superiors and are motivated by rewards, occasional punishments, and some involvement. Information flows both upward and downward in the organization. Upward communication is often accepted, though at times, it may be viewed with suspicion. Although broad policies and general decisions are made at the top of the organization, more specific decisions are made at lower levels.

- **System 4**—This style of management is characterized by complete trust and confidence in subordinates. Subordinates feel completely free to discuss their jobs with superiors and are motivated by such factors as economic rewards based on a compensation system developed through employee participation and involvement in goal setting. Information flows upward, downward, and horizontally. Upward communication is generally accepted—but even where it is not, employees' questions are answered candidly. Decision making is spread widely throughout the organization and is well coordinated.

Styles, Systems, and Productivity Likert has suggested that as management style moves from system 1 to system 4, the human needs of individuals within the organization tend to be more effectively satisfied over the long term. Thus, an organization that moves toward system 4 tends to become more productive over the long term.

Figure 17.7 illustrates the comparative long- and short-term effects of both system 1 and system 4 on organizational production. Managers may increase production in the short term by using a system 1 management style, because motivation by fear, threat, and punishment is generally effective in the short run. Over the long run, however, this style usually causes production to decrease, primarily because of the long-term nonsatisfaction of organization members' needs and the poor working relationships between managers and subordinates.

Conversely, managers who initiate a system 4 management style will probably face some decline in production initially but will see an increase in production over the long term. The short-term decline occurs because organization members must adapt to the new system management is implementing. The production increase over the long term materializes as a result of organization members' adjustment to the new system, greater satisfaction of their needs, and good working relationships that develop between managers and subordinates.

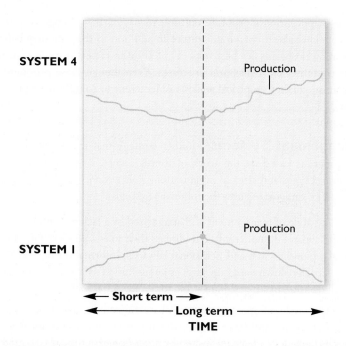

SYSTEM 4

Production

SYSTEM I

Production

◄— **Short term** —►

◄——————— **Long term** ———————►

TIME

FIGURE 17.7
Comparative long-term and short-term effects of system 1 and system 4 on organizational production

This long-term production increase under system 4 can also be related to decision-making differences in the two management systems. Because decisions reached in system 4 are more likely to be thoroughly understood by organization members than decisions reached in system 1, decision implementation is more likely to be efficient and effective in system 4 than in system 1.

Monetary Incentives   A number of firms make a wide range of money-based compensation programs available to their employees as a form of motivation. For instance, employee stock ownership plans (ESOPs) motivate employees to boost production by offering them shares of company stock as a benefit. Managers are commonly given stock bonuses as an incentive to think more like an owner and ultimately do a better job of building a successful organization. Other incentive plans include lump-sum bonuses—one-time cash payments—and gain-sharing, a plan under which members of a team receive a bonus when their team exceeds a goal. All of these plans link pay closely to performance.[53] Many organizations have found that by putting more of their employees' pay at risk, they can peg more of their total wage costs to sales, which makes expenses more controllable in a downturn.[54] Whatever approach a monetary incentive program takes, it is important that it be accompanied by communication to all employees, describing the organization's business goals and explaining how employees' behavior contributes to accomplishing those goals.[55]

how managers do it

Distributing Incentives at Comarco

Comarco CEO Sam Inman found an innovative way to inspire motivation among his employees through monetary incentives: he eliminated the annual review and automatic pay raises. Instead, Inman now distributes awards and raises on a random basis, after an employee has achieved a goal or delivered a project. Employees of Comarco, the maker of universal charge adapters, have also received spot rewards like gift certificates, plane tickets, and vacations for jobs well done.[56] ■

Nonmonetary Incentives   A firm can also keep its employees committed and motivated by nonmonetary means. For instance, some companies have a policy of promoting from within. They go through an elaborate process of advertising jobs internally before going outside to fill vacancies. Another nonmonetary incentive emphasizes quality, on the theory that most workers are unhappy when they know their work goes to producing a shoddy product.[57]

CHALLENGE CASE SUMMARY

Motivation is an inner state that causes individuals to act in certain ways that ensure the accomplishment of some goal. Jack Cooper in the Challenge Case seems to have an accurate understanding of the motivation process. He is focusing on influencing the behavior of his employees to enhance the success of his digital strategy program at Bristol-Myers Squibb. Cooper encourages employees within the company to be creative and efficient in implementing digital strategy. Cooper's focus on motivation should be a valuable tool in making his Internet strategy implementation efforts effective.

To motivate employees at Bristol-Myers Squibb, Cooper must keep five specific principles of human motivation clearly in mind: (1) felt needs cause behavior aimed at reducing those needs, (2) the degree of desire to perform a particular behavior is determined by an individual's perceived value of the result of performing the behavior and the perceived probability that the behavior will cause the result to materialize, (3) the perceived value of a reward for a particular behavior is determined by both intrinsic and extrinsic rewards that result in need satisfaction when the behavior is accomplished, (4) individuals can effectively accomplish a task only if they understand what the task requires and have the ability to perform the task, and (5) the perceived fairness of a reward influences the degree of satisfaction generated when the reward is received.

Jack Cooper undoubtedly understands the basic motivation principle that felt needs cause behavior. Before managers can have maximum impact on motivating their organization members, they must meet the more complex challenge of being thoroughly familiar with various individual human needs of their employees.

According to Maslow, people generally possess physiological needs, security needs, social needs, esteem needs, and self-actualization needs arranged in a hierarchy of importance. Argyris suggests that as people mature, they have increasing needs for activity, independence, flexibility, deeper interests, analyses of longer time perspectives, a position of equality with other mature individuals, and control over personal destiny. McClelland believes that the need for achievement—the desire to do something better or more efficiently than it has ever been done before—is a strong human need.

By guaranteeing every worker a position with no pay cuts as part of the Internet strategy implementation program, Cooper could focus on satisfying employee physiological and safety needs. Other possible features of Cooper's implementation program

to further motivate employees could be "Best Implementer of the Month" or "Best Implementation Idea of the Week" to focus on other needs that employees might have.

Once a manager understands that felt needs cause behavior, and is aware of people's different types of needs, he is ready to apply this information to motivating his workforce. From Cooper's viewpoint, motivating employees means furnishing them with the opportunity to satisfy their human needs by performing their jobs. This notion is especially important because successful motivation tends to increase employee productivity. If Cooper does not furnish his employees with an opportunity to satisfy their human needs while working, low morale within the company will eventually develop. Signs of this low morale might be only a few employees initiating new ideas, people avoiding the confrontation of tough situations, and employees resisting innovation.

What does the preceding information recommend that Cooper actually do to motivate employees involved in his digital strategy implementation efforts? One strategy he might follow is taking time to communicate with his employees. Manager–employee communication can help satisfy employee needs for recognition, belonging, and security. Another of Cooper's strategies might be based on McGregor's Theory X–Theory Y concept. In following this concept when dealing with employees, Cooper should assume that work is as natural as play; that employees can be self-directed in goal accomplishment; that the granting of rewards encourages the achievement of implementation objectives; that employees seek and accept responsibility; and that most employees are creative, ingenious, and imaginative. The adoption of such assumptions by Cooper can lead to satisfying many of the needs defined by Maslow, Argyris, and McClelland.

Jack Cooper could use two major job design strategies to motivate his employees at Bristol-Myers Squibb. With job enrichment, Cooper can incorporate into employee jobs such motivating factors as opportunities for achievement, recognition, and personal growth. Cooper's allowing workers to transfer back and forth among work teams and not work on just one product can be viewed as a type of job enrichment allowing workers opportunities for personal growth. However, for maximum success, hygiene factors at Bristol-Myers Squibb—company policy and administration, supervision, salary, and working conditions, for example—also should be perceived as desirable by employees.

The second major job design strategy that Cooper can use to motivate his employees is flextime. With flextime, his employees could have some freedom in scheduling the beginning and ending of workdays. This freedom could be somewhat limited by organizational factors such as the urgency of Internet strategy implementation or the availability of skilled employees to perform implementation jobs.

Jack Cooper can apply behavior modification to his situation at Bristol-Myers Squibb by rewarding appropriate employee behavior and punishing inappropriate employee behavior. Punishment has to be used carefully, however. If used continually, the working relationship between Cooper and his employees can be destroyed. For the behavior modification program to be successful, Cooper has to furnish employees with feedback on which behaviors are appropriate and inappropriate, to give workers different rewards depending on the quality of their performance, to tell workers what they were doing wrong, to punish workers privately, and to consistently give rewards and punishments when earned.

To use Likert's system 4 management style to motivate employees over the long term, Cooper has to demonstrate complete confidence in his workers and encourage workers to feel completely free to discuss problems with him. In addition, communication among those involved in digital strategy implementation at Bristol-Myers Squibb has to flow freely in all directions within the organization structure, with upward communication discussed candidly. Cooper's decision-making process under system 4 has to involve many employees. Cooper can use the principle of supportive relationships as the basis for his system 4 management style. No single strategy mentioned in this chapter for motivating organization members would necessarily be more valuable to managers such as Cooper than any of the other strategies. In reality, Cooper will probably find that some combination of all of these strategies is most useful in motivating Internet strategy implementation workers at Bristol-Myers Squibb.

MANAGEMENT SKILL ACTIVITIES

This section is specially designed to help you develop motivation skill. An individual's motivation skill is based on an understanding of motivation concepts and the ability to apply those concepts in management situations. The following activities are designed both to heighten your understanding of motivation fundamentals and to develop your ability to apply those concepts in various management situations.

UNDERSTANDING MOTIVATION CONCEPTS

 To check your understanding and to practice using the concepts in this chapter, go to www.mymanagementlab.com and explore the material associated with Chapter 17.

Know Key Terms

Understanding the following key terms is critical to your understanding of chapter material. Define each of these terms. Refer to the page(s) referenced after a term to check your definition or to gain further insight regarding the term.

Know How Management Concepts Relate

This section is comprised of activities that will further sharpen your understanding of management concepts. Answer essay questions as completely as possible. Also, remember that many additional true/false and multiple choice questions appear online at MyManagementLab.com to help you further refine your understanding of management concepts.

1. Write out the equation for the expectancy theory of motivation. How can you use this equation to improve your motivation skill? Be specific.
2. Is Maslow's hierarchy of needs useful to managers? Why?

3. Describe your maturity level according to Argyris's maturity-immaturity continuum. What insights about your human needs does this description give you?
4. Which strategy for motivating organization members presented in the chapter would you find easiest to implement? Why? Which would you find most difficult to use? Why?
5. Discuss your personal opinion about how to use positive reinforcement, negative reinforcement, and punishment in motivating organization members. Which of the three do you think is the most important ingredient of behavior modification? Explain.

DEVELOPING MANAGEMENT SKILLS

Learning activities in this section are aimed at helping you develop motivation skill. Learning activities include Exploring Your Management Skill: Parts 1 and 2, Experiential Exercises, Cases, and a VideoNet Exercise.

Exploring Your Management Skill: Part 1

Before studying this chapter, respond to the following questions regarding the type of advice you would give to Jack Cooper, a top manager at Bristol-Myers Squibb referenced in the Challenge Case. Then address the concerning motivation challenges that he presently faces within the company. You are not expected to be a motivation expert at this point. Answering the questions now can help you focus on important points when you study the chapter. Also, answering the questions again after you study the chapter will give you an idea of how much you have learned.

Record your answers here or go to MyManagementLab.com. Recording your answers in MyManagementLab will allow you to get immediate results and see how your score compares to your classmates. If you answer the questions in the book, the answers are located in the Exploring Your Management Skill Appendix at the end of the book.

FOR EACH STATEMENT CIRCLE:
• "Y" if you would give the advice to Cooper.
• "N" if you would NOT give the advice to Cooper.
• "NI" if you have no idea whether you would give the advice to Cooper.

Mr. Cooper, in meeting your motivation challenges at Bristol-Myers Squibb (BMS), you should...

Before After
Study Study

1. pay people more money if you want them to be more committed to their work.
Y, N, NI

2. know that the perceived value of the result of performing some behavior is the main determinant of motivation strength.
Y, N, NI

3. strive to make compensation equitable as perceived by workers, but normally not managers.
Y, N, NI

4. keep in mind that people generally desire to interact with one another.
Y, N, NI

5. give people opportunities to grow and develop in the workplace.
Y, N, NI

6. normally, help high achievers set goals for themselves.
Y, N, NI

7. remember that affiliation needs are more prevalent in organizations than needs for power.
Y, N, NI

8. sometimes, simply communicate with others as a tactic for keeping them motivated in the workplace.
Y, N, NI

9. rotate people through different jobs to make sure they're motivated over the longer term.
Y, N, NI

10. enrich jobs by filling them with hygiene factors.
Y, N, NI

11. remember that esteem needs represent hygiene factors related to a job but not motivators.
    Y, N, NI

12. use punishment and negative reinforcement in the same way.
    Y, N, NI

13. strive to use a System 1 management style to ensure long-run company success.
    Y, N, NI

14. remember that both monetary and nonmonetary incentives can be equally effective in ensuring organization members are appropriately motivated.
    Y, N, NI

15. keep in mind that both the long- and short-term effects of the System 4 and System 1 management styles are essentially the same.
    Y, N, NI

Exploring Your Management Skill: Part 2

As you recall, you completed Exploring Your Management Skill: Part 1 before you started to study this chapter. Your responses gave you an idea of how much you initially knew about motivation and helped you focus on important points as you studied the chapter. Answer the Exploring Your Management Skill questions again now and compare your score to the first time you took it. This comparison will give you an idea of how much you have learned from studying this chapter and pinpoint areas for further clarification before you start studying the next chapter. Record your answers within the text or go to MyManagementLab.com. Recording your answers in MyManagementLab will allow you to get immediate results and see how your score compares to your classmates. If you answer the questions in the book, the answers are located in the Exploring Your Management Skill Appendix at the end of the book.

Your Management Skills Portfolio

Your Management Learning Portfolio is a collection of activities especially designed to demonstrate your management knowledge and skill. By completing these activities online at MyManagementLab.com, you will be able to print, complete with cover sheet, as many activities as you choose. Be sure to save your work. Taking your printed portfolio to an employment interview could be helpful in obtaining a job.

The portfolio activity for this chapter is Motivating Workers at Honda of America. Read the highlight about Honda of America and answer the questions that follow.

In 1977 Honda, a Japanese company, announced plans to build a motorcycle manufacturing plant in the United States near Marysville, Ohio, and in 1980 announced plans to build an automobile manufacturing facility in the same area. Since these announcements, Honda's history has been nothing but impressive. To highlight this success, the Marysville Auto Plant now produces the Accord Coupe for export to Japan, Honda of America has become a leading auto exporter in the United States, and the motorcycle plant produced its one-millionth unit of the Gold Wing motorcycle. Many maintain that the following belief statement, which appears prominently on the Honda of America Web site, is a primary reason for the company's success: Why do people want to work for Honda? How does Honda achieve industry-leading quality year after year, making extremely complex products such as cars, trucks, motorcycles, and engines? The answer is in Honda's foundation principle—the tenant upon which all the other Honda philosophies are based. It's called Respect for the Individual.

Founders Soichiro Honda and Takeo Fujisawa believed in creating a workforce where each member's ideas received the full consideration and respect of the group. People are diverse and that's a good thing, Mr. Honda believed, because diversity of thought, skills, background, and experiences can enrich the workplace and the product, if the differences are allowed to generate ideas.

In order for the associates' best work to come forward, they must feel valued and comfortable speaking up and interacting with their work groups. That's where respect comes in. Only in an atmosphere of maximized respect and inclusion can a workforce reach its highest levels of achievement.

Activities

You have just been contacted to interview for the top management position at Honda of America. You would be responsible for both automobile and motorcycle manufacturing. Before you visit the Marysville facility for a series of face-to-face interviews, however, you have been asked to answer the following questions related to your own beliefs about how managers should handle people. Answer the following questions in preparation for your trip to Marysville.

1. What role do you think individual needs of people play in building a successful company?

2. What insights do you have about building employee commitment to the success of Honda of America?

3. Do you believe maintaining fair pay in Honda's Marysville plant is important? Why?

4. What is your personal philosophy about using "job design" as a tool for motivating Honda of America employees?

5. What management style would you use at Honda of America? Discuss its short- and long-term implications on production levels.

Experiential Exercises

1 Analyzing Study Results

Directions. Read the following scenario and then perform the listed activities. Your instructor may want you to perform the activities as an individual or within groups. Follow all of your instructor's directions carefully.

You are part of a special task force established by the human resources department of a farm equipment manufacturing company in the Midwest. The company has 2,200 employees, 405 of whom are managers at various organizational levels. The assignment of your task force is to analyze the results of a survey recently completed by managers within the company and to recommend whatever action might be necessary, if any, given your opinions about survey results.

The following chart summarizes survey results concerning manager beliefs about the amount of information they receive from others in the company regarding how well their job is being done, their job duties, organizational policies, pay and benefits, and how technology changes within the company affect their jobs. According to survey results, managers believe they need more information in all areas to do their job properly.

Activity

Your instructor will divide your class into small groups and appoint a discussion leader for each group. Assume the role of the task force and answer the following questions. After discussion has been completed, your instructor will lead the class in a discussion regarding the opinions of all groups.

1. Do you believe the results are having a negative effect within the company on the level of managers' commitment to attaining organizational success? Explain.

2. Given survey results and Maslow's hierarchy of needs, discuss the extent to which you believe managers' personal needs are being met within the organization. Explain.

3. Given your thoughts about questions 1 and 2, what action would you recommend (if any) should be taken to improve the level of organizational success? Explain. Be as specific as possible.

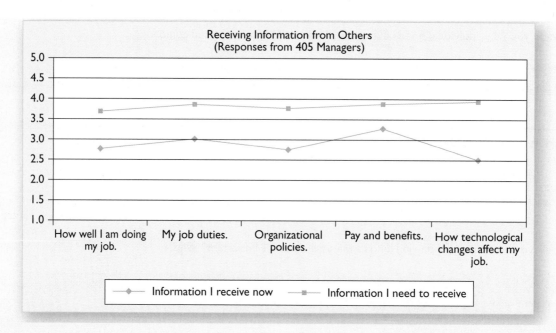

Receiving Information from Others
(Responses from 405 Managers)

— Information I receive now   — Information I need to receive

2 You and Your Career

Information in this chapter implies that punishment can be an effective tool in managing employee behavior. Eric Mangini, former manager of the New York Jets football team, had a team that commit few mistakes in games.[58] As evidence, the Jets ranked No. 3 in the league in fewest penalties and No. 2 in lowest penalty yardage assessed. How has the coach accomplished this feat? Mangini reinforced his message of playing smart by having players run extra penalty laps for practice infractions that fall under the category of penalties. One player, Rashad Washington, believed the punishment laps have a lot to do with the penalty-free nature of the team. According to Washington,

"Those things get tiring, especially after you've been practicing twice a day and you end up having to run a lap in the middle of practice, then come back and jump right back in. You try your best in practice not to make dumb penalties so you don't have to run, and it carries over to the game."

1. Would you want a manager to help build your career by using such punishment tactics on you? Explain.
2. As a manager, would you use punishment to help build the careers of your employees? Explain.
3. List two advantages and two disadvantages of punishment to build the careers of others.

VideoNet Exercise

Motivating Employees at KPMG

Video Highlights

When Bruce Pfau was hired as vice-chair of human resources at KPMG, the company was in trouble: Employee satisfaction was at an all-time low, and turnover was high. He had to turn the place around. A transformation this big could only happen with the full support of senior management. Bruce used employee surveys to find out what employees really wanted, and he delivered. While compensation matters, many folks develop a loyalty to KPMG because of other benefits. Working mom Liz Harper has a new lease on life thanks to her alternative work arrangement involving a flexible schedule and a shorter work week. (Liz had left KPMG 12 years ago because she wasn't able to juggle the demands of her job and her new family.) Other employees chime in about what makes them tick.

Discussion Questions

1. Which of the process theories of motivation explains the choice of benefits used by KPMG?
2. Using the job enrichment concept, does the benefit package offered by KPMG motivate people to work harder? Explain.
3. Does top management at KPMG hold Theory X or Theory Y assumptions about the nature of man? Explain.

Internet Activity

Go to the KPMG Web site at www.kpmg.com. Combining what you learned at the site with what you learned from the video, would you be a motivated worker at KPMG? Why?

CASES

1 MOTIVATION SAVVY MANAGEMENT AT BRISTOL-MYERS SQUIBB ENSURES CUTTING-EDGE INTERNET PRESENCE

"Motivation Savvy Management at Bristol-Myers Squibb Ensures Cutting-Edge Internet Presence" (p. 399) and its related Challenge Case Summary were written to help you better understand the management concepts contained in this chapter. Answer the following discussions about the Challenge Case to better understand how motivation concepts can be applied in a company such as Bristol-Myers Squibb.

1. Do you think it would be unusual for a manager such as Jack Cooper to spend a significant portion of his time motivating his workforce? Explain.

2. Which of the needs on Maslow's hierarchy of needs could implementing Internet strategy at Bristol-Myers Squibb help satisfy? Why? If you have omitted one or more of the needs, explain why the implementation would not satisfy those needs.

3. Is it possible for Cooper's efforts to be successful in motivating workers yet detrimental to organizational success? Explain.

2 MOTIVATION AT UNITED WAY

Read the case and answer the questions that follow. Studying this case will help you better understand how concepts relating motivation can be applied in an organization such as the United Way.

The United Way is a nonprofit organization that has been around since 1887. Founded to help charities raise funds, the United Way also provides grants and coordinates emergency relief services. It is one of the largest nonprofit agencies in the United States, with about 1,300 local organizations and a reach covering 46 countries.[59]

In a difficult economic climate, nonprofits such as the United Way—as well as the charities it supports—have found themselves in a trying situation. Donations to all kinds of charitable organizations have recently dropped precipitously. As people have less discretionary money available, they use what they have for their own need; and therefore, give less to charities. Simultaneously, more people desperately need assistance from others to make ends meet. In the most recent year, the United Way experienced a 68 percent increase in the number of requests for basic needs.[60] This is a clear sign individuals and families have been hit hard by the recession. With this increase of need and a decrease in donations, the organization is experiencing an incredible strain.

So how does a manager motivate employees and volunteers during tough economic environments?

Keeping a large staff of full-time employees as well as tens of thousands of volunteers motivated is not an easy task in even the best of times. Furthermore, for an organization that relies on the passion and dedication of those associated with the organization, motivation becomes even more challenging when financial incentives are out of the question. So, the United Way had to find a way to motivate its staff in a way that was also financially responsible. What it discovered was that training of employees and volunteers could be a key method of enriching professional lives. With 9,300 employees and countless volunteers, tackling this in an effective manner is challenging, but vital. Heidi Kotzian, director of marketing and national events at United Way, said the organization "will succeed only if our staff has the tools and knowledge they need to effect change."[61] Thus, training not only keeps people associated with the organization excited about their roles within the United Way, but also facilitates ongoing organizational performance.

Traditionally, training and development of employees is an area of an organization's budget that gets slashed in economic downturns. Broad-stroked budget cuts are the norm as both nonprofit and for-profit entities attempt to keep costs to a minimum. Often, training is seen as a luxury expense and is put on the back burner until the economic situation improves.

But the United Way is taking a different approach by stepping up its training efforts. Working with the marketing team, the training function was revamped and treated like a "brand"—something that could be readily recognized by employees and even eagerly sought out by those same employees. A catalog consisting of 34 pages of training opportunities is marketed to every employee in the organization.

Feedback from employee participants in various training sessions provides continuous improvement. The organization can determine what works and what doesn't. It also collects data on what topics employees desire from a training and development standpoint. This is important because meeting the needs of the staff is vital for maintaining motivation. For volunteers who do not receive a salary or wage, but rather devote sometimes countless hours of their time, maintaining a high degree of motivation is essential.

For Kotzian, the results speak for themselves. The organization has seen increased efficiencies, but also more teamwork and improved communication. "We have seen a boost internally," she said, "from those recognizing the benefits of reaching local United Way staff through learning courses and events."[62] (Johnson 2010).

QUESTIONS

1. Which theory of motivation do you think is most applicable in describing the United Way's use of training? Explain.

2. With a very limited budget, what other nonmonetary incentives can you identify to maintain employees' commitment to the United Way?

3. Thinking solely about United Way's volunteers, how would you motivate them given that they are unpaid, but still have a strong dedication to the work they do?

Endnotes

1. This description of the company Web site reflects data as of October 10, 2007.

2. Philip A. Rudolph and Brian H. Kleiner, "The Art of Motivating Employees," *Journal of Managerial Psychology* 4 (1989): i–iv; Carole L. Jurkiewicz, Tom K. Massey Jr., and Roger G. Brown, "Motivation in Public and Private Organizations: A Comparative Study," *Public Productivity & Management Review* 21, no. 3 (March 1998): 230–250.

3. For a useful discussion of motivation, see Thomas Wright, "What Every Manager Should Know: Does Personality Help Drive Employee Motivation?" *The Academy of Management Executive* 17 (2003): 131.

4. Mike DeLuca, "Motivating Your Staff Is Key to Your Success," *Restaurant Hospitality* (February 1995): 20; see also Sanford De Voe and Sheena Ivengar, "Managers' Theories of Subordinates: A Cross-Cultural Examination of Manager Perceptions of Motivation and Appraisal of Performance," *Organizational Behavior and Human Decision Processes* 93 (2004): 47.

5. For an overview of the field known as work motivation, see James M. Diefendorff and Megan M. Chandler, "Maintaining, Expanding, and Contracting the Organization," in Sheldon Zedeck (Ed.), *APA Handbook of Industrial and Organizational Psychology*, vol. 3. (Washington: American Psychological Association, 2011), 65–135.

6. Craig Miller, "How to Construct Programs for Teams," *Reward & Recognition* (August/September 1991): 4–6; Walter F. Charsley, "Management, Morale, and Motivation," *ManagementWorld* 17 (July/August 1988): 27–28.

7. Victor H. Vroom, *Work and Motivation* (New York: Wiley, 1964); Thomas L. Quick, "How to Motivate People," *WorkingWomen* 12 (September 1987): 15, 17.

8. J. Stacy Adams, "Towards an Understanding of Inequity," *Journal of Abnormal and Social Psychology* 67 (1963): 422–436. For a rationale linking expectancy and equity theories, see Joseph W. Harder, "Equity Theory Versus Expectancy Theory: The Case of Major League Baseball Free Agents," *Journal of Applied Psychology* (June 1991): 458–464. For group rewards as an alternative to individual rewards in human motivation, see Donald J. Campbell, Kathleen M. Campbell, and Ho-Beng Chia, "Merit Pay, Performance Appraisal, and Individual Motivation: An Analysis and Alternative," *Human Resource Management* 37, no. 2 (Summer 1998): 131–146.

9. Eric O'Keefe, "Executive Pay Proposals Rejected at AMR," *NewYork Times*, May 17, 2007, C5.

10. L. W. Porter and E. E. Lawler, *Managerial Attitudes and Performance* (Homewood, IL: Richard D. Irwin, 1968). For more information on intrinsic and extrinsic rewards, see Pat Buhler, "Rewards in the Organization," *Supervision* 50 (January 1989): 5–7.

11. Eunmi Chang, "Composite Effects of Extrinsic Motivation on Work Effort: A Case of Korean Employees," *Journal ofWorld Business* 38 (2003): 70.

12. For a recent study that assesses the effectiveness of intrinsic and extrinsic rewards, see R. C. Mahaney and A. Lederer, "The Effect of Intrinsic and Extrinsic Rewards for Developers on Information Systems Project Success," *Project Management Journal* 37 (2006): 42–54.

13. Eric G. Flamholtz and Yvonne Randle, "The Inner Game of Management," *Management Review* 77 (April 1988): 24–30.

14. Abraham Maslow, *Motivation and Personality*, 2d ed. (New York: Harper & Row, 1970). For an up-to-date discussion of the value of Maslow's ideas, see Edward Hoffman, "Abraham Maslow: Father of Enlightened Management," *Training* 25 (September 1988): 79–82.

15. "Maslow's Hierarchy of Needs Revisited," *Nursing Forum* 38 (2003): 3.

16. For a discussion of an empowerment tool managers can use to help employees satisfy esteem and self-actualization needs, see Chris Argyris, "Empowerment: The Emperor's New Clothes," *Harvard Business Review* 76, no. 3 (May/June 1998): 98–105.

17. For critiques of Maslow, see Jack W. Duncan, *Essentials of Management* (Hinsdale, IL: Dryden Press, 1975), 105; Hoffman, "Abraham Maslow: Father of Enlightened Management"; Dale L. Mort, "LeadYour Team to the Top," *Security Management* 32 (January 1988): 43–45.

18. For information about Maslow's revised hierarchy of needs, see M. Koltko-Rivera, "Rediscovering the Later Version of Maslow's Hierarchy of Needs: Self-Transcendence and Opportunities for Theory, Research, and Unification," *Review of General Psychology* 10 (2006): 302–317.

19. Clayton Alderfer, *Existence, Relatedness, and Growth* (New York: Free Press, 1972). For a reconstruction of Maslow's hierarchy, see Francis Heylighen, "A Cognitive-Systemic Reconstruction of Maslow's Theory of Self-Actualization," *Behavioral Science* (January 1992): 39–58.

20. Chris Argyris, *Personality and Organization* (New York: Harper & Bros., 1957). See also Charles R. Davis, "The Primacy of Self-Development in Chris Argyris's Writings," *International Journal of Public Administration* 10 (September 1987): 177–207.

21. Karen E. Klein, "Where an Inventor-Entrepreneur Finds Motivation," *Bloomberg BusinessWeek*, August 4, 2009, http://www.businessweek.com.

22. David C. McClelland and David G. Winter, *Motivating Economic Achievement* (New York: Free Press, 1969). See also Lawrence Holp, "Achievement Motivation and Kaizen," *Training and Development Journal* 43 (October 1989): 53–63; D. C. McClelland and David H. Burnham, "Power Is the Great Motivator," *Harvard Business Review* (January/February 1995): 126–139.

23. Michael Sanson, "Fired Up!" *Restaurant Hospitality* (February 1995): 53–64.

24. For an empirical investigation of the importance of a manager's ability to effectively communicate, see D. English, E. Manton, and J. Walker, "Human Resource Managers' Perception of Selected Communication Competencies," *Education* 127 (2007): 410–418.

25. Douglas McGregor, *The Human Side of Enterprise* (New York: McGraw-Hill, 1960). For an illustration of howTheory X–TheoryY relates to modern business, see Kenneth B. Slutsky, "Viewpoint: Why Not

Theory Z?" *Security Management* 33 (April 1989): 110, 112. For a discussion of theories X,Y, and Z as they relate to the adoption of new technology in organizations, see Richard T. Due, "Client/Server Feasibility," *Information Systems Management* (Summer 1994): 79–82.

26. Elizabeth A. Fisher, "Motivation and Leadership in Social Work Management: A Review of Theories and Related Studies," *Administration in Social Work* 33, no. 4 (October–December 2009): 347–367.

27. For further information about McGregor's TheoryY, see C. Carson, "A historical view of Douglas McGregor's TheoryY," *Management Decision* 43 (2005): 450–462.

28. For further information about applying Theory Z in the workplace, see Richard Daft, "Theory Z: Opening the Corporate Door for Participative Management," *Academy of Management Executive* 18 (2004): 117.

29. For further information about the possible usefulness of Theory X, see Michael Bobic and William Davis, "A Kind Word for Theory X: Or Why So Many Newfangled Management Techniques Quickly Fail," *Journal of Public Administration Research and Theory* 13 (2003): 239.

30. For more information on reducing boredom in the workplace, see Z. Bhadury and Z. Radovilsky, "Job Rotation Using the Multi-Period Assignment Model," *International Journal of Production Research* 44 (2006): 4431.

31. For more discussion on the implications of job rotation in organizations, see Alan W. Farrant, "Job Rotation Is Important," *Supervision* (August 1987): 14–16; see also Wipawee Tharmmaphornphilas and Bryan A. Norman, "A Quantitative Method for Determining Proper Job Rotation Intervals," *Annals of Operations Research* 128 (2004): 251.

32. Julia Weichel, Sanjin Stanic, José Alonso Enriquez Diaz, and Ekkehart Frieling, "Job Rotation – Implications for Old and Impaired Assembly Line Workers," *Occupational Ergonomics* 9, no. 2 (June 2010): 67–74.

33. L. E. Davis and E. S. Valfer, "Intervening Responses to Changes in Supervisor Job Designs," *Occupational Psychology* (July 1965): 171–190.

34. This section is based on Frederick Herzberg, "One More Time: How Do You Motivate Employees?" *Harvard Business Review* (January/February 1968): 53–62.

35. Katina W. Thompson, "Underemployment Perceptions, Job Attitudes, and Outcomes: An Equity Theory Perspective," *Academy of Management Proceedings* 2009, 1–6.

36. For an understanding of how job enrichment relates to other workplace factors, see L. Lapierre, R. Hackett, and S. Taggar, "A Test of the Links between Family Interference with Work, Job Enrichment, and Leader-Member Exchange," *Applied Psychology* 55 (2006): 489.

37. Scott M. Meyers, "Who Are Your Motivated Workers?" *Harvard Business Review* (January/February 1964): 73–88; Matt Oechsli, "Million Dollar Success Habits," *Managers Magazine* 65 (February 1990): 6–14; J. Barton Cunningham and Ted Eberle, "A Guide to Job Enrichment and Redesign," *Personnel* 67 (February 1990): 56–61.

38. Ray B. Williams, "How to Motivate Employees: What Managers Need to Know," *Psychology Today*, February 13, 2010, http://www.psychologytoday.com.

39. For an analysis of the strengths of implementing flextime in the workplace, see J. Haar, "Exploring the Benefits and Use of Flextime: Similarities and Differences," *Qualitative Research in Accounting and Management* 4 (2007): 69.

40. Bob Smith and Karen Matthes, "Flexibility Now for the Future," *HR Focus* (January 1992): 5.

41. D. A. Bratton, "Moving away from Nine to Five," *Canadian Business Review* 13 (Spring 1986): 15–17.

42. Douglas L. Fleuter, "Flextime—A Social Phenomenon," *Personnel Journal* (June 1975): 318–319; Jill Kanin-Lovers, "Meeting the Challenge of Workforce, 2000," *Journal of Compensation and Benefits* 5 (January/February 1990): 233–236.

43. B. F. Skinner, *Contingencies of Reinforcement* (New York: Appleton-Century-Crofts, 1969).

44. For an interesting discussion of accounting as a means of rewarding employees, see Mahmoud Ezzamel and Hugh Willmott, "Accounting, Remuneration, and Employee Motivation in the New Organization," *Accounting and Business Research* 28, no. 2 (Spring 1998): 97–110.

45. For further information about the use of positive reinforcement in the workplace, see D. Wiegand and S. Geller, "Connecting Positive Psychology and Organizational Behavior Management: Achievement Motivation and the Power of Positive Reinforcement," *Journal of Organizational Behavior Management* 24 (2004/2005): 3.

46. P. M. Padokaff, "Relationships between Leader Reward and Punishment Behavior and Group Process and Productivity," *Journal of Management* 11 (Spring 1985): 55–73.

47. For an understanding of the potential repercussions of excessive punishment, see Steven Schepman, and Lynn Richmond, "Employee Expectations and Motivation: An Application from the Learned Helplessness Paradigm," *Journal of American Academy of Business* 3 (2003): 405.

48. "New Tool: Reinforcement for Good Work," *Psychology Today* (April 1972): 68–69.

49. W. Clay Hamner and Ellen P. Hamner, "Behavior Modification on the Bottom Line," *Organizational Dynamics* 4 (Spring 1976): 6–8.

50. James K. Hickel, "Paying Employees to Control Costs," *Human Resources Professional* (January/February 1995): 21–24.

51. For more information about cognitive-behavior modification, see D. Boan, "Cognitive-Behavior Modification and Organizational Culture," *Consulting Psychology Journal: Practice and Research* 58 (2006): 51–61.

52. Rensis Likert, *New Patterns of Management* (New York: McGraw-Hill, 1961). For an interesting discussion of the worth of Likert's ideas, see Marvin R. Weisbord, "For More Productive Workplaces," *Journal of Management Consulting* 4 (1988): 7–14. The following descriptions are

based on the table of organizational and performance characteristics of different management systems in Rensis Likert, *The Human Organization* (New York: McGraw-Hill, 1967), 4–10.

53. For an empirical investigation of the effectiveness of monetary incentives, see H. McGee, A. Dickinson, B. Huitema, and K. Culig, "The Effects of Individual and Group Monetary Incentives on High Performance," *Performance Improvement Quarterly* 19 (2006): 107–130.

54. For a discussion of a novel monetary incentive program, see Charles A. Cerami, "Special Incentives May Appeal to Valued Employees," *HR Focus* (November 1991): 17. See also Reginald Shareef, "A Midterm Case Study Assessment of Skill-Based Pay in the Virginia Department of Transportation," *Review of Public Personnel Administration* 18, no. 1 (Winter 1998): 5–22.

55. "Create a Successful Incentive Program," *Journal of Financial Planning,* May/June 2010, 12–13.

56. Jena McGregor, "Will Ending Annual Reviews Make You More Like a Startup?" *BusinessWeek,* August 28, 2009, http://www.businessweek.com.

57. Marilyn Moats Kennedy, "What Makes People Work Hard?" *Across the Board* 35, no. 5 (May 1998): 51–52.

58. Crouse, "Punishment Laps Help Jets Kick Penalty Habit."

59. Johnson, Gordon. "Marketing Learning the United Way." *Chief Learning Officer* 9, no. 5 (2010): 42–47. www.unitedway.org

60. Kadlec, Dan. "The Nonprofit Squeeze," *Time* 173, no. 12 (2009): 49–50.3M.

61. See note 59 above.

62. See note 59 above.

chapter 18

Groups and Teams

Target Skill

team skill: the ability to manage a collection of people so that they influence one another toward the accomplishment of an organizational objective(s)

objectives

To help build my *team skill*, when studying this chapter, I will attempt to acquire:

1. A definition of the term *group* as used in the context of management

2. A thorough understanding of the difference between formal and informal groups

3. Knowledge of the types of formal groups that exist in organizations

4. An understanding of how managers can determine which groups exist in an organization

5. An appreciation for what teams are and how to manage them

CHALLENGE CASE

TEAMWORK SPREADS AT XEROX

XEROX CORPORATION IS A GLOBAL LEADER in providing document solutions that enhance business productivity. Company focus is on developing, manufacturing, marketing, servicing, and financing a complete range of document-processing products designed to make organizations more productive. The company's digital output includes color copiers and printers with production speeds ranging from 20 to 65 pages per minute.

Xerox manages an extremely complex logistics system that focuses on asset management, which entails tracking and coordinating thousands of pieces of equipment at hundreds of customer work locations. The company must keep track of the specific equipment requirements involving issues such as space, electricity, cooling, network connectivity, supplies, and maintenance. Solutions also have to be developed for helping customer organizations coordinate equipment service, related training, and ordering of supplies from almost anywhere in the world.

Asset management at Xerox also involves the proper billing of customers. Customers must be billed for every single piece of equipment based on its specific usage, and they need invoices that clearly delineate equipment usage costs but don't overwhelm with too much information.

Another component of Xerox's asset management includes providing outstanding service and support to customers who can call a toll-free number with questions, problems, and requests related to thousands of equipment assets. At Xerox, after equipment is sold or leased, the formidable challenge of technical support begins.

According to company officials, asset management at Xerox is a challenging and labor-intensive job. Alan Asher, one of the managers, believes that successful asset management requires a tremendous amount of coordination and is exceedingly difficult to pull off, because you must have processes in place that are really detailed and really tight, or things can fall through the cracks.

The Houston office has had some success because of a small, tightly knit work team, but it has had to confront a serious problem in operations: managing fleets of office equipment at multiple sites from a remote location. Evelyn Grubb, the customer account manager in Houston, explains: "We've got a group of people here that truly works together. It's really a family. Everyone works together. If we didn't have that spirit here, none of this would have happened."

Learning from the success of this team in Houston, Xerox management is encouraging the spread of teamwork into a number of different organizational areas. The company's recent use of teams to design successful new products for the marketplace has been particularly impressive.[1]

■ *Many of Xerox's most successful initiatives in asset management depend on the work of teams that cooperate closely to keep customers' document-processing products working effectively.*

425

EXPLORING YOUR MANAGEMENT SKILL

You can explore your level of team skill **before** studying the chapter by completing the exercise "Exploring Your Management Skill: Part 1" on page 443 and **after** studying this chapter by completing the exercise "Exploring Your Management Skill: Part 2" on page 444.

"Exploring Your Management Skill: Part 1" on page 443 and "Exploring Your Management Skill: Part 2" on page 444.

THE TEAM CHALLENGE

The Challenge Case highlights the important role that teams play in the success of operations at Xerox. The material in this chapter should help managers, such as those at Xerox, gain insights about how to successfully manage teams. This chapter (1) defines groups, (2) discusses the kinds of groups that exist in organizations, (3) explains what steps managers should take to manage groups appropriately, and (4) explains team management.

The previous chapters in Part 5 dealt with three primary activities of the influencing function: communication, leadership, and motivation. This chapter focuses on managing teams, the last major influencing activity to be discussed in this text. As with the other three activities, managing teams requires guiding the behavior of organization members in ways that increase the probability of reaching organizational objectives.

GROUPS

To deal with groups appropriately, managers must have a thorough understanding of the nature of groups in organizations.[2] As used in management-related discussions, a **group** is not simply a gathering of people. Rather, it is "any number of people who (1) interact with one another, (2) are psychologically aware of one another, and (3) perceive themselves to be a group."[3] Groups are characterized by frequent communication among members over time and a size small enough to permit each member to communicate with all other members on a face-to-face basis. As a result of this communication, each group member influences and is influenced by all other group members.

The study of groups is important to managers because the most common ingredient of all organizations is people and the most common technique for accomplishing work through these people is dividing them into work groups. In a classic article, Cartwright and Lippitt list four additional reasons why managers should study groups:[4]

1. Groups exist in all kinds of organizations.
2. Groups inevitably form in all facets of organizational existence.
3. Groups can cause either desirable or undesirable consequences within the organization.
4. An understanding of groups can help managers raise the probability that the groups with which they work will cause desirable consequences within the organization.[5]

KINDS OF GROUPS IN ORGANIZATIONS

Organizational groups are typically divided into two basic types: formal and informal.

Formal Groups

A **formal group** is a group that exists within an organization by virtue of management decree to perform tasks that enhance the attainment of organizational objectives.[6] Figure 18.1 is an organization chart showing a formal group. The placements of organization members in such areas as marketing departments, personnel departments, and production departments are examples of establishing formal groups.

Actually, organizations are made up of a number of formal groups that exist at various organizational levels. The coordination of and communication among these groups is the responsibility of managers, or supervisors, commonly called "linking pins."

Formal groups are clearly defined and structured. The next sections discuss the basic kinds of formal groups, examples of formal groups as they exist in organizations, and the four stages of formal group development.

Kinds of Formal Groups Formal groups are commonly divided into command groups and task groups. A **command group** is a formal group that is outlined in the chain of

FIGURE 18.1 A formal group

command on an organization chart. Command groups typically handle routine organizational activities.

A **task group** is a formal group of organization members who interact with one another to accomplish most of the organization's nonroutine tasks. Although task groups are usually made up of members on the same organizational level, they can consist of people from different levels in the organizational hierarchy.[7] For example, a manager might establish a task group to consider the feasibility of manufacturing some new product and include representatives from various levels of such organizational areas as production, market research, and sales.[8]

Examples of Formal Groups Two formal groups that are often established in organizations are committees and work teams. Committees are the more traditional formal group; work teams have only recently gained acceptance and support in U.S. organizations. The part of this text dealing with the managerial function of organizing emphasized command groups; however, the examples here emphasize task groups.

Committees A **committee** is a group of individuals charged with performing some type of specific activity and is usually classified as a task group. From a managerial viewpoint, committees are established for four major reasons:[9]

1. To allow organization members to exchange ideas
2. To generate suggestions and recommendations that can be offered to other organizational units
3. To develop new ideas for solving existing organizational problems
4. To assist in the development of organizational policies.

Committees exist in virtually all organizations and at all organizational levels. As Figure 18.2 suggests, however, the larger the organization, the greater the probability that it will use committees on a regular basis. The following two sections discuss why managers should use committees and what makes a committee successful.

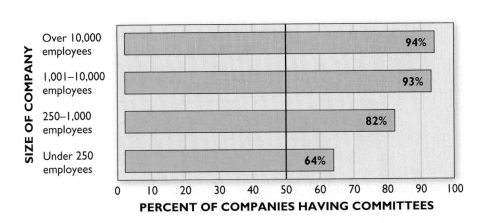

FIGURE 18.2
Percent of companies that have committees, by size of company

A committee is a team charged with a specific task. It is most successful when that task is clearly defined and the committee is given appropriate authority for decision making.

WHY MANAGERS SHOULD USE COMMITTEES Managers generally agree that committees have several uses in organizations.

- Committees can improve the quality of decision making. As more people become involved in making a decision, the strengths and weaknesses of various alternatives tend to be discussed in greater detail and the chances of reaching a higher-quality decision increase.

- Committees encourage the expression of honest opinions. Committee members feel protected enough to say what they really think because the group output of a committee cannot be associated with any one member of that group.

- Committees also tend to increase organization members' participation in decision making and thereby enhance the chances of widespread support of decisions. Another result of this increased participation is that committee members satisfy their social or self-esteem needs through committee work.

- Finally, committees ensure the representation of important groups in the decision-making process. Managers must choose committee members wisely, however, to achieve appropriate representation, for if a committee does not adequately represent various interest groups, any decision it comes to may well be counter to the interests of some important organizational group.

how managers do it

Committee for Recruitment at Red Robin Gourmet Burgers

Committees are often used to recruit new organization members. Consider, for example, the case of Red Robin Gourmet Burgers, a national chain of casual dining restaurants. Two activist investor groups that own nearly 8 percent of Red Robin stock filed a complaint with the Securities and Exchange Commission over the performance of the board and the company's chief executive. The company later announced several changes to its board structure. In addition, the board of directors agreed to form a search committee to identify a new chief executive. The search committee consists of the board chair and three new directors approved by the investor groups.[10] ■

Although executives vary somewhat in their enthusiasm about using committees in organizations, a study reported by McLeod and Jones concludes that most executives favor using committees. The executives who took part in this study said they got significantly more information from organizational sources other than committees, but found the information from committees more valuable than the information from any other source. Nevertheless, some top executives express only qualified support for using committees as work groups, and others had negative feelings toward committees. Still, the executives who feel positively about committees or who display qualified acceptance of them in general outnumber those who look upon committees negatively.

WHAT MAKES COMMITTEES SUCCESSFUL Although committees have become an accepted management tool, managerial action taken to establish and run them is a major variable in determining their degree of success.

Procedural Steps Several procedural steps can be taken to increase the probability that a committee will be successful:[11]

- The committee's goals should be clearly defined, preferably in writing, to focus the committee's activities and reduce the time members devote to discussing just what it is the committee is supposed to be doing.

- The committee's authority should be specified. Is it merely to investigate, advise, and recommend, or is it authorized to implement decisions?

- The optimum size of the committee should be determined. With fewer than 5 members, the advantages of group work may be diminished. With more than 10 or 15 members, the committee may become unwieldy. Although optimal size varies with circumstances, the ideal number of committee members for most tasks seems to be from 5 to 10.

- A chairperson should be selected on the basis of ability to run an efficient meeting—that is, the ability to keep committee members from getting bogged down in irrelevancies and to see to it that the necessary paperwork gets done.

- Appointing a permanent secretary to handle communications is often useful.

- The agenda and all supporting material for the meeting should be distributed before the meeting takes place. When members have a chance to study each item beforehand, they are likely to stick to the point and be prepared to make informed contributions.

- Meetings should start on time, and their ending time should be announced at the outset.

People-Oriented Guidelines In addition to these procedural steps, managers can follow a number of more people-oriented guidelines to increase the probability that a committee will succeed. In particular, a manager can raise the quality of committee discussions by doing the following:[12]

- **Rephrasing ideas already expressed**—This rephrasing ensures that the manager as well as other people on the committee clearly understand what has been said.

- **Bringing all members into active participation**—Every committee member is a potential source of useful information, so the manager should serve as a catalyst to spark individual participation whenever appropriate.

- **Stimulating further thought by members**—The manager should encourage committee members to think ideas through carefully and thoroughly, for only this type of analysis will generate high-quality committee output.

Groupthink Managers should also help the committee avoid a phenomenon called "groupthink." **Groupthink** is the mode of thinking that group members engage in when the desire for agreement so dominates the group that it overrides the need to realistically appraise alternative problem solutions.[13] Groups tend to slip into groupthink when their members become overly concerned about being too harsh in judging one another's ideas and lose their objectivity.[14] Such groups tend to seek complete support on every issue to avoid conflicts that might endanger the "we-feeling" atmosphere.[15]

Groupthink, a term initially established by Irving Janis, occurs in five stages. The first stage, antecedents, describes what precursors are associated with the development of groupthink. For example, a group with a high level of cohesiveness is likely to be susceptible to groupthink. The second stage, concurrence seeking, occurs when a group member agrees with the entire group's position, even when the group member might privately oppose the entire group's position. The third stage, symptoms of groupthink, occurs as group members feel pressure to conform and censor their own ideas. The fourth stage, decision-making defects, occurs when group members fail to make effective decisions. An example of decision-making defects occurs when a group does not collect the needed information to make an effective decision. The fifth stage, poor decision outcomes, occurs when the group performs poorly.

Often, managers unconsciously rely on the people they know best as a sounding-board for decision making. They look to their own small group of friends or colleagues in the workplace to help them analyze situations. Their regular interaction with this "informal network" may bias their thinking and create its own type of groupthink. Managers must be aware of how this phenomenon can affect their decisions. They need to recognize the different types and stages of groupthink so that they can be identified and rectified objectively in the workplace.[16]

Work Teams A **work team** is another example of a task group used in organizations. Contemporary work teams in the United States evolved out of the problem-solving teams—based on Japanese-style quality circles—that were widely adopted in the 1970s.[17] Problem-solving teams consist of 5 to 12 volunteer members from different areas of the department who meet weekly to discuss ways to improve quality and efficiency.

SPECIAL-PURPOSE AND SELF-MANAGED TEAMS Special-purpose teams evolved in the early to middle 1980s out of problem-solving teams. The typical special-purpose team consists of workers and union representatives meeting together to collaborate on operational decisions at all levels. The aim is to create an atmosphere conducive to quality and productivity improvements.

Special-purpose teams laid the foundation for the self-managed work teams that arose in the 1990s, and it is these teams that appear to be the wave of the future. Self-managed teams consist of 5 to 15 employees who work together to produce an entire product. Members learn all the tasks required to produce the product and rotate from job to job. Self-managed teams even take over such managerial duties as scheduling work and vacations and ordering materials. Because these work teams give employees so much control over their jobs, they represent a fundamental change in how work is organized. (Self-managed teams will be discussed in some detail later in this chapter.)

Employing work teams allows a firm to draw on the talent and creativity of all its employees, not just a few maverick inventors or top executives, to make important decisions. As product quality becomes more and more important in the business world, companies will need to rely more and more on the team approach to stay competitive. Consider a recent situation at Yellow Freight Systems, a shipping company whose management was intent on giving its customers excellent service. To address this concern, management established a work team made up of employees from many different parts of the company, including marketing, sales, operations, and human resources. The overall task of the work team was to run an excellence-in-service campaign that management had initiated.[18]

Stages of Formal Group Development Another requirement for successfully managing formal groups is understanding the stages of formal group development. In a classic book, Bernard Bass suggested that group development is a four-stage process that unfolds as the group learns how to use its resources.[19] Although these stages may not occur sequentially, for the purpose of clarity, the discussion that follows will assume that they do.

The Acceptance Stage It is common for members of a new group to mistrust one another somewhat initially. The acceptance stage occurs only after this initial mistrust melts and the group has been transformed into one characterized by mutual trust and acceptance.

The Communication and Decision-Making Stage Once they have passed through the acceptance stage, group members are better able to communicate frankly with one another. This frank communication provides the basis for establishing and using an effective group decision-making mechanism.

The Group Solidarity Stage   Group solidarity comes naturally as the mutual acceptance of group members increases and communication and decision making continue within the group. At this stage, members become more involved in group activities and cooperate, rather than compete, with one another. Members find belonging to the group extremely satisfying and are committed to enhancing the group's overall success.

The Group Control Stage   A natural result of group solidarity is group control. In this stage, group members attempt to maximize the group's success by matching individual abilities with group activities and by assisting one another. Flexibility and informality usually characterize this stage.

As a group passes through each of these four stages, it generally becomes more mature and effective—and therefore more productive. The group that reaches maximum maturity and effectiveness is characterized by the following traits in its members:

- **Members function as a unit**—The group works as a team. Members do not disturb one another to the point of interfering with their collaboration.

- **Members participate effectively in group effort**—Members work hard when there is something to do. They seldom loaf, even if they have the opportunity to do so.

- **Members are oriented toward a single goal**—Group members work for the common purpose; they do not waste group resources by moving in different directions.

- **Members have the equipment, tools, and skills necessary to attain the group's goals**—Members are taught the various parts of their jobs by experts and strive to acquire whatever resources they need to attain group objectives.

- **Members ask and receive suggestions, opinions, and information from one another**—A member who is uncertain about something stops working and asks another member for information. Group members generally talk to one another openly and frequently.

Informal Groups

Informal groups, the second major kind of group that can exist within an organization, are groups that develop naturally as people interact. An **informal group** is defined as a collection of individuals whose common work experiences result in the development of a system of interpersonal relations that extend beyond those established by management.[20]

As Figure 18.3 shows, informal group structures can deviate significantly from formal group structures. As is true of Supervisor A in the figure, an organization member can belong to more than one informal group at the same time. In contrast to formal groups, informal groups are not highly structured in procedure and, while generally they are not formally recognized by management, some organizations have seen the value of integrating informal groups into their corporate structure.[21]

FIGURE 18.3   Three informal groups that deviate significantly from formal groups within the organization

The next sections discuss the following subjects:

1. Various kinds of informal groups that exist in organizations
2. The benefits people usually reap from belonging to informal groups

Kinds of Informal Groups Informal groups are divided into two general types: interest groups and friendship groups. An **interest group** is an informal group that gains and maintains membership primarily because of a common concern members have about a specific issue. An example is a group of workers pressing management for better pay or working conditions. Once the interest or concern that instigated the formation of the informal group has been eliminated, the group will probably disband.

As its name implies, a **friendship group** is an informal group that forms in organizations because of the personal affiliation members have with one another. Such personal factors as recreational interests, race, gender, and religion serve as foundations for friendship groups. As with interest groups, the membership of friendship groups tends to change over time. Here, however, membership changes as friendships dissolve or new friendships are made.

Benefits of Informal Group Membership Informal groups tend to develop in organizations because of various benefits group members obtain:[22]

1. Perpetuation of social and cultural values that group members consider important
2. Status and social satisfaction that people might not enjoy without group membership
3. Increased ease of communication among group members
4. Increased desirability of the overall work environment

These benefits may be one reason that employees who are on fixed shifts or who continually work with the same groups tend to be more satisfied with their work than employees whose shifts are continually changing.

MANAGING WORK GROUPS

To manage work groups effectively, managers must simultaneously consider the effects of both formal and informal group factors on organizational productivity. This consideration requires two steps:

1. Determining group existence
2. Understanding the evolution of informal groups

Determining Group Existence

The most important step managers need to take in managing work groups is to determine what informal groups exist within the organization and who their members are. **Sociometry** is an analytical tool managers can use for this purpose. They can also use sociometry to get information on the internal workings of an informal group, including the identity of the group leader, the relative status of group members, and the group's communication networks.[23] This information on informal groups, combined with an understanding of the established formal groups shown on the organization chart, will give managers a complete picture of the organization's group structure.

Sociometric Analysis The procedure for performing a sociometric analysis in an organization is quite basic. Various organization members simply are asked, through either an interview or a questionnaire, to name several other organization members with whom they would like to spend free time. A **sociogram** is then constructed to summarize the informal relationships among group members. Sociograms are diagrams that visually link individuals

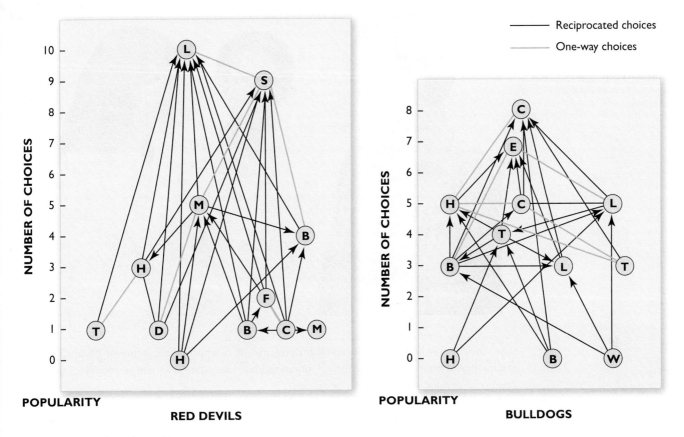

FIGURE 18.4   Sample sociograms

within the population queried according to the number of times they were chosen and whether the choice was reciprocated.

Applying the Sociogram Model   Figure 18.4 shows two sample sociograms based on a classic study of two groups of boys in a summer camp—the Bulldogs and the Red Devils. An analysis of these sociograms leads to several interesting conclusions. First, more boys within the Bulldogs than within the Red Devils were chosen as being desirable to spend time with. The implication is that the Bulldogs are a closer-knit informal group than the Red Devils. Second, the greater the number of times an individual was chosen, the more likely it was that the individual would be the group leader. Thus, individuals C and E in Figure 18.4 are probably Bulldog leaders, while L and S are probably Red Devil leaders. Third, communication between L and most other Red Devils members is likely to occur directly, whereas communication between C and other Bulldogs is likely to pass through other group members.

Sociometric analysis can give managers many useful insights concerning the informal groups within their organization. Managers who do not want to perform a formal sociometric analysis can at least casually gather information on what form a sociogram might take in a particular situation. They can pick up this information through normal conversations with other organization members as well as through observations of how various organization members relate to one another.

Understanding the Evolution of Informal Groups

As we have seen, the first prerequisite for managing groups effectively is knowing what groups exist within an organization and what characterizes the membership of those groups. The second prerequisite is understanding how informal groups evolve. This understanding will give managers

Informal groups like this one provide status, social satisfaction, and ease of communication among members, as well as other personal and organizational benefits.

some insights on how to encourage the development of appropriate informal groups, that is, groups that support the attainment of organizational objectives and whose members maintain good relationships with formal work groups.

Homans Model Perhaps the most widely accepted framework for explaining the evolution of informal groups was developed by George Homans.[24] Figure 18.5 broadly summarizes his theory. According to Homans, the informal group is established to provide satisfaction and growth for its members. At the same time, the sentiments, interactions, and activities that emerge within an informal group result from the sentiments, interactions, and activities that already exist within a formal group. Given these two premises, it follows that feedback on the functioning of the informal group can give managers ideas about how to modify the formal group so as to increase the probability that informal group members will achieve the satisfaction and growth they desire. The ultimate consequence will be to reinforce the solidarity and productiveness of the formal group—to the advantage of the organization.

Applying the Homans Model To see what Homans's concept involves, suppose that 12 factory workers are members of a formal work group that manufactures toasters. According to Homans, as these workers interact to assemble toasters, they might discover common personal interests that encourage the evolution of one or more informal groups that would maximize the satisfaction and growth of their members. Once established, these informal groups will probably resist changes in the formal work group that threaten the satisfaction and growth of the informal group's members. On the other hand, modifications in the formal work group that enhance the satisfaction and growth of the informal group's members will tend to be welcomed.

FIGURE 18.5
Homans's ideas on how informal groups develop

TEAMS

The preceding sections of this chapter discussed groups—what they are, what kinds exist in organizations, and how such groups should be managed. This section focuses on a special type of group: teams. It covers the following topics:

1. Difference between groups and teams
2. Types of teams that exist in organizations
3. Stages of development that teams go through
4. What constitutes an effective team
5. Relationship between trust and team effectiveness

Groups Versus Teams

The terms *group* and *team* are not synonymous. As we have seen, a group consists of any number of people who interact with one another, are psychologically aware of one another, and think of themselves as a group. A **team** is a group whose members influence one another toward the accomplishment of an organizational objective(s).

Not all groups in organizations are teams, but all teams are groups. A group qualifies as a team only if its members focus on helping one another accomplish organizational objectives.[25] In today's quickly changing business environment, teams have emerged as a requirement for success.[26] Therefore, good managers constantly try to help groups become teams.

how managers do it

Building a Team at Renaissance Executive Forums

A team-building exercise is a training tool for helping to transform a group into a team. For Ken Keller, the owner of Renaissance Executive Forums, it meant bringing his group to a Sonoma, California, vineyard, dividing people into teams, and challenging them to create their own wine. Teams had to collaborate to come up with a wine from the basic ingredients provided, then design a label and a marketing strategy. Keller says team-building exercises work because they require a group to focus on an unfamiliar task and work together to achieve a goal.[27] ■

Teams operate in all kinds of situations. The members of NASCAR driver Greg Biffle's pit crew must depend on one another to get the job done, with each contributing expertise in a particular task.

The questions of how teams plan, set goals, and make decisions continue to be the subject of much field research.[28] The following part of the chapter provides insights on how managers can facilitate the evolution of groups into teams.

Types of Teams in Organizations

Organizational teams take many different forms. The following sections discuss three types of teams commonly found in today's organizations: problem-solving teams, self-managed teams, and cross-functional teams.

Problem-Solving Teams

Problem-Solving Teams Management confronts many different organizational problems daily. Examples are production systems that are not manufacturing products at the desired levels of quality, workers who appear to be listless and uninvolved, and managers who are basing their decisions on inaccurate information.

For assistance in solving such formidable problems, management commonly establishes special teams. A team set up to help eliminate a specified problem within the organization is called a **problem-solving team**.[29] The typical problem-solving team has 5 to 12 members and is formed to discuss ways to improve quality in all phases of the organization, to make organizational processes more efficient, or to improve the overall work environment.[30]

After the problem-solving team reaches a consensus, it makes recommendations to management about how to deal with the specified problem. Management may respond to the team's recommendations by implementing them in their entirety, by modifying and then implementing them, or by requesting further information to assess them. Once the problem that management asked the problem-solving team to address has been solved, the team is generally disbanded.

Self-Managed Teams

Self-Managed Teams The **self-managed team**, sometimes called a *self-managed work group* or *self-directed team*, is a team that plans, organizes, influences, and controls its own work situation with only minimal intervention and direction from management.[31] This creative team design involves a highly integrated group of several skilled individuals who are cross-trained and have the responsibility and authority to perform some specified activity.

Activities typically carried out by management in a traditional work setting—creating work schedules, establishing work pace and breaks, developing vacation schedules, evaluating performance, determining the level of salary increases and rewards received by individual workers, and ordering materials to be used in the production process—are instead carried out by members of the self-managed team. Generally responsible for whole tasks as opposed to "parts" of a job, the self-managed team is an important new way of structuring, managing, and rewarding work.[32] Because these teams require only minimum management attention, they free managers to pursue other management activities such as strategic planning.

Reports of successful self-managed work teams are plentiful.[33] These teams are growing in popularity because today's business environment seems to require such work teams to solve complex problems independently, because American workers have come to expect more freedom in the workplace, and because the speed of technological change demands that employees be able to adapt quickly. Recent studies seem to suggest that the collective behavior of a self-managed team can make it more effective than the individual efforts of its team members.[34]

Not all self-managed teams are successful. To ensure the success of a self-managed team, the manager should carefully select and properly train its members.[35]

Cross-Functional Teams

Cross-Functional Teams A **cross-functional team** is a work team composed of people from different functional areas of the organization—marketing, finance, human resources, and operations, for example—who are all focused on a specified objective.[36] Cross-functional teams may or may not be self-managed, though self-managed teams are generally cross-functional. Because cross-functional team members are from different departments within the organization, the team possesses the expertise to coordinate all the department activities within the organization that affect its own work.[37]

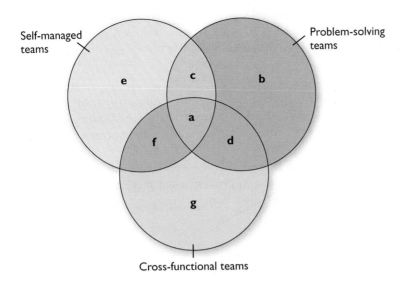

FIGURE 18.6
Possible team types based on various combinations of self-directed, problem-solving, and cross-functional teams

Some examples of cross-functional teams are teams established to choose and implement new technologies throughout the organization, teams formed to improve marketing effectiveness within the organization, and teams established to control product costs.[38]

This section discussed three types of teams that exist in organizations: problem-solving, self-directed, and cross-functional. It should be noted here that managers can establish various combinations of these three types of teams. Figure 18.6 illustrates some possible combinations that managers could create. For example, *a* in the figure represents a team that is problem-solving, self-directed, and cross-functional, while *b* represents one that is problem-solving, but neither cross-functional nor self-directed. Before establishing a team, managers should carefully study their own unique organizational situation and set up the type of team that best suits that situation.

STAGES OF TEAM DEVELOPMENT

More and more modern managers are using work teams to accomplish organizational tasks. Simply establishing such a team, however, does not guarantee it will be productive. In fact, managers should be patient when an established work team is not initially productive, for teams generally need to pass through several developmental stages before they become productive. Managers must understand this developmental process so they can facilitate it. The following sections discuss the various stages a team usually must pass through before it becomes fully productive.[39]

Forming **Forming** is the first stage of the team development process. During this stage, members of the newly formed team become oriented to the team and acquainted with one another. This period is characterized by exploring issues related to the members' new job situation, such as what is expected of them, who has what kind of authority within the team, what kind of people are team members, and what skills team members possess.

The forming stage of team development is usually characterized by uncertainty and stress. Recognizing that team members are struggling to adjust to their new work situations and to one another, managers should be tolerant of lengthy, informal discussions exploring team specifics and not regard them as time wasters. The newly formed team must be allowed an exploratory period if it is to become truly productive.

Storming After a team has formed, it begins to storm. **Storming**, the second stage of the team development process is characterized by conflict and disagreement as team members become more assertive in clarifying their individual roles. During this stage, the team seems to lack unity because members are continually challenging the way the team functions.

To help the team progress beyond storming, managers should encourage team members to feel free to disagree with any team issues and to discuss their own views fully and honestly. Most of all, managers should urge team members to arrive at agreements that will help the team reach its objective(s).

Norming When the storming stage ends, norming begins. **Norming**, the third stage of the team development process, is characterized by agreement among team members on roles, rules, and acceptable behavior while working on the team. Conflicts generated during the storming stage are resolved in this stage.

Managers should encourage teams that have entered the norming stage to progress toward developing team norms and values that will be instrumental in building a successful organization. The process of determining what behavior is and is not acceptable within the team is critical to the work team's future productivity.

Performing The fourth stage of the team development process is **performing**. At this stage, the team fully focuses on solving organizational problems and on meeting assigned challenges. The team is now productive: After successfully passing through the earlier stages of team development, it knows itself and has settled on team roles, expectations, and norms.

During this stage, managers should recognize the team's accomplishments regularly, for productive team behavior must be reinforced to enhance the probability that it will continue in the future.

Adjourning The fifth, and last, stage of the team development process is known as **adjourning**. Now the team is finishing its job and preparing to disband. This stage normally occurs only in teams established for some special purpose to be accomplished in a limited time period. Special committees and task groups are examples of such teams. During the adjourning stage, team members generally feel disappointment that their team is being broken up because disbandment means the loss of personally satisfying relationships or an enjoyable work situation.

During this phase of team development, managers should recognize team members' disappointment and sense of loss as normal and assure them that other challenging and exciting organizational opportunities await them. It is important that management then do everything necessary to integrate these people into new teams or other areas of the organization.

Although some work teams do not pass through every one of the development stages just described, understanding the stages of forming, storming, norming, performing, and adjourning will give managers many useful insights on how to build productive work teams. Above all, managers must realize that new teams are different from mature teams and that their challenge is to build whatever team they are in charge of into a mature, productive work team.[40]

Team Effectiveness

Earlier in this chapter, teams were defined as groups of people who influence one another to reach organizational targets. It is easy to see why effective teams are critical to organizational success. Effective teams are those that come up with innovative ideas, accomplish their goals, and adapt to change when necessary.[41] Their individual members are highly committed to both the team and organizational goals. Such teams are highly valued by upper management and recognized and rewarded for their accomplishments.[42] Recent research suggests that a high level of mutual trust within a team can have a positive effect on the team's performance and result in even more rewards from management.[43]

Figure 18.7 sketches the characteristics of an effective team. Note the figure's implications for the steps managers need to take to build effective work teams in organizations. *People-related steps* include the following: [44]

1. Trying to make the team's work satisfying
2. Developing mutual trust among team members and between the team and management
3. Building good communication—from management to the team as well as within the team

PEOPLE-RELATED FACTORS
• Personal work satisfaction
• Mutual trust and team spirit
• Good communication
• Low unresolved conflict and power struggle
• Low threat, fail-safe, good job security

ORGANIZATION-RELATED FACTORS
• Organizational stability and job security
• Involved, interested, supportive management
• Proper rewards and recognition of
  accomplishments
• Stable goals and priorities

TASK-RELATED FACTORS
• Clear objectives, directions, and project plans
• Proper technical direction and leadership
• Autonomy and professionally challenging work
• Experienced and qualified project/team personnel
• Team involvement and project visibility

EFFECTIVE TEAM PERFORMANCE
• Innovative ideas
• Goal(s) accomplished
• Adaptable to change
• High personal/team commitment
• Rated highly by upper management

FIGURE 18.7
Factors contributing to team effectiveness

4. Minimizing unresolved conflicts and power struggles within the team
5. Dealing effectively with threats toward and within the team
6. Building the perception that the jobs of team members are secure

Organization-related steps managers can take to build effective work teams include:

1. Building a stable overall organization or company structure that team members view as secure
2. Becoming involved in team events and demonstrating interest in team progress and functioning
3. Properly rewarding and recognizing teams for their accomplishments
4. Setting stable goals and priorities for the team

Finally, Figure 18.7 implies that managers can build effective work teams by taking six *task-related steps*:

1. Developing clear objectives, directions, and project plans for the team
2. Providing proper technical direction and leadership for the team
3. Establishing autonomy for the team and challenging work within the team
4. Appointing experienced and qualified team personnel
5. Encouraging team involvement
6. Building visibility within the organization for the team's work

Modern managers must focus on building the effectiveness of not only domestic teams, but global teams. In the past, the effectiveness of a global team depended chiefly on a company having staff and factories on the ground in various countries and corporate headquarters carefully and methodically coordinating their activities. Today, however, the challenge is much different. Globally dispersed teams must be built into highly effective, sometimes even self-managed teams. Because of the ever-changing and fast-moving nature of the competition, workers spread across the globe must be able to communicate and collaborate instantly. Fortunately for modern managers, the Internet is available to enable such collaboration. Managers must remember, however, that the availability of the Internet in itself does not guarantee that global teams will be effective. The appropriate use of the Internet by global teams, however, can be a significant contributor to their effectiveness.

class discussion highlight

MODERN RESEARCH AND TEAM SKILL

Which Individuals Most Influence Team Decisions?

All teams rely on input from multiple team members. Nonetheless, most individuals who have been in teams know that some team members have more influence than others. A team of researchers recently studied a number of teams to better understand the characteristics of those individuals who provided the most influence in team decisions.

One of the factors that the authors investigated is known as "trait dominance." As its name implies, trait dominance describes individuals who are dominant, assertive, and forceful. The study, then, examined the extent to which dominant individuals influenced team decisions. In addition, the researchers studied team members' opinions of dominant individuals.

What do you think the researchers found? Do you think the dominant individuals influenced team decision making? Do you think team members viewed dominant individuals positively or negatively? Why?

Source: Anderson, C. and Kilduff, G. J. "Why do Dominant Personalities Attain Influence in Face-to-Face Groups? The Competence-Signaling Effects of Trait Dominance," *Journal of Personality and Social Psychology* 96, no. 2 (2009): 491–503.

Trust and Effective Teams

Probably the most fundamental ingredient of effective teams is trust. Trust is belief in the reliance, ability, and integrity of another. Unless team members trust one another, the team leader, and management, managers may well find that building an effective work team is impossible.[45]

Today the concern is that management is not inspiring the kind of trust that is essential to team effectiveness. The lack of trust within a team is likely to discourage individuals on the team from contributing and participating in the growth of a creative, productive team.[46] In addition, subordinates' trust in their managers is critically low, and employee opinion polls indicate that it may well decline even further in the future. Without trust in its manager, a team would seem only marginally interested in building productive working relationships.

Management urgently needs to focus on reversing this trend.[47] Managers can use a number of different strategies to build trust within groups.[48]

how managers do it

Building Trust at Burberry

As an example of a manager communicating often with team members to build trust, consider Burberry president Angela Ahrendts. Burberry, the quintessential British fashion house, offers British fashion elegance throughout the world. Ahrendts has become known as a people-oriented manager, communicating often with members of her team. According to Stacey Cartwright, the company's chief financial officer, Ahrendts is collaborative, likes to gather her team around her, and seems energized by the debates within the team. Ahrendts knows that such communication with her team will almost certainly help build trust within the team, which should significantly contribute to team success.[49] ■

- **Communicate often to team members**—This is a fundamental strategy. Keeping team members informed of organizational news, explaining why certain decisions have been made, and sharing information about organizational operations are examples of how managers should communicate to team members.

- **Show respect for team members**—Managers need to show team members they are highly valued. They can demonstrate their respect for team members by delegating tasks to them, listening intently to feedback from the group, and acting on it appropriately.

- **Be fair to team members**—Team members must receive the rewards they have earned. Managers must therefore conduct fair performance appraisals and objectively allocate and distribute rewards. It should go without saying that showing favoritism in this area sows mistrust and resentment.

- **Be predictable**—Managers must be consistent in their actions. Team members should usually be able to forecast what decisions management will make before those decisions are made. Moreover, managers must live up to commitments made to team members. Managers who make inconsistent decisions and fail to live up to commitments will not be trusted by teams.

- **Demonstrate competence**—To build team trust, managers must show team members they are able to diagnose organizational problems and have the skill to implement solutions to those problems. Team members tend to trust managers they perceive as competent and distrust those they perceive as incompetent.

Effective teamwork is built on trust. When conductor Michael Tilson-Thomas works with an orchestra, he trusts the musicians to know their parts thoroughly, while they trust his vision of the music they are to perform.

CHALLENGE CASE SUMMARY

For managers to be able to manage work they need to understand the definition of the term *group*, and they need to understand that several types of groups exist in organizations. A group at Xerox or any other organization is any number of people who interact, who are psychologically aware of each other, and who perceive themselves as a group. A company such as Xerox is made up of formal groups, the groups that appear on the company's organization charts, such as the marketing department. Managers of groups act as the "linking pins" among departments. The ability of Xerox managers to coordinate and communicate with these groups and their success in dealing with their own departments are certainly important factors in the future success of the company as a whole.

At times, managers at Xerox can form new groups to handle some of the more nonroutine challenges. For example, management could form a task group by choosing two people from each of several different departments and getting them together on developing a new and more efficient system for improving company asset management procedures. Then, as with any other organization, Xerox also has informal groups (those that do not appear on the organization chart) to consider. More discussion on informal groups will follow later in this Challenge Case Summary.

Xerox management could decide to form a committee to achieve some specific goal. For example, a committee might be formed on how to enhance the quality of copiers offered by Xerox, which could allow various departments to exchange quality improvement ideas and generate related suggestions to management. Such a committee could improve Xerox decision making in general by encouraging honest feedback from employees about quality issues in the organization. It could also be used to get fresh ideas about enhancing product quality, and to encourage Xerox employees to participate more seriously in improving the quality of equipment offered by the company. This approach would help ensure that all appropriate departments are represented in important quality decisions, so when Xerox takes action to improve the quality of its copiers, for example, every important angle would be considered, including design, production, marketing, sales, and so on.

In managing such a quality committee at Xerox, management should encourage the members to take certain steps that can help the committee be successful, because a poorly run committee wastes a lot of time. For example, the committee should develop a clear definition of its goals and the limits of its authority: Is it just going to come up with quality improvement ideas, or should it also take the initial steps toward implementing its ideas?

In addition, the quality committee should not have too few or too many members. Issues such as appointing a secretary to handle communications and appointing a chairperson who is people-oriented must be addressed. Such a quality committee needs someone who can rephrase ideas clearly to ensure that everyone understands; and someone who can get members to participate and think about the issues while avoiding "groupthink": Original ideas should be generated by the committee, not by a unanimous opinion because everyone is trying to avoid conflict.

Managers in companies such as Xerox must be patient and understand that it will take some time for a new group to develop into a productive working unit. The members in any new work group must start by trusting and accepting one another and then begin communicating and exchanging ideas. Once this acceptance and communication increases, group solidarity and control come naturally. The group members get involved, cooperate, and try to maximize the group's success.

With the quality committee that is being used as an example, Xerox management must be patient and let it mature before maximum effectiveness and productivity can be expected. If given time to grow, the group will function as a unit, members will participate willingly and effectively, and the group will reach valuable decisions about what needs to be done to improve the quality of equipment that Xerox offers.

Other issues regarding informal groups could affect the success of work groups at Xerox. Employee groups get together at times because of certain issues. For example, certain minority employees could get together as a group to increase the opportunities for their professional growth at Xerox; and employees form friendship groups, which ease communication and provide feelings of satisfaction in a company. In general, such informal groups can improve the work environment for everyone involved, so it can be advantageous for management to encourage their development.

Perhaps Xerox management could accelerate the development of a quality committee into a productive unit by including individuals who already know and trust one another through membership in one or more informal groups at Xerox. For example, some members of the newly formed quality committee might know and trust one another immediately as a result of membership on a company bowling or softball team. Under such circumstances, a trust developed among employees through past informal group affiliations could help the formal quality committee to develop into a productive group more quickly.

For a company such as Xerox to be successful, managers must be able to consider how formal and informal groups affect organizational productivity, and they need to determine what informal groups exist, know who the group members are, and understand how these groups form. Armed with this information, Xerox management can strive to make their work groups more effective.

One way management can get information about the groups at Xerox is to use sociometry. A questionnaire can be designed asking employees with whom they spend time, and a sociogram can be constructed to summarize this information. Managers could also do a more casual analysis by just talking to their employees and observing how they interact with one another.

Managers in a company such as Xerox should try to understand how informal groups evolve and should be aware that an organization's formal structure influences how the informal groups develop within it. For example, assume that in one department at Xerox, 30 people work on copier design. Many of them are interested in sports, have become friends because of this common interest, and work well together as a result. If a manager needed to make some changes in such a department, he or she should try to accommodate such informal friendship groups to keep employees satisfied. Only with very good reason should a manager of such a department damage the existence of the productive friendship group by transferring any informal group members out of the design department.

Managers in a company such as Xerox should consider the four major factors that influence work-group effectiveness. First, the size of the work group can be important to its productivity. A 20-person quality committee would probably be somewhat large and would hamper the group's effectiveness. Remember also, however, that managers should consider informal groups before making changes in group size. The quality committee could end up being less productive without one or more of its respected members than it would be if it were slightly too large.

Another important factor that influences work group effectiveness is group cohesiveness, because a more cohesive group will tend to be more effective. The Challenge Case mentions that the cohesiveness of the asset management work group at Xerox's Houston office was instrumental in its success. Evelyn Grubb increased the cohesiveness of her formal asset management group by doing such things as allowing members to take breaks together or rewarding informal group members for a job well done.

Group norms, or appropriate behaviors required within the informal group, are a third factor that affects the productivity of formal group behavior. Because these norms affect profitability, managers must be aware of them and understand how to influence them within the formal group structure. For example, assume that a smaller informal group of workers within Xerox's asset management department normally maintains the quality of asset management by focusing mainly on tracking the durability of Xerox equipment. Unfortunately, because of this quality norm, the informal group members are taking too much time tracking durability and too little time servicing customer requests via e-mail feedback. Management could try to improve this situation by giving bonuses to group members who best service e-mail requests while tracking equipment durability. This reward would probably increase the formal group productivity while encouraging a positive norm within the informal group.

Status within the informal groups also affects work group productivity. For example, if Xerox managers want to increase productivity for a group, management should try to encourage the informal group's leaders, as well as the group's formal supervisor. Chances are that a targeted group will become more productive if its informal, high-status members support that objective.

Overall, if the company wants to maximize work group effectiveness, management must remember both the formal and informal dimensions of its work groups while considering the four main factors that influence work group productivity.

MANAGEMENT SKILL ACTIVITIES

This section is specially designed to help you develop team skill. An individual's team skill is based on an understanding of team concepts and the ability to apply those concepts in management situations. The following activities are designed to both heighten your understanding of team concepts and to develop the ability to apply those concepts in a variety of management situations.

UNDERSTANDING TEAM CONCEPTS

To check your understanding and to practice using the concepts in this chapter, go to www.mymanagementlab.com and explore the material associated with Chapter 18.

Know Key Terms

Understanding the following key terms is critical to your understanding of chapter material. Define each of these terms. Refer to the page(s) referenced after a term to check your definition or to gain further insight regarding the term.

group **426**
formal group **426**
command group **426**
task group **427**
committee **427**
groupthink **429**
work team **430**

informal group **431**
interest group **432**
friendship group **432**
sociometry **432**
sociogram **432**
team **435**
problem-solving team **436**

self-managed team **436**
cross-functional team **436**
forming **437**
storming **437**
norming **438**
performing **438**
adjourning **438**

Know How Management Concepts Relate

This section is comprised of activities that will sharpen your understanding of team concepts. Answer essay questions as completely as possible. Also, remember that additional true/false and multiple choice questions appear online at MyManagementLab.com to help you further refine your understanding of team concepts.

1. What is the difference between formal and informal groups? Explain how you would manage each type of group in helping an organization achieve success.

2. What is the difference between a group and a team?

3. As a manager, would you ever create a team that is both problem-solving and cross-functional? Explain.

4. What signs would you look for as a manager to indicate that a team in your organization is "storming"? What would you do if the team was indeed "storming"? Why?

5. What is the role of trust in building effective teams? As a manager, how would you build trust within a team?

DEVELOPING MANAGEMENT SKILLS

Learning activities in this section are aimed at helping you develop management skill. Learning activities include Exploring Your Management Skill: Parts 1 and 2, Your Management Skill Portfolio, Experiential Exercises, Cases, and a VideoNet Exercise.

Exploring Your Management Skill: Part 1

Before studying this chapter, respond to the following questions regarding the type of advice you would give to Xerox's Alan Asher, referenced in the Challenge Case. Then address the concerning team challenges managers face within the company. You are not expected to be a team expert at this point. Answering the questions now can help you focus on important points when you study the chapter. Also, answering the questions again after you study the chapter will give you an idea of how much you have learned.

Record your answers here or go to MyManagement Lab.com. Recording your answers in MyManagementLab will allow you to get immediate results and see how your score compares to your classmates. If you answer the questions in the book, the answers are located in the Exploring Your Management Skill Appendix at the end of the book.

FOR EACH STATEMENT CIRCLE:

- "Y" if you would give the advice to Asher.
- "N" if you would NOT give the advice to Asher.
- "NI" if you have no idea whether you would give the advice to Asher.

Mr. Asher, in meeting your team challenges at Xerox, you should . . .

Before   After

Study   Study

1. try to eliminate informal groups whenever possible.
Y, N, NI

2. incorporate "groupthink" into your team process to increase the accuracy of team decisions.
Y, N, NI

3. know that the acceptance stage of formal group development is characterized by group members communicating frankly to one another.
Y, N, NI

4. try to increase the overall desirability of the work environment by encouraging the development of informal groups.
Y, N, NI

5. try to apply the basic concepts of sociometry in attempting to determine the members of informal groups.
Y, N, NI

6. remember that informal groups commonly develop to provide safety and growth for their members, which is more difficult to obtain through formal group membership.
Y, N, NI

7. know that *groups* and *teams* are synonymous concepts.
Y, N, NI

8. understand that teams you establish can be self-managed as well as cross-functional.
Y, N, NI

9. help developing teams to work though "norming" before "performing."
Y, N, NI

10. try to bypass "storming" in the team development process.
Y, N, NI

11. sometimes enhance organizational stability and job security to enhance team effectiveness.
Y, N, NI

12. try to build effective work teams by developing clear objectives and deemphasizing technical direction.
Y, N, NI

13. build the trust a team has for you by being predictable.
Y, N, NI

14. sometimes demonstrate your competence to build the trust a team has for you.
Y, N, NI

15. focus on building trust as opposed to open communication in building team effectiveness.
Y, N, NI

Exploring Your Management Skill: Part 2

As you recall, you completed Exploring Your Management Skill before you started to study this chapter. Your responses gave you an idea of how much you initially knew about teams and helped you focus on important points as you studied the chapter. Answer the Exploring Your Management Skill questions again now and compare your score to the first time you took it. This comparison will give you an idea of how much you have learned from studying this chapter and pinpoint areas for further clarification before you start studying the next chapter. Record your answers within the text or go to MyManagementLab.com. Recording your answers in MyManagementLab will allow you to get immediate results and see how your score compares to your classmates. If you answer the questions in the book, the answers are located in the Exploring Your Management Skill Appendix at the end of the book.

Your Management Skills Portfolio

Your Management Learning Portfolio is a collection of activities especially designed to demonstrate your management knowledge and skill. By completing these activities online at MyManagementLab.com, you will be able to print, complete with cover sheet, as many activities as you choose. Be sure to save your work. Taking your printed portfolio to an employment interview could be helpful in obtaining a job.

The portfolio activity for this chapter is Using Committees and Teams in Accomplishing Florida Hospital's Mission. Read the following highlight about Florida Hospital and answer the questions that follow.[50]

Florida Hospital, a Christian-based Adventist Health System hospital, is an acute-care health care system with 3,025 beds throughout Central Florida. Florida Hospital treats more than one million patient visits each year. In fact, the Florida Hospital system is the busiest system in the country. For the last six years, *U.S. News & World Report* has recognized Florida Hospital as one of "America's Best Hospitals."

Florida Hospital offers a wide range of health services for the entire family, including many nationally and internationally recognized programs in cardiology, cancer, diabetes, and digestive health. Because Florida Hospital performs more complex cardiac procedures than any other facility in the country, MSNBC selected Florida Hospital as the premier focus of their hour-long special—"Heart Hospital."

Florida Hospital's mission statement appears in Exhibit 1.

EXHIBIT 1 Florida Hospital Mission Statement

To Our Patients
Our first responsibility as a Christian hospital is to extend the healing ministry of Christ to all patients who come to us. We endeavor to deliver high-quality service, showing concern for patients' emotional and spiritual needs, as well as their physical condition. It is our desire to serve patients promptly, with consideration and dignity.

To Our Employees
We are responsible to our employees and depend upon their teamwork. We show concern for the whole person, respecting each worker's individuality and listening to each one's concerns and suggestions. We pay fair wages and offer clean and safe working conditions. We provide opportunities for our employees' professional growth and development.

To Our Medical Staff
We are responsible to the doctors who are the leaders of the medical team. We provide them with a professional environment, state-of-the-art medical facilities and equipment, and trained support staff. We strive to process their requests for patient care accurately and in a timely manner.

To Our Community
We are responsible to our community both as an organization and as individuals. We must be a strong corporate citizen with interests in the total community welfare, not just those aspects in which we have a business interest. We maintain and use our buildings and grounds to enhance the interest of the community.

To Our Future
We are responsible for the future success and security of our institution's resources. We protect our financial investments through responsible fiscal management, strategic planning and effective marketing. We cultivate and protect the preferred patronage of patients, doctors and businesses.

To Our Religious Heritage
In response to the Seventh-day Adventist faith and heritage upon which Florida Hospital is built, we celebrate the healing ministry of our Lord, encourage preventive health care practices, respect the seventh-day Sabbath, and observe high moral and ethical standards.

To Our God
We are responsible to communicate through caring service that God is a loving, gracious and protecting Father who places infinite value on every individual and is worthy of our admiration, affection and willing commitment.

Learning Activity

Assume that you are the president of Florida Hospital and have decided to establish a hospital-wide committee to monitor and ensure the accomplishment of the hospital's mission. Answer the following questions to outline how you would form this committee and mold it into an effective work team.

1. What reason(s) could you use to explain to your employees why you are instituting this committee at Florida Hospital?

2. List four procedures you will have the committee follow as it does its work. Be sure to explain the value of each procedure.

Procedure 1:

Value of Procedure 1:

Procedure 2:

Value of Procedure 2:

Procedure 3:

Value of Procedure 3:

Procedure 4:

Value of Procedure 4:

3. Outline what you would say to the committee to encourage it to function as a team as opposed to a group.

4. Would you make the committee aware of the stages of team development? Explain.

5. How would you help the committee members develop trust for one another? Be as specific as possible.

Experiential Exercises

1 Planning Your Team Development Program

Directions. Your instructor will divide your class into small groups of about five and appoint a discussion leader for each group. Each group is to evaluate the Mountain Top Game that appears here as a team-building activity. Decide whether you would use the activity as a real manager trying to build a real team in your organization. You would be the instructor or the one actually administering the game. Be sure to explain why the group does or does not believe that the exercise would be useful. After all groups have finished discussion, the instructor will lead a discussion of the entire class focused on conclusion of the small groups.

Mountain Top Game[51]

Objective:

For group members to work together for the good of the group

Group Size:

8 to 15 is ideal

Materials:

- A rope hanging from the ceiling (i.e., gym climbing rope)
- Rope or other boundary marker
- 2 coffee cans or similar height blocks or cans
- 1 pole, stick, or piece of pipe about 1inch in diameter

Procedure for Administering the Game:

Set up the two coffee cans with a pole set horizontally across them about three or four feet to one side of the rope. On the other side of the rope, use a different piece of rope to make a circle that the whole group can stand in. For added challenge make the circle small so the group must work together to stand in it without falling out of the boundary. This circle should be about three to four feet from the rope as well.

Set this activity up by telling a story that requires the group to get from a cliff to a mountain top some distance away. Starting behind the "cliff" (pole) they must get hold of the climbing rope without stepping off the "cliff." Once they have the rope, they must swing across to the other side and land on the "mountain" (the rope circle). Only one person may go across at a time. If anyone steps out of the boundary, knocks the pole off of the cans, or touches the ground, the group must start over. For safety reasons, the leader should stand near the climbing rope to catch anyone who falls.

Possible Questions for Leading Discussion After the Game:

1. How did the group come up with a plan?

2. How did the order that you were in factor into the plan?

3. How did you ensure your teammates were safe during this activity?

4. How would this activity have been different if there was a real cliff and a real mountain top?

5. Would you trust your teammates if it were real? Why or why not?

6. How can you build trust as a team?

Variations:

- Give group members things to carry with them to the mountain for an added challenge.
- Set up a low platform for the group to stand on in place of the circle.

2 You and Your Career[52]

The Randstad Group is one of the largest temporary and contract staffing organizations in the world. The company has subsidiaries in Europe, North America, and Asia with about 13,000 employees. On average, the company places about 250,000 people in other companies every day. The company is trying to win the loyalty of its own young employees by pairing them in two-person teams with older, more experienced employees. Every new sales agent is assigned a partner to work with until their business has grown to a certain size, which usually takes a few years. Neither person is "the boss." Each employee is expected to teach the other. Then they both start over again with someone who has just joined the company. The company's motto is "Nobody should be alone."

Would you like to start your career in this program? Why? As an experienced hand, would you like to be involved in this program about mid-career? Why? Why do you think the company instituted this program?

CASES

1 TEAMWORK SPREADS AT XEROX

"Teamwork Spreads at Xerox" (p. 425) and its related Challenge Case Summary were written to help you better understand the management concepts contained in this chapter. Answer the following discussions about the Challenge Case to better understand how concepts relating to groups and teams can be applied in a company such as Xerox.

1. Describe the characteristics of an effective work team at Xerox.
2. As a manager at Xerox, what steps would you take to turn a work group into an effective team? Explain the importance of each step.

2 BEST BUY'S EXTREME TEAM BUILDING

Read the case and answer the questions that follow. Studying this case will help you better understand how concepts relating to team building can be applied in a company such as Best Buy.

When executives at the electronics retailing giant, Best Buy, decided they wanted to build teams while fostering innovation, they took an extreme move. Imagine telling a group of employees that they will have to set their lives—personal and professional—on hold for more than two months. Further, they'll have to spend that time with a group of strangers every single day and night. That's exactly what this Minnesota-based company did. And the payoff has been huge.

Best Buy is no stranger to innovation or success. Although the company started in 1966 under the name of Sound of Music, it wasn't until the 1980s that the chain really hit its stride with the development of the super store. This concept revolutionized how consumers purchased electronics. Rather than samples of items appearing on store shelves, Best Buy put all its stock on the floor, enabling customers to try out different products and ultimately take home what they liked without waiting for an employee to select a box from a warehouse inventory. The other major innovation was hiring and training store employees who didn't rely on commissions for their income. This practice created an impartial and very knowledgeable salesforce customers could rely on.

Thus, when executives wanted to sequester a team of store employees for 10 weeks, it took very few people at the company by surprise. The new CEO of Best Buy, Brian Dunn, knows how it feels to be a sales floor associate—he started his career at the company as one in 1985. He fully supports efforts that result in innovation and continues to build Best Buy's reputation as *the* place to go for consumers. "We want to become a digital playground," he said, "where people come in, experience it, try it, and find out how all these things can work together around their life." (Edwards)

So recently, the company tried something completely new. They chose groups of sales associates—all in their 20s and 30s—and put them up in an apartment complex in Los Angeles. In making a comparison to a popular program on MTV, one of the participants remarked, "My friends joked and said I was joining *Real World: Best Buy Edition*" (Jana). Indeed, the situation was very similar. These sales associates—strangers to one another—found themselves thrown together and had to establish bonds quickly. Naturally, since the team was in Los Angeles, some—of the time was spent at the beach, but they also found themselves working longer hours and talking about how Best Buy could improve.

The goal of the 10-week program was to develop ideas for the company. One of those ideas was Best Buy Studio. This new venture provides Internet consulting for small businesses. It enables entrepreneurs, who could not otherwise afford to hire full-time Web designers, to create Web sites. The idea, crafted during the 10 weeks, was approved and supported by top executives at Best Buy. So far, Best Buy Studio is only in a few West Coast stores, but could expand to other areas soon.

Dunn believes that team building situations like this foster ideas that may not emerge otherwise. "Employees don't need permission to create or innovate," he said. (Jana) But, incubators such as this one certainly create a climate where employees are free to pursue concepts that they may not have considered during the course of a busy workday. Participants are forced to get to know one another very rapidly and also understand that the time together is an opportunity to create something positive. Some of the ideas may not ever come to fruition, but those that do are likely to be very well-thought and have a great deal of buy-in from those involved in the creative process.

After Circuit City folded in 2009, Best Buy found itself in a strong position with few competitors, and they have continued to experience growth. The company has revenues of nearly $50 billion and has approximately 180,000 employees. Its success can be attributed to the innovative steps they take, but also the solid teamwork that is shared among associates. Dunn, who rose through the ranks of the company, feels that change and innovation are what keep the company not only alive, but thriving while other competitors have fallen by the wayside. "The easiest changes are when you are backed up against the corner and it's sort of 'change or perish,'" he said. "Now we're trying to change at a time when we are very, very successful" (Edwards).

QUESTIONS

1. Consider the 10-week incubator program Best Buy uses. Would you characterize this as a group or a team? Why?

2. If you were in charge of managing this 10-week program, how would you ensure that an effective team emerges? How would you help build trust among participants?

3. What challenges do you think might exist in thrusting a group of strangers together in isolation for 10 weeks? How would you overcome those challenges?

REFERENCES

Edwards, Cliff. "Why Tech Bows to Best Buy," *BusinessWeek* no. 4160 (2009): 50–56.

Jana, Reena. "Real Life Imitates Real World. (cover story)," *BusinessWeek* no. 4124 (2009): 42.

Endnotes

1. Nanette Byrnes, "Xerox New Design Team: Customers" *BusinessWeek,* May 07, 2007, 72.

2. For an article illustrating the importance of managing groups in organizations, see Gregory E. Kaebnick, "Notes from Underground: Walter Corbitt Talks about Monitoring Paperwork for 35,000 Underground Storage Tanks," *Inform* 3 (July/August 1989): 21–22, 48.

3. Edgar H. Schein, *Organizational Psychology* (Upper Saddle River, NJ: Prentice Hall, 1965), 67.

4. Dorwin Cartwright and Ronald Lippitt, "Group Dynamics and the Individual," *International Journal of Group Psychotherapy* 7 (January 1957): 86–102.

5. For insights into how to be more successful in dealing with people in groups, see Anonymous, "Becoming More Persuasive," *Association Management* 50, no. 7 (July 1998): 24–25.

6. Edgar H. Schein, *Organizational Psychology,* 2nd ed. (Upper Saddle River, NJ: Prentice Hall, 1970), 182.

7. For information on the role of gender in task groups, see S. Hysom and C. Johnson, "Leadership structures in same-sex task groups," *Sociological Perspectives* 49 (2006): 391–410.

8. For a study exploring diversity and task group processes, see Warren E. Watson, Lynn Johnson, and Deanna Meritt, "Team Orientation, Self-Orientation, and Diversity in Task Groups," *Group & Organization Management* 23, no. 2 (June 1998): 161–188.

9. To understand further the possible duties of a committee, see Stephanie Balzer, "Committee to Study $500M Civic Plaza Expansion," *The Business Journal* 21, no. 39 (June 22, 2001): 7.

10. Paul Ziobro, "Red Robin Forming Committee to Find New CEO," *Wall Street Journal,* March 5, 2010, http://online.wsj.com.

11. Cyril O'Donnell, "Group Rules for Using Committees," *Management Review* 50 (October 1961): 63–67. For an example of problems created by committees not doing their jobs, see Joann S. Lublin and Elizabeth MacDonald, "Management: Scandals Signal Laxity of Audit Panels," *Wall Street Journal,* July 17, 1998, B1.

12. These and other guidelines are discussed in "Applying Small-Group Behavior Dynamics to Improve Action-Team Performance," *Employment Relations Today* (Autumn 1991): 343–353.

13. For an analysis of the symptoms associated with groupthink, see D. Henningsen, M. Henningsen, J. Eden, and M. Cruz, "Examining the symptoms of groupthink and retrospective sensemaking," *Small Group Research* 37 (2006): 36–64.

14. Robert McMurry, "The Tyranny of Groupthink," *Harvard Business Review* 81 (2003): 120.

15. See Irving L. Janis, *Groupthink* (Boston: Houghton Mifflin, 1982). For insights on how to avoid groupthink, see Peter Kay, "Group Think," *Philadelphia Business Journal,* July 2–8, 1999, 11.

16. Rob Cross, Robert J. Thomas, and David A. Light, "How 'Who You Know' Affects What You Decide," *Sloan Review,* January 9, 2009, http://sloanreview.mit.edu.

17. For further information about independent work teams, see K. Roper and D. Phillips, "Integrating self-managed work teams into project management," *Journal of Facilities Management* 5 (2007): 22–36.

18. For suggestions on how to build a team, see "Teamwork Translates into High Performance," *HR Focus* 75, no. 7 (July 1998): 7; see also Sheila Webber and Richard Klimoski, "Crews: A Distinct Type of Work Team," *Journal of Business and Psychology* 18 (2004): 261.

19. Bernard Bass, *Organizational Psychology* (Boston: Allyn and Bacon, 1965), 197–198.

20. Raef T. Hussein, "Informal Groups, Leadership, and Productivity," *Leadership and Organization Development Journal* 10 (1989): 9–16.

21. Richard McDermott and Douglas Archibald, "Harnessing Your Staff's Informal Networks," *Harvard Business Review,* March 2010, http://hrb.org.

22. Keith Davis and John W. Newstrom, *Human Behavior at Work: Organizational Behavior* (New York: McGraw-Hill, 1985), 310–312.

23. For the importance of determining such information, see Dave Day, "New Supervisors and the Informal Group," *Supervisory Management* 34 (May 1989): 31–33.

24. Homans, *The Human Group.*

25. For information regarding the role of culture in workplace teams, see M. Uday-Riley, "Eight Critical Steps to improve workplace performance with Cross-Cultural Teams" *Performance Improvement* 45 (2006): 28.

26. William G. Dyer, *Teambuilding: Issues and Alternatives* (Reading, MA: Addison-Wesley, 1987): 4. See also Dawn R. Deeter-Schmelz and Rosemary Ramsey, "A Conceptualization of the Functions and Roles of Formalized Selling and Buying Teams," *Journal of Personal Selling & Sales Management* (Spring 1995): 47–60.

27. Nancy Mann Jackson, "Team-Building with a Purpose," *Entrepreneur,* April 17, 2009, http://www.entrepreneur.com.

28. For an interesting discussion of the role planning plays in the relationship between team goal orientation and performance, see Anju Mehta, Hubert Feild, Achilles Armenakis, and Nikhil

29. Mehta, "Team Goal Orientation and Team Performance: The Mediating Role of Team Planning," *Journal of Management* 35, no. 4 (August 2009): 1026–1046.

29. For a recent article describing effective team problem-solving techniques, see V. Tran and H. Latapie, "Developing virtual team problem-solving and learning capability using the case method," *The Business Review, Cambridge* 8 (2007): 27–33.

30. J. H. Shonk, *Team-Based Organizations* (Homewood, IL: Irwin, 1922).

31. For a study exploring the relationship between leadership and self-managed teams, see Vanessa Urch Druskat and Jane Wheeler, "Managing from the Boundary: The Effective Leadership of Self-Managing Work Teams," *Academy of Management Journal* 46 (2003): 435.

32. Jack L. Lederer and Carl R. Weinberg, "Equity-Based Pay: The Compensation Paradigm for the Re-Engineered Corporation," *Chief Executive* (April 1995): 36–39.

33. Kevin R. Zuidema and Brian H. Kleiner, "Self-Directed Work Groups Gain Popularity," *Business Credit* (October 1994): 21–26.

34. For a different perspective on the value of teams in inspiring collective behavior, see Michael J. Mauboussin, "When Individuals Don't Matter," *Harvard Business Review,* October 2009, http://www.hbr.org.

35. Sami M. Abbasi and Kenneth W. Hollman, "Self-Managed Teams: The Productivity Breakthrough of the 1990s," *Journal of Managerial Psychology* 9 (1994): 25–30.

36. For further information about the components of an effective cross-functional team, see Yvonne Athanasaw, "Team Characteristics and Team Member Knowledge, Skills, and Ability Relationships to the Effectiveness of Cross-Functional Teams in the Public Sector," *International Journal of Public Administration* 26 (2003): 1167.

37. For a recent article describing the role of positive feedback in cross-functional teams, see H. Peelle, "Appreciative Inquiry and Creative Problem Solving in Cross-Functional Teams," *Journal of Applied Behavioral Science* 42 (2006): 447–467.

38. For more information on cross-functional teams, see D. Michael D. Hutt, Beth A. Walker, and Gary L. Frankwick, "Hurdle the Cross-Functional Barriers to Strategic Change," *Sloan Management Review* (Spring 1995): 22–30; John Teresko, "Reinventing the Future," *Industry Week* (April 17, 1995): 32–38; Margaret L. Gagne and Richard Discenza, "Target Costing," *Journal of Business & Industrial Marketing* 10 (1995): 16–22.

39. Bruce W. Tuckman and Mary Ann C. Jensen, "Stages of Small Group Development Revisited," *Group and Organizational Studies* 2 (1977): 419–427.

40. For an empirical analysis of how to effective develop a team, see E. Chong, "Role Balance and Team Development: A Study of Team Role Characteristics Underlying High and Low Performing Teams," *Journal of Behavioral and Applied Management* 8 (2007): 202–217.

41. For further information on team effectiveness and leadership, see S. Baker and D. Gerlowski, "Team Effectiveness and Leader-Follower Agreement: An Empirical Study," *Journal of American Academy of Business, Cambridge* 12 (2007): 15–23.

42. Hans J. Thamhain, "Managing Technologically Innovative Team Efforts toward New Product Success," *Journal of Product Innovation Management* (March 1990): 5–18.

43. Kurt T. Dirks and Daniel P. Skarlicki, "The Relationship between Being Perceived as Trustworthy by Coworkers and Individual Performance," *Journal of Management* 35, no. 1 (February 2009): 136–157.

44. For insights about motivation and teams, see Gerben van der Vegt, Ben Emans, and Evert van de Vliert, "Motivating Effects of Task and Outcome Independence in Work," *Group & Organization Management* 23, no. 2 (June 1999): 124–143.

45. Jerre L. Stead, "People Power: The Engine in Reengineering," *Executive Speeches* (April/May 1995): 28–32.

46. Liz Wiseman and Greg McKeown, "Bringing out the Best in Your People," *Harvard Business Review,* May 2010, 117–121.

47. For information on building trust in the context of teams, see P. Greenberg, R. Greenberg, and Y. Antonucci, "Creating and sustaining trust in virtual teams," *Business Horizons* 50 (2007): 325.

48. Fernando Bartolome, "Nobody Trusts the Boss Completely—Now What?" *Harvard Business Review* (March/April 1989): 114–131.

49. Company Web site, http://www.burberryplc.com, accessed June 24, 2010; Peter Gumbel, "Burberry's New Boss Doesn't Wear Plaid," *Fortune,* October 15, 2007, 124–130.

50. Information for this exercise is based upon www.floridahospital.com.

51. This exercise is from www.teambuildingportal.com.

52. Susan Berfield, "Bridging the Generation Gap: Employment Agency Randstad Teams Newbies with Older Staff to Great Effect," *BusinessWeek,* September 17, 2007, 60.

Managing Organization Culture

Target Skill

organization culture skill: the ability to establish a set of shared values of organization members regarding the functioning and existence of their organization to enhance the probability of organizational success

objectives

To help build my *organization culture skill,* when studying this chapter, I will attempt to acquire:

1. A definition of *organization culture*

2. An understanding of the importance of organization culture in building organizational success

3. Insights regarding the functions of organization culture

4. An appreciation for various types of cultures that can exist in organizations

5. Thoughts about how to build a high-performance organization culture

6. Tactics for keeping an organization culture alive and well

CHALLENGE CASE

BP'S ATTEMPT TO ESTABLISH A SAFETY CULTURE FAILED[1]

BP WAS MOVING ALONG NICELY. The world's second-largest oil and gas company, BP produced about 3 percent of the oil and gas consumed in the world through operations in 100 countries. The company employed more than 104,000 employees around the world.[2]

On March 23, 2005, BP's good fortunes seemed to change for the worse. On that day, an explosion occurred at BP's Texas City, Texas, refinery. The explosion resulted in 15 deaths and 170 injuries.

The U.S. Chemical Safety Board's report on the explosion concluded that the company had failed to establish a "corporate safety culture." The Chemical Safety Board report also reprimanded BP for being too focused on personal injuries as a metric for success. Instead, companies should focus on "process safety metrics," which include the company's goals, the report said. For example, instead of measuring injuries, companies should set goals on how many safety meetings each plant has in a quarter, then measure how well each plant meets that goal. Managers should measure the drivers within BP that actually create a change in the culture. In addition, BP needs to create incentives so employees feel comfortable reporting accidents or the potential for accidents. According to the report, BP did not have a trusting and open environment to facilitate these kinds of discussions.

Almost exactly five years after the Texas explosion, on April 20, 2010, one of BP's oil rigs in the Gulf of Mexico exploded killing 11 rig workers and injuring several others. The rig was nearly 50 miles offshore and had just been completed and readied for pumping. As a result of the explosion, the drilled well started gushing oil, with BP seemingly helpless to stop the leak. Weeks turned into months; the leak continued. Estimates for the size of the leak were put as high as 60,000 barrels of oil per day. Outrage at BP spread throughout the United States like wildfire since the leak was easily the largest environmental disaster the country had ever experienced and growing significantly each day. Environmentalists predict the Gulf's ecosystem—and its thriving fishing industry—may have been permanently harmed.

Criticism of BP and Hayward was so relentless over the 2010 explosion that he was eventually replaced by Robert Dudley. In replacing Hayward, Dudley now faces the serious challenge of establishing a culture at BP that emphasizes safety and arms employees with specific actions to take in safety crisis situations.

■ *The Gulf of Mexico oil spill caused by BP is shown on a beach in Gulf Shores, Alabama.*

EXPLORING YOUR MANAGEMENT SKILL

You can explore your level of organization culture skill **before** studying the chapter by completing the exercise "Exploring Your Management Skill: Part 1" on page 469 and **after** studying this chapter by completing the exercise "Exploring Your Management Skill: Part 2" on page 470.

THE ORGANIZATION CULTURE CHALLENGE

The Challenge Case illustrates corporate culture challenges that BP must meet. The remaining material in this chapter explains corporate culture concepts and helps develop the corresponding corporate culture skill that you will need to meet such challenges throughout your career. After studying chapter concepts, read the Challenge Case Summary at the end of the chapter to help you relate chapter content to meeting corporate culture challenges at BP.

FUNDAMENTALS OF ORGANIZATION CULTURE

This first chapter section is an introduction to the concept of organization culture. Major topics in this section focus on discussing a definition of organization culture and the importance of organization culture. Overall, this section explains what organization culture is and tells why managing organization culture is a critical component of a manager's job.

Defining Organization Culture

Organization culture is a set of shared values that organization members have regarding the functioning and existence of their organization. The actual dimensions of a particular culture are often difficult to define. Even employees in the same organization may describe their culture differently. In part, this could be a reflection of their individual experiences and the meanings ascribed to them.[3]

Organization culture is not established at once by a manager, but evolves slowly over time. Basically, organization culture can be thought of as the personality of the organization, a description of how the organization functions. As such, organization culture has dimensions such as organizational rituals, special language, norms, and habits. Organization culture can be characterized in an organization by describing such dimensions. Management that understands the significance of all such dimensions can use them to develop an organization culture that is beneficial to the firm.[4]

At times, organization culture may seem to include an almost endless list of considerations, and managers can become frustrated trying to accurately define their cultures. As help to define a culture, research suggests that managers ask a few basic questions:[5]

1. Do people innovate and take risks?
2. Are people attentive to detail?
3. Are people focused on outcomes of what they do?
4. Is the organization sensitive to people?
5. Do people function as a team?
6. Are people in the organization aggressive?
7. Are people focused on maintaining the status quo?

Although discussions regarding organization culture seem to assume that only one culture exists within an organization, in fact, many subcultures can exist within an organization. An **organization subculture** is a mini-culture within an organization that can reflect the values and beliefs of a specific segment of an organization formed along lines such as established departments or geographic regions. Managers must be aware of subcultures that exist and how to manage them because subcultures can negatively or positively affect management efforts, such as organizational planning.[6] In managing organization culture, managers sometimes have a tendency to manage only the **dominant organization culture**, the shared values about organizational functioning held by the majority of organization members.[7] In managing organization culture, it's normally advisable for managers to consider the characteristics and potential influence of an organization's dominant organization culture as well as organization subcultures.

The Importance of Organization Culture

Understanding and managing organization culture have become extremely important issues for modern managers in achieving organizational success. According to Michael Porter, a professor at Harvard Business School, organization culture is such an important issue that managers should not merely be taking it seriously as a sound idea, but embedding it into organizational strategy to help build a competitive advantage.[8] Many management writers believe an important prerequisite to organizational success is a manager's thorough understanding of organization culture concepts. Only through such an understanding can a manager begin to have impact on encouraging behavior of organization members that will lead to organizational success.[9]

FUNCTIONS OF ORGANIZATION CULTURE

What purpose does organization culture play in an organization? In general terms, organization culture influences the behavior of everyone within an organization and, if carefully crafted, can have a significant positive impact on organizational success.[10] Organization culture influences the way people carry out organizational processes and can create immense pressure for organization members to act in ways consistent with the culture. As a result, organization culture should reflect values that are conducive to organizational goal attainment.

In more specific terms, organization culture has a variety of functions within an organization. First, organization culture can enhance organizational productivity. Organization members often become more productive as organization culture increases focus on such factors as rewarding performance and setting goals.[11] Second, organization culture can serve as a component of organizational strategy.[12] Following this line of reasoning, competitive advantage arises from complex combinations of tangible as well as intangible resources. One such intangible resource is a culture that enhances organizational success. Third, organization culture provides a rationale for staffing.[13] Management must make sure that new hires fit the organization's culture. The employment interview is a prime opportunity for managers to see whether applicants might fit within the organization culture and for applicants to assess whether the organization culture is a good fit for their personal needs and aspirations. Within the interview, employers are looking for clues to issues such as an applicant's work ethic and personality while job seekers want to learn more about company culture issues, including the allocation of rewards and promotions. Last, organization culture can act as a guideline for making operational decisions. Given an explicit organization culture, organization members tend to make decisions that are consistent with the values embedded in that culture.

Overall, organization culture functions to influence organization members to act in ways that are consistent with the accepted values of the organization. To assist organization members in identifying these beliefs and values, many organizations establish a code of conduct. A **code of conduct** is a document that reflects the core values of an organization and suggests how organization members should act in relation to them.

Once established, at times a code of conduct may need to be changed. For example, although a code of conduct was already in place at Austin, Texas–based Tocquigny, the interactive ad agency suffered an embarrassing lapse that involved Twitter. An unhappy prospective client confronted the chief executive: He had read that her agency was also courting one of his competitors. Hurriedly, Tocquigny amended the social media guidelines in its code of conduct to include an admonition about respecting the firm's confidential and proprietary information. The agency also established a measure of control by assigning responsibility for posting to one person.[14] ■

how managers do it

Amending the Code of Conduct at Tocquigny

Managers must remember, however, that simply possessing a code of conduct does not guarantee for the organization that its members will follow the code. Overall, management must not only work to establish a code of conduct within an organization, but take steps to ensure that behavior that follows the code is rewarded.

TYPES OF ORGANIZATION CULTURE

Based on the preceding discussion, we see that organization culture is made up of several different factors. Needless to say, putting all of these factors together into a meaningful rationale for describing a culture can be difficult and frustrating for managers.

Fortunately, a model developed by Cameron and Quinn called the Competing Values Framework presents a rationale that managers can use to categorize organization cultures.[15] The Competing Values Framework appears in Figure 19.1. According to the model, cultures differ with respect to two sets of opposite values. The first set of opposite values is organizational flexibility and discretion versus organizational stability, order, and control. The second set of opposite values is an internal organizational focus versus an external organizational focus. Depending on how a culture contains various combinations of the competing values represented by these two dimensions, cultures are divided into four types:

1. *Clan Culture.* As shown in Figure 19.1, **clan culture** is an organization culture characterized by a strong internal focus with a high degree of flexibility and discretion. The *clan culture* derives its name from the fact that this organization culture seems much like a family. This culture includes activities that reflect shared values and goals, cohesion among organization members, teamwork, and organization commitment to employees.

    The culture at Southwest Airlines is often used as an example of a clan culture. The following excerpt of a recent Thanksgiving Day message by Southwest Airlines president Colleen Barrett shows the emphasis of the Southwest culture on internal focus, flexibility, shared values and goals, and a high commitment to employees:

    > As a Company, we are blessed to have 33,000-plus Employees who continually amaze me with their ability to live the Southwest Way. In an industry where change doesn't happen gradually, it happens overnight—if you are lucky to have that much advance notice—our People adapt to change faster than a chameleon. Unlike chameleons, when Southwest Employees adapt, they never change their true colors. Their Warrior Spirit, Servant's Heart, and Fun-LUVing attitude are part of my Thanksgiving blessings.[16]

FIGURE 19.1

The Competing Values Framework model depicts four different kinds of organization culture

Source: Kim S. Cameron and Robert E. Quinn, *Diagnosing and Changing Organizational Culture* (Reading, MA: Addison Wesley 1999), 32.

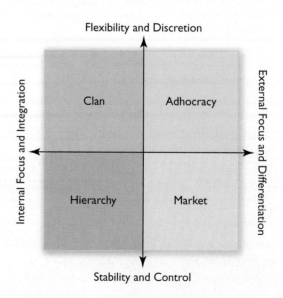

In a clan culture, leaders are seen more as mentors and perhaps even parent figures. And, as in any family, relationship issues can crop up, particularly as they involve mentoring.[17]

2. *Adhocracy Culture.* **Adhocracy culture** is an organization culture characterized by flexibility and discretion along with an external focus. As illustrated in Figure 19.1, an adhocracy is a culture reflecting an organization with a simple structure or lack of structure. In essence, adhocracy is the opposite of bureaucracy. Within the adhocracy culture one will find few rules or procedures. This culture is characterized by a creative workplace where people are entrepreneurial, taking risks to achieve success.

Google's organization culture has often been used as an example of an adhocracy culture. The following quote depicts the Google corporate culture as reflecting adhocracy characteristics:

> **Though growing rapidly, Google still maintains a small company feel. At the Googleplex headquarters almost everyone eats in the Google café (known as "Charlie's Place"), sitting at whatever table has an opening and enjoying conversations with Googlers from all different departments. Topics range from the trivial to the technical, and whether the discussion is about computer games or encryption or ad serving software, it's not surprising to hear someone say, "That's a product I helped develop before I came to Google."**

Google's emphasis on innovation and commitment to cost containment means each employee is a hands-on contributor. There's little in the way of corporate hierarchy and everyone wears several hats. The international webmaster who creates Google's holiday logos spent a week translating the entire site into Korean. The chief operations engineer is also a licensed neurosurgeon. Because everyone realizes they are an equally important part of Google's success, no one hesitates to skate over a corporate officer during roller hockey.[18]

3. *Hierarchy Culture.* Figure 19.1 shows that **hierarchy culture** is an organization culture characterized by an internal focus along with an emphasis on stability and control. The workplace within this type of culture is formal and structured. Leaders tend to focus on coordination and organization. Individuals within the workplace are concerned about efficiency and formal rules and policies govern how people operate.

McDonald's restaurants are commonly given as an example of a hierarchy culture. The typical McDonald's restaurant has younger employees with little significant experience and produces standardized products for customers. Restaurant success is built on efficient and fast food production. French fries are cooked for an established period and hamburgers are topped with exact amounts of toppings like mustard and ketchup. Employees are thoroughly trained in production rules covering all facets of restaurant operations, and management closely monitors employee behavior to make sure rules are precisely executed.

4. *Market Culture.* As indicated in Figure 19.1, **market culture** is an organization culture that reflects values that emphasize stability and control along with an external focus. An organization with a market culture is oriented toward all stakeholders in the market, not just customers. As such, this culture emphasizes relationships with all constituencies including customers, suppliers, contractors, government regulators, and unions. Leaders in this culture tend to be hard-driving. The organization is focused on winning and emphasizes achieving stretch goals and outpacing the competition.[19]

General Electric is often used as an example of a company with a market culture. The company operates under the premise that if any of its subsidiaries were not number one or two in market sales, the subsidiaries would be sold. As a result of this premise, the company has sold more than 300 businesses over the last few decades. The organization culture is highly competitive with a "results or else" mentality.

Research tells us that competent managers in each of these four organization cultures tend to act in different ways.[20] Figure 19.2 lists each type of culture and shows corresponding activities that competent managers within each of these cultures tend to emphasize. Studying this figure carefully will provide insight concerning how managers operating in each culture might act to increase the effectiveness of that culture.

CULTURE TYPE	ACTIVITIES MANAGERS TEND TO PERFORM
The Hierarchy Culture	… Make sure employees know exactly what is expected of them. … Standardize policies and procedures so employees know exactly how to get work accomplished. … Include in employee orientation a focus on tradition, values, and vision of the organization. … Give employees regular feedback on how well they are performing jobs. … Establish a monitoring system that shows how well employees are performing jobs.
The Market Culture	… Make sure everyone can name their three most critical customers. … Accept only world-class quality in products and services. … Give customers what they want the first time. … Track how competitors are performing. … Understand the keys to your competitors' success.
The Clan Culture	… Establish a clear goal for the work team. … Establish specific work targets with deadlines that the team can accomplish. … Empower others to perform. … Coach and counsel employees. … Celebrate the successes of work teams and individuals.
The Adhocracy Culture	… Hold people accountable for generating innovative ideas. … Talk to people about their new ideas and what they expect the results of ideas could be. … Reward those who come up with new ways to perform work. … Establish vehicles for trying out new ideas. … Make continuous improvement a feature of the workplace.

FIGURE 19.2

Four types of culture and corresponding activities managers can take to make them successful

BUILDING A HIGH-PERFORMANCE ORGANIZATION CULTURE

The development of culture within an organization is inevitable. In all organizations, culture can develop naturally over time as organization members interact with one another. Under these circumstances, the culture that develops may or may not facilitate or enhance organizational performance. On the other hand, the establishment and growth of culture within an organization can be influenced by specific actions taken by management. Under these circumstances, the culture that develops will generally have a higher probability of encouraging high performance within an organization than if left to developing naturally over time as organization members interact.

Figure 19.3 summarizes the steps managers can take to help build an organization culture that yields high performance.[21] Each of the steps is discussed here:

1. *Lead as Champion.* Leaders in organizations must champion organization climate. As such, leaders throughout the organization must explain repeatedly why the practices that help build organization culture are necessary and how such practices will benefit the organization. If the practices represent new practices, leaders must convince organization members that change is necessary.

2. *Link Work to Organizational Mission.* The purpose of organizational mission is to clarify the purpose(s) of the organization. The mission statement helps employees understand why their organization exists. Helping employees understand how their work contributes to accomplishing organizational mission is critical. Such understanding emphasizes the great importance of employee efforts to the success of the organization and helps to build a sense of pride in their jobs and the work they do. If employees understand how their efforts result in the accomplishment of organizational mission, commitment to working hard so the mission can be accomplished will normally grow.

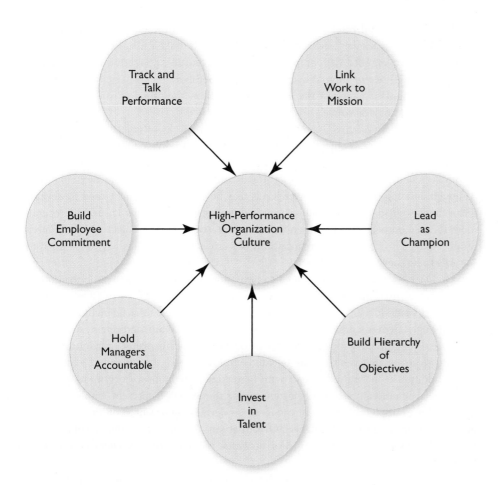

FIGURE 19.3
Steps managers can take to
build a high-performance
organization culture

3. *Track and Talk About Performance.* All organization members should always be thinking about their individual performance. What is excellent performance? How can performance be improved? Why is excellent performance necessary? Why should organization members strive to be excellent performers? Performance, by managers and nonmanagers alike,

General Electric's hard-driving market culture is highly competitive and focused on getting results. The parent company has sold 300 subsidiary units that failed to measure up.

should be defined and tracked to monitor how appropriately individuals are performing. As performance is tracked, corrective action should be taken, if necessary, to foster performance improvement. Also, employees generally like to know how well their organization as a whole is performing. When organization members receive regular communication regarding the performance of the entire organization, they tend to stay focused on contributing to that performance.

4. *Build a Hierarchy of Objectives.* As discussed earlier, a hierarchy of objectives is a set of objectives wherein the overall objectives of the organization are divided into subobjectives for all sections and levels of the organization. As objectives at lower levels of the organization are accomplished, they contribute to the attainment of objectives at the next higher level. Although defining objectives at lower levels may be difficult, the effort used to develop the hierarchy is well spent. Even employees at the lowest organizational levels will generally be more focused on performance when they see the cascading set of objectives in the hierarchy of objectives. Throughout the organization, objectives should be challenging and have clear rewards to be earned when reached.

5. *Invest in Talent.* Certain employees tend to have more talent to perform a job than others. As such, these talented individuals have a greater capacity for performance. Talented employees generally demand higher wages in the labor market than others. Management must recognize that although talented employees may be more expensive to hire and retain, such employees are normally an effective means to better organizational performance. In addition, managers must do whatever they can to retain talented employees once they are hired.

   In addition to hiring individuals with better talent to improve organizational performance, management can also invest in developing the talents of present employees. Through training, for example, management can focus on developing organization member abilities to improve organizational performance. Organizations that invest in and maintain employee work abilities send the message to all organization members that excellent performance is a top priority.

6. *Recognize and Reward.* Management needs to help employees *learn* to be high performers. As such, appropriate performance behavior needs to be reinforced or rewarded. Because research tells us that reinforced behavior tends to be repeated, as management reinforces appropriate performance, appropriate performance will tend to be repeated. Reinforcement can be monetary or nonmonetary. In certain instances a simple, nonmonetary certificate of high performance can be as powerful a reinforcement as a monetary cash bonus. Periodically, recognition and reward practices within any organization should be evaluated for possible improvement.

7. *Hold Managers Accountable.* The performance of managers should be tracked with job-related progress being communicated to them both formally and informally. Maintaining this performance contributes to ensuring the success of a manager's area of responsibility, which in turn contributes to the performance and success of the organization as a whole. Managers should understand what it takes for employees to be high performers and advise, coach, and counsel them in ways to improve performance and reach performance goals. Given the critical contribution that employee performance makes to organizational success, managers should be held accountable for managing that performance.

8. *Build Organizational Commitment.* **Organizational commitment** can be defined as the dedication of organization members to uphold the values of the organization and to make worthwhile contributions to fulfilling organizational purpose. Research indicates that one way to build organizational commitment is to maintain an organizational focus on providing excellent customer service. Such a focus seems to result in higher job satisfaction which, in turn, seems to help build stronger organizational commitment.[22] Overall, this increased commitment to the organization seems to raise the desire of employees to remain in the organization and focus on providing quality goods and services. Foundation studies in this area indicate that organizational commitment serves as a "psychological bond" that influences individuals to act in ways that are consistent with the interests of the organization.[23]

class discussion highlight

MODERN RESEARCH AND ORGANIZATION CULTURE SKILL

Understanding the factors that increase employee turnover (i.e., workers leave their jobs) is an important issue for managers. After losing employees, organizations must spend money to recruit, train, and develop new employees. Typical studies on employee turnover examine the role of factors such as employee pay satisfaction, job satisfaction, and job performance in understanding why workers leave their jobs.

A recent study, however, extended this research by examining the extent to which employees' intentions to leave their organizations are influenced by the organizational commitment of their co-workers. In other words, are employees more likely to leave their jobs if their co-workers are less committed to their employers (e.g., the co-workers are actively engaged in searching for new jobs)? The researchers studied employees in two organizations in attempt to better understand this issue. Do you think that the job search behaviors of an employee's co-workers influenced that employee's intention to leave the organization? Why or why not?

Source: W. Felps, T. R. Mitchell, D. R. Hekman, T. W. Lee, B. C. Holtom, and W. S. Harman. "Turnover contagion: How coworkers' job embeddedness and job search behaviors influence quitting," *Academy of Management Journal*, 2009, vol. 52, 545–561.

KEEPING ORGANIZATION CULTURE ALIVE AND WELL

Given the critical contribution that organization culture makes to organizational success, managers must keep organization culture alive and well in their organizations. Important steps in this process include establishing a vision for organization culture, building and maintaining organization culture through artifacts, integrating new employees within organization culture, and maintaining the health of organization culture. Each of these steps is discussed in the following sections.

Establishing a Vision of Organization Culture

Managing organization culture normally begins by establishing a vision of what the culture of an organization should be. In essence, this vision becomes a target at which management aims. Without such a target, management will not have a benchmark for modifying and improving organization culture over time.

Management should reflect on what type of culture would be appropriate given specific organizational circumstances. Given the complexity of circumstances for most modern organizations, most modern organization cultures tend to be multidimensional. Managers should strive to establish various dimensions in their own cultures that will best contribute to accomplishing organizational mission. Dimensions commonly observed in modern organization cultures include a focus on quality, ethics, innovation, spirituality, diversity, and customer. Not all organization cultures contain all of these dimensions. Instead, managers tend to decide which dimension(s) will best help enhance organizational success and then take steps to include that dimension as a major feature of organization culture. Each of these dimensions is discussed here.

Quality Dimension The **quality dimension of organization culture** is an element of organization culture that focuses on making sure a product, in the opinion of the customer, does what it is supposed to do. Organizations with such cultures tend to focus on communicating their focus on quality to customers and explaining how quality processes operate within the organization. Management generally hopes to benefit from such cultural emphasis by winning customer loyalty and repeat purchases through customer satisfaction with products or services. An example of an organization with a strong quality dimension of organization culture is KB Home, a home builder that operates mainly in 18 states in the southwest and southeast parts of the United

At KB home, quality is so important to organizational culture that on its web site the homebuilding company promises 100% customer satisfaction on 10 construction checkpoints.

States. KB Home uses its Web site to communicate its focus on quality to customers. At KB Home, the quality of houses produced is especially important to the company. The company has a "100% Satisfied Pledge," which offers home buyers 10 quality construction checkpoints.

Ethics Dimension The **ethics dimension of organization culture** is a facet of organization culture that focuses on making sure an organization emphasizes not only what is good for the organization, but what is good for other human beings. Until recently, an ethics dimension has been dangerously ignored. The debate about the ethics dimension now needs to move from whether it should exist in organizations to how to build it.[24]

Ethics training is arguably the most commonly used vehicle for developing the ethics dimension of organization culture.[25] Ethics training normally focuses on developing a common understanding throughout the organization of the role ethics plays in organizational operations. Ethics training will not guarantee that employees will choose the desired ethical behavior in every situation. Such training will, however, start useful dialogue about right and wrong behavior in various organizational situations. In essence, ethics training strives to give employees a worthwhile framework for ethical reasoning that will help them to make ethical choices in various organizational situations after training ends.

What can managers do to increase the probability that ethics training influences organization members to act ethically over time? First, after ethics training concludes, management can provide employees with a vehicle for making ethical queries anonymously. Some organizations provide a hotline that employees can call to get advice about ethical dilemmas. Management can also try to make sure organization members act ethically after ethics training concludes by establishing methods for the resurfacing of topics covered in ethics training. For example, a company can use its intranet, publish brochures, and even use screensavers to keep reminding employees about issues covered in ethics training. Another tactic management can use to try to ensure organization members act ethically after ethics training, is to promote employees who behave ethically. Rewarding ethical behavior of the past is a powerful vehicle for increasing the probability that organization members will act ethically in the future.

Innovation Dimension The **innovation dimension of organization culture** is an aspect of organization culture that encourages the application of new ideas to the improvement of organizational processes, products, or services. Innovation is a major source of organizational change and improvement. Once an innovation dimension is established, management cannot assume it will continue to exist over time. An innovation dimension of organization culture can become significantly weakened or even extinct if not properly nurtured.

The 3M Company is known for producing thousands of imaginative products, emerging from a culture widely regarded as innovative and creative. By its nature, invention is commonly a disorderly and inefficient process. Historically, 3M allowed researchers to spend years testing products with little regard for the efficiency of the process.

Consider 3M's invention of the Post-It note. The inventor, Art Fry, fiddled with the idea for several years before the product went into full production in 1980. But then, management began making changes to the culture to emphasize efficiency. What the company didn't realize was that, in emphasizing efficiency, innovation was also being squeezed out. Once 3M management realized this focus was being destroyed, it took steps to somewhat deemphasize the focus on efficiency and spend more on research and development in an effort to reinvigorate its culture of innovation, long considered to be the lifeblood of the company.[26] ■

how managers do it

Modifying Innovative
Cultural at 3M

Spirituality Dimension The **spirituality dimension of organization culture** is an aspect of organization culture that encourages organization members to integrate spiritual life and work life. A spiritual awakening seems to be occurring in the American workplace. Many managers are encouraging the development of this new trend.[27] Managers seem to be encouraging this trend because of their belief that a spiritually humanistic work environment is beneficial for both employees and the organization. According to the logic of such managers, a spiritually reflective work environment will be personally satisfying to organization members who will thereby become more productive and creative. On the other hand, such managers tend to believe that a workplace without a spiritual dimension will normally result in unsatisfied organization members who will become frustrated and thereby consistently absent from the workplace.[28] Organization cultures that have a spiritual emphasis typically do not focus on one specific type of spiritual belief or religion, but emphasize the acceptance of whatever spiritual focus organization member might possess. In emphasizing a spiritual focus, organizations create opportunities for spiritually based activities such as prayer, meditation, reading sacred texts, listening to worship music, and having objects in the workplace as reminders of spiritual beliefs.

Diversity Dimension The **diversity dimension of organization culture** is a component of organization culture that encourages the existence of basic human differences among organization members. Such differences can relate to ethnicity, religion, physical ability, or sexual orientation. The diversity dimension is a mainstay of modern organization culture mainly because managers are anxious to reap diversity-related advantages such as increased perspectives on how to solve problems and how to better relate to diverse customers.

Toyota's American division recently concluded that its corporate culture lacked diversity.[29] Organization members as a group were thought to be too homogeneous, thereby depriving management of the benefits of a diverse workforce. To solve this problem, Toyota is trying to make organization members as a whole more diverse by hiring more people from other industries and companies. These hirings, however, are being done carefully. Management does not want the addition of new people ruining its present and otherwise healthy corporate culture.

Customer Dimension The **customer dimension of organization culture** is a facet of organization culture that focuses on catering to the needs of those individuals who buy goods or services produced. One recent survey indicates that 80 percent of executives believe they are doing an excellent job of serving customers yet only 8 percent of their customers agree.[30] Perhaps because of such survey results along with the calamity that such results could cause in organizations, many managers are strengthening their organization culture focus on customers.

Some organizations, however, are well known for an enduring commitment to customer satisfaction, have achieved much success because of it, and are expected to continue benefiting from it in the future. For example, many believe that Apple's success over the years is primarily due to its enduring commitment to know what customers want even before customers know it. At General Electric, as another example, CEO Immelt has initiated "dreaming sessions" to brainstorm with key customers in order to have a forward-looking view of customer needs.

Building and Maintaining Organization Culture Through Artifacts

A **cultural artifact** is a dimension of an organization that helps to describe and reinforce the culture, or beliefs, values, and norms, in which an artifact exists. Cultural artifacts can change over time as organization culture changes, because what the artifacts represent, how they appear, how they are used, and why they are used are no longer pertinent given the new culture. Several cultural artifacts commonly used by modern managers are discussed here.[31]

Values   At the heart of any organization's culture, by definition, are its values. From a societal viewpoint, a **value** is a belief of a person or social group in which they have an emotional investment. In society, values can be "for" something, such as excellent health care for all society, or "against" something, such as violence among society members. In organizations, values can also be for things such as hiring talented workers, rewarding excellent performance, and developing leadership skills, or against things such as polluting the environment, discrimination in hiring practices, and maintaining the status quo.

Organizational values are reflected in organizational ingredients, including strategy, structure, and processes. Values are also reflected in the way leaders lead as well as in organizational rules, reward systems, policies, and procedures. More and more, modern managers are crafting value statements to clearly communicate held cultural values throughout the organization. A **values statement** is a formally drafted document that summarizes the primary values within the culture of a specific organization. A values statement gives managers the opportunity to communicate effectively and efficiently the values that drive an organization and thereby help increase the probability that appropriate values will influence organization member behavior. Figure 19.4 contains a statement of values for Microsoft.

Social psychologist Michael O'Malley studies organization culture and, in his spare time, practices beekeeping. Indulging in his hobby has led O'Malley to study the habits of bees and apply them to management practices in building organizational values in his book *The Wisdom of Bees: What the Hive Can Teach Business About Leadership*. For example, O'Malley says, older bees in the hive "mentor" younger bees. Culture is important to the hive's overall productivity and well-being, and when colonies from two hives occasionally merge, an "enculturation" process goes on to ensure the merger is successful.[32]

FIGURE 19.4
Statement of Values for Microsoft

Source: http://www.microsoft.com/about/en/us/default.aspx (accessed December 1, 2010).

> **Our Values**
>
> As a company, and as individuals, we value integrity, honesty, openness, personal excellence, constructive self-criticism, continual self-improvement, and mutual respect. We are committed to our customers and partners and have a passion for technology. We take on big challenges, and pride ourselves on seeing them through. We hold ourselves accountable to our customers, shareholders, partners, and employees by honoring our commitments, providing results, and striving for the highest quality.

Organizational Myths An **organizational myth** is a popular belief or story that has become associated with a person or institution that is considered to illustrate an organization culture ideal. Myths are used to explain organizational beginnings or events that are of great significance to the organization. Myths stimulate organization members to do well and provide the logic for action taken. The events contained in myths never actually happened, but act as an inspirational foundation for behavior. Organizational myths are commonly perpetuated in organizations to enhance organization member pride in belonging and overall commitment to the organization. In addition, myths are commonly perpetuated to build employee commitment reflected by the myth.

One of the most famous myths in business history centers on Lee Iacocca and how he "saved" Chrysler Corporation from bankruptcy.[33] Iacocca took over as chairman of Chrysler Corporation in 1979. At that time, Chrysler was in deep crisis. The company was losing money, had acquired unprofitable companies, and was producing low-quality products necessitating huge, expensive product recalls. Iacocca took bold, nontraditional action to save the company. He negotiated government backing of the company, took charismatic personal ads to the marketplace asking for customer support, and negotiated significant concessions with the United Auto Workers Union to dodge bankruptcy. Word began to quickly spread that Iacocca had single-handedly saved the company, which of course was not true. Many people were involved in saving Chrysler. The myth of Iacocca saving the company single-handedly, however, helped build the Chrysler cultural value of trust and support for Chrysler leadership.

Organizational Sagas An **organizational saga** is a narrative describing the adventures of a heroic individual or family significantly linked to an organization's past or present. In general, the purpose of a saga is to identify and perpetuate the organization's shared values. Organizational sagas usually reveal important historical facts about an organization relating to issues such as early organizational pioneers and products, past triumphs and failures of the organization, and the leaders who founded or transformed the company.

Mary Kay Ash is the founder of Mary Kay Cosmetics and one of the most successful entrepreneurs in the history of the United States. Information on the Web site of the company she founded outlines a saga related to Mary Kay Ash's company history. This information serves as an inspirational saga to all organization members that significant success is available to all within the company through hard work, dedication, and self-confidence.

Managers at all levels can become involved in **organizational storytelling**, the act of passing organizational myths and sagas to other organization members. Obviously, given the example about Mary Kay Ash, modern managers can tell stories not only via word of mouth, but also via the Internet.

Organizational Language The language used in organizations often points to the organization's shared values. Some companies reveal how they feel about the competition through repeatedly using phrases such as "let's be #1 in the marketplace," or how they feel about technology by repeatedly using phrases such as "win through technology." Still other organizations repeatedly use the phrase "customer is king" to emphasize how they feel about dealing with customer satisfaction. Language used at Walt Disney Companies reflects organizational values that are particularly interesting. At Walt Disney, rather than being called an employee, everyone is called a "member of the cast." This language emphasizes that rather than simply working, organization members should think of themselves as always being *on stage*, and always giving the best *performance* possible for customers. Many companies use slogans internally and externally through advertising to convey important organizational values. Figure 19.5 contains several well-known slogans and the companies that use them to convey important organizational values.

Organizational Symbols An **organizational symbol** is an object that has meaning beyond its intrinsic content. Symbols provide a roadmap for what is important in a particular organization. Some companies use impressive buildings to convey company strength. Other

COMPANY	SLOGAN	VALUE REFLECTED
Maytag	"The dependability people"	Maytag products are durable.
Petland	"Petland Pets Make Life Better!"	Petland pets improve lives.
Allstate Insurance Co.	"You're In Good Hands With Allstate"	Allstate takes care of customers.
Staples	"That was easy"	Staples solves problems easily.
Wal-Mart	"Always low prices. Always."	Wal-Mart has low prices every day.

FIGURE 19.5
Well-known companies, their slogans, and the values these slogans reflect

companies use logos, flags, and coats of arms to convey the importance they place on certain ideas or events. As examples, Prudential Life Insurance Company uses the Rock of Gibraltar as a symbol of the company's dependability, strength, and unchanging commitment to customers; and McDonald's uses the clown Ronald McDonald as a symbol of child-friendliness and fun within McDonald's restaurants.

Organizational Ceremonies An **organizational ceremony** is a formal activity conducted on important organizational occasions. Such occasions could include openings of new stores, anniversary dates for hiring of employees, and employee promotions. Perhaps one of the most well-known organizational ceremonies is the ceremony celebrating successful sales campaigns at Mary Kay Cosmetics. At Mary Kay Cosmetics sales celebrations, everything has a purpose—not just the decorations, but sales prizes, including the automobiles awarded.

Organizational Rewards Rewards tailor behavior in some way in most organizations.[34] Some rewards come from sources within the organization and can include compensation, satisfying work, and verbal recognition. Rewards can also come from outside the organization and can include comments from customers, competitors, and suppliers. Management should continually be involved with identifying and rewarding those individuals who uphold the values of the organization. Rewarding people for engaging in behavior that reflects important organization culture values is critical in increasing the probability of organizational success.

Integrating New Employees into the Organization Culture

The previous section discussed how to keep organization culture alive and well through the use of cultural artifacts. This section focuses on how to keep organization culture alive and well by appropriately integrating newly hired organization members within an existing organization culture.

Organizational socialization is the process by which management can appropriately integrate new employees within an organization's culture.[35] As the U.S. economy improves, it is

May Kay Cosmetics builds its company culture through inspirational stories, including that of founder Mary Kay Ash, organizational ceremonies, and rewards, including autos for topselling representatives.

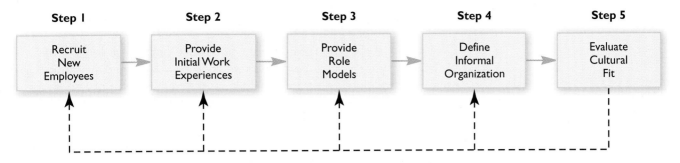

FIGURE 19.6 Possible steps of a socialization process

likely that employers will need to integrate more new employees. During periods of uncertainty and layoffs, employees who still have jobs tend to "stay put" even if they are dissatisfied with their position. However, as the economy improves, those same employees will begin to leave their jobs, requiring employers to recruit new employees.[36] The visual scheme in Figure 19.6 shows recommended steps for a socialization process and how the steps relate to one another. The following material discusses the process as a whole as well as each step in more detail.

As shown in Figure 19.6, the organizational socialization process can begin by carefully planning the organization's recruitment process. As part of this planning, management should determine what type of individual characteristics would best fit within the organization culture. Such characteristics might include an individual's determination to be successful in a job, commitment to personal ethics, and level of self-confidence and competitiveness. After such best-fit characteristics have been determined, management should use the recruitment process to identify individuals possessing those characteristics. Naturally, after management has identified individuals who possesses the characteristics, serious steps should be taken to hire the individuals.

Once individuals possessing the best-fit characteristics are hired, management should continue their socialization process (step 2) by carefully crafting meaningful experiences for them within the first four to six weeks of new recruits' lives within the organization. In this situation, experiences are meaningful if they expose new hires to important organization culture values and emphasize the importance of new individuals' commitment to them. Such values might include the importance of tackling challenging work, openness to training for handling new situations, and the importance of functioning as a team member. Such initial experiences can also involve new recruits observing and practicing new jobs with input from established organization members.

Once individuals with appropriate personal characteristics have been hired and have experienced meaningful activities within the first four to six weeks, management should continue with the socialization of these individuals by exposing the new recruits to appropriate role models (step 3). Management should be focused on connecting new recruits to role models who possess vital characteristics that would be valuable for new recruits. The role models should illustrate cultural values such as being productive, highly motivated, loyal to the organization, and having high trust in management.

As the next step of the organizational socialization process, management can help new recruits to understand various facets of the organization's informal structure and how it complements the formal structure. Helping new recruits infiltrate and become members of informal groups that uphold important organizational values can be especially important to management. On the other hand, ignoring this informal focus in the organizational socialization process could allow new recruits to unknowingly align with less productive facets of an organization's informal structure and thereby limit the contribution of the new recruits to organizational success.

As a final step in the organizational socialization process, management must control the cultural fit of new recruits. New recruits are generally considered new for about one year. During this first year within the organization, management must keep in mind that new recruits will be making mistakes and struggling to appropriately fit within organization culture. This struggle to acquire organizational fit can be frustrating to new recruits and lead to premature turnover if not handled sensitively by management. New recruits must be able to practice new jobs, at times employing trial and error, without fear of punishment or failure.

With more than 2,500 attorneys in office on four continents, Jones Day is one of the world's largest law firms. Like most large firms, it has a set of traits it looks for when recruiting new lawyers to its firm. For example, candidates must not exhibit a sense of entitlement or appear too focused on personal success. Also, because of its collaborative culture, the firm rules out candidates who would compete with their colleagues or are too interested in their peers' performance. Jones Day has what is called a "closed" compensation system, and even its partners are not privy to information about the salaries of their peers. While this kind of secrecy may be highly unusual, it seems to be accepted within the firm's culture. What's more, it doesn't appear to have adversely affected the firm's success: unlike many of its competitors, Jones Day did not lay off lawyers during the recent global recession.[37] ■

Management must also remember that not all recruits are ideal fits for organization culture and that some recruits my need to be weeded out to make room for other new recruits who may be a better fit. This weeding out can take place by either moving poor performers out of the organization or to jobs comprised of less critical roles. As this weeding out process occurs, management should reflect on any possible mistakes made during the organizational socialization process of the recruits and thereby come up with ideas on how to improve the process so that such mistakes will not be made in the future.

Maintaining the Health of Organization Culture

Arguably, the most important step management takes to maximize the success of an organization is to create a healthy culture within that organization. *Health* is defined in terms of the extent to which a culture facilitates the achievement of organizational mission and objectives. A **healthy organization culture** is an organization culture that facilitates the achievement of the organization's mission and objectives. An **unhealthy organization culture** is an organization culture that does not facilitate the accomplishment of the organization's mission and objectives.

Managers must continually analyze symptoms or signs related to the health of an organization and take action to build and maintain a healthy organization culture. *Healthy organization culture* is usually people oriented and contains the characteristics listed in Figure 19.7. A manager should keep the characteristics of a healthy organization climate in mind and focus on maintaining and building organization culture health whenever possible. For example, if managers believe that organization culture is healthy, they should take steps to improve this health wherever possible. Even though an organization culture might be considered healthy, increasing a cultural focus on risk-taking or excellence in job performance might make it even healthier. On the other hand, a manager might believe that his or her organization culture is unhealthy. In such a case, the manager must determine what factors are making the organization climate unhealthy, take steps to eliminate these factors, and introduce ingredients into the culture that will make it healthy.

That was the strategy implemented by Jonathan Ciano when he became CEO of Uchumi Supermarkets in Kenya, Africa. Soon after joining the company, Ciano saw obvious signs that organization culture was unhealthy. Staff theft and unregulated procurement systems led to record debt and uncertainty regarding the company's sustainability. To change the unhealthy culture into a healthy one, besides confronting the issues of theft and uncontrolled procurement, the new CEO initiated a culture in which employees were able to think for themselves on behalf of the company. As a result, Uchumi employees started making independent judgments and decisions.[38]

1. **Openness and humility from top to bottom of the organization**
   Arrogance kills off learning and growth by blinding us to our own weaknesses. Strength comes out of receptivity and the willingness to learn from others.

2. **An environment of accountability and personal responsibility**
   Denial, blame, and excuses harden relationships and intensify conflict. Successful teams hold each other accountable and willingly accept personal responsibility.

3. **Freedom for risk-taking within appropriate limits**
   Both extremes—an excessive, reckless risk-taking and a stifling, fearful control—threaten any organization. Freedom to risk new ideas flourishes best within appropriate limits.

4. **A fierce commitment to "do it right"**
   Mediocrity is easy; excellence is hard work, and there are many temptations for shortcuts. A search for excellence always inspires both inside and outside an organization.

5. **A willingness to tolerate and learn from mistakes**
   Punishing honest mistakes stifles creativity. Learning from mistakes encourages healthy experimentation and converts negatives into positives.

6. **Unquestioned integrity and consistency**
   Dishonesty and inconsistency undermine trust. Organizations and relationships thrive on clarity, transparency, honesty, and reliable follow-through.

7. **A pursuit of collaboration, integration, and holistic thinking**
   Turf wars and narrow thinking are deadly. Drawing together the best ideas and practices, integrating the best people into collaborative teams, multiplies organizational strength.

8. **Courage and persistence in the face of difficulty**
   The playing field is not always level, or life fair, but healthy cultures remain both realistic about the challenges they face and unintimidated and undeterred by difficulty.

FIGURE 19.7
Eight characteristics of a healthy organization culture
Source: Developed by the Institute for Business, Technology, and Ethics (IBTE); www.customerfocusconsult.com/articles/articles_template.asp?ID=36.

If Ciano's steps to make organization culture healthier are successful, he will start to see signs such as organization members fixing mistakes rather than rationalizing them, and new ideas and information will start to flow freely within the company. On the other hand, if the organization culture is not becoming healthier, the CEO will see signs that include employees blaming others when mistakes occur.

CHALLENGE CASE SUMMARY

For Robert Dudley, the new BP chief executive officer mentioned in the Challenge Case, to build a culture emphasizing safety within his organization, he must understand the fundamental concepts of organization culture. He must know that in building this safety focus, he is actually attempting to build shared values within BP so that organization members view safety as a critical organizational activity. Ultimately, building such a safety culture at BP could help the company avoid dealing with future explosions and other catastrophes and thereby contribute to greater organizational success. This safety-focused culture can serve such useful and valuable functions at BP as enhancing company productivity, becoming a part of the company's strategy for success, and providing a rationale for adding new staff.

In all likelihood, Dudley's organization culture challenges will extend beyond the issue of safety. It would probably be worthwhile for Dudley to determine what type of overall organization culture he would like to see at BP. He might consider establishing a clan culture, an adhocracy culture, a hierarchy culture, or a market culture. In making this determination, Dudley should consider the challenges facing BP and anticipate which culture or combination of cultures would best help BP meet these challenges.

Given information presented in the case, safety is one of the challenges that BP is facing. In facing the task of establishing a safety focus to BP's organization culture, Dudley should also plan for establishing a broader organization culture that encourages high performance. To create a high-performance culture, Dudley must lead as a champion. That is, he must explain repeatedly why organization culture values such as safety are critical for BP and take steps to encourage organization members to act in ways that are consistent with such cultural values. To create this high-performance culture, Dudley can also focus on linking work to BP's mission and recognize and reward those individuals whose actions are consistent with accomplishing BP's mission. In helping to build a high-performance culture, Dudley can also take actions that include investing in outstanding talent, holding managers accountable for their actions, and building the commitment of organization members to BP.

In planning to establish a safety dimension to BP's organization culture, Dudley should plan on keeping the culture alive and well once established. Keeping the culture alive and well actually starts with Dudley envisioning exactly what the culture should be. Without such a vision, Dudley will be unable to tweak the culture over time to make it consistent with this vision. In addition to a safety dimension, Dudley's vision of the culture could include a combination of dimensions focusing on areas such as quality, ethics, innovation, spirituality, diversity, or customer.

Once the vision for the BP culture is complete in Dudley's mind, the process of keeping BP's culture alive and well should probably focus on Dudley choosing the artifacts that he would like to use to establish and maintain BP's organization culture. Such artifacts might include a values statement outlining BP's key organization culture values, the development of organizational myths and sagas that can be used to perpetuate cultural values, special language and ceremonies to bring key ingredients of BP's cultural values to life, and organization rewards that reinforce and encourage behavior that is consistent with organization culture.

Bringing new organization members into BP's culture is a serious matter. Socializing new individuals into the culture will help ensure the culture stays alive and well over the long run. Steps that Dudley can take to appropriately socialize new organization members into BP's culture include carefully planning BP's recruitment process, providing significant experiences at BP once individuals are hired, exposing newcomers to appropriate BP role models, and changing organization members when individuals do not seem to be fitting well within the BP culture. Overall, Dudley must focus on establishing a healthy organization culture at BP, a culture that facilitates the achievement of BP's goals.

MANAGEMENT SKILL ACTIVITIES

This section is specially designed to help you develop organization culture skills. An individual's organization culture skill is based on an understanding of organization culture concepts and the ability to apply those concepts in management situations. The following activities are designed to both heighten your understanding of organization culture concepts and to develop the ability to apply those concepts in a variety of management situations.

UNDERSTANDING ORGANIZATION CULTURE CONCEPTS

To check your understanding and to practice using the concepts in this chapter, go to www.mymanagementlab.com and explore the material associated with Chapter 19.

Know Key Terms

Understanding the following key terms is critical to your understanding of chapter material. Define each of these terms. Refer to the page(s) references after a term to check your definition or to gain further insight regarding the term.

Know How Management Concepts Relate

This section is comprised of activities that will further sharpen your understanding of management concepts. Answer essay questions as completely as possible. Also, remember that many additional true/false and multiple choice questions appear online at MyManagementLab.com to help you further refine your understanding of management concepts.

1. Define *organization culture* and explain why organization culture skill is valuable to managers.

2. Explain the advantages and disadvantages of having a *clan culture* within an organization. As a manager, would this culture be hard for you to establish? Why?

3. Assume you are a professor teaching a management course. What vision would you have for the course culture? List three artifacts you would use to establish and maintain this vision. Be sure to explain why you chose each artifact.

4. List three challenges a manager might face in appropriately socializing new employees into an organization culture. What advice would you give managers for how to meet these challenges?

5. How would you turn an unhealthy organization culture into a healthy one? Be as specific as possible.

DEVELOPING MANAGEMENT SKILLS

Learning activities in this section are aimed at helping you develop organization culture skill. Learning activities include Exploring Your Management Skill: Parts 1 and 2, Your Management Skill Portfolio Exercise, Experiential Exercises, Cases, and a VideoNet Exercise.

Exploring Your Management Skill: Part 1

Before studying this chapter, respond to the following questions regarding the type of advice that you would give to BP's new CEO Richard Dudley, referenced in the Challenge Case. Then address the concerning organization culture challenges that he presently faces within the company. You are not expected to be an organization culture expert at this point. Answering the questions now can help you focus on important points when you study the chapter. Also, answering the questions again after you study the chapter will give you an idea of how much you have learned.

Record your answers here or go to MyManagementLab.com. Recording your answers in MyManagementLab will allow you to get immediate results and see how your score compares to your classmates. If you answer the questions in the book, the answers are located in the Exploring Your Management Skill Appendix at the end of the book.

FOR EACH STATEMENT CIRCLE:

- "Y" if you would give the advice to Dudley.
- "N" if you would NOT give the advice to Dudley.
- "NI" if you have no idea whether you would give the advice to Dudley.

Mr. Dudley, in meeting your organization culture challenges at BP, you should...

Before   After
Study   Study

1. aim at building shared values in organization members that will lead to organizational success.
   Y, N, NI

2. proceed with caution because the real value of establishing organization culture is still being debated vigorously.
   Y, N, NI

3. expect that once the culture is established, organization members will follow cultural artifacts like a code of conduct.
   Y, N, NI

4. strive to establish a clan culture if you want to focus on having a more regimented, stable organization.
   Y, N, NI

5. establish an adhocracy culture if you need an organization that is flexible, has an external focus, and where people exercise discretion.
   Y, N, NI

6. champion whatever culture you'd like to establish.
   Y, N, NI

7. use a hierarchy of objectives to help you encourage organization member performance.
   Y, N, NI

8. deemphasize building values because values often influence organization members to make somewhat emotional decisions.
   Y, N, NI

9. use sagas to emphasize historical issues of the past that can influence company success in the present.
   Y, N, NI

10. deemphasize using organizational symbols because they are too simplistic for building more complicated organizational values.

    Y, N, NI

11. reward organization members who perform behavior that reflects organization culture, beliefs, and values.

    Y, N, NI

12. consider applying organizational socialization concepts mainly for individuals who have been with the organization for more than five years.

    Y, N, NI

13. from time to time evaluate the cultural fit of new recruits.

    Y, N, NI

14. focus on monitoring and improving the health of organization culture.

    Y, N, NI

15. probably not consider emphasizing special dimensions of organization culture such as innovation or quality.

    Y, N, NI

Exploring Your Management Skill: Part 2

As you recall, you completed Exploring Your Management Skill before you started to study this chapter. Your responses gave you an idea of how much you initially knew about organization culture and helped you focus on important points as you studied the chapter. Answer the Exploring Your Management Skill questions again now and compare your score to the first time you took it. This comparison will give you an idea of how much you have learned from studying this chapter and pinpoint areas for further clarification before you start studying the next chapter. Record your answers within the text or go to MyManagementLab.com. Recording your answers in MyManagementLab will allow you to get immediate results and see how your score compares to your classmates. If you answer the questions in the book, the answers are located in the Exploring Your Management Skill Appendix at the end of the book.

Your Management Skills Portfolio

Your Management Learning Portfolio is a collection of activities especially designed to demonstrate your management knowledge and skill. By completing these activities online at MyManagementLab.com, you will be able to print, complete with cover sheet, as many activities as you choose. Be sure to save your work. Taking your printed portfolio to an employment interview could be helpful in obtaining a job.

The portfolio activity for this chapter is *Establishing Organization Culture at Eden's Fresh Company*. Read the highlight about Eden's Fresh Company and perform the skills activities that follow.

Brian Certo had just graduated from Rollins College with an MBA. Rather than entering the job market, he decided to open Eden's Fresh Company, a fast casual restaurant specializing in salads and wraps in Winter Park, Florida.

Brian began planning for the opening of Eden's by producing a spreadsheet reflecting all projected costs and revenues anticipated. Having developing a spreadsheet business model that seemed workable, Brian began taking steps to start his restaurant. His first step was to recruit a partner, Colin Knight, who had just graduated from the University of Florida. Together, Brian and Colin acquired funding, selected and renovated a site, interviewed and chose suppliers, designed the restaurant's décor, and purchased appropriate equipment and furnishings. As one of the last steps, they hired eight employees and began training.

Skills Activities

Assume you are opening Eden's. The last part of your planning is to plan for and implement the organization culture you would like to exist within the restaurant. Perform the organization culture planning tasks that follow:

1. Write a paragraph describing the type of organization culture you would like to establish at Eden's. Be sure to emphasize all of the values you would like to exist.

_____

_____

_____

_____

_____

_____

_____

2. List and discuss in detail five cultural artifacts you would use to implement and maintain the values contained in your organization culture vision.

    Artifact 1:

    _____

    _____

    _____

    What organization culture value does this artifact emphasize and how?

    _____

    _____

    _____

    _____

    Artifact 2:

    _____

    _____

    _____

    What organization culture value does this artifact emphasize and how?

    _____

    _____

    _____

    _____

    Artifact 3:

    _____

    _____

    _____

    What organization culture value does this artifact emphasize and how?

    _____

    _____

    _____

    _____

    Artifact 4:

    _____

    _____

    _____

    _____

What organization culture value does this artifact emphasize and how?

_____

_____

_____

_____

Artifact 5:

_____

_____

_____

_____

_____

What organization culture value does this artifact emphasize and how?

_____

_____

_____

_____

Experiential Exercises

1 Exploring the Values of New Recruits

Directions. Read the following scenario and then perform the listed activities. Your instructor may want you to perform the activities as an individual or within groups. Follow all of your instructor's directions carefully.

You are the head of the human resources department of a major real estate investment company involved in buying and selling commercial real estate property around the world. You have a new position opening and next week you will be going to the Kelly School of Business at Indiana University to interview prospective graduating students who might fill this position. Today you are meeting with a small group of human resource personnel to develop a plan for uncovering during a job interview the personal values that prospective job applicants might have. You and your team understand how important it is to discover such values as part of the organizational socialization process.

Directions. Your instructor will divide your class into small groups and designate who will be the head of human resources. This individual will lead the group in developing its plan. Later in the class your instructor might ask someone from each group to *actually conduct* the planned employment interview with someone outside the group. This interview might be videotaped and replayed in class for special discussion and learning opportunities.

Sales Executive Opening

Opening: Chicago Sales Executive

Company: Real Estate Sales Worldwide, 215 employees

Salary: USD 50,000/year, Benefits: Medical, Dental, Vision, 401(k), and Vacation

Industry: Real Estate

Location: Chicago, IL

Status: Full Time, Employee

Career: No Experience Necessary

Education Required: Bachelor's Degree

Expectation of Employee: Team-oriented individual will be successful in direct sales, possess time management skills, will contribute to overall marketing plan, will provide innovative ideas, and will increase sales volume in slow periods.

Essential Job Duties Include: Solicit new real estate buyers in the local market, follow furnished sales leads, design and execute strategies to meet sales goals, analyze market trends, attend networking events, attend trade shows, schedule property tours with customers, make sales presentations, and schedule customer meetings.

2 You and Your Career

You are looking for a job and see a position opening that piques your interest. You like the position and qualify for it. In preparing for your employment interview, you decide to ask three questions about culture within the organization that would be vital in assessing the likelihood of your career flourishing within the company. List the three questions you believe would help you assess the degree of career success you would expect within the company. Explain why you would ask each question.

Videonet Exercise

Organization Culture at Terracycle

Video Highlights

Picture the following and you begin to get a sense of the culture at TerraCycle. Most the employees are 25 and younger, and they're willing to work insane hours for minimal pay because they believe in the company. All of the desks, chairs, phones, and computers in the office are recycled or made out of recycled materials. The outside of the building is covered in graffiti. Every year, they have a graffiti jam in which they paint all the walls black again so new graffiti artists from all over the world can give the place a new look. In honor of their graffiti-rich workplace, they are launching a new line of pots covered in original graffiti as well. Culture can be hard to discern at a large corporation, but at TerraCycle, you can't miss it.

Discussion Questions

1. How does TerraCycle's use of graffiti support its organization culture?
2. Which of the primary mechanisms for reinforcing culture is used most by Tom Szaky, CEO and founder of TerraCycle?
3. How does the organization culture of TerraCycle contribute to the organization's success?

Internet Activity

Go to TerraCycle's home page at www.TerraCycle.net. How has it used its company products to build corporate culture? Explain.

CASES

1 BP'S ATTEMPT TO ESTABLISH A SAFETY CULTURE FAILED

"BP's Attempt to Establish a Safety Culture Failed" (p. 451) and its related Challenge Case Summary were written to help you better understand the management concepts contained in this chapter. Answer the following discussion questions about the Challenge Case to better understand how concepts relating to organization culture be applied in a company such as BP.

1. What first step would you advise Dudley to take in establishing the new safety focus in the organization culture at BP? Why would this be the first step you recommend?
2. Assuming you're Dudley, would you choose to establish a clan, market, hierarchy, or adhocracy culture at BP? Why?
3. Discuss how you would ensure that BP's organization culture is a high-performance culture.

2 HOW CINTAS DEFINES CULTURE

Read the case and answer the questions that follow. Studying this case will help you better understand how concepts relating to organization culture can be applied in a company such as Cintas.

Many may not have heard of Cintas, but its presence in American businesses of all types—restaurants, repair shops, service industries, and retail stores—is ubiquitous. Once known exclusively for uniform rentals, the company has grown tremendously in the last 30 years through steadfast business practices as well as more than 200 acquisitions.

So what is Cintas? Though the Cincinnati-based company is diversified in its offerings, all of its efforts are focused on business-to-business services. For most of the company's existence, it has been known for its uniform rental services. Every single day, approximately 5 million working people put on a uniform or other clothing provided by Cintas. However, the company is much more than just uniform rentals. Cintas has expanded its services to other areas through major acquisitions of existing companies. Today, Cintas assists organizations with facility maintenance, fire protection services, first aid and safety products, document shredding, and many other services. More than 30,000 employees work for this $4 billion company.[39]

The founder of the Cintas conglomerate and chairman of the board, Richard T. Farmer, feels the organization culture of the company is what drives this business. For him, the success of Cintas can be directly attributed to the culture that has been established over the decades. "A corporate culture of honesty and integrity is more valuable than cash in the bank," he said. "It is the glue that holds a company together and helps companies like Cintas do great things."[40]

Cintas' organization culture begins at the top. It is the kind of company where managers and executives are expected to have front-line experience. Rising through the ranks at Cintas is the norm and many career paths at the company were started at the lowest levels. "Each of the three CEOs who have led our company," Farmer said, "spent time early in his career driving trucks and working the plant floors."[41]

In addition, a sense of strong ethical business practices permeates the entire organization. Employees—they're called *partners* at Cintas—are encouraged to report any problems they see. If any staff member witnesses or experiences something perceived as counter to the ethical standards of the company, they have a responsibility to alert the management team—be it a vendor, a customer, or even another associate. "All of our partners," Farmer said, "can call a 1-800 number. Any claim that is made is investigated."[42] Essentially, it all comes down to respect and professionalism. Farmer added that respect "is evident in the fact that we live by the rules and recognize that no one is above them. We have a direct line to top management for partners to share any ethical concerns. We strive to keep our relationships and our environment professional at all times."[43]

Farmer acknowledges that Cintas is as successful as it is due to its employees and also extending the respect and professionalism to customers. From very early in Cintas' history, balancing the needs of all the company's constituents was set in stone. "At Cintas," Farmer said, "our culture starts with our principal objective, which is to maximize the long-term value of Cintas for its shareholders and working partners by exceeding our customers' expectations. We base every decision on that objective."[44]

Cintas has had incredible success with these philosophies. All kinds of accolades have been bestowed on the company including being named one of *Fortune* magazine's most admired companies. In addition, it has experienced a growth in profit and sales for more than 35 consecutive years. But, Cintas' success rides on a strong organization culture that is diligently maintained through training of new partners and constant reminders in the company's daily operational processes.

Recently, Farmer gave advice to other managers and business leaders when talking about the culture of Cintas and its unique success. "Work hard to define your values," he suggested, "put them into writing, communicate them, teach them, live them. Make sure every person at every level of your organization knows the standard—and the consequences of not following it."[45]

QUESTIONS

1. How would you define the organization culture of Cintas? Is it an environment where you would enjoy working?
2. Using the Competing Values Framework, what type of culture do you think exists at Cintas? Why?
3. Cintas' culture is based on the vision set forth by the founder, Richard T. Farmer. What happens to the culture of an organization when the founder or CEO who drives the culture departs or is no longer with the firm?

Endnotes

1. This case is based on: Jessica Marquez, "Creating a Culture of Safety: Out of Disaster Comes a Call for Creating a 'Safety Culture,'" *Workforce Management*, April 23, 2007, p. 1; Stanley Reed, Jessica Resnick Ault, Brian Swint, *Business Week*, New York: May 31, 2010. p. 1; Ian Urbina and Justin Gillis, *New York Times*, May 8, 2010. pg. A.1
2. Company Web site, http://www.bp.com, accessed November 25, 2007.
3. Maria A. Dixon and Debbie S. Dougherty, "Managing the Multiple Meanings of Organizational Culture in Interdisciplinary Collaboration and Consulting," *Journal of Business Communication* 47, no. 1 (January 2010): 3–19.
4. For notable research on the effects of organization culture on workplace performance, see Md. Zabid Abdul Rashid, Murali Sambasivan, and Juliana Johari, "The Influence of Corporate Culture and Organizational Commitment on Performance," *The Journal of Management Development*, 22 (2003): 708; see also Lynn Waters, "Cultivate Corporate Culture and Diversity," *Nursing Management* 35 (2004): 36.
5. J. Chatman and D. F. Caldwell, "People and Organizational Culture: A Profile Comparison Approach to Assessing Person-Organization Fit," *Academy of Management Journal*, September, 1991, 487–516.
6. Mary G. Locke and Lucy Guglielmino, "The Influence of Subcultures on Planned Change in a Community College," *Community College Review* 34, no. 2 (October 2006): 108–128.
7. For an interesting study exploring African female executives and dominant culture organizations see: Patricia S. Parker, "Negotiating Identity in Raced and Gendered Workplace Interactions: The Use of Strategic Communication by African American Women Senior Executives within Dominant Culture Organizations," *Communication Quarterly* 50, no. 3/4 (Summer 2002) 251.
8. Stefan Stern, "Wake Up and Smell the Coffee on Your Corporate Culture," *Financial Times*, March 27, 2007, 12.
9. Victor S. L. Tan, "Transforming Your Organization," *New Straits Times*, June 16, 2007, 58.
10. Cass Bettinger, "Use Corporate Culture to Trigger High Performance," *Journal of Business Strategies* (March/April 1989): 38–42. For an article devoted to corporate culture, see J. Lee Howard, "Building a Corporate Culture," *The Business Journal* 14, no. 31. (November 5, 1999): 19.
11. Mike Foster, "Be positive!" *Construction Distribution* 10, no. 2 (October/November 2007): 80.
12. Julie Verity, "Understanding Success: Economics and Human Nature," *Business Strategy Series* 8, no. 5 (2007): 330.
13. "Finding the Right Fit: Nearly Half of Workers Have Misjudged an Employer's Culture," *PR Newswire*, May 23, 2007.
14. Douglas MacMillan, "A Twitter Code of Conduct," *BusinessWeek*, May 8, 2009, http://www.businessweek.com.
15. Kim S. Cameron and Robert E. Quinn, *Diagnosing and Changing Organizational Culture* (Reading, MA: Addison Wesley, 1999).
16. Southwest.com, http://southwest.com/about_swa/?ref=abtsw_fgn (accessed November 26, 2007).
17. For an interesting discussion on the problems that can arise in mentoring relationships, see Dawn E. Chandler, Lillian Eby, and Stacy McManus, "When Mentoring Goes Bad," *MIT Sloan Management Review*, May 24, 2010, http://sloanreview.mit.edu.
18. www.google.com/corporate/culture.html (accessed November 26, 2007).
19. The environment in most professional services firms fits the description of a market culture. For a discussion of how a consulting firm intentionally challenged a tenet of that culture by instituting planned, uninterrupted time off, see Leslie A. Perlow and Jessica L. Porter, "Making Time Off Predictable—and Required," *Harvard Business Review*, October 2009, http://hbr.org.
20. Kim S. Cameron and Robert E. Quinn, *Diagnosing and Changing Organizational Culture* (Reading, MA: Addison Wesley, 1999), 186–201.
21. Howard Risher, "Fostering a Performance-Driven Culture in the Public Sector," *Public Manager* 36, no. 3 (Fall 2007): 51–56.
22. Yi-Jen Chen, "Relationships Among Service Orientation, Job Satisfaction, and Organizational Commitment in the International Tourist Hotel Industry," *Journal of American Academy of Business* 1 no. 2 (September, 2007): 71.
23. For an interesting discussion of what employers can do to enhance job satisfaction among their employees, see Paul Fairlie, "10 Ways to Make Work More Meaningful," *Workforce Management*, February 2010, http://www.workforce.com.
24. Paul Basson, "How Ethics Can Help Establish Unified Corporate Culture," *Financial Times*, August 24, 2006, 8.
25. The remainder of this section is based upon Jean Thilmany, "Supporting Ethical Employees," *HR Magazine* 52, no. 9 (September 2007): 105.
26. Brian Hindo, "At 3M, a Struggle Between Efficiency and Creativity; How CEO George Buckley Is Managing the Yin and Yang of Discipline and Imagination," *BusinessWeek*, June 11, 2007, 8.
27. Mathew L. Sheep, "Nurturing the Whole Person: The Ethics of Workplace Spirituality in a Society of Organizations," *Journal of Business Ethics* 66, no. 4 (2006): 357–375.
28. Jean-Claude Garcia-Zamor, "Workplace Spirituality and Organizational Performance," *Public Administration Review* 63, no. 3 (May/June 2003): 355.

29. Jeff Mortimer, "Help Wanted: New Blood, Ideas Must Fuel Inclusive, Expanding Corporate Culture," *Automotive News,* October 29, 2007, T184.

30. Betsy Morris, "New Rule: The Customer Is King," *CNNMoney.com,* July 11, 2006.

31. The following section draws heavily from M. Higgins, Craig Mcallaster, Samuel C. Certo, and James P. Gilbert, "Using Cultural Artifacts to Change and Perpetuate Strategy," *Journal of Change Management* 6, no. 4 (December 2006): 397–415.

32. Michelle V. Rafter, "The Hive Mind at Work," *Workforce Management,* May 2010, http://www.workforce.com.

33. This discussion is based on Harrison M. Trice and Janice M. Beyer (Upper Saddle River, NJ: Prentice Hall, 1993), 271–272.

34. J. Kerr and J. W. Slocum Jr., "Managing corporate culture through reward systems," *Academy of Management Executive* 19, no. 4 (2005): 130.

35. This section is based largely on Catherine Filstad, "How Newcomers Use Role Models in Organizational Socialization," *Journal of Workplace Living* 16 (2004): 396–410.

36. Michael Stewart, "The Road to Recovery: Four Crucial Steps to Regain Employees' Trust," *Workforce Management,* June 2010, http://www.workforce.com.

37. "That 'Unique' Organizational Culture at Jones Day: Actually Already the Prevailing Model in Social Media," *Law and More,* May 24, 2010, http://lawandmore.typepad.com Elie Mystal, "New Recruits at Jones Day Better Make Great Pets," *Above the Law,* May 24, 2010, http://abovethelaw.com Elie Mystal, "Jones Day: Secrecy Breeds Strength?" *Above the Law,* September 14, 2009, http://abovethelaw.com.

38. "Use of Corporate Culture to Spur Growth in a Firm," *Africa News,* October 16, 2007.

39. www.cintas.com

40. Farmer, Richard T. "Corporate Culture Defines a Company and Its Future." *Mid-American Journal of Business* 20, no. 2 (2005): 7–9.

41. Ibid.

42. Gottfried, Tatge, Mark, and Miriam. "Dirty Laundry." *Forbes* 178, no. 12 (2006): 120–125.

43. See note 40 above.

44. See note 40 above.

45. See note 40 above.

chapter 20

Encouraging Creativity and Innovation

Target Skill

creativity and innovation skill: the ability to generate original ideas or new perspectives on existing ideas and to take steps to implement these new ideas

objectives

To help build my *creativity and innovation skill*, when studying this chapter, I will attempt to acquire:

1. A definition of *creativity* and an awareness of its importance in organizations

2. Insights about the three components that comprise creativity in individuals

3. Guidelines for how to increase creativity in organizations

4. A definition of innovation and an understanding of the relationship between creativity and innovation

5. An awareness of the innovation process

6. An understanding of total quality as a base for spawning creative ideas

7. Insights about achieving quality and the quality improvement process

CHALLENGE CASE

FOSTERING CREATIVITY AND INNOVATION AT HORMEL FOODS

JEFFREY ETTINGER is the chief executive officer of Hormel Foods Corporation, a multinational manufacturer of meat and food products. The company has more than 15,600 employees and is headquartered in Austin, Minnesota.

Hormel Foods has long enjoyed a strong reputation for innovation. As an example, George A. Hormel, the founder of the company, encouraged his employees to "Originate, don't imitate." This philosophy, which continues today, is largely responsible for Hormel's products, which are highly regarded for quality, taste, nutrition, and value. Products include hams, bacon, sausages, franks, and canned luncheon meats. Perhaps the most easily recognized company label names are Fast 'n Easy, Always Tender, and Jennie-o-Turkey Store.

Probably the best known Hormel product is Spam. Developed in the 1930s by Jay C. Hormel, founder of the company, Spam was initiated as the result of a creative way to use pork shoulder meat left over from pork processing. The leftover pork shoulder was actually thrown away until Hormel came up with the idea for this product. Spam gained national attention during World War II, when it was served to U.S. troops morning, noon, and night. On the home front during the war, Spam became a popular standby when fresh meat was scarce.

Despite the company's long history, Hormel continues to innovate and produce new products. Recently, Hormel introduced a new line of meats that contain proprietary cook-in bags. These bags allow consumers to put the meat in the oven without actually touching the meat; this new packaging helps consumers keep their hands clean during the cooking process. This new packaging is a first for the meat category, and Hormel reports that initial sales have exceeded expectations.

In addition to the new products introduced by the company, Hormel has also used innovative techniques to improve the processes used in its manufacturing facilities. For example, engineers at Hormel recently began using personal digital assistants (PDAs) to monitor the performance of each manufacturing facility. Specifically, these engineers use their PDAs to record statistics about the quality of the company's products and employees. In addition, they use their PDAs to take pictures inside the plants if problems arise; these pictures help them communicate these issues to engineers in other plants.

Hormel Foods management remains committed to providing consumers with high-quality, high-value products that are flavorful, nutritional, and convenient. The company's century-old tradition of product excellence is valued today by management as much as ever before.[1]

■ *Hormel Foods has performed well over its long history by developing creative new products. One of their original products, Spam, continues to sell almost a century after its development.*

EXPLORING YOUR MANAGEMENT SKILL

You can explore your level of creativity and innovation skill **before** studying the chapter by completing the exercise "Exploring Your Management Skill: Part 1" on page 496 and

after studying this chapter by completing the exercise "Exploring Your Management Skill: Part 2" on page 496.

THE CREATIVITY AND INNOVATION CHALLENGE

The Challenge Case discusses how Hormel Foods is experiencing declining revenue caused by both decreasing product demand and lower prices being charged customers. The case emphasizes that company management is faced with the challenge of generating creative ways for dealing with this

declining revenue environment. This chapter covers concepts to help managers such as those at Hormel find creative ways to meet such organizational challenges. Topics covered are (1) creativity, (2) innovation, and (3) total quality management as a catalyst for creativity and innovation.

CREATIVITY

This chapter begins with a focus on *creativity*. Defining creativity, the importance of creativity in organizations, creativity in individuals, and increasing creativity in organizations are discussed in the following sections.

Defining Creativity

Creativity is the ability to generate original ideas or new perspectives on existing ideas.[2] In our modern society, the term *creativity* often sparks thoughts related to the arts or literature and highly original contributions such as those of Michelangelo and his work on the figure of *David*, or Herman Melville and his writing of *Billy Budd*.

Although how best to define creativity from a management viewpoint may be somewhat controversial, creativity in organizations does indeed relate to generating original ideas or new perspectives on existing ideas.[3] Originality or newness, however, is not enough when analyzing creativity from an organizational perspective. An idea must be useful and actionable. Overall, an idea must have a desirable impact on how organizational goals are accomplished. That is, an idea must be evaluated for positive impact on critical organizational factors such as productivity, communication, coordination, or product quality.

Importance of Creativity in Organizations

Creativity involves seeing issues from different angles and breaking away from old rules and norms that bind us to traditional methods of accomplishing tasks. Creativity allows us to be different and helps us find new answers and solutions to problems, both old and new.[4]

The relationship between breaking away from old rules and norms for accomplishing tasks and meeting critical organizational challenges is clear. For example, many managers face the daily challenge of motivating organization members and, as a result, are constantly searching for new ways to encourage employees to be more committed to their work. Additionally, managers often face the challenge of dealing more effectively with competitors and, as a result, commonly search for new ways to increase the quality of their products or develop new and more competitive products. Overall, meeting the challenges of motivating organization members or dealing more effectively with competitors is necessary for ensuring organizational success. Because creativity is the source of new ideas on how to meet such challenges, managers should view creativity as a vital element for ensuring organizational success.

Creativity in Individuals

Within each individual, creativity is a function of three components. These components are expertise, creative thinking skills, and motivation. Figure 20.1 illustrates these three components and depicts how, when overlapping, they result in creativity.

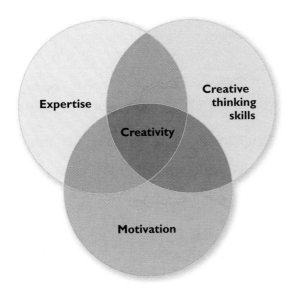

FIGURE 20.1
The three components of creativity

Expertise, as depicted in Figure 20.1, is everything an individual knows and can do in the broad domain of his or her work. This knowledge pertains to work-related techniques and procedures as well as a thorough understanding of overall work circumstances. Take, for example, a produce worker in a supermarket. Her expertise includes basic abilities in trimming and cleaning fresh fruits and vegetables, building appealing displays that encourage customers to buy products, and building customer relations. As with all organization members, the abilities of this produce worker can be acquired through formal education, experience, and interaction with peers and other professionals.

Creative thinking is the capacity to put existing ideas together in new combinations. Overall, creative thinking determines how flexibly and imaginatively individuals approach problems. For example, the produce worker will tend to be more creative if she feels comfortable disagreeing with people about how the produce department presently functions. Such disagreement will often result in new thoughts about how to improve the department, such as keeping produce fresher for longer periods. In addition, she will tend to have more creative success if she keeps plodding along to face and solve department problems, such as buying new technology to keep produce cool and not necessarily always looking for quick problem solutions. This enduring attention to problems will afford the produce worker the attention necessary to generate creative solutions to complex organizational problems.

Motivation, as depicted in Figure 20.1, refers to an individual's need or passion to be creative. If an individual feels a need to be creative, that individual is more likely to do so. Expertise and creative thinking are the individual's raw materials for being creative, but motivation determines whether an individual will actually be creative. An individual can be driven to be creative either extrinsically through organizational rewards and punishments, or intrinsically through personal interest and passion related to a situation.

Activision CEO Bobby Kotick is an example of an individual who is driven to succeed, both extrinsically and intrinsically. A video game enthusiast since childhood, Kotick bought video game company Activision while it was called Mediagenic. Not only did he restore the company's original name, he also restored its culture to one that rewards game developers for their creativity and diligence. Activision grows by acquiring other video game developers, all while striving to nurture and preserve the unique culture of each acquired company and its talented workforce.[5] ■

how managers do it

Promoting Creativity
at Activision

Normally, people will be most creative when motivated by personal interest, satisfaction, and the challenge of the work. Continuing with our supermarket example, the produce worker could have the expertise and critical thinking necessary to be creative, but unless she is motivated, she probably will not be creative. Generally, the produce worker will be more motivated to be creative if she is personally interested in supermarket problems, tends to be personally satisfied by solving these problems, and sees solving the problems as challenging.

Increasing Creativity in Organizations

As discussed, creativity is a critical ingredient for meeting challenges in organizations of all types. Accordingly, managers should conscientiously take specific action aimed at building creativity in organizations. To encourage creativity in organizations, managers can take the steps discussed in the following sections.[6]

Challenge Workers Of all of the steps managers can take to stimulate creativity, perhaps the most effective is providing organization members with an appropriate level of job-related challenge. When people feel appropriately challenged, they seem almost naturally to search for new creative ideas to help perform a job in an improved way. People should not be placed in jobs that are too simple or too difficult. If organization members have jobs that stretch their abilities too little, they can easily become bored on the job and distracted from being creative. If a job stretches worker abilities too much, workers can feel overwhelmed and therefore not inclined to generate creative solutions to job-related problems. Managers must struggle to understand both organization members and their jobs to make sure workers are challenged at a level that encourages creative solutions for meeting job challenges.

Establish Worker Autonomy People tend to be more creative in their jobs if they have some freedom to influence the process used to perform their jobs. Providing this freedom, of course, assumes that organization members have a clear understanding of work goals to be accomplished. Without such understanding, organization member creativity will lack the consistent direction needed to promote organizational success. Overall, creativity is promoted to the best advantage of organizations when members are clear on work goals to accomplish and can exercise some freedom in determining better ways of accomplishing these goals.

Afford Time for Accomplishing Work Appropriate time is commonly discussed as a critical resource that fuels creativity in organization members. Without enough time in which to perform a job appropriately, organization members can be so engaged with simply

In addition to providing plenty of challenging tasks and worker autonomy, Google also allows its employees sufficient time to accomplish their jobs. That includes down time that helps refresh their creative juices. Here, two Google employees use some down time to engage in a light saber duel at the office.

performing a job that generating creative solutions to job-related problems is curbed. Managers who use unnecessarily tight deadlines to push organization members to reach higher levels of production can simultaneously cause employees to feel overly controlled and helpless in terms of being creative.

In the past, many managers believed that organization members normally generated their best creative ideas when operating under tight time constraints. Based on this belief, managers imposed tight deadlines as a tactic for encouraging creativity in organizations. A recent stream of research, however, suggests that time pressures can actually affect creativity in different ways, depending on various other organizational conditions.[7]

The time-pressure/creativity matrix presented in Figure 20.2 illustrates how managers can either encourage or discourage the likelihood of creative thinking in organizations depending on how high and low time pressures are combined with various organizational factors. According to this matrix, given the condition of low time pressure, the likelihood of creativity in an organization could be low if workers feel they're *on autopilot* and get little encouragement to be creative from management. Under the same low time pressure condition, however, the likelihood of creativity in an organization could be high if people feel they're *on an expedition* and thereby are characterized by creativity slanted more towards exploring ideas.

Time Pressure

	Low	High
High	Creative thinking under low time pressure is more likely when people feel as if they are on an expedition. They: • show creative thinking that is more oriented toward generating or exploring ideas than identifying problems. • tend to collaborate with one person rather than with a group.	Creative thinking under extreme time pressure is more likely when people feel as if they are on a mission. They: • can focus on one activity for a significant part of the day because they are undisturbed or protected. • believe that they are doing important work and report feeling positively challenged by and involved in the work. • show creative thinking that is equally oriented toward identifying problems and generating or exploring ideas.
Low	Creative thinking under low time pressure is unlikely when people feel as if they are on autopilot. They: • receive little encouragement from senior management to be creative. • tend to have more meetings and discussions with groups rather than with individuals. • engage in less collaborative work overall.	Creative thinking under extreme time pressure is unlikely when people feel as if they are on a treadmill. They: • feel distracted. • experience a highly fragmented workday, with many different activities. • don't get the sense that the work they are doing is important. • feel more pressed for time than when they are "on a mission" even though they work the same number of hours. • tend to have more meetings and discussions with groups rather than with individuals. • experience lots of last-minute changes in their plans and schedules.

Likelihood of Creative Thinking (vertical axis label)

FIGURE 20.2 Time-pressure/creativity matrix

High time pressure is examined in Figure 20.2. Given the high time pressure condition, the likelihood of creativity in an organization could be high if people feel they're *on a mission* to discover solutions to job-related problems. Under the same high pressure condition, however, the likelihood of creativity in an organization could be low if people feel they're *on a treadmill* and commonly experience extensive last-minute changes to schedules and plans.

Establish Diverse Work Groups

Work groups that are characterized by members with a diversity of perspectives and backgrounds tend to be more creative than groups characterized by members who have similar backgrounds and perspectives. Diversity by itself, however, is simply not enough. To complement this diversity in generating creativity, members of a work group should share excitement for accomplishing the group's work goal(s), be willing to help each other through difficult periods and setbacks, and recognize and respect the differences of unique knowledge and perspective that each group member possesses.

Personally Encourage Workers

As with any other desirable behavior in organizations, managers should personally encourage organization members to be creative. Such encouragement may take many different forms and range from a simple, verbal "thank you," to awarding a Creative Achievement Certificate of Appreciation, to holding a creativity appreciation luncheon.

Because managers are extremely busy and under constant pressure for achieving results, they can be easily distracted from personally encouraging creativity. Organization members often find their work challenging and interesting and can display creativity in the shorter run without much personal encouragement from management. To sustain creativity in organization members over the longer run, however, encouragement from management is vital. Such encouragement assures organization members that creativity is important to the organization and that management values creative efforts, even those that at times may be unsuccessful.

Establish Systems Support

To complement the personal encouragement discussed, organizational systems and procedures should clearly support organization member creativity.[8] Such organizational support clearly identifies organization member creativity as a highly valued endeavor. Organizational procedures that promote information sharing and collaboration as related to solving organizational problems are examples of such a procedure. Additionally, research suggests that managers who are trustworthy and provide employees with developmental feedback help increase employee creativity.[9]

how managers do it

Supporting Employee Creativity at Coca-Cola Company

Coca-Cola Company is often cited for building organizational systems that support employee creativity. At Coca-Cola, being creative is considered an everyday activity, not an activity initiated by some new program or an activity focused on only from time to time. Instead, at Coca-Cola creativity is a constant theme supported throughout the very fabric of the company, including the way organization members interact through meetings and problem-solving collaboration.[10] ∎

Hire and Retain Creative People

As one last tactic for increasing creativity in organizations, managers can attempt to hire and retain organization members who are creative. Although this tactic may sound simple, it can be difficult to implement. Identifying people who are creative can be a formidable challenge. Retaining creative employees is particularly important given research suggesting that individuals' social structures can influence their creativity.[11] In other words, it may help to surround creative employees with other creative employees. To help managers identify creative people, Figure 20.3 contains a list of characteristics that creative people tend to possess.

Creative people tend to be...

...free spirited	...open to new opportunities
...unorthodox	...flexible decision makers
...quiet	...open to taking risk
...introverted	...persistent
...emotional	...tolerant of ambiguity
...challenging reality	...perceptive
...outrageous	...willing to grow
...intuitive	...willing to change
...playful	...tolerant of criticism
...humorous	...moderately concerned with failure
...different	...trying new things

FIGURE 20.3
Characteristics of creative people

INNOVATION

This second major chapter segment builds on the topic of creativity by discussing *innovation*. The discussion focuses on defining innovation, linking innovation and creativity, and the innovation process.

Defining Innovation

The term *innovation* can be defined in several different ways.[12] From a management viewpoint, **innovation** is the process of applying a new idea to the improvement of organizational processes, products, or services. Innovation is critical to the long-run success of virtually any organization. Deployed correctly, the "collective intelligence" of an organization has the power to spark innovation.[13] On the other hand, without innovation, organizations tend to become less competitive and less desirable to customers as well as organization members, and organizations that do not innovate tend to fail.[14] Many management theorists believe that innovation is so critical it not only can fuel the prosperity of organizations, but of nations.[15] To be sure, though, innovation starts with employees. In fact, a recent long-term study of new product development in two organizations reveals that social networks with strong relationships and active participation in decision making help foster innovation.[16] As Arthur Levinson, chairman and chief executive officer of Genentech, one of the world's leading biotechnology companies, has said, "If you want an innovative environment, hire innovative people, listen to them tell you what they want, and do it."[17]

Table 20.1 lists the top ten most innovative companies in the world.

Amazon is known as one of the world's most innovative companies because of its ability to diversify and grow the company in creative ways. Founded in 1994 as an online bookseller, Amazon soon expanded its product lines well beyond books. Today, customers can order electronics, office supplies, toys, and a host of other merchandise from the Amazon Web site—even groceries and automotive supplies. The company has also broadened and diversified its products and services. Its offerings include the Kindle 2 e-reader, an MP3 store, extensive cloud computing services, data storage and computing services, and more.[18]

how managers do it

Innovating for Success at Amazon

TABLE 20.1	The Top Ten Most Innovative Companies
1. Apple	
2. Google	
3. Microsoft	
4. IBM	
5. Toyota	
6. Amazon	
7. LG Electronics	
8. BYD	
9. General Electric	
10. Sony	

Source: Based on "The 50 Most Innovative Companies 2010," *BusinessWeek,* April 26, 2010, http://www.businessweek.com.

Linking Innovation and Creativity

Confusion often exists in organizations over the relationship between innovation and creativity.[19] Basically, innovation involves turning a new idea into new or improved processes, products, or services that promote the attainment of organizational goals. The ideas on which innovation is based come from creativity in the organization. Innovation is the process of turning those ideas into something tangible that benefits the organization. An organization that is creative but not innovative is characterized by a fertile source of good ideas, but lacking in the ability to make the ideas tangible. An organization that is innovative but not creative is characterized by the ability to turn ideas into tangible benefit, but lacking good ideas to make tangible. Figure 20.4 illustrates that organizations can be either creative or innovative, and makes the point that managers should strive to build organizations that are both a source of sound ideas and capable of turning the ideas into tangible benefits for the organization.

FIGURE 20.4

Managers should strive to build organizations that are both creative and innovative

class discussion highlight

MODERN RESEARCH AND CREATIVITY AND INNOVATION SKILL

Previous sections highlighted the importance of creativity and innovation in improving the performance of organizations. Surprisingly, however, there is little research examining the relationship between creativity and innovation. To address this void, researchers examined the relationship between these two concepts while studying a group of 99 entrepreneurs. Specifically, the researchers examined whether two characteristics of the entrepreneur—the entrepreneur's mood (i.e., is the entrepreneur active, enthusiastic, and excited?) as well as the entrepreneur's creativity—influenced his or her company's level of innovation.

What do you think the researchers found? What relationships would you expect between an entrepreneur's mood and creativity and the company's level of innovation? Why would you expect these relationships?

Source: R. A. Baron and J. Tang. In press. "The role of entrepreneurs in firm-level innovation: Joint effects of positive affect, creativity, and environmental dynamism," *Journal of Business Venturing* (2009).

The Innovation Process

Innovation process is defined as the steps managers take to implement creative ideas. In reality, the number of steps that specific implementations require may be debatable. Such steps can range from straightforward steps, such as issuing specific orders to production supervisors, to complicated steps that might include determining the potential value of a planned innovation under consideration. To make managing the innovation process more practical, however, managers can visualize the process as having five main steps: inventing, developing, diffusing, integrating, and monitoring. Each step is discussed here.[20]

STEP 1 **Inventing. Inventing** is defined as the step of the innovation process that establishes a new idea that could help the organization be more successful. The innovation process begins with the determination of some new idea. Consistent with the previous section of this chapter, creativity provides such ideas within organizations. Such ideas naturally vary from organization to organization but usually fall into one of the following categories: technology, product, process, and management.[21]

- **Technology ideas** are ideas that focus on invention that enhances the use of technology within organizations. Technology ideas can cover a broad array of topics and include ideas such as employing barcoding to better manage inventory or using videoconferencing to help organization members across the globe communicate more effectively.

- **Product ideas** are ideas that focus on invention that develops new products or services, or enhances existing products or services. Such ideas can include issues related to product pricing, promoting products in the marketplace, distributing products, packaging products, and advertising products.

- **Process ideas** are ideas that focus on inventions for improving a manufacturing process. Examples of process ideas include adopting robotics to make a manufacturing process more efficient, or redesigning work stations to make workers more productive.

- **Management ideas** are ideas that focus on invention relating to the way in which the organization is managed. These ideas involve management as a whole and center on improving human resource management, redesigning organizational structure, changing organizational leadership, or refining competitive strategy.

One interesting example of inventing in organizations involves a new idea in the photography equipment industry.[22] Eastman Kodak, a major company in this industry, has for decades successfully sold traditional photography products. Over the years, Kodak has been

The giant Boeing 787 Dreamliner passenger aircraft represents an innovative manufacturing process, in which parts are made in a number of different countries and then assembled at Boeing plants in the United States.

especially successfully manufacturing and selling disposable cameras employing traditional film. To better compete with the technology of digital photography in the marketplace, Kodak developed the idea of manufacturing and selling disposable digital cameras. This idea would probably be categorized as a product idea, since the new disposable digital camera is actually a modification of the existing disposable camera employing traditional film.

STEP 2 **Developing. Developing** is defined as that step of the innovation process that makes a new idea practical. After being established in step 1, an idea must next be developed, or made practical as a vehicle for enhancing organizational success. Some creative ideas defy practicality and should never be pursued.[23] On the other hand, some ideas are practical and can focus on diverse areas such as improving cell phone service to attract more customers,[24] adding attractions to a theme park to make it more competitive,[25] or better training to conquer the hurdle of getting professionals both comfortable and effective with operating newly purchased equipment.[26]

3M Company, formerly known as Minnesota Mining and Manufacturing Company, has become world famous for developing new ideas. Perhaps the most well-known 3M innovation is the Post-It note. 3M may have achieved this fame through a formal, simple, and well-established company policy that helps ensure that every idea that deserves to be developed is indeed developed. This policy encourages employees to see if managers in other parts of the company will help develop a new idea after the employee's immediate boss has rejected it.[27]

Eastman Kodak's new idea for establishing a new disposable digital camera illustrates step 1 of the innovation process. Step 2 of the innovation process indicates that this new camera idea must now be made practical. In essence, management must now determine feasible methods for manufacturing and selling the new camera. Such a determination would include where the camera will be manufactured, what suppliers will be involved in manufacturing the camera, and how the camera will be sold.

STEP 3 **Diffusing. Diffusing** is defined as that step of the innovation process that puts a new idea to use by end users or customers. Step 3 of the innovation process takes place after an idea has been established (step 1) and developed (step 2). If the idea is for an improvement to an organizational process, organization members who would be affected by the idea would explore using the idea to test its utility and worth. If the idea is for establishing a new product, perhaps certain customers would be given a prototype product to test the ultimate utility and worth of the product.

In the Eastman Kodak example, the idea for manufacturing and selling a disposable digital camera was established and the new product was made practical in innovation process steps 1 and 2, respectively. In step 3, customers would actually be given prototype disposable digital cameras to enable Kodak to determine camera utility and worth to customers. If customer

FIGURE 20.5 How steps of the innovation process relate to Eastman Kodak's disposable digital camera innovation

feedback is negative at this point, Kodak may wish to discontinue the disposable digital camera project or take additional time to improve the proposed product. If customer feedback is positive at this point, Kodak would probably proceed to the next step of the innovation process.

STEP 4 Integrating. Integrating is defined as that step of the innovation process that establishes an invention as a permanent part of the organization. If the invention focuses on a new organizational process, for example, management takes steps to make the new process standard operating procedure within the organization. If the invention focuses on a new product, management takes steps to start manufacturing and selling the new product to the marketplace.

In the example of relating Kodak's proposed disposable digital camera to the innovation process, the idea for the camera has been established, developed or made practical, and customers have verified the desirable value and worth of the product. Now, in step 4, Kodak management integrates the new idea or makes the new disposable digital camera an established component of the company's product line. In essence, management takes appropriate steps to start manufacturing and selling the new camera.

STEP 5 Monitoring. Monitoring is that step of the innovation process in which a newly implemented idea is tracked to determine if and when the idea should be improved or terminated. Management monitors newly implemented ideas to make sure contributions to organizational success generated by the ideas continues to accrue. As long as implemented ideas continue to make a contribution to organizational success, the useful lives of those ideas continue. When new ideas cease to make a contribution to organizational success, however, the ideas should be improved or terminated.

At this stage of the innovation process in the Kodak example, the idea for the camera was established, was made practical for use, customers endorsed the idea, and the camera is being built and sold. Now Kodak must monitor the contribution the new disposable digital camera makes to organizational success and improve or discontinue it when the contribution becomes unacceptable. Figure 20.5 summarizes the major steps of the innovation process discussed here and shows how the Eastman Kodak disposable digital camera example relates to each step.

This stage in the innovation process often includes *reverse innovation,* which involves taking a concept or a product created for a very specific use and extending it to a new, often larger, audience. For example, General Electric recently announced it would introduce two of its medical devices, formerly sold only in emerging markets, in the United States. The company's $1,000 handheld electrocardiogram device was originally created for physicians who practice in rural areas of India. Its portable, PC-based ultrasound machine was created for use in rural China. By selling these products in the United States, not only will GE realize a profit, it will also make health care more affordable.[28]

CATALYST FOR CREATIVITY AND INNOVATION: TOTAL QUALITY MANAGEMENT

As discussed earlier, creativity spawns new ideas to promote organizational success, and innovation makes those ideas a reality. As also discussed earlier, organization member expertise is normally a significant catalyst in spawning new creative ideas.

This section presents critical insights into building expertise in total quality management (TQM) for both managers and nonmanagers in organizations. This expertise is intended as a wellspring for generating new creative, quality-oriented ideas to promote organizational success. Major topics discussed are the essentials of total quality management and creative ideas based on TQM expertise.

Essentials of Total Quality Management (TQM)

This section outlines the fundamental principles of total quality management. Topics include defining total quality management, the importance of quality in organizations, established quality awards, and the quality improvement process.

Defining Total Quality Management

Quality is defined as how well a product does what it is supposed to do—how closely and reliably it satisfies the specifications to which it is built. Quality is presented as the degree of excellence on which products or services can be ranked on the basis of selected features.

Total quality management (TQM) is the continuous process of involving all organization members in ensuring that every activity related to the production of goods or services has an appropriate role in establishing product quality.[29] In other words, all organization members emphasize the appropriate performance of activities throughout the company to maintain the quality of products offered by the company. Under the TQM concept, organization members work both individually and collectively to maintain the quality of products offered to the marketplace.

Although the TQM movement actually began in the United States, its establishment, development, and growth throughout the world are largely credited to the Japanese. The Japanese believe that a TQM program should be companywide and must include the cooperation of all people within a company. Top managers, middle managers, supervisors, and workers throughout the company must strive together to ensure that all phases of company operations appropriately affect product quality. The company operations referred to include areas such as market research, research and development, product planning, design, production, purchasing, vendor management, manufacturing, inspection, sales, after-sales customer care, financial control, personnel administration, and company training and education.

The Importance of Quality

Many managers and management theorists warn that U.S. organizations without high-quality products will soon be unable to compete in the world marketplace. A 1990 book by Armand V. Feigenbaum put the problem succinctly:

> **Quality. Remember it? American manufacturing has slumped a long way from the glory days of the 1950s and 1960s when "Made in the U.S.A." proudly stood for the best that**

Total Quality Management is a robust quality process whose development is largely credited to Japanese managers. Here Motorola employees participate in a Total Quality Management training course.

industry could turn out.... While the Japanese were developing remarkably higher standards for a whole host of products, from consumer electronics to cars and machine tools, many U.S. managers were smugly dozing at the switch. Now, aside from aerospace and agriculture, there are few markets left where the U.S. carries its own weight in international trade. For American industry, the message is simple: Get Better or Get Beat.[30]

Producing high-quality products is not an end in itself. Rather, successfully offering high-quality goods and services to the marketplace typically results in three important ends for the organization: a positive company image, lower costs and higher market share, and decreased product liability costs.

POSITIVE COMPANY IMAGE A reputation for high-quality products creates a positive image for an organization, and organizations gain many advantages from having such an image. A positive image helps a firm recruit valuable new employees, accelerate sales of its new products, and obtain needed loans from financial institutions. To summarize, high-quality products generally result in a positive company image, which leads to numerous organizational benefits.[31]

LOWER COSTS AND HIGHER MARKET SHARE Activities that support product quality benefit the organization by yielding lower costs and greater market share. Figure 20.6 illustrates this point. As shown in the top half of this figure, greater market share or gain in product sales is a direct result of customer perception of improved product quality. As shown in the bottom half of the figure, organizational activities that contribute to product quality result in such benefits as increased productivity, lower rework and scrap costs, and lower warranty costs, which, in turn, result in lower manufacturing costs and lower costs of servicing products after they are sold. Figure 20.6 also makes the important point that both greater market share and lower costs attributed to high quality normally result in greater organizational profits.

FIGURE 20.6 TQM typically results in greater market share and lower costs

DECREASED PRODUCT LIABILITY COSTS Product manufacturers are increasingly facing costly legal suits over damages caused by faulty products. More and more frequently, organizations that design and produce faulty products are being held liable in the courts for damages resulting from the use of such products. To take one dramatic example, Pfizer, a company that develops mechanical heart valves, recently settled an estimated 180 lawsuits by heart-implant patients claiming that the valves used in their implants were faulty.[32] Successful TQM efforts typically result in improved products and product performance, and the normal result of improved products and product performance is lower product liability costs.

Established Quality Awards Recognizing all these benefits of quality, U.S. companies have placed significant emphasis on manufacturing high-quality products. Several major awards have been established in the United States and abroad to recognize those organizations that produce exceptionally high-quality products and services. The most prestigious international award is the Deming Award, established in Japan in honor of W. Edwards Deming, who introduced Japanese firms to statistical quality control and quality improvement techniques after World War II. The most widely known award in the United States is the Malcolm Baldrige National Quality Award, awarded by the American Society of Quality and Control. This award was established in 1988.[33]

As these examples suggest, quality is an increasingly important element in an organization's ability to compete in today's global marketplace.

The Quality Improvement Process Two approaches may be taken to improve quality. The first is the one advocated by most of the quality experts. This process can be described as "incremental improvement"—or improve one thing at a time. Actually, many incremental improvements may be undertaken simultaneously throughout an organization; recall Toyota's average of instituting 5,000 improvements per day in 1982.

The second approach, advocated by Michael Hammer, consists of completely reengineering a process.[34] This approach requires starting with a clean slate. Management looks at operations and asks, "If we were to start over today, how would we do this?"

Each approach is discussed in detail in the following sections.

THE INCREMENTAL IMPROVEMENT PROCESS Researchers and consultants have advocated a variety of incremental approaches to achieving excellent quality in products and processes. Despite their differences, almost all of these plans bear some remarkable similarities. Although a specific improvement process may not precisely follow the outline in Figure 20.7, most such processes at least approximate it.

- **Step 1: An area of improvement is chosen, which often is called the improvement "theme"**—Either management or an improvement team may choose the theme. Examples are:
  - Reduction in production cycle time
  - Increase in the percentage of nondefective units produced
  - Reduction in the variability of raw material going into production
  - Increase in on-time deliveries
  - Reduction in machine downtime
  - Reduction in employee absenteeism

    Many other examples are possible, of course, but these suffice to make the point that an improvement objective must be chosen.

    Consider a pizza company whose delivery business is lagging behind that of its competitors, chiefly because of slow deliveries. The improvement theme in this case may be a reduction in delivery time (i.e., cycle time).

- **Step 2: If a quality improvement team has not already been organized, one is organized**—Members of this team might include:
  - One or more associates directly responsible for the work being done
  - One or more customers receiving the benefits of the work

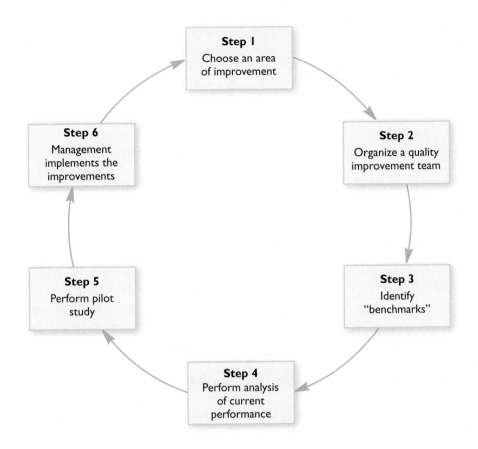

FIGURE 20.7
The incremental approach to improving quality

- One or more suppliers providing input into the work

- A member of management

- Perhaps one or more experts in areas particularly relevant to solving the problem and making the improvement

For the pizza delivery company, the team might include two pizza builders, a driver, a university student customer, a local resident customer, and a store manager.

- **Step 3: The team "benchmarks" the best performers—that is, identifies how much improvement is required to match the best performance**—For example, the pizza company may discover in this step that the benchmark (i.e., the fastest average time between the moment an order is taken until the moment of front-door delivery) established by a competitor is 20 minutes.

  Suppose the company's current average delivery performance is 35 minutes. That leaves a minimum possible improvement of 15 minutes on the average.

- **Step 4: The team performs an analysis to find out how current performance can be improved to meet, or beat, the benchmark**—Factors to be analyzed here include potential problems related to equipment, materials, work methods, people, and the environment, such as legal constraints, physical conditions, and weather. To return to the pizza delivery company, suppose the team discovered that the pizza-building process could be shortened by 4 minutes. Also suppose they found an average lag of 5 minutes between the time the pizza is ready and the time the delivery van picks it up. Finally, suppose the team discovered that a different oven could shorten cooking time by 7 minutes. Total potential savings in delivery time, then, would be 16 minutes—which would beat the benchmark by 1 minute.

  The popular phrase "Necessity is the mother of invention" serves as a reminder that, in some cases, constraints—both within and outside the organization—can actually provide the impetus for innovation.[35]

- **Step 5: The team performs a pilot study to test the selected remedies to the problem**—In the pizza case, suppose the team conducted a pilot program for a month, during which time the new pizza-building process was implemented, a new driver and van were added, and a new oven was rented. At the end of the month, suppose actual improvement was 17 minutes on average.

The question then becomes, "Is the improvement worth the cost?" In this case, the improved pizza-building process is improving other customer service as well, thereby increasing the company's overall sales capacity. By beating the benchmark, the company can establish a new delivery system standard—a significant marketing advantage. Suppose, then, that a cost–benefit study favors the changes.

- **Step 6: Management implements the improvements**—Making many such incremental improvements can greatly enhance a company's competitiveness. Of course, as more and more companies achieve better and better quality, the market will become more and more demanding. The key, therefore, is to continually improve both product and process.

REENGINEERING IMPROVEMENTS Hammer argues that significant improvement requires "breaking away from . . . outdated rules and . . . assumptions." It demands a complete rethinking of operations. He, too, recommends that management organize a team representing the functional units involved in the process to be reengineered, as well as other units that depend on the process.

One important reason for reengineering instead of attempting incremental improvements is the need to integrate computerized production and information systems. This change is expensive and one that is difficult to accomplish piecemeal through an incremental approach.

Hammer outlines seven principles of reengineering:

- **Principle 1: Organize around outcomes, not tasks**—Traditionally, work has been organized around different tasks, such as sawing, typing, assembling, and supervising. This first principle of reengineering would, instead, have one person or team performing all the steps in an identified process. The person or team would be responsible for the outcome of the total process.

- **Principle 2: Have those who use the output of the process perform the process**—For example, a production department may do its own purchasing, and even its own cost accounting. This principle would require a broader range of expertise from individuals and teams, and a greater integration of activities.

- **Principle 3: Subsume information-processing work into the real work that produces the information**—Modern computer technology now makes it possible for a work process to process information simultaneously. For example, scanners at checkout counters in grocery stores both process customer purchases and update accounting and inventory records at the same time.

- **Principle 4: Treat geographically dispersed resources as though they were centralized**—Hammer uses Hewlett-Packard as an example of how this principle works. Each of the company's 50 manufacturing units had its own purchasing department, which prevented the company from achieving the benefits of scale discounts. Rather than centralize purchasing, which would have reduced responsiveness to local manufacturing needs, Hewlett-Packard introduced a corporate unit to coordinate local purchases, so that scale discounts could be achieved. That way, local purchasing units retained their decentralized authority and preserved their local responsiveness.

- **Principle 5: Link parallel activities instead of integrating their results**—Several processes are often required to produce products and services. Too often, though, companies segregate these processes so that the product comes together only at the final stage. Meanwhile, problems may occur in one or more processes, and those problems may not become apparent until too late, at the final step. It is better, Hammer says, to coordinate the various processes so that such problems are avoided.

- **Principle 6: Put the decision point where the work is performed and build control into the process**—Even though traditional bureaucracies separate decision authority from the work, this principle suggests that the people doing the work are the ones who should make the decisions about that work. The salesperson should have the authority and responsibility to approve credit, for example. This principle saves time and allows the organization to respond more effectively and efficiently to customer needs.

Some managers worry that this principle will reduce control over the process. However, control can be built into the process. In the example cited, criteria for credit approval can be built into a computer program, so the salesperson has guidance for every credit decision.

- **Principle 7: Capture information once and at the source**—Computerized online databases help make this principle achievable. It is now easy to collect information when it originates, store it, and send it to those who need it.

Reengineering allows major improvements to be made all at once. Although reengineering can be an expensive way to improve quality, today's rapidly changing markets sometimes demand such a drastic response—even and especially when firms experience poor performance.[36]

Creative Ideas Based on TQM Expertise

Expertise in TQM—understanding TQM principles—can serve as a foundation for generating creative ideas in organizations. Indeed, the number of creative ideas that can be spawned by TQM expertise seems limitless. Keep in mind, however, that an idea that may seem new and creative in one organization may not seem new and creative in another because it has already been considered.

The following sections discuss several possible new ideas for organizations based on the work of Phillip B. Crosby and W. Edwards Deming, two internationally acclaimed quality experts.[37]

Possible Creative Ideas Based on Crosby's Work Philip B. Crosby is known throughout the world as an expert in the area of quality and is considered a pioneer of the quality movement in the United States.[38] His work provides managers with valuable insights on how to achieve product quality. According to Crosby, organizational integrity, systems, communications, operations, and policies must all be consistent with achieving product quality before significant progress in reaching product quality can be reached and maintained. Several possible creative ideas based on Crosby's work for how to achieve quality in organizations are listed in Figure 20.8.

Possible Creative Ideas Based on Deming's Work W. Edwards Deming, who originally trained as a statistician and began teaching statistical quality control in Japan shortly after World War II, is recognized internationally as a primary contributor to Japanese quality improvement programs. Deming advocated that the way to achieve product quality is continuously to improve the design of a product and the process used to manufacture it.[39] According to Deming, management has the primary responsibility for achieving product quality. Several possible creative ideas based on Deming's work for how to achieve quality in organizations are listed in Figure 20.9.

FIGURE 20.8
Possible creative ideas for enhancing organizational success based on Crosby's thoughts about TQM

1. Dedicate the quality management function to measuring conformance to requirements and reporting and differences accurately.
2. Continually inform all employees about the progress of quality improvement and related successes.
3. Begin each management meeting with a factual and financial review of quality.
4. Create relevant policies on quality management that are clear and unambiguous.
5. Educate suppliers to ensure that they will deliver quality materials in a dependable fashion.
6. Dedicate top management to having customers receive products as promised.
7. Dedicate all managers to getting jobs done correctly the first time.
8. Develop communication systems that allow employees to inform management immediately about any observed deviations from quality.
9. Develop communications systems that allow managers to respond immediately to quality issues.
10. Establish an organizational bias toward handling quality issues immediately.

1. Publish quality goals for all workers so they know exactly what they are expected to do.

2. Use product inspections to improve the manufacturing process and to reduce costs.

3. Choose your suppliers on the basis of how they can support your quality goals.

4. Train for maintaining quality.

5. Drive out fear of reporting mistakes.

6. Build teams (not just individuals) that focus on quality.

7. Eliminate production processes based simply on producing a quota.

8. Create production processes based upon learning how to improve the processes.

9. Build pride for maintaining quality.

10. Encourage self-development of workers as more useful players in maintaining quality.

FIGURE 20.9
Possible creative ideas for enhancing organizational success based on Deming's thoughts about TQM

CHALLENGE CASE SUMMARY

The Challenge Case points out that Hormel Foods management is faced with finding creative ways to deal with declining revenue. In essence, Hormel management must seek original ideas or ideas based on existing conditions at Hormel that will help management meet this challenge. The ideas must not only be original, but also be useful and actionable. That is, the ideas must help Hormel as a company become more productive, communicate more effectively, achieve better coordination, and enhance product quality. Such ideas are important because they will help Hormel break away from old rules and norms about accomplishing tasks. At Hormel, the expertise, motivation level, and creative thinking skills of organization members will be the foundation on which creative ideas will be conceived.

Earlier information provides insights to managers such as those at Hormel regarding how to encourage creativity within the company. For example, managers at Hormel can encourage creativity by making sure workers are challenged just enough. Worker abilities should be stretched, but not so overwhelmed that workers give up on being creative. As another example, Hormel managers should make sure workers have an appropriate level of freedom in their jobs. Workers with such freedom are prone to experiment somewhat to find creative solutions to job challenges.

One of the most important steps Hormel managers can take to encourage creativity in organization members is to manage time pressure carefully. Depending on whether Hormel organization members feel they're on autopilot, on an expedition, on a mission, or on a treadmill, time pressure can either encourage or discourage creativity. Hormel managers must find the right combination of time pressure and other organizational conditions to make sure creativity is encouraged within the company.

Hormel management should focus not only on searching for creative ideas, but on innovation, or putting those ideas into action. As an example, assume that to meet its low revenue trend challenge, the company has generated the creative idea of establishing a new class of fast-cooking pork loin products with various flavoring, including spicy Western barbecue and teriyaki.

Based on the earlier discussion of the innovation process, this concept of a new class of pork loin products would indeed be an invention—a new idea. Additionally, the idea would be a *product idea*, or invention that focuses on developing new products. After generating this new product idea, Hormel management must develop the idea, or make it practical. Management must focus on where the new product will be manufactured, who will sell the product, and how the best product flavors will be developed. Once the idea is made practical, it must be diffused, or market tested. Management must assess the true potential of the new product. After the new pork loin product has been market tested with favorable results, the new product must be integrated, or made available to the marketplace. Once integrated, the new pork loin product must be monitored to make sure its contribution to organizational success continues.

Based on earlier information, Hormel management must realize that expertise in total quality management can serve as a stimulus for generating creative ideas within the company. As such, Hormel management should take steps to educate itself as well as other organization members about what TQM entails. All Hormel organization members should know that product quality, and adherence to specifications, must be maintained throughout the product lines. The new pork loin products being offered as a new idea must have specifications regarding issues such as weight, thickness, and freshness that must be constantly maintained. Hormel organization members should realize that TQM within the company should be a continuous process involving everyone within the company, from management to salespeople to meat cutters.

Hormel has much to gain from maintaining product quality. Through product quality, Hormel will gain a positive image both inside and outside the organization. Such an image can be especially valuable when trying to recruit new and talented management. High product quality can also help Hormel lower costs and gain market share. Gaining market share would be particularly valuable in Hormel's present declining revenue environment. Last, Hormel's high product quality can decrease liability costs. Consumers' legal suits over tainted meat, for example, can be minimized. To maximize the benefit of high product quality, Hormel management may opt to apply for the Malcolm Baldrige Award.

Hormel management can deliberate on improving quality either incrementally or through reengineering. Incremental improvement would focus on improving Hormel quality slowly and over time. Reengineering improvement would focus on improving Hormel quality through more drastic improvement in the nearer term.

Assume that Hormel management has decided to focus on improving quality at Hormel incrementally. Improving quality incrementally would involve steps such as targeting an area at Hormel for quality improvement, establishing a quality improvement team to effect desired improvements, identifying benchmarks or standards for quality, comparing current Hormel operations with the benchmarks, and performing a pilot study to see that formulated improvement activities are effective and efficient. Naturally, if the activities actually work, management would opt to adopt the activities as normal operating procedure.

Hormel management can study the work of both Crosby and Deming to gain possible new ideas for implementing and maintaining the company quality improvement process. Such ideas could include building an organization culture that has a bias for handling quality issues quickly and emphatically, dedicating top management to having customers receive all products as promised, and training organization members in how to build product quality.

MANAGEMENT SKILL ACTIVITIES

This section is specially designed to help you develop creativity and innovation skill. An individual's creativity and innovation skill is based on an understanding of creativity and innovation concepts and the ability to apply those concepts in management situations. As a result, the following activities are designed both to heighten your understanding of creativity and innovation concepts and to help you gain facility in applying these concepts in various management situations.

UNDERSTANDING CREATIVITY AND INNOVATION CONCEPTS

 To check your understanding and to practice using the concepts in this chapter, go to www.mymanagementlab.com and explore the material associated with Chapter 20.

Know Key Terms

Understanding the following key terms is critical to your understanding of chapter material. Define each of these terms. Refer to the page(s) referenced after a term to check your definition or to gain further insight regarding the term.

creativity **478**
innovation **483**
innovation process **485**
inventing **485**

developing **486**
diffusing **486**
integrating **487**
monitoring **487**

quality **488**
total quality management (TQM) **488**

Know How Management Concepts Relate

This section is comprised of activities that will further sharpen your understanding of management concepts. Answer essay questions as completely as possible. Also, remember that many additional true/false and multiple choice questions appear online at MyManagementLab.com to help you further refine your understanding of management concepts.

1. Define and describe the relationships between expertise, creative thinking skills, motivation, and creativity.

2. Explain the differences between creativity and innovation.
3. Describe five ways that organizations might increase creativity.
4. Describe the five steps of the innovation process.
5. Define total quality management (TQM), and describe the relationship between TQM and innovation.

DEVELOPING MANAGEMENT SKILLS

Learning activities in this section are aimed at helping you develop your creativity and innovation skill. Learning activities include Exploring Your Management Skill: Parts 1 and 2, Experiential Exercises, Cases, and a VideoNet Exercise.

Exploring Your Management Skill: Part 1

Before studying this chapter, respond to the following questions regarding the type of advice you would give to Hormel Food's Jeffrey Ettinger, referenced in the Challenge Case. Then address the concerning creativity and innovation challenges that he presently faces within the company. You are not expected to be a creativity and innovation expert at this point. Answering the questions now can help you focus on important points when you study the chapter. Also, answering the questions again after you study the chapter will give you an idea of how much you have learned.

Record your answers here or go to MyManagementLab.com. Recording your answers in MyManagementLab will allow you to get immediate results and see how your score compares to your classmates. If you answer the questions in the book, the answers are located in the Exploring Your Management Skill Appendix at the end of the book.

FOR EACH STATEMENT CIRCLE:

- "Y" if you would give the advice to Ettinger.
- "N" if you would NOT give the advice to Ettinger.
- "NI" if you have no idea whether you would give the advice to Ettinger.

Mr. Ettinger, in meeting your creativity and innovation challenges at Hormel Foods, you should...

Before   After
Study   Study

1. reward Hormel's employees for extending old ideas and discourage them from producing new ideas.
    Y, N, NI

2. increase employee creativity by encouraging employees to ignore organizational goals.
    Y, N, NI

3. understand that creativity and motivation are distinct concepts that bear little relationship.
    Y, N, NI

4. establish and encourage worker autonomy to promote creativity within Hormel.
    Y, N, NI

5. establish support systems within Hormel that encourage creativity.
    Y, N, NI

6. limit diversity within work groups to encourage creativity.
    Y, N, NI

7. reinforce to Hormel's employees that creativity and innovation are interchangeable terms that have the same meaning.
    Y, N, NI

8. understand the first step in Hormel's innovation process is monitoring.
    Y, N, NI

9. recognize that one of the important steps in the innovation process is integrating, which entails establishing a new product or process as a permanent part of Hormel.
    Y, N, NI

10. promote total quality management within Hormel as a technique that complements creativity and innovation.
    Y, N, NI

11. encourage innovation at Hormel, as innovation turns sound ideas into tangible benefit.
    Y, N, NI

12. understand that total quality management will address the quality of Hormel's products but will not address the quality of the firm's processes.
    Y, N, NI

13. recognize that total quality management is particularly important in the United States, because the principles of TQM were initially developed in the United States.
    Y, N, NI

14. promote total quality management within Hormel, because it has the ability to simultaneously increase market share and lower costs.
    Y, N, NI

15. view TQM as a quick fix to remedy any production processes at Hormel.
    Y, N, NI

Exploring Your Management Skill: Part 2

As you recall, you completed Exploring Your Management Skill before you started to study this chapter. Your responses gave you an idea of how much you initially knew about creativity and innovation and helped you focus on important points as you studied the chapter. Answer the Exploring Your Management Skill questions again now and compare your score to the first time you took it. This comparison will give you an idea of how much you have learned from studying this chapter and pinpoint areas for further clarification before you start studying the next chapter. Record your answers within the text or go to MyManagementLab.com. Recording your answers in MyManagementLab will allow you to get immediate results and see how your score compares to your classmates. If you answer the questions in the book, the answers are located in the Exploring Your Management Skill Appendix at the end of the book.

Your Management Skills Portfolio

Your Management Learning Portfolio is a collection of activities especially designed to demonstrate your management knowledge and skill. By completing these online at MyManagement.com, you will be able to print, complete with cover sheet, as many activities as you choose. Be sure to save your work. Taking your printed portfolio to an employment interview could be helpful in obtaining a job.

The portfolio activity for this chapter is Innovating at Electronic Arts. Study the information and complete the exercises that follow.[40]

Although creativity and innovation are important for all companies, these terms are the essence of many companies. An example of such a company is Electronic Arts (EA), a company based in Redwood City, California, that develops, produces, markets, and distributes video games such as Tiger Woods PGA Golf, Medal of Honor, and Madden NFL.

EA is currently interested in diversifying its product line to include more video games for younger children. EA's management team views this age group as a prime target market for new video games. Specifically, EA wants you to develop a game that helps preschool through elementary school-aged children further develop their math skills. In other words, your mission is to develop a new product idea.

In the following sections, record your answers as you walk through the five steps of the innovation process.

1. *Inventing:* Describe the main characteristics of your new video game (i.e., What will the children do in the new game? How will it help them develop their math skills?).

2. *Developing:* Describe how you can make the new video game practical for EA.

3. *Diffusing:* How would you test the new video game's utility and worth?

4. *Integrating:* How would you make the new video game a permanent part of the organization?

5. *Monitoring:* Describe how you monitor the new video game and determine the extent to which the new game is helping EA.

Experiential Exercises

1 Using Your Creativity and Innovation

Creativity and innovation are important for organizational success. NBC has contacted your group to help create a new comedy series that will consist of five-minute episodes that NBC will broadcast on its Web site. NBC's executives want this comedy series to appeal to college-aged individuals. To be clear, NBC does not want your group to create this new series—NBC has the employees necessary to approach this project. Instead, NBC's executives want your group to outline the most important techniques it can use to foster the creativity and innovation it needs within its company. In your group, create five different recommendations (and provide examples) to help NBC foster creativity within the organization. Be prepared to present these recommendations in class.

2 You and Your Career

The previous sections have highlighted the importance of creativity for organizational success. As such, organizations will continue to search for creative employees. How would you rate your own creativity skills? What evidence do you have to support your rating? Think about an interview with a potential employer who is searching for creative employees. How would you use examples from your life to demonstrate your creative skills? In addition to helping you obtain a job, your creative skills might help you advance in an organization. If you currently hold a job, how might you demonstrate your creative skills to your manager?

VideoNet Exercise

Change and Innovation at TerraCycle

Video Highlights

TerraCycle is coming out with several new products, one of which is a new fire log—a more earth-friendly, pressed log made out of shredded wax cardboard (e.g., recycled milk and juice containers), scrap wood chips from furniture manufacturers, and recycled glycerin. It will be wrapped in recycled newspaper, and the only "new" part of this product will be its sticker. Tom gets orders for products that are still in development and often only has a few months to deliver. What's the method behind the madness, or is there one? Why is innovation so critical to the company's success? How does a small company like TerraCycle have an edge over many larger companies when it comes to product development cycles?

Discussion Questions

1. How does TerraCycle encourage creativity in its organization?
2. How does TerraCycle manage to successfully link innovation and creativity?
3. How important is creativity in achieving success at TerraCycle? Why?

Internet Activity

Go to TerraCycle's home page at www.TerraCycle.net. Learn more about the different products offered by this company. Can the innovation process discussed in the chapter be applied to the development of the different types of products offered by this firm? Explain.

CASES

1 CREATIVE SOLUTIONS AT HORMEL FOODS

"Fostering Creativity and Innovation at Hormel Foods" (p. 477) and its related Challenge Case Summary sections were written to help you better understand the management concepts contained in this chapter. Answer the following discussions about the Challenge Case to better understand how the concepts of creativity and innovation can be applied in a company such as Hormel.

1. Is creativity or innovation more important to Hormel management in facing a declining revenue environment? Explain fully.
2. If you were the top manager at Hormel, name two organizational systems you would establish to encourage organization member creativity. Be as specific as possible. Why are these systems important to the future success of Hormel?
3. List three creative ideas based on your TQM expertise that, if implemented, would ensure Hormel's future success. Be sure to explain how each idea would contribute to that success.

2 INVENTABLES SELLS INNOVATION

Read the case and answer the questions that follow. Studying this case will help you better understand how concepts relating to innovation can be applied in a company such as Inventables.

Today's organization relies heavily on innovation. Development of new products, finding efficient means to deliver services to customers, or simply improving manufacturing processes are all innovative practices sought by companies. But one firm has crafted a business out of innovation itself.

Inventables, a Chicago-based company, helps other firms solve problems in a very unique way. Inventables connects sellers of innovative materials and technologies to businesses. The firm does not actually manufacture anything. In fact, it even *sells* new technologies and materials. It simply provides a venue for creative marketers and engineers to reach out to inventors.

When the company first started in 2003, Inventables mailed a huge package of items to big name companies like Nike, BMW, Boeing, Motorola, and Procter & Gamble. The idea was to inspire creative teams at these firms to use new-to-the-market ideas. These businesses eagerly paid the $63,000 subscription fee to garner these packages from Inventables. However, that business model has changed. Now, companies simply visit the Inventables Web site and see what's available.

Co-founded by college buddies, Zach Kaplan and Keith Schacht, the company has grown to become an international venture with "technology hunters" who scour the world for undiscovered innovations. Some of these ideas could almost be perceived as science fiction. Inventables has a textured glass that changes color as the temperature changes. It also represents a steel foil that is transparent. Or how about a surface coating that is resistant to ice, corrosion, and bacteria? Or consider a substance that looks like glass and breaks like glass, but feels like rubber. These and hundreds more are available through Inventables.[41]

The application for each new idea may not be readily apparent, but that's part of Inventables' charm—give companies material and technologies and let the creative process happen. "The unexpected property expands your understanding of what's possible," said Kaplan, the CEO of Inventables.[42]

On Inventables' Web site, one can view—free of charge—many of the innovative products the company has found. Savvy inventors who want a wider audience are encouraged to approach the Inventables team and have their ideas showcased on the Web site. These inventors pay only when they decide to pursue a lead generated through the site. In other words, Inventables serves as a clearinghouse for ideas and does not profit from the actual sale of those ideas. According to Kaplan, "We're really creating the platform to get people communicating. We create a common language and increase the chance that the exchange will be worth the user's time."[43]

An example of a company that has benefited from a partnership with Inventables is Antoine Amrani Chocolates. Inventables provided the chocolate company with an edible substance that adds a decorative shimmer to chocolate, thereby attracting more customers. It's something quite simple, but it provides enough differentiation for the company to stand out among competitors.

Another example is the Palm Treo Pro. The cradle for this state-of-the-art smartphone uses a micro-suction tape. On the tape's surface are thousands of tiny suction cups. These barely perceptible suction cups replace adhesives. Thanks to Palm's partnership with Inventables, users of the Palm Treo Pro can now set their smartphone cradle on most surfaces and it won't slip or slide, and it never leaves a sticky residue.

While many companies are closely guarding their innovations and new product developments, Inventables is making available all manner of new ideas to the marketplace. In addition,

it is providing a venue for inventors to gain a foothold in what could be a very lucrative environment. At one time, if an inventor developed a new material or technology, he or she had to also identify an application for it. But, through Inventables, the inventor only has to show the idea and let other firms determine how best to apply that idea.

QUESTIONS

1. How has Inventables changed the innovation process in American businesses?

2. Discuss how creativity and innovation are linked at Inventables.

3. If you were Zach Kaplan, how would you innovate Inventables even further?

Endnotes

1. This case based on Lauren R. Hartman, "Flat-Bottomed Pouch Is Oven-Ready," *Packaging Digest* 44, no. 5 (2007): 64–66; and Rod R. Kekkonen, "Hormel Gets Technical," *Industrial Engineer* 39, no. 7 (2007): 38–43.

2. For an excellent review of research on creativity, see Mark Runco, "Creativity," *Annual Review of Psychology* 55 (2004): 657–687.

3. Cameron M. Ford, "Creative Developments in Creativity Theory," *The Academy of Management Review* 25, no. 2 (April 2000): 284–285. For an interesting study examining creativity in the advertising industry, see Andrew Von Nordneflycht, "Is public ownership bad for professional service firms? Ad agency ownership, performance, and creativity," *Academy of Management Journal* 50, no. 2 (2007): 429–445.

4. David K. Carson, "The Importance of Creativity in Family Therapy: A Preliminary Consideration," *Family Journal* 7, no. 4 (October 1999): 326–334.

5. Jeff Cork, "Bobby Kotick Traces His Roots, Announces Indie Game Competition," *Game Informer*, February 18, 2010, http://gameinformer.com.

6. This section is based on Theresa M. Amabile, "How to Kill Creativity," *Harvard Business Review* 76, no. 5 (September–October 1998): 77–89.

7. Teresa M. Amabile, Constance N. Hadley, and Steven J. Kramer, "Creativity Under the Gun," *Harvard Business Review* 80, no. 8 (August 2002): 52–61. See also Markus Baer & Greg R. Oldham, "The curvilinear relation between experienced creative time pressure and creativity: Moderating effects of openness to experience and support for creativity," *Journal of Applied Psychology* 91, no. 4 (2006): 963–970.

8. For more information on the cross-level factors that foster creativity, see Giles Hirst, Daan Van Knippenberg, and Jing Zhou. A cross-level perspective on employee creativity: Goal orientation, team learning behavior, and individual creativity. *Academy of Management Journal*, 52, no. 2 (2009): 280–293.

9. Jennifer M. George and Jing Zhou, "Dual tuning in a supportive context: Joint contributions of positive mood, negative mood, and supervisory behaviors to employee creativity," *Academy of Management Journal* 50, no. 3 (2007): 605–622.

10. John J. Kao, "The Art & Discipline of Business Creativity," *Strategy & Leadership* 25, no. 4 (July/August 1997): 6–11.

11. Jill E. Perry-Smith, "Social yet creative: The role of social relationships in facilitating individual creativity," *Academy of Management Journal* 49, no. 1 (2006): 85–101.

12. Howard Schlossberg, "Innovation: An Elusive Commodity with Many Definitions," *Marketing News* 25, no. 8 (April 15, 1991): 11.

13. For an interesting discussion of how some organizations use collective intelligence to innovate effectively, see "A Billion Brains Are Better Than One," *MIT Sloan Management Review*, March 18, 2010, http://sloanreview.mit.edu.

14. James M. Higgins, *Innovate or Evaporate: Test & Improve Your Organization's IQ* (Winter Park, FL: The New Management Publishing Company, 1995). See also Shalini Khazanchi, Marianne Lewis, and Kenneth Boyer, "Innovation-supportive culture: The impact of organizational values on process innovation," *Journal of Operations Management* 25, no. 4 (2007): 871–884.

15. John Kao, *Innovation Nation* (New York: Free Press, 2007).

16. Bob Kijkuit and Jan van den Ende, "With a Little Help from Our Colleagues: A Longitudinal Study of Social Networks for Innovation," *Organization Studies* 31, no. 4 (2010): 451–479.

17. Jena McGregor, "Special Report: 25 most innovative companies," *BusinessWeek*, May 14, 2007, 52–60.

18. Chuck Salter, "Most Innovative Companies 2010," *Fast Company*, February 17, 2010, http://www.fastcompany.com.

19. For more information on the link between creativity and innovation, see Bob Kijkuit and Jan van den Ende, "The Organizational Life of an Idea: Integrating Social Network, Creativity and Decision-Making Perspectives," *Journal of Management Studies* 44, no. 6 (2007): 863–882.

20. This discussion is based on D. R. Nayak and J. M. Ketteringham, *Breakthroughs* (New York: Rawson Associates, 1986).

21. James Higgins, *101 Creative Problem Solving Techniques: The Handbook of New Ideas for Business* (Winter Park, FL: The New Management Publishing Company, 1994), 9–10.

22. John C. Dvorak, "Razors with No Blades," *Forbes*, October 18, 1999, 168.

23. Claire Beale, "Strategic Thinking Will Never Rescue a Poor Creative Idea," *Campaign*, August 24, 2001, 14.

24. Tim Hanrahan, "New Cellphone Service Helps Find Friends and Place to Hang Out," *Wall Street Journal*, May 22, 2003, B1.

25. Bruce Orwall, "Universal's Anxious Summer," *Wall Street Journal*, May 22, 2003, B1.

26. Kristinha McCort, "Learning a New Definition," *Millimeter* 29, no. 11 (November 2001): 29–32.

27. Frances Horibe, "Innovation, Creativity, and Improvement," *The Canadian Manager* 28, no. 2 (Spring 2003): 20.

28. Jeffrey R. Immelt, Vijay Govindarajan, and Chris Trimble, "How GE Is Disrupting Itself," *Harvard Business Review*, October 2009, http://hbr.org.

29. For more information on these three contributions, see Charles H. Fine and David H. Bridge, "Managing Quality Improvement," *Quest for Quality: Managing the Total System*, ed. by M. Sepheri (Norcross, GA: Institute of Industrial Engineers, 1987), 66–74. See also Klaus J. Zinc, "From total quality management to corporate sustainability based on stakeholder management," *Journal of Management History* 13, no. 4 (2007): 394–401.

30. For some of Crosby's more notable books in this area, see Philip B. Crosby, *Quality Is Free* (New York: McGraw-Hill, 1979); *Quality without Tears* (New York: McGraw-Hill, 1984); *Let's Talk Quality: 96 Questions You Always Wanted to Ask Phil Crosby* (New York: McGraw-Hill, 1989); and *Leading* (New York: McGraw-Hill, 1990).

31. "The Push for Quality," *BusinessWeek*, June 8, 1987, 131. For a study assessing the importance of total quality management in the workplace, see Thomas J. Douglas and William Q. Judge Jr., "Total Quality Management Implementation and Competitive Advantage: The Role of Structural Control and Exploration," *Academy of Management Journal* 44, no. 1 (February 2001): 158–169.

32. A. V. Feigenbaum, *Total Quality Control* (New York: McGraw-Hill, 1983).

33. For a broadening discussion of a positive image, see Susan Watkins, "A Positive Image Is Not Just the Business of Business," *Public Management* 82, no. 7 (July 2000): 8–10.

34. From Michael Schroeder, "Heart Trouble at Pfizer," *BusinessWeek*, February 26, 1990, 47–48.

35. Michael Gibbert and Philip Scranton, "Constraints as Sources of Radical Innovation? Insights from Jet Propulsion Development," *Management & Organizational History* 4, no. 4 (2009): 385–399.

36. Scott F. Latham and Michael Braun, "Managerial Risk, Innovation, and Organizational Decline," *Journal of Management* 35, no. 2 (March 2009): 258–281.

37. For a discussion of companies that have recently won the Malcolm Baldrige National Award, see Karen Bemowski, "1994 Baldrige Award Recipients Share Their Expertise," *Quality Progress* (February 1995): 35–40.

38. Michael Hammer, "Reengineering Work: Don't Automate, Obliterate," *Harvard Business Review* (July/August 1990): 104–112.

39. See Deming's 14 Points (January 1990 revision) from W. Edwards Deming, *Out of Crisis* (Cambridge, MA: MIT Center for Advanced Engineering Study, 1986).

40. This case was based on information obtained from EASports.com.

41. www.inventables.com.

42. Lambert, Emily. "Gadgets to Go." *Forbes* 177, no. 12 (2006): 69–70.

43. Deligio, Tony. "Interactive Materials Marketplace Helps Engineers and Resin Suppliers Connect." *Plastics Today*. May 10, 2010.

Controlling, Information, and Technology

Target Skill

controlling skill: the ability to use information and technology to ensure that an event occurs as it was planned to occur

objectives

To help build my *controlling skill*, when studying this chapter, I will attempt to acquire:

1. A definition of control

2. A thorough understanding of the controlling subsystem

3. Insights into the relationship between power and control

4. An understanding of the steps required to increase the quality of a controlling subsystem

5. An understanding of the relationship between data and information

6. Insights regarding the main factors that influence the value of information

7. An understanding of the importance of an information system (IS) to an organization

8. Insights regarding how to manage an IS effectively

CHALLENGE CASE

SPERRY VAN NESS: HARNESSING TECHNOLOGY FOR BUSINESS SUCCESS

COMPANIES THAT HANDLE INVENTORY often rely on information-gathering systems to help them in the controlling process. For commercial real estate brokerage firms, the "inventory" consists of real estate listings. Commercial real estate brokerage Sperry Van Ness uses the power of wireless technology to track inventory and maintain its competitive position.

Sperry Van Ness was founded in 1987 in Irvine, California, and since that time the organization has grown rapidly. Today, its nearly 1,000 real estate professionals work in the more than 150 Sperry Van Ness locations in the United States and overseas. The company offers a full range of real estate services, including brokerage, consulting, asset management, property management, leasing, accelerated marketing, and auction services.

The recent global economic downturn has had a chilling effect on the real estate market. For nearly two years, commercial lending in the United States has slowed almost to a stop, creating a weak market with more sellers anxious to unload properties than buyers interested in purchasing them. A construction boom that ended with the downturn resulted in a glut of office and commercial space, much of it now standing vacant while builders attempt to recoup their investments.

Sperry Van Ness has addressed the market challenges by using technology to better control its inventory, which will hopefully spur sales. It recently became one of the first organizations in the commercial real estate industry to adopt a mobile marketing platform called Qonnect.mobi. Working through the use of two-dimensional barcodes, Qonnect enables Sperry Van Ness to manage its commercial property listings. By scanning the barcodes with a smartphone, users can gain immediate handheld access to Sperry Van Ness's commercial listings around the world, including comprehensive information about the property, images, video, and more.

The Sperry Van Ness office in Chicago was the first to implement the new technology, using it to market 13,000 square feet of restaurant and retail space in a luxury high-rise development in Chicago's trendy Fulton River district.

Here's how the process works. As soon as a contract is signed, the Sperry Van Ness broker uses Qonnect to list the property. The listing becomes available instantaneously via mobile phone to brokers and investors, who can access all the information they might need about the property.

During a challenging economy, quick turnaround becomes an even more critical factor in real estate. For that reason, the Qonnect platform represents a competitive advantage for Sperry Van Ness. Said company president and CEO Kevin Maggiacomo, "This new mobile marketing platform is a result of our efforts to improve our efficiencies in marketing our listings."[1]

■ *Sperry Van Ness offers brokerage services for commercial real estate such as this retail and office space available for sale of lease.*

EXPLORING YOUR MANAGEMENT SKILL

You can explore your level of controlling skill **before** studying the chapter by completing the exercise "Exploring Your Management Skill: Part 1" on page 521 and **after** studying this chapter by completing the exercise "Exploring Your Management Skill: Part 2" on page 522.

THE CONTROLLING CHALLENGE

According to the Challenge Case, issues at Sperry Van Ness involve maintaining and improving the speed of operations, internal communication, and communication with clients and prospects. The management function called *control* can help professionals at Sperry Van Ness and other organizations improve such issues, and the material in this chapter explains why these activities would be considered controlling. The following material also elaborates on the control function as a whole. Major topics in this chapter are (1) fundamentals of controlling, (2) power and control, (3) information, and (4) information systems.

THE FUNDAMENTALS OF CONTROLLING

As the scale and complexity of modern organizations grow, so does the problem of control in organizations. Prospective managers, therefore, need a working knowledge of the essentials of the controlling function.[2] To this end, the following sections provide a definition of control, a definition of the process of controlling, and a discussion of the various types of control that can be used in organizations.

Defining Control

Stated simply, **control** entails ensuring that an event occurs as it was planned to occur.[3] As implied by this definition, planning and control are virtually inseparable functions.[4] In fact, these two functions have been called the Siamese twins of management. According to Robert L. Dewelt:

> The importance of the planning process is quite obvious. Unless we have a soundly charted course of action, we will never quite know what actions are necessary to meet our objectives. We need a map to identify the timing and scope of all intended actions. This map is provided through the planning process.
>
> But simply making a map is not enough. If we don't follow it or if we make a wrong turn along the way, chances are we will never achieve the desired results. A plan is only as good as our ability to make it happen. We must develop methods of measurement and control to signal when deviations from the plan are occurring so that corrective action can be taken.[5]

Murphy's Law is a lighthearted adage making the serious point that managers should continually control—that is, check to see that organizational activities and processes are going as planned. According to Murphy's Law, anything that can go wrong will go wrong.[6] This law reminds managers to remain alert for possible problems, because even if a management system appears to be operating well, it might be eroding under the surface. Managers must always seek feedback on how the system is performing and make corrective changes whenever warranted.

Defining Controlling

Controlling is the process managers go through to control. According to Roberto Mockler, controlling is

> a systematic effort by business management to compare performance to predetermined standards, plans, or objectives to determine whether performance is in line with these standards and presumably to take any remedial action required to see that human and other corporate resources are being used in the most effective and efficient way possible in achieving corporate objectives.[7]

Objectives
The controller (or comptroller) is responsible for all accounting activities within the organization.

Functions
1. *General accounting*—Maintain the company's accounting books, accounting records, and forms.

    a. Preparing balance sheets, income statements, and other statements and reports
    b. Giving the president interim reports on operations for the recent quarter and fiscal year to date
    c. Supervising the preparation and filing of reports to the SEC

2. *Budgeting*—Prepare a budget outlining the company's future operations and cash requirements.
3. *Cost accounting*—Determine the cost to manufacture a product and prepare internal reports for management of the processing divisions.

    a. Developing standard costs
    b. Accumulating actual cost data
    c. Preparing reports that compare standard costs to actual costs and highlight unfavorable differences

4. *Performance reporting*—Identify individuals in the organization who control activities and prepare reports to show how well or how poorly they perform.
5. *Data processing*—Assist in the analysis and design of a computer-based information system. Frequently, the data-processing department is under the controller, and the controller is involved in management of that department as well as other communications equipment.
6. *Other duties*—Other duties that may be assigned to the controller by the president or by corporate bylaws include:

    a. Tax planning and reporting
    b. Service departments such as mailing, telephone, janitors, and filing
    c. Forecasting
    d. Corporate social relations and obligations

FIGURE 21.1
Specific components of the controlling subsystem

For example, production workers generally have daily production goals. At the end of each working day, the number of units produced by each worker is recorded so weekly production levels can be determined. If these weekly totals are significantly below weekly goals, the supervisor must take corrective action to ensure actual production levels equal planned ones. If, on the other hand, production goals are being met, the supervisor should allow work to continue as it has in the past.[8]

The following sections discuss the controlling subsystem and provide more details about the control process itself.

The Controlling Subsystem As with the planning, organizing, and influencing functions described in earlier chapters, controlling can be viewed as a subsystem of the overall management system. The purpose of this subsystem is to help managers enhance the success of the overall management system through effective controlling. Figure 21.1 shows the specific components of the controlling subsystem.

The Controlling Process As Figure 21.2 illustrates, there are three main steps in the controlling process:

1. Measuring performance
2. Comparing measured performance to standards
3. Taking corrective action

MEASURING PERFORMANCE Before managers can determine what must be done to make an organization more effective and efficient, they must measure current organizational performance.[9] However, before they can take such a measurement, they must establish some unit

FIGURE 21.2   The controlling subsystem

of measure that gauges performance and observe the quantity of this unit as generated by the item whose performance is being measured.[10]

- *How to Measure.* A manager who wants to measure the performance of five janitors, for example, first must establish units of measure that represent janitorial performance—such as

This pharmacist studies an inventory list in the pharmacy store room. Understanding what to measure in inventory is a critical step in the control process.

the number of floors swept, the number of windows washed, or the number of light bulbs changed. After designating these units of measure, the manager has to determine the number of each of these units accomplished by each janitor. The process of determining both the units of measure and the number of units associated with each janitor furnishes the manager with a measure of janitorial performance.

- *What to Measure.* Managers must always keep in mind that a wide range of organizational activities can be measured as part of the control process. For example, the amounts and types of inventory on hand are commonly measured to control inventory, while the quality of goods and services being produced is commonly measured to control product quality. Performance measurements can relate as well to various effects of production, such as the degree to which a particular manufacturing process pollutes the atmosphere.

The degree of difficulty in measuring various types of organizational performance, of course, is determined primarily by the activity being measured. For example, it is far more difficult to measure the performance of a highway maintenance worker than to measure the performance of a student enrolled in a college-level management course.

COMPARING MEASURED PERFORMANCE TO STANDARDS Once managers have taken a measure of organizational performance, their next step in controlling is to compare this measure against some standard. A **standard** is the level of activity established to serve as a model for evaluating organizational performance.[11] The performance evaluated can be for the organization as a whole or for some individuals working within the organization.[12] In essence, standards are the yardsticks that determine whether organizational performance is adequate or inadequate.[13]

Studying operations at General Electric (GE) will give us some insights into the different kinds of standards managers can establish. GE has established the following standards:

1. **Profitability standards**—In general, these standards indicate how much money GE would like to make as profit over a given period—that is, its return on investment. More and more, GE is using computerized preventive maintenance on its equipment to help maintain profitability standards. Such maintenance programs have reduced labor costs and equipment downtime and thereby have helped raise company profits.

2. **Market position standards**—These standards indicate the share of total sales in a particular market that GE would like to have relative to its competitors. GE market position standards were set by company chairman John F. Welch, Jr., in 1988, when he announced that henceforth any product his company offers must achieve the highest or second-highest market share compared to similar products offered by competitors or it would be eliminated or sold to another firm.

3. **Productivity standards**—How much various segments of the organization should produce is the focus of these standards. Management at GE has found that one of the best ways to convince organization members to commit themselves to increasing company productivity is simply to treat them with dignity and make them feel they are part of the GE team.

4. **Product leadership standards**—GE intends to assume a leading position in product innovation in its field. Product leadership standards indicate what must be done to attain such a position. Reflecting this interest

how managers do it

Establishing Standards
at General Electric

(continued)

in innovation, GE has pioneered the development of synthetic diamonds for industrial use. In fact, GE is considered the leader in this area, having recently discovered a method for making synthetic diamonds at a purity of 99.9 percent. In all probability, such diamonds will eventually be used as a component of super-high-speed computers.

5. **Personnel development standards**—Standards in this area indicate the type of training programs GE personnel should undergo to develop properly. GE's commitment to sophisticated training technology is an indication of the seriousness with which the company takes personnel development standards. Company training sessions are commonly supported by sophisticated technology such as large-screen projection systems, computer-generated visual aids, combined video and computer presentations, and laser videos.

6. **Employee attitudes standards**—These standards indicate what types of attitudes GE managers should strive to inculcate in GE employees. Like many other companies today, GE is trying to build positive attitudes toward product quality in its employees.

7. **Social responsibility standards**—GE recognizes its responsibility to make a contribution to society. Standards in this area outline the level and types of contributions management believes GE should make. One recent activity that reflects social responsibility standards at GE is the renovation of San Diego's Vincent de Paul Joan Kroc center for the homeless, accomplished by work teams made up of GE employees. These teams painted, cleaned, and remodeled a building to create a better facility for some of San Diego's disadvantaged citizens.

8. **Standards reflecting the relative balance between short- and long-range goals**—These standards express the relative emphasis that should be placed on attaining various short- and long-range goals. GE recognizes that short-range goals exist to enhance the probability that long-range goals will be attained. ■

(Continued)

Successful managers pinpoint all important areas of organizational performance and establish corresponding standards in each area.[14] Managers at American Airlines, for example, have set two specific standards for appropriate performance of its airport ticket offices: (1) at least 95 percent of the flight arrival times posted should be accurate, meaning that actual arrival times do not deviate more than 15 minutes from posted times, and (2) at least 85 percent of customers coming to the airport ticket counter should not have to wait more than 5 minutes to be serviced.

TAKING CORRECTIVE ACTION After actual performance has been measured and compared with established performance standards, the next step in the controlling process is to take corrective action if necessary. **Corrective action** is managerial activity aimed at bringing organizational performance up to the level of performance standards.[15] In other words, corrective action focuses on correcting organizational mistakes that are hindering organizational performance. Before taking any corrective action, however, managers should make sure the standards they are using were properly established and their measurements of organizational performance are valid and reliable.[16]

• *Recognizing Problems.* At first glance, it seems a fairly simple proposition that a manager should take corrective action to eliminate a **problem**—any factor within an organization that is a barrier to organizational goal attainment.[17] In practice, however, it often proves difficult to pinpoint the problem causing some undesirable organizational effect. Let us suppose that a performance measurement indicates a certain worker is not adequately passing on critical information to fellow workers. If the manager is satisfied that the communication standards are appropriate and that the performance measurement information is both valid and reliable, the manager should take corrective action to eliminate the problem causing this substandard performance.

- *Recognizing Symptoms.* What exactly is the problem causing substandard communication in this situation? Is it that the worker is not communicating adequately simply because he or she doesn't want to communicate? Is it that the job makes communication difficult? Is it that the worker does not have the necessary training to communicate in an appropriate manner? Before attempting to take corrective action, the manager must determine whether the worker's failure to communicate is a problem in itself or a **symptom**—a sign that a problem exists.[18] For example, the worker's failure to communicate adequately could be a symptom of inappropriate job design or a cumbersome organizational structure.

Once the problem has been properly identified, corrective action can focus on one or more of the three primary management functions of planning, organizing, and influencing. That is, corrective action can include such activities as modifying past plans to make them more suitable for future organizational endeavors, making an existing organizational structure more suitable for existing plans and objectives, or restructuring an incentive program to ensure that high producers are rewarded more than low producers. Note that because planning, organizing, and influencing are closely related, it is likely that corrective action taken in one area will necessitate some corresponding action in one or both of the other two areas.

Many organizations use technology to help support their controlling activities. At discount retailer Stein Mart, for example, store managers use Oracle Retail, a suite of merchandising and planning tools, to help them minimize merchandising errors and take corrective action. Stein Mart management recently purchased and implemented the Oracle system to help the company carry out its goals to deliver fresh merchandise to every store and gain a thorough understanding of its unique customer base.[19] ■

how managers do it

Using Technology to Support Planning at Stein Mart

POWER AND CONTROL

To control successfully, managers must understand not only the control process, but also how organization members relate to it. Up to this point, the chapter has emphasized the nonhuman variables of controlling. This section focuses on power, perhaps the most important human-related variable in the control process. The following sections present a definition of power, elaborate on the total power of managers, and list the steps managers can take to increase their power over other organization members.

A Definition of Power

Perhaps the two most often confused terms in management are *power* and *authority*. Authority was defined in Chapter 12 as the right to command or give orders. The extent to which an individual is able to influence others so they respond to orders is called **power**.[20] The greater this ability, the more power an individual is said to have.

Power and control are closely related. To illustrate, after comparing actual performance with planned performance and determining that corrective action is necessary, a manager usually gives orders to implement this action. Although the orders are issued by virtue of the manager's organizational authority, they may or may not be followed precisely, depending on how much power the manager has over the individuals to whom the orders are addressed.

Business and management scholar and Stanford University professor Jeffrey Pfeffer claims managers must learn how to wield power in order to advance their organization's agenda. In fact, he says, many highly competent professionals have floundered in management careers because they are uncomfortable using power.[21] In the following sections, we describe the different types of power and describe steps managers may take to increase their power.

Total Power of a Manager

The **total power** a manager possesses is made up of two different kinds of power: position power and personal power. **Position power** is power derived from the organizational position a manager holds.[22] In general, a manager moving from lower-level management to upper-level management accrues more position power. **Personal power** is power derived from a manager's relationships with others.[23]

Steps for Increasing Total Power

Managers can increase their total power by enhancing either their position power or their personal power, or both. Position power is generally enhanced by a move to a higher organizational position, but most managers have little personal control over when they will move up in an organization. Managers do, however, have substantial control over the amount of personal power they hold over other organization members. John P. Kotter stresses the importance of developing personal power:

> To be able to plan, organize, budget, staff, control, and evaluate, managers need some control over the many people on whom they are dependent. Trying to control others solely by directing them and on the basis of the power associated with one's position simply will not work—first, because managers are always dependent on some people over whom they have no formal authority, and second, because virtually no one in modern organizations will passively accept and completely obey a constant stream of orders from someone just because he or she is the "boss."[24]

To increase personal power, a manager should attempt to develop the following attitudes and beliefs in other organization members:[25]

1. **A sense of obligation toward the manager**—If a manager succeeds in developing this sense of obligation, other organization members will allow the manager to influence them within certain limits. The basic strategy suggested for creating this sense of obligation is to do personal favors for people.

2. **A belief that the manager possesses a high level of expertise within the organization**—In general, a manager's personal power increases as organization members perceive that the manager's level of expertise is increasing. To raise perceptions of their expertise, managers must quietly make their significant achievements visible to others and build up a successful track record and a solid professional reputation.

3. **A sense of identification with the manager**—The manager can strive to develop this identification by behaving in ways that other organization members respect and by espousing goals, values, and ideals commonly held by them. The following description illustrates how a certain sales manager took steps to increase the degree to which his subordinates identified with him:

> One vice president of sales in a moderate-sized manufacturing company was reputed to be so much in control of his sales force that he could get them to

Steve Jobs, Apple's CEO, gains a large part of his management power from his acknowledged technological expertise. Here he unveils the new iPad at the Yerba Buena Center for the Arts in San Francisco.

respond to new and different marketing programs in a third of the time taken by the company's best competitors. His power over his employees was based primarily on their strong identification with him and what he stood for. Immigrating to the United States at age seventeen, this person worked his way up "from nothing." When made a sales manager in 1965, he began recruiting other young immigrants and sons of immigrants from his former country. When made vice president of sales in 1970, he continued to do so. In 1975, 85 percent of his sales force was made up of people whom he hired directly or who were hired by others he brought.[26]

4. **The perception that they are dependent on the manager**—The main strategy here is to clearly convey the amount of authority the manager has over organizational resources—not only those necessary for organization members to do their jobs, but also those organization members personally receive in such forms as salaries and bonuses. This strategy is aptly reflected in the managerial version of the Golden Rule: "He who has the gold makes the rules."

Making Controlling Successful

In addition to avoiding the potential barriers to successful controlling mentioned in the previous section, managers can perform certain activities to make the control process more effective. To increase the quality of the controlling subsystem, managers should make sure controlling activities take all the following factors into account.

Specific Organizational Activities Being Focused On Managers should make sure the various facets of the control process are appropriate to the control activity under consideration. For example, standards and measurements concerning a line worker's productivity are much different from standards and measurements concerning a vice president's productivity. Controlling ingredients related to the productivity of these individuals, therefore, must be different if the control process is to be applied successfully.

Different Kinds of Organizational Goals Control can be used for such different purposes as standardizing performance, protecting organizational assets from theft and waste, and standardizing product quality.[27] Managers should remember that the control process can be applied to many different facets of organizational life and that, if the organization is to receive maximum benefit from controlling, each of these facets must be emphasized.

Timely Corrective Action Some time will necessarily elapse as managers gather control-related information, develop necessary reports based on this information, and decide what corrective action should be taken to eliminate a problem. However, managers should take the corrective action as promptly as possible to ensure that the situation depicted by the information gathered has not changed. Unless corrective actions are timely, the organizational advantage of taking them may not materialize.

Communication of the Mechanics of the Control Process Managers should take steps to ensure people know exactly what information is required for a particular control process, how that information is to be gathered and used to compile various reports, what the purposes of the various reports actually are, and what corrective actions are appropriate given those reports. The lesson here is simple: For control to be successful, all individuals involved in controlling must have a working knowledge of how the control process operates.[28]

ESSENTIALS OF INFORMATION

As mentioned in the previous sections, *controlling* is the process of making things happen as planned. Of course, managers cannot make things happen as planned if they lack information on the manner in which various events in the organization occur. The remainder of this chapter

L.L.Bean retail operations have grown from its original catalog business to include a Web site and a few retail stores like this one. Managers of each retail arm require different kinds of information. For instance, data about shoppers' access to technology and their privacy concerns are important to the company's Web site manager, while the demographics of the local labor supply matter to managers of the telephone centers and retail outlets.

discusses the fundamental principles of handling information in an organization by first presenting the essentials of information and then examining both information technology and information systems (IS).

The process of developing information begins with gathering some type of facts or statistics, called **data.** Once gathered, data typically are analyzed in some manner. In general terms, **information** refers to details about a project or the set of conclusions derived from data analysis. In management terms, however, information refers to the set of conclusions derived from the analysis of data that relate to the operation of an organization. Before a project commences, then, it is important for team members to reach agreement on what the term *information* will mean to them. In this way, they will be assured of operating from a mutual understanding.[29]

As examples to illustrate the relationship between data and information, managers gather data regarding pay rates that individuals are receiving within industries to collect information about how to develop competitive pay rates, data regarding hazardous-materials accidents to gain information about how to improve worker safety, and data regarding customer demographics to gain information about product demand in the future.[30] Large organizations often use information systems to help them spot market trends and respond quickly and efficiently.[31] In addition, many successful organizations are using the power of information systems to change the way they approach innovation.[32]

The information that managers receive heavily influences managerial decision making, which, in turn, determines the activities that will be performed within the organization, which, in turn, dictates the eventual success or failure of the organization. Some management writers consider information to be of such fundamental importance to the management process that they define *management* as the process of converting information into action through decision making.[33] The next sections discuss the factors that influence the value of information and how to evaluate information.

Factors Influencing the Value of Information

Some information is more valuable than other information.[34] The value of information is defined in terms of the benefit that can accrue to the organization through its use.[35] The greater this benefit, the more valuable the information.

Four primary factors determine the value of information:

1. Information appropriateness
2. Information quality
3. Information timeliness
4. Information quantity

CHARACTERISTICS OF INFORMATION	OPERATIONAL CONTROL	MANAGEMENT CONTROL	STRATEGIC PLANNING
Source	Largely internal	⟶	External
Scope	Well defined, narrow	⟶	Very wide
Level of aggregation	Detailed	⟶	Aggregate
Time horizon	Historical	⟶	Future
Currency	Highly current	⟶	Quite old/historical
Required accuracy	High	⟶	Low
Frequency of use	Very frequent	⟶	Infrequent

FIGURE 21.3

Characteristics of information appropriate for decisions related to operational control, management control, and strategic planning

In general, management should encourage generation, distribution, and use of organizational information that is appropriate, of high quality, timely, and of sufficient quantity. Following this guideline will not necessarily guarantee sound decisions, but it will ensure that important resources necessary to make such decisions are available.[36] Each of the factors that determines information value is discussed in more detail in the paragraphs that follow.

Information Appropriateness **Information appropriateness** is defined in terms of how relevant the information is to the decision-making situation the manager faces. If the information is quite relevant, then it is said to be appropriate. Generally, as the appropriateness of information increases, so does the value of that information.

Figure 21.3 shows the characteristics of information appropriate for the following common decision-making situations:[37]

1. Operational control
2. Management control
3. Strategic planning

Operational Control, Management Control, and Strategic Planning Decisions *Operational control decisions* relate to ensuring that specific organizational tasks are carried out effectively and efficiently. *Management control decisions* relate to obtaining and effectively and efficiently using the organizational resources necessary to reach organizational objectives. *Strategic planning decisions* relate to determining organizational objectives and designating the corresponding action necessary to reach them.

As Figure 21.3 shows, characteristics of appropriate information change as managers shift from making operational control decisions to making management control decisions to making strategic planning decisions. Strategic planning decision makers need information that focuses on the relationship of the organization to its external environment, emphasizes the future, is wide in scope, and presents a broad view. Appropriate information for this type of decision is generally not completely current, but more historical in nature. In addition, this information does not need to be completely accurate because strategic decisions tend to be characterized by some subjectivity and focus on areas that are difficult to measure, such as customer satisfaction.

Information appropriate for making operational control decisions has dramatically different characteristics from information appropriate for making strategic planning decisions. Operational control decision makers need information that focuses, for the most part, on the internal organizational environment, emphasizes the performance history of the organization, and is well-defined, narrow in scope, and detailed. In addition, appropriate information for this type of decision is both highly current and highly accurate.

Information appropriate for making management control decisions generally has characteristics that fall somewhere between the extreme of appropriate operational control information and appropriate strategic planning information.

Information Quality

The second primary factor that determines the value of information is **information quality**—the degree to which information represents reality. The more closely information represents reality, the higher the quality and the greater the value of that information. In general, the higher the quality of information available to managers, the better equipped managers are to make appropriate decisions and the greater the probability that the organization will be successful over the long term.

Perhaps the most significant factor in producing poor-quality information is *data contamination.* Inaccurate data gathering can result in information that is of low quality—a poor representation of reality.[38]

Information Timeliness

Information timeliness, the third primary factor that determines the value of information, is the extent to which the receipt of information allows decisions to be made and action to be taken so the organization can gain some benefit from possessing the information. Information received by managers at a point when it can be used to the organization's advantage is said to be timely.

For example, a product may be selling poorly because its established market price is significantly higher than the price of competitive products. If this information is received by management after the product has been discontinued, the information will be untimely. If, however, it is received soon enough to adjust the selling price of the product and thereby significantly increase sales, it will be timely.

Information Quantity

The fourth and final determinant of the value of information is **information quantity**—the amount of decision-related information managers possess. Before making a decision, managers should assess the quantity of information they possess that relates to the decision being made. If this quantity is judged to be insufficient, more information should be gathered before the decision is made. If the amount of information is judged to be as complete as necessary, managers can feel justified in making the decision.

There is such a thing as *too* much information. According to Rick Feldcamp of Century Life of America, information overload—too much information to consider properly—can make managers afraid to make decisions and result in important decisions going unmade. Information overload is generally considered to be the major cause of indecision in organizations—commonly referred to as "paralysis by analysis."[39]

Evaluating Information

Evaluating information is the process of determining whether the acquisition of specified information is justified. As with all evaluations of this kind, the primary concern of management is to weigh the dollar value of benefit gained from using some quantity of information against the cost of generating that information.

Identifying and Evaluating Data

According to the flowchart in Figure 21.4, the first major step in evaluating organizational information is to ascertain the value of that information by pinpointing the data to be analyzed, and then determine the expected value or return to be received from obtaining perfect information based on these data. Then this expected value is reduced by the amount of benefit that will not be realized because of deficiencies and inaccuracies expected to appear in the information.

Evaluating the Cost of Data

Next, the expected value of organizational information is compared with the expected cost of obtaining that information. If the expected cost does not exceed the expected value, the information should be gathered. If it does exceed the

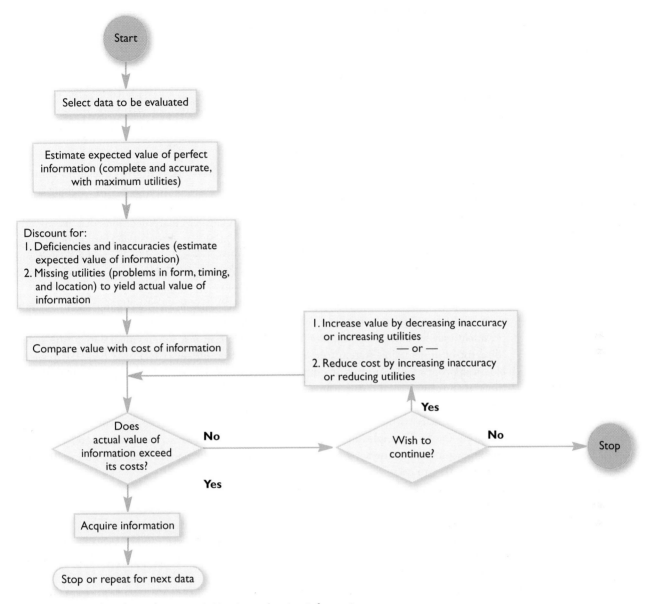

FIGURE 21.4 Flowchart of main activities in evaluating information

expected value, managers either must increase the information's expected value or decrease its expected cost before the information gathering can be justified. If neither of these objectives is possible, management cannot justify gathering the information.

INFORMATION TECHNOLOGY

Technology consists of any type of equipment or process that organization members use in the performance of their work. This definition includes tools as old as a blacksmith's anvil and tools as new and innovative as virtual reality. This section discusses one segment of technology, **information technology (IT)**, which is technology such as computers and telecommunication devices that focus on the use of information in the performance of work.

THE INFORMATION SYSTEM (IS)

In simple terms, an **information system (IS)** is a network of applications established within an organization to provide managers with information that will assist them in decision making.[40] The following, more complete definition of an IS was developed by the Management Information System Committee of the Financial Executives Institute:

> A system designed to provide selected decision-oriented information needed by management to plan, control, and evaluate the activities of the corporation. It is designed within a framework that emphasizes profit planning, performance planning, and control at all levels. It contemplates the ultimate integration of required business information subsystems, both financial and nonfinancial, within the company.[41]

The typical IS is a formally established organizational network that gives managers continual access to vital information. For example, the IS normally provides managers with ongoing reports relevant to significant organizational activities such as sales, worker productivity, and labor turnover. Based on information they gain via an IS, managers make decisions that are aimed at improving organizational performance. Because the typical IS is characterized by computer usage, managers can use an IS to gain online access to company records and condensed information in the form of summaries and reports. Overall, the IS is a planned, systematic mechanism for providing managers with relevant information in a systematic fashion.[42]

The title of the specific organization member responsible for developing and maintaining an IS varies from organization to organization. In smaller organizations, a president or vice president may have this responsibility. In larger organizations, an individual with a title such as "director of information systems" or "chief information officer (CIO)" may be solely responsible for appropriately managing an entire IS department. The term *IS manager* is used in the sections that follow to indicate the person within the organization who has the primary responsibility for managing the IS. The term *IS personnel* is used to designate the nonmanagement individuals within the organization who possess the primary responsibility for actually operating the IS. Examples of nonmanagement individuals are computer operators and computer programmers. The sections that follow describe an IS more fully and outline the steps managers take to establish an IS.

Describing the IS

The IS is perhaps best described by a summary of the steps necessary to properly operate it,[43] and by a discussion of the different kinds of information various managers need to make job-related decisions.

Operating the IS   IS personnel generally need to perform six sequential steps to properly operate an IS.[44] Figure 21.5 summarizes the steps and indicates the order in which they are performed. The first step is to determine what information is needed within the organization, when it will be needed, and in what form it will be needed. Because the basic purpose of the IS is to assist management in making decisions, one way to begin determining management information needs is to analyze the following:

1. Decision areas in which management makes decisions
2. Specific decisions within these decision areas that management must actually make
3. Alternatives that must be evaluated to make these specific decisions.

For example, insights regarding what information management needs in a particular organization can be gleaned by understanding that management makes decisions in the area of plant and equipment, that a specific decision related to this area involves acquiring new equipment, and that two alternatives that must be evaluated relating to this decision are buying newly developed, high-technology equipment versus buying more standard equipment that has been around for some time in the industry.

The second major step in operating the IS is pinpointing and collecting data that will yield needed organizational information. This step is just as important as determining information

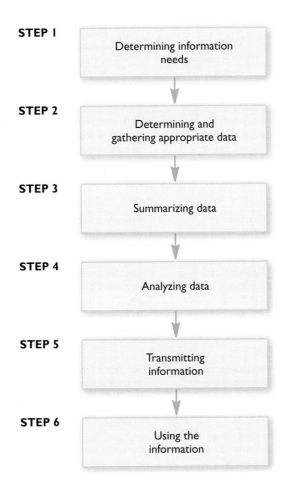

STEP 1 Determining information needs

STEP 2 Determining and gathering appropriate data

STEP 3 Summarizing data

STEP 4 Analyzing data

STEP 5 Transmitting information

STEP 6 Using the information

FIGURE 21.5
The six steps necessary to operate an IS properly in order of their performance

needs of the organization. If collected data do not relate properly to information needs, it will be impossible to generate needed information.

After information needs of the organization have been determined and appropriate data have been pinpointed and gathered, summarizing the data and analyzing the data are, respectively, the third and fourth steps IS personnel generally should take to properly operate an IS. It is in the performance of these steps that IS personnel find computer assistance of great benefit.

The fifth and sixth steps are transmitting the information generated by data analysis to appropriate managers and getting the managers to actually use the information. The performance of these last two steps results in managerial decision making. Although each of the six steps is necessary if an IS is to run properly, the time spent on performing each step will naturally vary from organization to organization.

Different Managers Need Different Kinds of Information For maximum benefit, an IS must collect relevant data, transform that data into appropriate information, and transmit that information to the appropriate managers. Appropriate information for one manager within an organization, however, may not be appropriate information for another. Robert G. Murdick suggests that the degree of appropriateness of IS information for a manager depends on the activities for which the manager will use the information, the organizational objectives assigned to the manager, and the level of management at which the manager functions.[45] All of these factors are closely related. Murdick's thoughts on this matter are best summarized in Figure 21.6. As you can see from this figure, because the overall job situations of top managers, middle managers, and first-line managers are significantly different, the kinds of information these managers need to satisfactorily perform their jobs are also significantly different.

Organizational Level	Type of Management	Manager's Organizational Objectives	Appropriate Information from IS	How IS Information Is Used
1. Top management	CEO, president, vice president	Survival of the firm, profit growth, accumulation and efficient use of resources	Environmental data and trends, summary reports of operations, exception reports of problems, forecasts	Corporate objectives, policies, constraints, decisions on strategic plans, decisions on control of the total company
2. Middle management	Middle managers in such areas as marketing, production, and finance	Allocation of resources to assigned tasks, establishment of plans to meet operating objectives, control of operations	Summaries and exception reports of operating results, corporate objectives, policies, constraints, decisions on strategic plans, relevant actions and decisions of other middle managers	Operating plans and policies, exception reports, operating summaries, control procedures, decisions on resource allocations, actions and decisions related to other middle managers
3. First-line management	First-line managers whose work is closely related	Production of goods to meet marketing needs, supplying budgets, estimates of resource requirements, movement and storage of materials	Summary reports of transactions, detailed reports of problems, operating plans and policies, control procedures, actions and decisions of related first-line managers	Exception reports, progress reports, resource requests, dispatch orders, cross-functional reports

FIGURE 21.6   Appropriate IS information under various sets of organizational circumstances

Managing Information Systems

The effectiveness of an organization's IS depends largely on the ability of individuals within the organization to properly manage the IS. Three activities that improve IS effectiveness are managing user satisfaction, managing the IS workforce, and managing IS security. To the extent that employees are able to manage these activities, organizations will reap rewards in the form of IS effectiveness.

how managers do it

Scaling Data Systems for New Users at Sage

Just as different managers may require different kinds of information, not all information systems are appropriate for all organizations. For example, for-profit firms gauge their success in terms of profitability: do they make more money than they spend? And while nonprofits and government entities also track how their organizations use their funds, they evaluate their performance against different criteria, such as how well their stakeholders are served. To support the operations of nonprofits and government agencies, Sage North America developed its MIP Fund Accounting financial management software. Sage's recent introduction of HR modules to complement the software system enables users to automate their human resources activities with employee self-service, payroll, and tax compliance capabilities.[46] ■

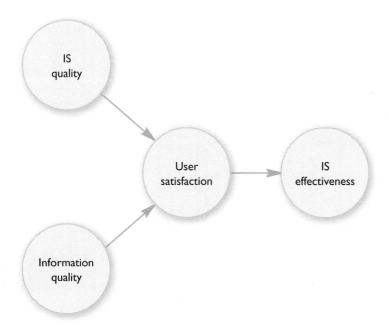

FIGURE 21.7
A model of IS effectiveness

Managing User Satisfaction[47] One of the most important determinants of IS effectiveness is the degree to which employees, or users, are satisfied with the IS. User satisfaction, which denotes the degree of user satisfaction with the IS, is determined by two main factors: (1) the quality of the IS and (2) information quality. The quality of the IS refers to its ease of use. If a company's employees consider an IS easy to use, that IS would be labeled a high-quality IS. Information quality, on the other hand, measures the degree to which the information produced by the IS is accurate and in a format required by the user. Taken together, then, users are satisfied with the IS when the IS is of high quality and provides high-quality information.

User satisfaction is important because of its direct influence on IS effectiveness. When users are satisfied with the IS, the IS will be more integrated in the user's work routine, and the user will become more dependent on the IS. Stated differently, when employees are satisfied with the IS, they will use the IS in their work routines. As users become dependent on the IS and integrate the IS into their routines, the IS becomes effective. These relationships are depicted in Figure 21.7.

Managing the IS Workforce In recent years, executives have faced different obstacles in managing the IS workforce. During the economic and technological boom of the late 1990s, executives faced tremendous hurdles in terms of hiring and retaining IS employees.[48] During that period, as compared to other professionals, IS professionals were considered more difficult to hire and retain because the economic and technological boom created a multitude of job prospects for IS professionals. Moreover, executives found it quite expensive to replace IS professionals who left; some estimates suggest that the cost of replacing an IS employee is 1 to 2.5 times their annual salary.[49]

In more recent years, however, companies have started to use workers in other countries to staff IS departments—and many expect this trend to continue. Although approximately 27,000 IS jobs in the United States were outsourced to other countries in 2000, experts expect this number to increase to almost 500,000 by 2015.[50] A recent survey indicated that almost half of firms outsource work to workers in other countries to reap cost advantages.[51] Specifically, the cost of IS employees in international countries is much less than for IS employees in the United States (see Figure 21.8). This issue of lower costs partly explains why EDS, a Texas-based firm that offers its clients IT-based solutions, employs about 1,000 IS workers in India but expects this number to increase to nearly 20,000 in the near future.

Despite the cost advantages associated with these international workers, this practice creates other problems such as integrating domestic and nondomestic workforces, managing international languages and cultures, and defining global work expectations. In addition, U.S. firms could face a backlash from their customers for outsourcing IS work to other countries, as some customers could view the practice as being unpatriotic.

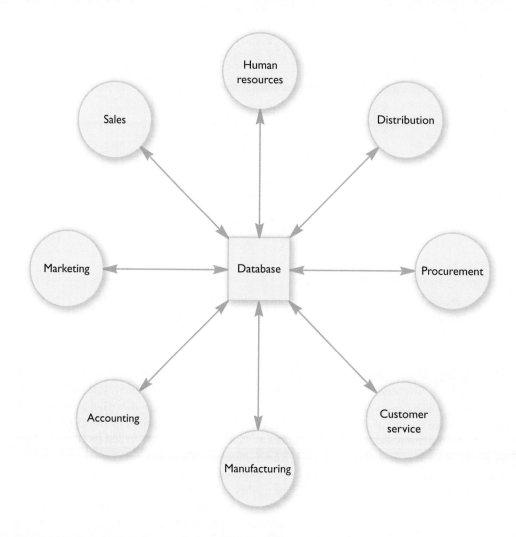

FIGURE 21.8
Centralized databases:
An illustration

class discussion highlight

MODERN RESEARCH AND CONTROLLING SKILL

Managing IS Road Warriors

Organizations must find ways to stay current with the most recent technological advances. Due to this need, the IS consulting industry has continued to develop in recent years. These consulting companies will send to a given organization an individual or team of consultants to help the organization implement the most advanced information systems. These consultants will often travel to new cities and stay for days, weeks, or months at a time.

Although this practice of employing IS consultants continues to grow, little is known about the consultants who travel to work with other organizations. To better understand these individuals, Professor Ahuha and colleagues examined a sample of 171 "road warriors." According to their framework,

road warriors are consultants who spend most of the week in a different city working with another organization and then return home for the weekend.

The researchers were particularly interested in the factors that influence the road warriors' commitment to their home organizations as well as their general levels of exhaustion. As you think about this unique set of individuals, which factors might influence their overall level of work exhaustion? Which factors might influence their commitment to their home organization (i.e., the consulting firms)? Why?

Source: This discussion is based on M. K. Ahuja, K. M. Chudoba, C. J. Kacmar, D. H. McKnight, and J. F. George, "IT Road Warriors: Balancing Work-Family Conflict, Job Autonomy, and Work Overload to Mitigate Turnover Intentions," *MIS Quarterly* 31, no. 1 (2007): 1–17.

TABLE 21.1	GASSP's Key Principles for Maintaining Information Security
Accountability principle	Organizations must clearly define and acknowledge information security accountability and responsibility.
Ethics principle	Organizations should use information and execute information security in an ethical manner.
Timeliness principle	Organizations should act in a timely manner to prevent or respond to breaches of and threats to information systems.
Assessment principle	Organizations should periodically assess the risks to information and information systems.
Equity principle	Management shall respect the rights of all employees when setting policy regarding security measures.

Managing IS Security As corporations rely more heavily on information systems, they become more susceptible to security issues involving these systems. In particular, companies may lose valuable financial, employee, or customer data due to security breaches involving IS. In addition, companies become increasingly vulnerable to viruses, worms, and trojan horses designed to paralyze information systems. As technology continues to change rapidly, it becomes more difficult for IS employees to prevent and eliminate these security threats.

In response to the increasing threat of security issues to information systems, private and public organizations around the world came together in 1992 to form the International Information Security Foundation. This committee produced a document known as the Generally Accepted System Security Principles (GASSP), which included a set of best practices for IS managers.[52] The best practices listed within the GASSP provide a good starting point for managers when they are attempting to prevent security threats. Table 21.1 provides an overview of some of the broad principles outlined in the GASSP.

CHALLENGE CASE SUMMARY

The information in this chapter supports the notion that the efficient use of technology actually should be categorized as a control problem. Control is making things happen at Sperry Van Ness in a way they were planned to happen. Going one step further, the process of controlling is the action that management takes to control. Ideally, this process at Sperry Van Ness, as within any company, would include a determination of company plans, standards, and objectives so steps can be taken to eliminate company characteristics that caused deviation from these factors.

In theory, Sperry Van Ness management should view controlling activities within the company as a subsystem of the organization's overall management system. For management to achieve organizational control, the controlling subsystem requires a portion of the people, money, and other resources available within the company.

The process portion of the controlling subsystem at Sperry Van Ness involves three steps:

1. Measuring the performance levels of various selling units
2. Comparing these performance levels to predetermined performance standards for these units

3. Taking any corrective action necessary to make sure that planned performance levels are consistent with actual performance levels

Based on information in the Challenge Case, one area in which management should emphasize standards is in the arena of desired profitability. Management is initiating a new set of processes to ensure Sperry Van Ness and its real estate advisors in the field are working with the same information.

As the company gathers more information and considers potential corrective actions, management must be certain the action is aimed at organizational problems rather than at symptoms of problems. For Sperry Van Ness's management to be successful in controlling, they have to be aware not only of the intricacies of the control process itself, but also of how to deal with people as they relate to the control process. With regard to people and control, managers must consider the amount of power they hold over organization members.

The total amount of power that Sperry Van Ness management possesses comes from the positions they hold and from their personal relationships with other organization members. For example, the top managers already have more position power than any other managers in the organization. Therefore, to increase their total power, they would have to develop their personal power. Top management might attempt to expand personal power by developing:

1. A sense of obligation in other organization members toward top managers
2. The belief in other organization members that top management has a high level of task-related expertise
3. A sense of identification that other organization members have with top management
4. The perception in organization members that they are dependent on top management

Information at Sperry Van Ness can be defined as conclusions derived from the analysis of data relating to the way in which the company operates. The case implies that managers at Sperry Van Ness will be better able to make sound decisions, including better control decisions, because of the successful data handling achieved by its information system. One important factor in evaluating the overall worth of Sperry Van Ness's information handling system would be the overall impact of the system on the value of information that company managers would receive. A manager such as Kevin Maggiacomo must see that investing in technology at a reasonable cost can enhance the value of information he receives and improve the appropriateness of decisions. That is, investments in improving information system components can enhance the appropriateness, quality, timeliness, and quantity of information that Maggiacomo can use to make decisions. Maggiacomo must believe and act on the notion that the benefits of making investments in technology will significantly improve his decisions.

For a company such as Sperry Van Ness to get maximum benefit from computer assistance, management must appropriately build each main ingredient of its IS. The IS the organizational network established to provide managers with information that helps them make job-related decisions. Such a system would normally necessitate the use of several IS personnel who would help determine information needs at the company, help determine and collect appropriate Sperry Van Ness data, summarize and analyze these data, transmit analyzed data to appropriate Sperry Van Ness managers, and generally help managers in interpreting received IS information.

To make sure managers get appropriate information, Sperry Van Ness's IS personnel must appreciate how different managers need different kinds of information. As an example, a top manager would normally need information that summarizes trends in consumer tastes, competitor moves, and summary reports for productivity and costs related to various organizational units. Middle managers would need information that focuses more on specific operating units within the company, such as all specifics regarding the performance of a specific office. More lower-level managers would normally need information about sales goals.

Assume that Maggiacomo has just decided to establish a new IS. Sperry Van Ness, like any other company, would probably gain significantly by carefully planning the way in which its IS would be established. For example, perhaps the answers to the following questions, such as those that arise during the planning stage of Sperry Van Ness's IS, would be useful: Is an appropriate computer-based system being acquired and integrated? Does the company need new IS personnel, or will present personnel require further training to operate the new IS? Will managers need additional training to operate the new IS?

About the design and implementation stages of Sperry Van Ness's new IS, Maggiacomo should seek answers to such questions as: How do we design the new IS based on managerial decision making? How can we ensure the new IS as designed and implemented will actually exist and be functional?

Maggiacomo as well as IS personnel should continually try to improve the new IS. All users of the IS should be aware of the symptoms of an inadequate IS and should constantly attempt to pinpoint and eliminate corresponding weaknesses. Suggestions for improving the new IS could include (1) building additional cooperation between IS managers, IS personnel, and line managers; (2) stressing that the purpose of the IS is to provide managers with decision-related information; (3) using cost–benefit analysis to evaluate IS activities; and (4) ensuring that the IS operates in a people-conscious manner.

MANAGEMENT SKILL ACTIVITIES

This section is specially designed to help you develop controlling skill. An individual's controlling skill is based on an understanding of controlling concepts and the ability to apply those concepts in management situations. As a result, the following activities are designed both to heighten your understanding of controlling concepts and to help you gain facility in applying these concepts in various management situations.

UNDERSTANDING CONTROLLING CONCEPTS

To check your understanding and to practice using the concepts in this chapter, go to www.mymanagementlab.com and explore the material associated with Chapter 21.

Know Key Terms

Understanding the following key terms is critical to your understanding of chapter material. Define each of these terms. Refer to the page(s) referenced after a term to check your definition or to gain further insight regarding the term.

control 502
controlling 502
standard 505
corrective action 506
problem 506
symptom 507
power 507

total power 508
position power 508
personal power 508
data 510
information 510
information appropriateness 511
information quality 512

information timeliness 512
information quantity 512
technology 513
information technology (IT) 513
information system (IS) 513

Know How Management Concepts Relate

This section is comprised of activities that will further sharpen your understanding of management concepts. Answer essay questions as completely as possible. Also, remember that many additional true/false and multiple choice questions appear online at MyManagementLab.com to help you further refine your understanding of management concepts.

1. Describe the three main steps in the controlling process.

2. Define power and describe the determinants of an individual's power within an organization.
3. What is the difference between a problem and a symptom? Use an example to support your response.
4. Describe the six steps involved with information system performance.
5. What are the determinants of information system effectiveness?

DEVELOPING MANAGEMENT SKILLS

Learning activities in this section are aimed at helping you develop your controlling skill. Learning activities include Exploring Your Management Skill: Parts 1 and 2, Experiential Exercises, Cases, and a VideoNet Exercise.

Exploring Your Management Skill: Part 1

Before studying this chapter, respond to the following questions regarding the type of advice you would give to Sperry Van Ness CEO Kevin Maggiacomo, referenced in the Challenge Case. Then address the concerning controlling challenges that he presently faces within the company. You are not expected to be a controlling expert at this point. Answering the questions now can help you focus on important points when you study the chapter. Also, answering the questions again after you study the chapter will give you an idea of how much you have learned.

Record your answers here or go to MyManagementLab.com. Recording your answers in MyManagementLab will allow you to get immediate results and see how your score compares to your classmates. If you answer the questions in the book, the answers are located in the Exploring Your Management Skill Appendix at the end of the book.

FOR EACH STATEMENT CIRCLE:
• "Y" if you would give the advice to Maggiacomo.
• "N" if you would NOT give the advice to Maggiacomo.
• "NI" if you have no idea whether you would give the advice to Maggiacomo.

Mr. Maggiacomo, in meeting your controlling challenges at Sperry Van Ness, you should...

Before   After
Study   Study

1. understand that the planning and controlling functions at Sperry Van Ness are clearly separate.
Y, N, NI
2. recognize that controlling is primarily an organization-level concept and is not particularly relevant for lower-level employees.
Y, N, NI
3. realize that the first step in the controlling process is measuring performance.
Y, N, NI
4. understand that Sperry Van Ness must develop its own standards, which may or may not be the same standards as its competitors'.
Y, N, NI
5. emphasize to Sperry Van Ness's employees that problems and symptoms are often the same thing.
Y, N, NI
6. understand that managerial power is a function of an individual's position and personal relationships with others.
Y, N, NI
7. understand that conveying a high level of expertise will increase the level of power that Sperry Van Ness employees will associate with managers who demonstrate such expertise.
Y, N, NI

8. understand that information has value that depends on the appropriateness, quality, timeliness, and quantity of the information.

Y, N, NI

9. use the terms *data* and *information* interchangeably, because they are virtually the same.

Y, N, NI

10. update information systems as needed to ensure that Sperry Van Ness's managers have access to the information they need to make quality decisions.

Y, N, NI

11. recognize that the first step needed to operate an IS effectively entails summarizing data.

Y, N, NI

12. distribute all important information to all of Sperry Van Ness's managers, because these managers all need access to the same information.

Y, N, NI

13. not worry about an information system's ease of use; evidence suggests that users will learn to use even difficult systems if such use is necessary for their job performance.

Y, N, NI

14. recognize that the world is filled with IS professionals, and as such, traditional human resource management techniques are unnecessary for Sperry Van Ness's IS employees.

Y, N, NI

15. understand that information security continues to represent an important factor for companies such as Sperry Van Ness to consider as they maintain their information systems.

Y, N, NI

Exploring Your Management Skill: Part 2

As you recall, you completed Exploring Your Management Skill before you started to study this chapter. Your responses gave you an idea of how much you initially knew about controlling and helped you focus on important points as you studied the chapter. Answer the Exploring Your Management Skill questions again now and compare your score to the first time you took it. This comparison will give you an idea of how much you have learned from studying this chapter and pinpoint areas for further clarification before you start studying the next chapter. Record your answers within the text or go to MyManagementLab.com. Recording your answers in MyManagementLab will allow you to get immediate results and see how your score compares to your classmates. If you answer the questions in the book, the answers are located in the Exploring Your Management Skill section at the end of the book.

Your Management Skills Portfolio

Your Management Learning Portfolio is a collection of activities especially designed to demonstrate your management knowledge and skill. By completing these online at MyManagement.com, you will be able to print, complete with cover sheet, as many activities as you choose. Be sure to save your work. Taking your printed portfolio to an employment interview could be helpful in obtaining a job.

The portfolio activity for this chapter is Controlling at Merrill Lynch. Study the information and complete the exercises that that follow.[53]

Merrill Lynch provides a number of financial services to corporations and individuals. One of Merrill Lynch's primary activities involves providing advisory services to individual investors. To provide these services, financial planners work with clients and provide advice regarding potential investment decisions. In exchange for this advice, the financial planners earn money for the company based on commissions and other fees. Financial planners at Merrill Lynch work with different numbers of clients, and these clients vary dramatically in terms of their total assets.

John Thain, Merrill Lynch's CEO, has contacted you to help him think of ways to improve the performance of the many financial planners working for the company. His specific task for you involves making the controlling process relevant to the financial planners. In the following sections, answer the various questions as they pertain to Merrill Lynch. Visiting the company's Web site (www.ml.com) might help you as you think about this process.

1. The first step in the controlling process involves measuring performance. If you were John Thain, how would you measure the performance of the financial planners? Be specific.

_____

_____

_____

2. The second step in the controlling process entails comparing measured performance to standards.

a. What types of standards would you develop to help assess performance of these financial planners?

_____

_____

b. What information sources would you use for developing these standards?

3. The final step in the controlling process involves taking corrective actions if necessary.

   a. What types of corrective actions would you take to help control the performance of financial planners?

   b. How would you determine whether corrective actions were necessary?

Experiential Exercises

1 Working with Information

Directions. Read the following scenario and then perform the listed activities. Your instructor may want you to perform the activities as an individual or within groups. Follow all of your instructor's directions carefully.

Perhaps the most critical aspect of an information system is determining what information a given organization needs to operate effectively. When an organization understands what information is needed, leaders can design an information system that will allow them to collect this information efficiently. In this exercise, your group should choose a local restaurant and then assume you are the top management team for this restaurant. With this restaurant in mind, determine the primary pieces of information you need to ensure the restaurant operates effectively. If possible, group these different pieces of information into logical categories.

2 You and Your Career

In the previous sections we provided an overview of the controlling process, which involves measuring performance, comparing performance to standards, and taking corrective action if necessary. During your career in both management and nonmanagement roles, you will deal with performance standards. How have standards played a role in your life so far? Examples might include your academic career, your current or previous employer, or even extracurricular activities such as participation in sports. Until now, who has defined the standards that apply to you, and what role have you played in this process? How might your familiarity with standards influence your career in the future?

Videonet Exercise

Controlling and Technology: Platinum Autobody

Video Highlights

Platinum Autobody is a small, family-owned business focusing on custom body and mechanical jobs. The co-owners discuss how the four functions of management apply to their business: planning, organizing, leading, and controlling. In the video, the co-owners define their managerial roles and division of responsibilities.

Discussion Questions

1. Saboor and Kawa Hatef divide responsibilities for running Platinum Autobody. What are the advantages of such specialization?
2. How is Platinum Autobody using technology to improve its business?

3. Why would Platinum Autobody compare its prices to those charged by competitors?

Internet Activity

Browse the Platinum Autobody site at platinumab.com. Click on the ASE Certified link and read about the company's facilities and personnel. Now that you know a little more about the company, discuss the four functions, such as how planning applies to expanding the business, how organization benefits from technology, how leading provides motivation for employees, and how controlling applies to all operations of the shop. How do the ASE and I-Car certifications contribute to the controlling aspect of Platinum Autobody?

CASES

1 SPERRY VAN NESS: HARNESSING TECHNOLOGY FOR BUSINESS SUCCESS

"Sperry Van Ness: Harnessing Technology for Business Success" (p. 501) and its related Challenge Case Summary sections were written to help you better understand the management concepts contained in this chapter. Answer the following discussion questions about this Challenge Case to further enrich your understanding of chapter content:

1. List three decisions an improved IS could help Sperry Van Ness president and CEO Kevin Maggiacomo make. For each decision, describe the data that must be in the database to provide such help.

2. The main steps of the controlling process are measuring performance, comparing performance to standards, and taking corrective action. Discuss the possible role of an IS at Sperry Van Ness in each of these steps.

3. In addition to commercial real estate, some of Sperry Van Ness's chief competitors also handle residential real estate. Because of this additional area of operation, do you think Sperry Van Ness's IS should differ from that of its competitors? Why?

2 TECHNOLOGY HELPS NIKE RACE TOWARD HIGHER PERFORMANCE

Read the case and answer the questions that follow. Studying this case will help you better see how your understanding of information technology can be applied in a company such as Nike.

Nike takes a step forward in its race for sales and profits every time it sells a pair of sneakers. The Oregon-based company has a commanding lead over Adidas and other rivals because of its 32 percent share of the global athletic shoe market. Still, CEO Philip Knight and his executive team know they must sell a lot of shoes and sports apparel to expand beyond the current $12 billion in yearly sales and hike the gross profit margin above 43 percent (the highest margin in company history). They have to estimate how well each product will sell, allow enough time to manufacture the right quantities, get the products to the right place at the right time at the right cost, and reach out to the right customers. The unpredictability of fashion trends makes their decisions even more challenging.

So how does Nike do it? With technology, a healthy dose of human expertise, and patience. The company was using 27 different information systems to handle sales forecasting, factory orders, and deliveries to retailers worldwide when management began planning for a single, integrated IS. One goal was to slash, from nine months to six months, the time needed to get shoes and other items from the design stage to store shelves. Another goal was closer coordination with the Asian factories that manufacture Nike's shoes as a way to minimize inventory. This coordination would help the company avoid some of the financial risks of catering to fashion-conscious customers whose

tastes can change overnight. Finally, management wanted a single, centralized system for forecasting and ordering that managers and employees could learn to use efficiently and effectively.

Months of preparation went into the project, as company managers worked with specialists to customize software to Nike's unique situation and then implemented the system before a new corporate-wide IT project took effect. At first, the forecasting/ordering system struggled to handle the more than 10 million stock numbers needed to track all product variations; it also operated more slowly than expected when tied to the existing IT network. Then the system issued factory orders for too many of some models and too few of others, causing Nike to lose an estimated $100 million worth of sales.

The project managers created workarounds to make data available for planning purposes while they analyzed what had happened, revamped the system design, and got ready to implement it more gradually. "Once we got into this, we quickly realized that what we originally thought was going to be a two-to-three-year effort would be more like five to seven [years]," observes Roland Wolfram, Nike's vice president of global operations and technology. In fact, the new system was phased in, area by area, over the next two years, and users received intensive training in advance. As a double check, Nike managers carefully scrutinize system output "to make sure it makes sense," says Wolfram; they also ask retailers for input when forecasting demand for new items. Now, six years after the original project began, the system is working so well that Nike managers have set a new goal of reducing the lead time for orders even further.

The Internet plays a major role in Nike's plans for communicating with customers to build brand loyalty and stimulate demand. For example, Nike keeps its trademark "swoosh" symbol in front of soccer fans by inviting them to log onto the company's Web site and participate in multiplayer games such as Football Olé. It has teamed up with MSN Europe to create an Instant Messenger version of the same game that can be played by people across the continent. In addition, Nike has developed a series of Web sites tailored to the interests of specific customer groups, such as www.nikegoddess.com for women, www.nikerunning.com for runners, and www.nikebasketball.com for basketball fans. Watch for more technological innovation as Nike continues its never-ending race for higher sales and higher profits.

QUESTIONS

1. Why are information quality and timeliness particularly important to Nike's success?

2. What security issues do you think Nike management should take into account when planning, designing, and implementing a system for sales forecasting and factory orders? Why?

3. What else should Nike do to use the World Wide Web for communicating with customers?

Endnotes

1. Allison Landa, "Sperry Van Ness Implements New Mobile Marketing Technology," *Commercial Property Executive,* March 30, 2010, http://www.cpexecutive.com; Kristen Tatti, "Two Years Later, Sperry Van Ness Still Growing," *Northern Colorado Business Report,* April 23, 2010, http://www.ncbr.com; Chris Wood, "Sperry Van Ness Brokers Go Mobile," *Multifamily Executive,* April 8, 2010, http://www.multifamilyexecutive.com.

2. For an illustration of the complexity of control in an international context, see Jean-Francois Hennart, "Control in Multinational Firms: The Role of Price and Hierarchy," *Management International Review,* Special Issue 1991, 71–96. See also "Defining Controls," *The Internal Auditor* 55, no. 3 (June 1998): 47.

3. For insights about control in the international arena, see John Volkmar, "Context and Control in Foreign Subsidiaries: Making a Case for the Host Country National Manager," *Journal of Leadership and Organizational Studies* 10 (2003): 93.

4. K. A. Merchant, "The Control Function of Management," *Sloan Management Review* 23 (Summer 1982): 43–55.

5. Robert L. Dewelt, "Control: Key to Making Financial Strategy Work," *Management Review* (March 1977): 18. For discussion relating planning and controlling to leadership, see Sushil K. Sharma and Savita Dakhane, "Effective Leadership: The Key to Success," *Employment News* 23, no. 10 (June 6–12, 1988): 1, 15.

6. For more discussion on Murphy's Law, see Grady W. Harris, "Living with Murphy's Law," *Research-Technology Management* (January/February 1994): 10–13.

7. Robert J. Mockler, ed., *Readings in Management Control* (New York: Appleton-Century-Crofts, 1970), 14.

8. For insights about the process that Delta Air Lines uses to control distribution costs, see Perry Flint, "Delta's 'Shot Heard 'Round the World,'" *Air Transport World* (April 1995): 61–62.

9. Francis V. McCrory and Peter Gerstberger, "The New Math of Performance Measurement," *Journal of Business Strategy* (March/April 1991): 33–38; L. Bielski, "KPI: Your metrics should tell a story," *ABA Banking Journal* 99, no. 10 (2007): 66–68; B. Hirtle, "The impact of network size on bank branch performance," *Journal of Banking & Finance* 31, no. 12 (2007): 3782–3805.

10. For an article focusing on challenges associated with measuring the performance of physicians, see T. G. Ferris, J. Marder, C. S. Sennett, and E. G. Campbell, "TRENDS: Physician Specialty Societies and the Development of Physician Performance Measures," *Health Affairs* 26, no. 6 (2007): 1712–1719.

11. For discussion of quality-oriented performance standards, see Perry Rector and Brian Kleiner, "Performance Standards: Defining Quality Service in Community-Based Organizations," *Management Research News* 26 (2003): 161.

12. James M. Bright, "A Clear Picture," *Credit Union Management* (February 1995): 28–29.

13. For a discussion of how standards are set, see James B. Dilworth, *Production and Operations Management: Manufacturing and Nonmanufacturing* (New York: Random House, 1986), 637–650. For more information on various facets of standards and standard setting, see Len Eglo, "Save Dollars on Maintenance Management," *Chemical Engineering* 97 (June 1990): 157–162.

14. For an example of a company surpassing performance standards, see Peter Nulty, "How to Live by Your Wits," *Fortune,* April 20, 1992, 19–20.

15. To better understand the importance of corrective action, see Zheng Gu, "Predicting Potential Failure, Taking Corrective Action Are Keys to Success," *Nation's Restaurant News* 33, no. 25 (June 21, 1999): 31–32.

16. For more about corrective action in developing countries, see Martin Brownbridge and Samuel Maimbo, "Can Prompt Corrective Action Rules Work in the Developing World?" *Journal of African Business* 4 (2003): 47.

17. For a review of other common problems in organizations, see Robert E. Quinn, Regina M. O'Neill, and Lynda St. Clair, *Pressing Problems in Modern Organizations (That Keep Us Up at Night): Transforming Agendas for Research and Practice* (New York: AMACOM): 1999.

18. For an illustration of the problem/symptom relationship, see Elizabeth Dougherty, "Waste Minimization: Reduce Wastes and Reap the Benefits," *R&D* 32 (April 1990): 62–68.

19. "Stein Mart Selects Oracle Retail Merchandising and Planning Applications," *Trading Markets,* April 22, 2010, http://www.tradingmarkets.com.

20. To explore the relationship between nonverbal behavior and power, see Herman Aguinis, Melissa M. Simonsen, and Charles A. Pierce, "Effects of Nonverbal Behavior on Perceptions of Power Bases," *The Journal of Social Psychology* 138, no. 4 (August 1998): 455–469.

21. Jeffrey Pfeffer, "Power Play," *Harvard Business Review* 88, no. 7/8 (July/August 2010): 84–92.

22. For more information on position power, see S. R. Giessner and T. W. Schubert, "High in the Hierarchy: How Vertical Location and Judgments of Leaders' Power are Interrelated," *Organizational Behavior and Human Decision Processes* 104, no. 1 (2007): 30–44.

23. See Amitai Etzioni, *A Comparative Analysis of Complex Organizations* (New York: Free Press, 1961), 4–6. To better understand the potential negative outcomes associated with power, see T. B. Lawrence and S. L. Robinson, "Ain't Misbehavin: Workplace Deviance as Organizational Resistance," *Journal of Management* 33, no. 3 (2007): 378–394.

24. John P. Kotter, "Power, Dependence, and Effective Management," *Harvard Business Review* (July/August 1977): 128.

25. Kotter, "Power, Dependence, and Effective Management," 135–136. For a discussion on how empowering subordinates can increase the power of a manager, see Linda A. Hill, "Maximizing Your Influence," *Working Woman* (April 1995): 21–22.

26. Kotter, "Power, Dependence, and Effective Management," 131.

27. W. Jerome III, *Executive Control: The Catalyst* (New York: Wiley, 1961), 31–34. See also William Bruns Jr. and E. Warren McFarlan, "Information Technology Puts Power in Control Systems," *Harvard Business Review* (September/October 1987): 89–94.

28. For an article emphasizing the importance of management understanding and being supportive of organizational control efforts, see Richard M. Morris III, "Management Support: An Underlying Premise," *Industrial Management* 31 (March/April 1989): 2–3.

29. The term *information* has been defined in various ways in academic and professional literature. For a classification of the various definitions, see Earl H. McKinney Jr., "Information about Information: A Taxonomy of Views," *MIS Quarterly* 34, no. 2 (June 2010): 329–A5.

30. Garland R. Hadley and Mike C. Patterson, "Are Middle-Paying Jobs Really Declining?" *Oklahoma Business Bulletin* 56 (June 1988): 12–14; A. Essam Radwan and Jerome Fields, "Keeping Tabs on Toxic Spills," *Civil Engineering* 60 (April 1990): 70–72; Dean C. Minderman, "Marketing: Desktop Demographics," *Credit Union Management* 13 (February 1990): 26.

31. Carol Davis and Edmund Haefele, "A Practical and Tested Infrastructure Design for Large Business Warehouse Systems," *Business Information Review* 27, no. 1 (2010): 43–55.

32. Michael S. Hopkins, "The Four Ways IT Is Revolutionizing Innovation," *Sloan Management Review,* (Spring 2010), 51–56.

33. Henry Mintzberg, "The Myths of MIS," *California Management Review* (Fall 1972): 92–97; Jay W. Forrester, "Managerial Decision Making," in *Management and the Computer of the Future,* ed. Martin Greenberger (Cambridge, MA and New York: MIT Press and Wiley, 1962), 37.

34. The following discussion is based largely on Robert H. Gregory and Richard L. Van Horn, "Value and Cost of Information." in J. Daniel Conger and Robert W. Knapp (Eds.), *Systems Analysis Techniques* (New York; Wiley, 1974), 473–489.

35. To better understand how information systems can improve the quality of an organization's information, see B. S. Butler and P. H. Gray, "Reliability, Mindfulness, and Information Systems," *MIS Quarterly* 30, no. 2 (2006): 211–224.

36. John T. Small and William B. Lee, "In Search of MIS," *MSU Business Topics* (Autumn 1975): 47–55.

37. G. Anthony Gorry and Michael S. Scott Morton, "A Framework for Management Information Systems," *Sloan Management Review* 13 (Fall 1971): 55–70.

38. Stephen L. Cohen, "Managing Human-Resource Data Keeping Your Data Clean," *Training & Development Journal* 43 (August 1989): 50–54.

39. Michael A. Verespej, "Communications Technology: Slave or Master?" *Industry Week* (June 19, 1995): 48–55; John C. Scully, "Information Overload?" *Managers Magazine,* May 1995, 2.

40. T. Mukhapadhyay and R. B. Cooper, "Impact of Management Information Systems on Decisions," *Omega* 20 (1992): 37–49. For more information on information systems in developing countries, see G. Walsham, D. Robey, and S. Sahay, "Foreword: Special Issue on Information Systems in Developing Countries," *MIS Quarterly* 31, no. 2 (2007): 317–326.

41. Robert W. Holmes, "Twelve Areas to Investigate for Better MIS," *Financial Executive* (July 1970): 24. A similar definition is presented and illustrated in Jeffrey A. Coopersmith, "Modern Times: Computerized Systems Are Changing the Way Today's Modern Catalog Company Is Structured," *Catalog Age* 7 (June 1990): 77–78.

42. Kenneth C. Laudon and Jane Price Laudon, *Management Information Systems: Organization and Technology* (New York: Macmillan, 1993), 38.

43. For an article discussing how a well-managed MIS promotes the usefulness of information, see Albert Lederer and Veronica Gardner, "Meeting Tomorrow's Business Demands through Strategic Information Systems Planning," *Information Strategy: The Executive's Journal* (Summer 1992): 20–27.

44. This section is based on Richard A. Johnson, R. Joseph Monsen, Henry P. Knowles, and Borge O. Saxberg, *Management Systems and Society: An Introduction* (Santa Monica, CA: Goodyear, 1976), 113–120; James Emery, "Information Technology in the 21st Century Enterprise," *MIS Quarterly* (December 1991): xxi–xxiii.

45. Robert G. Murdick, "MIS for MBO," *Journal of Systems Management* (March 1977): 34–40; see also A. S. Dunk, "Innovation budget pressure, quality of IS information, and departmental performance," *The British Accounting Review* 39, no.2 (2007): 115–124

46. "Sage North America Expands HR Management Software Choices for Nonprofit and Government Organizations," *MarketWire,* April 1, 2010, http://smart-grid.tmcnet.com.

47. The discussion is based on A. Rai, S. S. Lang, and R. B. Welker, "Assessing the Validity of IS Success Models: An Empirical Test and Theoretical Analysis," *Information Systems Research* 13, no. 1 (2002): 50–69.

48. For more information on the turnover of IT workers, see D. Joseph, K. Ng, C. Koh, and S. Ang, "Turnover of Information Technology Professionals: A Narrative Review, Meta-Analytic Structural Equation Modeling, and Model Development," *MIS Quarterly* 31, no. 3 (2007): 547–577.

49. C. O. Longenecker and J. A. Scazzero, "The Turnover and Retention of IT Managers in Rapidly Changing Organizations," *Information Systems Management* (Winter 2003): 58–63.

50. S. Overby, "The Future of Jobs and Innovation: Scenario One," *CIO,* December 15, 2003, www.cio.com.

51. J. King, "IT's Global Itinerary," *Computerworld,* September 15, 2003, www.computerworld.com.

52. M. R. Gramaila and I. Kim, "An Undergraduate Business Information Security Course and Laboratory," *Journal of Information Systems Education* 13, no. 3 (2003): 189–196.

53. This exercise was based on www.merrilllynch.com, as well as Jena McGregor, "Room & Board Plays Impossible to Get," *BusinessWeek,* October 1, 2007, 80.

Production and Control

Target Skill

production skill: the ability to transform organizational resources into products

To help build my *production skill*, when studying this chapter, I will attempt to acquire:

1. Definitions of production, productivity, and quality

2. An understanding of the importance of operations and production strategies, systems, and processes

3. Insights into the role of operations management concepts in the workplace

4. An understanding of how operations control procedures can be used to control production

5. Insights into operations control tools and how they evolve into a continual improvement approach to production management and control

CHALLENGE CASE

DELTA ATTEMPTS TO BOOST PRODUCTIVITY[1]

DELTA AIR LINES PROVIDES AIR TRANSPORTATION for travelers and cargo throughout the world. Although Delta derives most of its revenues from the United States, the company also flies to more than 30 foreign countries. Despite these many markets, the company has struggled in recent years to maintain profitability. To help remedy Delta's troubles, the board of directors recently named Richard Anderson as the company's new chief executive officer.

Improving Delta's performance will entail increasing customer satisfaction. Recent Delta surveys of passengers revealed they had grown tired of the time required to board Delta's planes. In addition, industry surveys suggest travelers can tolerate about 17 minutes of waiting, but after that mark satisfaction declines substantially for every 5 additional minutes of standing in line.

In response to this survey, Delta invested approximately $200 million to speed up the check-in process. A large portion of this $200 million will support Delta's new strategy of using self-service kiosks that help passengers check in more quickly. With these kiosks, which Delta has already installed in more than 80 airports, passengers can check in by themselves. After inserting either credit cards or Delta frequent flier cards as identification, passengers can use the kiosks to identify their flights and choose their seats. At the end of the process, the kiosks print out boarding passes, and baggage labels are printed out at nearby locations where Delta employees attach the labels to the luggage.

Delta has also made other changes to speed up the check-in process. For example, Delta is now installing telephones in airports under banners entitled "Delta Direct." When passengers need to make changes to their itineraries, they simply pick up one of the telephones. These telephones, in turn, will connect them to service agents in Tampa who specialize in making such itinerary changes. Delta processes about 500,000 such requests per month through this important function. With these phone banks, Delta reduces the number of employees needed at airport counters to respond to these passenger requests.

Delta has enjoyed some early success with these changes. According to the company, the check-in process at the kiosks usually takes about two minutes. In addition, this self-service process requires fewer employees, which means the kiosk-system improves Delta's productivity. This new process may help to explain why Delta believes that soon 80 percent of passengers will check in someplace other than the traditional ticket counter.

Delta needs the productivity increases from these changes desperately if it wants to survive. Due in part to this need for increased productivity, Delta recently merged with Northwest Airlines. By combining operations with Northwest, Delta might be able reduce costs and increase productivity. If the merger works as planned, Delta might just regain its position as the leader of U.S. airline industry.

■ *Management at Delta Air Lines is focusing on eliminating waiting lines for passenger check-in.*

EXPLORING YOUR MANAGEMENT SKILL

You can explore your level of production skill **before** studying the chapter by completing the exercise "Exploring Your Management Skill: Part 1" on page 551 and **after** studying this chapter by completing the exercise "Exploring Your Management Skill: Part 2" on page 552.

THE PRODUCTION CHALLENGE

The Challenge Case describes the changes that Delta is implementing to improve productivity. Specifically, it explains how Delta is making changes in airports in an effort to reduce the time it takes passengers to board their flights. This chapter is designed to help managers in companies such as Delta increase productivity.

This chapter emphasizes the fundamentals of production control—ensuring that an organization produces goods and services as planned. The primary discussion topics in the chapter are (1) production, (2) operations management, (3) operations control, and (4) selected operations control tools.

PRODUCTION

To reach organizational goals, all managers must plan, organize, influence, and control to produce some type of goods or services. Naturally, these goods and services vary significantly from organization to organization. This section of the chapter defines production and productivity and discusses the relationship between quality and productivity and automation.

Defining Production

Production is the transformation of organizational resources into products.[2] In this definition, *organizational resources* are all assets available to a manager to generate products, *transformation* is the set of steps necessary to change these resources into products, and *products* are various goods or services aimed at meeting human needs. Inputs at a manufacturing firm, for example, would include raw materials, purchased parts, production workers, and even schedules. The transformation process would encompass the preparation of customer orders, the design of various products, the procurement of raw materials, and the production, assembly, and (perhaps) warehousing of products. Outputs, of course, would consist of products fit for customer use.

"Production" occurs at service organizations as well. Inputs at a hospital, for instance, would include ambulances, rooms, employees (doctors, nurses, administrators, receptionists), supplies (medicines, bandages, food), and (as at a manufacturer) funds, schedules, and records. The transformation process might begin with transporting patients to the facility and end with discharging them. In between, the hospital would attend to patients' needs (nursing and feeding them, administering their medication, recording their progress). The output here is health care.

Productivity

Productivity is an important consideration in designing, evaluating, and improving modern production systems.[3] We can define **productivity** as the relationship between the total amount of goods or services being produced (output) and the organizational resources needed to produce them (input). This relationship is usually expressed by the following equation:[4]

$$\text{productivity} = \frac{\text{outputs}}{\text{inputs}}$$

The higher the value of the ratio of outputs to inputs, the higher the productivity of the operation.

Managers should continually strive to improve their production processes.[5] As an example, Duke Energy has committed to investing $1 billion over five years in smart grid technology. The new technology promises to save energy, lower operating costs, and reduce the world's carbon footprint. Under the plan, Duke is replacing conventional electric meters with digital meters that allow remote meter reading, connections, and disconnections.[6] ∎

It is no secret that over the past several years workers in the United States have been among the world's most productive.[7] Some of the more traditional strategies for increasing productivity are as follows:[8]

1. Improving the effectiveness of the organizational workforce through training
2. Improving the production process through automation
3. Improving product design to make products easier to assemble
4. Improving the production facility by purchasing more modern equipment
5. Improving the quality of workers hired to fill open positions

Intel is an example of an organization that has taken steps to improve worker productivity by changing the way it designs offices.[9] Although Intel was initially credited with the popularization of cubicles, Intel executives have reconsidered the costs and benefits of cubicle arrangements, which block worker visibility while failing to reduce noise. Intel is now testing alternative office arrangements in several locations. One such arrangement involves using large tables that employees can sit around in groups with notebook computers. Intel is hopeful that this new arrangement will help to boost both morale and productivity.

Quality and Productivity

Quality can be defined as how well a product does what it is intended to do—how closely it satisfies the specifications to which it was built.[10] In a broad sense, quality is the degree of excellence on which products or services can be ranked on the basis of selected features or characteristics. It is customers who determine this ranking, and customers define quality in terms of appearance, performance, availability, flexibility, and reliability.[11] Product quality determines an organization's reputation.

Printed circuits are made to exacting standards, so production quality is a primary concern of these technicians, who are checking over their work.

During the last decade or so, managerial thinking about the relationship between quality and productivity has changed drastically. Many earlier managers chose to achieve higher levels of productivity simply by producing a greater number of products given some fixed level of available resources. They saw no relationship between improving quality and increasing productivity. Quite the contrary: They viewed quality improvement as a controlling activity that took place toward the end of the production process and largely consisted of rejecting a number of finished products that were too obviously flawed to be offered to customers. Under this approach, quality improvement efforts were generally believed to *lower* productivity.

Focus on Continual Improvement Management theorists have more recently discovered that concentrating on improving product quality throughout all phases of a production process actually improves the productivity of the manufacturing system.[12] U.S. companies were far behind the Japanese in making this discovery. As early as 1948, Japanese companies observed that continual improvements in product quality throughout the production process normally resulted in improved productivity. How does this improvement happen? According to Dr. W. Edwards Deming, a world-renowned quality expert, a serious and consistent quality focus normally reduces nonproductive variables such as the reworking of products, production mistakes, delays and production snags, and inefficient use of time and materials.

Deming believed that for continual improvement to become a way of life in an organization, managers need to understand their company and its operations. Most managers feel they do know their company and its operations, but when they begin drawing flowcharts, they discover that their understanding of strategy, systems, and processes is far from complete. Deming recommended that managers question every aspect of an operation and involve workers in discussion before they take action to improve operations. He maintained that a manager who seriously focuses on improving product quality throughout all phases of a production process will initiate a set of chain reactions that benefits not only the organization, but also the society in which the organization exists.

Focus on Quality and Integrated Operations Deming's flow diagram for improving product quality (see Figure 22.1) contains a complete set of organizational variables. It establishes the customer as part of the operations process and introduces the idea of continually refining knowledge, design, and inputs into the process to constantly increase customer satisfaction. The diagram shows the operations process as an integrated whole, from the first input

FIGURE 22.1
Deming's flow diagram for improving product quality

to actual use of the finished product; a problem at the beginning of the process will affect the whole process and the end product. Deming's scheme eliminates barriers between the company and the customer, between the customer and suppliers, or between the company and its employees. Because the process is unified, the greater the harmony among all its components, the better the results will be.

An organization's interpretation of quality is expressed in its strategies. If a company does not incorporate quality into its strategic plan, customers may look for other solutions.

Wal-Mart's continuous focus on "everyday low prices" has led some consumers to equate the retailer with low quality.[13] Because of these perceptions, Wal-Mart's sales growth decreased when some Wal-Mart customers started shopping at stores such as Target, which is associated with higher quality. The following sections elaborate on the relationship between quality and production by discussing quality assurance and quality circles as part of organizational strategy. ■

how managers do it

Balancing Quality and Low Prices at Wal-Mart

Quality Assurance **Quality assurance** is an operations process involving a broad group of activities aimed at achieving the organization's quality objectives.[14] Quality assurance is a continuum of activities that starts when quality standards are set and ends when quality goods and services are delivered to the customer. Although the precise activities involved in quality assurance vary from organization to organization, activities such as determining the safest system for delivering goods to customers and maintaining the quality of parts or materials purchased from suppliers are part of most quality assurance efforts.[15]

Statistical Quality Control Statistical quality control is a much narrower concept than quality assurance. **Statistical quality control** is the process used to determine how many products should be inspected to calculate a probability that the total number of products will meet organizational quality standards. An effective quality assurance strategy reduces the need for quality control and subsequent corrective actions.

"No Rejects" Philosophy Quality assurance works best when management adopts a "no rejects" philosophy. Unfortunately, such a philosophy is not economically feasible for most mass-produced products. What is possible is training employees to approach production with a "do not make the same mistake" mind-set. Mistakes are costly, and detecting defective products in the final quality control inspection is expensive. Emphasizing quality in the early stages—during product and process design—will reduce rejects and production costs.

Quality Circles The recent trend in U.S. organizations is to involve all company employees in quality control by soliciting their ideas for judging and maintaining product quality. This trend developed out of a successful Japanese control system known as *quality circles*. Although many U.S. corporations are now moving beyond the concept of the quality circle to that of the work team, as discussed in Chapter 18, many ideas generated from quality circles continue to be valid.[16]

A **quality circle** is a small group of workers that meets to discuss quality assurance of a particular project and to communicate their solutions to these problems to management directly at a formal presentation session.[17] Figure 22.2 shows the quality circle problem-solving process.

Most quality circles operate in a similar manner. The circle usually has fewer than eight members, and the circle leader is not necessarily the members' supervisor. Members may be workers on the project and/or outsiders. The focus is on operational problems rather than interpersonal ones. The problems discussed in the quality circle may be ones assigned by management or ones uncovered by the group itself.

FIGURE 22.2   The quality circle problem-solving process

Automation

The preceding section discussed the relationship between quality and productivity in organizations. This section introduces the topic of automation, which shows signs of increasing organizational productivity in a revolutionary way.[18]

Automation is defined as the replacement of human effort by electromechanical devices in such operations as welding, materials handling, design, drafting, and decision making. It includes robots—mechanical devices built to perform repetitive tasks efficiently—and **robotics**, which is the study of the development and use of robots.

Automation replaces human effort with electromechanical devices, like this police department robot.

Over the past 20 years, a host of advanced manufacturing systems have been developed and implemented to support operations. Most of these automated systems combine hardware-industrial robots and computers—and software. The goals of new automation include reduced inventories, higher productivity, and faster billing and product distribution cycles. So far, the industrialized Asian countries appear to be doing the best job of making optimal use of company resources through automation.

Strategies, Systems, and Processes

According to Kemper and Yehudai, an effective and efficient operations manager is skilled not only in management, production, and productivity, but also in strategies, systems, and processes. A *strategy* is a plan of action. A *system* is a particular linking of organizational components that facilitates carrying out a process. A *process* is a flow of interrelated events toward a goal, purpose, or end. Strategies create interlocking systems and processes when they are comprehensive, functional, and dynamic—when they designate responsibility and provide criteria for measuring output.[19]

OPERATIONS MANAGEMENT

Operations management deals with managing the production of goods and services in organizations. The sections that follow define *operations management* and discuss various strategies managers can use to make production activities more effective and efficient.

Defining Operations Management

According to Chase and Aquilano, **operations management** is the performance of managerial activities that involve selecting, designing, operating, controlling, and updating production systems.[20] Figure 22.3 describes these activities and categorizes them as either periodic or continual. The distinction between periodic and continual activities is one of relative frequency of performance: Periodic activities are performed from time to time, while continual activities are performed essentially without interruption.

FIGURE 22.3   Major activities performed to manage production

Operations Management Considerations

Overall, *operations management* is the systematic direction and control of operations processes that transform resources into finished goods and services.[21] The concept conveys three key notions:

* Operations management involves managers—people who get things done by working with or through other people.

* Operations management takes place within the context of objectives and policies that drive the organization's strategic plans.

* The criteria for judging the actions taken as a result of operations management are standards for effectiveness and efficiency.

Effectiveness is the degree to which managers attain organizational objectives: "doing the right things." **Efficiency** is the degree to which organizational resources contribute to productivity: "doing things right." A review of organizational performance based on these standards is essential to enhancing the success of any organization.

Several years ago a researcher studied how workers at a Domino's Pizza placed pepperoni on a pizza to keep it from sliding into the center when the pizza was put into the oven. Their technique was widely shared among Domino's franchises and helped assure greater operational efficiency. The sharing of best practices is one way an organization can ensure enhanced productivity.[22]

Operations strategies—capacity, location, product, process, layout, and human resources—are specific plans of action designed to ensure that resources are obtained and used effectively and efficiently. An operational strategy is implemented by people who get things done with and through people. It is achieved in the context of objectives and policies derived from the organization's strategic plan.

Capacity Strategy   **Capacity strategy** is a plan of action aimed at providing the organization with the right facilities to produce the needed output at the right time. The output capacity of the organization determines its ability to meet future demands for goods and services. *Insufficient capacity* results in loss of sales that, in turn, affects profits. *Excess capacity* results in higher production costs. A strategy that aims for *optimal capacity*, where quantity and timing are in balance, provides an excellent basis for minimizing operating costs and maximizing profits.

Capacity flexibility enables the company to deliver its goods and services to its customers in a shorter time than its competitors. This component of capacity strategy involves having flexible plants and processes, broadly trained employees, and easy and economical access to external capacity, such as suppliers.

Managers use capacity strategy to balance the costs of overcapacity and undercapacity. The difficulty of accurately forecasting long-term demand makes this balancing task risky. Modifying long-range capacity decisions while in production is both hard and costly. In a highly competitive environment, construction of a new high-tech facility might take longer than the life cycle of the product. Correcting overcapacity by closing a plant saddles management with high economic costs and even higher social costs—such as lost jobs that devastate both employees and the community in which the plant operates—that will have a long-term adverse effect on the firm.

The traditional concept of economies of scale led management to construct large plants that tried to do everything. The more modern concept of the focused facility has shown management that better performance can be achieved in more specialized plants that concentrate on fewer tasks and are therefore smaller.

Five Steps in Capacity Decisions Managers are more likely to make sound strategic capacity decisions if they adhere to the following five-step process:

1. Measure the capacity of currently available facilities.
2. Estimate future capacity needs on the basis of demand forecasts.
3. Compare future capacity needs and available capacity to determine whether capacity must be increased or decreased.
4. Identify ways to accommodate long-range capacity changes (expansion or reduction).
5. Select the best alternative based on a quantitative and qualitative evaluation.

Location Strategy **Location strategy** is a plan of action that provides the organization with a competitive location for its headquarters, manufacturing, services, and distribution activities. A competitive location results in lower transportation and communication costs among the various facilities. These costs—which run as high as 20 to 30 percent of a product's selling price—greatly affect the volume of sales and amount of profit generated by a particular product. Many other quantitative and qualitative factors are important when formulating location strategy.

Factors in a Good Location A successful location strategy requires a company to consider the following major factors in its location study:

* Nearness to market and distribution centers
* Nearness to vendors and resources
* Requirements of federal, state, and local governments
* The character of direct competition
* The degree of interaction with the rest of the corporation
* The quality and quantity of labor pools
* The environmental attractiveness of the area
* Taxes and financing requirements
* Existing and potential transportation
* The quality of utilities and services

The dynamic nature of these factors could make what is a competitive location today an undesirable location in five years.

Product Strategy **Product strategy** is an operational plan of action outlining which goods and services an organization will produce and market.[23] Product strategy is a main component of an organization's operations strategy—in fact, it is the link between the operations strategy and the other functional strategies, especially marketing and research and development. In essence, product, marketing, and research and development strategies must fit together if management is to be able to build an effective overall operations strategy. A business's product and operations strategies should take into account the strengths and weaknesses of operations, which are primarily internal, as well as those of other functional areas concerned more with external opportunities and threats.

Cooperation and coordination among its marketing, operations, and research and development departments from the inception of a new product are strongly beneficial to a company. At the very least, it ensures a smooth transition from research and development to production, because operations people will be able to contribute to the quality of the total product, rather than merely attempt to improve the quality of the components. Even the most sophisticated product can be designed so that it is relatively simple to produce, thus reducing the number of units that must be scrapped or reworked during production, as well as the need for highly trained and highly paid employees. All of these strategies lower production costs and hence, increase the product's price competitiveness or profits or both.

Process Strategy **Process strategy** is a plan of action outlining the means and methods the organization will use to transform resources into goods and services. Materials, labor, information, equipment, and managerial skills are resources that must be transformed. A competitive process strategy will ensure the most efficient and effective use of these organizational resources.

Types of Processes All manufacturing processes may be grouped into three different types. The first is the *continuous process,* a product-oriented, high-volume, low-variety process used, for example, in producing chemicals, beer, and petroleum products. The second is the *repetitive process,* a product-oriented production process that uses modules to produce items in large lots. This mass-production or assembly-line process is characteristic of the auto and appliance industries.

The third type of manufacturing process is used to produce small lots of custom-designed products such as furniture. This high-variety, low-volume system, commonly known as the *job-shop process,* includes the production of one-of-a-kind items as well as unit production. Spaceship and weapons systems production are considered job-shop activities.

Organizations commonly employ more than one type of manufacturing process at the same time and in the same facility.

Process strategy is directly linked to product strategy. The decision to select a particular process strategy is often the result of external market opportunities or threats. The corporation decides what it wants to produce, then selects a process strategy to produce it. The product takes center stage and the process becomes a function of the product.

The function of process strategy is to determine what equipment will be used, what maintenance will be necessary, and what level of automation will be most effective and efficient. The type of employees and the level of employee skills needed are dependent on the process strategy chosen.

Layout Strategy **Layout strategy** is a plan of action that outlines the location and flow of all organizational resources around, into, and within production and service facilities. A cost-effective and cost-efficient layout strategy is one that minimizes the expenses of processing, transporting, and storing materials throughout the production and service cycle.

Layout strategy—which is usually the last part of operations strategy to be formulated—is closely linked, either directly or indirectly, with all other components of operations strategy: capacity, location, product, process, and human resources. It must target capacity and process requirements. It must satisfy the organization's product design, quality, and quantity requirements. It must target facility and location requirements. Finally, to be effective, the layout strategy must be compatible with the organization's established quality of work life.

A **layout** is the overall arrangement of equipment, work areas, service areas, and storage areas within a facility that produces goods or provides services.[24] Three basic types of layouts are used for manufacturing facilities:

1. A **product layout** is designed to accommodate high production volumes, highly specialized equipment, and narrow employee skills. It is appropriate for organizations that produce

The right facilities layout strategy can help streamline the work of this candymaker, who is pouring melted fudge at a Rocky Mountain Chocolate factory. The design of his workplace must take into account the distance the fudge travels between the cooking area and the marble table shown here, the weight of the vats, the temperature and humidity of the work area, the next step in the manufacturing process, and many other factors.

and service a limited number of different products. It is not appropriate for an organization that experiences constant or frequent changes of products.

2. A **process (functional) layout** is a layout pattern that groups together similar types of equipment. It is appropriate for organizations involved in a large number of different tasks. It best serves companies whose production volumes are low, whose equipment is multipurpose, and whose employees' skills are broad.

3. The **fixed-position layout** is one in which the product is stationary while resources flow. It is appropriate for organizations involved in a large number of different tasks that require low volumes, multipurpose equipment, and broad employee skills. A *group technology layout* is a product layout cell within a larger process layout. It benefits organizations that require both types of layout.

Figure 22.4 illustrates the three basic layout patterns. Actually, most manufacturing facilities are a combination of two or more different types of layouts. Various techniques are available to assist management in designing an efficient and effective layout that meets the required specifications.

Human Resources Strategy *Human resources* is the term used for individuals engaged in any of the organization's activities. Two human resource imperatives are as follows:

1. It is essential to optimize individual, group, and organizational effectiveness.
2. It is essential to enhance the quality of organizational life.

A **human resources strategy** is an operational plan to use the organization's human resources effectively and efficiently while maintaining or improving the quality of work life.[25] As discussed in Chapter 13, human resource management is about employees—who

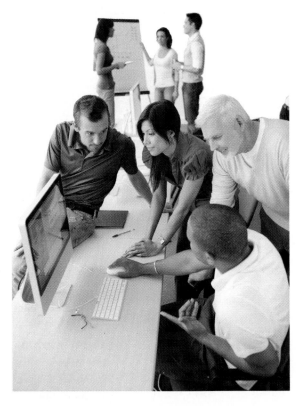

Hiring the right people for every job and training them to be productive is a human resources strategy with implications for management control.

FIGURE 22.4
Three basic layout patterns

PROCESS LAYOUT IN A HEALTH CARE CLINIC

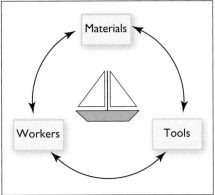

PRODUCT LAYOUT IN FURNITURE MANUFACTURING

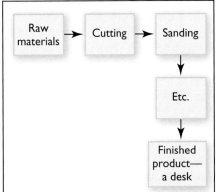

FIXED-POSITION LAYOUT IN BUILDING A SHIP

Chrysler Corporation recently adapted its human resources strategy after its acquisition by Italian automaker Fiat. Specifically, Chrysler hired 600 engineers—200 of them with a background in quality processes—to help it fill the supply pipeline with vehicles. Working from a clean slate, Chrysler identified skilled designers who could adapt Fiat platforms to cars and trucks to be marketed under brands like Chrysler, Dodge, Jeep, and Ram.[26] ■

are the best means of enhancing organizational effectiveness. Whereas financial management attempts to increase organizational effectiveness through the allocation and conservation of financial resources, human resource management (personnel management) attempts to increase organizational effectiveness through such factors as the establishment of personnel policies, education and training, and procedures.

Operational Tools in Human Resources Strategy Operations management attempts to increase organizational effectiveness by employing the methods used in the manufacturing and service processes. Human resources, one important factor of operations, must be compatible with operations tasks.

Labor force planning is the primary focus of the operations human resources strategy. It is an operational plan for hiring the right employees for a job and training them to be productive. This process is lengthy and costly. A human resources strategy must be founded on fair treatment and trust. The employee, not operations, must take center stage. Yet, the recent economic decline has had a significant impact on the workforce, with widespread layoffs and many jobs moved offshore. As the economy recovers, the process of strategic workforce planning will become even more critical and will force employers to revisit some of their conventional assumptions about hiring.[27]

Job design is an operational plan that determines who will do a specific job and how and where the job will be done. The goal of job design is to facilitate productivity. Successful job design takes efficiency and behavior into account. It also guarantees that working conditions are safe and that the health of employees will not be jeopardized in the short or the long run. When executed effectively, job design sets the state for a successful recruitment and retention program.[28]

Work methods analysis is an operational tool used to improve productivity and ensure the safety of workers. It can be performed for new or existing jobs. **Motion-study techniques** are another set of operational tools used to improve productivity.

Work measurement methods are operational tools used to establish labor standards. These standards are useful for planning, control, productivity improvements, costing and pricing, bidding, compensation, motivation, and financial incentives. In measuring organizational characteristics (e.g., pricing, quality, etc.), managers must ensure that their methods are integrated with the organization's objectives.[29]

OPERATIONS CONTROL

Once a decision has been made to design an operational plan of action, resource allocations are considered. After management has decided on a functional operations strategy, using marketing and financial plans of action, it determines what specific tasks are necessary to accomplish functional objectives. This process is known as *operations control*.

Operations control is defined as making sure operations activities are carried out as planned. The major components of operations control are just-in-time inventory control, maintenance control, cost control, budgetary control, ratio analysis, and materials control. Each of these components is discussed in detail in the following sections.

Just-in-Time Inventory Control

Just-in-time (JIT) inventory control is a technique for reducing inventories to a minimum by arranging for production components to be delivered to the production facility "just in time" to be used.[30] The concept, developed primarily by the Toyota Motor Company of Japan, is also called "zero inventory" or *kanban*—the latter a Japanese term referring to purchasing raw materials by using a special ordering form.[31]

JIT is based on the management philosophy that products should be manufactured only when customers need them and only in the quantities customers require in order to minimize the amounts of raw materials and finished goods inventories manufacturers keep on hand. It emphasizes maintaining organizational operations by using only the resources that are absolutely necessary to meet customer demand.

Best Conditions for JIT JIT works best in companies that manufacture relatively standardized products that experience consistent demand. Such companies can comfortably order materials from suppliers and assemble products in small, continuous batches. The result is a smooth, consistent flow of purchased materials and assembled products, with little inventory buildup.

However, JIT is not always the best choice for every organization. Companies that manufacture nonstandardized products that experience sporadic or seasonal demand, however, generally face more irregular purchases of raw materials from suppliers, more uneven production cycles, and greater accumulations of inventory.[32]

Advantages of JIT When successfully implemented, JIT enhances organizational performance in several important ways. First, it reduces the unnecessary labor expenses generated by manufacturing products that are not sold. Second, it minimizes the tying up of monetary resources in purchases of production-related materials that do not result in timely sales. Third, it helps management hold down inventory expenses—particularly storage and handling costs. Better inventory management and control of labor costs, in fact, are the two most commonly cited benefits of JIT.

Characteristics of JIT Experience indicates that successful JIT programs have certain common characteristics:[33]

1. **Closeness of suppliers**—Manufacturers using JIT find it beneficial to use raw materials suppliers who are based only a short distance from them. When a company is ordering smaller quantities of raw materials at a time, suppliers must sometimes be asked to make one or more deliveries per day. Short distances make multiple deliveries per day feasible. Nonetheless, relying on one large supplier may present disadvantages as well. For example, an earthquake once caused one of Toyota's piston suppliers to temporarily suspend its operations. Because the automaker practices JIT, the resulting shortage of pistons caused a delay in the delivery of about 55,000 vehicles.[34]
2. **High quality of materials purchased from suppliers**—Manufacturers using JIT find it especially difficult to overcome problems caused by defective materials. Because they keep their materials inventory small, defective materials purchased from a supplier may force them to discontinue the production process until another delivery from the supplier can be arranged. Such production slowdowns can be disadvantageous, causing late delivery to customers or lost sales.
3. **Well-organized receiving and handling of materials purchased from suppliers**—Companies using JIT must be able to receive and handle raw materials effectively and efficiently. Materials must be available for the production process where and when they are needed, because if they are not, extra costs will be built into the production process.
4. **Strong management commitment**—Management must be strongly committed to the concept of JIT. The system takes time and effort to plan, install, and improve—and is therefore expensive to implement. Management must be willing to commit funds to initiate the JIT system and support it once it is functioning.

Maintenance Control

Maintenance control is aimed at keeping the organization's facility and equipment functioning at predetermined work levels. In the planning stage, managers must select a strategy that will direct personnel to fix equipment either before it malfunctions or after it malfunctions. The first strategy is referred to as a **pure-preventive maintenance policy**—machine adjustments, lubrication, cleaning, parts replacement, painting, and needed repairs and overhauls are done regularly, before facilities or machines malfunction. At the other end of the maintenance control continuum is the **pure-breakdown (repair) policy**, which decrees that facilities and equipment be fixed only after they malfunction.

Most organizations implement a maintenance strategy somewhere in the middle of the maintenance continuum. Management usually tries to select a level and frequency of maintenance that minimize the cost of both preventive maintenance and breakdowns (repair). Because no level of preventive maintenance can eliminate breakdowns altogether, repair will always be an important activity.

Whether management decides on a pure-preventive or pure-breakdown policy, or on something in between, the prerequisite for a successful maintenance program is the availability of maintenance parts and supplies or replacement (standby) equipment. Some organizations choose to keep standby machines to protect themselves against the consequences of breakdowns. Plants that use special-purpose equipment are more likely to invest in standby equipment than those that use general-purpose equipment.

Cost Control

Cost control is broad control aimed at keeping organizational costs at planned levels.[35] Because cost control relates to all organizational costs, it emphasizes activities in all organizational areas, such as research and development, operations, marketing, and finance. If an organization is to be successful, costs in all organizational areas must be controlled. Cost control is therefore an important responsibility of all managers in an organization.

Operations activities are cost-intensive—perhaps the most cost-intensive of all organizational activities—so when significant cost savings are realized in organizations, they are generally realized at the operations level.

Operations managers are responsible for the overall control of the cost of goods or services sold. Producing goods and services at or below planned cost levels is their principal objective, so operations managers are commonly evaluated primarily on their cost control activities. When operations costs are consistently above planned levels, the organization may need to change its operations management.

Stages in Cost Control   The general cost control process has four stages:

1. Establishing standard or planned cost amounts
2. Measuring actual costs incurred
3. Comparing planned costs to incurred costs
4. Making changes to reduce actual costs to planned costs when necessary

Following these stages for specific operations cost control, the operations manager must first establish planned costs or cost standards for operations activities such as labor, materials, and overhead. Next, the operations manager must actually measure or calculate the costs incurred for these activities. Third, the operations manager must compare actual operations costs to planned operations costs, and fourth, take steps to reduce actual operations costs to planned levels if necessary.

Budgetary Control

As described in Chapter 10, a budget is a single-use financial plan that covers a specified length of time. An organization's **budget** is its financial plan outlining how funds in a given period will be obtained and spent.

In addition to being a financial plan, however, a budget can be the basis for *budgetary control*—that is, for ensuring that income and expenses occur as planned. As managers gather information on actual receipts and expenditures within an operating period, they may uncover significant deviations from budgeted amounts. If so, they should develop and implement a control strategy aimed at bringing actual performance in line with planned performance. This effort, of course, assumes that the plan contained in the budget is appropriate for the organization. The following sections discuss some potential pitfalls of budgets and human relations considerations that may make a budget inappropriate.

Potential Pitfalls of Budgets To maximize the benefits of using budgets, managers must avoid several potential pitfalls. Among these pitfalls are the following:

1. **Placing too much emphasis on relatively insignificant organizational expenses**— In preparing and implementing a budget, managers should allocate more time for dealing with significant organizational expenses and less time for relatively insignificant organizational expenses. For example, the amount of time managers spend on developing and implementing a budget for labor costs typically should be much more than the amount of time they spend on developing and implementing a budget for office supplies.

2. **Increasing budgeted expenses year after year without adequate information**— It does not necessarily follow that items contained in last year's budget should be increased this year. Perhaps the best-known method for overcoming this potential pitfall is zero-base budgeting.[36] **Zero-base budgeting** is a planning and budgeting process that requires managers to justify their entire budget request in detail rather than simply referring to budget amounts established in previous years.

   Some management theorists believe that zero-base budgeting is a better management tool than traditional budgeting—which simply starts with the budget amount established in the prior year—because it emphasizes focused identification and control of each budget item. It is unlikely, however, that this tool will be implemented successfully unless management adequately explains what zero-base budgeting is and how it is to be used in the organization. One of the earliest and most commonly cited successes in implementing a zero-base budgeting program took place in the Department of Agriculture's Office of Budget and Finance.

3. **Ignoring the fact that budgets must be changed periodically**—Managers should recognize that such factors as costs of materials, newly developed technology, and product demand change constantly and that budgets must be reviewed and modified periodically in response to these changes.

A special type of budget called a *variable budget* is sometimes used to determine automatically when such changes in budgets are needed. A **variable budget**, also known as a *flexible budget,* outlines the levels of resources to be allocated for each organizational activity according to the level of production within the organization. It follows, then, that a variable budget automatically indicates an increase in the amount of resources allocated for various organizational activities when production levels go up and a decrease when production goes down.

Human Relations Considerations in Using Budgets Many managers believe that although budgets are valuable planning and control tools, they can result in major human relations problems in an organization. A classic article by Chris Argyris, for example, shows how budgets can build pressures that unite workers against management, cause harmful conflict between management and factory workers, and create tensions that result in worker inefficiency and worker aggression against management.[37] If such problems are severe enough, a budget may result in more harm than good to the organization.

Reducing Human Relations Problems Several strategies have been suggested to minimize the human relations problems caused by budgets. The most often recommended strategy is to design and implement appropriate human relations training programs for finance personnel, accounting personnel, production supervisors, and all other key people involved in the formulation and use of budgets. These training programs should emphasize both the advantages and disadvantages of applying pressure on people through budgets and the possible results of using budgets to imply that an organization member is a success or a failure at his or her job.

Ratio Analysis

Another type of control uses ratio analysis.[38] A *ratio* is a relationship between two numbers that is calculated by dividing one number into the other. **Ratio analysis** is the process of generating information that summarizes the financial position of an organization through the calculation of ratios based on various financial measures that appear on the organization's balance sheet and income statements.

The ratios available to managers for controlling organizations, shown in Table 22.1, can be divided into four categories:

1. Profitability ratios
2. Liquidity ratios
3. Activity ratios
4. Leverage ratios

Using Ratios to Control Organizations Managers should use ratio analysis in three ways to control an organization:[39]

- **Managers should evaluate all ratios simultaneously.** This strategy ensures that they will develop and implement a control strategy appropriate for the organization as a whole rather than one that suits only one phase or segment of the organization.

- **Managers should compare computed values for ratios in a specific organization with the values of industry averages for those ratios.** (The values of industry averages for the ratios can be obtained from Dun & Bradstreet; Robert Morris Associates, a national association of bank loan officers; the Federal Trade Commission; and the Securities and Exchange Commission.) Managers increase the probability of formulating and implementing appropriate control strategies when they compare their financial situation to that of competitors in this way.

- **Managers' use of ratios should incorporate trend analysis.** Managers must remember that any set of ratio values is actually only a determination of relationships that existed in a specified time period (often a year). To employ ratio analysis to maximum advantage, they need to accumulate ratio values for several successive time periods to uncover specific organizational trends. Once these trends are revealed, managers can formulate and implement appropriate strategies for dealing with them.

Materials Control

Materials control is an operations control activity that determines the flow of materials from vendors through an operations system to customers. The achievement of desired levels of product cost, quality, availability, dependability, and flexibility heavily depends on the effective and

TABLE 22.1 Four Categories of Ratios

Type	Example	Calculation	Interpretation
Profitability	Return on investment (ROI)	$\dfrac{\text{Profit after taxes}}{\text{Total assets}}$	Productivity of assets
Liquidity	Current ratio	$\dfrac{\text{Current assets}}{\text{Current liabilities}}$	Short-term solvency
Activity	Inventory turnover	$\dfrac{\text{Sales}}{\text{Inventory}}$	Efficiency of inventory management
Leverage	Debt ratio	$\dfrac{\text{Total debt}}{\text{Total assets}}$	How a company finances itself

efficient flow of materials. Materials management activities can be broadly organized into six groups or functions: purchasing, receiving, inventorying, floor controlling, trafficking, and shipping and distributing.

Procurement of Materials

More than 50 percent of the expenditures of a typical manufacturing company are for the procurement of materials, including raw materials, parts, subassemblies, and supplies. This procurement is the responsibility of the purchasing department. Actually, purchases of production materials are largely automated and linked to a resources requirement planning system. Purchases of all other materials, however, are based on requisitions from users. The purchasing department's job does not end with the placement of an order; order follow-up is just as crucial.

Receiving, Shipping, and Trafficking

Receiving activities include unloading, identifying, inspecting, reporting, and storing inbound shipments. Shipping and distribution activities are similar and may include preparing documents, packaging, labeling, loading, and directing outbound shipments to customers and to distribution centers. Shipping and receiving are sometimes organized as one unit.

A traffic manager's main responsibilities are selection of the transportation mode, coordination of the arrival and departure of shipments, and auditing freight bills.

Inventory and Shop-Floor Control

Inventory control activities ensure the continuous availability of purchased materials. Work-in-process and finished-goods inventory are inventory control subsystems. Inventory control specifies what, when, and how much to buy. Held inventories buffer the organization against a variety of uncertainties that can disrupt supply, but since holding inventory is costly, an optimal inventory control policy provides a predetermined level of certainty of supply at the lowest possible cost.

Shop-floor control activities include input/output control, scheduling, sequencing, routing, dispatching, and expediting.

Although many materials management activities can be programmed, the human factor is the key to a competitive performance. Skilled and motivated employees are therefore crucial to successful materials control.

class discussion highlight

DOES QUALITY CONTROL MATTER?

This chapter highlights how a company's operations management is important, but do these management techniques ultimately help managers improve the performance of their firms? To answer this question, Professors Tan, Kannan, and Narasimhan examined the influence of quality control and just-in-time strategies on firm performance.

The researchers designed a survey to better understand how operations management techniques influence firm performance, and they received more than 500 responses from operations management professionals. Do you think the authors found support for relationships between quality control and just-in-time strategies and firm performance? Why or why not? If managers share your beliefs, what are the implications for organizations and their budgets?

Source: C. Tan, V. R. Kannan, and R. Narasimhan, "The Impact of Operations Capability on Firm Performance," *International Journal of Production Research* 45, no. 21 (2007): 5135–5156.

SELECTED OPERATIONS CONTROL TOOLS

In addition to understanding production, operations management, and operations control, managers also need to be aware of various operations control tools that are useful in an operations facility. A **control tool** is a specific procedure or technique that presents pertinent organizational information in a way that helps managers and workers develop and implement an appropriate control strategy. That is, a control tool aids managers and workers in pinpointing the organizational strengths and weaknesses on which a useful control strategy must focus. This section discusses specific control tools for day-to-day operations as well as for longer-run operations.

Using Control Tools to Control Organizations

Continual improvement of operations is a practical, not a theoretical, managerial concern. It is, essentially, the development and use of better methods. Different types of organizations have different goals and strategies, but all organizations struggle daily to find better ways of doing things. This goal of continual improvement applies not just to money-making enterprises, but to those with other missions as well. Because organizational leaders are continually changing systems and personal styles of management, everyone within the organization is continually learning to live with change.

Inspection

Traditionally, managers believed that if you wanted good quality, you hired many inspectors to make sure an operation was producing at the desired quality level. These inspectors examined and graded finished products or components, parts, or services at any stage of operation by measuring, tasting, touching, weighing, disassembling, destroying, and testing. The goal of inspection was to detect unacceptable quality levels before a bad product or service reached a customer. Whenever a lot of defects were found, management blamed the workers and hired more inspectors.

To Inspect or Not to Inspect   Today, managers know that inspection cannot catch problems built into the system. The traditional inspection process does not result in improvement and does not guarantee quality. In fact, according to Deming, inspection is a limited, grossly overused, and often misused tool. He recommended that management stop relying on mass inspection to achieve quality, and advocated instead either 100 percent inspection in those cases where defect-free work is impossible or no inspection at all where the level of defects is acceptably small.

Management by Exception

Management by exception is a control technique that allows only significant deviations between planned and actual performance to be brought to a manager's attention. Management by exception is based on the *exception principle,* a management principle that appears in early management literature.[40] This principle recommends that subordinates handle all routine organizational matters, leaving managers free to deal with nonroutine, or exceptional, organizational issues.

Establishing Rules   Some organizations rely on subordinates or managers themselves to detect the significant deviations between standards and performance that signal exceptional issues. Other organizations establish rules to ensure that exceptional issues surface as a matter of normal operating procedure. Setting rules must be done carefully to ensure that all true deviations are brought to the manager's attention.

Two examples of rules based on the exception principle are the following:[41]

1. A department manager must immediately inform the plant manager if actual weekly labor costs exceed estimated weekly labor costs by more than 15 percent.
2. A department manager must immediately inform the plant manager if actual dollars spent plus estimated dollars to be spent on a special project exceed the funds approved for the project by more than 10 percent.

Although these two rules happen to focus on production-related expenditures, detecting and reporting significant rules deviations can be established in virtually any organizational area.

If appropriately administered, the management-by-exception control technique ensures the best use of managers' time. Because only significant issues are brought to managers' attention, the possibility that managers will spend their valuable time working on relatively insignificant issues is automatically eliminated.

Of course, the significant issues brought to managers' attention could be organizational strengths as well as organizational weaknesses. Obviously, managers should try to reinforce the first and eliminate the second.

Management by Objectives

In management by objectives, which was discussed in Chapter 7, the manager assigns a specialized set of objectives and action plans to workers and then rewards those workers on the basis of how close they come to reaching their goals. This control technique has been implemented in corporations intent on using an employee-participative means to improve productivity.

Break-Even Analysis

Another production-related control tool commonly used by managers is break-even analysis. **Break-even analysis** is the process of generating information that summarizes various levels of profit or loss associated with various levels of production. The next sections discuss three facets of this control tool: basic ingredients of break-even analysis, types of break-even analysis available to managers, and the relationship between break-even analysis and controlling.

Basic Ingredients of Break-Even Analysis
Break-even analysis typically involves reflection, discussion, reasoning, and decision making relative to the following seven major aspects of production:

1. **Fixed costs**—A **fixed cost** is an expense incurred by the organization regardless of the number of products produced. Some examples are real estate taxes, upkeep to the exterior of a business building, and interest expenses on money borrowed to finance the purchase of equipment.
2. **Variable costs**—An expense that fluctuates with the number of products produced is a **variable cost.** Examples are costs of packaging a product, costs of materials needed to make the product, and costs associated with packing products to prepare them for shipping.
3. **Total cost**—The **total cost** is simply the sum of the fixed and variable costs associated with production.
4. **Total revenue**—**Total revenue** is all sales dollars accumulated from selling manufactured products or services. Naturally, total revenue increases as more products are sold.
5. **Profit**—**Profit** is defined as the amount of total revenue that exceeds the total costs of producing the products sold.

6. **Loss**—**Loss** is the amount of the total costs of producing a product that exceeds the total revenue gained from selling the product.
7. **Break-even point**—The **break-even point** is the level of production at which the total revenue of an organization equals its total costs—that is, the point at which the organization is generating only enough revenue to cover its costs. The company is neither gaining a profit nor incurring a loss.

Types of Break-Even Analysis
Two somewhat different procedures can be used to determine the same break-even point for an organization: algebraic break-even analysis and graphic break-even analysis.

Algebraic Break-Even Analysis
The following simple formula is commonly used to determine the level of production at which an organization breaks even:

$$BE = \frac{FC}{P - VC}$$

where

BE = the level of production at which the firm breaks even
FC = total fixed costs of production
P = price at which each individual unit is sold to customers
VC = variable costs associated with each product manufactured and sold

In using this formula to calculate a break-even point, two sequential steps must be followed. First, the variable costs associated with producing each unit must be subtracted from the price at which each unit will sell. The purpose of this calculation is to determine how much of the selling price of each unit sold can go toward covering total fixed costs incurred from producing all products. Second, the remainder calculated in the first step must be divided into total fixed costs. The purpose of this calculation is to determine how many units must be produced and sold to cover fixed costs. This number of units is the break-even point for the organization.

Say a book publisher faces the fixed and variable costs per paperback book presented in Table 22.2. If the publisher wants to sell each book for $12, the break-even point could be calculated as follows:

$$BE = \frac{\$88,800}{\$12 - \$6}$$

$$BE = \frac{\$88,800}{\$6}$$

$$BE = 14,800 \text{ copies}$$

TABLE 22.2 Fixed Costs and Variable Costs for a Book Publisher

Fixed Costs (Yearly Basis)		Variable Costs per Book Sold	
1. Real estate taxes on property	$1,000	1. Printing	$2.00
2. Interest on loan to purchase equipment	5,000	2. Artwork	1.00
3. Building maintenance	2,000	3. Sales commission	.50
4. Insurance	800	4. Author royalties	1.50
5. Salaried labor	80,000	5. Binding	1.00
Total fixed costs	$88,800	Total variable costs per book	$6.00

FIGURE 22.5
Break-even analysis for a book publisher

* Note that drawing the variable costs line on top of the fixed costs line means that variable costs have been added to fixed costs. Therefore, the variable costs line also represents total costs.

This calculation indicates that if expenses and selling price remain stable, the book publisher will incur a loss if book sales are fewer than 14,800 copies, will break even if book sales equal 14,800 copies, and will make a profit if book sales exceed 14,800 copies.

Graphic Break-Even Analysis Graphic break-even analysis entails the construction of a graph showing all the critical elements in a break-even analysis. Figure 22.5 is such a graph for the book publisher. Note that in a break-even graph, the total revenue line starts at zero.

Advantages of Using the Algebraic and Graphic Break-Even Methods
Both the algebraic and the graphic methods of break-even analysis for the book publisher result in the same break-even point—14,800 books produced and sold—but the processes used to arrive at this point are quite different.

Which break-even method managers should use is usually determined by the situation they face. For a manager who desires a quick yet accurate determination of a break-even point, the algebraic method generally suffices. For a manager who wants a more complete picture of the cumulative relationships between the break-even point, fixed costs, and escalating variable costs, the graphic break-even method is more useful. For example, the book publisher could quickly and easily see from Figure 22.5 the cumulative relationships of fixed costs, escalating variable costs, and potential profit and loss associated with various levels of production.

Control and Break-Even Analysis Break-even analysis is a useful control tool because it helps managers understand the relationships between fixed costs, variable costs, total costs, and profit and loss within an organization. Once these relationships are understood, managers can take steps to modify one or more of the variables to reduce deviation between planned and actual profit levels.[42]

Increasing costs or decreasing selling prices has the overall effect of increasing the number of units an organization must produce and sell to break even. Conversely, the managerial strategy for decreasing the number of products an organization must produce and sell to break even entails lowering or stabilizing fixed and variables costs or increasing the selling price of each unit. The exact break-even control strategy a particular manager should develop and implement is dictated primarily by that manager's unique organizational situation.

Other Broad Operations Control Tools

Some of the best-known and most commonly used operations control tools are discussed in the following sections. The primary purpose of these tools is to control the production of organizational goods and services.[43]

Decision Tree Analysis **Decision tree analysis,** as you recall from Chapter 8, is a statistical and graphical multiphased decision-making technique that contains a series of steps showing the sequence and interdependence of decisions. Decision trees allow a decision maker to deal with uncertain events by determining the relative expected value of each alternative course of action. The probabilities of different possible events are known, as are the monetary payoffs that result from a particular alternative and a particular event. Decision trees are best suited to situations in which capacity decisions involve several capacity expansion alternatives and the selection of the alternative with the highest expected profit or the lowest expected cost is necessary.

Process Control Statistical process control, known as **process control,** is a technique that assists in monitoring production processes. Production processes must be monitored continually to ensure that the quality of their output is acceptable. The earlier the detection of a faulty production process can occur, the better. If detection occurs late in the production process, the company may find parts that do not meet quality standards, and scrapping or reworking these units is a costly proposition. If a production process results in unstable performance or is downright out of control, corrective action must be taken. Process control can be implemented with the aid of graphical charts known as control charts.

Value Analysis **Value analysis** is a cost control and cost reduction technique that helps managers control operations by focusing primarily on material costs. The goal of this analysis, which is performed by examining all the parts and materials and their functions, is to reduce costs by using cheaper components and materials in such a way that product quality or appeal is not affected. Simplification of parts—which lowers production costs—is also a goal of value analysis. Value analysis can result not only in cost savings, but in an improved product.

Value analysis requires a team effort. The team, if not companywide, should at least include personnel from operations, purchasing, engineering, and marketing.

Computer-Aided Design **Computer-aided design (CAD)** systems include several automated design technologies. *Computer graphics* is used to design geometric specifications for parts, while *computer-aided engineering (CAE)* is employed to evaluate and perform engineering analyses on a part. CAD also includes technologies used in process design. CAD functions to ensure the quality of a product by guaranteeing not only the quality of parts in the product, but also the appropriateness of the product's design.

Computer-Aided Manufacturing **Computer-aided manufacturing (CAM)** employs computers to plan and program equipment used in the production and inspection of manufactured items. Linking CAM and CAD processes through a computer is especially beneficial when production processes must be altered, because when CAD and CAM systems can share information easily, design changes can be implemented in a short period of time.

CHALLENGE CASE SUMMARY

Increasing productivity at Delta, as described in the Challenge Case, is mainly a matter of integrating resources such as people, equipment, and materials to provide better customer service.

Although the level of productivity at Delta was far from disastrous, management decided it was necessary to lower operating costs through improved productivity to stay competitive in the increasingly combative airline carrier business. One of Delta's first moves involved installing self-service kiosks that help passengers move through the airports more quickly. To increase productivity at Delta even further, managers might also take such actions as implementing more effective training programs for employees and being more selective in hiring people.

To maintain and improve the quality of customer service, Delta management could establish a quality assurance program that continually monitors services to ensure that they are at acceptable levels. Quality circles could be established to involve employees in the effort to improve customer service both in the specific area of reducing check-in times and in more general terms.

In attempting to reduce the time it takes its passengers to reach their planes, Delta's management is involved in operations management. Most of the issues mentioned in the Challenge Case pertain to the "periodic updating" segment of operations management activities—revising systems to provide better customer service. Delta's periodic updating should focus on the appropriate use of company resources such as ticket agents, caterers, fuel trucks, and ramp agents. Once established, the new operations procedure must be continually monitored by Delta's management for both effectiveness—"doing the right things"—and efficiency—"doing things right."

Factors that Delta's management must consider in making operations decisions include *capacity strategy*, making sure that the airline has appropriate resources to perform needed functions at appropriate times; *location strategy*, making sure that airline resources are appropriately postured for work when the work must be performed; *product strategy*, making sure appropriate customer services are targeted and provided; *process strategy*, making sure that Delta is employing appropriate steps in providing various customer services; *layout strategy*, making sure that the flow of Delta's resources in the process of providing customer services is desirable; and *human resources strategy*, making sure that Delta has appropriate people providing services to customers.

Operations control activities help Delta's management make certain that customer services are carried out as planned. *Just-in-time inventory control*, for example, would ensure that enough self-service kiosks are in place and available just when customers need them. Putting money into large surpluses of these kiosks, however, would needlessly tie up company resources and reduce company profitability. *Maintenance control* would ensure that equipment (e.g., baggage conveyors) needed to provide customer service is operating at a desirable level. *Cost control* would ensure that Delta is not providing services to customers too expensively. *Budgetary control* would focus on acquiring company resources and using them to provide customer services as stipulated by Delta's financial plan.

Operations control at Delta can also include ratio analysis, or determining relationships between various factors on Delta's income statement and balance sheet to arrive at a good indication of the company's financial position. Through ratio analysis, Delta's management could monitor issues such as customer services to determine their overall impact on company profitability, liquidity, and leverage. To assess the impact of providing various customer services on the financial condition of Delta, management would track ratios over time to discern trends.

Finally, operations control at Delta would need to include materials control to ensure that materials purchased from suppliers are flowing appropriately from vendors to customers in the form of customer services. For example, the goal of monitoring the drinks, snacks, and meals that caterers are providing to Delta's passengers would be to improve the quality of such items in terms of temperature, freshness, and nutritional value.

Several useful production control tools are available to Delta's management to ensure that various services are provided to customers as planned. First, management can have customer services inspected to determine which, if any, services should be improved and how to improve them. Second, Delta can use management by exception to control customer services. In this case, Delta's workers would handle all routine customer service issues and bring only exceptional matters to management's attention. To successfully use management by exception at Delta, it would be necessary to implement a number of carefully designed rules. One such rule might be that when 5 percent or more of passengers are late for a given flight, a customer service representative must report this fact to a supervisor. The supervisor would then carefully inspect the check-in process to see why so many passengers are late—perhaps because the airport does not offer enough self-service kiosks—and management would take steps to correct the situation.

Delta might prefer to use management by objectives to control customer service issues. For example, management could set such customer service objectives as answering a ticket counter phone within three rings or ticketing a passenger within five minutes. If such objectives are deemed both worthwhile and realistic, yet Delta's employees are not reaching them consistently, management would take steps to ensure that they are met.

Another control tool Delta's management might find highly useful is break-even analysis. Break-even analysis would furnish management with information about the various levels of profit or loss associated with various levels of revenue. To use this tool, Delta would have to determine the total fixed costs necessary to operate the airline, the price at which flights are sold, and the variable costs associated with various flights.

For example, if management wanted to determine how many tickets had to be sold before the company would break even on a particular flight, it could arrive at this break-even point algebraically by following three steps. First, all fixed costs attributable to operating the flight—for example, airport facility rent—would be totaled. Second, all the variable costs of furnishing a flight to a passenger would be totaled, and from this total, management would subtract the revenue that a ticket will generate. Variable costs include such expenses as meal costs, fuel costs, and labor needed to furnish the flight. Finally, the answer calculated in step 2 would be divided into the answer derived in step 1, and this figure would tell management how many tickets must be sold at the projected revenue level to break even.

Delta's management also could choose to determine the break-even point by constructing a graph showing fixed costs, variable costs, and revenue per flight. Such a graph would probably give managers a more useful picture for formulating profit-oriented flight plans.

Decision tree analysis, process control, value analysis, computer-aided design, and computer-aided manufacturing were presented in the text as broader operations tools that are highly useful to managers exercising the control function. Of all these tools, value analysis would have the most application to Delta's service-oriented operation. Delta's management could use this cost control and cost reduction technique to examine the cost and worth of every component of customer service. To gain a complete picture of customer service components and their usefulness, Delta might establish a team comprising members from different customer service areas.

For instance, a team composed of a ticket agent, a flight attendant, a maintenance supervisor, and a baggage handler might explore different options for establishing comfortable cabin temperature while a plane is being loaded but before it taxis to the runway to await takeoff. If this team concludes, for example, that expediting the baggage-handling process would expose passengers to uncomfortable temperatures for shorter periods of time, management could take steps to speed up the process. Implementation of more efficient ways of handling baggage would result not only in better customer service, but in lower airline operating costs.

MANAGEMENT SKILL ACTIVITIES

This section is specially designed to help you develop production and control skill. An individual's production and control skill is based on an understanding of production and control concepts and the ability to apply those concepts in management situations. The following activities are designed to both heighten your understanding of production and control concepts and to develop the ability to apply those concepts in a variety of management situations.

UNDERSTANDING PRODUCTION AND CONTROL CONCEPTS

To check your understanding and to practice using the concepts in this chapter, go to www.mymanagementlab.com and explore the material associated with Chapter 22.

Know Key Terms

Understanding the following key terms is critical to your understanding of chapter material. Define each of these terms. Refer to the page(s) referenced after a term to check your definition or to gain further insight regarding the term.

production **528**	quality **529**	statistical quality control **531**
productivity **528**	quality assurance **531**	quality circle **531**

Know How Management Concepts Relate

This section is comprised of activities that will sharpen your understanding of team concepts. Answer essay questions as completely as possible. Also, remember that additional true/false and multiple choice questions appear online at MyManagementLab.com to help you further refine your understanding of team concepts.

1. Describe the relationship between quality and productivity.

2. Define capacity strategy and describe the five steps involved with making capacity decisions.

3. Describe the advantages and disadvantages associated with just-in-time inventory control.

4. Compare and contrast the following operations controls: maintenance control, cost control, budgetary control, and ratio analysis.

5. What is operations management?

DEVELOPING MANAGEMENT SKILLS

Learning activities in this section are aimed at helping you develop your production and control skill. Learning activities include Exploring Your Management Skill: Parts 1 and 2, Experiential Exercise, Cases, and a VideoNet Exercise.

Exploring Your Management Skill: Part 1

Before studying this chapter, respond to the following questions regarding the type of advice you would give to Delta's Richard Anderson, referenced in the Challenge Case. Then address the concerning production and control challenges that he presently faces within the company. You are not expected to be a production expert at this point. Answering the questions now can help you focus on important points when you study the chapter. Also, answering the questions again after you study the chapter will give you an idea of how much you have learned.

Record your answers here or go to MyManagementLab.com. Recording your answers in MyManagementLab will allow you to get immediate results and see how your score compares to your classmates. If you answer the questions in the book, the answers are located in the Exploring Your Management Skill Appendix at the end of the book.

FOR EACH STATEMENT CIRCLE:
- "Y" if you would give the advice to Anderson.
- "N" if you would NOT give the advice to Anderson.
- "NI" if you have no idea whether you would give the advice to Anderson.

Mr. Anderson, in meeting your production management challenges at Delta Air Lines, you should...

Before   After
Study   Study

1. understand that the production process involves all those activities needed to transform organizational resources into products.

Y, N, NI

2. encourage Delta's employees to increase productivity by maximizing the inputs necessary to create a given output (product).
Y, N, NI

3. focus more on productivity and less on quality, because quality efforts undermine productivity.
Y, N, NI

4. use quality circles as a mechanism to gain insights from Delta's employees regarding ways to improve productivity.
Y, N, NI

5. realize that Delta's operations management is mostly quantitative and does not require managerial decision making.
Y, N, NI

6. realize that when formulating Delta's capacity strategy, it's better to error on the side of having excess capacity, because having excess capacity imposes no costs on the company.
Y, N, NI

7. ignore just-in-time strategies, because such techniques to not apply to Delta.
Y, N, NI

8. understand that if Delta does choose to pursue just-in-time strategies, the company will need to work closely with its suppliers.
Y, N, NI

9. realize that pure-preventive maintenance and pure-breakdown maintenance control policies would have similar effects on Delta's operations.
Y, N, NI

10. understand that budgetary controls have virtually no pitfalls and are the safest operations controls.
Y, N, NI

11. recognize that relying on budgetary controls limits potential human relations problems, because such controls are purely quantitative in nature.
Y, N, NI

12. realize that when using ratio analysis, the different ratios communicate information regarding different components of Delta's operations.
Y, N, NI

13. encourage employees to continuously inspect all aspects of Delta's operations to improve productivity.
Y, N, NI

14. rely on break-even analysis to understand those aspects of Delta's operations that do not involve profit or loss.
Y, N, NI

15. consider only transportation and communication costs when reviewing Delta's location strategy.
Y, N, NI

Exploring Your Management Skill: Part 2

As you recall, you completed Exploring Your Management Skill before you started to study this chapter. Your responses gave you an idea of how much you initially knew about production and control and helped you focus on important points as you studied the chapter. Answer the Exploring Your Management Skill questions again now and compare your score to the first time you took it. This comparison will give you an idea of how much you have learned from studying this chapter and

pinpoint areas for further clarification before you start studying the next chapter. Record your answers within the text or go to My ManagementLab.com. Recording your answers in MyManagementLab will allow you to get immediate results and see how your score compares to your classmates. If you answer the questions in the book, the answers are located in the Exploring Your Management Skill Appendix at the end of the book.

Your Management Skills Portfolio

Your Management Learning Portfolio is a collection of activities especially designed to demonstrate your management knowledge and skill. By completing these online at MyManagement.com, you will be able to print, complete with cover sheet, as many activities as you choose. Be sure to save your work. Taking your printed portfolio to an employment interview could be helpful in obtaining a job.

The portfolio activity for this chapter is Improving Production and Control at Nissan. Study the information and complete the exercises that follow.

In recent years, Nissan—a car manufacturer based in Japan—has established a positive reputation with respect to the quality of its cars. Much of this reputation is based on the company's new CEO, Carlos Ghosn, and the strategies and tactics he has employed as the CEO of Nissan. Ghosn is largely responsible for an increased reputation for both Nissan and Infiniti, which is one of Nissan's subsidiaries.

Ghosn believes strongly that a large driver of the company's success is derived from its production and control processes. In fact, he believes so strongly in this notion that he plans to distribute a 500-word memo to all new employees highlighting the benefits of production and control processes. As Ghosn's personal assistant, your task is to prepare a first draft of this memo. This memo should include an overview of the importance of productivity, quality, and the relationship between these two concepts. In addition, the memo should also contain brief descriptions of some techniques that Nissan might use to increase quality.

Remember the audience for this memo—new employees—knows little about production and control. Your task requires you to communicate these ideas in a way that this audience will understand.

Experiential Exercises

1 Defining Management by Exception

Directions. Read the following scenario and then perform the listed activities. Your instructor may want you to perform the activities as an individual or within groups. Follow all of your instructor's directions carefully.

The owner of a small business in your community has contacted your group to help him with his organization. The owner recently encountered the term *management by exception* in a magazine article, but he is not clear about what it means or how organizations implement this practice. Your assignment involves searching the Internet for examples of how companies implement management by exception. Prepare a five-minute presentation that defines this term and then includes examples of how organizations use management by exception.

2 You and Your Career

This chapter highlights the role of productivity—the relationship between outputs produced and the inputs needed to produce them—in determining organizational success. Given the importance of productivity, it is clear that organizations continuously strive to hire productive employees. In addition, when facing difficult choices about laying off workers, organizations seek to retain the most productive employees. Given the importance of this topic, then, it will be important for you to highlight your productivity to future employers. Think about your current job (or a past job). How would you define productivity in this job? Would you describe yourself as "productive" in that job? Why or why not? Can you identify any factors that helped or diminished your productivity? Explain how this experience might improve your productivity in future jobs.

Videonet Exercise

Production and Control: Sound in Motion

Video Highlights

Sound in Motion provides DJs who entertain at events. The partners discuss how the four functions of management (planning, organizing, leading, and controlling) apply to their business.

Discussion Questions

1. What does Adrian Cavlan say about the benefits of hands-on experience in the early stages of the business?
2. Describe the role of meetings at Sound in Motion.
3. Describe the two actions that Sound in Motion uses when it is necessary to improve an employee's performance.

Internet Activity

Browse the Sound in Motion site at www.simdjs.com. Look around the site at the services offered and some of the upcoming events. Now, click on the links within the "About" section. Read about who they are, what they do, and what they believe makes them different. The owners describe themselves with the following statement that appears on the main page: "A passion for music, a commitment to quality." How does this statement relate to the managerial functions of leading and controlling? Do you think the partners enjoy managing their business? What evidence can you provide to support your answer?

CASES

1 DELTA ATTEMPTS TO BOOST PRODUCTIVITY

"Delta Attempts to Boost Productivity" (p. 527) and its related Challenge Case Summary were written to help you better understand the management concepts contained in this chapter. Answer the following discussion questions about the Challenge Case to better see how your understanding of production and control can be applied in a company such as Delta.

1. Why is Delta attempting to raise productivity? From your personal experience with airlines, in what other ways do you think the company could increase productivity?

2. List three concepts discussed in this chapter that could help Delta's management increase productivity. Be sure to explain how each concept could help.

3. Which concept listed in question 2 do you think would have the most positive impact on increasing productivity? Explain fully.

2 HOW MICHAEL'S ON EAST MAINTAINS COST CONTROLS

Read the case and answer the questions that follow. Studying this case will help you better understand how concepts relating to cost controls can be applied in a company such as Michael's on East.

As the recent recession impacted many consumers' wallets, it also directly affected businesses that have relied on the discretionary income of those very consumers. The restaurant industry has certainly been no exception. Americans curbed their penchant for dining out or traded down to lower priced restaurant options. For higher end restaurants, the loss of business has been devastating.

Enter Al Massa.

Massa is executive chef of the Florida-based restaurant, Michael's on East. Menu items include veal chops, racks of lamb, Cornish game hens, filet mignon, lobster, salmon, sea bass, and swordfish. The elegant dining room, complete with piano bar has become known as Sarasota, Florida's "gastronomic sanctuary."[44] It is a place to enjoy a fine dinner with an equally fine glass of wine.

But Massa had a difficult challenge on his hands: maintain a high quality menu of offerings while controlling rising costs. It was not easy. Loyal customers of the restaurant had come to expect a certain degree of quality in the menu but were reluctant to continue paying the same prices they had in previous years. Slashing prices, however, was not the answer. And sacrificing the quality of ingredients was not an option. "The idea isn't to just cut costs, it's to build sales," Massa said.[45]

The true difficulty lay in how Massa could craft a menu that exhibits quality, but is still sensitive to the cost concerns of restaurant patrons. In the fast-food industry, 99-cent and dollar menus have become a mainstay for value-conscious consumers. Though it would not have been prudent for Michael's on East to offer one-dollar steaks and lobsters, it could still borrow from the fast-food industry in its costing and pricing strategies. "We took a value approach to combat food costs," said Massa. Three years ago, the restaurant offered a three-course dinner for $25 and a two-course lunch offering for $15. "It was so successful," Massa said, "that we made it a regular part of our operation." The first summer Michael's on East attempted this strategy, it sold 2,000 more meals than the previous summer.[46]

Another way Massa is controlling his costs is through portion size. "Instead of serving our normal eight- to nine-ounce slab of swordfish, we'll do six ounces, cut into medallions," he said.[47] When served, customers don't notice the very slight difference in size of the entrée.

Even the curried chicken—a best seller at the restaurant—has received Massa's cost-trimming attention. For Michael's on East, the chicken only costs the restaurant $2 to serve, but by pairing it with delicious, but lower-cost side dishes, the profit margin increased. "If we can sell 120 of those at a food cost of 25 percent," Massa calculated, "that's how we're going about reducing our food cost—by having some of our lead sellers be our value menu selections."[48]

Traditional menu items such as steak have also been carefully scrutinized. When Massa realized that the restaurant could not cut portion size or price, he devised a unique plan: offer just the steak with no sides. Called simply "steak on a plate," if a customer wants a baked potato or other side, those are purchased a la carte. "We worried customers would balk at not getting their potato and vegetable, but they didn't skip a beat."[49]

It would probably have been easier to gradually slash menu prices by 10 percent or even 20 percent and try to make up the lost profit margin through increased volume. But restaurants such as Michaels on East have a particular image to uphold, and a drastic drop in price sometimes conveys a loss of quality in the mind of the customer. And, Massa could also have opted for cheaper ingredients and cutting corners on the quality of steaks and fish purchased, but patrons may have detected the difference. Instead, Massa's approach to maintain very high quality raw ingredients and combine it with a value approach to the menu has enabled the restaurant to continue its success in a tough economic climate.

QUESTIONS

1. How would you evaluate Massa's cost control strategies?
2. What potential challenges do you see in Massa's cost control strategies? How would you recommend overcoming those challenges?
3. If you were Massa, what other cost controls would you try and implement?

Endnotes

1. C. Dade, "Changing Pilots," *Wall Street Journal*, October 4, 2007, A1; D. McDougall, "Hurry up and Wait," *CMA Management* 81, no. 5 (2007): 42–44; M. Esterl, "Delta's Full Integration of Northwest Gets Final Clearance," *Wall Street Journal*, January 4, 2010, B1.

2. James B. Dilworth, *Production and Operations Management: Manufacturing and Non-Manufacturing* (New York: Random House, 1986), 3.

3. For a better understanding of the relationship between employee knowledge and productivity, see M. R. Hass and M. T. Hansen, "Different knowledge, different benefits: Toward a productivity perspective on knowledge sharing in organizations," *Strategic Management Journal* 28, no. 11 (2007):1133–1153.

4. John W. Kendrick, *Understanding Productivity: An Introduction to the Dynamics of Productivity Change* (Baltimore: Johns Hopkins University Press, 1977), 114. For useful discussion on how to motivate people to do more to enhance productivity, see Geoffrey Colvin, "What Money Makes You Do," *Fortune*, August 17, 1998: 213–214. For a recent article assessing the role of productivity within a company, see Michael H. Moskow, "Productivity: Key to the Economic Future," *Executive Speeches* 15, no. 6 (June/July 2001): 24–28.

5. E. Magnani, "The Productivity Slowdown, Sectoral Reallocations and the Growth of Atypical Employment Arrangements," *Journal of Productivity Analysis* 20 (2003): 121.

6. Raju Shanbhag, "Duke Energy Invests $1 Billion on Smart Grid Technology," *TMCnet*, February 25, 2010, http://www.tmcnet.com.

7. Justin Lahart, "Moment of Truth for U.S. Productivity Boom," *Wall Street Journal*, May 5, 2010 (accessed July 6, 2010, www.wsj.com).

8. For an example of virtual offices created to increase worker productivity, see Michael K. Takagawa, "Turn Traditional Work Spaces into Virtual Offices," *Human Resources Professional* (March/April 1995):11–14.

9. This example is based on D. Clark, "Theory & Practice: Why Silicon Valley Is Rethinking the Cubicle Office," *Wall Street Journal*, October 15, 2007, B9.

10. For more information regarding the interplay between quality and production, see J. Voros, "The dynamics of price, quality and productivity improvement decisions," *European Journal of Operational Research* 170, no. 3 (2006): 809–823.

11. For more information on how customers might improve productivity, see I. Anitsal and D. W. Schumann, "Toward a conceptualization of customer productivity: The customer's perspective on transforming customer labor into customer outcomes using technology-based self-service options," *Journal of Marketing Theory and Practice* 15, no. 4 (2007): 349–363.

12. W. Edwards Deming, *Out of the Crisis* (Boston: MIT Centre for Advanced Engineering Study, 1986).

13. Gary McWilliams, "Wal-Mart Era Wanes Amid Big Shifts in Retail; Rivals Find Strategies to Defeat Low Prices; World Has Changed," *Wall Street Journal,* October 3, 2007, A.1.

14. John J. Dwyer Jr., "Quality: Can You Prove It?" *Fleet Owner* (April 1995): 36. For coverage of quality assurance, see "Quality Assurance," *Manufacturing Engineering* 125, no. 2 (August 2000): 270–291.

15. "Key Ratings: Developing a Quality Assurance Framework for In-Service Training and Development," *Measuring Business Excellence* 7 (2003): 99.

16. Gerry Davidson, "Quality Circles Didn't Die—They Just Keep Improving," *CMA Magazine,* February 1995, 6.

17. M. Beyer, F. Gerlach, U. Flies, and R. Grol, "The Development of Quality Circles/Peer Review Groups as a Method of Quality Improvement in Europe: Results of a Survey in 26 European Countries," *Family Practice* 20 (2003): 443.

18. John Peter Koss, "Plant Robotics and Automation," *Beverage World* (April 1995): 108; Rob Spencer, "A Driving Force: Use of Robotics Remains Strong in Auto Industry," *Robotics World* 19, no. 1 (January/February 2001): 18–21.

19. Robert E. Kemper and Joseph Yehudai, *Experiencing Operations Management: A Walk-Through* (Boston: PWS-Kent Publishing Company, 1991), 48.

20. Richard B. Chase and Nicholas J. Aquilano, *Production and Operations Management: A Life Cycle Approach* (Homewood, IL: Richard D. Irwin, 1981), 4. For a worthwhile discussion of forecasting product demand as a continual operations management activity, see Jim Browne, "Forecasting Demand for Services," *Industrial Engineering* (February 1995): 16–17.

21. Roger W. Schmenner, "Operations Management," *Business Horizons* 41, no. 3 (May/June, 1998): 3–4; M. Rungtusanatham, T. Choi, D. Hollingworth, Z. Wu, and C. Forza, "Survey Research in Operations Management: Historical Analyses," *Journal of Operations Management* 21 (2003): 475.

22. Michelle V. Rafter, "Researcher Delivers a New Flavor of Management Courtesy of Domino's," *Workforce Management,* June 2010, http://www.workforce.com.

23. For a thorough discussion of product strategy, see Olav Sorenson, "Letting the Market Work for You: An Evolutionary Perspective on Product Strategy," *Strategic Management Journal* 21, no. 5 (May 2000): 577–592.

24. For an example of the kinds of layout issues that concern printers in Europe, see Jill Roth, "Molto Bene," *American Printer* (March 1994): 54–58.

25. For ways to ensure that human resource strategy is progressive, see Kevin Barksdale, "Why We Should Update HR Education," *Journal of Management Education* 22, no. 4 (August 1998): 526–530.

26. Bradford Wernle, "Chrysler Rushes to Hire As It Refills Product Pipeline," *Workforce Management,* January 13, 2010, http://www.workforce.com.

27. For two perspectives on labor force planning during a period of economic uncertainty, see John Zappe, "Dissatisfied Workers + Recovery = Workforce Planning," *ERE.net,* January 19, 2010, http://www.ere.net; and Fay Hansen, "Strategic Workforce Planning in an Uncertain World," *Workforce Management,* July 2009, http://www.workforce.com.

28. For a step-by-step description of job design, see the Rutgers University website, "How to Design a Job," http://uhr.rutgers.edu, accessed July 1, 2010.

29. Sergio Sousa and Elaine E. Aspinwall, "Development of a Performance Measurement Framework for SMEs," *Total Quality Management & Business Excellence* 21, no. 5 (May 2010): 475–501.

30. For a review of JIT and lean production, see M. Holweg, "The genealogy of lean production," *Journal of Operations Management* 25, no. 2 (2007): 420–437.

31. Lee J. Krajewski and Larry P. Ritzman, *Operations Management: Strategy and Analysis* (Reading, MA: Addison-Wesley, 1987), 573. Albert F. Celley, William H. Clegg, Arthur W. Smith, and Mark A. Vonderembse, "Implementation of JIT in the United States," *Journal of Purchasing and Materials Management* (Winter 1987): 9–15. See also, Y. Matsui, "An empirical analysis of just-in-time production in Japanese manufacturing companies," *International Journal of Production Economics* 108 (2007): 153–164.

32. Jeremy N. Smith, "What Comes after Just-in-Time?" *World Trade* 22, no. 4 (April 2009): 22–26.

33. John D. Baxter, "Kanban Works Wonders, but Will It Work in U.S. Industry?" *Iron Age* (June 7, 1982): 44–48.

34. Amy Chozick, "Toyota Sticks by 'Just in Time' Strategy After Quake," *Wall Street Journal,* July 24, 2007, A2

35. For discussion of cost control focusing on corporate jets, see Mel Mandell, "Why Sharing Jets Is Cost Effective," *World Trade* 11, no. 7 (July 1998): 85.

36. George S. Minmier, "Zero-Base Budgeting: A New Budgeting Technique for Discretionary Costs," *Mid-South Quarterly Business Review* 14 (October 1976): 2–8. See also Peter A. Phyrr, "Zero-Base Budgeting," *Harvard Business Review* (November/December 1970): 111–121; E. A. Kurbis, "The Case for Zero-Base Budgeting," *CA Magazine,* April 1986, 104–105; Linda J. Shinn and M. Sue Sturgeon, "Budgeting from Ground Zero," *Association Management* 42 (September 1990): 45–48; Gregory E. Becwar and Jack L. Armitage, "Zero-Base Budgeting: Is It Really Dead?" *Ohio CPA Journal* 48 (Winter 1989): 52–54.

37. Chris Argyris, "Human Problems with Budgets," *Harvard Business Review* (January/February 1953): 108.

38. This section is based primarily on J. Fred Weston and Eugene F. Brigham, *Essentials of Managerial Finance,* 7th ed. (Hinsdale, IL: Dryden Press, 1985). See also J. Pearce, "The Value of Corporate Financial Measures in Monitoring Downturn and Managing Turnaround: An Exploratory Study," *Journal of Managerial Issues* 19, no. 2 (2007): 253–270.

39. For an excellent discussion of ratio analysis and its alternatives, see W. Chen & L. McGinnis, "Reconciling ratio analysis and DEA as performance assessment tools," *European Journal of Operational Research* 178, no. 1 (2007): 277–291.

40. Lester R. Bittle, *Management by Exception* (New York: McGraw-Hill, 1964); Frederick W. Taylor, *Shop Management* (New York: Harper & Bros., 1911), 126–127.

41. These two rules are adapted from *Boardroom Reports* 5 (May 1976): 4.

42. Robert J. Lambrix and Surenda S. Singhvi, "How to Set Volume-Sensitive ROI Targets," *Harvard Business Review* (March/April 1981): 174.

43. For a listing and discussion of quantitative tools and their appropriate uses, see Kemper and Yehudai, *Experiencing Operations Management,* 341–355. For a clear discussion, illustrations, and examples of linear programming, break-even analysis, work measurement, acceptance sampling, payoff tables, value analysis, computer-aided design (CAD), computer-aided engineering (CAE), computer-aided manufacturing (CAM), manufacturing resource planning (MRP), program evaluation and review technique (PERT), capacity requirements planning (CRP), and input/output control, see Jay Heizer and Barry Render, *Production and Operations Management: Strategies and Tactics* (Needham Heights, MA: Allyn and Bacon, 1993).

44. www.michaelsoneast.com

45. "Less is more at Michael's on East." *Restaurant Business* 108, no. 12 (December 2009): 26–31.

46. Ibid.

47. Ibid.

48. Ibid.

49. Ibid.

Exploring Your Management Skill Answers

Chapter 1
1. Y
2. N
3. N
4. N
5. Y
6. Y
7. Y
8. N
9. Y
10. N
11. Y
12. N
13. N
14. N

Chapter 2
1. Y
2. N
3. Y
4. N
5. Y
6. N
7. Y
8. Y
9. N
10. N
11. N
12. Y
13. Y
14. N
15. Y

Chapter 3
1. Y
2. N
3. N
4. N
5. Y
6. Y
7. Y
8. N
9. Y
10. N
11. Y
12. N
13. Y
14. Y
15. N

Chapter 4
1. Y
2. N
3. N
4. Y
5. Y
6. N
7. Y
8. N

Chapter 5
1. N
2. N
3. Y
4. N
5. Y
6. N
7. Y
8. Y
9. Y
10. N
11. N
12. Y
13. Y
14. Y
15. N

Chapter 6
1. N
2. Y
3. N
4. Y
5. Y
6. N
7. Y
8. Y
9. N
10. N
11. N
12. Y
13. N
14. N
15. Y

Chapter 7
1. N
2. N
3. N
4. Y
5. Y
6. N
7. N
8. N
9. Y
10. N
11. Y
12. N
13. Y
14. N
15. N

9. N
10. N
11. Y
12. N
13. Y
14. N
15. N

Chapter 8
1. N
2. Y
3. N
4. N
5. N
6. N
7. Y
8. N
9. Y
10. N
11. Y
12. N
13. N
14. Y
15. N

Chapter 9
1. N
2. N
3. Y
4. N
5. N
6. Y
7. Y
8. Y
9. N
10. N
11. Y
12. N
13. Y
14. N
15. Y

Chapter 10
1. Y
2. N
3. N
4. N
5. Y
6. N
7. Y
8. N
9. Y
10. N
11. N
12. NI
13. N
14. N
15. Y

Chapter 11
1. N
2. Y
3. N
4. Y
5. N
6. N
7. N

8. Y
9. N
10. N
11. Y
12. N
13. N
14. Y
15. N

Chapter 12
1. Y
2. N
3. Y
4. N
5. Y
6. Y
7. N
8. N
9. N
10. Y
11. Y
12. N
13. Y
14. N
15. Y

Chapter 13
1. N
2. N
3. N
4. Y
5. Y
6. N
7. N
8. N
9. Y
10. Y
11. Y
12. N
13. Y
14. Y
15. Y

Chapter 14
1. N
2. Y
3. N
4. N
5. Y
6. N
7. Y
8. Y
9. N
10. N
11. N
12. N
13. N
14. N
15. N

Chapter 15
1. N
2. Y
3. N
4. N
5. Y
6. Y
7. Y
8. Y
9. N
10. N
11. N
12. N
13. Y
14. Y
15. N

Chapter 16
1. N
2. N
3. N
4. Y
5. N
6. N
7. N
8. N
9. Y
10. Y
11. Y
12. N
13. Y
14. Y
15. Y

Chapter 17
1. N
2. N
3. N
4. Y
5. Y
6. Y
7. N
8. Y
9. N
10. N
11. N
12. N
13. N
14. Y
15. N

Chapter 18
1. N
2. N
3. N
4. Y
5. Y
6. Y
7. N

8. Y
9. Y
10. N
11. Y
12. N
13. Y
14. Y
15. N

Chapter 19
1. Y
2. N
3. N
4. N
5. Y
6. Y
7. Y
8. N
9. Y
10. N
11. N
12. N
13. N
14. Y
15. N

Chapter 20
1. N
2. N
3. N
4. Y
5. N
6. N
7. N
8. N
9. Y
10. Y
11. Y
12. N
13. N
14. Y
15. N

Chapter 21
1. N
2. N
3. Y
4. Y
5. N
6. Y
7. Y
8. Y
9. N
10. Y
11. N
12. N
13. N
14. N
15. Y

Chapter 22
1. Y
2. N
3. N
4. Y
5. N
6. N
7. N
8. Y
9. N
10. N
11. N
12. Y
13. N
14. N
15. N

Glossary

Accountability refers to the management philosophy whereby individuals are held liable, or accountable, for how well they use their authority or live up to their responsibility of performing predetermined activities.

Achievement behavior is aimed at setting challenging goals for followers to reach and expressing and demonstrating confidence that they will measure up to the challenge.

Activities are specified sets of behavior within a project.

Adhocracy culture is an organization culture characterized by flexibility and discretion along with an external focus.

Adjourning, the fifth and last stage of the team development process, is the stage in which the team finishes its job and prepares to disband.

Affirmative action programs are organizational programs whose basic purpose is to eliminate barriers against and increase employment opportunities for underutilized or disadvantaged individuals.

Alderfer's ERG theory is an explanation of human needs that divides them into three basic types: existence needs, relatedness needs, and growth needs.

Allocating skill is the ability to provide the organizational resources necessary to implement a strategy.

Angel investor is a wealthy individual who provides capital to new companies.

Appropriate human resources are the individuals in the organization who make a valuable contribution to management system goal attainment.

Argyris's maturity-immaturity continuum is a concept that furnishes insights into human needs by focusing on an individual's natural progress from immaturity to maturity.

Assessment center is a program in which participants engage in, and are evaluated on, a number of individual and group exercises constructed to simulate important activities at the organizational levels to which they aspire.

Authority is the right to perform or command.

Automation is the replacement of human effort by electromechanical devices.

Avoiding is a conflict management technique whereby managers simply ignore the conflict.

Bank financing occurs when an entrepreneur obtains financing from a financial institution in the form of a loan.

Behavior modification is a program that focuses on encouraging appropriate behavior by controlling the consequences of that behavior.

Behavioral approach to management is a management approach that emphasizes increasing production through an understanding of people.

Bias refers to departures from rational theory that produce suboptimal decisions.

Bicultural stress is stress resulting from having to cope with membership in two cultures simultaneously.

Bounded rationality refers to the fact that managers are bounded in terms of time, computational power, and knowledge when making decisions.

Brainstorming is a group decision-making process in which negative feedback on any suggested alternative to any group member is forbidden until all group members have presented alternatives that they perceive as valuable.

Break-even analysis is the process of generating information that summarizes various levels of profit or loss associated with various levels of production.

Break-even point is that level of production where the total revenue of an organization equals its total costs.

Budget is a control tool that outlines how funds in a given period will be spent, as well as how they will be obtained.

Bureaucracy is the term Max Weber used to describe a management system characterized by detailed procedures and rules, a clearly outlined organizational hierarchy, and impersonal relationships among organization members.

Business portfolio analysis is an organizational strategy formulation technique that is based on the philosophy that organizations should develop strategy much as they handle investment portfolios.

Buyer power refers to the power that customers have over the firms operating in an industry; as buyer power increases, the attractiveness of an industry decreases.

Capacity strategy is an operational plan of action aimed at providing the organization with the right facilities to produce the needed output at the right time.

Career is a sequence of work-related positions occupied by a person over the course of a lifetime.

Career plateauing is a period of little or no apparent progress in the growth of a career.

Cash cow is an SBU with a large share of a market that is growing only slightly.

Centralization refers to the situation in which a minimal number of job activities and a minimal amount of authority are delegated to subordinates.

Change agent is an individual inside or outside the organization who tries to modify an existing organizational situation.

Change-related activities are management efforts aimed at modifying organizational components.

Changing an organization is the process of modifying an existing organization to increase organizational effectiveness.

Clan culture is an organization culture characterized by a strong internal focus with a high degree of flexibility and discretion.

Classical approach to management is a management approach that emphasizes organizational efficiency to increase organizational success.

Closed system is one that is not influenced by, and does not interact with, its environment.

Coaching is leadership that instructs followers on how to meet the special organizational challenges they face.

Code of conduct is a document that reflects the core values of an organization and suggests how organization members should act in relation to them.

Code of ethics is a formal statement that acts as a guide for making decisions and acting within an organization.

Command group is a formal group that is outlined in the chain of command on an organization chart. Command groups handle routine activities.

Commercial entrepreneurship involves individuals or corporations that pursue entrepreneurial opportunities for the purposes of generating sales and profits.

Commitment principle is a management guideline that advises managers to commit funds for planning only if they can anticipate, in the foreseeable future, a return on planning expenses as a result of long-range planning analysis.

Committee is a task group that is charged with performing some type of specific activity.

Communication is the process of sharing information with other individuals.

Communication macrobarriers are factors hindering successful communication that relate primarily to the communication environment and the larger world in which communication takes place.

Communication microbarriers are factors hindering successful communication that relate primarily to such variables as the communication message, the source, and the destination.

Communication skill is the ability to direct the behavior of others toward the accomplishment of objectives.

Competitive dynamics refers to the process by which firms undertake strategic and tactical actions and how competitors respond to these actions.

Competitor awareness refers to how mindful a company is of its competitor's actions.

Competitor capability refers to a firm's ability to undertake an action.

Competitor motivation refers to the incentives that an organization has to take action.

Comprehensive management skill is the ability to collectively apply concepts from various major management approaches to performing a manager's job.

Compromise means the parties to the conflict settle on a solution that gives both of them *part* of what they wanted.

Computer-aided design (CAD) is a computerized technique for designing new products or modifying existing ones.

Computer-aided manufacturing (CAM) is a technique that employs computers to plan and program equipment used in the production and inspection of manufactured items.

Conceptual skills are skills involving the ability to see the organization as a whole.

Conflict is defined as a struggle that results from opposing needs or feelings between two or more people.

Consensus is an agreement on a decision by all the individuals involved in making that decision.

Consideration behavior is leadership behavior that reflects friendship, mutual trust, respect, and warmth in the relationship between leader and followers.

Content theories of motivation are explanations of motivation that emphasize people's internal characteristics.

Contingency approach to management is a management approach emphasizing that what managers do in practice depends on a given set of circumstances—a situation.

Contingency theory of leadership is a leadership concept that hypothesizes that, in any given leadership situation, success is determined primarily by (1) the degree to which the task being performed by the followers is structured, (2) the degree of position power possessed by the leader, and (3) the type of relationship that exists between the leader and the followers.

Control entails ensuring that an event occurs as it was planned to occur.

Control tool is a specific procedure or technique that presents pertinent organizational information in a way that helps managers to develop and implement an appropriate control strategy.

Controlling is the process managers go through to control. It is a systematic effort to compare performance to predetermined standards, plans, or objectives to determine whether performance is in line with those standards or needs to be corrected.

Controlling skill is the ability to use information and technology to ensure that an event occurs as it was planned to occur.

Coordination is the orderly arrangement of group effort to provide unity of action in the pursuit of a common purpose. It involves encouraging the completion of individual portions of a task in an appropriate, synchronized order.

Corporate entrepreneurship is the process in which an individual or group of individuals in an existing corporation create a new organization or instigate renewal or innovation within that corporation.

Corporate social responsibility is the managerial obligation to take action that protects and improves both the welfare of society as a whole and the interests of the organization.

Corporate social responsibility skill is the ability to take action that protects and improves both the welfare of society and the interests of the organization.

Corrective action is managerial activity aimed at bringing organizational performance up to the level of performance standards.

Cost leadership is a strategy that focuses on making an organization more competitive by producing products more cheaply than competitors can.

Creativity is the ability to generate original ideas or new perspectives on existing ideas.

Creativity and innovation skill is the ability to generate original ideas or new perspectives on existing ideas and to take steps to implement these new ideas.

Critical path is the sequence of events and activities within a program evaluation and review technique (PERT) network that requires the longest period of time to complete.

Critical question analysis is a strategy development tool that consists of answering basic questions about the present purposes and objectives of the organization, its present direction and environment, and actions that can be taken to achieve organizational objectives in the future.

Cross-functional team is an organizational team composed of people from different functional areas of the organization who are all focused on a specified objective.

Cultural artifact is a dimension of an organization that helps to describe and reinforce the culture, or beliefs, values, and norms in which an artifact exists.

Culture is the set of characteristics of a given group of people and their environment.

Customer dimension of organization culture is a facet of organization culture that focuses on catering to the needs of those individuals who buy goods or services produced.

Data are facts or statistics.

Decentralization refers to the situation in which a significant number of job activities and a maximum amount of authority are delegated to subordinates.

Decision is a choice made between two or more available alternatives.

Decision-making skill is the ability to choose alternatives that increase the likelihood of accomplishing objectives.

Decision tree is a graphic decision-making tool typically used to evaluate decisions involving a series of steps.

Decision tree analysis is a statistical and graphical multiphased decision-making technique that contains a series of steps showing the sequence and interdependence of decisions.

Decline stage is the fourth and last stage in career evolution; it occurs near retirement age, when individuals of about 65 years of age show declining productivity.

Decoder/destination is the person or persons in the interpersonal communication situation with whom the source is attempting to share information.

Delegation is the process of assigning job activities and related authority to specific individuals within the organization.

Delphi technique is a group decision-making process that involves circulating questionnaires on a specific problem among group members, sharing the questionnaire results with them, and then continuing to recirculate and refine individual responses until a consensus regarding the problem is reached.

Demographics are statistical characteristics of a population.

Department is a unique group of resources established by management to perform some organizational task.

Departmentalizing is the process of establishing departments within the management system.

Developing is that step of the innovation process that makes a new idea practical.

Differentiation is a strategy that focuses on making an organization more competitive by developing a product or products that customers perceive as being different from products offered by competitors.

Diffusing is that step of the innovation process that puts a new idea to use by end users or customers.

Direct investing is using the assets of one company to purchase the operating assets of another company.

Directive behavior is aimed at telling followers what to do and how to do it.

Discrimination is the act of treating an issue, person, or behavior unjustly or inequitably on the basis of stereotypes or prejudices.

Diversity refers to characteristics of individuals that shape their identities and the experiences they have in society. Major areas of diversity are gender, race, ethnicity, religion, social class, physical ability, sexual orientation, and age.

Diversity dimension of organization culture is a component of organization culture that encourages the existence of basic human differences among organization members.

Diversity skill is the ability to establish and maintain an organizational workforce that represents a combination of assorted human characteristics appropriate for achieving organizational success.

Diversity training is a learning process designed to raise managers' awareness and develop their competencies to deal with the issues endemic to managing a diverse workforce.

Divestiture is a strategy adopted to eliminate a strategic business unit that is not generating a satisfactory amount of business and has little hope of doing so in the near future.

Division of labor is the assignment of various portions of a particular task among a number of organization members. Division of labor calls for specialization.

Dog refers to an SBU that is a dog; it has a relatively small share of a low-growth market. They may barely support themselves; in some cases, they actually drain off cash resources generated by other SBUs. Examples of dogs are SBUs that produce typewriters or cash registers.

Domain definition occurs when a firm proactively seeks to create a new product market position that competitors have not recognized.

Domestic organization is an organization that essentially operates within a single country.

Dominant organization culture is the shared values about organizational functioning held by the majority of organization members.

Downside loss refers to the resources (i.e., money, relationships, etc.) that the entrepreneur could lose if the opportunity does not succeed.

Economics is the science that focuses on understanding how people of a particular community or nation produce, distribute, and use various goods and services.

Effectiveness is the degree to which managers attain organizational objectives; it is doing the right things.

Efficiency is the degree to which organizational resources contribute to production; it is doing things right.

Emotional intelligence is the capacity of people to recognize their own feelings and the feelings of others, to motivate themselves, and to manage their own emotions as well as the emotions in relationships with others.

Employee-centered behavior is leader behavior that focuses primarily on subordinates as people.

Entrepreneur is an individual who identifies, evaluates, and exploits opportunities.

Entrepreneurial alertness refers to an individual's ability to notice and be sensitive to new information about objects, incidents, and patterns of behavior in the environment.

Entrepreneurial leadership is leadership that is based on the attitude that the leader is self-employed.

Entrepreneurial opportunities are occasions to bring into existence new products and services that allow outputs to be sold at a price greater than their cost of production.

Entrepreneurial risk is the likelihood and magnitude of the opportunity's downside loss.

Entrepreneurship refers to the identification, evaluation, and exploitation of opportunities.

Entrepreneurship skill involves the identification, evaluation, and exploitation of opportunities.

Environmental analysis is the study of the organizational environment to pinpoint environmental factors that can significantly influence organizational operations.

Equal Employment Opportunity Commission (EEOC) is an agency established to enforce federal laws prohibiting discrimination on the basis of race, color, religion, sex, and national origin in recruitment, hiring, firing, layoffs, and all other employment practices.

Equity theory is an explanation of motivation that emphasizes the individual's perceived fairness of an employment situation and how perceived inequities can cause certain behaviors.

Establishment stage is the second stage in career evolution; individuals of about 25 to 45 years of age typically start to become more productive, or higher performers.

Esteem needs are Maslow's fourth set of human needs—including the desires for self-respect and respect from others.

Ethics is the capacity to reflect on values in the corporate decision-making process, to determine how these values and decisions affect various stakeholder groups, and to establish how managers can use these observations in day-to-day company management.

Ethics dimension of organization culture is a facet of organization culture that focuses on making sure that an organization emphasizes not only what is good for the organization, but what is good for other human beings.

Ethnocentric attitude reflects the belief that multinational corporations should regard home-country management practices as superior to foreign-country management practices.

Ethnocentrism is the belief that one's own group, culture, country, or customs are superior to that of others.

Events are the completions of major project tasks.

Existence need is the need for physical well-being.

Expatriate is an organization member who lives and works in a country where he or she does not have citizenship.

Expected value (EV) is the measurement of the anticipated value of some event, determined by multiplying the income an event would produce by its probability of producing that income (EV = I $\times$ P).

Exploitation refers to the activities and investments committed to gain returns from the new product or service arising from the opportunity.

Exploration stage is the first stage in career evolution; it occurs at the beginning of a career, when the individual is typically 15 to 25 years of age, and it is characterized by self-analysis and the exploration of different types of available jobs.

Exporting is selling goods or services to another country.

Extrinsic rewards are rewards that are extraneous to the task accomplished.

Feasibility analysis is analysis that helps entrepreneurs understand whether an idea is practical.

Feedback is, in the interpersonal communication situation, the destination's reaction to a message.

Five Forces Model outlines the primary forces that determine competitiveness within an industry and illustrates how those forces are related; perhaps the best-known tool for industry analysis, it was developed by internationally acclaimed strategic management expert Michael E. Porter.

Fixed costs are expenses incurred by the organization regardless of the number of products produced.

Fixed-position layout is a layout plan in which the product is stationary while resources flow. It is appropriate for organizations involved in a large number of different tasks that require low volumes, multipurpose equipment, and broad employee skills.

Flextime is a program that allows workers to complete their jobs within a workweek of a normal number of hours that they schedule themselves.

Focus is a strategy that emphasizes making an organization more competitive by targeting a particular customer.

Forcing is a technique for managing conflict in which managers use authority to declare that conflict is ended.

Forecasting is a planning tool used to predict future environmental happenings that will influence the operation of the organization.

Formal group is a group that exists within an organization by virtue of management decree to perform tasks that enhance the attainment of organizational objectives.

Formal organizational communication is organizational communication that follows the lines of the organization chart.

Formal structure is defined as the relationships among organizational resources as outlined by management.

Forming is the first stage of the team development process, during which members of the newly formed team become oriented to the team and acquainted with one another as they explore issues related to their new job situation.

Friendship group is an informal group that forms in organizations because of the personal affiliation members have with one another.

Functional authority consists of the right to give orders within a segment of the management system in which the right is normally nonexistent.

Functional similarity method is a method for dividing job activities in the organization.

Gantt chart is a scheduling tool composed of a bar chart with time on the horizontal axis and the resource to be scheduled on the vertical axis. It is used for scheduling resources.

Gender-role stereotypes are perceptions about people based on what our society believes are appropriate behaviors for men and women.

General environment is the level of an organization's external environment that contains components normally having broad long-term implications for managing the organization; its components are economic, social, political, legal, and technological.

Geocentric attitude reflects the belief that the overall quality of management recommendations, rather than the location of managers, should determine the acceptability of management practices used to guide multinational corporations.

Global management skill is the ability to manage global factors as components of organizational operations.

Graciunas's formula is a formula that makes the span-of-management point that as the number of a manager's subordinates increases arithmetically, the number of possible relationships between the manager and the subordinates increases geometrically.

Grapevine is the network of informal organizational communication.

Grid organization development (grid OD) is a commonly used organization development technique based on a theoretical model called the managerial grid.

Group is any number of people who (1) interact with one another, (2) are psychologically aware of one another, and (3) perceive themselves to be a group.

Groupthink is the mode of thinking that group members engage in when the desire for agreement so dominates the group that it overrides the need to realistically appraise alternative problem solutions.

Growth is a strategy adopted by management to increase the amount of business that a strategic business unit is currently generating.

Growth need is the need for continuing personal growth and development.

Healthy organization culture is an organization culture that facilities the achievement of the organization's mission and objectives.

Heuristics are simple rules of thumb used to make decisions.

Hierarchy culture is an organization culture characterized by an internal focus along with an emphasis on stability and control.

Horizontal dimensioning of an organization refers to the extent to which firms use lateral subdivisions or specialties within an organization.

Host country is the country in which an investment is made by a foreign company.

Host-country national is an organization member who is a citizen of the country in which the facility of a foreign-based organization is located.

Human relations movement is a people-oriented approach to management in which the interaction of people in organizations is studied to judge its impact on organizational success.

Human relations skill is the ability to work with people in a way that enhances organizational success.

Human resource inventory is information about the characteristics of organization members; the focus is on past performance and future potential, and the objective is to keep management up to date about the possibilities for filling a position from within.

Human resource management skill is the ability to take action in the form of recruitment, selection, training, and performance appraisal that increases the contributions of individuals within the organization toward the organization's goal attainment.

Human resource planning involves reflecting on organizational objectives to determine overall human resource needs; comparing these needs to the existing human resource inventory to determine net human resource needs; and, finally, seeking appropriate organization members to meet the net human resource needs.

Human resources strategy is an operational plan to use the organization's human resources effectively and efficiently while maintaining or improving the quality of work life.

Human skills are skills involving the ability to build cooperation within the team being led.

Hygiene, or maintenance, factors are items that influence the degree of job dissatisfaction.

Illusion of control exists when entrepreneurs overestimate the extent to which they can control the outcome of an opportunity.

Importing is buying goods or services from another country.

Industry environment is the level of an organization's external environment that contains components normally having relatively specific and immediate implications for managing the organization.

Influencing is the process of guiding the activities of organization members in appropriate directions.

Informal group is a collection of individuals whose common work experiences result in the development of a system of interpersonal relations that extend beyond those established by management.

Informal organizational communication is organizational communication that does not follow the lines of the organization chart.

Informal structure is defined as the patterns of relationships that develop because of the informal activities of organization members.

Information is the set of conclusions derived from data analysis.

Information appropriateness is the degree to which information is relevant to the decision-making situation the manager faces.

Information asymmetry refers to the fact that individuals vary in terms of the information to which they have access.

Information quality is the degree to which information represents reality.

Information quantity is the amount of decision-related information a manager possesses.

Information system (IS) is a network of applications established within an organization to provide managers with information that will assist them in decision making. An IS gets information to where it is needed.

Information technology (IT) is technology that focuses on the use of information in the performance of work.

Information timeliness is the extent to which the receipt of information allows decisions to be made and action to be taken so the organization can gain some benefit from possessing the information.

Innovation is the process of applying a new idea to the improvement of organizational processes, products, or services.

Innovation dimension of organization culture is an aspect of organization culture that encourages the application of new ideas to the improvement of organization processes, products, or services.

Innovation process is defined as the steps that managers take to implement creative ideas.

Input planning is the development of proposed action that will furnish sufficient and appropriate organizational resources for reaching established organizational objectives.

Integrating is that step of the innovation process which establishes an invention as a permanent part of the organization.

Intensity of rivalry refers to the intensity of competition among the organizations in an industry; as the intensity of rivalry increases, the attractiveness of an industry decreases.

Interacting skill is the ability to manage people during implementation.

Interest group is an informal group that gains and maintains membership primarily because of a common concern members have about a specific issue.

Internal environment is the level of an organization's environment that exists inside the organization and normally has immediate and specific implications for managing the organization.

International joint venture is a partnership formed by a company in one country with a company in another country for the purpose of pursuing some mutually desirable business undertaking.

International management is the performance of management activities across national borders.

International market agreement is an arrangement among a cluster of countries that facilitates a high level of trade among these countries.

International organization is an organization based primarily within a single country but having continuing, meaningful transactions in other countries.

Intrinsic rewards are rewards that come directly from performing a task.

Intuition refers to an individual's inborn ability to synthesize information quickly and effectively.

Inventing is that step of the innovation process that establishes a new idea that could help the organization to be more successful.

Job analysis is a technique commonly used to gain an understanding of what a task entails and the type of individual who should be hired to perform that task.

Job-centered behavior is leader behavior that focuses primarily on the work a subordinate is doing.

Job description is a list of specific activities that must be performed to accomplish some task or job.

Job design is an operational plan that determines who will do a specific job and how and where the job will be done.

Job enlargement is the process of increasing the number of operations an individual performs in order to enhance the individual's satisfaction in work.

Job enrichment is the process of incorporating motivators into a job situation.

Job rotation is the process of moving workers from one job to another rather than requiring them to perform only one simple and specialized job over the long term.

Job specification is the characteristics of the individual who should be hired to perform a specific task or job.

Jury of executive opinion method is a method of predicting future sales levels primarily by asking appropriate managers to give their opinions on what will happen to sales in the future.

Just-in-time (JIT) inventory control is a technique for reducing inventories to a minimum by arranging for production components to be delivered to the production facility "just in time" to be used.

Labor force planning is an operational plan for hiring the right employees for a job and training them to be productive.

Law of small numbers occurs when individuals rely on a small sample of information to inform their decisions.

Layout is the overall arrangement of equipment, work areas, service areas, and storage areas within a facility that produces goods or provides services.

Layout strategy is an operational plan that determines the location and flow of organizational resources around, into, and within production and service facilities.

Leader flexibility is the idea that successful leaders must change their leadership styles as they encounter different situations.

Leader–member relations is the degree to which the leader feels accepted by the followers.

Leadership is the process of directing the behavior of others toward the accomplishment of objectives.

Leadership skill is the ability to direct the behavior of others toward the accomplishment of objectives.

Leadership style is the behavior a leader exhibits while guiding organization members in appropriate directions.

Learning organization is an organization that does well in creating, acquiring, and transferring knowledge, and in modifying behavior to reflect new knowledge.

Lecture is primarily a one-way communication situation in which an instructor trains an individual or group by orally presenting information.

Level dimension of a plan is the level of the organization at which the plan is aimed.

License agreement is a right granted by one company to another to use its brand name, technology, product specifications, and so on in the manufacture or sale of goods and services.

Life cycle theory of leadership is a leadership concept that hypothesizes that leadership styles should reflect primarily the maturity level of the followers.

Line authority consists of the right to make decisions and to give orders concerning the production-, sales-, or finance-related behavior of subordinates.

Location strategy is an operational plan of action that provides the organization with a competitive location for its headquarters, manufacturing, services, and distribution activities.

Loss is the amount of the total costs of producing a product that exceeds the total revenue gained from selling the product.

Maintenance stage is the third stage in career evolution; individuals of about 45 to 65 years of age show either increased performance (career growth), stabilized performance (career maintenance), or decreased performance (career stagnation).

Majority group refers to that group of people in the organization who hold most of the positions that command decision-making power, control of resources and information, and access to system rewards.

Management is the process of reaching organizational goals by working with and through people and other organizational resources.

Management by exception is a control tool that allows only significant deviations between planned and actual performance to be brought to a manger's attention.

Management functions are activities that make up the management process. The four basic management activities are planning, organizing, influencing, and controlling.

Management inventory card is a form used in compiling a human resource inventory. It contains the organizational history of an individual and indicates how that individual might be used in the organization in the future.

Management manpower replacement chart is a form used in compiling a human resource inventory. It is people oriented and presents a composite view of individuals management considers significant to human resource planning.

Management responsibility guide is a tool that is used to clarify the responsibilities of various managers in the organization.

Management science approach is a management approach that emphasizes the use of the scientific method and mathematical techniques to solve operational problems.

Management skill is the ability to carry out the process of reaching organizational goals by working with and through people and other organizational resources.

Management system is composed of a number of parts that function interdependently to achieve a purpose; its main parts are organizational input, organizational process, and organizational output.

Managerial effectiveness refers to management's use of organizational resources in meeting organizational goals.

Managerial efficiency is the proportion of total organizational resources used during the production process.

Managerial grid is a theoretical model based on the premise that concern for people and concern for production are the two primary attitudes that influence management style.

Market culture is an organization culture that reflects values that emphasize stability and control along with an external focus.

Materials control is an operational activity that determines the flow of materials from vendors through an operations system to customers.

McClelland's acquired needs theory is an explanation of human needs that focuses on the desires for achievement, power, and affiliation that people develop as a result of their life experiences.

Mechanistic structures are formal organizational structures.

Message is encoded information that the source intends to share with others.

Message interference refers to stimuli that compete with the communication message for the attention of the destination.

Minority group refers to that group of people in the organization who are fewer in number than the majority group or who lack critical power, resources, acceptance, or social status.

Mission statement is a written document developed by management, normally based on input by managers as well as nonmanagers, that describes and explains what the mission of an organization actually is.

Monitoring is that step of the innovation process in which a newly implemented idea is tracked to determine if and when the idea should be improved or terminated.

Monitoring skill is the ability to use information to determine whether a problem has arisen that is blocking implementation.

Motion study finds the best way to accomplish a task by reducing each job to the most basic movements possible.

Motion-study techniques are operational tools that are used to improve productivity.

Motivating factors, or **motivators,** are items that influence the degree of job satisfaction.

Motivation is the inner state that causes an individual to behave in a way that ensures the accomplishment of some goal.

Motivation skill is the ability to create organizational situations in which individuals performing organizational activities are simultaneously satisfying personal needs and helping the organization attain its goals.

Motivation strength is an individual's degree of desire to perform a behavior.

Moving average method utilizes historical data to predict future sales levels.

Multinational corporation is a company that has significant operations in more than one country.

Need for achievement is the desire to do something better or more efficiently than it has ever been done before.

Need for affiliation is the desire to maintain close, friendly, personal relationships.

Need for power is the desire to control, influence, or be responsible for others.

Needs-goal theory is a motivation model that hypothesizes that felt needs cause human behavior.

Negative reinforcement is a reward that consists of the elimination of an undesirable consequence of behavior.

Nominal group technique is a group decision-making process in which every group member is assured of equal participation in making the group decision. After each member writes down individual ideas and presents them orally to the group, the entire group discusses all the ideas and then votes for the best idea in a secret ballot.

Nonprogrammed decisions are typically one-shot decisions that are usually less structured than programmed decisions.

Nonverbal communication is the sharing of information without using words.

Norming, the third stage of the team development process, is characterized by agreement among team members on roles, rules, and acceptable behavior while working on the team.

On-the-job training is a training technique that blends job-related knowledge with experience in using that knowledge on the job.

Open system is one that is influenced by, and is continually interacting with, its environment.

Operations control is making sure that operations activities are carried out as planned.

Operations management is performance of managerial activities entailed in selecting, designing, operating, controlling, and updating production systems.

Organic structures are less formal organizational structures and represent loosely coupled networks of workers.

Organization chart is a graphic illustration of organizational structure.

Organization culture is a set of shared values that organization members have regarding the functioning and existence of their organization.

Organization culture skill is the ability to establish a set of shared values of organization members regarding the functioning and existence of their organization to enhance the probability of organizational success.

Organization development (OD) is the process that emphasizes changing an organization by changing organization members and bases these changes on an overview of structure, technology, and all other organizational ingredients.

Organization subculture is a mini-culture within an organization that can reflect the values and beliefs of a specific segment of an organization formed along lines such as established departments or geographic regions.

Organizational ceremonies are formal activities conducted on important organizational occasions.

Organizational change skill is the ability to modify an organization in order to enhance its contribution to reaching company goals.

Organizational commitment can be defined as the dedication of organization members to uphold the values of the organization and to make worthwhile contributions to fulfilling organizational purpose.

Organizational communication is interpersonal communication within organizations that directly relates to the goals, functions, and structure of human organizations.

Organizational mission is the purpose for which, or the reason why, an organization exists.

Organizational myth is a popular belief or story that has become associated with a person or institution that is considered to illustrate an organization culture ideal.

Organizational objectives are the targets toward which the open management system is directed. They flow from the organization's mission.

Organizational purpose is what the organization exists to do, given a particular group of customers and customer needs.

Organizational rejuvenation involves improving the firm's ability to execute strategies and focuses on new processes instead of new products.

Organizational resources are all assets available for activation during the production process; they include human resources, monetary resources, raw materials resources, and capital resources.

Organizational saga is a narrative describing the adventures of a heroic individual or family significantly linked to an organization's past or present.

Organizational socialization is the process by which management can appropriately integrate new employees within an organization's culture.

Organizational storytelling is the act of passing organizational myths and sagas to other organization members.

Organizational symbols are objects that have meanings beyond their intrinsic content.

Organizing is the process of establishing orderly uses for resources within the management system.

Organizing skill is the ability to establish orderly uses for resources within the management system.

Overlapping responsibility refers to a situation in which more than one individual is responsible for the same activity.

Paradox of choice is having too many alternatives, which may actually demotivate decision makers, which harms decision making.

Parent company is the company investing in international operations.

Participative behavior is aimed at seeking suggestions from followers regarding business operations to the extent that followers are involved in making important organizational decisions.

Path–goal theory of leadership is a theory of leadership that suggests that the primary activities of a leader are to make desirable and achievable rewards available to organization members who attain organizational goals and to clarify the kinds of behavior that must be performed to earn those rewards.

People change is a type of organizational change that emphasizes increasing organizational effectiveness by changing certain aspects of organization members.

People factors are attitudes, leadership skills, communication skills, and all other characteristics of the organization's employees.

People-related activities are management efforts aimed at managing people in organizations.

Perception is an individual's interpretation of a message.

Performance appraisal is the process of reviewing individuals' past productive activity to evaluate the contribution they have made toward attaining management system objectives.

Performing, the fourth stage of the team development process, is characterized by a focus on solving organizational problems and meeting assigned challenges.

Personal power is the power derived from a manager's relationships with others.

Physiological needs are Maslow's first set of human needs—for the normal functioning of the body, including the desires for water, food, rest, sex, and air.

Plan is a specific action proposed to help the organization achieve its objectives.

Planning is the process of determining how the organization can get where it wants to go, and what it will do to accomplish its objectives.

Planning skill is the ability to take action to determine the objectives of the organization as well as what is necessary to accomplish those objectives.

Planning tools are techniques managers can use to help develop plans.

Planning tools skill is the ability to employ the qualitative and quantitative techniques necessary to help develop plans.

Plant facilities planning involves determining the type of buildings and equipment an organization needs to reach its objectives.

Pluralism refers to an environment in which differences are acknowledged, accepted, and viewed as significant contributors to the entirety.

Policy is a standing plan that furnishes broad guidelines for taking action consistent with reaching organizational objectives.

Polycentric attitude reflects the belief that because foreign managers are closer to foreign organizational units, they probably understand them better, and therefore foreign management practices should generally be viewed as more insightful than home-country management practices.

Porter–Lawler theory is a motivation theory that hypothesizes that felt needs cause human behavior and that motivation strength is determined primarily by the perceived value of the result of performing the behavior and the perceived probability that the behavior performed will cause the result to materialize.

Position power is power derived from the organizational position a manager holds.

Position replacement form is used in compiling a human resource inventory. It summarizes information about organization members who could fill a position should it open up.

Positive reinforcement is a reward that consists of a desirable consequence of behavior.

Power is the extent to which an individual is able to influence others so that they respond to orders.

Prejudice is a preconceived judgment, opinion, or assumption about an issue, behavior, or group of people.

Probability theory is a decision-making tool used in risk situations—situations in which decision makers are not completely sure of the outcome of an implemented alternative.

Problem-solving team is an organizational team set up to help eliminate a specified problem within the organization.

Problems are factors within an organization that are barriers to organizational goal attainment.

Procedure is a standing plan that outlines a series of related actions that must be taken to accomplish a particular task.

Process control is a technique that assists in monitoring production processes.

Process (functional) layout is a layout pattern based primarily on grouping together similar types of equipment.

Process strategy is an operational plan of action outlining the means and methods the organization will use to transform resources into goods and services.

Process theories of motivation are explanations of motivation that emphasize how individuals are motivated.

Product layout is a layout designed to accommodate a limited number of different products that require high volumes, highly specialized equipment, and narrow employee skills.

Product life cycle is the five stages through which most products and services pass: introduction, growth, maturity, saturation, and decline.

Product stages method predicts future sales by using the product life cycle to better understand the history and future of the product.

Product strategy is an operational plan of action outlining which goods and services an organization will produce and market.

Production is the transformation of organizational resources into products.

Production skill is the ability to transform organizational resources into products.

Productivity is the relationship between the total amount of goods or services being produced (output) and the organizational resources needed to produce them (input).

Profits are the amount of total revenue that exceeds the total costs of producing the products sold.

Program is a single-use plan designed to carry out a special project in an organization that, if accomplished, will contribute to the organization's long-term success.

Program evaluation and review technique (PERT) is a scheduling tool that is essentially a network of project activities showing estimates of time necessary to complete each activity and the sequence of activities that must be followed to complete the project.

Programmed decisions are decisions that are routine and repetitive and that typically require specific handling methods.

Programmed learning is a technique for instructing without the presence or intervention of a human instructor. Small pieces of information requiring responses are presented to individual trainees, and the trainees determine from checking their responses against provided answers whether their understanding of the information is accurate.

Punishment is the presentation of an undesirable behavior consequence or the removal of a desirable one that decreases the likelihood that the behavior will continue.

Pure-breakdown (repair) policy is a maintenance control policy that decrees that machine adjustments, lubrication, cleaning, parts replacement, painting, and needed repairs and overhaul will be performed only after facilities or machines malfunction.

Pure-preventive maintenance policy is a maintenance control policy that tries to ensure that machine adjustments, lubrication, cleaning, parts replacement, painting, and needed repairs and overhauls will be performed before facilities or machines malfunction.

Quality is the extent to which a product reliably does what it is intended to do.

Quality assurance is an operations process involving a broad group of activities aimed at achieving the organization's quality objectives.

Quality circles are small groups of workers that meet to discuss quality-related problems on a particular project and to communicate their solutions to these problems to management at a formal presentation session.

Quality dimension of organization culture is an element of organization culture that focuses on making sure that a product, in the opinion of the customer, does what it is supposed to do.

Question mark is an SBU with a small share of a high-growth market.

Ratio analysis is a control tool that summarizes the financial position of an organization by calculating ratios based on various financial measures that appear on the organization's balance sheet and income statements.

Rational decision-making process comprises the steps the decision maker takes to arrive at a choice.

Recruitment is the initial attraction and screening of the supply of prospective human resources available to fill a position.

Regression method predicts future sales by analyzing the historical relationship between sales and time.

Relatedness need is the need for satisfying interpersonal relationships.

Relevant alternative is an alternative that is considered feasible for solving an existing problem and for implementation.

Repatriation is the process of bringing individuals who have been working abroad back to their home country and reintegrating them into the organization's home-country operations.

Repetitiveness dimension of a plan is the extent to which the plan is to be used over and over again.

Resolving is a technique for managing conflict by working out the differences between managers and employees.

Responsibility is the obligation to perform assigned activities.

Responsibility and delegation skill is the ability to understand one's obligation to perform assigned activities and to enlist the help of others to complete these activities.

Responsibility gap exists when certain organizational tasks are not included in the responsibility area of any individual organization member.

Retrenchment is a strategy adopted by management to strengthen or protect the amount of business a strategic business unit is currently generating.

Reverse discrimination is the term used to describe inequities affecting members of the majority group as an outcome of programs designed to help underrepresented groups.

Risk refers to situations in which statistical probabilities can be attributed to alternative potential outcomes.

Robotics is the study of the development and use of robots.

Role conflict is the conflict that results when a person has to fill competing roles because of membership in two cultures.

Role overload refers to having too many expectations to comfortably fulfill.

Rule is a standing plan that designates specific required action.

Salesforce estimation method predicts future sales levels primarily by asking appropriate salespeople for their opinions of what will happen to sales in the future.

Satisfice occurs when an individual makes a decision that is not optimal but is "good enough."

Scalar relationships refer to the chain-of-command positioning of individuals on an organization chart.

Scheduling is the process of formulating a detailed listing of activities that must be accomplished to attain an objective, allocating the resources necessary to attain the objective, and setting up and following timetables for completing the objective.

Scientific management emphasizes the "one best way" to perform a task.

Scope dimension of a plan is the portion of the total management system at which the plan is aimed.

Scope of the decision is the proportion of the total management system that a particular decision will affect. The broader the scope of a decision, the higher the level of the manager responsible for making that decision.

Security, or safety, needs are Maslow's second set of human needs—reflecting the human desire to keep free from physical harm.

Selection is choosing an individual to hire from all those who have been recruited.

Self-actualization needs are Maslow's fifth, and final, set of human needs—reflecting the human desire to maximize personal potential.

Self-managed team is an organizational team that plans, organizes, influences, and controls its own work situation with only minimal intervention and direction from management.

Serial transmission involves the passing of information from one individual to another in a series.

Servant leadership is an approach to leading in which leaders view their primary role as helping followers in their quests to satisfy personal needs, aspirations, and interests.

Signal is a message that has been transmitted from one person to another.

Single-use plans are plans used only once—or, at most, several times—because they focus on unique or rare situations within the organization.

Site selection involves determining where a plant facility should be located. It may use a weighting process to compare site differences.

Situational approach to leadership is a relatively modern view of leadership that suggests that successful leadership requires a unique combination of leaders, followers, and leadership situations.

Social audit is the process of measuring the present social responsibility activities of an organization. It monitors, measures, and appraises all aspects of an organization's social responsibility performance.

Social entrepreneurship involves the recognition, evaluation, and exploitation of opportunities that create social value as opposed to personal or shareholder wealth.

Social needs are Maslow's third set of human needs—reflecting the human desire to belong, including longings for friendship, companionship, and love.

Social networks represent individuals' patterns of social relationships.

Social obligation approach is an approach to meeting social obligations that considers business as having primarily economic purposes and confines social responsibility activity mainly to existing legislation.

Social responsibility approach is an approach to meeting social obligations that considers business as having both and economic and societal goals.

Social responsiveness is the degree of effectiveness and efficiency an organization displays in pursuing its social responsibilities.

Social responsiveness approach is an approach to meeting social obligations that considers business as having both societal and economic goals as well as the obligation to anticipate potential social problems and work actively toward preventing their occurrence.

Social value refers to the basic long-standing needs of society and has little to do with profits.

Social values are the relative degrees of worth society places on the manner in which it exists and functions.

Sociogram is a sociometric diagram that summarizes the personal feelings of organization members about the people in the organization with whom they would like to spend free time.

Sociometry is an analytical tool that can be used to determine what informal groups exist in an organization and who the leaders and members of those groups are.

Source/encoder is the person in the interpersonal communication situation who originates and encodes information to be shared with others.

Span of management is the number of individuals a manager supervises.

Spirituality dimension of organization culture is an aspect of organization culture that encourages organization members to integrate spiritual life and work life.

Stability is a strategy adopted by management to maintain or slightly improve the amount of business that a strategic business unit is generating.

Staff authority consists of the right to advise or assist those who possess line authority as well as other staff personnel.

Stakeholders are all those individuals and groups that are directly or indirectly affected by an organization's decisions.

Standard is the level of activity established to serve as a model for evaluating organizational performance.

Standing plans are plans that are used over and over because they focus on organizational situations that occur repeatedly.

Star is an SBU that has a high share of a high-growth market and typically needs large amounts of cash to support rapid and significant growth.

Statistical quality control is the process used to determine how many products should be inspected to calculate a probability that the total number of products will meet organizational quality standards.

Stereotype is a positive or negative assessment of members of a group or their perceived attributes.

Storming, the second stage of the team development process, is characterized by conflict and disagreement as team members try to clarify their individual roles and challenge the way the team functions.

Strategic business unit (SBU) is, in business portfolio analysis, a significant organizational segment that is analyzed to develop organizational strategy aimed at generating future business or revenue. SBUs vary in form, but all are a single business (or collection of businesses), have their own competitors and a manager accountable for operations, and can be independently planned for.

Strategic control is the last step of the strategy management process and consists of monitoring and evaluating the strategy management process as a whole to ensure that it is operating properly.

Strategic management is the process of ensuring that an organization possesses and benefits from the use of an appropriate organizational strategy.

Strategic planning is long-range planning that focuses on the organization as a whole.

Strategic planning skill is the ability to engage in long-range planning that focuses on the organization as a whole.

Strategic renewal occurs when a firm attempts to alter its own competitive strategy.

Strategy is a broad and general plan developed to reach long-term objectives; it is the end result of strategic planning.

Strategy formulation is the process of determining appropriate courses of action for achieving organizational objectives and thereby accomplishing organizational purpose. Strategy development tools include critical question analysis, SWOT analysis, business portfolio analysis, and Porter's Model for Industry Analysis.

Strategy implementation is the fourth step of the strategy management process and is putting formulated strategy into action.

Stress is the bodily strain that an individual experiences as a result of coping with some environmental factor.

Stressor is an environmental demand that causes people to feel stress.

Structural change is a change aimed at increasing organizational effectiveness through modifications to the existing organizational structure.

Structural factors are organizational controls, such as policies and procedures.

Structure refers to the designated relationships among resources of the management system.

Structure behavior is leadership activity that (1) delineates the relationship between the leader and the leader's followers or (2) establishes well-defined procedures that the followers should adhere to in performing their jobs.

Suboptimization is a condition wherein subobjectives are conflicting or not directly aimed at accomplishing the overall organizational objectives.

Successful communication refers to an interpersonal communication situation in which the information the source intends to share with the destination and the meaning the destination derives from the transmitted message are the same.

Succession planning is the process of outlining who will follow whom in various organizational positions.

Superleadership is leading by showing others how to lead themselves.

Supplier power denotes the power that suppliers have over the firms operating in an industry; as supplier power increases, industry attractiveness decreases.

Supportive behavior is aimed at being friendly with followers and showing interest in them as human beings.

Sustainability is the degree to which a person or entity can meet its present needs without compromising the ability of other people or entities to meet their needs in the future.

Sustainable organization is an organization that has the ability to meet its present needs without compromising the ability of future generations to meet their needs.

Sustained regeneration occurs when firms develop new cultures, processes, or structures to support new product innovations in current markets as well as with existing products into new markets.

SWOT analysis is a strategic development tool that matches internal organizational strengths and weaknesses with external opportunities and threats.

Symptom is a sign that a problem exists.

System is a number of interdependent parts functioning as a whole for some purpose.

System approach to management is a management approach based on general system theory—the theory that to understand fully the operation of an entity, the entity must be viewed as a system.

Tactical planning is short-range planning that emphasizes the current operations of various parts of the organization.

Task group is a formal group of organization members who interact with one another to accomplish nonroutine organizational tasks. Members of any one task group can come from various levels in the organizational hierarchy.

Task-related activities are management efforts aimed at carrying out critical management-related duties in organizations.

Task structure is the degree to which the goals—the work to be done—and other situational factors are outlined clearly.

Team is a group whose members influence one another toward the accomplishment of an organizational objective(s).

Team skill is the ability to manage a collection of people so that they influence one another toward the accomplishment of an organizational objective(s).

Technical skills are skills involving the ability to apply specialized knowledge and expertise to work-related techniques and procedures.

Technological change is a type of organizational change that emphasizes modifying the level of technology in the management system.

Technological factors are any types of equipment or processes that assist organization members in the performance of their jobs.

Technology consists of any type of equipment or process that organization members use in the performance of their work.

Testing is examining human resources for qualities relevant to performing available jobs.

Theory X is a set of essentially negative assumptions about human nature.

Theory Y is a set of essentially positive assumptions about human nature.

Theory Z is the effectiveness dimension that implies that managers who use either Theory X or Theory Y assumptions when dealing with people can be successful, depending on their situation.

Third-country national is an organization member who is a citizen of one country and who works in another country for an organization headquartered in still another country.

Threat of new entrants refers to the ability of new firms to enter an industry; as the threat of new entrants increases, the attractiveness of an industry decreases.

Threat of substitute products refers to the extent to which customers may use products or services from another industry instead of the focal industry. As the threat of substitutes increases, which implies that customers have more choices, the attractiveness of an industry decreases.

Time dimension of a plan is the length of time the plan covers.

Tokenism refers to being one of few members of your group in the organization.

Total costs are the sum of fixed costs and variable costs.

Total power is the entire amount of power an individual in an organization possesses. It is made up of position power and personal power.

Total quality management (TQM) is the continuous process of involving all organization members in ensuring that every activity related to the production of goods or services has an appropriate role in establishing product quality.

Total revenue is all sales dollars accumulated from selling manufactured products or services.

Training is the process of developing qualities in human resources that will enable them to be more productive and thus to contribute more to organizational goal attainment.

Training needs are the information or skill areas of an individual or group that require further development to increase the productivity of that individual or group.

Trait approach to leadership is an outdated view of leadership that sees the personal characteristics of an individual as the main determinants of how successful that individual could be as a leader.

Transformational leadership is leadership that inspires organizational success by profoundly affecting followers' beliefs in what an organization should be, as well as their values, such as justice and integrity.

Transnational organization, also called a global organization, takes the entire world as its business arena.

Triangular management is a management approach that emphasizes using information from the classical, behavioral, and management science schools of thought to manage the open management system.

Triple bottom-line emphasizes that managers should focus on building organizations that are sustainable in economic, environmental, and societal activities.

Uncertainty refers to situations where the probability that a particular outcome will occur is not known in advance.

Unhealthy organization culture is an organization culture that does not facilitate the accomplishment of the organization's mission and objectives.

Unity of command is the management principle that recommends that an individual have only one boss.

Unsuccessful communication refers to an interpersonal communication situation in which the information the source intends to share with the destination and the meaning the destination derives from the transmitted message are different.

Value analysis is a cost control and cost reduction technique that examines all the parts, materials, and functions of an operation to help managers control operations.

Values are the beliefs of a person or social group in which they have an emotional investment.

Values statement is a formally drafted document that summarizes the primary values within the culture of a specific organization.

Variable budget (also known as a flexible budget) is one that outlines the levels of resources to be allocated for each organizational activity according to the level of production within the organization.

Variable costs are expenses that fluctuate with the number of products produced.

Verbal communication is the sharing of information through words, either written or spoken.

Venture capitalist is a firm that raises money from investors and then uses this money to make investments in new firms.

Vertical dimensioning refers to the extent to which an organization uses vertical levels to separate job responsibilities.

Virtual corporation is an organization that goes significantly beyond the boundaries and structure of a traditional organization by comprehensively "tying together" a company's stakeholders—employees, suppliers, and customers—via an elaborate system of e-mail and other Internet-related vehicles such as videoconferencing.

Virtual office is a work arrangement that extends beyond the structure and boundaries of the traditional office arrangement.

Virtual organization is an organization having the essence of a traditional organization, but without some aspect of traditional boundaries and structure.

Virtual teams are groups of employees formed by managers that go beyond the boundaries and structure of traditional teams by having members in geographically dispersed locations meeting via real-time messaging on an intranet or the Internet to discuss special or unanticipated organizational problems.

Virtual training is a training process that goes beyond the boundaries and structure of traditional training.

Vroom expectancy theory is a motivation theory that hypothesizes that felt needs cause human behavior and that motivation strength depends on an individual's degree of desire to perform a behavior.

Vroom–Yetton–Jago (VYJ) model of leadership is a modern view of leadership that suggests that successful leadership requires determining, through a decision tree, what style of leadership will produce decisions that are beneficial to the organization and will be accepted and committed to by subordinates.

Whistle-blower is the employee who reports the alleged activities of suspected misconduct or corruption within an organization.

Whistle-blowing is the act of an employee reporting suspected misconduct or corruption believed to exist within an organization.

Work measurement methods are operational tools that are used to establish labor standards.

Work methods analysis is an operational tool used to improve productivity and ensure the safety of workers.

Work team is a task group used in organizations to achieve greater organizational flexibility or to cope with rapid growth.

Workplace bullying refers to individuals being isolated or excluded socially and having work efforts devalued.

Zero-base budgeting requires managers to justify their entire budget request in detail rather than simply referring to budget amounts established in previous years.

Photo Credits

Chapter 1, page 3, Alamy Images; page 12, Benis Arapovic/Shutterstock; page 17, StockLite/Shutterstock.

Chapter 2, page 27, Richard Levine/Alamy Images; page 32, Leah-Anne Thompson/Shutterstock; page 34, Walter Hodges/Getty Images, Inc./Stone Allstock.

Chapter 3, page 51, © Richard Levine/Alamy; page 53, Douglas Healey/The New York Times; page 57, Taras Vyshnya/Shutterstock.

Chapter 4, page 81, wavebreakmedia ltd/Shutterstock; page 85, Mark Richards/PhotoEdit Inc; page 89, Jeff Greenbergy/PhotoEdit Inc; page 95, erwinova/Fotolia, LLC–Royalty Free.

Chapter 5, page 109, © MING MING/Reuters/Corbis; page 113, Robert Fried/robertfriedphotography.com; page 117, iStockphoto.com; page 120, Erica Lanser/Black Star.

Chapter 6, page 139, Ben Margo/AP Wide World Photos; page 141, Klaus Tiedge/BlendImages/TIPS Images North America; page 142, CHUCK FADELY/MIAMI HERALD/Newscom; page 146, Image Source Pink/Alamy Images– Royalty Free; page 149, zumawireworld-photos/Newscom.

Chapter 7, page 159, DTO/Shutterstock; page 166, © KIMBERLY WHITE/Reuters/Corbis; page 172, Girish Menon/Shutterstock.

Chapter 8, page 181, RoidRanger/Shutterstock; page 185, © Reuters/Corbis; page 189, Debra Reid/AP Wide World Photos.

Chapter 9, page 203, Vladru/Shutterstock; page 207, Ed Wray/AP Wide World Photos; page 211, © (Ramin Talaie)/Corbis All Rights Reserved; page 214, Bob Daemmrich/PhotoEdit Inc.

Chapter 10, page 227, NetPhotos/Alamy Images; page 228, AP Wide World Photos; page 232, Stephen Oliver © Dorling Kindersley; page 235, Manish Swarup/AP Wide World Photos; page 239, David Young-Wolff/PhotoEdit Inc.

Chapter 11, page 249, Paul Sakuma/AP Wide World Photos; page 252, Michael Rosenfeld/Stone/Getty Images; page 256, Jagadeesh/Reuters/Corbis; page 260, Mario Tama/Getty Images, Inc.

Chapter 12, page 273, Jose Gil/Shutterstock; page 275, Jeff Greenberg/PhotoEdit Inc; page 279, © Bettmann/Corbis All Rights Reserved; page 285, © Dorling Kindersley.

Chapter 13, page 295, Hiroko Masuike/The New York Times/Redux Pictures; page 301, Michael Newman/PhotoEdit Inc;

page 305, Gautam Singh/AP Wide World Photos; page 308, JHDT Stock Images LLC/Shutterstock.

Chapter 14, page 319, Robert Lawson/Photolibrary Royalty Free; page 324, Antonio Calanni/AP Wide World Photos; page 328, JOERG BOETHLING/Photolibrary/Peter Arnold, Inc; page 332, HYPESTOCK/Shutterstock.

Chapter 15, page 345, Tupungato/Shutterstock. com; page 350, Jiang Jin/SuperStock, Inc; page 355, Hakimata Photography/Shutterstock; page 356, © STR/Reuters/Corbis.

Chapter 16, page 369, © MIKE NELSON/epa/Corbis; page 371, Ted S. Warren/AP Wide World Photos; page 373, Stone/Getty Images; page 483, © 2003 Randy Pench/Sacramento Bee/Zuma Press; page 486, Terry Vine/Getty Images, Inc.–Stone Allstock.

Chapter 17, page 399, © James Leynse/Corbis; page 404, Nam Y. Huh/AP Wide World Photos; page 407, Ben Baker/Redux Pictures; page 411, Getty Images–Stockbyte, Royalty Free.

Chapter 18, page 425, Yuri Acurs/Shutterstock.com; page 428, Dmitriy Shironosov/Shutterstock.com; page 434, StockLite/Shutterstock.com; page 435, AP Wide World Photos; page 441, Georg Anderhub/Lebrecht Music & Arts Photo Library.

Chapter 19, page 451, Danny E Hooks/Shutterstock.com; page 457, Lisa Turay/Shutterstock.com; page 460, sculpies/Shutterstock.com; page 464, Daily Press, Buddy Norris/AP Wide World Photos.

Chapter 20, page 477, Nick Wright/Photolibrary; page 480, © Eros Hoagland/Redux; page 486, Robert Sorbo/CORBIS–NY; page 488, Michael L. Abramson/Getty Images/Time Life Pictures.

Chapter 21, page 501, Mark Winfrey/Shutterstock.com; page 504, PHANIE/Photo Researchers, Inc.; page 508, © Paul Chinn/San Francisco Chronicle/Corbis; page 510, Susan Van Etten/PhotoEdit Inc.

Chapter 22, page 527, Mike Simons/Newscom; page 529, Stephen Coburn/Shutterstock; page 533, GRANT, SPENCER/Photo Researchers, Inc.; page 536, Myrleen Ferguson Cate/PhotoEdit Inc; page 537, auremar/Shutterstock.com.

Book icon in Class Discussion Highlight boxes, D Kvarfordt/Shutterstock.

Name Index

A

ABC, 181
Ackoff, Russell L., 216
Activision, 479
Adams, J. Stacy, 402
Advantage Fitness Products, 148
Adventist Health System, 444
Aetna, 309
AFL-CIO Amalgamated Transit Union, 404f
Ahrendts, Angela, 440
Ahuja, M. K., 518
Akers, John F., 63
Alabama Department of Public Safety, 304t
Alderfer, Clayton, 405
Alexis, Marcus, 185
Amazon.com, 148, 166f, 189f, 217,
          218–219, 484
American Airlines, 6, 403, 506
American Association of University Women, 5
American Can Company, 66
American Heart Association, 17
American Society of Quality and Control, 490
AMP, Inc., 110–111
Anderson, RIchard, 527, 551
Anheuser-Busch InBev, 356
Apple, 148, 230, 370, 462, 508
Apple MacWorld Conference, 508
Aquilano, Nicholas J., 533
Arch Chemicals, 52
Argyris, Chris, 405, 415, 541
Arpey, Gerard J., 403
Arthurs, J. D., 145
Ash, Mary Kay, 463, 464f
Asher, Alan, 425, 443–444
AT&T, 303
Atlantic Richfield, 55
Auburn Farms, 119
Avery, Derek R., 94
azTeen Magazine, 24
Azure, 227

B

Bach, Robbie, 198–199
Backman, Michael, 124
Banana Republic, 76
Barenburg, Max, 74
Barnard, Chester, 187
Barnes & Noble, 217
Barrett, Colleen, 454
Barrett, Dermot, 357
Bass, Bernard, 430
Baughn, Christopher, 15
Bavelas, Alex, 357
Bayless, Maggie, 25
Beacon Sweets & Chocolates of South Africa, 119
Becker, William, 308
Bell, Ella, 88
Bellamy, Sarah, 365
Ben & Jerry's, 223, 384
Beresford, Peter, 360
Berkowitz, Seth, 269
Bernard, Chester, 32, 278
Bertanlanffy, Ludvig von, 38
Best Buy, 200, 244, 265, 448–449
Bestfoods, 223
Bethlehem Steel Co., 28–29
Bezos, Jeff, 166f
Biffle, Greg, 435f
B.J.'s Men's Clothing, 238
Black, John, 365

Black, Stewart, 95
Black & Decker, 215
Blackberry, 365
Blind Pig Bar, 22–24
Blockbuster, 142
Boeing, 486f
Bond, Sir John, 178
Boston Boxing and Fitness, 154
Boston Scientific and Aboott Laboratories, 142
Brammer, S., 55
Branson, Richard, 172f
Brin, Sergey, 150, 150–151
Bristol-Myers Squibb, 399–400, 399f, 415–416, 421
British Petroleum (BP), 451–452, 467–468
Brito, Carlos, 356
BRK Electronics, 114
Brooklyn Union Gas, 17
Brown, Alvin, 32
Brown, Jeff, 186
Bruch, Helka, 371
Buchanan, Bruce, 345–346, 361–363, 366
Buckley, George W., 269
Bugaloo Strollers Company, 74
Burberry, 440
Burger King, 16, 27, 27f, 28, 42–44, 47, 153–154
Burgess, Michelle, 24
Burns, Ursula, 211f
Busenitz, L. W., 145
BusinessWeek, 369

C

Cadbury, 208
Callin, Victor J., 327
Calvin Klein, 223
Cameron, Kim S., 454
Campbell, Michael E., 52
Campus MovieFest, 47
CaringWorks, 105
Carlisle, Howard M., 263
Carnegie Mellon Summer Academy, 99
Carrefour Hypermarkets, 228f
Cartwright, Dorwin, 426
Cartwright, Stacy, 440
Castagna, Heather, 184
Caterpillar, Inc., 324
C.Crane, 406
The Center for Health, Environment and Justice, 54
Century Life of America, 512
Certo, Brian, 470
Cescau, Patrick, 224
Chambers, John, 295
Chapman, Matt, 341
Chapman, Mike, 341
Chase, Richard B., 533
Chemical Bank, 66
Chevron Texaco Company, 61, 61f
Chidsey, John, 27, 42–43, 44
Chouinard, Yvon, 407f
Chronicle of Higher Education, 301
Chrysler Corporation, 463, 538
Ciano, Jonathan, 466
Circuit City, 265, 448
Cisco Systems, 295–296, 295f, 301, 310, 315
Coca-Cola Company, 54, 124, 237, 482
Cohen, Bennett, 384
Colgate-Palmolive, 223
Collard, Carol S., 105
Colorado Department of Health and Public
          Environment, 67
Comarco, 414

Coney Island Hospital, 260f
Connolly, Terry, 308
ConocoPhillips, 167
Control Data Corporation, 55, 63
Cooper, Jack, 399–400, 415–416, 421
Corning Corporation, 41, 83
Crane, Bob, 406
Crocs, Inc., 45–46
Crosby, Phillip B., 493, 495

D

Dale, Ernest, 185
Danone, 223
Dao, Thi Thanh Lam, 15
Darden Graduate School of Business, University of
          Virginia, 356
Darden Restaurants, 176
Davis, Keith, 53, 72–74, 359
Dayton-Hudson, 55
De Cremer, David, 283
Dean Foster Associates, 12
Deepwater Horizon, 164
Dell, 200, 222, 263, 314
Dell, Michael, 200, 222
Delta Air Lines, 527–528, 527f, 549–552, 553
Deming, W. Edwards, 490, 495, 530, 544
Dennison, Henry, 32
Denver Museum of Nature and Science, 67
Dewelt, Robert L., 502
Diller, Barry, 300
Dillinger, John, 155
Disney World, 20
DiTomaso, Nancy, 84
Domino's Pizza, 20, 534
Don Cesar Beach Resort, 177
Donaldson and Scannell, 98
Dove, 223
Drucker, Peter F., 5, 167, 169
Dudley, Robert, 451, 467–468
Duke Energy, 529
Dun & Bradstreet, 542
Dunn, Brian, 448
DuPont, 72f, 114

E

Eastman Kodak, 119, 485–486, 487f
eBay, 301, 366
Ebony, 214
Eden's Fresh Company, 470
Edwards, Cliff, 448
Einstein, Albert, 254
Eisner, Michael, 300
Eitelto, Maria, 57
Elizabeth Arden, 223
Elms, Heather, 210
eMachines, 200
Emery Worldwide, 412
Energy*Solutions*, 261
Enron Corporation, 67, 68
Ericson, 340–341
Ericsson, 356
Ettinger, Jeffrey, 477, 496
European Union (EU), 121f, 124
Exxon, 297

F

Facebook, 39, 315, 395
Famous Amos, 215
Fayol, Henri, 11, 26, 28, 29, 32–33, 44, 235, 250
Federated Department Store, 16
Feigenbaum, Armand V., 488

Subject Index